# AMERICAN
# RELIGION

## LITERARY SOURCES
## &
## DOCUMENTS

Plate 12: Norman Rockwell, detail from *Freedom to Worship*, 1943 .

# AMERICAN RELIGION

LITERARY SOURCES & DOCUMENTS

*Edited and with an Introduction by*
## David Turley

## Volume III
## Modern American Religion
## since the Late Nineteenth Century

HELM INFORMATION

Selection and editorial matter
© 1998 Helm Information Ltd
The Banks,
Mountfield,
near Robertsbridge,
East Sussex TN32 5JY,
U.K.

ISBN 1-873403-21-6

A CIP catalogue record for this book
is available from the British Library.

Frontispiece: Norman Rockwell, detail from *Freedom to Worship*, 1943.
Reprinted by permission of the Norman Rockwell Family Trust.


Printed on neutral-sized ('acid-free') paper and
bound by MPG Books, Bodmin, Cornwall.

# Contents

## VOLUME III
## Modern American Religion since the Late Nineteenth Century

### Scene Setting: Urban Revivalism and Immigrant Religiosity

### New Immigrants: Catholicism

## New Immigrants: Judaism

## Religion in Urban Industrial Society

## Moral Behaviour and Political Action: Religion and Prohibition

## Faith in a Changing World

## New Thought and Therapeutic Religion

# Black Churches and Sects

# Religion and Race Relations

# Eastern Religions in America

## Modern Evangelism, Radical and Conservative Christianity

# List of Illustrations

# Volume III:
# Modern American Religion
# since the late
# Nineteenth Century

# Scene Setting:
# Urban Revivalism and
# Immigrant Religiosity

Plate 13: *Moody and Sankey addressing a rally in Brooklyn, c. 1880s .*

# From Church to Opera House: A Change of Tactics

## DELAVAN LEONARD PIERSON

Arthur Tappan Pierson (1837–1911) became a significant figure in the transatlantic conservative evangelical movement of the late nineteenth century. An associate of Dwight L. Moody, Pierson, like his fellow revivalists, was driven by deep anxieties to try to restore the influence of Bible-based Christianity. They feared the corrosive effects on faith of science, migration to the cities and new forms of industrial life. The desire to reach all classes with the gospel took Pierson away from grand church buildings to modern urban equivalents of mission halls and camp meetings. He also eventually freed himself from denominational loyalties.

S uccess had thus far crowned Dr. Pierson's efforts. As the popular pastor of one of the leading churches in the Middle West he occupied an enviable position. His congregation was large, cultured, influential and wealthy; his people were harmonious, devoted and enthusiastic; his work was well organized and aggressive and the various departments of church activity seemed to be in a healthy condition. He had received the degree of Doctor of Divinity, his salary had been increased, and there were other tokens of appreciation and esteem. His fame had spread abroad, in city, state and nation so that he had many remunerative opportunities to lecture, and he was recognized as a power in civic and ecclesiastical affairs, especially as a leader in religious and missionary enterprises. God's blessing seemed to rest upon him so that he had very nearly reached the summit of his ambition, but still he was far from being satisfied. What lacked he yet? Some pastors might have been content to settle down with a consciousness of achievement. They would have cared for no greater sign of success than a well-filled and well-organized church. But this did not satisfy the soul of Dr. Pierson. Most of the additions to the church were by letter or were children from the

Source: Delavan Leonard Pierson, 'From Church To Opera House—A Change Of Tactics', *Arthur T. Pierson*, New York, 1912, pp. 127–47.

Sunday-school, and while he rejoiced over these, he longed to see men and women born anew and manifesting their new birth by a new nature and a new life. His dissatisfaction grew as he saw and heard of multitudes converted under the simple preaching of comparatively unlettered evangelists. He realized that there was a power of God of which he knew nothing. There were promises of blessing which were not being fulfilled. He believed in God's Word and in His power, but something must be standing in the way.

While this burden was lying heavily upon him, God sent to Detroit two of His servants, Major D. W. Whittle and his associate, P. P. Bliss, the singing evangelist. They began gospel meetings on Tuesday, October 6, 1874, and continued their Detroit campaign for six weeks. Dr. Pierson gladly sat at their feet, as a learner. He attended the services, studied their methods and observed the results. He learned three things: (1) The power of simple gospel preaching in contrast to that which emphasized literary style; (2) the power of God's Word when used to unfold the great Christian doctrines in contrast to non-Biblical preaching; and (3) the power of gospel song in contrast to elaborate music rendered chiefly for artistic effect.

Mr. Bliss wrote his music, as Major Whittle prepared his sermons, solely for spiritual impression, and when Dr. Pierson wrote for them a song, "With Harps and with Viols," he was impressed to see Mr. Bliss withdraw for a season of prayer before composing the music. All they did was "sanctified by the Word of God and by prayer."

The evangelists were entertained for a month in the Pierson home and their very presence was a benediction. The calm peace and joy in the Holy Spirit that pervaded their lives spoke even more loudly than their sermons and songs. Their host longed to experience more of the fullness of God's abiding presence and power in his own personal life and ministry.

One night after a meeting of unusual power, the pastor of the Methodist church, in which it was held, entered his lecture room and found Dr. Pierson alone with his head bowed on his hands, deeply moved. On being asked the cause of his distress he replied:

"I feel that I have never been truly converted nor have I preached the Gospel as I ought."

By many external leadings and by the inward "Still small voice" God was calling him to larger, more fruitful service. Just before the evangelists left the city, Major Whittle said to his host, with great earnestness:

"Brother Pierson, Bliss and I are firmly convinced that God would mightily use you if you were wholly consecrated to Him. We have agreed to pray for you daily that you may be fully surrendered."

These words were not easy to forget, but for over a year they apparently bore no fruit. He became restless amid his worldly success until he finally felt that he must face the issue or give up his commission. The conviction had been growing upon him that before he could be used as he wished for the conversion of men he must be more fully consecrated to God. At his suggestion a room was fitted up in the church tower and thither he went for uninterrupted Bible study, meditation, self-examination and communion with God. On November 12, 1875, a day appointed by the Synod of Michigan for fasting and prayer, he was convinced that the great obstacle to his spiritual growth and power was his ambition for literary glory. This conviction had been slowly growing, but he had almost unconsciously fought against it. Now he asked God to deal with this ambition in His own way. He was brought to the depths of humiliation and almost despair. The steps by which he began to come out of the slough of despond, he describes as follows:

> I began to pray aloud in private and found this a great help to my realization of the presence of God, and I learned what real prayer meant. Then I was impressed with the necessity for honesty, absolute candour with God in asking what I really wanted, and what I was willing to give up everything else to obtain. I saw that my life had been full of self-seeking and idolatry, such as I had never realised. Next I felt the need of present faith in the sure Word of God which promises answer to such prayer. God gave me this assurance in the preparation of a special sermon to my people. Finally I saw that I must give up every ambition and every idol, and must place myself unreservedly in the hands of God. It was a terrible battle, but at last I said, with all my heart, "Lord, let me be nothing, but use me if Thou wilt to save souls and to glorify Thee."
>
> From that day I was conscious of the presence of the Holy Spirit in my life and work in a way that I had before never known. The text, 1 John v. 4, "I have overcome the world," was revealed to me in a new light and instead of depending upon my energy and ability to overcome the world. I saw that God must do it and all the glory was to be His, not mine.
>
> Just at this time the remarkable biography of Charles G. Finney was put into my hands and from it I saw how God's spirit could use a man wholly absorbed in the work of saving souls. From the hour that I nailed my ambition for literary honours and applause to the Cross of Christ, I began to feel a deep and solemn conviction that God, in answer to prayer, was about to commission me to a new work for Christ. Within one year this expectation was marvellously fulfilled.

One Sabbath morning, March 19, 1876, he preached on "The New Birth with a keen sense of the help of the Holy Spirit. The impression made on the hearers was deep and solemn. The pastor felt that many would have arisen for prayer but for the atmosphere and traditions of the congregation, which restrained him from making any such innovation. Inquirers were asked to come to the lecture room and two men responded and gave themselves to God. At the evening service the pastor began a series of sermons suggested by facts in Finney's life, and there was evidence of still deeper interest.

The next Friday evening, March 24th, was unusually stormy, but seventy-five gathered for prayer and the pastor took his people into his confidence. He spoke plainly and tenderly of the barriers that he felt stood between the church and larger ingatherings. He told them of his own surrender and asked the church to join him in a determination to remove any obstacles that might be due to tradition, prejudice, fashion, over-attention to the aesthetic or to lack of sympathy with the masses. The very character of the church building, with its imposing architecture, beautiful furnishings, and rented pews, was suggested as a possible hindrance to drawing the poorer classes. God's promises to answer prayer and to give power for service were quoted from His Word. Then pastor and people knelt down (this act itself was an innovation) and prayed that at all costs their church might be used to give the Bread of Life to the unsaved multitudes of the city.

While that prayer was being breathed out to God the church building was burning. As they rose from their knees smoke was noticeable in the room and some of the officers sought the cause but without success. They concluded that contrary winds were blowing the smoke down the chimney, and after a careful investigation they went home. The next morning the beautiful temple was in ashes. The fire had started in a defective flue and had crept along between the walls, so that in the early dawn the whole building burst into flame. When the fire engines arrived the interior was a roaring furnace.

In spite of the financial loss and the grief due to the devastation of the place so full of hallowed associations, Dr. Pierson saw in this seeming calamity the hand of God. The tower study, in which were a thousand books, and two thousand sermons—the work of twenty years,—was destroyed, but even he felt that the spiritual lessons and experiences were beyond the reach of the flames. He wrote to D. L. Moody:

> I felt as if God had laid His hand on my shoulder and said, "I am thy God; henceforth be a man of prayer and faith and give thyself to the work of saving souls." I replied, "Lord, by Thy grace, I will."

Immediately the church officers were called together and at their pastor's earnest request decided to hire the large "Whitney's Opera House," and to open it freely for evangelistic services, with gospel hymns and a volunteer choir.

This was a great step for the aristocratic, exclusive church to take. At the same time their pastor discarded forever the use of written sermons, for he saw in the loss of his manuscripts a call to abandon what he believed to be the hindrance to direct preaching of God's message to the people. His first sermon in the Opera House was sought on his knees and he was led to preach on the words: "The fire shall try every man's work of what sort it is."

A newspaper writer of the day thus describes the first service in the Opera House:

> The audience began to assemble long before the doors were open and stood patiently reading the billboards, which announced the play "The Black Crook." As the people began to fill the house from the pit to top gallery, two theatre men who dropped in out of curiosity remarked that such an audience would bring a good sum at fifty cents a head. When the audience joined in singing "Praise God from whom all blessings flow," it made the house ring as it never had rung before even for the grandest opera chorus. Some of the people, who were more accustomed to the opera than to church, were impressed by the singing that they began to applaud. A hushed stillness pervaded the vast audience during the prayer and they listened sympathetically to the sermon on "The Ordeal of Fire." Two actors who came in at the stage door to look for their baggage stood behind the flies, with hats in hand, listening with rapt attention to the man who stood where they had performed the evening before.

The preacher seemed inspired as he gave what was reported to be "one of the most startling, plain spoken discourses a nineteenth century audience ever listened to."

The power of God was immediately manifest in the Opera House not only at the preaching services but in the two Bible readings and two prayer-meetings held each week. God touched His servant's lips with a live coal from off the altar and his words burned their way into men's hearts. Hundreds rose for prayer and remained for personal conversation. Men and women, who had not been in church for years, began to attend; even standing room was taken, and often on pleasant evenings from 800 to 1,000 were turned away. In the next sixteen months Dr. Pierson saw more souls converted then in the previous sixteen years of his ministry.

In a letter to Mr. Moody he expressed his own convictions:

> I pray especially that neither I nor any one else may attribute these results to any human instrument. It is so plainly the work of God that I am comparatively lost sight of, as I desire to be, but I have a deep conviction that God is anointing me for some new service, new at least in some respects. . . . Pray that I may be wholly emptied of self and filled with Him.

On the second Sabbath the pastor preached another stirring discourse on "The Church and the Masses" (Luke xiv. 23), in the course of which he said:

> Men give three kinds of excuses to avoid coming into the kingdom of God: First there is the excuse of property, second of preoccupation, and third of domestic ties. Similar hindrances stand in the way of the churches that would minister to the unsaved. When churches are ornate and have rented pews, poor men will not come to be guests of the rich.... When Christian people are not willing to sacrifice their tastes for art, architecture, music and oratory in the house of God they do not reach the masses. A kid glove is often a non-conductor between man and man.... But the Church *must* have the people or it will die. The Church needs them as much as they need the Church.

Thus from the beginning of the new era Dr. Pierson spoke plainly to his people and urged them to prepare to follow God's leading and to build a simple tabernacle in which all classes would feel at home in the worship of God. He asked for a church building adapted to this purpose and for an unworldly administration.

One of his sermons presents some of his convictions on the church and free pews.

> 1. We must magnify the idea of the *Lord's* House by some system that discourages all exclusive human rights of property in the sanctuary and discountenances all invidious social distinctions.
>
> 2. The support of the ministry should be on the basis of voluntary contributions so as to promote true independence on the part of the Lord's ambassador.
>
> 3. We must study economy according to the principles and practice of the Apostolic Church and be an example to other churches.
>
> 4. We must so plan as to bring the Gospel into contact with the unsaved multitudes about us. Attendance at the house of worship should be as free as is consistent with the necessary cost of maintaining the work.

The pastor himself felt, with Paul, "Woe is me if I preach not the Gospel." He proclaimed with earnestness and power not only the attractive aspects of the Gospel but the sterner doctrines as well. He was never a prophet of smooth things. Sin was denounced and mercy was offered. The result was one of the greatest religious revivals the city ever experienced. Scores of converts were added to many churches and some of the most prominent men of the city date their conversion from the Opera House services.

These converts were not like paper, caught up and carried along only for a brief moment by the whirl of a passing enthusiasm. Twenty-one years later an investigation was made and it was found that of 294 members received into Fort Street Church on confession of faith as a result of these meetings 229 were satisfactorily accounted for as faithful to their Christian vows.

When the question arose as to the rebuilding of the church, Dr. Pierson urged his officers to aim to make it not so much "a model of art as a model of a church"—a building not for display but for work and worship, without unnecessary extravagance but adequately equipped for service. He asked not for a colossal tabernacle but for an auditorium adapted to work for the masses, planned for comfort but not for luxury.

He was also opposed to a church debt and exclaimed,

"Better a frame chapel free from debt with Christian ideas, upheld with Christian manhood, than a stately temple built and controlled by the money of ungodly men, or obtained by bowing to those who do not bow the knee to Christ as Saviour and Lord."

The officers of the church listened patiently and courteously to their pastor's arguments and appeals, but while they loved and respected him they were not convinced. The church was rebuilt more beautiful than ever, but by way of compromise the pews were made free for the evening services. The pastor was disappointed and felt that they were not *wholly* following the Lord's leading. He however threw himself into the effort to win men to Christ by the use of such equipment as he had. Both pastor and people had been radically changed by their experience in the Opera House, and when they returned to their renovated temple after sixteen months' absence, a different spirit and atmosphere prevailed. Instead of formality and comparative coldness to strangers there was a warmth and cordial welcome for all.

The congregational singing took on a new life and the mottoes "Preach the Gospel" and "Pray without ceasing" on either side of the pulpit were put into practice with new fervour. Many members had acquired a taste for soul winning, and every week young men visited hotels, saloons, and street corners to distribute invitations. "After meetings" were held each Sunday night and missionary work was carried on in neglected quarters of the city. Earnest men and women went out to hold cottage prayer-meetings, Sunday-schools and preaching services, and more than one new church grew up as a result. Dr. Pierson's motto for his people was "Let every hearer become a herald."

But with the return to the new and stately building it was found impossible to preserve the hold upon non-churchgoers, though the pewholders sought to make strangers welcome and the sermons continued to be simple, practical, and extemporaneous. The preacher did not disregard his talents and literary style, but he made them subservient to the one great end of reaching men.

During this period Dr. Pierson learned many lessons in dealing with inquirers. He himself testified that he had up to that time depended on argument in place of on the Holy Spirit. He thought he could interpret anything or solve any difficulty. He used to lay his plans to capture men as he would capture a fortress, but he too often found that when he had taken one stronghold the garrison had fled to another. Now he learned that when he kept Christ in the foreground and depended on the Sword of the Spirit, God gave the victory. The heart cannot be captured by attacking the head, and spiritual difficulties must be overcome by spiritual weapons. The one dependence in this warfare is on the guidance and power of the Holy Spirit.

Some of the experiences of the inquiry room were of unique interest and permanent value as examples of effective methods in leading men to Christ. One of these Dr. Pierson described as follows:

> At the close of a sermon on "Abiding in Christ", according to my custom, I invited any person present who was impressed with his need of Christ to meet me in the inquirer's room.
>
> One young man of about thirty responded. He was tall, stalwart of frame, intelligent, and would have been fine looking but for a cloud that seemed to abide upon his countenance. In fact, his face seemed scarred and furrowed, as though his life had been a battle with sin and care, and he had been terribly worsted in the contest. I said to him:
>
> "I take it, sir, that you are here to talk with me about your spiritual interests. Will you let me into the very heart of your trouble or difficulty?"
>
> "Well, sir," said he, "I suppose you would consider my case a desperate one. I am a follower of Robert Ingersoll. I am an unbeliever, a disbeliever, an infidel."
>
> "But I suppose there are some things you believe. You believe the Bible to be the Book of God?"
>
> "No, sir."
>
> "You believe Jesus Christ to be the Son of God?"
>
> "No, sir."
>
> "Well, at least you believe in God!"
>
> "There may be a God; I cannot say that I believe there is, but there may be; I do not know."
>
> "Then why are you here? I do not see what you want of me, if you do not believe in the Bible nor in Christ, and are not even sure there is any God."
>
> "I heard you preach to-night, and it seems to me that you must believe something and that it gives you peace and comfort."
>
> "You are quite right"
>
> "Well, I don't believe anything, and am perfectly wretched; if you can show me the way to believe anything and to get happiness in believing, I wish you would. If you can help me, do it quickly, for I have been carrying this burden as long as I can. I am a law student, but I am so wretched I cannot study nor sit still. I wandered over here to-night, and heard the organ playing in your church, and went in expecting to hear some fine music. I heard nothing but simple congregational singing, but curiosity led me to remain and hear what you

had to say, and one thing impressed me, —that you have faith in somebody or something, and you are happy in believing. My envy of you brings me in here."

I lifted my heart to God for special guidance, and drew my chair up close to this unhappy man and involuntarily put my arm around him.

"Tell me something to read", he said.

"I would have you read nothing but the Bible. You have been reading too much; that is partly what is the matter with you. You are full of the misleading, plausible sophistries of the skeptics. Read the Word of God."

"But what is the use when I do not believe it to be the Word of God?"

Opening my Bible, I turned to John v. 39, and with my finger on the verse slowly read: "Search the Scriptures; for in them ye think ye have eternal life and they are they which testify of Me and ye will not come unto Me that ye may have life." "Now," said I, "it is God's testimony and my experience that he who diligently searches the Scriptures will find that they contain the witness to their own divine origin and inspiration, and to the divinity of the Lord Jesus Christ."

"Well," said he, "I'll read the Bible, but what beside?"

Turning to Matthew vi. 6. I pointed to the words:

"Enter into thy closet, and when thou hast shut thy door, pray to thy Father which is in secret, and thy Father which seeth in secret Himself shall reward thee." "If that means anything, it means that if you sincerely pray to God He will reveal Himself to you."

"But of what use to pray to God if you don't believe there is a God?"

For an instant I was perplexed. But a thought flashed across me, and although I never had given such counsel to any man before, I gave utterance to it, for I felt guided.

"It makes no difference," I replied, "provided you are sincere. God will not disregard any genuine effort to draw near to Him. Go and pray, if only like the famous Thistlewood conspirator: 'Oh, God, if there be a God, save my soul, if I have a soul.'"

"Anything more?" said he.

"Yes,"and I opened to John vii. 17, and read:

'If any man will do His will, he shall know of the doctrine.' That means that if you act up to whatever light you have, you shall have more light. In God's school, we never are taught a second lesson till we practice the first. 'Then shall we know if we follow on to know the Lord.'

I have given you three texts already to ponder and study. I wish to add one more: Matt. xi. 28, 29, 30, 'Come unto Me, all ye that labour and are heavy laden, and I will give you rest.' That means that if you come directly to Jesus Christ, He will give you rest. Now notice these four texts. One bids you to search the scriptures; one, to pray in secret; one, to put in practice whatever you know; and the last, to come to Jesus Christ as your personal Saviour."

"Is that all?" he inquired.

"That is all. Will you promise me to go and follow this simple prescription?"

"I will."

After kneeling in prayer together, this Ingersollite left me. Two weeks later, at the close of service, I gave a similar invitation to inquirers. The congregation was scarcely half out of the house, when this same man came towards me, with both hands extended and his face beaming. "I have found God and Christ, and I am a happy man!"

He sat beside me and told me the fascinating story. He had gone home that Sunday night, taken out from his trunk the Bible his mother had put there when he left home; had opened it knelt before the unseen God. He simply, sincerely asked that if there were a God at all, and if the Bible were the Word of God,

12

and Jesus Christ His Son and the Saviour of man, it might be shown to him plainly. As he read and prayed and sought for light, light was given; he humbly tried to follow every ray and to walk in the light, and the path became clearer and plainer and the light fuller and brighter, until his eyes rested in faith upon Jesus.

At about this time—in 1878—another remarkable influence came into Dr. Pierson's life and another teaching of the Scripture was revealed to him. It was in connection with the visit of the sainted George Müller of Bristol, England, to America. These two men who were to be so closely associated in later years had never met. It chanced that, in the providence of God, Dr. Pierson had been invited to accompany a party to the Pacific Coast for rest and recuperation for a severely overstrained body. While in San Francisco he learned that George Müller was on the coast and would start East on Friday or Saturday. He was somewhat astonished, as this would involve travelling on the Sabbath and, as it was his only opportunity for the coveted interview, he was sorely tempted to break his own rule by taking the same train. After prayerful consideration he decided not to do so, however, and was rewarded by discovering on reaching Ogden that Mr Müller was on the same train. He had not travelled on the Sabbath but had rested at Ogden. Together they journeyed to Chicago and afterwards Mr Müller accepted an invitation to visit Detroit.

Up to this time Dr. Pierson had been an earnest advocate of what is known as the "Post-Millennial" view of the Lord's Second Coming. Many times he had addressed the Presbytery and other bodies on the subject and had set forth what seemed to him unanswerable arguments in the support of this view. Now, however, he was led through Mr Müller to make a new and more careful study of the subject. He says:

> Mr. Müller listened patiently to my objections and then said, with his celestial smile: "The only thing I can say is that none of your arguments are founded on *Scripture*. It makes no difference what *we* think but *what does God's Word say?*" For ten days he came to my study every day and opened up the truth to me. Ever since that time I have been looking for the Lord's personal return and it has been the inspiration of my life."

This doctrine came to be to him a key with which to unlock many perplexing difficulties in Biblical theology. He says:

> Two-thirds of the Book which had been sealed to me were opened by this key, and I was permitted to enter and walk through marvellous chambers of mystery.

Although Mr. Müller was thirty-two years older than his friend and although the days actually spent in each other's companionship through life would not aggregate one year, it is impossible to estimate all that the friendship meant to Dr. Pierson. Mr. Müller came into his life at a critical time and they were irresistibly drawn to each other. Daily for twenty-eight years they remembered each other in prayer until the older man went to his reward. Only those who have studied the prayer life of Mr. Müller and know what power he had with God can estimate the results of this prayer covenant.

Meanwhile God seemed to be stirring the nest and there were thorns that made it uncomfortable. Dr. Pierson was impressed with the thought that he should work more systematically for the masses. Gradually the church work seemed to be getting back into old ruts, and he found that he could not carry out his ideas for simplicity in worship. In spite of the pastor's musical talent, the elaborate anthems by the choir were irksome to him and too often seemed out of harmony with the sermons. He believed in congregational singing and said, "God never intended four or forty people to stand in a choir and do the singing for all the people." He also had an unconquerable aversion to anything that seemed to him like formal ritualism or liturgy in a church service. With characteristic faithfulness he presented his views to his congregation, for he could not endure the bondage involved in shaping his course to meet the preferences of men. Freedom and truth demanded that he deliver his message as he believed it came from God.

It was natural that many, especially among non-Christians, should be offended by some of his outspoken utterances as he declaimed against Sabbath desecration, intemperance, ritualism, rationalism and worldliness. Efforts were made to attack his character and to discredit him in the eyes of the public, but without avail. His reputation and his character were in the hands of God.

A year before he left the Fort Street Church Dr. Pierson wrote a long pastoral letter to his people which he printed and distributed. This letter set forth the history of God's dealings with him and with the church since his coming. It spoke of his own temptations to ambitions and self-glory and the entire revolution in his own convictions and ideas. After rehearsing the story of the fire and the experiences and lessons of the Opera House meetings, he went on to say:

> My conviction was strong that such a church building as ours hinders access to the common people. The very elegance of its architecture, its furniture, the high rate of its pew rents and the air of exclusiveness that seemed to outsiders to hang about it would repel a poor man.
>
> I do not mean to say that my beloved people are to blame for the impressions, often unjust, which keep the masses out of our place of worship, but it does seem to me that if we are really aiming to reach those who neglect the Gospel we would build and run our places of worship accordingly. Formerly I justified costly church edifices, and when our former house was remodelled, I helped to plan its artistic completeness, but I believe that God has taught me that the present system of building and conducting churches is a real hindrance in saving souls. When, however, the congregation determined to rebuild in the same style as before the fire, I forbore to obtrude my views on the people.
>
> Next I tried to show that the rental and reserving of pews would repel the poor and I offered to serve without guaranteed salary if the seats were made free.... After presenting my views and supporting them on Scriptural basis, I left you, my dear people, to decide without any attempt or desire to fetter your action.... You decided to maintain the former system of pew rents but to make them free in the evening. I worked hard, and during the summer after our return to our new church building I took no vacation but maintained the Sunday preaching services, the inquiry meetings and prayer-meetings. Yet, as you know, from the day of entering our new edifice the work of God's grace in conversion

14

has steadily declined. There have been marked cases of spiritual growth among disciples, but the number of converts has become smaller each year.

With perfect frankness, I wish to lay down plank by plank the platform of Bible principles, as I see them, on this subject:

1. The Church of God exists on earth in great part to rescue unsaved souls.

2. The more destitute souls are, the greater is the obligation of the church towards them.

3. Practical indifference to the salvation of the unevangelized forfeits the claim of the church to God's blessing or even to a place among His Golden Candlesticks.

4. The twofold work of evangelization and edification must go on side by side.

5. Everything in the church should be adapted to these two ends—the salvation of the unsaved and the building up of believers.

Now as a church are we reaching the results that God's promises lead us to expect?....

I write this letter only that I may put you into the full possession of facts, and that I many impart to you any light that I may have received. I could not be faithful to you or to God without telling you how I look on these matters. I have no plans only to follow Him patiently step by step....

We must stand by each other and by God in the firm resolve to elevate the standard of holy living. I am ready to "cross the stream and burn the bridge behind me."

When the large influx of converts received in the Opera House services did not continue, Dr. Pierson grew impatient for contact with the masses. Sermons on the subject of the "Ideal Church" and the "Mission of the Church" were followed by remonstrances from his officers who decided that it was unwise either to erect another branch of the church or to do away with the ownership of pews. The officers expressed their love and admiration for their pastor and he reciprocated their cordial feeling, but they did not see eye to eye with him in these matters of church policy, and he saw that it would be difficult for either to yield. It was inevitable therefore that he should listen to the overtures of another church that seemed to offer larger opportunities to reach the multitudes. It cost him unspeakable sorrow to sunder ties that bound him to his people, and it was a difficult matter to pull up the roots that had run wide and deep in the interests of city and state, but he felt the call of God to leave, and on July 19, 1882, after thirteen years in Detroit, he resigned his charge to accept a call to the Second Presbyterian Church of Indianapolis.

# ☙112☙

# The Reporter's Conversion

## DWIGHT L. MOODY

Perhaps part of the success of Dwight L. Moody (1837–1899), the most famous evangelist of his time, arose from his own experience in moving from country to city and making his way as a salesman. He understood his audiences particularly well and how to reach them. Revival crusades relied on organization, promotion and publicity about successful conversions. Anecdotes of the winning over of hardened scoffers became a staple item of such publicity.

---

One of the most conspicuous persons at the Brooklyn Rink was a man of over fifty years, a reporter, apparently of a sensational sort. One of my friends entered into conversation with him the second evening, and found him partially intoxicated, ribald, sneering and an infidel. Inquiring further concerning him, we found that he had been several times in the city jail for drunken brawls, although originally a man of culture and polish. Time passed, and on our last day at Brooklyn the same man, conspicuous by his commanding figure, sat in a back seat in the Simpson Church. My friend accosted him once more, and this was the answer:

> I am waiting to thank Mr. Moody, who, under God, has been the greatest blessing of my life to me. I have given up my engagement, the temptations of which are such as no Christian can face. And I am a Christian—a new creature; not reformed, you can't reform a drunkard; I tried that a hundred times; but I am regenerated, born again by the grace and power of God. I have reported sermons many a time, simply to ridicule them, but never had the least idea what true religion meant till I heard Mr. Moody's address on "Love and Sympathy", ten days ago, and I would not have believed there could be so much sweetness in a lifetime as has been condensed into those ten days. My children know the change; my wife knows it; I have set up the family altar, and the appetite for liquor has been so utterly taken away, that I only loathe what I used to love.

Source: Dwight L. Moody, 'The Reporter's Conversion', from *Arrows and Anecdotes*, London, 1876, pp. 58–9.

"Let him that standeth take heed least he fall," suggested my friend.

"No, not while I stand so close to the cross as I do to-day;" and he opened a small hymn-book, on the fly leaf of which was written: "I have set my face like a flint, and I know that I shall not be ashamed."

# ⊰113⊱

# The New Immigration: Churches

## PETER ROBERTS

Between 1880 and the immigration restriction legislation of 1921, nearly 25 million migrants entered the United States. Increasingly they came from the empires of Central and Eastern Europe and the countries of Southern Europe. Thus, while there were Protestants amongst them, they added hugely to the Catholic and Jewish population. By the beginning of the twentieth century, greater religious variety existed in America than ever before in a society transformed by industry and cities.

In foreign-speaking colonies of 10,000 population and over, many magnificent churches are built. Religion forms an essential part of life of the southeastern European, and much money is spent on church edifices where the faithful may worship. In Shenandoah, Pa., the foreigners have invested no less than $100,000 in church property and the total population is a little over 30,000 of whom 80 per cent are either foreign-born or descendants of foreign-born parents. In Buffalo the most imposing church building is that of St. Stanislaus, built by the Poles. The churches built by the foreigners on the South Side of Pittsburgh are far more magnificent than any built by their predecessors—the men of the old immigration. The same is true of towns and cities in New Jersey and New England. A church in Pawtucket, R.I., has mural decorations that are superb. It is impossible to state how much money the peoples of southeastern Europe have put into stone and wood, in window and altar, in art and music, for the purpose of worshiping God, but it is safe to put it at $10 per capita, which would make a sum of not less than $75,000,000.[1] When they come, they are poor, having less than $16 each; they get the lowest wage in the industries of America, but when the appeal for funds is made to put up a church to worship God, these people respond. And it is absurd to say that all this wealth molded into sacred structure is forced out of the people by ecclesiastical terror. The foreigner is not long in America before he knows that

Source: Peter Roberts, 'Churches', The New Immigration, New York, 1912, pp. 200-15.

there is no connection between the government and the church and that the faith of his fathers and the service of God must be preserved and propagated by voluntary contributions, and no priest could compel the people to give freely of their substance to this purpose if their religious faith and love of sacred ideals did not impel them.

## Roman Catholics Coming

When the immigration stream runs at the rate of 1,000,000 a year, more than 600,000 of the total landed in America are Roman Catholics. During the last twenty years, the total number of immigrants entering the United States, adherents of the Roman Catholic Church, cannot be less than 10,000,000 souls. Never in the history of the world has a religious organization faced an obligation such as that confronting the Roman Catholic Church of the United States, because of the incoming tide from Europe. To shepherd these millions of souls speaking thirty different tongues, each race having its own idiosyncrasies that make it difficult for ecclesiastical leaders trained in English-speaking countries to understand how best to adjust the machinery to the church to meet their needs in the new world; to house them in churches; to soothe racial prejudice so that men who cherish antipathies and hatred may sit in the same pew and worship under the same priest; to secure an adequate number of priests of the various nationalities; to reconcile them to superiors having different ideas from those in authority in Europe; to make it possible for the priests of eight different nations in one city to coöperate that the Roman Catholic Church of that city may be one and not divided—these are the problems that no ecclesiastical body before, in the history of the Christian faith, has been called upon to solve. They have precipitated questions and difficulties which have put a strain and stress upon the Roman Catholic leaders in America that none outside of that circle can understand or appreciate. Many educated and intelligent men, outside the pale of that church, have criticized its shortcomings in meeting this great need—they should rather study the problem and sympathize with the men who face so grave a responsibility. The Catholic church has done and is still doing a great work for the foreign-speaking people in America; if its beneficent influence were removed, the millions of the new immigration would be far more lawless and reckless than they are. The teachings and leadings of this religious organization are a defense to both the secular and moral institutions of the country.

## Replacement of Worshipers

The foreigners in cities, as before stated, occupy sections once inhabited by the English-speaking, and the religious edifices in them, formerly used by the men of the old immigration, often pass into the hands of the new. A section in Chicago, once occupied by Germans and Scandinavians, is now taken up by Jews and Poles, and in the place of Protestant churches are found synagogues and Roman Catholic edifices. The situation in South Side, Pittsburgh, is typical of hundreds of other places where this change takes place. The Servians bought out the building used by the German Lutherans, the Slovaks bought out the church building of the Methodist Protestants, the Croatians bought out the edifice of the Methodists, the Lithuanians bought out another building of the same denomination, the Greeks bought out the building of the Lutherans, while the churches of the Baptists and Congregationalists have been purchased by other peoples of southeastern Europe, now residing in this part of the city. In every city of industrial importance in the North Atlantic and North Central states, this transference of sacred edifices goes on. Instances are found in New York, Philadelphia, Chicago, etc., of Protestant denominations honestly trying to hold the fort and adapt their work to the need of the new immigrants. These are exceptions, however. The rule is to abandon the field and give way to religious forms better adapted to meet the taste of the newcomers.

## All Romanists do not Agree

It is not always easy to meet the tastes of the foreign-speaking in forms of worship. In a town in New England, a group of foreigners had the privilege of using the edifice of the Irish-Americans. When the aliens built a church of their own, members of the English-speaking congregation were very happy, for one of them said, "You couldn't leave a pocket handkerchief or a pocketbook on the seat but a foreigner would immediately pick it up." An English-speaking priest in New Jersey, whose duty it was to look after the foreigners in his parish, was greatly concerned about their spiritual interest and said, "I want to bring a foreigner to confess these people before Easter, so that they may come to communion." The Uniates, such as the Lithuanians, Ruthenians, etc., give more concern to ecclesiastical authorities than do the Romanists, such as the Poles, the Slovaks, Magyars, etc. The Uniates recognise the supremacy of the Pope of Rome, but retain the rites and doctrines of the Greek church, to which communion they formerly belonged. Hence in these churches, the cup is given the laity in the sacrament, the priests marry, divorces are granted in certain cases, the mass is celebrated in the language the people can understand, and the priest is called and dismissed by the board of directors. These usages were once condemned by the Pope, but when the Jesuits brought certain peoples of the Greek Orthodox church into the Roman fold, the compromise was agreed to—if they recognized the Pope they could retain the Greek usages. As long as these people remained in Europe, in close proximity to the Greek church, the discrepancies between them and their Catholic co-religionists were not apparent; but when they come to America, exercising the privileges granted them by the compromise, and still call themselves Roman Catholics, the differences become very embarrassing, hard to explain to the faithful, and obnoxious to priests who are staunch believers in the canonical law. The Croats are faithful Catholics, but they insist that the mass be said in "Old Slavic" or "Glagolitza," and every effort made to have them adopt the Latin litany has

20

failed. Ecclesiastical authority has, in its effort to introduce Latin form, gone as far as to close their church; the people have preferred that to taking away the Old Slavic tongue. The Ruthenians and the Wallachians are affected by this inharmonious relation more than any other people; it has led to many disputes, lawsuits, and schisms in this country.[2] Friction, because of these differences, accounts for the independent Greek church of Canada, which has some eighty congregations made up wholly of Ruthenians. The movement is Roman Catholic in form, but Protestant in spirit. The priests insist upon ordination, they retain the seven sacraments, the Greek rites are used, but the government is Presbyterian, they expound the Scripture and do preaching, but they also remember the patriarch of Jerusalem in their prayers. Sometimes Roman Catholic priests serve men of the Greek Orthodox faith. When the Servians first came to Pittsburgh, they had no priest, so they were served by the Catholic clergy, who possibly did not know that they served men of a different faith. They used to bury their dead in the German Catholic cemetery, but when a Servian priest came on field, the practice was at once changed.

## The Greek Orthodox

Greek Orthodox congregations are found in the country. There are three types: the Servian, which recognizes the headship of the Servian church, an autonomous body, although in usage identical with the Russian church; the Greek, which recognizes the headship of the Patriarch of Constantinople, but its rites and ceremonies are similar to those of the Servians and Russians; the Russian, which recognizes the headship of the Patriarch of St. Petersburg and the Czar of Russia. The Bulgarians are like the Servians in religious usages, but turn their faces more to Constantinople than to St. Petersburg. In these congregations the title of property rests in the board of trustees, and the congregations also have a voice in the selection and dismissal of the priest. When in Milwaukee we asked the Greek priest for the use of the vestry to hold a meeting on a week night for a group of Greeks, he referred us to the head of the Greek congregation, who was the authorised party to give permission. This was very different from the attitude of the Slovak priest interviewed on precisely the same service, who said, "I would give it you gladly, but if the Bishop came to know of it, I would get in trouble."

## Foreigners have Many Faiths

We have representatives of many other faiths among the new immigration. One of these is the Nazarites, a sect resembling the Bogomiles of Russia, and not unlike the Quakers. A congregation of them in Barberton, Ohio, is led by a man of superior ability and refinement. The meekness and simplicity he exhibited while explaining the faith of which he was proud were worthy of imitation by men of large religious influence. Many Slovaks and Magyars are Protestants, but the majority of them are lost to Christian influence, because of the preponderating number of Catholics in the communities where they live. They are carried with the tide away from the faith of their childhood into no faith. Protestant missionaries are sent to labor among these peoples, but their labors are rather unsatisfactory because of the difficulties of the work. Protestantism in southeastern Europe differs greatly from the type found in America. The pastor of a Magyar church will, on a Sunday evening, sit with his board smoking cigarettes and drinking black coffee, while a moving picture show goes on in the church. Another foreign-speaking clergyman was busy on a Sunday evening going from house to house collecting his salary while the church doors were closed—the Lord's day being an opportune occasion to catch all the men. Some of these ministers have high regard for the auditorium although it may be nothing more than a rented store. An Italian missionary in Chicago, held services in a rented storeroom which was simply furnished, but he was not willing to have the room used for social work. "The place was dedicated for the worship of God." A Magyar congregation, in Yonkers, wanted communion, but had no service for the occasion. The pastor in whose church they worshiped said, "You can have the use of the service used by our church." But the leaders said, "We can't take communion from a borrowed service"; they bought one of their own. But this high idealism is far from common. Some churches hold picnics at which cigars and beer are sold, dancing and gambling are indulged in— anything to catch the dollar. Some Protestant missionaries, working among the foreigners, put the cross over the church. I asked one of these why he placed the symbol over his mission, and his answer was, "To refute the words of Catholics who say that we do not believe in Christ." When I asked a Slav Catholic what he thought of the symbol over the mission, he said, "It's a ruse to induce us to enter the building."

## Foreigners are very Religious

The immigrants from southeastern Europe are very religious; indeed, it may be said that they are too religious, and are given to much superstition. They are not long in the country, however, before the spirit of America soon works a perceptible change. Men who are thoroughly Americanized do not have the same deference to the priesthood nor the same servile attitude to the church as they once had. In a city in New York, accompanied by an Americanized Pole, I called on the Polish priest. In the office at the time sat a Pole recently come from Europe. As soon as the priest appeared the recent immigrant rose, bowed reverently, took his proffered hand, kissed it devoutly, and resumed his seat at a sign from the Father; the older immigrant rose, did not bow, said, "Good evening, Father," shook his hand, and resumed his seat. When in Brooklyn interviewing the Lithuanians, I asked one of them if his people went to church. "Greenies go," he replied, "but Lithuanians in America five or eight years don't go; they, like Protestants, no go to church." One of the comforting and promising sights in a Slavic or Lithuanian colony is he number attending divine service on Sundays. In a Lithuanian church on the South Side of Pittsburgh, the number of persons attending mass on Sunday was about

1500 souls, nine-tenths of whom were males—young men in the heyday of their strength. Half a dozen gray heads were seen in the throng and I asked, "Are those gray-haired people Lithuanians?" "No," was the reply, "they are Irish and German—too old to go to their own church, they come here to worship." What a contrast this was to the average Protestant congregation in which four females may be counted for every male. The scene around a Greek church on festive days is worth witnessing. When the images of the Virgin and the saints are carried around the church, the devout kneel on the pavement, on the lawn, on the street, anywhere, as they bow reverently before the sacred symbol. The spirit of worship in these people is a phenomenon that cannot be found elsewhere in any community. The men of the new immigration flock to the churches and support their priests fairly well. This is especially true of the Slav. The Italian is more indifferent. Italian men will not attend church. In communities of 5000 Italians, one church can hardly be supported, whereas in a similar colony of Slavs, two could be amply sustained. In an Italian church in the city in New York state, the majority of the congregation was Irish. I asked a prominent Catholic, "How is it the Irish worship in the Italian church?" "Well," said he, "most of them are shirkers—they can get religion cheap there, but they have to pay for it in their own church," In a small town in the same state, the Italians petitioned the Bishop for a church. He replied that the place was too small to support two churches, that they should worship in the Roman Catholic church of the town. The Irish-Americans objected, however, for the reason that the Italians "won't pay pew rent."

## No State Church not Understood

The foreign-speaking men of southeastern Europe cannot understand why it is necessary to support the church in America by voluntary contributions. In the fatherland, the priest was paid by the government, the church was built by the government, current expenses were provided by the landed gentry or the government. The poor man contributed nothing and took all the privileges offered. Here it is wholly different; church and state are separated, but many of these ignorant and illiterate immigrants cannot understand it. Many Italian priests cannot get a living out of the people whom they serve, because of this very reason. The intelligent members of the flock understand the situation, but the ignorant shake their heads and say, "It is buying religion." The priest tries to explain, but to no purpose,—"it is wrong for a priest to want money." In one of the towns not far from New York City, the priest posts a notice on the church door stating that every one coming into that church must pay 5 cents for his seat. In the city of Utica, the Italians are supposed to be between 12,000 and 15,000 souls, and one Italian church can hardly be maintained. An intelligent Italian in Montpelier, Vt., explained why he did not go to church: "Mother fed me too much religion in Italy and my stomach is against it." Another Italian said, "The conduct of many priests in Italy accounts for the indifference of the Italians to the church." The penuriousness of the Italian also accounts for this conduct. The only time they open the strings of their purses is on festas. On these occasions they spend money freely and take great delight in the parade. The image of the Virgin or that of a saint carried through the streets of Little Italy, in the Empire City, will be covered with dollar greenbacks, and the priest must look to it that he makes the best of the money then received, for little else will he get until another festa comes around. The Slavs are very different; they attend and support their churches admirably. Their conception of religion may not differ from that of the Italian, but they support the church. The vast majority of the men of the new immigration look upon the ceremonies of the church in a simple straightforward way, ask blessings on home, and work on the *quid pro quo* principle; but the Italians take it in large doses on festive days, while the Slavs are constant and steadfast in their attendance on church ceremonies. A Lithuanian priest in Kenosha, Wis., who had served among Mexicans in San Antonio, said, "Mexicans are funny; they come to church thrice in their life—to be baptized, married and buried—give me the Lithuanians." Many Italians in America wholly forsake the church and get along without the service of the priest or preacher. In Barre, Vt., 3000 Italians are found and no religious services of any kind are held among them. They do not baptize their children, the young people are married by the magistrate, and they bury their dead without religious ceremony. All the colony is made up of northern Italians.

## Drifting from the Church

Many of the new immigrants leave the faith of their fathers when they come to this country. No statistics are available upon the question, but it is safe to say that the percentage of men among Catholics, Protestants, and Jews giving up the faith of their fathers is large. Especially is this true of the young men of every nation. Among the younger men from Scandinavia and Finland, Russia, and Italy, the teachings of Socialism have a great attraction. A college young man working with a group of Jewish boys, was assisted by a young Hebrew, and discussing the work one evening, the Gentile said, "I don't teach Christianity to the boys." "Why not?" asked the Jew. "Well, I don't think it is right," replied the college man. "You can teach it," said the Hebrew, "it won't make any difference—I don't believe in Judaism or Christianity—I'm a socialist." An Italian, in Baltimore, broke away from his church, but found great difficulty with his wife, who was a loyal adherent of the Catholic faith. There was no peace at home and hence he resolved to convert her. He locked her in a room, placed a Protestant Bible on a table, and said, "Here you'll stay and you can't come out until you are a Protestant." The man apparently effected his purpose and celebrated his victory by placing a card over the door of the house on which was written, "This is the house of a Christian, no blasphemy, no drink, no gambling can take place in it." His friends forsook him, for he was unsafe.

## Men who leave their Church

When foreign-born men of Catholic antecedents come over to the Protestant faith, it is hard telling what they'll do. A fellow in Chicago began to read his Bible very diligently when he was converted. He came across a the passage describing the gift of tongues; he became enthusiastic, pronounced some jargon, fell into spasms and twistings, and believed he got the "powers." He came to the mission church with his discovery; his enthusiasm was contagious; soon the congregation was under the spell of the "gift of tongues," and held protracted meetings; the residents in the neighborhood of the mission complained and the authorities interfered to preserve the peace of the community. Among some peoples, to leave the church of their fathers is identical with forsaking one's nation. A Greek, in Chicago, left the Greek church, and was employed by one of the denominations to do missionary work among his countrymen. When the Greeks heard that he was a turncoat from the Greek Orthodox church, they called him "devil," "traitor," "renegade," "betrayer," etc., and his influence was gone. When a Greek was asked, why this was, he said, "Protestant is all right for you; you were born Protestant, but he was born Greek." "A Greek is born to his religion just as he is to his nationality. It would be hard to find one who would not profess to be a Christian."[3] A young Russian, in one of the cities of the West, left the Greek church and was thrown out of his boarding house by his co-religionists. These people at once communicated with his elder brother in Russia, who immediately came to America to bring the wanderer home. He went to the house in which the young man stayed and threatened to kill him if he did not return to the faith of his fathers, for, said he, "The family is shamefully disgraced." He could not persuade his brother to return, and so he went to the police and said that "the young man was detained in his boarding house contrary to his will." The police officer secured the young man and was taking him to the courthouse, when the missionary in the case appeared on the scene and gave security for the appearance of the young convert in court. When the case was called, the judge soon grasped the situation and proceeded to tell the brother that he was in America now and not in Russia. Sometimes the priests throw out of beneficial organizations those who leave the faith. A foreign-born man, residing in Astoria, N.Y., left the church and was thrown out of the society. He secured damages on the ground that a society holding a charter from the state had no right to discriminate against men because of creed or religion. Priests don't like to lose members of their church and try to guard against this. A group of Bulgarians, coming to America, were called into church by the priest the night before they started, and made to swear solemnly that they would never enter a church in America. The attitude of Rev. Iwanawski, in Erie, Pa., was far more intelligent than that. He wanted a man trained in gymnastics so as to be able to lead the boys and young men of his parish. He sent him to the Young Men's Christian Association gymnasium for training. The secretary, in making the arrangement, said: "Father, you need not fear we'll turn him Protestant." "Oh," said the priest, "you leave that to me; I'll see to that."

## The Priests are Capable

The shepherds of the foreign-speaking flocks are on the whole good men, hard workers, rendering good service. They are not all good men. There are some bad men among them, as among spiritual leaders of English-speaking peoples. The priests of the twentieth century are not perfect any more than the Apostles of the first were, but the vast majority are spiritual leaders of the right kind, who render service to their countrymen in America which cannot be computed. A prince bishop who was profane excused his profanity by saying that he swore as a prince and not as a bishop, but one of the peasants asked him, "If the prince is damned, what will become of the bishop?" A priest in New Jersey adopted a two-fold standard and excused himself on like grounds. He was wholly unworthy of the priesthood, and his mother protested that he should be a better man, but he said, "I'm a priest only when in church, on the road I'm like other men." A Protestant missionary among the Portuguese was very little better. He exhorted his people to pray and told them, "If you want anything, pray for it and you'll get it." He visited a home that was very poor, and told the man to pray for bread and God would answer him. The man fell on his knees and prayed. The fellow went out, bought a loaf of bread, put it at his door and told the man it was a miraculous answer to his prayer. Some priests experience difficulty in managing certain members of their congregation. A priest located in a city of New York, was threatened by a band of ruffians from among his people. He appealed to the court and the judge gave him the right to carry a revolver; he also entered suit against his persecutors. The Father believed in fighting with other than spiritual weapons. Another priest of the Greek faith was shamefully abused by some of his congregation because he would not acquiesce to their demand. When foreign-speaking ruffians rise against the priest, there is nothing too savage for them to do. Of course, some priests give cause for violent action. A priest in the neighborhood of Pittsburgh, was guilty of crime for which men have been lynched, and if he were among Americans, his villainy could not be hid. A priest, in Detroit, instilled the spirit of lawlessness into his congregation that neither canonical nor secular law had much effect among the people of his parish. But these are exceptions. The army of clergymen doing work among the foreign-speaking peoples of America are capable and worthy men.

## Fanatical Converts

Some priests, having abandoned their vows, become missionaries of the Protestant faith for foreign-speaking peoples. In a city of the Middle West, one of these converts kept his sacred robes of office, and, when called upon to baptize the child of a foreigner, would carry out the ceremony in every detail as his custom was when a priest of the Catholic church. He believed in making himself all things to all men as a Protestant missionary. Another convert from the priesthood was rabid in his attacks upon the Roman Catholic church. While in a town in Texas, making one of his tirades, he was assaulted by Catholics and to this day carries on his body the marks of the attack. Another missionary of the same type goes from place to place attacking the Catholic church, "challenging priests to public debate that he may tell them things they ought to know." When an ex-priest visited Berwick, Pa., a falsehood was circulated that he was thrown out of one of the saloons, too drunk to walk home; and in the neighborhood of Pittsburgh, where colporteurs sell Bibles, it is stated that some foreign-speaking priests boast of how many Protestant Bibles they have found among their people which they have confiscated. All this fanaticism is out of place in America and should not be countenanced by either Protestants or Catholics. Religious antagonism, debates as to the merit of the various systems of Christian faith, lying and deceiving for the sake of the faith are all out of date in the twentieth century and out of sympathy with the American spirit. The Republic stands for religious toleration, and the converts from either faith should, in this country, understand that freedom of conscience is a fundamental principle which all true Americans honor.

## A Sure Cure

An ex-priest in New York State, in a very efficient manner burnt the bridges behind him. One of his reasons for leaving the Catholic church was that he found the canonical law in America very different from what it was in Europe. His friends and relatives were greatly concerned about his action, and spared no effort to induce him to return to the fold. Their solicitations caused him some anxiety and he resolved to marry. He had a friend in the drug business to whom he told his trouble and begged of him to find him a wife. The druggist agreed to do so. Two weeks later, the ex-priest came to the store and asked him, "Have you filled out my prescription?" "What do you mean?" asked the pharmacist. "A wife, of course." "Are you in earnest?" asked the friend. "Yes," said the bachelor. "Very well, I'll try," and they parted. Two weeks latter, the ex-priest was called to the store and introduced to the woman who is to-day his wife.

## Protestant Pastors

Many Protestant pastors among the foreign-speaking suffer many privations. The number of Protestants in the new immigration is small, hence the congregations are weak, and widely scattered. The missionaries must travel a great deal if they minister to the needs of the men of their faith. The Letts are Protestants and small groups are found in Baltimore, Philadelphia, and Boston, and only one pastor to supply their spiritual needs in the language they love. In Fairport and other port towns on Lake Erie, there are Protestant Magyars and Slovaks, but no minister to serve their spiritual needs. Many missionaries sent among these people live on very small rations and carry on their work. Some of these men in first-class cities minister to the foreign-speaking on a salary of $50 a month. How they can live on such a salary is beyond comprehension.

## Harmony Needed

In Hungary, we were told that the Protestants and Roman Catholics live side by side in peace, and that it is not unusual for the Roman Catholic priest to arrange with a Protestant schoolmaster to give the children of his parish the necessary instruction to prepare them for their first communion. We have not come to this in America, and still the trend is in that direction. An Irishman, in Utica, said, "I hated the Protestants in Ireland, but in this country I can't do it—I don't know why." That man had caught the American spirit. One of the worst evils arising from the antagonism and strife between Protestants and Catholics is the discord which comes into homes having mixed marriages. When parents quarrel about their religion it is at the sacrifice of the children. Many Catholic wives with Protestant husbands, and *vice versa*, for the sake of peace in the home, keep their children away from religious services. If parents, having these difficulties, could agree upon the essentials of the Christian faith, and have their children taught and trained in them, it would be better for the home and for the offspring. This can only be done when priests and pastors, who worship the same Master, come to a common understanding as to what are the essentials in his teachings, and put these in a form that could be used in such homes.

## Agree in doing Good

Rousseau uttered a profound maxim when he said, "It is by doing good that we become good." Catholics and Protestants, Greeks and Jews are concerned in doing good, and when they meet in practical service, they agree and work harmoniously. When leaders of all creeds feel the burdens which men bear to-day, see the motives and impulses which move men in this twentieth century, bring to the clear the sense of justice, the obligations of affection, the respect due of law and order, then they lose sight of their differences in united action. Before the great spiritual awakening comes, men of all creeds must come together, and the only ground upon which this can be done is practical service to men. But when intelligent men feed the people on lies, raise the trivial and accidental above the essential and fundamental, and emphasize more creed than conduct, then faith languishes and the church decays. A keen observer says, "My observation in England and America has been that religion is to non-Russian peoples merely a respectable habit, a method of civil decency." How far is the judgement of the Slav justified? Is there more genuine religion in the simple Slav than in the polished Anglo-Saxon? The religion of Christ came to peoples of varied tongues and it welded the most diverse elements into one. Has it not, in the twentieth century, the vital power to bring about the same among the people of the new immigration? The simple truths of the Nazarene, if divested of ecclesiastical drapery, have in them the breath of life when applied to the problems of this country. None who know the people of these United States will deny that political and religious skepticism is daily spreading among the masses; the Church of God, that once was so powerful in meeting the needs of men, seems to be bankrupt when facing the problems of to-day. While we preach human unity, the visible expression of the religion in which that truth has its basis—the church—is not the embodiment of true democracy. One branch is autocratic and does not believe in the power of the people for self-government; the other is out of relation with the rank and file of workingmen and has no real message for them. It is not true that the men of this nation deny God. Religion and religious truths lie dormant in the hearts of the people—there they await the voice of the prophet. When he comes, speaking as a man of authority, the people will hear him gladly and will follow him. When religious faith and life again come to their own in America, the foreigners will be a potent factor in the awakening for righteousness and justice. They are children who have not been spoiled by sophistry and tradition. Give them the real message from God, and they, the children of the backward nations of Europe, will respond and give to the spiritual life of America strength and power such as they freely give to-day to the production of our material wealth.

## Notes

1. In the diocese of Boston, Greater New York, Philadelphia, Buffalo, Cleveland, and Milwaukee, 356 churches are devoted to the religious worship of men of the new immigration. This does not give all the buildings dedicated to their services, for the returns in the Catholic Directory do not always specify the nationality worshiping in a church, while two or three nationalities may worship in the same church.

2. The Greek Catholic churches or congregations enjoyed considerable freedom before the arrival of a Greek Catholic Bishop, in 1907. They were incorporated, their affairs were managed by boards of directors and trustees, composed wholly of lay members. The priest was called and removed by the directors and the voice of the congregation was supreme in all matters. Since the coming of the Bishop, many congregations have given up their charters so that the property and the management of affairs are in the hands of the Bishop and the priests. Many congregations, however, resent this transference of property and authority, and discontentment is the result.

3. "Greek Immigrants in the United States," p.46.

# New Immigrants:
# Catholicism

*Plate 14: A Polish Catholic Parish Church in Chicago, c. 1900.*

# ⧼114⧽

# American Priests for
# Italian Missions

## JOHN T. MacNICHOLAS

The Irish were the first Catholics in America in substantial numbers and had assumed dominance in the higher reaches of the Church by the time the new immigrant Catholics arrived. Thus the argument advanced here is, in effect, for the existing Irish priesthood to guide the faithful through the shoals of a potentially hostile culture rather than entrust them to their own priests, themselves inexperienced in American life. This attitude and practice caused considerable ethnic tension within the American Catholic Church.

---

Who are the priests best suited for the work of caring for the Italians in this country? The native Italian diocesan priest is not, I think, the best qualified, in all cases, to work as a missionary among immigrants from Italy. In the first place, the Italians cannot be regarded as representing one nation. "United Italy" is an ironical designation. Between a northern Italian and the Neapolitan or Sicilian there exists hardly any bond of sympathy. On the contrary, they often bear each other a racial hatred stronger than that which separates the Irish and the English. When Americans speak of an Italian priest working among his own people, they rarely give any thought to the question whether he be from the North or the South of Italy. Yet to the Italian priest and people it means more than we can appreciate. Unfortunately it must be said that a number of native Italian diocesan priests, abstracting from racial prejudices are not disposed to work among what we call "their own people." They prefer to labor among other nationalities. And the pronounced tendency of many to work for pecuniary interests has given this entire class of priests the reputation of being lacking in zeal.

Nor is the native Italian religious necessarily the best qualified missionary for the immigrants from his own country. First, as in the case of the diocesan native priest, because he is apt to have or suffer from the racial antipathies above alluded

Source: John T. MacNicholas, 'American Priests for Italian Missions', *Ecclesiastical Review*, December 1908.

to; and these are apt to destroy the zeal we expect to find in him. Again, these priests can rarely understand the spirit of liberty which people enjoy in this country, nor have their habits been adapted or their character formed to appreciate the necessity of the constant activity which marks the life of the truly zealous American priest. It must be expected that fitting adjustment to our liberty and activity, when one is advanced in life, will be slow, and not always attended with the desired results. Lastly, there are those American diocesan and religious priests who go to Rome or Italy in the expectation of fitting themselves for advancement, with an ultimate view of honors and titles. They generally return as Doctors of Philosophy or of Divinity and are regarded as representative men in their respective dioceses. They are hardly the men to expect to be sent to insignificant parishes, with the task of working among the poorest from whom little pecuniary compensation can be expected and still less received. This is true especially of the secular clergy who study in Rome. The American religious priest or student who is sent abroad "causa studiorum" is usually intended by his superiors for the work of teaching in his Order or Congregation.

There remains one class of priests that the writer ventures to suggest as best qualified to work among the Italians in the United States. They are diocesan and religious American priests chosen by our bishops and religious superiors definitively for this work. They need to be priests not so much of big heads as of big hearts, not so much of noble intellects as men of deep religious sentiment and zealous activity, men not destined for degrees, but eager to learn the language and to familiarize themselves fairly with the dialects of Italy, especially the Neapolitan and Sicilian; men who are anxious to acquire sympathy for the Italian people without which no work can be done; in fine, men who are willing to sacrifice themselves in their own country, for the sake of the hundreds of thousands of souls they can be instrumental in saving to the Church in the United States.

In the case of diocesan clergy, it may be necessary to make special provisions for priests assigned to labor in what might be called "the Italian missions" of the country. For some time to come the revenues from distinctly Italian parishes must be small; but if the Italians be given a little time, they will no doubt prove their generosity. With regard to priests of Religious Orders, the solution is much easier. Their vow of poverty gives them peculiar advantages in this work. Most of the religious priests, during their course of preparation in the many cities of Italy where they would study the different manners and customs of the people, could live with their brethren. On taking up the work after their return to America, if their Order or Congregation has a house in or near the locality where the congested Italian districts are, three or four Fathers could be maintained by the community at very little expense, to serve the Italian missions. The various Religious Orders, once their attention is drawn to the subject, can hardly escape the obligation of taking up the work, and a refusal to do so might revive the often-stated charge made against religious bodies, namely that they will not coöperate in such a field because there is no pecuniary remuneration.

We have many movements in the interest of Catholicity, but none seems more important than this, and none seems easier of success. The American diocesan and regular priests whom I propose for this task as the most fitted and attainable, would have no racial prejudices to contend with and they would be assured of a respect rarely accorded the native Italian priest. In justice it must be said of the Italian that he has inborn respect for the "forestieri." He will show courtesies to the stranger that he will not extend to his own countrymen. These American diocesan and regular priests who go to Italy for the purpose of qualifying themselves to do this work would get correct notions of the many peoples there, and thus be much better qualified to Americanize the Italians who come to us. These Italians are far from being representative. They came from the poorest classes; they have had no educational advantages. Oppression and unjust taxation have given those who are not simple peasants an inborn hatred of government. The Italians in this country often continue for years under the misapprehension that the Church and her officials here are supported by the government, as is the case in Italy. . . .

Can we spare a sufficient number of priests, both diocesan and regular, who will go to Italy to prepare themselves for this work? However overcrowded a diocese is, however numerous a religious community, there is always a demand for zealous, active priests. The supply of such priests will never equal the demand until the end of time. In this sense a scarcity of priests, both diocesan and religious, will always exist. Very probably in many of our large dioceses, where most of the Italians live in congested districts, a few zealous, diocesan clergymen could be spared. Can ten large dioceses spare four priests each? This would total forty priests. Can the many religious Orders and Congregations in the country assign sixty religious to the work? Two years in Italy would fit these priests admirably for the great task. Their duties would be first, to study the language and people, acquiring a sympathy for them; secondly, to prepare sermons and instructions. In caring for foreigners of their dioceses some few bishops and individual members of Religious Orders have adopted this plan with excellent results. In New York State there are 600,000 Italians. In the city of Philadelphia there are over 100,000. Naturally in these large centers the greatest number of workers will be required. While each organization and body looks on its own interests and strives to impress on others the importance or its claims, seeking help to carry on its propaganda, all of which is permissible and commendable, yet the great and vital interests of the entire Church in the United States must not be lost sight of. All should be willing to bear their share of the burden.

# ❦·115·❧

# The American Mission of
# Frances Xavier Cabrini

## JAMES J. WALSH

Rome was not always content with the development of the American Church. In the case of the first, mainly male, Italian immigrants, the Pope was fearful that without attention of a culturally familiar kind, they would fall away from the faith. In 1889, Leo XIII sent Mother Frances Xavier Cabrini to provide welfare for the immigrants and to sustain their faith. Despite an initial rebuff from Archbishop Corrigan of New York, she eventually established schools, orphanages and charitable hospitals across the country.

═══════════════════════════════

If ever there was a social problem so complex as to seem almost hopelessly insoluble and so many-sided as to perplex and bewilder the best intentioned, it was the welfare of the Italian immigrant in this country during the past twenty-five years. Not only schools for the poor were needed, but for the better classes as well, where they might find sympathy with their national aspirations and character; hospitals also were necessary to prevent the pitiable condition of sufferers coming to dispensaries and city hospitals with little or no knowledge of English and subject to being unfortunately misunderstood to their own detriment. The hard manual labor in which their fathers were engaged, involved numerous accidents, left many orphan children to be cared for, and in a thousand other ways also, these willing workers bearing so many difficult burdens of the country, demanded sympathetic assistance. The question was where would one begin, and having begun how carry on and diffuse any social work widely enough to cover these needs not alone in the coast cities of the East, but everywhere where the Italian immigrant had gone or had been brought by others.

Many people, even Catholics, feel that very little has been done, especially by Catholics, for the solution of this vast problem, although it mainly concerns our Italian Catholic brethren. Such a thought, however, betrays ignorance of an

Source: James J. Walsh, 'The American Mission of Frances Xavier Cabrini',
*The Catholic World*, April 1918.

immense work that has been developing around us during the last twenty years. The recent death of Mother Frances Xavier Cabrini at the Columbus Hospital, Chicago (December, 1917), has emphatically called attention to the fine results secured in this important matter by her congregation of the Missionary Sisters of the Sacred Heart. Not quite seventy when she died, she had established over seventy houses of her religious. Her institute, less than forty years old, numbers its members by thousands. From Italy, where her foundation was made, it has spread to North, South and Central America, as well as France, Spain and England. No wonder that at her death, she was honoured by those who knew her work as a modern apostle whose influence for good proved that the arm of the Lord had not been shortened: that He still raised up great personalities to meet the special needs of the Church in all generations.

Mother Frances Xavier Cabrini was born at St. Angelo di Lodi, July 16, 1850. Her parents belonged to the Italian nobility. From her early years she gave evidence of devout piety, and at the age of thirty undertook the organization of a congregation that would devote itself to teaching especially the children of the poor and of training school teachers. Her first house was founded at Codogno in 1880. A series of houses sprang up, during the following years, in and around Milan, and her work having attracted the attention of Leo XIII., she was invited to open a Pontifical School at Rome. This succeeded so admirably, that the Pope saw in it a great agency for the benefit of Italians all over the world. This great Pontiff had been very much attracted by Mother Cabrini's character and her enthusiastic zeal, which overcame obstacles that to many seemed insurmountable.

Accordingly when the foreign missionary spirit developed among her Sisters, Mother Cabrini, knowing the blessing that always accrued to a congregation for missionary work, applied to the Pope for permission to send her Sisters into the Orient. Pope Leo suggested that her mission lay in exactly the opposite direction. He recommended the Americas, North and South, as a fertile field for the labors of the Missionary Sisters of the Sacred Heart. Mother Cabrini receiving the suggestion as a command from God, proceeded to carry it out. A few months later she embarked for America with her Sisters, and assumed charge of a school for the children of Italian immigrants which was opened in New York in connection with the Church of St. Joachim.

Immigration was then at its height, the social problems of the Italians were at a climax, Americans had scarcely awakened to the need of doing anything, the Italian government was aroused to the necessity of accomplishing something, but politics were blocking the way, and it looked as though a little band of Italian Sisters could accomplish very little. Yet in a few years it became evident that this mustard seed was destined to grow into a large tree whose branches would shelter the birds of the air.

Mother Cabrini very soon realized that despite the importance of teaching, there were other crying needs of our Italian population that must be met if there was to be a solid foundation for the solution of social problems among them. Ailing and injured Italians needed the care that could properly be given them only by their own. Seeing in the celebration of the five hundredth anniversary of the discovery of America by Columbus, then impending, an auspicious moment, Mother Cabrini, in 1892, opened Columbus Hospital in New York. It had an extremely humble beginning in two private houses and with such slender support as would surely have discouraged anything less than the zeal of this foundress, convinced that she was doing God's work on a mission indicated by the Pope himself. Before long, the fortunes of the hospital began to brighten, until now it is one of the recognized institutions in New York, situated in a commodious building that brings it conspicuously to the notice of New Yorkers. Before the outbreak of the War [World War I], plans had been drawn for a ten-story building which should have been finished before this, and would have been one of the most complete hospitals in the country.

But Columbus Hospital was only the beginning. Mother Cabrini's great work of schools for Italian children of the poorer and better classes, was not neglected, but it was now evident that hospitals offered the best chance to win back adult Italians who had abandoned their faith and to influence deeply those who could be brought in no other way under Christian influences. After an Italian had been under the care of these devoted Italian Sisters, it was, indeed, hard for him to neglect his religion as before, and many a family returned to the devout practice of the faith when the father had had his eyes opened to the practical virtues of religion by his stay in the hospital. Hence, in 1905, Columbus Hospital, Chicago, was founded under extremely difficult conditions. For some time the failure of this enterprise seemed almost inevitable, and Reverend Mother Cabrini's heart was heavy at the prospect of her beloved poor deprived of skilled care. She did not lose courage, however, and she was rewarded, after a particularly trying time in which her greatest consolation and help was prayer, by the assured future of the hospital.

A little later, a branch hospital known as Columbus Extension Hospital, was established for the very poor in the heart of an Italian district in Chicago, at Lytle and Polk Streets. Five years later, Columbus Hospital and Sanitarium in Denver was founded and a few years later Columbus Hospital, Seattle. All of these were in excellent condition, with abundant promise of future usefulness, and healthy development at the time of Mother Cabrini's death. This holy woman brought to the service of her zeal for religion such good sound common sense and business acumen and efficiency, as to call forth the admiration of all who knew her and who realized what she was accomplishing in the face of unlooked-for and almost insurmountable difficulties. . . .

At the time of her death there were, as we had said, more houses of her Congregation than she counted years, though her work as a foundress had not begun until nearly half of her life was run. It is said that as a young woman she had in her zeal for missionary labor asked her confessor for permission to join an order of missionary sisters that would take her far from home, so that home ties should count for little in life, and should surely not disturb her complete devotion to her vocation. Her confessor replied that he knew of none. There were no missionary sisters in the strict sense of the word and so Mother Cabrini founded the Congregation of the Missionary Sisters of the Sacred Heart, which has flourished so marvelously. . . .

Everywhere she emphasized the Italian origin and spirit of her work. No wonder then that the Ambassador from Italy deeply concerned with the problem of making Italian people here as happy and contented as possible, but above all of keeping them from being imposed upon in any way, called her his "precious collaborator." "While I may be able to conserve the interests of the Italians," he said, "by what I am able to accomplish through those who are in power, she succeeds in making herself loved and esteemed by the suffering, the poor, the children, and thus preserves these poor Italians in a foreign country."

In spite of her devoted Italian sentiments, she drew her postulants from practically every nationality in the country. Many an Irish girl, after looking into Mother Cabrini's wonderful eyes, felt it her vocation to help this wonderful little woman in the work she had in hand. She won all hearts to herself, but only for the sake of the Master, and so it is that in the course of scarcely more than twenty-five years, her Congregation counts nearly five hundred members here in America. It has some three thousand throughout the world, all intent on accomplishing the social work that has been placed in their care, and of solving the problems brought about by the huge Italian immigration to the Americas in the eighties and nineties of the last century.

When the Italians entered the War, Mother Cabrini, by cable, mobilized her Sisters in Italy for the aid of their native country in every way possible. The houses of the Congregation were transformed into hospitals and refuges for the convalescent, as well as asylums for the sons and daughters of those who had fallen on the field of battle. Her devotion to her Italian people was so great, *Il Carroccio*, or as it is called in English, *The Italian Review*, published in New York, compares her to Florence Nightingale, for what she has accomplished both in peace and in war. Nor may anyone who knows all the circumstances of her work, deny that the comparison is more than justified.

# ❧116❧

# The Poles

## PETER ROBERTS

Polish Catholic immigrants were renowned for the fervour of their religion. In their homeland, the Church had been the core of their nationality under Russian rule. It remained central to maintaining their cohesiveness as a group in the New World. Hence the institutional density of the Poles as a religious community.

---

In Polish-American society the parish is the center of community life, but the formation of the colony precedes the formation of the parish. Wherever Poles are collected for work, other Poles join them from the old country, and the colony grows spontaneously. The first organization is a mutual aid society. It is only when the colony has grown in numbers that a priest is called. But when the parish is established in America, it has a much larger social function than it has in Poland. It assumes, to a degree, the character of a commune.

139. Just as the benefit society is much more than a mutual insurance company, so the Polish-American parish is much more than a religious association for common worship under the leadership of a priest. The unique power of the parish in Polish-American life, much greater than in even the most conservative peasant communities in Poland, cannot be explained by the predominance of religious interests, which, like all other traditional social attitudes, are weakened by emigration, though they seem to be the last to disappear completely. The parish is, indeed, simply the old primary community reorganized and concentrated. In its concrete totality it is a substitute for both the narrower but more coherent village group and the wider but more diffuse and vaguely outlined *okolica*. In its institutional organization it performs the functions which in Poland are fulfilled by both the parish and the commune. It does not control the life of its members as efficiently as did the old community, for, first of all, it seldom covers a given territory entirely and is unable to compel everyone living within this territory to belong to it; secondly, its stock of socially recognized rules and forms of behavior is much poorer; thirdly, the attitudes of its members evolve too rapidly in the new conditions; finally, it has no backing for its coercive measures in the wider society of which it is part. But its activities are much broader and more complex than those of a parish or of a commune in the old country.[1]

Source: Peter Roberts, 'The Poles', *The New Immigration*, New York, 1912, pp. 211-19.

40

The priest and the parish committee are careful to select a site for the church as close as possible to the centres where Poles work, and in a locality where rent is low and land is cheap. There follows a further territorial concentration of Poles. The original population—Italians, Germans, Irish—slowly moves out as the neighborhood becomes predominantly Polish. The parish thus becomes the community. Polish business is developed, associations of the type enumerated in document 140 are formed, affording their members economic advantages, social entertainment, a field for economic co-operation, educational opportunities, help in expressing and realizing their political ideals, and a congenial social milieu in which the desires for recognition and response are satisfied. Even Poles who are not religious are thus drawn into the parish institutions.

The following document, 140, is an enumeration of the organizations connected with the largest Polish parish in America—St. Stanislaw Kostka, in Chicago; document 141 characterizes one of these organizations.

140. Zuaves of St. Stanislaw Kostka; Society of the Virgins of the Holy Rosary; Brotherhood of the Young Men of St. Joseph; Citizens' Club of Thaddeus Kosciuszko; Theater and Dramatic Club; the Parochial School; the Parish Committee; the Association of Altar Boys; the Marshals of the Lower Church; the Arch-sorority of the Immaculate Heart of Mary (two groups); the Women of the Holy Rosary (four groups) the Arch-brotherhood of the Saints; the Third Order of St. Francis; the Choirs of the Upper Church; the Choirs of the Lower Church; the Club of Ladies of Queen Labrowska; the Society of the Alumni of the Parish School; the Musical and Literary Society of Leo XIII; the Needlework Club of St. Rose of Lima; the Polish Roman Catholic Union (central office); the Society of St. Cecilia (No. 14 of the R. C. Union); the Society of King John III Sobieski under the patronage of the Most Holy Virgin Mary; Queen of the Polish Crown (No. 16 of the R. C. Union); the Society of the Most Holy Name of Mary (No. 2 of the R. C. Union); the Society of St. Stanislaw the Bishop (No. 31 of the R. C. Union); the Society of St. Walenty (No. 847 of the R. C. Union); the Society of the Heart of Jesus (No. 32 of the R. C. Union); the Society of St. Stefan (No. 318 of the R. C. Union); the Society of St. Nicolas (No. 42 of the R. C. Union); the Society of Polish Women of God's Mother of Czestochowa (No. 53 of the R. C. Union); the Society of Priest Wincenty Barzynski (No. 91 of the R. C. Union); the Society of Polish Women of St. Cecilia (No. 219 of the R. C. Union); the Society of St. Bernard the Abbot (No. 320 of the R. C. Union); the Society of St. Andrew the Apostle (No. 233 of the R. C. Union); the Society of Polish Women of St. Agnes (No. 256 of the R. C. Union); the Society of the Polish Crown (No 296 of the R. C. Union); the Society of Polish Women of St. Lucia (No. 378 of the R. C. Union); the Society of Polish Women of St. Anna (No. 480 of the R. C. Union); the Society of Polish Women of St. Apolonia (No. 482 of the R. C. Union); the Society of St. Helena (No.924 of the R. C. Union); the Society of Polish Women of Queen Wanda (No. 525 of the R, C. Union); the Polish Alma Mater (central office); the Branch of St. Kazimierz the King's Son (No. 1 of the Alma Mater); the Branch of St. Kinga (No. 12 of the Alma Mater); the Branch of St. Monica (No. 25 of the Alma Mater); the Branch of St. Clara (No. 26 of the Alma Mater); the Branch of St. Cecilia (No. 92 of the Alma Mater); the Branch of St. Joseph (No. 49 of the Alma Mater); the Court of Pulaski (No. 482 of the Union of Catholic Foresters); the Court of God's Mother of Good Advice (No. 91 of Catholic Foresters); the Court of St. Vincent of Ferrara (No.

174 of Catholic Foresters); the Court of St. Stanislaw Kosta (No. 255 of Catholic Foresters); the Court of Priest Barzynski (No. 995 of Catholic Foresters); the Court of St. Walenty (No. 1,001 of Catholic Foresters); the Court of St. Irene (No. 445 of Catholic Foresters); the Court of Frederic Chopin (No. 1,391 of Catholic Foresters); the Court of St. John (No. 864 of Catholic Foresters); the Court of Leo XIII (No. [?] of Catholic Foresters); the court of St. Martin the Pope (No. 1,143 of Catholic Foresters); the Society of the Guardianship of St. Joseph (Group 115 of the Polish Association in America); the Society of St. George the Martyr (Group 96 of the Polish Association); the Society of St. Roch (Group 71 of the Polish Association); the Society of St. John of Nepomuk (Group 26 of the Polish Association); the Society of the Heart of Jesus (Group 124 of the Polish Association); the Society Pearl of Mary (Group 152 of the Polish Association); the Society of St. Wojcieck (Group 104 of the Polish Association); the Society of Young Men of St. Kazimierz (Independent Mutual Help Association); the Society of Ladies of Queen Jadwiga (Mutual Help Association); the Loan and Savings Association of St. Joseph No. 3; the Building Loan and Savings Association of Pulaski; the Building Loan and Savings Association of St. Francis; the Press Committee; the College of St. Stanislaw Kostka; the Novice's Convent of the Resurrectionist; the Convent of the Sisters of St. Francis; the Chicago *Daily News* (Polish)—74 in all.[2]

141. *Zuaves of St. Stanislaus Kostka.*The Zuaves were organized into an association May 1, 1915, by Rev. Franciszek Dembinski, the present rector of the parish. They wear uniforms, helmets, and swords on the model of the Papal Guard in the Vatican. These little knights participate in large celebrations like New Year's, the Forty Hours' Divine Service, Pentecost, Christmas, the first communion of the school children: they stand on guard at the grave of Lord Jesus (before Easter), take part in the processions on Easter and Corpus Christi. The Zuaves drill in the school courtyard. The drill is taught by the well-known captain of the Cavalry of Stanislaw, Mr. Franciszek Gorzynski. The Zuaves are composed of thirty members chosen from the Society of Altar Boys.... They are sons of parents who have belonged to the parish for many years and have been educated in the parochial school. They are obliged to shine as models of devotion, to partake regularly of the Holy Sacraments and thereby to be sons of their dear parents, to know the history of their ancestors, the great men of Poland, to talk Polish among themselves and at home. In a word, the Zuaves are expected to be the guardians of everything that is divine and Polish in order to grow to be real Polish patriots and defenders of the Christian faith. [Picture of the group and names of the members given.][3]

Document 142 illustrates the formation of a small parish, and document 143 shows the condition of the same parish after twenty-five years, under the leadership of an exceptionally energetic priest.

142. The first Pole who came to New Britain was Mr. Tomasz Ostrowski. After him others began to arrive and in September, 1889, a mutual help society under the patronage of St. Michael the Archangel was established. [All the officers enumerated....] In 1894 Priest Dr. Misicki, rector of the parish in Meriden, Connecticut, came every Sunday to celebrate the holy mass in New Britain in the old Irish church in Myrtle Street, at a yearly salary of $500. Then the society, together with other noble-minded Poles, began to think about the establishing a Polish parish, which was organized under the patronage of St. Kazimierz....

In September, 1895, Rev. Lucyan Bójnowski.... was appointed rector of the parish.... and a wooden church was built under the patronage of the Sweetest Heart of Jesus.... First of all Priest Bójnowski made efforts to turn the people from drink, from getting married in court, from indecent dress, from holding balls on Saturdays and nightly revelries, from playing cards, loafing in saloons, fighting in their homes, immoral life, conjugal infidelity, theft, bad education of children, indecent behavior on the street, and disorderly conduct at weddings and christenings. Instead, he encouraged them to go to confession and communion, to participate in various divine services, to belong to fraternities, etc....[4]

143.(1) The old church now contains schoolrooms and the rectorate. It is worth $25,000. (2) The new church (the largest in New Britain) cost $150,000 when built, and is now worth $300,000. (3) The new school was built in 1904 at the cost of $150,000. It is now worth twice as much. (4) A house for the teaching nuns is worth $15,000. The parish has a cemetery worth $25,000. There are no debts on all these buildings and lots. (6) In 1889 a co-operative bakery was established with an original capital of $6,000 contributed by 5 associations. At present its property is worth $60,000. (7) In 1904 a Polish orphanage was founded. It owns now 4 houses, 146 acres within the limits of the town, 107 acres outside the limits, 30 head of cattle, 7 horses, 70 hogs, 500 hens; total value over $200,000. No debts. (8) There is a parochial printing office. The lot, the building, and the machinery are worth $35,000. There is a debt of $5,000. (9) The Polish Loan and Industrial Corporation, founded in 1915, has a capitalization of $50,000, and owns $45,000 worth of houses. (10) The Polish Investment and Loan Corporation, founded in 1915, has a capitalization of $75,000, and real estate worth $10,000. (11) The People's Savings Bank, founded in December, 1916, has $496,000 deposited. (12) The New Britain Clothing Corporation, founded in 1919, capitalized at $50,000, has merchandise worth $100,000 and real estate worth $140,000. (13) The White Eagle Factory, established in 1919, capitalized at $25,000, produces cutlery. All of the above are co-operative organizations. (14) We gave 750 soldiers to the American army and 301 to the Polish army. (15) We have contributed to the Polish Relief Fund and to the Polish Army Fund, up to this moment, $110,672.36. (16) The parish counts now nearly 9,000 souls, including children. In 1894 there were only 700, counting Lithuanians, Slovaks, and Poles. (17) The parochial school has 35 teachers and an attendance of 1,736 children.

## Notes

1. Florian Znaniecki, *Study of Polish Institutions in America*, (manuscript).
2. Listed and described in *Album Pamiatkowe z Okazyi Zlotego Jubileuszy Parafii Sw. Stanislawa Kostka* (Memorial Album of the Celebration of the Golden Jubilee of the Parish of St. Stanislaus Kostka.
3. Album of the Parish of St. Stanislaus Kostka, p. 95.
4. From a history of the parish of New Britain, written by Priest Bójnowski, and published in 1902.

# ❧117❧

# Perils—Romanism

## JOSIAH STRONG

The presence of a growing Catholic population prompted a resurgence of anti-Catholicism amid charges that loyalty to Rome was in contradiction to attachment to American principles and ways. This hostility was expressed both in organizations favouring restriction of immigration, like the American Protective Association, and in efforts to maintain Protestant dominance, particularly in the swelling cities. Josiah Strong (1847–1916), as a well-known publicist and, from 1886, General Secretary of the Evangelical Alliance, was prominent in portraying Catholicism as an element in the social crisis which could only be met by a socially and politically progressive inter-denominational Protestantism.

---

## I

We have made a brief comparison of some of the fundamental principles of Romanism with those of the Republic. And,

1. We have seen the supreme sovereignty of the Pope opposed to the sovereignty of the people.

2. We have seen that the commands of the Pope, instead of the constitution and laws of the land, demand the highest allegiance of the Roman Catholics in the United States.

3. We have seen that the alien Romanist who seeks citizenship swears true obedience to the Pope instead of "renouncing forever all allegiance to any foreign prince, potentate, state or sovereignty," as required by our laws.

4. We have seen that Romanism teaches religious intolerance instead of religious liberty.

5. We have seen that Rome demands the censorship of ideas and of the press, instead of the freedom of the press and of speech.

6. We have seen that she approves the union of church and state instead of their entire separation.

7. We have seen that she is opposed to our public school system.

Source: Josiah Strong, 'Perils—Romanism', *Our Country*, New York, 1885, (1963 ed.)
pp. 73–80.

Manifestly there is an irreconcilable difference between papal principles and the fundamental principles of our free institutions. Popular government is self-government. A nation is capable of self-government only as far as the individuals who compose it are capable of self-government. To place one's conscience, therefore, in the keeping of another, and to disavow all personal responsibility in obeying the dictation of another, is as far as possible from *self*-government, and, therefore, wholly inconsistent with republican institutions, and, if sufficiently common, dangerous to their stability. It is the theory of absolutism in the state that man exists for the state. It is the theory of absolutism in the church that man exists for the church. But in republican and Protestant America it is believed that church and state exist for the people and are to be administered by them. Our fundamental ideas of society, therefore, are as radically opposed to Vaticanism as to imperialism, and it is as inconsistent with our liberties for Americans to yield allegiance to the Pope as to the Czar. It is true the Third Plenary Council in Baltimore denied that there is any antagonism between the laws, institutions and spirit of the Roman church and those of our country, and in so doing illustrated the French proverb that "To deny is to confess." No Protestant church makes any such denials.

History fully justifies the teaching of philosophers that civil and political society tends to take the form of religious society. Absolutism in religion cannot fail in time to have an undermining influence on political equality. Already do we see its baneful influence in our large cities. It is for the most part the voters who accept absolutism in their faith who accept the dictation of their petty political popes, and suffer themselves to be led to the polls like so many sheep.

Says the eminent Professor de Laveleye: "To-day we can prove to demonstration that which men of intellect in the eighteenth century were only beginning to perceive. The decisive influence which forms of worship bring to bear on political life and political economy had not hitherto been apparent. Now it breaks forth in the light, and is more and more closely seen in contemporary events." "Representative government is the natural government of Protestant populations. Despotic government is the congenial government of Catholic populations."

## II

Look now very briefly at the attitude or purpose of Romanism in this country. In an encyclical letter of November 7, 1885, Leo XIII., as reported by cable to the *New York Herald*, said: "We exhort all Catholics to devote careful attention to public matters, and take part in all municipal affairs and elections, and all public services, meetings and gatherings. All Catholics must make themselves felt as active elements in daily political life in countries where they live. All Catholics should exert their power to cause the constitutions of states to be modeled on the principles of the true church." "If Catholics are idle," says the same Pope, "the reins of power will easily be gained by persons whose opinions can surely afford little prospect of welfare. Hence, Catholics have just reason to enter into political life; . . . having in mind the purpose of introducing the wholesome life-blood of Catholic wisdom and virtue into the whole system of the state. All Catholics who are worthy of the name must. . . . work to the end, that every state be made conformable to the Christian model we have described." That Catholic authority, Dr. Brownson, in his Review for July, 1864, declared: "Undoubtedly it is the intention of the Pope to possess this country. In this intention he is aided by the Jesuits and all the Catholic prelates and priests." And in some cases expectation is as eager as desire. Father Hecker in his last work, published in 1887, says, "The Catholics will out-number, before the close of this century, all other believers in Christianity put together in the republic."

## III

Many of our Roman Catholic fellow citizens undoubtedly love the country, and believe that in seeking to Romanize it they are serving its highest interests, but when we remember, as has been shown, that the fundamental principles of Romanism are opposed to those of the Republic, that the difference between them does not admit of adjustment, but is diametric and utter, it becomes evident that it would be *impossible to "make America Catholic,"* (which the archbishop of St. Paul declared at the late Baltimore Congress to be the mission of Roman Catholics in this country) *without bringing the principles of that church into active conflict with those of our government, thus compelling Roman Catholics to choose between them, and in that event, every Romanist who remained obedient to the Pope, that is, who continued to be a Romanist, would necessarily become disloyal to our free institutions.*

## IV

It is said, and truly, that there are two types of Roman Catholics in the United States. They may be distinguished as those who are "more Catholic than Roman," and those who are "more Roman than Catholic." The former have felt the influence of modern thought, have been liberalized, and come into a large measure of sympathy with American institutions. Many are disposed to think that men of this class will control the Roman church in this country and already talk of an "American Catholic Church." But there is no such thing as an American or Mexican or Spanish Catholic Church. It is the Roman Catholic Church in America, Mexico and Spain, having one and the same head, whose word is law, as absolute and as unquestioned among Roman Catholics here as in Spain or Mexico. "The archbishops and bishops of the United States, in Third Plenary Council assembled," in their Pastoral Letter "to their clergy and faithful people," declare: "We glory that we are, and, with God's blessing, shall continue to be, not the American Church, nor the Church in the United states, nor a Church in any other sense, exclusive or limited, but an integral part of the one, holy, Catholic and Apostolic Church of Jesus Christ."

The Roman Catholics of the United States have repudiated none of the utterances of Leo XIII. or of Pius IX., nor have they declared their political independence of the Vatican. On the contrary, the most liberal leaders of the church here vehemently affirm their enthusiastic loyalty to the Pope. The Pastoral Letter issued by the Third Plenary Council of Baltimore (December 7, 1884), and signed by Cardinal Gibbons, "In his own name and in the name of all the Fathers," says: "Nor are there in the world more devoted adherents of the Catholic Church, the See of Peter, and the Vicar of Christ, than the Catholics of the United States." Says a writer on the recent Roman Catholic Congress at Baltimore: "It was well that Masonic pseudo-Catholics, compromisers of the papal authority, persecutors of the clergy, anti-jesuits, social revolutionalists, legal robber of church property, lay educationalists, anti-clericals, should learn once for all, that the *Catholic laymen of America are proud of being pro-papal without compromise*; that they are proud of the Jesuits from those chaste loins the church in the United States drew its vigorous life." This writer is not quoted as a representative of moderate Romanism, but, as one who very justly expresses the sentiment of loyalty to the Pope, which characterized the Baltimore Congress, and which, so far as we can judge, was shared by all alike.

It is undoubtedly safe to say that there is not a member of the hierarchy in America, who does not accept the infallibility of the Pope and who has not sworn to obey him. Now this dogma of papal infallibility as defined by the Vatican Council and interpreted by Puis IX. and Leo XIII. carries with it logically all of the fundamental principles of Romanism which have been discussed. Infallibility is necessarily intolerant. It can no more compromise with a conflicting opinion than could a mathematical demonstration. Truth cannot make concessions to error. Infallibility represents absolute truth. It is as absolute as God himself, and can no more enter into compromise than God can compromise with sin. And if infallibility is as intolerant as the truth, it is also as authoritative. Truth may be rejected, but even on the scaffold it is king, and has the right and always must have the right to rule absolutely, to control utterly every reasoning being. If I believed the Pope to be the infallible vicar of Christ, I would surrender myself to him as unreservedly as to God himself. How can a true Roman Catholic do otherwise? A man may have breathed the air of the nineteenth century and of free America, enough to be out of sympathy with the absolutism and intolerance of Romanism, but if he accepts the Pope's right to dictate his beliefs and acts, of what avail are his liberal sympathies? He is simply the instrument of the absolute and intolerant papal will. His sympathies can assert themselves and control his life only as he breaks with the Pope, that is, ceases to be a Roman Catholic. I fear we have little ground to expect that many would thus break with the Pope, were a distinct issue raised. Everyone born a Roman Catholic is suckled on authority. His training affects every fiber of his mental constitution. He has been taught that he must not judge for himself, nor trust to his own convictions. If he finds his sympathies, his judgement and convictions conflict with a papal decree, it is the perfectly natural result of his training for him to distrust himself. His will, accustomed all his life to yield to authority without question, is not equal to the conflict that would follow disobedience. How can he withstand a power able to inflict most serious punishment in this life, and infinite penalties in the next? Only now and then will one resist and suffer the consequences, in the spirit of the Captain in Beaumont and Fletcher's poem "The Sea Voyage." Juletta tells the Captain and his company:

"Why, slaves, 'tis in our power to hang ye."

The Captain replies:

"Very likely, 'Tis in our powers, then, to be hanged and scorn ye."

Modern times afford an excellent illustration of what may be expected when liberal prelates, strongly opposed to ultramontanism, are brought to the crucial test. Many members of the Vatican Council (1870) vigorously withstood the dogma of papal infallibility, among who, says Professor Schaff, "were the prelates most distinguished for learning and position." Many of them spoke and wrote against the dogma. Archbishop Kendrick, of St. Louis published in Naples an "irrefragable argument" against it. The day before the decisive vote was to be taken, more than a hundred bishops and archbishops, members of the opposition, left the council and departed from Rome rather than face defeat. But these moderate and liberal Romanists, including several American prelates who had belonged to the opposition, all submitted, and published to their respective flocks the obnoxious decree which some of them had shown to be contrary to history and to reason. It must be remembered that these men were the most liberal and among the most able in the church. In view of the fact that their opposition thus utterly collapsed, what reason have we to expect that liberal Romanists in this country, who have already assented to the infallibility to the Pope, will ever violate their oath of obedience to him? If the liberality of avowed opponents of ultramontanism yielded to papal authority, what reason is there to think the liberality of avowed ultramontanists will ever resist it?

Moreover it should be borne in mind that the more moderate Roman Catholics in the United States are generally those who in childhood had the benefit of our public schools, and their intelligence and liberality are due chiefly to the training there received. In the public schools they learned to think and were largely Americanized by associating with American children. But their children are being subjected to very different influences in the parochial schools. They are there given a training calculated to make them narrow and bigoted; and, being separated as much as possible from all Protestant children, they grow up suspicious of Protestants, and so thoroughly sectarianized and Romanized as to be well protected against the broadening and Americanizing influences of our civilization in after life.

# The Catholic Publication Society

## WALTER ELLIOTT

Himself a convert to Catholicism, Father Isaac Hecker (1819–1888) became known as one of the most ardent propagandists for Catholicism against what he regarded as the misrepresentation of such as Strong. He fostered a Catholic press and in 1866 founded the Catholic Publication Society whose tracts, in the popular form illustrated below, he used vigorously to assert the Catholic version of the truth.

## The Catholic Publication Society

The Catholic Publication Society was begun a year after *The Catholic World* was started, its aim being to turn to the good of religion, and especially to the conversion of non-Catholics, all the uses the press is capable of. It was a missionary work in the broadest sense seeking to enlist not only the clergy but especially the laity in an organized Apostolate of the Press, to enlighten the faith of Catholics and to spread it among their Protestant fellow-citizens. Its first work was to be the issuing of tracts and pamphlets telling the plain truth about the Catholic religion. Local societies, to be established throughout the country, were to buy these publications at a price less than cost, and to distribute them gratis to all classes likely to be benefited. To catch the eye of the American people, to affect their hearts, to supply their religious wants with Catholic truth, were objects kept in view in preparing the tracts. Although some of them were addressed to Catholics, enforcing important religious duties, nearly all of them were controversial. More than seventy different tracts were printed first and last, and many hundreds of thousands, indeed several millions, of them distributed in all parts of the country, public, charitable, and penal institutions being, of course, fair field for this work. They were all very brief, few of them covering more than four small-sized pages. "Three pages of truth have before now overturned a life-time of error," said Father Hecker. The tract *Is it Honest?* though only four pages

Source: Walter Elliott, 'The Catholic Publication Society', *The Life of Father Hecker*, New York, 1891, pp. 352–4.

of large type, or about twelve hundred words, created a sensation everywhere, and was answered by a Protestant minister with over fifty pages of printed matter, or about fifteen times more than the tract itself. One hundred thousand copies of this tract were distributed in New York City alone. It is printed herewith as a specimen, both as to style and matter, of what one may call the aggressive-defensive tactics in Catholic controversy:

### Is It Honest

*To say the Catholic Church prohibits the use of the Bible—*
When anybody who chooses can buy as many as he likes at any Catholic bookstore, and can see on the first page of any one of them the approbation of the Bishops of the Catholic Church, with the Pope at their head, encouraging Catholics to read the Bible, in these words: "The faithful should be excited to the reading of the Holy Scriptures," and that not only for the Catholics of the United States, but also for those of the whole world besides?

### Is It Honest

*To say that Catholics believe that man by his own power can forgive sin—*
When the priest is regarded by the Catholic Church only as the agent of our Lord Jesus Christ, acting by the power delegated to him, according to these words, "Whose sins you shall forgive, they are forgiven them; and whose sins you shall retain, they are retained?" (St. John xx. 23).

### Is It Honest

*To repeat over and over again that Catholics pay the priest to pardon their sins—*
When such a thing is unheard of anywhere in the Catholic Church—
When any transaction of the kind is stigmatized as a grievous sin, and ranked along with murder, adultery, blasphemy, etc., in every catechism and work on Catholic theology?

### Is It Honest

*To persist in saying that Catholics believe their sins are forgiven merely by the confession of them to the priest, without a true sorrow for them, or a true purpose to quit them—*
When every child finds the contrary distinctly and clearly stated in the catechism, which he is obliged to learn before he can be admitted to the sacraments? Any honest man can verify this statement by examining any Catholic catechism.

### Is It Honest

*To assert that the Catholic Church grants any indulgence or permission to commit sin—*
When an "indulgence," according to her universally received doctrine, was never dreamed of by Catholics to imply, in any case whatever, any permission to commit the least sin: and when an indulgence has no application whatever to sin until after sin has been repented of and pardoned?

### Is It Honest

*To accuse Catholics of putting the Blessed Virgin or the Saints in the place of God or the Lord Jesus Christ—*

When the Council of Trent declares that it is simply useful to ask their intercession in order to obtain favor from God, through his Son, Jesus Christ our Lord, who alone is our Saviour and Redeemer—

When "asking their prayers and influence with God" is exactly of the same nature as when Christians ask the pious prayers of one another?

## Is It Honest

*To accuse Catholics of paying divine worship to images or pictures, as the heathen do—*

When every Catholic indignantly repudiates any idea of the kind, and when the Council of Trent distinctly declares the doctrine of the Catholic Church in regard to them to be, "that there is no divinity or virtue in them which should appear to claim the tribute of one's veneration"; but that "all the honor which is paid to them shall be referred to the originals whom they are designed to represent?" (Sess. 25).

## Is It Honest

*To make these and many other similar charges against Catholics—*

When they detest and abhor such false doctrines more than those do who make them, and make them, too, without ever having read a Catholic book, or taken any honest means of ascertaining the doctrines which the Catholic Church really teaches?

Remember the commandment of God, which says: "Thou shalt not bear false witness against thy neighbor."

Reader, would you be honest, and do no injustice? Then examine the doctrines of the Catholic Church; read the works of Catholics. See both sides. Examine, and be fair; for AMERICANS LOVE FAIR PLAY.

# ⟨119⟩

# Church, State and School

## JOSEPH V. TRACY

A common accusation by critics of Catholicism in the United States was that Catholics wished to overturn the constitutional separation of Church and State and that, in creating religious schools, the Church separated the faithful from the values of the common school system in which American citizenship was grounded. Here is an attempt, from 1890, to put in a clear light the Catholic conception of the relationship between Church and State and, in justification of separate schools, the purpose of education.

---

The idea of complete separation of the state from religion is something worthy of careful consideration. Imagine a state appealing to is citizens upon the grounds altogether unreligious! The best thing in the way of motive the civil organism can present is "the general good." The general good is a purely negative quality; namely, securing the conditions without which happiness would be out of the question. And if this be the secular power's highest motive, its greatest sanction is on the side of reward, civil protection, worldly prosperity; and on the side of punishment, reformatories, jails and scaffolds. Imagine a society made up of men into whose lives, *as citizens*, no other motive nor sanction but these entered! It is not easy to form the concept of, in Mallock's word, a thoroughly *dereligionized* state. Such, however, would be one entirely separated from religion. The fact is that the motives and sanctions of religion are those which most move men in the right-minded fulfilment of civic duties. "Man's primary duty is towards God; his secondary duty is towards his brother-men; and it is only from the filial relation that the fraternal springs." On this fraternity the Christian state is based. The union between church and state which the Catholic Church reaches out for, and the separation of them which she condemns, were well summarized by Dr. Brownson in this magazine, May, 1870:

> For ourselves, we are partial to our American system, which, unless we are blinded by our national prejudices, comes nearer to the realization of the true union as well as distinction of church and state than has hitherto or elsewhere

Source: Joseph V. Tracy, 'Church, State and School', *The Catholic World*, January 1890.

been effected; and we own we should like to see it, if practicable there, introduced, by lawful means only, into the nations of Europe. The American system may not be practicable in Europe; but, if so, we think it would be an improvement. Foreigners do not generally, nor even do all Americans themselves, fully understand the relation of church and state as it really subsists in the fundamental constitution of American society. Abroad and at home there is a strong disposition to interpret it by the theory of European liberalism, and both they who defend and they who oppose the union of church and state regard it as based on their total separation. But the reverse of this, as we understand it, is the fact. American society is based on the principle of their union; and union, while it implies distinction, denies separation. Modern infidelity, or secularism, is no doubt, at work here as elsewhere to effect their separation; but as yet the two orders are distinct, each with its distinct organization, sphere of action, representative, functions, but not separate. Here the rights of neither are held to be grants from the other. The rights of the church are not franchises or concessions from the state, but are recognized by the state as held under a higher law than its own, and therefore rights prior to and above itself, which it is bound by the law constituting it to respect, obey, and, whenever necessary, to use its physical force to protect and vindicate. . . . We note here that this view condemns alike the absorption of the state in the church, and the absorption of the church in the state, and requires each to remain distinct from the other, each with its own organization, organs, faculties, and sphere of action. It favors, therefore, neither what is called theocracy, or clerocracy, rather, to which Calvinistic Protestantism is strongly inclined, nor the supremacy of the state, to which the age tends, and which was assumed in all the states of gentile antiquity, whence came the persecutions of Christians by pagan emperors. We note further that the church does not make the law; she only promulgates, declares, and applies it, and is herself as much bound by it as the state itself. The law itself is prescribed for the government of all men and nations by God himself as Supreme Lawgiver, or the end or final cause of creation, and binds equally states and individuals, churchmen and statesmen, sovereigns and subjects. Such, as we have learnt it, is the Catholic doctrine of the relation of church and state, and such is the relation that in the divine order really exists between the two orders, and which the church has always and everywhere labored with all her zeal and energy to introduce and maintain in society.

Many well-meaning non-Catholics think that an establishment, or concordat, or agreement by which church authorities should hold secular power, constitutes the ideal union which Catholics have longed for. On the contrary, Catholics know that the church was never more wronged than when dealt with as an establishment or tied up by a concordat. In every such case the tendency has been towards the assumption of church control by the civil power. Whatever advantages the church seemed to acquire from these alliances, her deprivation was generally, if not always, far in excess of her gain. Through the middle ages, when it is commonly supposed she possessed greatest civil authority, "she enjoyed not a moment's peace, hardly a truce, and was obliged to maintain an unceasing struggle with the civil authority against its encroachments on the spiritual order, and for her own independence and freedom of action as the Church of God."

These considerations are apt to throw some light on the Catholic aspects of the problem, which, briefly, is that both institutions were intended to act in harmony, each within its distinct province; one looking to man's temporal welfare, the other to his spiritual. Withal, though the province of each to distinct, the proximate—earthly prosperity—must not antagonize the ultimate end of man, happiness hereafter.

The history of civilization tells us the value of religion to society considered apart from its governmental functions. Industry, the arts, the sciences, sanitation, commerce, discovery have received their strongest impulse from her. If there be any advance which man has made in which positive dogmatic religion has had no hand, then that advance is not yet catalogued.

It is, moreover, entirely to the church that society owes the Home, where man finds his purest and completest earthly bliss.

But it is in the moral sphere that the church has rendered society untold benefits. It is popular to speak of religion in one breath and morality in another. Separate them, and what have you on the moral side? At best Utilitarianism. This could no more produce the high standard of actions religious motives put before men than the cracked, kernelless acorn-shell could grow the oak-tree. Sun would shine, rain fall in vain, the germ of life would be wanting. A moral code without inwardness, with a temporary value and without absoluteness, so that it would be within "the competence of any man or all men to alter or abolish it," would certainly be a sorry standard of social virtue, a veritable dummy togged out in "the clothes religion." To such a standard, to this kind of a god alone, has society a right if it be separated from religion.

Still, it has been objected that the union of religion and society tends either to corrupt the former "by debasing the spiritual to the love of luxurious ease, as in the case of the monastic orders," or to disorganize the latter "by proclaiming beggary [voluntary poverty?], the symbol of its ruin, more honored than productive industry." To confuse beggary with voluntary poverty the proximate cause of the greatest philanthropic industries the world has seen, is to outrage language; as well call property theft.

Could such results as those objected come to pass, they would be the effect of pure accident, and could be quoted no more fairly as reason why the church and society should be entirely cut asunder than a child's destructive carelessness in handling matches could be urged as ground sufficient for the prohibition of their manufacture. It is true that "each institution has its essential place and function," but this does not disprove their mutual usefulness. As religion makes of the individual more than a worm of earth, and of his life more than "an idiot's dream," so does it, and must it, lift society up out of the slough of natural satisfactions on to the highlands of spiritual endeavor. If in performing this duty the church would stoop to functions unworthy of itself, or run a risk of debasement, then would it be inherently unfit for the work it was to do; namely, to make the natural a path to that which is above nature and rounds out man's happiness, the divine.

So much by way of introduction to what we have to say of religion and education.

"The ultimate end of education," says Professor Huxley, "is to promote morality and refinement, by teaching men to discipline themselves, and by leading them to see that the highest, as it is the only content, is to be attained not by grovelling in the rank and steaming valleys of sense, but by continually striving towards those high peaks where, resting in eternal calm, reason discerns the undefined but bright idea of the highest good—'a cloud by day, a pillar of fire by night. °" The quotation is pertinent, because it defines the position of the "advanced" scientific school of the day as to the work education should do. This school, of course, regards religion as a detected superstition of no future influence. The work it did is, under the new *regime*, the province of education. The inference is an easy one: granting religion, it and education should go hand-in-hand, since their ultimate end is the same, raising men up out of "the rank and steaming valleys of sense."

In other words, the object of education is the formation of character; character is a matter of principle, of motive; these are subjects of the spiritual order; consequently, they belong to this order's authoritative representative, organized religion. It is begging the question to claim for the state absolute control of education because its own protection and the public good require educated citizens. It has already been shown that for the same reasons the state needs religious citizens. Should it, therefore, usurp a spiritual function?

The core of the matter is, secular society is unable to discharge its proper functions without the co-operation and aid of the spiritual society. Civic virtues no more than personal are the proper effects of purely secular training; uprightness, honesty (except as advantageous policy), fidelity, loyalty, respect for authority are not direct consequences of reading, 'riting, and 'rithmetic. Secular studies are undeniably valuable auxiliaries to spiritual progress, for religion, being a revelation of God, requires an intellectual worshipper. Of all religions the Catholic most thoroughly realized this truth; else why is her history the history of universities? The bearing of knowledge on religious truth is the subject of Dr. Newman's "Eighth Discourse on University Teaching," of which the following extracts are too pertinent to this article's purpose to be omitted:

> It is obvious, [he says] that the first step pastors of the church have to effect in the conversion, of man and the renovation of his nature is his rescue from that fearful subjection to sense which is his ordinary state. To be able to break through the meshes of that thraldom, and to disentangle and disengage its ten thousand holds upon the heart, is to bring it, I might almost say, half-way to heaven. Here even divine grace, to speak of things according to their appearances, is ordinarily baffled, and retires, without expedient or resource, before this giant fascination. Religion seems too high and unearthly to be able to exert a continued influence upon us; its effort to arouse the soul and the soul's effort to co-operate are too violent to last. . . . What we then need is some expedient or instrument which at least will obstruct and stave off the approach of our spiritual enemy, and which is sufficiently congenial and level with our nature to maintain as firm a hold upon us as the inducements of sensual gratification. It will be our wisdom to employ nature against itself. . . . Here, then, I think, is the important aid which intellectual cultivation furnishes to us in rescuing the victims of passion and self-will. It does not supply religious motives; it is not the cause or proper antecedent of anything supernatural; it is not

meritorious of heavenly aid or reward; but it does a work at least materially good (as theologians speak), whatever be its real and former character. It expels the excitements of sense by the introduction of those of the intellect. . . . Nor is this all. Knowledge, the discipline by which it is gained, and the tastes which it forms, have a natural tendency to refine the mind and to give it an indisposition, simply natural, yet real; nay, more than this, a disgust and abhorrence towards excesses.

If the church neglected education, she would deprive herself of the surest means of self-development; for her progress, nay, her existence, if you will, depends on her members having a secular education deficient in not an iota to that which others would possess. Fostering of ignorance by the church would be suicidal. There need be no apprehension that the church will play into the enemies' hands by doing her self what they have been struggling in vain to accomplish time out of mind.

However, to hold that secular schools in which religion is neglected or tabooed are not *godless*, in the sense Catholics use the term, because secular knowledge prepares the way for religious, or because therein truths of nature are taught, and all truth is God's, is quibbling unworthy serious minds. "The truth of mathematics," writes a present-day sophist, "the truth of history, the truth of science, truth anywhere round the globe, is just a word of God; and just in so far as children are taught that truth they are taught religion. . . . At any rate, by taking away from the schools all formal teaching concerning religion, suppose they are *godless*, they are at least harmless as far as they go." The assertion anent "the truth of mathematics," etc., proves altogether too much; namely, the utter impossibility of an atheistical school of science. Unfortunately for the proposition's defender, there have been such schools.

And the trend of "advanced" scientific teaching at present, is it for or against God? Is the whole truth or a half-truth taught when the fundamental principle of things is left as a matter of conjecture, of opinion? If the visible things of the world reveal the invisible, can the explanation of the one be given without any reference to the other? And will such reference be either theistic or atheistic? Such reference *must* be made, or the existence of God treated as an *unnecessary* fact. And is not that just how it is treated? Then how can schools of this complexion be harmless? Can there be a harmless neutral stand in regard to God, or materialism, or positivism?

Moreover, truth as expressed in things or principles, objective truth, apart from its concept by the human mind, is certainly God's truth; nobody questions the declaration that facts are facts. It is with the attempted statement and explanation of phenomena and principles, though with truth as a subjective element; truth modified or corrupted by opinion, and by theory, and by natural bent of disposition and by one-sided mental development, and by dyspepsia, by all the ingredients that go to make up human fallibility—with truth in this sense it is the schools have to do. Consequently, the teaching of truth depends altogether on the view the teachers take of it. Maybe now the adjective *godless* as applied by Catholics to schools distinctively secular may be understood, and the quibble as to its use estimated at its proper worth.

What would be the strongest ground on which the separation of secular and religious studies could be pressed would be that of their inborn incompatibility. Professor Harris, in the *Andover Review*, states the proposition as follows:

> The methods of religious instruction are of necessity different from the methods in secular education. In the secular branches the good method of instruction trains the intellect to keep all its powers awake and alert. The thought must be trained to be critical. The pupil must not take the words of his textbook on faith merely. He must question and verify, demanding proofs and investigating their validity. . . . In religion, on the other hand, faith is the chief organ. . . . Religious truth is revealed in allegoric and symbolic form, having both a literal sense and a spiritual sense. The analytical understanding is necessarily hostile and sceptical in its attitude towards religious truth. But such attitude is entirely appropriate to the study of science and history. It is obvious that the mind must not be changed abruptly from secular studies to religious contemplation. A lesson on religious dogmas just after a lesson in mathematics or physical science has the disadvantage that the mind brings with it the bent or proclivity of the latter study to the serious detriment of the former.

This view of religion and this method of religious criticism and investigation may satisfy a Protestant, but the Catholic church demands thorough rationalness in all religious inquiries. That reason proves the existence of God is with her a dogma; and she lays it down as incontrovertible that the reasoning faculty rightly exercised leads to the Catholic faith. John Henry Newman, on the day of his reception into her fold, wrote to his friend, T. W. Allies: "May I have only one-tenth as much faith as I have intellectual conviction where the truth lies!"

Catholic theology is a development of reasoning on the highest subjects. The acceptance of truths on the properly-tested authority of others (the fundamental principle of revealed religion) is a problem of pure reason. If reason has already demonstrated the existence of God, the fact that he is the authority on which truths are taken as such does not lift the problem out of reason's sphere, when the *fact* of the revelation can be proved by the same criterion as other facts accepted on authority—that is, by the testimony of witnesses qualified to give testimony as to the actual happening itself, no matter what be their qualifications for a right conception or explanation of the happening's meaning.

The man of strong eye-sight is best fitted for fine work at the telescope. Burnham, who by naked eye distinguished double stars which to others seemed a single point of light, with a small telescope discovered hundreds of them that blinked in vain for recognition by lenses twice the size of his. The illustration fits the Catholic Church's position as to the relationship of Reason and Revelation. Reason is the mental eyesight; the clearer, stronger, more critical it is the better use can it make of Revelation, the God-given telescope, by which it looks beyond the stars far into infinity.

While religion is held unable to bear the sharpest scrutiny from legitimate metaphysical inquiry it is belittled, turned into the lawful butt of infidel sarcasm. Hence the self-same methods are fitted for the introduction and guidance of youth in the spiritual as in the natural world of thought and fact. In one, as in the other, the method of imparting knowledge is progressive, proportioned to the age and abilities of the learner. Take the child in the primaries: it learns as it eats, on the authority of an older person declaring what is and what isn't good for it. How absurd to hold that a beginner must assimilate the Rule of Three through an acquaintance with the abstractions of calculus! Why, then, is religion to be taught backwards? A child sees a picture of Bucephalus and Alexander; another of Christ blessing children. For the teacher to state one fact in a method differing from a statement of the other would be an outrage on common sense. There is just as much need in the one case of a *critical* explanation as to why Alexander and his horse are of more interest than John Smith and his donkey as there is in the other case of a *philosophical* inquiry into the mode of union between the two natures in Christ. The facts come first; the realization of their full meaning grows in direct ratio with the development of mental capacity and the acquirement of knowledge. Religion alone, therefore, must not be made for the child a darkened chamber in which mystery and indistinctness overwhelm with awe, and which is sure to be treated as a hobgoblin room of the imagination when reason develops and memory recalls its terrors. On the contrary, the principle that religion is "the light that enlightens every man that cometh into the world" should be acted on. It should be made not the Mystifier, but the Illuminatrix of Reason, which bends the more reverently in worship of God and abasement of itself the more clearly it perceives his unspeakable perfections.

As a corollary to what has been written, it follows that the lesson in the catechism is not what differentiates the Catholic from the secular school. A half-hour daily in Catholic schools of the grammar grade, an hour or two weekly in higher schools, is given to this study. Though this brief time were turned to other use, the Catholic would yet differ *in toto* from the public school. Catechism, as a recitation, is as the other studies, simply an intellectual exercise. The Catholic school, however, has to do with more than the child's intelligence. The public school cannot pretend to train the conscience or will: its province is the intellect and memory, and even here it has to stop short within fixed limits. Beyond this province it may not go without positivizing as to religious truths, and positivize it cannot: it must suit equally infidel, pagan, Jew, Buddhist, Unitarian, Trinitarian, and the rest.

In the Catholic school, on the other hand, all the achievements of the intellect and memory are grouped about a common centre, inasmuch as all have their relations to the interests of Revealed Truth; besides this, a set of principles for the guidance of will-action, as authoritative in their department as the rules of the syllogism in theirs, is acted upon, not merely understood, by teachers and pupils. Hence the different results of the systems.

It remains to ask, Would this "sectarian" teaching bring about a condition of things similar to that of the middle ages, so that the majority might proclaim the profession of other beliefs than its own an overt act of treason? Comparing the nineteenth century with those days, the question bears its absurdity on its face. Anyway, for Catholics Dr. Brownson answered it years ago:

58

This union of church and state [see the first part of this article] supposes nothing like a competency on the part of the state [he is speaking of the American state] to authoritatively declare which church represents the spiritual order. The responsibility of that decision it does and must leave to its citizens, who must decide for themselves and answer to God for the rectitude of their decision. Their decision is law for the state, and it must respect and obey it in the case alike of majorities and minorities; for it recognizes the equal rights of all its citizens and cannot discriminate between them. The church that represents for the state the spiritual order is the church adopted by its citizens; and as they adopt different churches, it can realize and enforce, through the civil courts, the canons and decrees of each only on its own members, and on them only so far as they do not infringe on the equal rights of others.

But if not from a political stand-point, from that of private life would not separate schools beget separation and distrust of fellow-citizens? Since within one's own church are the elect, the loved of God, how can I, his friend, but hate those without, who are his enemies?

In answer to this we have to say that the contact the children in the common schools have with one another is so slight and superficial and short-lived as to be unworthy the exaggerated emphasis now put upon it. Up to the present this contact has rather strengthened than lessened social and religious distinctions, and it has done so in not the pleasantest of ways for both parties concerned. It is to the ties of neighborhood, labor, recreation, business, social equality, literary associations, politics, patriotism, that the spirit of kinship in us all owes its constant sustenance and consequent growth.

Furthermore, why is it to be taken for granted that in parochial schools children are not to be taught patriotically? What an insulting insinuation to Catholic Americans the objection cloaks!

For the Catholic school explicitly or implicitly to inculcate distrust or hatred of neighbors because of religious differences would be for it to contradict every applicable principle of Catholic theology. The Catholic Church was founded for the purpose of benefiting those whom the objector would wish us to style "the enemies of God." No man is God's enemy; it is the sin within a man that comes between himself and his Maker. *Its* destruction is the objective point of Christian endeavor. The church has ever distinguished between the sinner and the sin. Hence her asylums, hospitals, missions, good works of all sorts for the avail of sinners, heretics, and pagans.

The phases of the discussion touched upon in this article, with others of still more practical import, await the future development which from the force of circumstances they must receive. Much as has been written on the school question, the case is as yet but well opened. As the controversy advances Catholics will appreciate more and more the logicalness of the position their church has assumed. It is simply a matter of time and active controversy until the best Protestant opinion swings into line with the church, for right must win, at least in America.

The school movement just now is in a state of being analogous to that of the

Home Rule movement in England a few years since. Wait for half a decade, until the mists of prejudice and sophism have been scattered, and through a clear atmosphere American Christians with their own eyes see the masked spectre of infidelity, which, all unknown, has been making them dance to his music—wait, and see how thoroughly the demon will be "laid"!

# ❧120❧

# The American Nationality

## ANTON WALBURG

An important source of Protestant hostility to Catholic immigrants was fear that they would fragment American nationality. This fear was intensified by the proposal from German Catholic sources that the American Church be organized in ethnic parishes to maintain immigrant loyalty. Anton Walburg, a German immigrant priest in the Middle West, agreed with the proposal but saw it as an expression of 'true Americanism' which would ultimately enrich the content of American nationality.

*Now the broad shield complete, the artist crowned*
*With his last hand, and poured the ocean round;*
*In living silver seemed the waves to roll,*
*And beat the buckler's verge and bound the whole.*

*Westward the course of empire takes its way,*
*The four first acts already past;*
*A fifth shall close the drama of the day,—*
*Time's noblest offspring is the last.*

With regard to Americanism we make a distinction. There is a true and a false Americanism. True Americanism consists in the promotion of the peace, the happiness, and the prosperity of the people, and in the advancement of the public good and the general welfare of the country. As virtue is the principle, and the chief support of a Republic, true Americanism aids and encourages whatever promotes the growth of virtue and morality. It makes no distinction between natives and foreigners, considering all born free and equal, all entitled to the enjoyment of life, liberty, and happiness, and extends the hand of welcome to all nations. There is an analogy between true Americanism and the Catholic Church. She, too, invites all to enter her fold, is established for all nations and all times, and makes no distinction of color, rank, condition, or nationality. And, since the Catholic religion promotes virtue, piety, and

Source: Anton Walburg, 'The American Nationality', *The Question of Nationality in Its Relation to the Catholic Church in the United States*, St. Louis, 1889, pp. 39-62.

morality, true Americanism must desire the growth and spread of the Catholic Church.

False Americanism is a spirit of pride and self-conceit, and looks with contempt upon other nationalities. It is a boasting, arrogant spirit. It glories in the biggest rivers, the tallest trees, the grandest scenery, and considers this country superior to every other country on the face of the globe. It is a pharisaical, hypocritical spirit, putting on the garb of virtue when all is hollowness and rottenness within. It is a spirit of infidelity and materialism. False Americanism is mammon worship. It adores the golden calf and is directed to the accumulation of wealth with ardor which is unquenchable and with an energy which never tires. The eagerness for wealth is paramount and controls every other feeling. The ideal set before every American youth is money. Money is not only needful, but is the one thing needful. Money is a power everywhere, but here it is the supreme power. Abroad, there is the nobility, the pride of ancestry. This is vanity artificial and empty, yet it is not so degrading as money. Abroad, eminent worth counts for something. But here, we acknowledge only one god, and his name is Mammon. Who is the distinguished man in any village, town, city, or metropolis? Is it the learned man, the skilled mechanic, the creative artist, the great lawyer? No! the preference is given to the richest man. No matter how he acquired his wealth, no matter how miserly he is, he is observed, the pointed out, the envied one. All render him homage. The eminent lawyer, the wise physician, the man of learning, show him deference and attention even to the point of servility. This is the great evil of false Americanism, the curse of our society. It is demoralizing us. The hunger and the thirst after money consume like a raging fire all warmer sympathies, all better feelings of our nature. It dwarfs all higher aspirations. What are moral excellence, culture, character, manhood, when money-bags outweigh them all? How can better sentiments be impressed upon the children, when all about them teach them that these are of no value without money? Hence the startling dishonesty in the race for riches. Hence the bribery of officers, the purchase of office, the corruption and jobbery, the general demoralization, that threaten our institutions.

And with its vaunted independence, this spurious Americanism, in its ostentatious display of wealth, stoops to Foreignism, copies European fashions, imports a Parisian cook, and considers itself fortunate to exchange its wealth for the musty title of some needy descendant of the nobility.

In Europe, a man enjoys his competence; but here, no one has enough. No laborer is satisfied with his wages; no millionaire, however colossal his fortune, ceases in his greed for more. From the first dawn of manhood to the evening of old age, the gold fever continues to increase in strength and violence, till death puts an ends to the raging malady.

The American nationality, properly so-called, is the Anglo-Saxon or the Anglo-American nationality, the descendants of early settlers who came from England. These can justly claim the honoroble distinction of being called the American nationality. We were, in the beginning, substantially an English people. The first settlers in this country, the Pilgrim Fathers, were English. They had a long and bloody struggle to maintain against the Indians and suffered untold privations and hardships in effecting a firm and permanent foothold in this country. Notwithstanding all obstacles, the first colonies improved, and by dint of perseverance, courage, and industry, became very prosperous. They resisted British tyranny and oppression. They severed their allegiance to the British crown, declared the United Colonies to be free, independent, and sovereign states, at the same time mutually pledging to each other for the support of this declaration, their lives, their fortunes, and their sacred honor, and thus created the American nation. They founded the government of the United States, framed the Federal Constitution, and the Anglo-American nationality have been the directing and ruling power in this country till the present time. All real American history centres in and clusters around them. Although the Irish, the German, and other nationalities, proved to be valuable accessions to our population, yet our forefathers were English, and the rank and position we hold among nations is due to the Anglo-American nationality, which is therefore entitled to the honor and glory of being called the American nationality.

Notwithstanding this pre-eminence, and the fact that whatever is honorable in our history and worthy of esteem in our institutions, is owing chiefly to our forefathers; who, it is often said, builded better than they knew, nevertheless the American nationality, when tried by the test of true Americanism will in many respects be found wanting. It is often the hotbed of fanaticism, intolerance, and radical, ultra views on matters of politics and religion. All the vagaries of spiritualism, Mormonism, free-loveism, prohibition, infidelity, and materialism, generally breed in the American nationality. Here, also, we find dissimulation and hypocrisy. While the Irishman will get drunk and engage in an open street fight, and the German drink his beer in a public beer-garden, the American, pretending to be a total abstainer, takes his strong drink secretly and sleeps it off on a sofa or in a club-room. Who are the trusted employes, the public officers, that enjoyed the unlimited confidence of the people, and turned out to be hypocrites, impostors, and betrayers of trust? As a rule they are not Irish or Germans, but Americans. Who are the devotees at the shire of mammon? Who compose the syndicates, trusts, corporations, pools, and those huge monopolies that reach their tentacles over the nation, grinding down the poor and fattening in immense wealth? They are not Germans or Irish, but Americans. Who are the wild and reckless bank speculators, the forgers, the gamblers, and the defaulting officials? They are not the Irish or Germans, but Americans. Read the list of the refugees to Canada and you will find it made up of American names. We meet here also all species of refined wickedness. The educated villain, the expert burglar, the cool, calculating, deliberate criminal, generally belongs to the American nationality. Where the foreigners are corrupt that have in great measure been corrupted by the example of Americans. A republic that is not based upon morality and religion, where virtue is depressed, is ripe for an ignoble grave.

The Anglo-Saxon nationality has always been in England and in this country the bulwark of Protestantism and the main-stay of the enemies of the faith. It is so puffed up with spiritual pride, so steeped in materialism, that it is callous, and impervious to the spirit and the doctrines of the Catholic religion. It is true there are eminent converts in England and a few in this country; but they have no followers; the bulk of the people are as remote as ever from entering the Church.

Where are the doctors, the lawyers, the statesmen, the politicians, the bankers, the capitalists, the mechanics, the laborers, the farmers, the manufacturers, of the Anglo-Saxon nationality who have embraced the faith? Probably not as many of these can be found in the whole body of the Catholic Church as there are Catholics in the smallest diocese. Religion seems to make no impression upon them; they are as hostile as ever to the Church, and, though they perhaps wish it well as doing its share to keep the turbulent foreign element in check, they have not the remotest ideas of becoming Catholics themselves. And now we are asked to assimilate with this element, to adopt its usages, customs, feelings, and manners. That can not but prove detrimental to the Church. Are we going to lead our simple, straight-forward, honest Germans and Irish into this whirlpool of American life, this element wedded to this world, bent upon riches, upon political distinction, where their consciences will be stifled, their better sentiments trampled under foot?

But, it will be said, religion will keep them from rushing to this end, will sustain them in the path of virtue and rectitude. Nonsense! Denationalization is demoralization. It degrades and debases human nature. A foreigner who loses his nationality is in danger of losing his faith and character. When the German immigrant, on arriving in this country, seeks to throw aside his nationality and to become "quite English you know", the first word he learns is generally a curse, and the rowdy element is his preference to the sterling qualities of the Puritans. A German aping American customs and manners is, in his walk, talk, and appearance, in most cases, an object of ridicule and contempt. Like as the Indians in coming into contact with the whites adopted the vices rather than the virtues of the latter, so the effort to Americanize the foreigner will prove deteriorating. It has been observed, that the most noisy, disorderly, unruly class are the native, would-be American, Germans, and often, for that matter, too, the young Catholic Germans.

A man, in giving up his nationality, shows a lack of character. No educated German of any standing will deny his nationality, and such men as Carl Schurz and J. B. Stallo, who have gained national reputation, also remain intensely German. But it may be said, the Irish lost their language without losing their faith. The Irish, however, did not lose their nationality, and they were simply robbed of their language; they did not willingly abandon it. There are men here in Cincinnati who make the Irish language a special study, and an Irish sermon was preached here lately with marked success. Let but an effort be made to revive the Irish language, and it will be hailed with satisfaction by a large number of Irish in the United States.

The deleterious effects of Americanizing the foreign elements, show themselves in our Colleges. In the educational department of the Cincinnati Centennial Exposition, was exhibited a list of the students of Farmers' College, a small, insignificant institution in the neighborhood of the city, now gone into bankruptcy. Among the few pupils who attended this college in one and the same year were found the names of Benjamin Harrison, now President of the United States, Murat Halstead, Editor of the *Cincinnati Commercial Gazette*, the Nixon Brothers, Publishers of the *Chicago Inter Ocean*, Bishop J. M. Walden of the Methodist Church, all men of national reputation. Our flourishing Catholic colleges, with hundreds of students, after fifty years of existence, have hardly a man of note on the list of their alumni. The defect lies not so much in the lack of imparting knowledge as of forming character, and is probably to be accounted for in part from the fact that our colleges are engaged in the education of children and youths of foreign nationalities. It may be a point deserving the consideration of our educators as to whether or not education in parochial schools and colleges should be exclusively in the hands of religious, and as to whether or not they who are separated from the world are always best fitted to give the proper training for a life in the world.

Protestantism pervades the nature, the character, and the literature of the English language, and greatly impairs its power and fitness for the proper and full expression of Catholic thought and feeling. This is illustrated by the use of the second person singular in addressing the Deity. In the German language, for instance, the word "*thou*" is customary between parents and children, and intimate friends, and conveys a meaning of affection and familiar companionship. When the Protestant, who looks upon God as the Supreme Lord and Ruler of the universe, says, "*Thou* great and glorious God," the phrase is natural and appropriate; but to the Catholic, who conceives God under the sublime and lovely ideal of a good kind father, and Jesus Christ, of a dear friend and brother, the words, "I love *thee*, O God," sound strange and unnatural. These words in German convey a depth of feeling which the English language is inadequate to express. And, in praying to the Blessed Virgin, "We fly to *thee* weeping and sorrowing," how strained this phrase seems to express our confidence in that motherly love and tenderness beaming upon us, ready to shield and guard us, and to console our drooping hearts. Let any one, thoroughly conversant with both languages, take, say a chapter of St. Thomas a Kempis, and read the same in English and German, and he will readily perceive from which he derives the greater spiritual satisfaction, unction, and devotion. The English classics are Protestant, and our best Catholic writers, who are converts, such as Cardinal Newman, Cardinal Manning, Father Faber, and Dr. Brownson, naturally retain, in the culture of their taste and the formation of their style, a coloring of their early Protestant training.

The Church has made marvelous progress in this country. This has, however, not been brought about by Americanizing the heterogeneous elements of our incoming population, but by sustaining and keeping alive the languages and the nationalities of the foreign elements. Though not so flattering to our vanity it might prove more profitable to us to examine the losses we have sustained instead of rejoicing over the gains we have seemingly made. Gen. Von Steinwehr, an excellent statistician, gives the following estimates of the various nationalities for the year 1870:

Anglo-Saxons, 8,340,000; Irish, 10,255,000; Germans, 8,930,000; Italian and French, 1,016,000; Dutch and Scandinavians, 728,000; other nationalities 4,236,000. Total population in 1870, 33,595,000. The present population of the United States is estimated to be 60,000,000.

In the same proportion, as given above for 1870, we would have at present about 20,000,000 Irish-born and 16,000,000 German-born population.

Now there ought to be about 18,000,000 Irish Catholics, about one-third of the Germans, say nearly, 5,000,000, Americans, Poles, Italians, etc., 2,000,000,—total, 25,000,000.

According to Hoffmann's Directory the number of Catholics for the present year, 1889, is 8,157,676.

This shows a loss of two thirds of the Catholic population to the faith. The loss of this immense number can, in a great measure, be attributed to the fact that they have been Americanized, that they have lost their nationality, and with their nationality their religion. According to a census gathered by Father Enzleberger, we have 1,500,000 German Catholics, and our loss from the above estimate is therefore 3,500,000.

The comparative census for Cincinnati in the years 1846, 1850, and 1880, is as follows:

|  | Churches | | Population | |
|---|---|---|---|---|
|  | Irish. | German. | Irish. | German. |
| 1846 | 4 | 3 | 12,117 | 25,912 |
| 1850 | 5 | 7 | 13,616 | 30,628 |
| 1880 | 9 | 21 | 15,077 | 46,157 |

This shows an astonishing increase in the number of German churches and the German Catholic population, which is owing to the fact that the Germans have retained their language and nationality, even though many of them have joined the English-speaking congregations.

A similar result is observed in the German Protestant churches. In the year 1842, a certain Frederick Rammelsberg maintained that the German language would soon die out in this country and that everyone should speak English. He established an English-speaking congregation among the German Lutherans. And what was the result? While his church scarcely survives, the German-speaking Lutheran churches have increased from five at that time to twenty-five at the present time.

From the flourishing condition of the German Catholics in Cincinnati, let us look to New York, which has the third largest German population of any city in the world, ranking next to Hamburg and Berlin. Of the population of New York, which is 1,206,299, about one-third, or 400,000, are Germans, and of these about 125,000 ought to be Catholics. Now there are eleven German churches in New York with a probable membership of 30,000, which shows the frightful loss of three-fourths of the German Catholic population.

Dr. William H. Egle, Historian of Central Pennsylvania, in his "Notes and Queries," gives numerous instances where Irish Catholic families, — even whole Catholic settlements, — forsook their faith, and became Methodists, Baptists, Presbyterians, etc. Further investigation would show that they Americanized, that they were no longer Irish, and therefore no longer Catholics.

The annual immigration of German Catholics is about 50,000, of Irish Catholics about the same. 100,000 Italians arrived here in the last 18 months, 100,000 French Canadians are expected in the Eastern States this season, and a large number of Poles, Hungarians, and Catholics of other nationalities come every year. These all have still the embers of faith smoldering in their hearts which might be fanned into active life by nursing their nationality. A nucleus of the more wealthy and educated classes in each nationality could be formed, and annual conventions held in different cities where they would hear addresses in their native language, sing their native songs, keep up their old associations, and in other ways keep alive their nationality. The interest that the Church would thus take in them would not be without reward. While the American nationality is said to be deteriorating, we would, by retaining a hold upon the foreign nationalities who are multiplying, as with the blessing that rested upon the children of Israel in Egypt, in the course of time possess the land. These conventions or gatherings would certainly be productive of good results. Nor is there any danger of interference in diocesan regulations, for no king or potentate is so sure of the respect and obedience of his subjects, as is a Catholic bishop, provided they are good Catholics.

The Protestant sects show considerable zeal in proselyting the immigrants. In the last report of the Presbyterian Synod some interesting data were furnished by the Committee on Immigrant Population. The statistics of the report show that in the seven years of the present decade, 1881 to 1887, the immigrants have numbered 3,724,237, so that the total for this decade will exceed five million, or half as many as came over in all the years from the foundation of the government to 1880. There are in this denomination 111 German churches with 9,314 members and in addition there are churches, composed of persons from twelve other nationalities, 183 in number, and containing about 5,000 members. The resolutions appended to the report were in the main a recommendation that the Presbyterian Church should more thoroughly organize its work for the immigrant population. Though the Presbyterian Church has scarcely any members in Germany, we see that it has succeeded in gaining quite a foot-hold among the Germans in this country. Every church that looks to future prosperity must consider this immense, steady stream of immigration as one of its main sources of increase.

The German government is meeting with strong opposition from the inhabitants of Alsace and Lorraine, who are all Catholics, in introducing the German language in these provinces. The Catholic party, the bishops and priests in Germany, are giving the Government no aid, directly or indirectly, in enforcing this measure. Yet, by lending their assistance, they might gain the good will of the

Government and obtain valuable concessions. Such a course, however, would no doubt estrange many from the Church, who would rather abandon the faith than give up the French, their native language. Still the language of the country is German and ought to be spoken, for the same reason that the English ought to prevail here because it is the language of this country.

An illustration of the beneficial effects of keeping a nationality isolated and preserving its language, can be found in Canada. The writer of this, some time ago noticed, much to his astonishment, that the altar boys in the Montreal Cathedral could speak no word of English. Here the children were kept in total ignorance of the language of the country. Recent developments, however, show the wisdom of this policy. The following extracts from a newspaper article furnish an account of the Canadian situation and outlook:

> Canada is now in a ferment over the recognition of the claims of the Jesuits of the Province of Quebec to several hundred thousand dollars. All the Protestant denominations are justifying their name by protesting against this endowment. They fear that the already greatly preponderating influence of the Church of Rome will be greatly increased by this endowment, and sectarian antipathies are fast becoming intense. If it is extravagant to apprehend, as does the Reformed Episcopal Bishop of Toronto, the danger of civil war, there may at least be formidable riots. The stronghold of the French Catholic elements is in Quebec, yet as we have seen, an ecclesiastic in the principal city of Ontario is getting nervous. Moreover the Jesuits feel confident of their position in the Western Province, and have sued for libel the editor of the *Toronto Mail*. That paper claimed that their secret oath involved a repudiation of allegiance to all sovereigns except the Pope. This is denied. We do not think the Fathers will get the $50,000 damages which they claim, but the expenses of a lawsuit and the impossibility of procuring unquestionable evidence, will doubtless render editorial critics of the Order more cautious in the future.
>
> Be the rights and usages of the case what they may, more than a century and a quarter of British domination has failed to merge into one nationality the descendants of early English and Scotch colonists and those of the habitans who were scattered along the shores of the St. Lawrence in 1759. Different languages and religions are always formidable obstacles to the unification of stranger races. Of these two factors of alienation and separation, religion is doubtless the stronger. The French-Norman invasion of England in 1066, was effected by a people of strange language, but of a common faith. In a few centuries Norman and Saxon were blended, and our mother tongue was the result of the union.
>
> It is reasonable to affirm that the French Latins have a greater inveteracy of custom and habit than belongs to the English. The settlers of the lower provinces are obedient to their ecclesiastical superiors and their zealous supporters in all the frequent collisions of the Church with the civil power. But the faithful are not the only ones who are held to obedience. The quarrels between the clergy and the civil authorities have been constant, and the latter thus far, within recent years at least, have invariably yielded. An enumeration of the usurping and the recalcitrant acts of the Church in Quebec during the past fifty years, would fill a column or two, and we therefore content ourselves with the general statement which all interested can verify. England may have taken Canada in Wolfe's days; in our own time the French Canadians are altogether too much for English statesmanship. In one point only have the French-speaking Canadians obstinately

disobeyed their spiritual rulers. The high wages attainable in the United States have proved too strong a temptation. They are deaf to the injunctions to remain at home and preserve their ancestral faith against the seductive influences of the Union. In the beginning, and still now in many instances, they left home with the intention of making a little money and then returning. The more intelligent have discovered, however, that, in more ways than one, the Union offers advantages not attainable in the Dominion. Higher wages, more fertile farms, better schools, and a more genial climate, are inducements not easy to resist.

The American phase of the Canadian question is beginning to have its influence in New England politics, and unless the influx from the North is checked, it is destined to exert still more. Just now, however, the main point of interest lies beyond our borders. The results of the present disturbances are likely to affect materially the movements for Canadian annexation, for its forerunner is the establishment of a more liberal system of intercommunication. We can well desire the annexation of the immense forest ranges and wheat-producing prairies of the Dominion. but the devout habitans taken in *en masse*, would hardly be a desirable addition to our citizenship.

The condition of the French Catholics in the United States, as compared with the gratifying results of the Canadian policy, is not very encouraging. Except in New Orleans, where French sermons are still preached in the Cathedral, they are mostly infidels or merely nominal Catholics. That overflowing French population which is inundating our Eastern States from Canada, is in danger of losing its faith when it becomes Americanized. The religious question in Canada, however, is of easy solution. It was a fortunate thing that the Catholics were all French, and belonged to one and the same nationality, and could therefore be easily held together and maintain themselves. They were thus kept from marriages and associations with heretics and unbelievers. If they had been divided, if, for instance, the Irish, German, and Polish nationalities had been represented among them, each nationality might and probably would have struggled for the mastery, and hence rivalry and bitter feeling would have been ganerated. The result probably would have been that each faction in turn would have yielded to English influence, agreed to drop their own distinctive nationality and to enter the English camp.

The School Committee of Haverhill, Massachusetts, some time ago discovered a school taught by the Franciscan Fathers and attended almost exclusively by children of the French Candians, who are now swarming in the manufacturing towns of New England. The Committee discovered that the general grade of instruction was far below the general average of the State schools; that some of the teachers did not understand English; that the teaching was largely in French; and, finally, that the history of Canada, not that of the United States, was being taught. On the strength of these defects, and, fortified by a statute to do so, the Committee closed the school for general worthlessness.

Thus far they had not exceeded their powers. A little later they found that some of the late pupils were attending no school and were thus violating the truant law. Their parents were arraigned for the offense of neglecting the schooling of their children, and the whole subject was passed upon by the Police Court of the city.

The trial resulted in the acquittal of the parents, solely through the vagueness of one of the provisions of law, intended to be very definite and peremptory.

Now these Franciscan Fathers must have come to the conclusion, after their experience, that Americanism is a delicate tender plant, since it could not endure the teaching of a few children in the French language and in Canadian history, especially as, in view of the prospective annexation of Canada, the history of that country would also be part of United States history, they were really anticipating and ahead of the times. And when they reflected that millions of immigrants, ignorant of United States history and of the English language, were naturalized, that the elective franchise and full-fledged citizenship was given to 4,000,000 negroes—this mass of ignorance—they must have suspected that other motives were at the bottom than the pretended danger to our institutions, and that the School Committee, profiting by the experience of Great Britain in Canada, had determined to nip French education in the bud.

The French Canadians in the Eastern States met with little encouragement and assistance from their brethren in the faith, who agree with the School Committee that United States history and the English language must be taught. It cannot but lessen their attachment to the Church and the country, to be deprived, in this boasted land of freedom, of the liberty they enjoy in Canada, and thus to be prevented by legal process, from following their own plans in educating their children and preserving them in the faith.

From the foregoing we can conclude that religion and nationality go hand in hand, that religion sustains nationality, and nationality is an aid to religion. We have seen, that where the Irish, German, and French were isolated, their language and nationality encouraged and fostered, they were kept true to the faith, and that they generally lost their faith in proportion as they Americanized.

Whither are we drifting and what will be the result, when in the course of time this vast country has but one language and one nationality? We will miss the cheerful, unrestrained, and innocent enjoyment of the Germans, their refreshment-rooms where they sit drinking coffee and beer and enjoying life and the society of their fellows, their musical and singing societies, their public gardens, where all classes of society meet and mingle on terms of equality and drop the rigid forms of social etiquette. We will miss the refinement, elegance, grace, and charm of French life, society, and manners. We will miss that variety which constitutes one of the chief pleasures of the tourist abroad, who finds, sometimes in adjoining villages, differences of the dialect, fashions, and other peculiarities of the people. With these elements of variety taken out of them, our hearts will have but the hard metallic ring of money, our amusement will be some national game like base-ball or horse-racing which degenerates into gambling and creates undue excitement. Throughout the length and breadth of this vast country there will be but one language, a sameness and monotonous uniformity in the cities and villages and the style of architecture, so that, more than ever will the present saying be true, "When you see one American city, you have seen them all."

The torrent of Americanism is rushing forward and, aided by favorable conditions in the Church and state, is invading, undermining, and sweeping away the languages, customs, and strongholds of Foreignism, so that all foreign nationalities will finally be molded into one American nationality. An American writer says:

> The constant importation into this country of the lowest orders of people from abroad to dilute the quality of our natural manhood, is a sad and beggarly prostitution of the noblest gift ever conferred on our people. Who shall respect a people who do not respect their own blood? And how shall a national spirit, or any determinate and proportionate character, arise out of so many low-bred associations and coarse-grained temperaments, imported from every clime? It was indeed in keeping that Pan, who was the son of everybody, was the ugliest of the Gods.

A difference may here be noted between Catholic and Protestant nations. When a Catholic nation establishes itself in a foreign country, it seeks to spread the light of the Gospel by converting and civilizing the natives, and, believing all men to be of one blood, readily amalgamates with them. This can be observed in Mexico and the South American states, which were conquered by Catholics. The English, however, drove the Indians from their land, exterminated them, and planted their civilaization on the ruins of the aborigines of the country. With their immense colonial possessions in parts of the world, the English keep their own nationality intact, and rarely intermarry with the natives.

Nationalities are divided into two distinct families, the Germanic and the Romanic order. The Germans, English, Dutch, Scandanavians, and the Teutonic nations, are said to belong to the Germanic order, and the Irish,—or Celts,—French, Italians, and all so-called Latin nations, are said to belong to the Romanic order. Naturally those nationalities which belong to one and the same family with the English and American, will more readily assimilate and Americanize. The Germans are soon absorbed by other nationalities, and one of their writers calls them the fertilizers of other nations. When once settled in a country, they soon forget their fatherland, and take little interest in its affairs. The cause of this indifference can, in some measure, be attributed to the fact, that the Germans, until recently, before they were consolidated into one grand empire, did not feel as one people, had no political unity, no common country, but were divided into a number of principalities and petty kingdoms, sometimes warring with one another. There is scarcely a patriotic sentiment to be found in the works of Goethe, the greatest of German writers. Though the Germans cling tenaciously to their language and peculiar customs, they have little national feeling. With all their wealth and numbers, the German Catholics contributed only $60,000 to the Leo House, which is established in New York for German Catholic immigrants, and designed, by its founders, to be the grand national monument of German American Catholicity. Even the German nuns have caught the American spirit. They aim to adapt themselves to the customs of the country, and have, for the most part, given up their language and national peculiarities. On the other hand, the Little Sisters of the Poor, a French Order, send all their novices to *la belle France* to be educated, and continue to use the French language in their community.

It is doubtful whether the object of the originators and supporters of the movement to strengthen and perpetuate the German nationality in the Church in this country can be attained. This nationality has deserved well of the Church, dotted the land with churches, schools, and institutions, and is therefore justified in making lawful efforts to prolong its life and maintain its existence. The Germans stand second to none as loyal, faithful children of the Church, and it seems unjust to reprove them for showing signs of vitality and arousing their energies in the great cause for which they have so successfully labored. When, in the course of time, the German nationality should come to an end, and when its days are numbered by the years that are past, may the children of the German pioneers, who follow them in another, the American nationality, cherish and preserve as the richest legacy, the spiritual title-deed of their holy religion.

No foreign nationality can permanently maintain itself in this country. It is, of course, natural that immigrants should wish to find again their fatherland in this land of their adoption, but they will Americanize in spite of themselves. The American nationality will prevail. It assimilates the children of foreigners, and is strengthened by contributions from foreign sources. Foreign nationalities will be absorbed by it and flow in the current of American life.

However, the transition from one nationality to another, is always a dangerous process, and it will not do to hasten it and to force foreigners to Americanize. For the present we should remember that the American nationality counts for little or nothing in the American Church, and if it is ever to be converted, it must be done by the clergy and population already Catholics. The most efficient portion of our Catholic body are of foreign birth and training, and will be for some time to come. However we may work for non-Catholics, we must carry with us the sympathies and affections of the Catholic body. This body is composed of various nationalities with peculiarities of languages, habits, and prejudices. If these are opposed, and the national sensitiveness wounded, they may become irritated and indifferent, and lose their affection for the Church. We cannot move much in advance of the public sentiment of our own body. We must hold a tight rein, check the impatience to Americanize, and, though there may be some wrangling among conflicting nationalities, if we move slowly we will finally land in the American nationality with the Catholic body under full control and faithful to the Church.

The Church is not trammeled by nationalities and is adapted to all nations. She does not take part in the idiosyncracies, in the antagonism and war, of races. All are placed on a footing of equality, and a Hindoo or a Hottentot can be as good a Catholic as a Frenchman or an Italian. The various nationalities, with their differences of race, color, manners, habits, and usages, form a beautiful mosaic in her glorious temple.

The American nation is yet to be added as another rich gem in her crown. It is true we are one hundred years old. But what is one hundred years in the life of a nation, or the life of the Church? We are still laying the foundation of national greatness and prosperity; the Church is still sowing the seed that is to penetrate the living mass of American society, and subject it to the truth and sanctity of the Gospel. Let us then continue to sow, it may be in tribulation and sorrow, that future generations may reap in joy a rich and abundant harvest.

> *And all the clouds that lowered upon our house*
> *In the deep bosom of the ocean buried.*

# ❧·121·❧

# Testem Benevolentiae

## POPE LEO XIII

Some Catholic leaders in the United States publicly celebrated American institutions as providing a model framework for the future development of the Church more generally. Conservative elements in Rome came to associate this view with a number of doctrinal positions they disliked, a combination termed 'Americanism'. The Pope, mindful of the influence such ideas might have elsewhere, issued the following encyclical in 1899 to warn the American Church of the dangers it was running. The effect was to encourage American Catholics to concentrate on practical issues, even though the Vatican's belief that Americans wanted to see their Church develop differently from elsewhere was misplaced.

We send you this letter as a testimony of that devoted affection in your regard, which during the long course of Our Pontificate, We have never ceased to profess for you, for your colleagues in the Episcopate, and for the whole American people, willingly availing Ourselves of every occasion to do so, whether it was the happy increase of your church, or the works which you have done so wisely and well in furthering and protecting the interests of Catholicity. The opportunity also often presented itself of regarding with admiration that exceptional disposition of your nation, so eager for what is great, and so ready to pursue whatever might be conducive to social progress and the splendor of the State. But although the object of this letter is not to repeat the praise so often accorded, but rather to point out certain things which are to be avoided and corrected, yet because it is written with that same apostolic charity which We have always shown you, and in which We have often addressed you, We trust that you will regard it likewise as a proof of Our love; and all the more so as it is conceived and intended to put an end to certain contentions which have arisen lately among you, and which disturb the minds, if not of all, at least of many, to the no slight detriment of peace.

Source: Pope Leo XIII, *Testem Benevolentiae*, 1899, rptd in John Tracy Ellis, ed., *Documents of American Catholic History*, Milwaukee, 1953.

You are aware, beloved Son, that the book entitled "The Life of Isaac Thomas Hecker," chiefly through the action of those who have undertaken to publish and interpret it in a foreign language, has excited no small controversy on account of certain opinions which are introduced concerning the manner of leading a Christian life. We, therefore, on account of Our apostolic office, in order to provide for the integrity of the faith, and to guard the security of the faithful, desire to write to you more at length upon the whole matter.

The principles on which the new opinions We have mentioned are based may be reduced to this: that, in order the more easily to bring over to Catholic doctrine those who dissent from it, the Church ought to adapt herself somewhat to our advanced civilization, and, relaxing her ancient rigor, show some indulgence to modern popular theories and methods. Many think that this is to be understood not only with regard to the rule of life, but also to the doctrines in which the *deposit of faith* is contained. For they contend that it is opportune, in order to work in a more attractive way upon the wills of those who are not in accord with us, to pass over certain heads of doctrines, as if of lesser moment, or to so soften them that they may not have the same meaning which the Church has invariably held. Now, Beloved Son, few words are needed to show how reprehensible is the plan that is thus conceived, if we but consider the character and origin of the doctrine which the Church hands down to us. On that point the Vatican Council says:

> The doctrine of faith which God has revealed is not proposed like a theory of philosophy which is to be elaborated by the human understanding, but as a divine deposit delivered to the Spouse of Christ to be faithfully guarded and infallibly declared.... That sense of the sacred dogmas is to be faithfully kept which Holy Mother Church has once declared, and is not to be departed from under the specious pretext of a more profound understanding" (*Const. de Fid. cath.*, c. iv).

Nor is the suppression to be considered altogether free from blame, which designedly omits certain principles of Catholic doctrine and buries them, as it were, in oblivion. For there is the one and the same Author and Master of all the truths that Christian teaching comprises: *The only-begotten Son who is in the bosom of the Father* (John, i, 18). That they are adapted to all ages and nations is plainly deduced from the words which Christ addressed to His apostles: *Going therefore teach ye all nations: teaching them to observe all things whatsoever I have commanded you: and behold I am with you all days even to the consummation of the world* (*Matthew*, xxviii, 19). Wherefore the same Vatican Council says:

> By the divine and Catholic faith those things are to be believed which are contained in the word of God either written or handed down, and are proposed by the Church whether in solemn decision or by the ordinary universal magisterium, to be believed as having been divinely revealed (*Const. de Fid. cath.*, c. iii).

Far be it, then, for any one to diminish or for any reason whatever to pass over anything of this divinely delivered doctrine; whosoever would do so, would rather wish to alienate Catholics from the Church than to bring over to the Church those who dissent from it. Let them return; indeed, nothing is nearer to Our heart; let all those who are wandering far from the sheepfold of Christ return; but let it not be by any other road than that which Christ has pointed out.

The rule of life which is laid down for Catholics is not of such a nature as not to admit modifications, according to the diversity of time and place. The Church, indeed, possesses what her Author has bestowed on her, a kind and merciful disposition; for which reason from the very beginning she willingly showed herself to be what Paul proclaimed in his own regard: *I became all things to all men, that I might save all* (*Corinthians*, ix, 22). The history of all past ages is witness that the Apostolic See, to which not only the office of teaching but also the supreme government of the whole Church was committed, has constantly adhered *to the same doctrine, in the same sense and in the same mind* (Conc. Vatic., *ibid.*, c. iv): but it has always been accustomed to so modify the rule of life that, while keeping the divine right inviolate, it has never disregarded the manners and customs of the various nations which it embraces. If required for the salvation of souls, who will doubt that it is ready to do so at the present time? But this is not to be determined by the will of private individuals, who are mostly deceived by the appearance of right, but ought to be left to the judgment of the Church. In this all must acquiesce who wish to avoid the censure of Our predecessor Pius VI, who proclaimed the 18th proposition of the Synod of Pistoia "to be injurious to the Church and to the Spirit of God which governs her, inasmuch as it subjects to scrutiny the discipline established and approved by the Church, as if the Church could establish a useless discipline or one which would be too onerous for Christian liberty to bear."

But in the matter of which we are now speaking, Beloved Son, the project involves a greater danger, inasmuch as the followers of these novelties judge that a certain liberty ought to be introduced into the Church, so that, limiting the exercise and vigilance of its powers, each one of the faithful may act more freely in pursuance of his own natural bent and capacity. They affirm, namely, that this is called for in order to imitate that liberty which, though quite recently introduced, is now the law and the foundation of almost every civil community. On that point We have spoken very much at length in the Letter written to all the bishops about the constitution of States; where We have also shown the difference between the Church, which is of divine right, and all other associations which subsist by the free will of men. It is of importance, therefore, to note particularly an opinion which is adduced as a sort of argument to urge the granting of such liberty to Catholics. For they say, in speaking of the infallible teaching of the Roman Pontiff, that after the solemn decision formulated in the Vatican Council, there is no more need of solicitude in that regard, and, because of its being now out of dispute, a wider field of thought and action is thrown open to individuals. A preposterous method of arguing, surely. For if anything is suggested by the infallible teaching of the Church, it is certainly that no one should wish to withdraw from it; nay, that all should strive to be thoroughly imbued with and be guided by its spirit, so as to be the more easily preserved from any private error whatsoever. To this we may add that those who argue in that wise quite set aside the wisdom and providence of God; who when He desired it especially in order the more efficaciously to guard the minds of Catholics from the dangers of the present times. The license which is commonly confounded with liberty; the passion for saying and reviling everything; the habit of thinking and of expressing everything in print, have cast such deep shadows on men's minds, that there is now greater-utility and necessity for this office of teaching than ever before, lest men should be drawn away from conscience and duty. It is far, indeed, from Our intention to repudiate all that the genius of time begets; nay, rather, whatever the search for truth attains, or the effort after good achieves, will always be welcomed by Us, for it increases the patrimony of doctrine and enlarges the limits of public prosperity. But all this, to possess real utility, should thrive without setting aside the authority and wisdom of the Church.

We come now in due course to what are adduced as consequences from the opinions which We have touched upon; in which if the intention seem not wrong, as We believe, the things themselves assuredly will not appear by any means free from suspicion. For, in the first place, all external guidance is rejected as superfluous, nay even as somewhat of a disadvantage, for those who desire to devote themselves to the acquisition of Christian perfection; for the Holy Ghost, they say, pours greater and richer gifts into the hearts of the faithful now than in times past; and by a certain hidden instinct teaches and moves them with no one as an intermediary. It is indeed not a little rash to wish to determine the degree in which God communicates with men; for that depends solely on His will; and He Himself is the absolutely free giver of His own gifts. *The Spirit breatheth where He will* (John, iii, 8). *But to every one of us is given grace according to the measure of the giving of Christ* (Ephesians, iv, 7). For who, when going over the history of the apostles, the faith of the rising Church, the struggles and slaughter of the valiant martyrs, and finally most of the ages past so abundantly rich in holy men, will presume to compare the past with the present times and to assert that they received a lesser outpouring of the Holy Ghost? But, aside from that, no one doubts that the Holy Ghost, by His secret incoming into the souls of the just, influences and arouses them by admonition and impulse. If it were otherwise, any external help and guidance would be useless. "If any one positively affirms that he can consent to the saving preaching of the Gospel without the illumination of the Holy Ghost, who imparts sweetness to all to consent to and accept the truth, he is misled by a heretical spirit" (*Conc. Arausic.*, II, can. vii). But as we know by experience these promptings and impulses of the Holy Ghost for the most part are not discerned without the help, and, as it were, without the preparation of an external guidance. In this matter Augustine says: "It is he who in good trees co-operates in their fruiting, who both waters and cultivates them by any servant whatever from without, and who by himself gives increase within" (*De grat. Christi*, c. xix). That is to say, the whole matter is according to the common law by which God in His infinite providence has decreed that men for the most part should be saved by men: hence He has appointed that those whom He calls to a loftier degree of holiness should be led thereto by men, "in order that," as Chrysostom says, "we should be taught by God through men" (*Hom. i. in Inscr. altar.*). We have an illustrious example of this put before us in the very beginning of the Church, for although Saul, who was *breathing threatenings and slaughter* (*Acts*, c. ix), heard the voice of Christ Himself, and asked from Him, *Lord what wilt Thou have me to do?* he was nevertheless sent to Ananias at Damascus: *Arise and go into the city, and there it shall be told thee what thou must do.* It must also be kept in mind that those who follow what is more perfect are by the very fact entering upon a way of life which for most men is untried and more exposed to error, and therefore they, more than others, stand in need of a teacher and guide. This manner of acting has invariably obtained in the Church. All, without exception, who in the course of ages have been remarkable for science and holiness have taught this doctrine. Those who reject it, assuredly do so rashly and at their peril.

For one who examines the matter thoroughly, it is hard to see, if we do away with all external guidance as these innovators propose, what purpose the more abundant influence of the Holy Ghost, which they make so much of, is to serve. In point of fact, it is especially in the cultivation of virtue that the assistance of the Holy Spirit is indispensable; but those who affect these novelties extol beyond measure the natural virtues as more in accordance with the ways and requirements of the present day, and consider it an advantage to be richly endowed with them, because they make a man more ready and more strenuous in action. It is hard to understand how those who are imbued with Christian principles can place the natural ahead of the supernatural virtues, and attribute to them greater power and fecundity. Is nature, then, with grace added to it, weaker than when left to its own strength? and have the eminently holy men whom the Church reveres and pays homage to, shown themselves weak and incompetent in the natural order, because they have excelled in Christian virtue? Even if we examine the sometimes splendid acts of the natural virtues, how rate is the man who really possesses the habit of these natural virtues? Who is there who is not disturbed by passions, sometimes of a violent nature, for the persevering conquest of which, just as for the observance of the whole natural law, man must needs have some divine help? If we scrutinize more closely the particular acts We have above referred to, we shall discover that often times they have more the appearance than the reality of virtue. But let us grant that these are real. If we do not wish *to run in vain*, if we do not wish to lose sight of the eternal blessedness to which God in His goodness has destined us, of what use are the natural virtues unless the gift and strength of divine grace be added? Aptly does St. Augustine say: "Great power, and a rapid pace, but out of the course" (*In Ps.*, xxxi, 4). For as the nature of man, because of our common misfortune, fell into vice and dishonor, yet by the assistance of grace is lifted up and borne onward with new honor and strength; so also the virtues which are exercised not by the unaided powers of nature, but by the help of the same grace, are made productive of a supernatural beatitude and become solid and enduring.

With this opinion about natural virtue, another is intimately connected, according to which all Christian virtues are divided as it were into two classes, passive as they say, and active; and they add the former were better suited for the past times, but the latter are more in keeping with the present. It is plain what is to be thought of such division of the virtues. There is not and cannot be a virtue which is really passive. "Virtue," says St. Thomas, "denotes a certain perfection of a power; but the object of a power is an act; and an act of virtue is nothing else than the good use of our free will" (I. II. a. I), the divine grace of course helping, if the act of virtue is supernatural. The one who would have Christian virtues to be adapted, some to one age and others to another, has forgotten the words of the Apostle: *Whom he foreknew he also predestinated to be made conformable to the image of His Son* (Romans, viii, 29). The Master and exemplar of all sanctity is Christ, to whose rule all must conform who wish to attain to the thrones of the blessed. Now, then, Christ does not at all change with the progress of the ages, but is *yesterday and to-day, and the same forever* (Hebrews, xiii, 8). To men of all ages, the phrase is to be applied: *Learn of Me because I am meek, and humble of heart* (Matthew, xi, 29) and at all times Christ shows Himself to us as becoming *obedient unto* death (Philippians, ii, 8) and in every age also the word of the Apostle holds: *And they that are Christ's have crucified their flesh with the vices and concupiscence* (Galatians, v, 24). Would that more would cultivate those virtues in our days, as did the holy men of bygone times! Those who by humbleness of spirit, by obedience and abstinence, were *powerful in word and work*, were of the greatest help not only to religion but to the State and society.

From this species of contempt of the evangelical virtues, which are wrongly called *passive*, it naturally follows that the mind is imbued little by little with a feeling of disdain for the religious life. And that this is common to the advocates of these new opinions we gather from certain expressions of theirs about the vows which religious orders pronounce. For, say they, such vows are altogether out of keeping with the spirit of our age, inasmuch as they narrow the limits of human liberty; are better adapted to weak minds than to strong ones; avail little for Christian perfection and the good of human society, and rather obstruct and interfere with it. But how false these assertions are, is evident from the usage and doctrine of the Church, which has always given the highest approval to religious life. And surely not undeservedly. For those who, not content with the common duties of the precepts, enter of their own accord upon the evangelical counsels, in obedience to a divine vocation, present themselves to Christ as His prompt and valiant soldiers. Are we to consider this a mark of weak minds? In the more perfect manner of life is it unprofitable or hurtful? Those who bind themselves by the vows of religion are so far from throwing away their liberty that they enjoy a nobler and fuller one—that, *by which Christ has set us free* (Galatians, iv, 31).

What they add to this—namely, that religious life helps the Church not at all or very little—apart from being injurious to religious orders, will be admitted by no one who has read the history of the Church. Did not your own United States receive from the members of religious orders the beginning of its faith and civilization? For one of them recently, and it redounds to your credit, you have decreed that a statue should be publicly erected. And at this very time, with what alacrity and success are these religious orders doing their work wherever we find them! How many of them hasten to impart to new lands the life of the Gospel and to extend the boundaries of civilization with the greatest earnestness of soul and amid the greatest dangers! From them no less than from the rest of the clergy the Christian people obtain preachers of the Word of God, directors of conscience, instructors of youth, and the entire Church examples of holy lives. Nor is there any distinction of praise between those who lead an active life and those who, attracted by seclusion, give themselves up to prayer and mortification of the body. How gloriously they have merited from human society, and do still merit, they should be aware who are not ignorant of how *the continual prayer of a just man* (*James*, v, 16) especially when joined to affliction of the body, avails to propitiate and conciliate the majesty of God.

If there are any, therefore, who prefer to unite together in one society without the obligation of vows, let them do as they desire. That is not a new institution in the Church, nor is it to be disapproved. But let them beware of setting such associations above religious orders; nay rather, since mankind is more prone now than heretofore to the enjoyment of pleasure, much greater esteem is to be accorded to those *who have left all things and have followed Christ.*

Lastly, not to delay too long, it is also maintained that the way and the method which Catholics have followed thus far for recalling those who differ from us is to be abandoned and another resorted to. In that matter, it suffices to advert that it is not prudent, Beloved Son, to neglect what antiquity, with its long experience, guided as it is by apostolic teaching, has stamped with its approval. From the word of God we have it that it is the office of all to labor in helping the salvation of our neigbor in the order and degree in which each one is. The faithful indeed will most usefully fulfil their duty by integrity of life, by the works of Christian charity, by instant and assiduous prayer to God. But the clergy should do so by a wise preaching of the Gospel, by the decorum and splendor of the sacred ceremonies, but especially by expressing in themselves the form of doctrine which the apostles delivered to Titus and Timothy. So that if among the different methods of preaching the word of God, that sometimes seems preferable by which those who dissent from us are spoken to, not in the church but in any private and proper place, not in disputation but in amicable conference, such method is indeed not to be reprehended; provided, however, that those who are devoted to that work by the authority of the bishop be men who have first given proof of science and virtue. For We think that there are very many among you who differ from Catholics rather through ignorance than because of any disposition of the will, who, perchance, if the truth is put before them in a familiar and friendly manner, may more easily be led to the one sheepfold of Christ.

Hence, from all that We have hitherto said, it is clear, Beloved Son, that We cannot approve the opinions which some comprise under the head of Americanism. If, indeed, by that name be designated the characteristic qualities which reflect honor on the people of America, just as other nations have what is special to them; or if it implies the condition of your commonwealths, or the laws and customs which prevail in them, there is surely no reason why We should deem that it ought to be discarded. But if it is to be used not only to signify, but even to commend the above doctrines, there can be no doubt but that our Venerable Brethren the bishops of America would be the first to repudiate and condemn it, as being especially unjust to them and to the entire nation as well. For it raises the suspicion that there are some among you who conceive of and desire a church in America different from that which is in the rest of the world. One in the unity of doctrine as in the unity of government, such is the Catholic Church, and, since God has established its centre and foundation in the Chair of Peter, one which is rightly called Roman, for where Peter is there is the Church. Wherefore he who wishes to be called by the name of Catholic ought to employ in truth the words of Jerome to Pope Damasus, "I following none as the first except Christ am associated in communion with your Beatitude, that is, with the Chair of Peter; upon that Rock I know is built the Church; whoever gathereth not with thee scattereth" (S. Ambr. in Ps., xi, 57).

What We write, Beloved Son, to you in particular, by reason of Our office, we shall take care to have communicated to the rest of the bishops of the United States, expressing again that love in which we include your whole nation, which as in times past has done much for religion and bids fair with God's good grace to do still more in the future.

To you and all the faithful of America We give most lovingly as augury of divine assistance Our Apostolical Benediction.

# ❧122❧

# The Church and the Republic

## CARDINAL JAMES GIBBONS

Archbishop James Gibbons (1834–1921), who became the American Church's second Cardinal in 1886 and its most influential figure, was able to use his position, good relations with non-Catholics and close links with the Pope to clarify the position of American Catholicism both to the Vatican and to non-Catholics at home. In this passage, he unambiguously identifies the Church with American institutions and Catholics as patriots.

This form of religious propaganda Catholics know to be abhorrent to the spirit of every true American; and on that spirit they rely to nullify the spasmodic efforts of bigotry; for, though a large proportion of the non-Catholics do not sympathize with Catholic doctrines, this dissent is not carried over into political or social life. Men have learned in this country to disagree profoundly without rancor or bitterness. With no compromise of principle on either side, moral worth, sterling character, kindly qualities of mind and heart bind together in good-will, admiration and friendship the lives of those who do not worship at the same altar. The non-Catholic American would receive with a contemptuous smile or an indignant gesture any suggestion that his Catholic friend, or business associate, carried hidden in his heart some sinister tenet that gave the lie to his life, and might at any moment oblige him to turn traitor to the Republic.

The Catholic himself feels, as he has learned from the lips of his own revered and trusted teachers of religion, that the more faithful he is to his religion, the better and nobler citizen will he be. That religion and patriotism could ever come into conflict in his bosom, seems to him an utter impossibility; and in the religious principles which he has received in common with his fellow-Catholics, he sees the surest defense of the State against the forces of disorder and lawlessness, and the insidious influences that work for the overthrow of our Christian moral standards in private and public life.

Such are the conditions that exist, in themselves admirable, and gratifying to

Source: Cardinal James Gibbons, 'The Church and the Republic', A *Retrospective of Fifty Years*, Baltimore, 1916, pp. 212-21.

the statesmen, to the churchman, to the lover of religion and country; to all who rejoice in the spread of good-will and peace among men. Who would dare to introduce religious strife among us, to disturb this peace, and set the torch to the Temple of Concord?

## II

Of this body of American citizens living such a life and imbued with such sentiments (of which there are almost as many proofs as there are Catholics), two synods of Protestant ministers have deemed it just and wise to proclaim to the country that Catholics cannot be trusted with political office; that they cannot sincerely subscribe to the Federal Constitution; that their loyalty is illogical, being contrary to the teaching of the Church; that their religion is opposed to American liberties; and that they themselves, kept in the dark by their religious guides, are ignorant of the true nature of their Church's doctrines. In sounding forth these charges to American Catholics, and to the country in general, they declare themselves inspired, not by religious antagonism or the desire to profit by a good opportunity, but solely by patriotic solitude for the permanence of American institutions.

Charges so contrary to the abiding convictions of American Catholics, and so hurtful to their deepest affections, are naturally resented; yet they do not appear to have excited any commotion among us. It would indeed be a grave matter if these utterances expressed the judgment of the American nation, indicated its sentiments towards our Catholic citizens, and preluded a departure from the national policy of religious liberty and equality before the law. Happily, we know this is very far from the fact. The truth is, we believe, these ministers not only do not represent the American attitude towards us, but would meet with determined opposition if they attempted to carry with them even their own congregations. They have good cause to complain, as they do, of the apathy of their co-religionists. Catholics are convinced that the nation recognizes its own voice in President Roosevelt's letter to Mr. J. C. Martin rather than in the pronouncements if provoked. There they hear the ring of genuine Americanism; and they catch in the other the echo of old cries, of which they have long grown weary.

## III

It can be pleasant to none of us to be called upon, not only to prove our title to convictions which have guided us through life, but to show cause why we should not be deprived of the common political rights of human beings in our own native land. However, I feel obliged to speak out; and if I should speak with warmth on one or two points, it will be because I feel the proposal made deserves the strongest reprobation, and is, moreover, entirely unworthy of men in the position of those from whom it emanated. I have no desire to inflict pain, but cannot avoid characterizing the action of the synods as it deserves. Against the gentlemen themselves I can feel no animosity. They are excellent men in many respects, no doubt, and mean to be good citizens. I am sure, though their spirit does not tend to sweeten American life as much as we might desire, they help to purify and raise its tone, and to keep religion alive in the hearts of their people, and I can only wish them well.

The Catholic religion, as they understand it, is in conflict with the Federal Constitution, and with the object of our institutions; Catholics, then, ought not to be trusted with political office. Accordingly, Americans should seek to exclude Catholics from the chair of the President, who is called upon to enforce the Constitution; from the Supreme Bench, whose duty it is to interpret it; from the Senate and the House of Representatives, which have the power to change it. And as the chief evil dreaded from Catholics is a modification of the existing relations between Church and State, a power theoretically reserved to our State Governments, no Catholic should be chosen Governor, State legislator or judge of a supreme State court. This is the scope of their meaning, though not all explicitly avowed. It would logically be desirable to deny Catholics the right to vote, and with men in the frame of mind their attitude suggests, the realization of this desire in the statute books, and of their complete programme, would only be a matter of their possessing sufficient power and judging the act politically expedient.

Now this proposal to exclude Catholics from office—for it is no mere theory, but a practical programme earnestly recommended to the American public by two solemn assemblies—is advocated expressly in the interest of religious liberty and for the sake of preserving the Federal Constitution. That document says: "No religious test shall ever be required as a qualification to any office or public trust under the United States." Just understand here, however, remark these Lutheran and Baptist synods, an amendment, or rather let us say, a little clause which brings out the sense with admirable clearness: "Provided, of course, that this provision be not understood to apply to Roman Catholics."

Such restrictions on religion have always been felt to be incompatible with American ideas, and have fallen, though sometimes only after a long struggle, before the force of the real American spirit.

> When the Constitution came before the State Conventions, . . . in Massachusetts alone was a dread of liberty expressed. Major Lusk "shuddered at the idea that Roman Catholics, Papists and Pagans might be introduced into office, and that Popery and the Inquisition may be established in America." "Who", answered the Rev. Mr. Shute, "shall be excluded from natural trusts? Whatever answer bigotry may suggest, the dictates of candor and equality, I conceive, will be, none.¨

The Puritan clergyman carried his point, and Massachusetts endorsed the Federal Constitution. Most of the State constitutions, however, were not at first characterized by the same perfect liberty. Seven of them debarred Catholics from office or citizenship; six expressly, one by requiring naturalized citizens to abjure any foreign ecclesiastical allegiance. Unitarians in one State, Jews and unbelievers in several, were likewise subjected to civil disabilities. But in the course of time all restrictions against adherents of any religion were swept away. The removal of these civil disabilities has always, I believe, been considered a triumph of the American spirit; and the Lutheran and Baptist synods will find it difficult to persuade the public to write their synodical concept of religious liberty and civil equality upon our statute books. They will not attempt it. I have sufficient confidence in the enlightenment and good will of our American citizens, to be convinced that the clauses discriminating against Catholics which had been incorporated in some State constitutions in Colonial times, and which have been since expurged, shall never be revived, but shall forever lie buried in their ignominious graves.

That Americans in general do not believe in these synodical principles is shown at every election, when, as Mr Roosevelt has pointed out, districts predominantly Catholic have repeatedly elected Protestants to office, and visa versa, Catholics have been chosen by several strongly Protestant States as their Chief Magistrates, or as their representatives in the Senate. Presidents of the United States have shown no lack of confidence in them, calling them into their cabinet, designating two of them to the exalted post of Chief Justice of the United States, and charging them with important posts at home and abroad. Religious issues have sometimes been injected into campaigns; never, however, by Catholics, so far as I can recall; but everyone has a feeling that it is unfortunate and un-American. It has been done mostly in secret, for its authors were ashamed of the light.

It is a new thing, for the present generation at least, to see the chief authorities of important religious bodies advocating the exclusion of loyal American citizens from office on the sole ground of their religious allegiance. This act will be writ indellibly in the annals of our country in the chapter entitled "Religious Intolerance." And in the same chapter, history ought to record that the action, entirely clerical in origin, received no manifestation of sympathy with its aim or spirit from the laity, who thus earned the blame of their leaders (in things spiritual, but not in politics), and the approbation of the American people.

There must be no tampering with the delicate machinery by which religious liberty and equality are secured, and no fostering of any spirit which would tend to destroy that machinery. Religious passions are deep and strong; and any man in his senses who knows human nature or knows the history of Europe, and has at heart the future peace and happiness of our country, whatever his belief, will do nothing to introduce religious strife into politics of America. Religious tolerance is not the easy superficial virtue it seems in these placid days; intolerance in the dominating party tends to produce intolerance in the injured party. Then religious peace is near an end, unless strong restraints be used. The spirit of the country has changed much in half a century, and it would be very difficult to arouse such fanaticism as I saw in the Know-Nothing days. Prudent men, men who are far-sighted, especially if they are in positions of responsibility, will work for peace and harmony. Such has always been the attitude of our Catholic hierarchy, and, with few exceptions, of our priesthood. I know not what to think of men, putting themselves forward as the leaders of large religious bodies, who counsel the American people to depart from that policy which has promoted peace and goodwill among us and has made us illustrious among nations for our spirit of liberty and liberality. What good can they hope to accomplish?

They say Catholicism and loyalty are logically incompatible; but if, as they acknowledge, they are felt *in fact* to be compatible, should they not rejoice? Do they wish to force Catholics to be disloyal? Or do they—ah! perhaps the motive lies here—do they wish to force Catholics to renounce the Pope and became good Protestants? But no, their motive is purely patriotic. Taking Catholicism even at their worst estimate of it, then, should they be willing to introduce into American life all the bitter and hard feeling that a political war on Catholics would certainly precipitate? Willing to incur great and inevitable present evils to ward off a danger centuries hence that they cannot believe real? Willing to punish henceforth and forever honest good Catholics whom they themselves acknowledge to be loyal Americans, because their descendants of the dim distant future might have an opportunity—they would not grasp it, confess even these fearful ones—to overturn American liberties? We may well smile at the shuddering of Major Lusk; but the proposal of these men in this age is inexcusable.

I am speaking in no tone of deprecation. We have nothing to fear for ourselves. We are strong, not only in our own union and strength, but in the broad American spirit of fair play and love of liberty; and, I may be permitted to add, in our confidence that God destines the Catholic Church in this country to be the bulwark of law and order, of liberty, of social justice and purity. But I speak that I may put forth whatever strength I have to crush this detestable spirit of intolerance which, if it gained strength, would wreck the peace of the country and root out charity from the hearts of men.

"Let us uncover the hatchet!" shouts an excited Lutheran organ. Brothers, bury it. Far better for you and for the country if, when well out of sight of the Fatherland, you had silently dropped your hatchet into the deep.

Still, I do not deny that among some men who would oppose political discrimination against Catholics as unjust, unwise and unnecessary there remains a certain dread of Catholicism. They acknowledge that the Catholic Church in this country is an immense force for the public welfare, raising up native Catholics as patriotic Americans and moulding her foreign-body elements into a homogeneous people. The very sense of her strength, indeed, is in great part the cause of the dread; they fear the danger of a collision between the State and a Church whose head is a foreigner, and believes himself the representative of God upon earth. Catholic teaching, American principles of Government and the existing facts will show how baseless is the apprehension.

# New Immigrants:
# Judaism

# ❧123❧

# The Spirit of the Ghetto

## HUTCHINS HAPGOOD

This account of Jewish religion within the context of the recent immigrant community of the Lower East Side of New York as it was in 1902 raises the question of cultural adaptation by comparing generations. It is a sensitive rendering provided by an outsider, though Hutchins Hapgood (1869–1944), Harvard graduate and newspaperman of Midwestern origin, received aid from his fellow journalist, Abraham Cahan, who was familiar with the ghetto milieu from within.

When the Jew comes to America he remains, if he is old, essentially the same as he was in Russia. His deeply rooted habits and the "worry of daily bread" make him but little sensitive of the conditions of his new home. His imagination lives in the old country and he gets his consolation in the old religion. He picks up only about a hundred English words and phrases, which he pronounces in his own way. Some of his most common acquisitions are "vinda" (window), "Zieling" (ceiling), "never mind," "alle right," "that'll do," "politzman" (policeman); "*ein schön kind, ein reg'lar pitze!*" (a pretty child, a regular picture). Of this modest vocabulary he is very proud, for it takes him out of the category of the "greenhorn," a term of contempt to which the satirical Jew is very sensitive. The man who has been three weeks in this country hates few things so much as to be called a "greenhorn." Under this fear he learns the small vocabulary to which in many years he adds very little. His dress receives rather greater modification than his language. In the old country he never appeared in a short coat; that would be enough to stamp his as a "free-thinker." But when he comes to New York and his coat is worn out he is unable to find any garment long enough. The best he can do is to buy a "cut-away" or a "Prince Albert," which he often calls a "Prince Isaac." As soon as he imbibes the fear of being called a "greenhorn" he assumes the "Prince Isaac" with less regret. Many of the old women, without diminution of piety, discard their wigs, which are strictly required by the orthodox in Russia,

Source: Hutchins Hapgood, from *The Spirit of the Ghetto*, New York, 1902, pp. 10-37.

and go even to the synagogue with nothing on their heads but their natural locks.

The old Jew on arriving in New York usually becomes a sweat-shop tailor or push-cart peddler. There are few more pathetic sights than an old man with a long beard, a little black cap on his head and a venerable face—a man who had been perhaps a Hebraic or Talmudic scholar in the old country, carrying or pressing piles of coats in the melancholy sweat-shop; or standing for sixteen hours a day by his push-cart in one of the dozen crowded streets of the Ghetto, where the great markets are, selling among many other things apples, garden stuff, fish and second-hand shirts.

This man also becomes a member of one of the many hundred lodges which exist on the east side. These societies curiously express at once the old Jewish customs and the conditions of the new world. They are mutual insurance companies formed to support sick members. When a brother is ill the President appoints a committee to visit him. Mutual insurance societies and committees are American enough, and visiting the sick is prescribed by the Talmud. This is a striking instance of the adaptation of the "old" to the "new." The committee not only condoles with the decrepit member, but gives him a sum of money.

Another way in which the life of the old Jew is affected by his New York environment, perhaps the most important way as far as intellectual and educative influences are concerned, is through the Yiddish newspapers, which exist nowhere except in this country. They keep him in touch with the world's happenings in a way quite impossible in Europe. At the Yiddish theatres, too, he sees American customs portrayed, although grotesquely, and the old orthodox things often satirized to a degree; the "greenhorn" laughed to scorn and the rabbi held up to derision.

Nevertheless these influences leave the man pretty much as he was when he landed here. He remains the patriarchal Jew devoted to the law and to prayer. He never does anything that is not prescribed, and worships most of the time that he is not at work. He has only one point of view, that of the Talmud; and his aesthetic as well as his religious criteria are determined by it. "This is a beautiful letter you have written me"; wrote an old man to his son, "it smells of Isaiah." He makes of his house a synagogue, and prays three times a day; when he prays his head is covered, he wears the black and white praying-shawl, and the cubes of the phylactery are attached to his forehead and left arm. To the cubes are fastened two straps of goat-skin, black and white; those on the forehead hang down, and those attached to the other cube are wound seven times about the left arm. Inside each cube is a white parchment on which is written the Hebrew word for God, which must never be spoken by a Jew. The strength of this prohibition is so great that even the Jews who have lost their faith are unwilling to pronounce the word.

Besides the home prayers there are daily visits to the synagogue, fasts and holidays to observe. When there is a death in the family he does not go to the synagogue, but prays at home. The ten men necessary for the funeral ceremony, who are partly supplied by the Bereavement Committee of the Lodge, sit seven days in their stocking-feet on foot-stools and read Job all the time. On the Day of

Atonement the old Jew stands much of the day in the synagogue, wrapped in a white gown, and seems to be one of a meeting of the dead. The Day of Rejoicing of the Law and the Day of Purim are the only two days in the year when an orthodox Jew may be intoxicated. It is virtuous on these days to drink too much, but the sobriety of the Jew is so great that he sometimes cheats his friends and himself by shamming drunkenness. On the first and second evenings of the Passover the father dresses in a big white robe, the family gather about him, and the youngest male child asks the father the reason why the day is celebrated; whereupon the old man relates the whole history, and they all talk it over and eat, and drink wine, but in no vessel which has been used before during the year, for everything must be fresh and clean on this day. The night before the Passover the remaining leavened bread is gathered together, just enough for breakfast, for only unleavened bread can be eaten during the next eight days. The head of the family goes around with a candle, gathers up the crumbs with a quill or a spoon and burns them. A custom which has almost died out in New York is for the congregation to go out of the synagogue on the night of the full moon, and chant a prayer in the moonlight.

In addition to daily religious observances in his home and in the synagogues, to fasts and holidays, the orthodox Jew must give much thought to his diet. One great law is the line drawn between milk things and meat things. The Bible forbids boiling a kid in the milk of its mother. Consequently the hair splitting Talmud prescribes the most far-fetched discrimination. For instance, a plate in which meat is cooked is called a meat vessel, the knife with which it is cut is called a meat knife, the spoon with which one eats the soup that was cooked in a meat pot, though there is no meat in the soup, is a meat spoon, and to use that spoon for a milk thing is prohibited. All these regulations, of course, seem privileges to the orthodox Jew. The sweat-shops are full of religious fanatics, who, in addition to their ceremonies at home, form Talmudic clubs and gather in tenement-house rooms, which they convert into synagogues.

In several of the cafés of the quarter these old fellows gather. With their long beards, long black coats, and serious demeanor, they sit about little tables and drink honey-cider, eat lima beans and jealously exclude from their society the socialists and freethinkers of the colony who, not unwillingly, have cafés of their own. They all look poor, and many of them are, in fact, peddlers, shop-keepers or tailors; but some, not distinguishable in appearance from the proletarians, have "made their pile." Some are Hebrew scholars, some of the older class of Yiddish journalists. There are no young people there, for the young bring irreverence and the American spirit, and these cafés are strictly orthodox.

In spite, therefore, of his American environment, the old Jew of the Ghetto remains patriarchal, highly trained and educated in a narrow sectarian direction, but entirely ignorant of modern culture; medieval, in effect, submerged in old tradition and outworn forms.

# The Boy

The shrewd-faced boy with the melancholy eyes that one sees everywhere in the streets of New York's Ghetto, occupies a peculiar position in our society. If we could penetrate into his soul, we should see a mixture of almost unprecedented hope and excitement on the one hand, and of doubt, confusion, and self-distrust on the other hand. Led in many contrary directions, the fact that he does not grow to be an intellectual anarchist is due to his serious racial characteristics.

Three groups of influences are at work on him—the orthodox Jewish, the American, and the Socialist; and he experiences them in this order. He has either been born in America of Russian, Austrian, or Roumanian Jewish parents, or has immigrated with them when a very young child. The first of the three forces at work on his character is religious and moral; the second is practical, diversified, non-religious; and the third is reactionary from the other two and hostile to them.

Whether born in this country or in Russia, the son of orthodox parents passes his earliest years in a family atmosphere where the whole duty of man is to observe the religious law. He learns to say his prayers every morning and evening, either at home or at the synagogue. At the age of five, he is taken to the Hebrew private school, the "chaider," where, in Russia he spends most of his time from early morning till late at night. The ceremony accompanying his first appearance in "chaider" is significant of his whole orthodox life. Wrapped in a "talith," or praying shawl, he is carried by his father to the school and received there by the "melamed," or teacher, who holds out before him the Hebrew alphabet on a large chart. Before beginning to learn the first letter of the alphabet, he is given a taste of honey, and when he declares it to be sweet, he is told that the study of the Holy Law, upon which he is about to enter, is sweeter than honey. Shortly afterwards a coin falls from the ceiling, and the boy is told that an angel dropped it from heaven as a reward for learning the first lesson.

In the Russian "chaider" the boy proceeds with a further study of the alphabet, then of the prayer-book, the Pentateuch, other portions of the Bible, and finally begins with the complicated Talmud. Confirmed at thirteen years of age, he enters the Hebrew academy and continues the study of the Talmud, to which, if he is successful, he will devote himself all his life. For his parents desire him to be a rabbi, or Talmudical scholar, and to give himself entirely to a learned interpretation of the sweet law.

The boy's life at home, in Russia, conforms with the religious education received at the "chaider." On Friday afternoon, when the Sabbath begins, and on Saturday morning, when it continues, he is free from school, and on Friday does errands for his mother or helps in the preparation for the Sabbath. In the afternoon he commonly bathes, dresses freshly in Sabbath raiment, and goes to "chaider" in the evening. Returning from school, he finds his mother and sisters dressed in their best, ready to "greet the Sabbath." The lights are glowing in the candlesticks, the father enters with "Good Shabbas" on his lips, and is received by the grandparents, who occupy the seats of honor. They bless him and the children in turn. The father then chants the hymn of praise and salutation; a cup of wine or cider is passed from one to the other; every one washes his hands; all arrange themselves at table in the order of age, the youngest sitting at the father's right hand. After the meal they sing a song dedicated to the Sabbath, and say grace. The same ceremony is repeated on Saturday morning, and afterwards the children are examined in what they have learned of the Holy Law during the week. The numerous religious holidays are observed in the same way, with special ceremonies of their own in addition. The important thing to notice is, that the boy's whole training and education bear directly on ethics and religion, in the study of which he is encouraged to spend his whole life.

In a simple Jewish community in Russia, where the "chaider" is the only school, where the government is hostile, and the Jews are therefore thrown back upon their own customs, the boy loves his religion, he loves and honors his parents, his highest ambition is to be a great scholar—to know the Bible in all its glorious meaning, to know the Talmudical comments upon it, and to serve God. Above every one else he respects the aged, the Hebrew scholar, the rabbi, the teacher. Piety and wisdom count more than riches, talent and power. The "law" outweighs all else in value. Abraham and Moses, David and Solomon, the prophet Elijah, are the kind of great men to whom his imagination soars.

But in America, even before he begins to go to our public schools, the little Jewish boy finds himself in contact with a new world which stands in violent contrast with the orthodox environment of his first few years. Insensibly—at the beginning—from his playmates in the streets, from his older brother or sister, he picks up a little English, a little American slang, hears older boys boast of prize-fighter Bernstein, and learns vaguely to feel that there is a strange and fascinating life on the street. At this tender age he may even begin to black boots, gamble in pennies, and be filled with a "wild surmise" about American dollars.

With his entrance into the public school the little fellow runs plump against a system of education and a set of influences which are at total variance with those traditional to his race and with his home life. The religious element is entirely lacking. The educational system of the public schools is heterogeneous and worldly. The boy becomes acquainted in the school reader with fragments of writings on all subjects, with a little mathematics, a little history. His instruction, in the interests of a liberal non-sectarianism, is entirely secular. English becomes his most familiar language. He achieves a growing comprehension and sympathy with the independent, free, rather sceptical spirit of the American boy; he rapidly imbibes ideas about social equality and contempt for authority, and tends to prefer Sherlock Holmes to Abraham as a hero.

The orthodox Jewish influences, still at work upon him, are rapidly weakened. He grows to look upon the ceremonial life at home as rather ridiculous. His old parents, who speak no English, he regards as "greenhorns." English becomes his habitual tongue, even at home, and Yiddish he begins to forget. He still goes to "chaider," but under conditions exceedingly different from those obtaining in Russia, where there are no public schools, and where the boy is consequently shut up within the confines of Hebraic education. In America, the "chaider" assumes a position entirely subordinate. Compelled by law to go to the American public school, the boy can attend "chaider" only before the public school opens in the morning or after it closes in the afternoon. At such times the Hebrew teacher, who dresses in a long black coat, outlandish tall hat, and commonly speaks no English, visits the boy at home, or the boy goes to a neighboring "chaider."

Contempt for the "chaider's" teaching comes the more easily because the boy rarely understands his Hebrew lessons to the full. His real language is English, the teacher's is commonly the Yiddish jargon, and the language to be learned is Hebrew. The problem before him is consequently the strangely difficult one of learning Hebrew, a tongue unknown to him, through a translation into Yiddish, a language of growing unfamiliarity, which, on account of its poor dialectic character, is an inadequate vehicle of thought.

The orthodox parents begin to see that the boy, in order to "get along" in the New World, must receive a Gentile training. Instead of hoping to make a rabbi of him, they reluctantly consent to his becoming an American business man, or, still better, an American doctor or lawyer. The Hebrew teacher, less convinced of the usefulness and importance of his work, is in this country more simply commercial and less disinterested than abroad; a man generally, too, of less scholarship as well as of less devotion.

The growing sense of superiority on the part of the boy to the Hebraic part of his environment extends itself soon to the home. He learns to feel that his parents, too, are "greenhorns." In the struggle between the two sets of influences that of the home becomes less and less effective. He runs away from the supper table to join his gang on the Bowery, where he is quick to pick up the very latest slang; where his talent for caricature is developed often at the expense of his parents, his race, and all "foreigners"; for he is an American, he is "the people," and like his glorious countrymen in general, he is quick to ridicule the stranger. He laughs at the foreign Jew with as much heartiness as at the "dago"; for he feels that he himself is almost as remote from the one as from the other.

"Why don't you say your evening prayer, my son?" asks his mother in Yiddish.

"Ah, what yer givin' us!" replies, in English, the little American-Israelite as he makes a beeline for the street.

The boys not only talk together of picnics, of the crimes of which they read in the English newspapers, of prize-fights, of budding business propositions, but they gradually quit going to synagogue, give up "chaider" promptly when they are thirteen years old, avoid the Yiddish theatres, seek the up-town places of amusement, dress in the latest American fashion, and have a keen eye for the right thing in neckties. They even refuse sometimes to be present at supper on Friday evenings. Then, indeed, the sway of the old people is broken.

"Amerikane Kinder, Amerikane Kinder!" wails the old father, shaking his head. The trend of things is indeed too strong for the old man of the eternal Talmud and ceremony.

An important circumstance in helping to determine the boy's attitude toward his father is the tendency to reverse the ordinary and normal educational and economical relations existing between father and son. In Russia the father gives the son an education and supports him until his marriage, and often afterward, until the young man is able to take care of his wife and children. The father is, therefore, the head of the house in reality. But in the New World the boy contributes very early to the family's support. The father is in this country less able to make an economic place for himself than is the son. The little fellow sells papers, blacks boots, and becomes a street merchant on a small scale. As he speaks English, and his parents do not, he is commonly the interpreter in business transactions, and tends generally to take things into his own hands. There is a tendency, therefore, for the father to respect the son.

There is many a huge building on Broadway which is the external sign (with the Hebrew name of the tenant emblazoned on some extended surface) of the energy and independence of some ignorant little Russian Jew, the son of a push-cart peddler or sweat-shop worker, who began his business career on the sidewalks, selling newspapers, blacking boots, dealing in candles, shoe-strings, fruit, etc., and continued it by peddling in New Jersey or on Long Island until he could open a small basement store on Hester Street, than a more extensive establishment on Canal Street—ending perhaps as a rich merchant on Broadway. The little fellow who starts out on this laborious climb is a model of industry and temperance. His only recreation, outside of business, which for him is a pleasure in itself, is to indulge in some simple pastime which generally is calculated to teach him something. On Friday or Saturday afternoon he is likely, for instance, to take a long walk to the park, where he is seen keenly inspecting the animals and perhaps boasting of his knowledge about them. He is an acquisitive little fellow, and seldom enjoys himself unless he feels that he is adding to his figurative or literal stock.

The cloak and umbrella business in New York is rapidly becoming monopolized by the Jews who began in the Ghetto; and they are also very large clothing merchants. Higher, however, than a considerable merchant in the world of business, the little Ghetto boy, born in a patriarchal Jewish home, has not yet attained. The Jews who as bankers, brokers, and speculators on Wall Street control millions never have been Ghetto Jews. They came from Germany where conditions are very different from those in Russia, Galicia, and Roumania, and where, through the comparatively liberal education of a secular character which they were able to obtain, they were already beginning to have a national life outside of the Jewish traditions. Then, too, these Jews who are now prominent in Wall Street have been in this country much longer than their Russian brethren. They are frequently the sons of Germans who in the last generation attained commercial rank. If they were born abroad, they came many years before the Russian immigration began and before the American Ghetto existed, and have consequently become thoroughly identified with American life. Some of them began, indeed, as peddlers on a very small scale; travelled, as was more the habit with them then than now, all over the country; and rose by small degrees to the position of great financial operators. But they became so only by growing to feel very intimately the spirit of

American enterprise which enables a man to carry on the boldest operation in a calm spirit.

To this boldness the son of the orthodox parents of our Ghetto has not yet attained. Coming from the cramped "quarter," with still a tinge of the patriarchal Jew in his blood, not yet thoroughly at home in the atmosphere of the American "plunger," he is a little hesitant, though very keen, in business affairs. The conservatism instilled in him by the pious old "greenhorn," his father, is a limitation to his American "nerve." He likes to deal in ponderable goods, to be able to touch and handle his wares, to have them before his eyes. In the next generation, when in business matters also he will be an instinctive American, he will become as big a financial speculator as any of them, but at present he is pretty well content with his growing business on Broadway and his fine residence up-town.

Altho as compared with the American or German-Jew financier who does not turn a hair at the gain or loss of a million, and who in personal manner maintains a phlegmatic, Napoleonic calm which is almost the most impressive thing in the world to an ordinary man, the young fellow of the Ghetto seems a hesitant little "dickerer," yet, of course, he is a rising business man, and, as compared to the world from which he has emerged, a very tremendous entity indeed. It is not strange, therefore, that this progressive merchant, while yet a child, acquires a self-sufficiency, an independence, and sometimes an arrogance which not unnaturally, at least in form, is extended even toward his parents.

If this boy were able entirely to forget his origin, to cast off the ethical and religious influences which are his birthright, there would be no serious struggle in his soul, and he would not represent a peculiar element in our society. He would be like any other practical, ambitious, rather worldly American boy. The struggle is strong because the boy's nature, at once religious and susceptible, is strongly appealed to by both old and new. At the same time that he is keenly sensitive to the charm of his American environment, with its practical and national opportunities, he has still a deep love for his race and the old things. He is aware, and rather ashamed, of the limitations of his parents. He feels that the trend and weight of things are against them, that they are in a minority; but yet in a real way the old people remain his conscience, the visible representative of a moral and religious tradition by which the boy may regulate his inner life.

The attitude of such a boy toward his father and mother is sympathetically described by Dr. Blaustein, principle of the Educational Alliance:

> Not knowing that I speak Yiddish, the boy often acts as interpreter between me and his exclusively Yiddish-speaking father and mother. He always shows great fear that I should be ashamed of his parents and tries to show them in the best light. When he translates, he expresses, in his manner, great affection and tenderness toward these people whom he feels he is protecting; he not merely turns their Yiddish into good English, but modifies the substance of what they say in order to make them appear presentable, less outlandish and queer. He also manifests cleverness in translating for his parents what I say in English. When he finds that I can speak Yiddish and therefore can converse heart to heart with

the old people, he is delighted. His face beams, and he expresses in every way that deep pleasure which a person takes in the satisfaction of honoured protégés.

The third considerable influence in the life of the Ghetto boy is that of the socialists. I am inclined to think that this is the least important and the least desirable of the three in its effect on his character.

Socialism as it is agitated in the Jewish quarter consists in a wholesale rejection, often founded on a misunderstanding, of both American and Hebraic ideals. The socialists harp monotonously on the relations between capital and labor, the injustice of classes, and assume literature to comprise one school alone, the Russian, at the bottom of which there is a strongly anarchistic and reactionary impulse. The son of a socialist laborer lives in a home where the main doctrines are two: that the old religion is rubbish and that American institutions were invented to exploit the workingman. The natural effects on such a boy are two: a tendency to look with distrust at the genuinely American life about him, and to reject the old implicit piety.

The ideal situation for this young Jew would be that where he could become an integral part of American life without losing the seriousness of nature developed by Hebraic tradition and education. At present he feels a conflict between these two influences: his youthful ardor and ambition lead him to prefer the progressive, if chaotic and uncentred, American life; but his conscience does not allow him entire peace in a situation which involves a chasm between him and his parents and their ideas. If he could find along the line of his more exciting interests—the American—something that would fill the deeper need of his nature, his problem would receive a happy solution.

At present, however, the powers that make for the desired synthesis of the old and the new are fragmentary and unimportant. They consist largely in more or less charitable institutions such as the University Settlement, the Educational Alliance, and those free Hebrew schools which are carried on with definite reference to the boy as an American citizen. The latter differ from the "chaiders" in several respects. The important difference is that these schools are better organized, have better teachers, and have as a conscious end the supplementing of the boy's common school education. The attempt is to add to the boy's secular training an ethical and religious training through the intelligent study of the Bible. It is thought that an acquaintance with the old literature of the Jews is calculated to deepen and spiritualize the boy's nature.

The Educational Alliance is a still better organized and more intelligent institution, having much more the same purpose in view as the best Hebrew schools. Its avowed purpose is to combine the American and Hebrew elements, reconcile fathers and sons by making the former more American and the latter more Hebraic, and in that way improve the home life of the quarter. With the character of the University Settlement nearly everybody is familiar. It falls in line with Anglo-Saxon charitable institutions, forms classes, improves the condition of the poor, and acts as an ethical agent. But, tho such institutions as the above may do a great deal of good, they are yet too fragmentary and external, are too little a vital growth from the conditions, to supply the demand for a serious life which at the same time shall be American.

But the Ghetto boy is making use of his heterogeneous opportunities with the greatest energy and ambition. The public schools are filled with little Jews, the night schools of the east side are practically used by no other race. City College, New York University, and Columbia University are graduating Russian Jews in numbers rapidly increasing. Many lawyers, indeed, children of patriarchal Jews, have very large practices already, and some of them belong to solid firms on Wall Street; although as to business and financial matters they have not yet attained to the most spectacular height. Then there are innumerable boys' debating clubs, and literary clubs in the east side; altogether there is an excitement in ideas and an enthusiastic energy for acquiring knowledge which has interesting analogy to the hopefulness and acquisitive desire of the early Renaissance. It is a mistake to think that the young Hebrew turns naturally to trade. He turns his energy to whatever offers the best opportunities for broader life and success. Other things besides business are open to him in this country, and he is improving his chance for the higher education as devotedly as he has improved his opportunities for success in business.

It is easy to see that the Ghetto boy's growing Americanism will be easily triumphant at once over the old traditions and the new socialism. Whether or not he will be able to retain his moral earnestness and native idealism will depend not so much upon him as upon the development of American life as a whole. What we need at the present time more than anything else is a spiritual unity such as, perhaps, will only be the distant result of our present special activities. We need something similar to the spirit underlying the national and religious unity of the orthodox Jewish culture.

# ✥124✥

# Living Judaism

## LEO JUNG

The pressures on immigrants to adapt their cultures, including religion, to the American environment—the process contemporaries called 'Americanization'—posed difficult problems for them. How far did their new loyalties require them to modify old beliefs and practices? How far could they do so without losing what was most preciously distinctive in their lives? In the case of Jews, anxieties were most acute amongst the orthodox.

## Orthodox Judaism

### I

Thus, we too must ask the question, "What is the position of Torah-true Judaism in the United States of America?" If the watchmen are honest and farsighted the answer will at first seem most pessimistic. "In the darkness," they will reply. We who put the question in an institution dedicated to the harmonization of the American civilization with Jewish culture, who have succeeded in creating for ourselves an oasis in which our children may rest in safety and enjoy the fruits of our labors, must yet never allow ourselves to be confined to a narrow horizon, to view the outlook for Judaism through rosy glasses just because we have built ourselves a strong fortress of our faith. For, as we proceed on the right, we will be told that Torah-true Judaism is dead, and on the left, that it is not fit for modern life; and if we leave the city and travel in any direction, we shall find that, "Orthodoxy has apparently become an unpalatable affair, a system of life good enough for decrepit old age, but the object of indifferent contempt to the youth."

A superficial observer will say, "The orthodox Jews have lost courage after having lost their self-respect; and they have lost their self-respect after having been overconfident" (what the prophet describes as *shaananim*). No doubt there has been a terrific lifelessness in our camp. The few rabbis, teachers and laymen who

Source: Leo Jung, from *Living Judaism*, New York, 1927, pp. 208-12, 217-22.

know what Orthodoxy is, are preaching in a voice that calls out in a wilderness. Their sermons are drowned by the hubbub of the compromiser and by the shouts of the deliberate destroyer. The old are too feeble to exert any influence on their milieu, and those few who are young are too solitary, and very frequently they suffer from a subconscious sense of despair. They have lost the vista of their mission—so that appearances would justify the blackest prognostications. And *yet I want to say that once we shall understand clearly what the scope of orthodox Judaism is, what is its nature, what are its objects, what are the agencies whereby its problems may be solved and how these agencies have been used until now in this country—we shall have every reason to be optimistic.*

A short time ago a leading reform rabbi said to me, "I admit that reform Judaism is a failure, but you will have to admit that orthodox Judaism is one, too"; and I replied, "I do not wish to argue about the failure of the former; it has had every opportunity and you admit that it has failed. But as for orthodoxy,— it has never had any opportunity. It has had no chance to be known in its theory by the American Jew, and to be seen in practice in its full strength and beauty and therefore it has not failed. Reform Judaism has at its disposal, and makes full use of the leaders of the general daily, and to a great extent the weekly Jewish press. Its champions are captains of commerce and industry, pillars of society, friends of men in high places. At their beck are millions of dollars, legions of orators—they have all the advantages of a sturdy first comer. But orthodoxy hitherto has been neither articulate nor organized, nor representative of itself in any meaning of this word. It hasn't even begun to appear in its clear light. American Jewry has never rejected orthodox Judaism, for American Jewry has never seen what orthodox Judaism is."

Orthodox Judaism, or, as we prefer to call it, Torah-true Judaism, is the genuine historical faith of our people which is to express itself through the medium of a true Jewish life. It is as a kingdom of priests and a holy nation that we were called into being, and the great truths of the Fatherhood of God and of the Brotherhood of Man were to be expressed by the mode of life which the Torah prescribes and counsels.

In order that we may translate the ideals of the Torah into living reality, we are bid to be ever alive to these postulates:

1. Taskilu Bekhol asher taassu which means, "Do all that you do in the most intelligent manner." Even the greatest idea will lose its force and effectiveness if it is brought before men in a clumsy, thoughtless fashion.
2. Our rabbis tell us that it is a definite religious duty, *hithnach lefanav bemitzvoth*—which means, "To fulfill His commands in the most esthetic manner." The most perfect dish will become repulsive if it is served on a musty plate. The most soul-stirring melody will fail on a defective instrument. The great ideas and ideals of true Judaism will fail in their appeal if they are presented in ugly form.
3. The ladder of Jacob, we are told, with its top reached heaven, but its foot rested firmly on the ground. Moses, it is true, spent forty days and nights with Eternity, but he taught us that religion was not above in Heaven, nor beyond

the sea, but on earth, in human speech and in human hearts. The editor of the Mishnah, Rabbi Judah the Prince, bids us choose a path of life which will also be beautiful in the sight of man: *Vetifereth lo min ha-adam.*

These principles of conduct and method are commended to us Jews not only as pleasant ways of self-expression, but as essential conditions for the success of our labors for Judaism. Orthodox Jews, therefore, are not doing their duty as orthodox Jews if they are satisfied with anything less than this.

If, in American orthodox Jewry, these principles would have been acted upon, if the American youth would have seen such genuine Orthodoxy in every department of Jewish activity and would then have decided to reject it deliberately, definitely, and uncompromisingly,—then indeed our hopes would appear buried and we should have to look to the future with despairing eyes. But what has been the actual situation?

## The Synagogue

The orthodox Synagogue, in accordance with the law of Judaism, should be a place of which we think with reverence; in which the message of the Torah is given in clear terms, in Jewish *Kavanah* (devotion) and *Hithlahabuth* (enthusiasm), in which decorum and the spirit of holiness prevails; which our elders enter with such detachment from the manner and thoughts of the world without that the children would have borne upon them the fact that they are approaching God, communing with their Maker, uttering the prayers into which historic Israel has poured his hopes and his woes, his tears and his joys.

But what did and what does the average orthodox synagogue represent? A disheartening spectacle of disorder. The Jewish message came in a foreign tongue, Yiddish, and in a foreign method, and therefore did not reach the youth. The average orthodox synagogue, however orthodox in all other respects, is utterly unorthodox in this lack of an inspiring word to the younger generation, utterly unorthodox in its uncleanliness, utterly unorthodox in its lack of decorum, utterly unorthodox in the crude behavior of the worshippers. If the parents of our youth had made it their set purpose to drive their children away from the Jewish synagogue, they could have employed no better method for that end than the management and the conduct prevalent in the average "shul." A place dedicated to the worship of God, which the parents enter with a cheap sense of being-at-home, without any respect for its sacredness, in which the prayers are accompanied by promiscuous conversation, could not but become repulsive to the inner feelings of reverence in our boys and girls. If our young people refuse to go to synagogue, they do not do so because they reject Orthodoxy. They keep away from the synagogue not because of what is orthodox in it but precisely because of such of its elements as are non-orthodox; its lack of Jewish training for the child, its noise, its indecorum. Our youth here drift away not because the message of the synagogue is distasteful to them, but because they have never received it. We know that these defects of the American orthodox Synagogue are but a Galuth weakness. We know that many of our people under the Czarist regime had no opportunity for self-expression, that the street and the public places, by the tyranny of a bigoted bureaucracy, were so cribbed and confined as to frustrate a free vent to individual or collective feeling; that the synagogue, therefore, naturally did become the place in which the Jew discussed and lived over his experiences.

We understand that such a heritage cannot be easily overcome. It is the ballast which even a free generation can not throw overboard without much ado. But whatever the cause of synagogue noise may be, its effects unfortunately have proved very damaging to the interest of our faith.

We also know that the immigrant, both layman and rabbi, found so many problems awaiting him here, so much to be readjusted, so much to be revalued, so little time left after the sweat-shop hours, that physiologically and psychologically he was unable to plant virile Judaism into his institutions, to translate himself into American life and language, and to present in this new garb the old message to his youth. But the fact remains even after we know all contributary causes. We have expressed Judaism in the average orthodox synagogue not to its advantage but in a most disagreeable and unsatisfactory manner.

## II

Earlier discussion has brought out the point that Orthodoxy in the United States has come to a sorry pass because in this country it has hitherto failed in its three organs of expression: the synagogue, the school and the home. The obvious result of such failure can be seen today in the fact that the pulpit, the home, and the synagogue, in so far as they are controlled by the new generation, are usually non and frequently anti-orthodox. Hence a great deal of present-day pessimism:

> How can we, with our lack of efficient messengers of the Torah, revive genuine Jewishness in our country, as against the united vociferous efforts of hostile and indifferent pulpits, classrooms, and homes?

## Signs of the Dawn

That question was justified even as late as two years ago, and it has some of its force still. But between that time and today there yawns a chasm, happily unbridgeable. For last year the Rabbi Isaac Elchanan Yeshivah, the Academy of Orthodox Judaism, was yet in the fastnesses of East Broadway.

The Jewish Center school and system has done splendid pioneer work and has blazed the trail for the new era, but it represented too isolated an instance to justify general optimism.

The Yeshivah, heroically shouldering a task under which it managed to just avoid bankruptcy, charged with a mountain of responsibilities, which crushed its very striving, was a pitiful physical torso of a beautiful spiritual monument.

We must make the Torah appeal to the American youth. We must win over the American boy and girl. We must change them from indifferent Jewish boys into inspired young Jews, from pleasure-mad, shallow girls, into happy daughters of Israel. Not only the middle aged rabbi, but even the young Yeshivah graduate has often proved incapable of doing this. As the building, so did the "musmach" (diplomé) rushing forth from its portals, lack the outward grace, that double "hayn" of which the prophet speaks.

Judaism does not stand for the milieu of East Broadway. Unfortunately Galuth conditions have brought about such habitation of the Torah. But so far as Judaism is concerned, it is at home only in a place of bright rooms, wide vistas, and limitless fresh air. We do live on earth, though our ideas connect us with heaven. The Torah itself was written in the language of man, because it has been given to man and not to the ministering angels. Our children in public school and high school are taught a view of life which makes them appreciate the Jewish diction that "cleanliness is next to godliness," that fresh air and bright rooms are essentials of religion.

## The New Yeshivah

The Yeshivah, potentially the savior of American Jewry, has hitherto failed in these points, and with it suffered the prospects of upright Jewishness. All because of its unattractive garb and backward system. The Yeshivah thus offered the peg on which the multitude would hang its ready prejudices. In the mind of the average Jew it is ugly from without and unorganized from within, an institution probably noble in its aim, but hopelessly adequate in method. But all that will soon be a matter of the past. For the men at the helm at last have aroused themselves. At last they have realized that the Yeshivah, to be able to recreate the organs of public expression, the organized mouthpiece of faithful Israel, needs first of all an attractive exterior to develop its potentialities; must move from its obscure place on the Lower East Side to its rightful place as the mother of American Israel.

The men who guide its present destiny have seen that the time for petty effort and routine has passed, and that Orthodoxy must rise to the occasion. Orthodox Jews have outgrown the leadership of charity Judaism and have decided to apply themselves not only to the healing of the sick, but especially to the preventive health service of the Torah.

"Torah im Derech Erelz" implies a great number of things. At the Yeshivah it must imply the combination of modern method applied to the ancient limud (scholarship), through teachers, laymen and rabbis who will in themselves embody the harmonious synthesis of western achievement and Jewish asset: Modern civilization refined and made more enduring by Jewish principles; Judaism taught and spread by the workmanship of our best educators and our most honest thinkers.

The rabbi trained in the new rejuvenated Yeshivah college and seminary will be eminently fit to inspire the young Jew with the glory of Judaism.

The New Yeshivah thus represents the hope, and a very justified one, in the steady rebirth of American Jewish consciousness, of the collective and individual God-consciousness of Israel. The very boldness of the plan guarantees the rediscovery of our creative genius which has enriched so many foreign vineyards and distant fields. Once the orthodox Jew is aroused, once he has been taught to look up again, to look upon himself as the seed from which the tree of full Jewish life may grow up, once the Orthodox Jew has been guided to a broader vista, the glorious potentialities of the Torah, this building will assume proportions undreamed of even now. The orthodox Jew is just about to discover himself. He has not yet tapped his energies. Of his tremendous reserve powers, of his endless wealth and deathless energies, he himself has but dim notions. We know that the orthodox Jew is the mainstay of his people only when he is truly orthodox. That means manful, active; that means struggling, worrying, anxious about the future of his children. Let us teach the orthodox Jew, therefore, the courage of his convictions, to think consistently and to act upon his consistent thought. That differentiates the Orthodox from his fellow coreligionists. Zangwill admits that Orthodoxy is the only hope for the Jewish future. The essential difference between us and Jews of his type lies in the fact that the Orthodox Jew thinks logically to a conclusion and adopts Jewish life to recreate Jewish values.

Great is the task before us. The Yeshivah is expecting many willing hearts and open hands. The Yeshivah cannot fail to appeal and to appeal strongly and to appeal enduringly to that in us which is still Jewish, virile, clear-minded. We know that the solution of our problem is near. We know that its successful solution depends upon the willingness of the orthodox Jew to wrench himself away from all incumbrances, and hindrances, from selfishness and narrow-heartedness, from the spirit of over-confidence and the spirit of despondency, that it demands of him that he arouse himself and put his shoulder to the wheel.

## Forces Arousing the Dawn

It is obvious that whereas the building of the new Yeshivah College does promise to inaugurate a new epoch in American Jewry, the fact of that plan in itself is an indication of some rearousal, some reawakening in the orthodox camp.

Conditions in the Yeshivah have been deplorably unsatisfactory for quite a time, and yet the orthodox Jew seemed incapable of arousing himself to some definite action. Yet he seemed incapable of thinking for himself, planning for his own future.

The moment in which the Jewish Center rallied round the flag of Torah to defend it against the pompous folly of its betrayers, was the beginning of the new epoch. The men who then stood upright and braved the fury and the blows of uncovered dissent, have inscribed their names in golden letters into the records of loyal American Israel. But this new spirit in the "machneh Israel" (the camp of loyal Israel) is happily apparent in a number of directions. The Union of Orthodox Jewish Congregations is now working, battling, and emerging in many a field of Jewish endeavor. The academic youth in New York is flocking in large numbers to the Collegiate Branch of that Union. Many men and women, merchants and professionals, rabbis of learning, culture and fresh energies have definitely allied themselves to its cause, and it is going slowly but definitely from strength to strength.

# ❦125❧

# The Jewish Reform Movement in the United States

## DAVID PHILIPSON

The American Reform Movement in Judaism arose amongst Jews who were open to modern intellectual currents and were willing to make changes in their faith in the light of their understanding of American conditions. In effect such changes were also an attempt to bridge the differences in experience and outlook between the immigrant generation and their American-born children and grandchildren. This did not mean a wholesale abandonment of tradition but it did entail reception of some of the norms of religious worship in the larger culture such as organ music and the sermon. Philipson traces this process historically through the lives and ideas of its early leaders.

═══════════════════════════════════

## The Leaders of the Reform Movement

Every movement among men, in order to issue successfully, requires ability, conviction, and enthusiasm in its leaders. Without any doubt, the reform movement took such firm hold in the United States because in its early days it was led and directed by men of great ability, strong purpose, deep conviction, earnest enthusiasm, and scholarly aims. The first attempt in Charleston collapsed because it was not headed by a capable leader. The earnest men who composed that first "Reformed Society of Israelites" failed to succeed because there was no one to direct them. It was fortunate for the success of the movement elsewhere that a number of strong men, dissatisfied with conditions in Europe and despairing of accomplishing their cherished aims there, emigrated to America and shaped the policy of the congregations. As we have seen, the people themselves were ready for the reforms; the people themselves had organized

Source: David Philipson, from 'The Jewish Reform Movement in the United States', *Jewish Quarterly Review*, October, 1897.

106

reform societies, but these languished until they were taken in hand by men who stand as the true and tried leaders of those formative days. Mentioning them in the order of their appearance in American Jewish life, these will ever be regarded as the great pioneer preachers and workers in the cause of reform; Max Lilienthal, who arrived in New York in 1845; Isaac M. Wise, who came the following year, in 1846; David Einhorn, whose work began in Baltimore in 1855; Samuel Alder, who was called to New York in 1857; Bernard Felsenthal, whose *Kol Kore Bamidbar*, "the voice in the wilderness," was raised in Chicago in 1858; and Samuel Hirsch, who took charge of the congregation in Philadelphia in 1866.

It is not my purpose to give a biographical sketch of these men; space will not permit it. But, in order to show how clearly they understood and defined the issues, I shall, in extracts taken from words spoken or written in those early years of their work, let them speak for themselves. In one form or another, they express what to them are the essentials and characteristics of the reform movement. In sermons of burning eloquence, or in disquisitions of calm reasoning, they published forth the faith that was in them.

Max Lilienthal (1814–1882) arrived in America in 1845. He was elected rabbi of three orthodox congregations of New York city, in which capacity he served for several years, but severed the connexion on account of the differences that had arisen between his views and those of his constituencies. His opinions were changing and taking a decided trend towards the principles of reform. He was one of the most active spirits in the organization of the "Verein der Lichtfreunde," a society formed in 1849 for the discussion and the spreading of the teachings of the reform movement. In a lecture delivered before this society in that year, he said: "The bridge between the past and the present is broken off." He retired from the ministry for a number of years, and opened a school. In the year 1854, however, he again entered the area of active Jewish life by writing for *The Asmonean*; in a number of articles published in the columns of this paper, and in *The Israelite*, shortly thereafter, he declared strongly for reform. In 1855 he was elected rabbi of the congregation B'ne Israel, Cincinnati, which office he filled to the day of his death. He led the congregation along the path of reform. Characteristic was the statement he made shortly after assuming office in Cincinnati, when refusing to conduct the traditional service of lamentation on the ninth day of Ab; he said that he considered the destruction of Jerusalem a reason for rejoicing rather than mourning, as it was the cause of the Jews spreading all over the world and carrying the light of monotheism everywhere. In one of the early articles on reform, alluded to above, he wrote:—

> We are tired of seeing men violating the Sabbath until they have accumulated an independent fortune, and calling themselves orthodox nevertheless; we are disgusted at seeing men transgressing every religious ceremony in public life, and yet clothing themselves with the halo of sanctification. We wish to see this contradiction solved: we wish to know when religious ceremonies have to yield to the necessities of life and when they have to be kept at any price, subjugating life and its exigencies. In a word, we wish to know what in our law is God's

command and what is the transient work of mortal man. Such an investigation will solve the contradiction between life and religion; will raise the Mosaic law to its divine purity; will do away with all the unfounded conglomerations of different ages; and will surely reunite the now distracted body of Israel in peace and harmony....

Reform has tried and tries to raise the dignity of our worship. No one will deny that the worship as conducted in the old synagogues is unsatisfactory.... How many prayers are there unbecoming the country we live in; unfit for our mode of thinking, totally antagonistic to the changed views and feelings! Reform tries to find a remedy for all these abuses and to make the house of the Lord a house of true prayer and devotion....

Whether agreed to or not, it is a fact that the belief in a great many things, that fifty years ago were considered holy and sacred, has been greatly shaken. No one will be quieted by such sentences as "the Minhag of Israel is as binding as the law of Moses." Men of learning and profound reasoning have clearly shown the historical development of so many of our ceremonies, and the belief that the rabbinical law, from A to Z, has come down from Sinai, has totally disappeared. Scientific researchers have proved that all nations and times have added to the store of our religious observances, and that all therefore cannot be as holy as the Bible. Further researches will restore our religion to its primitive purity and simplicity; will remove each and every contest; and unite us again in the firm belief in the Holy One, for whom our fathers suffered and for whom also we, their descendants, are ready to make every sacrifice.... We are no reformers from inclination, no reformers for fashion's sake, but reformers from conviction. We do not belong to that frivolous or arrogant class that do away and abolish because it suits them just now. No; what we assert we intend to prove; and where we shall move the abolition of any ceremony, we shall not do it without showing that the religious codes themselves entitle us to demand such a change and such a reform.

Isaac M. Wise (b. 1819) who, at the age of seventy-eight, is still active in his chosen field of labor, may well be considered the great organizer and indefatigable worker in the cause. From the moment almost of his landing on these shores he became a power in American Judaism. It is not too much to say that, more than any other man, he has stamped his individuality upon the history and development of Jewish life in the United States. Restless, untiring, zealous, his is the most prominent name in American Jewry. His activity of over half a century as organizer, editor, preacher, educator, spans the history of the reform movement. In an article written in the year 1854, he said:—

Our religion contains better elements than a mere controversial and casuistical rabbinism, and these better elements must be considered the primary cause of its self-preservation. The Jew had the consciousness that he alone possesses the most philosophical views of the existence and nature of the Deity; of the nature, duties, and hopes of mankind; of justice, equity, and charity; of the several relations between God and his creatures, and between man and his fellow-man. With this sublime conviction he first stood in the midst of degraded and superstitious heathenism, then by the side of persecuting Catholicism, and finally opposed to a ridiculous mysticism.... The Jew, however, felt conscious of the verities of his religion, and therefore he loved them better than his life and worldly interests; he saw himself alone in the world, alone with his sublime ideas, and therefore he lived in his faith and for it, and the thousand forms which he observed only led him to his sublime ideas. It was this elevating and inspiring consciousness, and not rabbinism, which preserved Judaism. But now the idea, the sublime cardinal elements, are almost lost sight of in the multitude of thoughtless observances of rabbinical forms.... Judaism has become a set of unmeaning practices, and the intelligent Jew either mourns for the fallen daughter of Zion or has adopted a course of frivolity and indifference. Therefore we demand reforms. All unmeaning forms must be laid aside as outworn garments. The internal spirit of Judaism must be expounded, illustrated, and made dear again to the Jew. We must inform our friends and opponents that there is a Judaism independent of its forms, and that this is Judaism emphatically. It is therefore our principle of reform: "All forms to which no meaning is attached any longer are an impediment to our religion, and must be done away with." Before we propose to abolish anything we should inquire, What is its practical benefit? If there is none it is time to renounce it, for one dead limb injuries the whole body. Another principle of reform is this: "Whatever makes us ridiculous before the world as it now is, may safely be and should be abolished," for we are in possession of an intelligent religion, and the nations from our precept and example should be led to say, "This is a wise and intelligent people."

A third principle of reform is this, "Whatever tends to the elevation of the divine service, to inspire the heart of the worshipper and attract him, should be done without any unnecessary delay," for the value of divine service must be estimated according to its effect upon the heart and understanding.

A fourth principle of reform is this, "Whenever religious observances and the just demands of civilized society exclude each other, the former have lost their power;" for religion was taught for the purpose "to live therein and not to die therein;" our religion makes us active members of civilized society, hence we must give full satisfaction to its just demands.

Last, or rather first, it must be remarked, the leading star of reform must be the maxim, "Religion is intended to make man happy, good, just, active, charitable, and intelligent." Whatever tends to this end is truly religious, and must be retained or introduced if it does not yet exist. Whatever has an effect contrary to the above must be abolished as soon a possible.

David Einhorn (1809–1879), the prophet of the movement in many an inspiring sermon expressed the fundamental principles of reform. His words ring with the earnestness of conviction, and are eloquent with the enthusiastic outpourings of a spirit akin to that of the prophets of old. Israel's Messianic mission, Judaism's true inwardness, these form the frain and refrain of the remarkable utterances of this man, whose lips were touched with the coal of living fire taken from the altar of God. In the very first sermon that he preached in the United States, his inaugural address before the Har Sinai congregation in Baltimore, he stated in broad and clear lines his conception of Judaism. From that sermon the subjoined paragraphs are taken as indicative of his thought:—

Like man himself, the child of God, the divine law has a perishable body and an imperishable spirit. The body is intended to be the servant of the spirit, and must disappear as soon as bereft of the latter. This spirit is the doctrinal and moral law of Scripture, whose fundamental principles the Ten Commandments set forth exclusively; to them belongs also the Sabbath, which has a symbolical significance only in reference to the choice of the day. The Decalogue is the essence of the covenant between God and man; it is therefore binding for all times, places, and peoples, and was destined to become from the very beginning the common possession of mankind through Israel.... All other divine ordinances, on the other hand, are only *signs* of the covenant—guards and protections of the eternal and universal law....; these, from their very nature, cannot remain always and everywhere the same, nor acquire the force of eternal or general obligations. Not that man will ever be able to dispense altogether with visible signs, but the expression and form of these must necessarily change with different stages of culture, national customs, industrial, social, and civil conditions, in short with the general demands of the inner and outer life. As little as the ripe fruit can be forced back into the bud or the butterfly into the chrysalis, so little can the religious idea in its long process from generation to maturity be bound to one and the same form. And if the inner growth of the religious idea in Judaism demands such a transformation, the contact with the world callS for it none the less urgently.... The Israel which nestled on Mount Zion, more or less isolated among the neighbouring peoples, that, ocean-like, surrounded it, could and did fortify itself with quite different bulwarks than the Israel which traverses this ocean in all directions, which wanders through all districts with its spiritual possessions, and, willy nilly, cannot but recognize the demands made upon it to coalesce with the peoples round about. And, in truth, the historical development of our religion has effected so great a change in the biblical ordinances, that during the space of two thousand years the observance of the greater portion of them has disappeared from Jewish life.

It is true, the piety of our fathers sought to retain a hold on these forms as long and as well as it could possibly be done; they lamented sore as though in their loss Judaism had sustained a fatal wound, and they comforted themselves with the thought that these laws were only in a state of suspended animation. Not forever and for aye, so mused they, would the glorious house of David, the magnificent temple with its sacrifices, and priests, and Levites be sunk into the dust; not forever and for aye would Israel remain an outcast from its ancestral home! At some future day the Lord would once again erect the fallen tabernacle of David, gather the scattered tribes of Israel into the old home, and let the sanctuary of Zion rise in all its glory! But the lamentation as well as the consolation rested on the same untenable foundation, viz. the *equalization*, or more correctly the *confounding*, of the religious form with the religious spirit. Hence both were invested with immutability, and instead of striving to spiritualize the form, the spirit was formalized and a ceremonial standard applied even to the moral law.

Long ago those prophetical voices had been silenced which, with unwearied enthusiasm, had extolled the *spirit* of the divine law as the true banner of Israel, about which all people would some day rally, and, compared with which, all sacrifice and fasting would appear worthless. Those prophets would have proclaimed at the destruction of the second temple: "Comfort ye! the old forms are and will remain dead, but out of their grave the freed spirit rises to spread its pinions over all the earth; out of the ashes of the destroyed temple of isolated Israel will gradually emerge that gigantic temple, whereof the Lord hath said העמים ביתי בית תפלה יקרא לכל. My house shall be called a house of prayer for all peoples; from the ruins of Judah a Messianic world will arise! Yes, often will you be forced to cement the stones of this structure with your heart's blood; but such a mission merits such sacrifices, and these sacrifices are worth more than thousands of rams and goats!" Thus, I claim, our old prophets would have spoken; and truly at the present time we are called upon most urgently to work earnestly and effectively in the spirit of the prophets, to proceed to make the proper modification of our outer and our inner religious life. Judaism has reached a turning-point when all such customs and usages as are lifeless must be abolished, partly with the object of retaining its own followers, partly to protect from moral degeneracy. In consequence of the insuperable conditions of life there has set in a violent antagonism between practice and religious conviction which will eventually cease to distress the conscience. The continuance of such a state of affairs would be the greatest misfortune that could befall Israel. On the one hand, the most important ceremonial laws are violated daily, laws which are still considered incumbent upon the Israelite; on the other hand, religious wishes and hopes are expressed in prayer which do not awaken the least response in the heart, and stand in absolute contradiction to the true spirit of the Sinaitic doctrine. This must necessarily lead to one of two things, either that the religious sentiment will become completely dulled or take refuge in the bosom of some other faith. Experience has shown the futility of all attempts to breathe life into the obsolete and dead. Even those praiseworthy attempts to win back for the public service some of the old attractiveness by establishing an outward harmony must and will remain fruitless as long as, at bottom, they serve merely to hide the inner decay. There is at present a rent in Judaism which affects its very life, and which no covering however glittering can repair. The evil which threatens to corrode gradually all the healthy bone and marrow must be completely eradicated, and this can be done only if, in the name and in the interest of the religion, we remove from the sphere of our religious life all that is corrupt and untenable, and solemnly absolve ourselves from all obligations toward it in the future; thus we may achieve the liberation of Judaism for ourselves and for our children, so as to prevent the estrangement from Judaism.

The renunciation of antiquated religious notions and customs must direct our attention the more singly and completely to the essence of God's word, which is exalted above the change of times and places, and will be potent even through the earth wax old as a garment and the heavens vanish like smoke. No, no! we do not desire a self-made cult, our wish is not for a Judaism manufactured to meet the demands of aestheticism; no planing off of the Israelitish emblem, no excursions into the empty void; but, on the contrary, an Israelitism that is rooted in Sinai and wishes to bring forth new blossoms and fruits on the mighty height of a history of four thousand years.... The more ceremonialism loses its import and extent among us, the more necessary it becomes to grasp the Jewish belief in its uniqueness, a uniqueness which separates Judaism from all other faiths, even after the abolition of its whole ceremonial law.

These, then, are the beliefs which are the source of our strength, the fundamental reason of our unexampled endurance, the trophy of our historical struggle—the belief in the one and only God, who, eternal, invisible and incorporeal, reveals Himself to man alone in His wonderful works, but especially in man himself, pervading everything alike, the earth and the heavens, the perishable and the imperishable, the body and the spirit;—the belief in the innate goodness and purity of every created being, and especially of the godlike creatures gifted with reason, whose free self-sanctification no original sin prevents, and whose redemption and salvation no other mediation than their own free activity can effect;—the belief in one humanity, all of whose members, being of the same heavenly and earthly origin, possess a like nobility of birth and a claim to equal rights, equal laws, and an equal share of happiness;—the belief that all will partake of this happiness here on earth by the eventual amalgamation of all peoples into one people of God, from whose midst the Lord, according to the prophetical promise, אקח לבהנים ללוים ונם מהם, will choose also non-Israelitish priests and Levites; this people will recognize the Lord of the universe alone as its king והיה יי למלך על כל הארץ. Then shall the blood-stained purple of earthly dominion be buried forever, and with it the whole illusion of glittering falsehood, selfishness, and persecution. These and like teachings, whose first promulgation had to take place within the pale of the narrow Jewish nationality for the fear lest mankind at large might have been blinded by their splendour, are Israel's still to-day; the possession thereof is its pride, their future acknowledgment its only hope. Each of these doctrines contains treasures of world-redeeming thoughts, and it is our sacred mission to draw forth these treasures more and more from out the deep mine of our literature, to show them forth in all their glory, to make them practicable for active life, and through them enrich heart and soul.

Samuel Adler (1809–1891), the student and scholar, was active in the city of New York, where he served as Rabbi of Temple Emmanuel for nineteen years. He came to this country from Alzei in 1857. His sermon on the last day of Passover in that year clearly indicated that a new leader had been gained for the cause of Reformed Judaism in America.

> Our situation is like unto that of the Israelites immediately after their deliverance from Egypt. Behind us lies Egypt, the Middle Ages, before us the sea of Talmudic legalism, whereof it may truly he said, all streams and rivulets discharge themselves into the sea, which is nevertheless never filled nor yet ever cleansed through flood. Let then the rod be raised to cleave it! backwards we cannot go, to stand still means death. Then let us forward, forward across the sea. Reason holds the rod, reason is the leader. The Torah itself calls itself our wisdom and our understanding in the eyes of the nations. A violent east wind is being wafted, and dries up the sea in this land of freedom. The spirit indwelling here in the West, the spirit of freedom, is the newly-born Messiah.

Shortly before the Sinai congregation of Chicago was organized, its promoters addressed a series of questions to Dr. Adler, one of which was, "What course should a reformed congregation pursue?" His answer in part was as follows:—

> The answer to this question would quite fill a book, and cannot be even fully indicated in a letter. However, in order not to leave you without any satisfaction, I would state that the first and most important step for such a congregation to take is to free its service of shocking lies, to remove from it the mention of things and wishes which we would not utter if it had to be done in an intelligible manner. Such are, the lamentation about oppression and persecution, the petition for the restoration of the sacrificial cult, for the return of Israel to Palestine, the hope for a personal Messiah, and for the resurrection of the body. In the second place, to eliminate fustian and exaggeration; and, in the third place, to make the service clear, intelligible, instructive, and inspiring.

Samuel Adler was essentially a scholar, and preferred the quiet of the study to the excitement of active life. He spent the last sixteen years of his life in honoured retirement.

Bernard Felsenthal (b. 1822), who is now living in scholarly seclusion, was the most active spirit in the inauguration of the reform movement in Chicago.

As rabbi of Sinai and later of Zion congregation of that city, his voice and his pen were ever active in the service of reform. Firm and consistent, he has never wavered in his advocacy of, and allegiance to, that interpretation of Judaism which he set forth in the very first years of his activity. In the pamphlet *Kol Kore Bamidbar*, which, a clarion call, he addressed to the friends of reform in the year 1859, he speaks with no uncertain tone. From this pamphlet a number of paragraphs are herewith taken:—

> There is a time to tear down and a time to build up. Thus speaks the holy book imbued with the spirit of God. Our age, in as far as it concerns itself with Jewish religious life, is evidently intended rather to build up than to tear down. But what shall be built up, what shall be constructed anew? The inner, deep-seated belief in God, the moral sense in all the relations of life, the attachment to and love for Judaism, the teaching of Moses freed of all heathenism and foolishness; with this must be combined the excision of all statutes and observances intended for other times, places, and conditions.
>
> There is but one class of laws which, biblical or post-biblical, have eternal validity, and these are the moral laws, engraved by the finger of God with ineradicable letters in the spiritual nature of man.
>
> A religious law, which has not its root in the spiritual or physical nature of man, is of binding force only so long as it is able to exert a hallowing influence on mind and heart, on the sentiments and actions of the devotee.
>
> By virtue of our mind, which we recognize as a revelation of God in common with the rest of nature, we distinguish the treasures of eternal truth in sacred Scripture from that which is the result of the deficient conceptions of early times and the incorrect ideas concerning the world and life, as well as from those laws which were intended for past and transient conditions.
>
> Holding this doctrine concerning the Bible, we the more certainly assume the right to subject the post-biblical religious sources and institutions to investigation, and to separate that which we consider true in principle and worthy of retention from that which is evidently unsound in doctrine and antiquated or irrelevant in practice. But we recognize our mission to consist much more in nurturing and building up than in abolishing and removing. Doctrines which we have recognized as true, but which have lost in great part their hold on our contemporaries, must be implanted anew and more firmly; institutions which have a hallowing influence on the religious nature, and which are like to enhance the religious life, must be retained, suitably changed, or, when necessary, created anew, according to the needs and circumstances.

Samuel Hirsch (1815-1889) was the philosopher of the movement. Although he did not come to the United States till 1866, yet, with his clearness of purpose and positiveness of conviction, he became a strong factor in the work of Reform Judaism, not alone in Philadelphia, but in wider circles. In his various books, *Die Religions-philosophie der Juden, Die Messiaslehre der Juden in Kanzelvorträgen, Das Judenthum, der christliche Staat und die moderne Kritik, Die Humanität als Religion*, he had fully and explicitly expounded his views on religion, explained the principles of Judaism, and set forth his interpretation of the meaning and symbolism of the ceremonies and laws. As an expression of his thought, I have selected the closing paragraphs of his dissertation *Die Reform im Judenthum*, where he gives the conclusions of his reasoning:—

The need of the time is the highest law of Judaism; all ceremonies are but means for the fulfilment of this highest law; the means must however everywhere be subservient to the end, therefore also in Judaism. The demand that everything which hinders us from working for the maintenance and prosperity of civil society, with all our spiritual and material powers, be removed from our ceremonial practice is therefore religiously justified.... It is a serious misdemeanor against, and not an indifferent action towards, the spirit of Judaism if anything be retained which in any way prevents us from the fulfilment of duties incumbent upon the citizen as such. It matters not whether any ceremony which is not to be retained for the above-mentioned reason be prescribed in the Bible or the Talmud.... Even the most biassed cannot deny that in the regulation of the ceremonial law the Bible had only the Jewish state in view. True, it foresees the downfall of the Jewish state as a divine punishment, but it conceives the event to have been possible of prevention by the Jews through a change in conduct, and therefore it gives no precepts as to how the religious life was to be arranged thereafter. When the Jewish state disappeared, the people, as Hodheim correctly remarks, had no guiding principle to determine what, under the changed circumstances, should be retained and what must be abrogated. . . .

The ceremonies became meaningless, i.e. their meaning was no longer understood, and they passed current as the incomprehensible commands of God. Therefore to observe as many of the prescribed ceremonies as possible became the one and important principle. What was no longer possible of observance, as the temple service and everything connected with the possession of Palestine, naturally had to be relinquished. Yet this was regarded only as a punishment of God. God has abolished our sacrifices, our Sabbath and jubilee-years, because we are unworthy to fulfil these commands. Therefore the ever-repeated sigh, "Lead us back to Palestine in order that"— possibly to found there a state that should serve for the glorification of God? No, but—"we may pay our penalty there, that we may offer the prescribed number of sacrifices, &c." This is always and again the heathenish conception (so opposed to our time as well as to the Jewish spirit), that by the practice of ceremonies a service is rendered to God, and as though only the service in the temple at Jerusalem could be perfect because only there everything that God commands could be carried out. But our standpoint to-day is entirely different. We, and the world with us, have arrived at the threshold of the future that the prophets foresaw. A world-temple must be built unto God, for His name shall be praised from the rising of the sun to the setting thereof. The freedom of every man must be not merely proclaimed but realized, for all were created in the image of God. The sanctity of labour must be declared, for man has been placed on earth to work, to employ and develop his powers. God's activity in the history of the individual and of nations must be recognized and acknowledged. God gives the individual and nations the opportunity to use their powers rightly. If they undertake this high task they will live; if not, and they prefer mental sloth and material luxury to hard work, they will go to ruin.

Finally, we must bear testimony to the world, through our cult and through appropriate symbols and ceremonies, that this truth is confirmed in sacred history, inasmuch as there is shown in it how, in a rude, material age, a people, ruder and more sensual than others, was trained until it recognized and taught for all time to come the rule of spirit over nature, and how the spirit can retain this superiority only by free, spiritual activity. Therefore symbols must be retained in Judaism, symbols which shall give this testimony in a fitting manner both to the Jews and to the world. But the Jews of the present day must, before all else, participate in the work of the age with all their powers; for this work is the object of Jewish history, yes, it is the be-all and the end-all of Judaism. The high aim sanctified by time and by Judaism is, that all men be free, all recognize God, all employ their spiritual and material powers with full and free desire, so that a throne be built for truth and justice on this earth, a throne which shall adorn the lowliest hut as well as the most glorious palace. Therefore no symbol can hereafter pass as Jewish which prevents the Jew from participating in and working towards the fulfilment of this object with all his powers. He may not be a mere spectator of the work of the modern age, but must give himself heart and soul to it, for this is the command of the God of his fathers, who only wishes to have right and love realized on earth, and therefore called Abraham from the other side of the river, and desired to make him and his descendants a blessing for the world through their deeds and their sufferings.

These men were the leaders to whose influence is due the decided trend that Judaism in this country took towards reform. Their work was, in the nature of the case, largely individual, but in one instance they, with others, met in conference and gave expression to a declaration of principles. It is this and other conferences of rabbis that will now engage our attention.

## Rabbinical Conferences.

The first conference of rabbis of the reform school in this country was held in the city of Philadelphia, Nov. 3 to 6, 1869. Thirteen years before that, in 1856, there had been a conference at Cleveland, O.; this, however, aimed to be a conference of all the rabbis of the country of all shades of opinion. The articles upon which the rabbis assembled at Cleveland agreed were—

"1. The Bible, as delivered to us by our fathers, and as now in our possession, is of immediate divine origin, and the standard of our religion.

"2. The Talmud contains the traditional legal and logical exposition of the biblical laws, which must be expounded and practised according to the comments of the Talmud."

The second article called forth strong protests from the Har Sinai congregation of Baltimore and the Emmanuel congregation of New York; on the other hand, the conference did not go far enough for the rigidly orthodox. The results of this conference were most unfortunate. The house of the reformers was divided; two factions arose, one in the eastern, the other in the western, part of the country. This division continued for years with resultant controversies and dissensions, but the breach has been happily healed, as shall be seen later on.

The decade following the Cleveland conference, being the years of the civil war and intense political excitement which overshadowed all other interests, witnessed no further effort at a meeting of this kind. In the years 1867–1868, however, the subject was re-agitated in the columns of the *Israelite*, but before the meeting was called a conference was convened by the Eastern reformers in Philadelphia in 1869. This conference was attended by the leading reformers from both sections of the country. The conference adopted the following principles, the first public statement made by a body of reformers on this side of the

Atlantic;—

1. The Messianic aim of Israel is not the restoration of the old Jewish state under a descendant of David, involving a second separation from the nations of the earth, but the union of all the children of God in the confession of the unity of God, so as to realize the unity of all rational creatures and their call to moral sanctification.

2. We look upon the destruction of the second Jewish commonwealth not as a punishment for the sinfulness of Israel, but as a result of the divine purpose revealed to Abraham, which, as has become ever clearer in the course of the world's history, consists in the dispersion of the Jews to all parts of the earth, for the realization of their high priestly mission, to lead the nations to the true knowledge and worship of God.

3. The Aaronic priesthood and the Mosaic sacrificial cult were preparatory steps to the real priesthood of the whole people, which began with the dispersion of the Jews, and to the sacrifices of sincere devotion and moral sanctification, which alone are pleasing and acceptable to the Most Holy. These institutions, preparatory to higher religiosity, were consigned to the past, once for all, with the destruction of the second temple, and only in this sense—as educational influences in the past—are they to be mentioned in our prayers.

4. Every distinction between Aaronides and non-Aaronides, as far as religious rites and duties are concerned, is consequently inadmissible, both in the religious cult and in life.

5. The selection of Israel as the people of religion, as the bearers of the highest idea of humanity, is still, as ever, to be strongly emphasized, and for this very reason, whenever this is mentioned it shall be done with full emphasis laid on the world-embracing mission of Israel and the love of God for all His children.

6. The belief in the bodily resurrection has no religious foundation, and the doctrine of immortality refers to the after-existence of the soul only.

7. Urgently as the cultivation of the Hebrew language, in which the treasures of divine revelation are given and the immortal remains of a literature that influences all civilized nations are preserved, must be always desired by us in fulfilment of a sacred duty, yet has it become unintelligible to the vast majority of our co-religionists; therefore it must make way, as is advisable under existing circumstances, to intelligible language in prayer, which, if not understood, is a soulless form.

The conference, after adopting a number of resolutions in reference to marriage and divorce, adjourned to meet in Cincinnati the following year. The meeting, however, did not take place, because some of the men who were most prominent in the Philadelphia conference failed to appear. In the year 1871 a conference did take place in Cincinnati, after preliminary meetings in Cleveland and New York; this conference is chiefly memorable because it gave the impulse to the organization of the Union of American Congregations and the subsequent founding of the Hebrew Union College. I shall consider this in its place in telling the story of these two institutions.

In the year 1885, in the month of November, from the sixteenth of the eighteenth days of the month, the memorable Pittsburg conference was held. It adopted the following declaration of principles, the clearest expression of the reform movement that had ever been published to the world:—

116

1. We recognize in every religion an attempt to grasp the Infinite, and in every mode, source, or book of revelation held sacred in any religious system the consciousness of the indwelling of God in man. We hold that Judaism presents the highest conception of the God-idea as taught in our Holy Scriptures and developed and spiritualized by the Jewish teachers, in accordance with the moral and philosophical progress of their respective ages. We maintain that Judaism preserved and defended, midst continual struggles and trials and under enforced isolation, this God-idea as the central religious truth for the human race.

2. We recognize in the Bible the record of the consecration of the Jewish people to its mission as the priest of the one God, and value it as the most potent instrument of religious and moral instruction. We hold that the modern discoveries of scientific researches in the domain of nature and history are not antagonistic to the doctrines of Judaism, the Bible reflecting the primitive ideas of its own age, and at times clothing its conception of divine Providence and Justice dealing with man in miraculous narratives.

3. We recognize in the Mosaic legislation a system of training the Jewish people for its mission during its national life in Palestine, and to-day we accept as binding only its moral laws, and maintain only such ceremonies as elevate and sanctify our lives, but reject all such as are not adapted to the views and habits of modern civilization.

4. We hold that all such Mosaic and rabbinical laws as regulate diet, priestly purity, and dress originated in ages and under the influence of ideas entirely foreign to our present mental and spiritual state. They fail to impress the modern Jew with a spirit of priestly holiness; their observance in our days is apt rather to obstruct than to further modern spiritual elevation.

5. We recognize, in the modern era of universal culture of heart and intellect, the approaching of the realization of Israel's great Messianic hope for the establishment of the kingdom of truth, justice, and peace among all men. We consider ourselves no longer a nation, but a religious community, and therefore expect neither a return to Palestine, nor a sacrificial worship under the sons of Aaron, nor the restoration of any of the laws concerning the Jewish state.

6. We recognize in Judaism a progressive religion, ever striving to be in accord with the postulates of reason. We are convinced of the utmost necessity of preserving the historical identity with our great past. Christianity and Islam being daughter religions of Judaism, we appreciate their provisional mission to aid in the spreading of monotheistic and moral truth. We acknowledge that the spirit of broad humanity of our age is our ally in the fulfilment of our mission, and therefore we extended the hand of fellowship to all who operate with us in the establishment of the reign of truth and righteousness among men.

7. We reassert the doctrine of Judaism that the soul is immortal, grounding this belief on the divine nature of the human spirit, which forever finds bliss in righteousness and misery in wickedness. We reject, as ideas not rooted in Judaism, the beliefs both in bodily resurrection and in Gehenna and Eden (Hell and Paradise) as abodes for everlasting punishment and reward.

8. In full accordance with the spirit of Mosaic legislation, which strives to regulate the relation between rich and poor, we deem it our duty to participate in the great task of modern times, to solve, on the basis of justice and righteousness, the problems presented by the contrasts and evils of the present organization of society.

This platform aroused the usual storm of opposition in the conservative and orthodox camps, but it still stands as the utterance most expressive of the teachings of reformed Judaism.

There have been a number of local conferences which, after an existence of a few years, were dissolved. Two such were the Jewish Ministers' Association, organized in January, 1885, in the city of New York, and comprising the rabbis in the eastern section of the country; and the Conference of Rabbis of Southern Congregations, organized in April. 1885, in the city of New Orleans. These conferences have scarcely a place in the history of reformed Judaism as they included in their membership rabbis of both schools.

In July, 1889, the Central Conference of American Rabbis was organized in the city of Detroit. It has met in regular conference every year since then. It comprises in its membership, with scarcely an exception, all the rabbis of the reform school in the country. Although it does not exclude from the membership any rabbi, the third article of its constitution reading, "All active and retired rabbis of congregations, and professors of rabbinical seminaries, shall be eligible for membership," yet it is a well-known and accepted fact that it is a body of reform rabbis. It is truly representative, including as it does in its membership, according to its last report, one hundred and thirty-three rabbis located all over the country, from ocean to ocean and from lake to gulf. The president from the beginning has been the venerable rabbi, Isaac M. Wise. In his annual address delivered at the meeting of the conference held at Milwaukee, Wis., in July, 1896, the president summed up what the Central Conference had accomplished. The eight years' work of the conference, he said,

> records the end of the feuds and controversies of thirty-three years' duration, from 1856 to 1889, among the American rabbis and writers, and the closer union of at least one hundred and fifty of us in a covenant of peace and considerable unanimity.

The notable achievements of the conference are the production and publication of the *Union Prayer Book for Jewish Worship*, its success in representing Judaism at the World's Parliament of Religions held at Chicago during the World's Fair, its declaration on the requirements for the admission of proselytes[5], and, above all, its uniting in one body the reform leaders of the country. It has even extended into Canada, and the meeting of 1897 was held in Montreal. It has published six year-books, which contain, besides the record of the proceedings, a large number of addresses and learned papers read at the sessions.

The principles of the men forming the conference were so well known that there was not thought to be any necessity for making a declaration of principles, notably as at its second meeting the conference passed a resolution to the effect that all the declarations of reform adopted at previous rabbinical conferences in Europe and this country be collected and recorded in the year-book, and be understood as the working basis of this conference.

At the meeting held in Rochester, N. Y., in July, 1895, the president, in his address, proposed for discussion and decision several questions, one of which, bearing on the attitude of reformed Judaism, must be referred to here notably as it involved a far-reaching issue and concerned a question of principle. "What is our relation in all religious matters to our own post-biblical, our patristic literature, including the Talmud, casuits, responses, and commentaries?" The committee to whom this was referred reported as follows:—

> Your committee, to whom that part of the president's message was referred which reads, "What is our relation in all religious matters to our own post-biblical, our patristic literature, including the Talmud, casuists, responses, and commentaries," begs leave to report that, from the standpoint of Reform Judaism, the whole post-biblical and patristic literature, including the Talmud, casuists, responses, and commentaries, is, and can be considered as, nothing more or less than "religious literature." As such it is of inestimable value. It is the treasure-house in which the successive ages deposited their conceptions of the great and fundamental principles of Judaism, and their contributions to the never-ceasing endeavour to elucidate the same. Consciously or unconsciously, every age has added a wing to this great treasure-house, and the architecture and construction of each wing bear the indelible marks of the peculiar characteristics of the time in which it was erected. Our age is engaged in the same task. We too have to contribute to the enlargement of this treasure-house; but we have to do it in our own way, as the spirit of our time directs, without any slavish imitation of the past.
>
> To have awakened the consciousness of this historic fact is the great merit of Reform Judaism; and the more this consciousness grows upon our mind, the more the conditions and environments of our modern life force it upon us, the more persistently we have to assert: that our relations in all religious matters are in no way authoritatively and finally determined by any portion of our post-biblical and patristic literature.

This report was considered at the last session of the conference. Many of the members had left for their homes, so that only twenty were present. The report called forth long and warm discussion. A number of the most pronounced reformers took the ground that the report did not go far enough, and that it ought to have stated the attitude also in reference to the biblical books. They declared that in the stream of tradition the biblical books must be considered with the post-biblical, that the two cannot be separated. Therefore they voted against the report of the committee, which was carried by the narrow margin of eleven to nine. This action of the conference called forth great excitement. The conservative press naturally interpreted the vote as an almost equal declaration in favour of the binding authority of the Talmud, misrepresenting altogether the opinions of those who had voted in the negative. In his address at the opening of the next conference in July, 1896, the president referred to the matter as follows:—

> [The vote of eleven to nine] placed the conference on record that nine out of twenty hold the post-biblical or patristic literature as authoritative and final for us in all religious matters. So the vote was generally understood by outsiders, and this placed the conference in a ridiculous position of inconsistency, the same which I. M. Jost charges on German conferences in his time. As this was positively not the import of that vote, it places the nine of the opposition in a false light before the world as being adherents and advocates of orthodox

rabbinism. It will therefore be necessary that a reconsideration of the said vote be moved by some one who voted on it in the affirmative. We must sustain the position we took from the beginning: that this conference consists of the reform element only and exclusively, and its standpoint is historical Judaism, that is the Judaism of all ages, and not that of one period, class, or people. We cannot submit to the legalism of the Talmud, the Kabbalism of the Sohar, the literalism of the Karaites, or even rationalism of Maimonides and Mendelssohn, because either of them was a child of his respective age and not of the Judaism of all ages. And this only and exclusively is our basis.

The president's address was, as usual, referred to a committee of three; two of these were among the nine that had voted in the negative at the preceding conference. In their report they stated in reference to this part of the address:—

Those who were present at the conference held last year in Rochester, and who heard the discussion of the report of the Committee on Post-Biblical Literature, know full well that the nine who voted against it as it was presented and adopted had no intension of declaring in favour of the Talmud and the later codifications as an authority in religious matters, and if their vote was so construed, it was certainly misunderstood.

This was unanimously adopted by the conference, and thus its tendency of thought as a reform body once again emphasized.

## The Prayer Book

The public expression of a faith is its public service. That reforms were necessary here was the conviction of all the early reformers. The language of prayer, albeit the sacred tongue, was unintelligible to most of the worshippers. Customs were in vogue at the service that detracted much from making it devotional and reverential. In the prayers hopes were given expression to, and petitions directed to the throne of divine grace, which were not living hopes and petitions. Doctrines were expressed that were no longer the beliefs of the people. Naturally, attention was almost immediately given to making the public service a true reflection of the changes that had come upon men's thoughts. The traditional service was modified and changed. We have already seen how radically the first reformed congregation changed the order of service. The first attempt at a new prayer book in this country, however, was that made by the Rev. Dr. L. Merzbacher, and adopted as its ritual by the Emmanual congregation of New York in 1854. This prayer book greatly abbreviated the traditional service, and although not as thoroughly and consistently reformed as it might have been, was yet a great step forward at the time. In the year 1856, shortly after landing in this country, Dr. David Einhorn published the first part of his *Olath Tamid: a Prayer Book for Jewish Reform Congregations*. At the same time he set forth clearly the principles that had guided him in writing the book. He expressed the matter well when he wrote—

It is a clear and undeniable fact that the traditional service has no charm for the present generation; the old prayers have become for the most part untruths for present conditions and views, and neither the organ nor the choir, nor yet youthful memories that cluster about the synagogue, are sufficient to cover the bareness, to banish the lack of devotion, to fill again the vacant places. Salvation will come only from a complete reform of the public service which, founded on principle, will enable the worshipper to find himself and his God in the sacred halls.... Dogmatically, this prayer book is differentiated from the traditional order by the omission of prayers for the restoration of the sacrificial cult and the return to Palestine, i.e. the re-institution of the Jewish kingdom, as well as the change of the doctrine of bodily resurrection into the idea of a purely spiritual immortality.

Although the book followed the traditional order of prayers in a measure, and retained a number of prayers in the Hebrew, yet the greater part of the ritual was in the vernacular. In the Hebrew text, too, such changes as were necessitated by the changes of belief indicated above were made.

There now appeared from time to time a number of prayer books, such as the *Minhag America*, by Isaac M. Wise, adopted by most of the congregations in the southern and western sections of the country; the *Abodath Yisrael*, by B. Szold and M. Jastrow; the *Hadar Hattefillah*, by A. Huebsch; besides these, quite a number of congregations had individual prayer books prepared by their ministers for their use. There was thus a wondrous variety. As time wore on it was felt that there was a great need for a prayer book that could be adopted by the reformed congregations everywhere. There were obstacles in the way of taking any one of the existing books. At the meeting of the Central Conference of American Rabbis held in Baltimore in 1891, the subject of a Union Prayer Book was first broached. A ritual committee was appointed that laboured for three years, and at the meeting in Atlantic City in July, 1894, the book as submitted by the committee was ratified. This book expresses in its prayers and meditations the doctrines of reformed Judaism. In the report accompanying the MS. of the second part of the prayer book, the services for New Year's Day and the Day of Atonement, the Ritual Committee stated the principle that had guided it in its work:—

> Imbued with the earnestness of the task that was laid upon us, we endeavoured to conform the ritual for these two great holidays to the spirit and principle of the first part of our Union Prayer Book, to unite the soul-stirring reminiscences of the past with the urgent demands of the present, and to enhance the solemnity of the service by combining the two essential elements, the ancient time-honoured formulas with modern prayers and meditations in the vernacular.

That the book has met the requirements and the expectations of the congregations may be gathered from the fact that within the short space of three years one hundred and ten congregations, among them many of the largest and most influential in the land, have adopted it as their ritual. This has been the most decided step towards a real union that the reformed congregations of the country have yet taken.

# ❦126❧

# The Problem of
# Religious Education

## SOLOMON SCHECHTER

Solomon Schechter (1850-1915), educated in Central Europe and Germany, after an academic post at Cambridge was appointed head of the Jewish Theological Seminary in New York. There, this scholar, deeply attached to Jewish traditions, yet open to modern currents of thought, convinced that the Reform tendency was cutting away too much and concerned to provide a Jewish educational framework for the new immigrants, spoke for what became Conservative Judaism. To adapt, but not to sacrifice what was valuable, was the the larger purpose behind Schechter's emphasis in his Commencement Address to the Seminary in 1907.

M y Friends: It is now the fourth time that we meet in this hall to participate in the commencement exercises of this Seminary. Our pleasant task will be to do honor to those to whom honor is due, conferring the degree of Rabbi on some, the degree of Doctor on others, and awarding prizes to those who, by their particular industry and devotion to learning deserve this distinction. It is, to my knowledge, the first time that the Seminary confers the Doctor Degree for work done, upon which occasion I congratulate both the faculty and the directors. The importance of this degree consists in the fact that it shows that our students do not rest satisfied with that title which enables them to perform the necessary functions in their respective Synagogues, but that they endeavor to continue their studies, the foundations of which were laid at the Seminary.

In a previous graduation address, I had occasion to speak of the various activities of the Rabbi and the different needs of the community which a Rabbi is expected to superintend. I propose to offer a few remarks on this solemn occasion on the subject of Talmud Torah. By Talmud Torah I do not mean the

Source: Solomon Schechter, 'The Problem of Religious Education, an address delivered at the Graduating Exercises of the Seminary, 2 June, 1907', *Seminary Addresses and Personal Papers*, Cincinnati, 1915, pp. 106-18.

study of Jewish literature as pursued by the Rabbi and the few professional students. The Talmud Torah of which I wish to speak on this occasion is the study of the Torah, extended to the humblest member of the community, reaching the very babes: or, as the term is commonly used as a synonym of the בית הספר (the public school). In this capacity the Talmud Torah is one of the main objects for which synagogues are built and Rabbis are appointed. Thus, Judges 5:11 is paraphrased by an ancient Rabbi,

> Here is a small settlement in Israel. And they rose and built a synagogue and appointed a sage and engaged teachers for the children. The good example is followed by another city in its neighborhood. They also built a synagogue and engaged teachers. And so the schools increase in Israel, in which the righteous acts of the Lord are rehearsed even in the very villages.

The establishment of a school for children, or the erection of the Talmud Torah, and equipping it with the necessary staff is here regarded as the main function of the synagogue. This was the rule which was followed by Israel almost throughout its long history. No community was too small to provide for the instruction of the young, and no sacrifice was too great.

How deeply this sentiment took root in Israel may be seen by the various references to bequests for the Talmud Torah scattered over the *Responsa* of the Middle Ages and other historical records. In a *Responsum* dating from the sixteenth century, mention is made of a single bequest of one hundred thousand *lebenim* for educational purposes. This would be a princely donation even in our own times, considering the purchasing value of money in the sixteenth century, which was about fifteen times as much as the present. The first task, again, which the Jewish community at Amsterdam, entirely consisting of refugees from various parts of Europe, set to itself was the building up of a model school. Rabbi Sheftel Horwitz, of Frankfort, a place more distinguished at that period for its piety and erudition than for system and method, shed tears of joy when he visited the school, with its fine building, its graded schedule, and its excellent discipline, and recommended it as a model to his fellow-countrymen, the German Jews. The community of Cracow, again, in the sixteenth century, after passing through terrible epidemics, took the first opportunity after its return to normal conditions to reorganize its schools, which, coinciding with the distress of the times, was only done at a great sacrifice on the part of its members.

However, it is not my intention to dwell here upon the history of the Talmud Torah and its various improvements, which may easily be found in a number of books dealing with this subject. All I want to urge is, first, that the Talmud Torah is an essential adjunct to the Synagogue. Secondly, that it is just after great historical catastrophes that the importance of the Talmud Torah is even more realized than before, and forms a main feature in the programme of the newly settled or reorganized congregations. The school children are, as the Rabbis suggest, the very "flower and blossom of the Courts of our Lord," so that the synagogue and the establishment of the Talmud Torah in a sorely tried community means a new pledge for the rejuvenation of Israel. The conditions of a great part of Jewry in America are in many respects not dissimilar to those of the Amsterdam community. Our numbers consist chiefly of immigrants fleeing from conditions resembling those of Europe in the seventeenth century, and like those refugees, we are also engaged in the process of the creation of our institutions. Much has been done of which every American Jew can be truly proud. Our places of worship and our charitable institutions, which are constantly increasing in number and in weight, bear comparison with those of the oldest communities in Europe and Asia. But there is one point which requires the serious attention of our leaders, and that is the Talmud Torah. I by no means overlook the fact that we are already in possession of institutions set apart for the purpose of training Rabbis and devoted to the cause of higher Jewish learning. To those already in existence, a new one is to be added by the munificence of the late Moses A. Dropsie, at Philadelphia, under the direction of experienced guides and trusted leaders, whose work, I have no doubt, will likewise contribute to magnify the cause of Jewish learning and to make it glorious.

Yet it must be stated that as long as we have no proper Talmud Torah, the higher learining will always remain without a basis and never take root on American soil. The normal conditions in olden times seem to have been that of a thousand persons entering the Talmud Torah, the largest number obtained a fair knowledge of the Bible, a smaller number became acquainted with the Mishnah and certain fraction even acquired a knowledge of the Talmud; whilst it was only one of a thousand who was considered capable of giving decisions, or as we would say, of exercising the functions of the Rabbi in the widest sense of the word. We have fairly provided for the one in a thousand, but have done very little for the remaining nine hundred and ninety-nine. I by no means ignore the existence of our Sunday Schools, in addtion to a certain number of Talmud Torah schools and a large number of private tutors in religion, or Melamdim, but they are quite out of proportion to the numbers which are left without any religious instruction. In a conversation lately with a gentleman familiar with the statistics of New York, I learned to my suprise that there must be at least 150,000 Jewish children in New York, and that the provision for religious instruction, by rough calculation, hardly amounts to the relief even of the third part of this number. These are alarming conditions. But what is worse is that we could hardly supply the deficiency even if we had the will, for we are still to a large extent lacking in everything indispensable for the building up of the Talmud Torah.

The first difficulty under which we labor is the great dearth of trained teachers. The old private tutor, or Melamed, is an impossibility in this country for any length of time. Judging by results which held good for many centuries, it would be hazardous to say that his method was entirely wrong. However, great as the results may have been to which he can point in former generations and under different conditions, it is not likely that he will be able to maintain his status much longer. Neither his medium of instruction nor his method is to be recommended in the case of boys brought up in an American public school. It is especially his medium of instruction which is a thing impossible in this country, and sooner or later it must give way to the English language, the language of our fellow-citizens, the language of public schools, and the language of all other institutions of learning. The American teacher, with his knowledge of the English language and his familiarity with the best educational methods, will thus in the end prove to be the only fit person to instruct also in religion, but unfortunately he is not always sufficiently equipped with a knowledge of Hebrew things in general and the Hebrew language in particular, to enable him to accomplish his duties in a satisfactory manner. A thorough and sound knowledge of Hebrew is an indispensable qualification of every teacher in a Jewish religious school. It is the sacred language, it is the language of the Bible, it is the language of the Prayer Book and the despository of all the sublimest thoughts and noblest sentiments that Israel taught and felt for more than three thousand years. It is the tie that unites us with millions of worshippers in the same sacred language, who are our brothers and our brethren in spite of all the latest theological discoveries and ethnological hypotheses. It is the natural language of the Jew when in communion with his God; he divines more than he is able to explain. Translations are a poor makeshift at best, and more often a miserable caricature. For more than twenty-three centuries the world has been busy with the interpretation and translation of the Scriptures, and yet no agreement has been reached as to the exact rendering of the fourth verse of the sixth chapter of Deuteronomy containing the confession of Israel's creed. But the Jew reads the ישראל שמע and does know it. He cannot translate it, but he feels it and *is* it. For, as the mystics have it, to be a thing is to know a thing and to know a thing is to be a thing.

I am aware that there are some well-meaning persons who maintain that the fate of religion should not be made dependent on a certain language. The real question is what we mean by religion. If we are indifferent as to the nature of the religion (confusing it with religiosity) any language will do. It may blossom out into an ethical cult, it may develop into the worship of the beautiful and the sublime, or may take the shape of the Service of Man. Constituted, however, as human nature is, with its hankering after the mysterious and its tendency towards the worship of Sorrow, it is more probable that this "distilled religion" will sooner or later evaporate into a sort of Spiritualism or Christian Science. Of this possibility the signs are not wanting even at the present moment. But whatever shape it may take, it will certainly not be Judaism. When the last sound of Hebrew will have disappeared from our synagogues, the last trace of Judaism will also have gone.

We must thus insist upon Hebrew. But for this we require proper training schools. All our means at present are of a perfunctory nature and accomplish very little. The Seminary has with inadequate means tried to cope with this difficulty, but I do not think that it will ever accomplish this mission without increasing its staff of teachers for this purpose, and extending its curriculum and the number of hours of instruction. But above all, no training can be perfect without the help of a model school in which the teachers should impart instruction for a certain number of years under the supervision of their professors.

The second crying meed is the almost utter lack of text-books. Through some cause or other, the English language is the poorest in this kind of literature. We have as yet no Jewish history fit to place in the hands of a teacher or pupil, no readers for the different grades, and no commentary to the Bible written in a Jewish spirit. I am glad to announce on this occasion that the Jewish Publication Society, recognizing this last want, is now engaged in the preparation of such a commentary as will undoubtedly have the effect of bringing the Bible back to the Jew. We must have a whole series of primers and readers and text-books and histories extending at least over a course of eight years, commencing with the Hebrew alphabet and culminating somewhere in the later Hebrew literature. I cannot refrain on this occasion from paying my tribute to our brethren in Russia, who amidst all the persecutions by which these last decades have been marked, have produced a large educational literature covering almost all the subjects fit for instruction, which excites the envy and admiration of every student. It is humiliating to think that with all the means at our disposal and our various Societies constantly discussing the topic I am just dealing with, we should be in this respect behind our brethren in the East, the poorest among the poor, and engaged in a deadly struggle with all the powers of darkness.

But it is only when we have provided for the needs of the nine hundred and ninety-nine, by well-equipped training schools for teachers and proper text-books in the English language, fit to be put in the hands of the so-called laity, that the mission of the thousandth (that of the Rabbi) will be accomplished. Without this broad basis of the congregation at large, and its hearty co-operation, the work of the Rabbi will never be effective. The knowledge of the one will never be able to grapple successfully with the ignorance of the many. The old saying was, "Knowledge is Power." Paradox as it may seem, everyone will admit that Ignorance is a greater Power—on the side of destruction. I do not hesitate for a moment to maintain that the excesses in the camp of Judaism which we witness, and this unceasing succession of spiritual amputations which is going on before our very eyes, is mainly owing to the insufficient acquaintance with the tenets of Judaism, its traditions of the past and its aspirations and hopes for the future on the part of the nine hundred and ninety-nine. Never before were the words of the Prophet so fully realized,

> My people are destroyed for lack of knowledge: because thou hast rejected knowledge, I will also reject thee, that thou shalt be no priest to me: seeing that thou has forgotten the Law of thy God, I will also forget thy children. (Hos. 4:6)

We are laboring under the peculiar idea that we shall benefit Judaism by removing the last vestige of the Sabbath, by abolishing the Day of Atonement, or robbing it of its most essential features, by banishing the Sefer Torah from the place of worship, and by removing the last shreds of the sacred language. This seems to be the programme of the twentieth century, and this is what we call progress in Judaism. Nay, we hail it as hastening the day in which "the upright shall exult, and the saints triumphantly rejoice,"—the day which formed one of Israel's brightest visions and the object of Israel's prayers for thousands of years.

It never occurs to us that this irreverence for the past, this perpetual battering away at institutions considered sacred by the great majority of mankind, this worship of individualism which in most cases is nothing more than thinly disgised selfishness and vanity, and this disregard of authority and the utter absence of the qualities of submission and obedience are, in part at least, responsible for the rampant materialism and unrighteousness which we all so much deplore.

A great European thinker somewhere remarked, "America, with its lack of high culture, is the only nation in our day which has been able to furnish soil for new religions." This is a malicious libel. A country which has given to the world men of the stamp of Emerson, Channing, Lowell, Motley, and so many other celebrities, can in all respects compare favorably with any part of the Old World; but I cannot help saying that my heart fails me when I see the mushroom religions springing up around us, the constant travesties and caricatures of the Bible which we are witnessing, and the assurance with which men offer their undigested thoughts as substitutes for religion. As to the experiments to which Judaism is often subjected, the least one can say is that they show that our knowledge of religion and the great historical forces at work in the spiritual world are of an amateur order. Be an idea ever so absurd, be it ever so incompatible with all the laws of history and philosophy, ever so antagonistic to the spirit of Judaism and its teachings, it will always find a response among us, provided it has eloquence and smartness on its side, and is uttered with that certainty and assurance which ignorance alone can command.

My young friends, ere long you will be active in Jewish communities. Your activities will be arduous and manifold. Holiness as understood by Judaism, and righteousness as understood by Judaism and by the large bulk of humanity will be the subjects that will occupy your attention. But never forget the Talmud Torah. Do apply yourselves to the training of the nine hundred and ninety-nine, so that they may be in time your equals in the knowledge of Judaism. Be not afraid that a universal knowledge of the Scriptures and of the important works embodying Jewish tradition and Jewish history will in any way curtail your authority. The Sabbath preceding the Day of Atonement and the one preceding the Passover were, as you know, the fete days of the Synagogue, when the Rabbi would give lengthy discourses on some complicated Halachic subjects. Both the pupils and the members of the Congregation were permitted to take part in the discussion, but none felt prouder than the Rabbi if one of his congregants would stop him with the words, "Master, you have overlooked a paragraph in Maimonides' Code," or, "Master, according to your argument this or that passage in the Novelae of Rabbi Solomon ben Adereth would be quite unintelligible," for such contradiction on the part of the so-called "laity" showed that the work of the Rabbi was effective, and that he and his predecessors had done their duty by the community with regard to Talmud Torah. This is the pride which you ought to cultivate, and make it the goal of your ambition. It is a poor sort of authority which derives its infallibility from the helplessness of the majority. The authority that maintains itself by the ignorance of the masses is not worth having.

One of the most important characteristics of the synagogue was its democratic constitution, placing everybody under the law and making the knowledge of the law accessible to all. Under the law, we are all equals; outside of the law, or, as it is called, above the law, is anarchy and confusion, resulting in tyranny. In politics, we are overwhelmed by the dragoon; in the spiritual world, we are crushed by the talker. My friends, restore to the synagogue its democratic spirit. Remain in the service of the law, and do not aspire to be above the law. This is not spirituality; this is conspiracy. In the synagogue everybody taught, everybody learned, everybody contributed his or her share in its building up, in its aspect as a collection of institutions making for the sanctification of life in its various manifestations. To hand over one's conscience and things most sacred to a single individual, be he ever so great, brands one as a "slave by his own compulsion," or as indifferent to the cause of religion. This is neither American nor Jewish. Remember, my friends, the words of Maimonides:

> The guarantee for the survival of Judaism is the continuance of the knowledge of God's Torah and the acquaintance with His word among us.

With the disappearance of the Torah, the synagogue itself can become a danger to itself and a playground for all the forces of destruction. It may cease to be a Beth Hakneseth, suggestive of the Keneseth Israel, where the spirit of Catholic Israel dwells, and become a בית עַם (the House of the Plebs), where multitudes enjoy "intellectual treats," even at the very expense of Judaism. Only knowledge of Judaism can ward off this danger. For thus it is written:

> They shall not hurt nor destroy in all my holy mountain: for the earth shall be full of the knowledge of the Lord, as the waters cover the sea.

# The Duty of American Jews

## LOUIS LIPSKY

Modern Zionism, under the stimulus of Theodor Herzl's plan for a Jewish State in Palestine (1896), became a source of controversy amongst American Jews. In concentrated form the debate posed the question of who Jews in America were, by juxtaposing the idea of a Jewish nation with the ideal of Americanism. Louis Lipsky (1876–1963), a journalist and editor of Jewish publications, who became active in national and international Zionist organisations, here puts a case which he hopes will appeal beyond Orthodox Jews.

Zionism is not merely a solution of the Jewish question. It is not like the atomic theory, or Darwinian theory. It is not merely an argument which logically proves a certain thing, and which you must, as a logical being, accept and cease combatting. If you see the truth of it you are not saved. It is not merely a program. If it were, discussion, education, argument, etc. would be the simple method of propaganda, and it could get along without orators, songs or displays, without appeals to the imagination, without poetry or enthusiasm.

Theodor Herzl expressed it right when he said that a return to Judaism would precede the realization of the object of Zionism, but by the word Judaism, I take it, Herzl meant a return to the fervor and enthusiasm, a return to faithfulness, which has always been associated with religion in its larger sense.

Before Zionism, which is the means of escape from the *Galuth*, can become a reality, it must be preceded by the rebirth of emotion, which, among Jews, will take the form of religious enthusiasm. You may talk for centuries of theories, of certain truths—as Reform Jews talk of the Jewish mission—but until the souls of the persons appealed to have been quickened, until the idea has become related to their own being, the idea, or the theory, or the truth, is just so much junk in the intellectual treasury of the world and nothing more.

An annual exhibition of spiritual and intellectual squinting and dodging is

Source: Louis Lipsky, 'The Duty of American Jews', 1909, repr. in *Memoirs in Profile*, Philadelphia, 1975, pp. 328–35. © 1975 by The Jewish Publications Society.

given by the Central Conference of American Rabbis, who also speak of truths, Jewish ideals, etc. It is not many years since that dignified body of wanderers in the desert of barren ideas and empty phrases declared that the Jews do not constitute a nation, that Washington is our Jerusalem and the United States our Zion, and yet, that idea, unrelated to the life and thought of the Jewish people, actually untrue to Jewish life, has floated about the United States, the object of ridicule, a gratuitous fling at the aspiration of loyal sons of the Jewish people, a useless impudent, foolish idea, for it never had a basis in the lives of Jews who have the right to speak as Jews. The force of spiritual necessity has even brought into the fold of Zionism a large number of the very men who at the time stood by and passively permitted the rabbinical stupidity to speak.

The Jewish mission has dwindled down to a mere whisper, and is heard now only in apologetic terms, for the force of circumstances has swept it off the boards, and it is now properly taking its place in the archives of American Jewish history, which our alert American Jewish Committee is compiling for the edification of future generations. It was an artificial thing from the start, but it was puffed up into the semblance of life by the army of ranters, who contrive to hold the right to the pulpits of Jewish temples.

The trouble with the Jewish mission was that it was an unreal interpretation of the meaning of Jewish life, promulgated with a dishonorable motive. In their souls the Jewish missionaries knew that the theory that the Jews were chosen by God to live in *golus* and to be a light to the nations, to whom they were to preach a pure monotheism, was an audacious brag, an artificial imposition on Jewish history, a contrivance to permit Jewish life to be sapped by assimilation without a struggle on the part of the victims. It was a contrivance to prolong the Jewish Galuth by inertia. It was a conception which struck truth at no point in its career. It was something to which no honest, unprofessional Jew would subscribe. The Jewish mission was an apology for existence, which no dignified man or race or nation would ever consent to make. The mission of any individual, race or nation, is, first and last, to be true to its own self, which from the start was denied by the mission theorists.

Nor are the rabbinical exponents of race and national dishonor the only organized body in the field, pretending to speak for the Jews. The Union of American Hebrew Congregations met last month and again the empty pretence was pressed to the fore by the same class of professional Jews, who have never understood the people whom they are supposed to represent, that the Jews are not a race or a nation, but a religious community. If the Jewish mission means anything, it should aim to express not only Jewish principles of religion, but the Jewish principles of governing all the relations of man, yet every opportunity they see to limit the Jewish mission to something more ethereal, more unrelated to life, they grasp with the enthusiasm of makeshift statesmen.

When the Union of American Hebrew Congregations makes a declaration like that it does not go back to the records for proof of its assumption; it does not consult the Jewish religion to see whether it is consistent with it on that subject, for its primary object is to lull to rest the slumbering national and racial feelings among the Jews, and thus make easier, from a crass material point of view, their present existence. When it speaks of religion, so obtuse are these professed theologians that they do not see that they are speaking of religion in the Christian sense, as a creed, which the Jewish religion never was, for it has always considered religion and life one and indivisible.

Whatever you see Jewish life in its undiluted, unassimilated state, no matter how deformed or abnormal it may be, it is always bounded in every detail by the Jewish religion, and there is no more un-Jewish conception than that the Jews can eliminate all national and racial elements in their lives and actually remain exponents of Judaism. In every genuine Jewish town, or community, the Jewish religion means law, civil and criminal, hygiene, charity and philanthropy, education; in fact, all of life is governed by this version of the Jewish religion, for the value of Judaism, its future development, as well as its past, lies in just this combination of law and life, which has made it an indispensable factor in the civilization of the world, and which the Zionist Movement has come into being in order to conserve for future uses.

Dr. M. H. Harris, of New York, who for a brief period was regarded as somewhat of a nationalist, but who has since retired to reconsider the question and to listen to the dictates of an enlightened conscience, recently said that all Jews who have no faith in Judaism and do not practice it, should get out of the fold. That was a bold thing to say for a rabbi whose congregation stands close to the precipice of advanced reform. Dr. Harris' audacity has not been denounced as it should be. His impertinence has not been called by its right name, and, although his views have appeared in print, not one of the many rabbis and prominent Jews of this city have been keen enough to take offense at the insulting, un-Jewish, inquisitorial proposition made by Dr. Harris in the statement that if Jews cannot or do not believe in what he calls the Jewish faith, and do not practice Judaism, it were better that their children be brought up at least in the Christian faith.

This teacher of ethics and religion, who writes books on Jewish history where he condemns the efforts of Jews to maintain their own nationality against the Romans, forgets, however, that while there are many Jews who cannot utter the words of prayer, and who cannot regulate their lives according to the statutes of an arrested nationality, these same Jews wish to base their lives in Jewish thought, Jewish religion, Jewish tradition, but the conditions of life hamper the expression of their desires, and because they cannot get out of the fold without repudiating the Jewish brotherhood, which they hold dear, they prefer to reserve to their own homes the expression of the religion they believe in. They are not as glib as rabbis are, who so easily compromise with even the trivial incidents of life, who so easily formulate a pallid, empty monotheism, modelled on Christian forms. Jews who are Zionists are not so facile in forming their religion to suit the exigencies of a professional career.

We Zionists face Jewish life, see the abnormality of our position, admit that the Judaism we know cannot live in *golus* unless we create a national center in

Palestine, observe the demoralizing effect of the *golus* spirit, the insidious inroads of assimilation, the dilution of Jewish ideas by alien forces, and we demand of the Jewish people that they assert their national or racial strength in order to give reality to our projects and to destroy these abnormalities and dangers. We are not so positive even that the Jewish people will respond. When Bar Kochba took up arms against a magnificent Roman army, he was not so certain that his brethren would respond to his call to arms; but his cause was just, it was necessary, and he was bound to take up the fight. We are not victims of self-deception; we are not dreamers in that sense. We expect that there will be thousands of assimilating Jews, who, shortsighted and complacent, will take up arms against us, and denounce us, but we hope and we have the right to expect that they will have the decency not to invoke the Jewish religion or Jewish tradition against us.

A double dilemma confronts every American Jew, the Zionist as well, who is not orthodox. He sees before him an immobile Judaism. The law decisions and the statutes of an arrested nationality, congealed in a religious form in order to conserve the Jewish people, are repugnant to democracy and especially to the American youth filled with impulses to have life reflect his own individuality. The hygienic regulations of the Jewish state, which have also become enslaved to religion, he would have scrutinized by science and rejected if they do not stand the test.

The detailed methods of worship, the legislation that prescribes every movement on the Sabbath, cannot have any actual authority, wherever the Jew is free, and inner pressure does not demand it for ulterior reasons. Even the ideal of God, who once selected the Jews as his bearers of light and law cannot, unless there are reasons of national interest, be accepted without a protest against the arrogance of the claim, the absence of humility in it. Unless you admit the national authority, you are bound to deny the validity of Jewish law. Those who deny the existence of the Jewish nation, and live the Jewish traditional life, are like the blind fish in the mammoth cave in Kentucky who would insist having eyes, where there is nothing to see.

The traditional law was effective while the world erected barriers against us, and we could not escape from the Jewish world. Here in America the barriers have been removed. But you cannot touch the traditional religion without destroying the form that had been created to preserve the Jewish future. You dare not remove one form of Jewish life, without creating another.

Before you can be free to create your own religion, with variations on the Jewish original, as it must be, you must free the Jewish religion of all its national elements, allowing those national elements to develop under normal conditions. Jewish life must be made to mean more than Judaism, in order that Judaism may not tremble at every danger which affects Jewish life.

Therefore the Jewish youth of America, who are not materialists, who are not atheists, who have faith though it does not conform, who hope to reconcile the phenomena of life with their religious hopes, are unable to go very far without an encounter with this peculiar situation. On the one hand the American Jew sees an anomalous form of arrested religion, and, on the other, a form of religion which has repudiated all those national elements without which Jewish life becomes a ghost without a habitation, without which our heritage from our fathers is given away, denied, compromised, for the sake of conformity, assimilation, adjustment, etc. He has the choice of subduing his natural longing to have religion express his conception of truth, his relation to God and man, or repudiating all those things in his own soul, which he has had from his forefathers, and which he does not wish to deny, give away, compromise or lose.

That is the religious dilemma of every progressive, thinking young Jew. The rabbis may not wish to see it, but we choose not to pass it over with pretence and hypocrisy. The American Jew must meet the issue. When life in all its complexity confronts him, he must get out of the dilemma, he must state his relation to the problem, he must adjust his life to the great past, which holds him, not in bondage, as so many think, but as a willing servant, in order to realize the best in his own individuality, and pass on to his children something of the heritage of which he is proud.

Nor is the religious cause the only one that must prompt the American Jew to become a Zionist.

There is plain, ordinary, every-day gratitude to your parents, and through them to your ancestors. You are compelled to an interest in all the difficulties of the race, whose son you are. Not because they are over there and suffer, but because you yourself are so much less in value, as they are reduced in value. It is not altruism; it is ennobled self-respect. You bear the name Jew, and wherever a Jew is ill-treated, oppressed, contemned, despised, you are ill-treated, oppressed, despised. You feel their hurts, just as you feel the hurt of your own natural brother when he is hounded and maltreated. They strike you when they strike him. You cannot hold you head erect here, while over there Jews are being thrown to the ground and trampled upon. You may live far from the scene, but you cannot live your own life unless you have righted your brothers' wrong.

Your parents have implanted in you certain affections, certain hates, certain aspirations. They have breathed into you the traditions of Jewish life, of Jewish lore, of Jewish conceptions of nobility, of virtue, of dignity. Wherever those virtues, that dignity, that nobility is attacked, your own dignity, your own nobility, your own virtue vibrates in sympathy, and is seriously affected. The destruction of the Jewish people means the destruction of everything you hold to be noble in life, which you hope to transmit to your children. You cannot live a full life without having lifted your hand to redress the wrongs which the Jewish people endure, *for your own personal interests are at stake.* These interests may not be your own bread and butter, your goods, but they are the higher interests of your individuality, which, if you are a Jewish nobleman, you will defend at the cost of your life, if need be.

Judaism is one of the manifestations of Jewish life. It is not the only manifestation when Zionism has entered into Jewish life. Judaism has preserved the identity of the Jewish people; it has been the form of communal unity, which held all that was valuable in Jewish life. Until we have re-established Jewish life on the model of its former national life, we Zionists shall not raise a finger to minimize or destroy the Judaism which has performed such a valuable function in Jewish life heretofore, but we shall devote ourselves to the enlargement of Jewish life so that it will be possible for all Jews who feel the ties of brotherhood to be included in the ranks of the Jewish people.

If you are Jewish noblemen, American citizens, you are bound to heed the call to defend the interests of Jewish character, of Jewish ideas, of Jewish aspirations. And when you see the victims who have suffered in those interests, it is not only sympathy you feel, but also a feeling of greatness, for you will find that the outraged kinsmen who are about you here, as they are over there, are not the victims of diseased ideals, not dumb beasts, not the scum of the world, but men and women who have been everlastingly treated unjustly, and it thus becomes not only your duty, but also your willing mission, in order to relieve the everlasting injuries of your people, to become a part of them, to merge all your interests with theirs, to take into yourself all that they have to teach of the ideas of life, which have been perpetuated among the Jewish people, not merely in response to a caprice of nature, but in order that some day it may obtain its freedom and develop under normal, natural conditions.

When you are once under these influences, as all self-respecting American Jews are bound to come, then you are on the road to become a full-fledged Zionist. You open your soul to the waves of life which Jewish national life has set in motion. You take your knowledge and culture from your own people, for you know that your own people have produced that which best adjusts itself to your individuality. You gradually permit yourself to be enveloped in Jewish life, and you naturally arrive at the Zionist solution, for you see that all these abnormalities in Jewish life, all the dilemmas of your soul, can never be adjusted while the Jews are in exile or are not in a land which they feel is their own, in an environment where only Jewish influences are radiated, where a political form of life shuts off, for a time, the intrusive alien ideas.

And thus, if you open your soul, your taste for Jewish literature is developed. You do not, naturally, take it at its face value, for you understand that it reflects, for the most part, the abnormality of Jewish life. But you appreciate that this reflects also the normal, and you hope for the day of redemption when literature shall become a free expression of the aspirations of the Jewish people.

You will see nothing incompatible in Zionism with the ideals of an American republic. Rather, you will find in American history analogies to confirm your faith in Zionism. You will see in the migration of the Pilgrim fathers the same impulse which animates Zionists. You will see in the American revolution the ideal of freedom for which men have fought and died and thus there will be nothing visionary or fanciful in the Zionist ambition to sacrifice material gains if need be in order to acquire those spiritual rewards for which, in many diverse ways, the Jews have died during the ages of exile. Zionists demand a separate national territory for those who by long tradition, by a common religion, by a common culture, have acquired certain traits that can best develop and purify themselves in a territory governed by representatives of that culture, tradition and ideals. That is compatible with American tradition, with democratic principles, with present American citizenship.

Let those who call themselves American Jews take warning. It is vital to the future of the Jews that they be honest with themselves. The difficulties, the alterations in character, which I have attempted to describe to you, are real, and the arrival at the ultimate solution cannot be stopped. Not all the resolutions of a central conference of Reform rabbis, or a union of American Hebrew congregations, or the utterances of shortsighted time-servers who occupy pulpits, will alter, in the least, the revolution in Jewish life which is going on in American Jewry. If these people were honest with themselves, they would confess that the troubles of life are their own troubles, that the religious dilemma, the racial dilemma, the national dilemma affects them also, and instead of trying to beat back the ocean waves, they will lend a hand to our movement, help to sweep away the brush of the forest, make the path to Zion easy, and aid Jews who wish to establish a nucleus of free independent Jewish life in Palestine. Instead of denying Jewish nationality and making desperate efforts to meet Jewish immigration problems by diverting it to Texas, Mexico, or North Africa, they would be among the first to aid us in our work of regenerating the Jewish nation in Palestine. They will find, from year to year, that the inevitable progress of Zionism, without an adequate relief in Palestine, will still further embitter their lives, and imperil their efforts to be the first of all the peoples coming to this country to jump into the melting pot which Israel Zangwill has imported into the United States.

The more our opponents protest, the stronger will Zionism become, for as their protests lose the value of novelty, and investigation proves that they are based on an unreal conception of Jewish life, the American Jew is bound to become a Zionist, and these assimilationists will be left as the unhonored remnant that refused to leave the flesh-pots for Egypt for the Land of Promise because they had become victims of their own social aberrations.

# ᠊᠊128᠊᠊

# Palestinian or American Judaism?

## KAUFMANN KOHLER

Reform Judaism initially provided the fewest recruits to Zionism. This was not only because Reform Jews had made the most adjustments to American life, but also because they were powerfully influenced by the idea that, as a religious community rather than a nation, it was their calling to labour amongst the nations to establish a world of justice and righteousness. Kaufmann Kohler (1843-1926) as a New York rabbi and, from 1903, president of Hebrew Union College, was one of the most polemically vigorous Reform spokesmen. His opposition to Zionism came from seeing America as a great new field for "realization of these Messianic expectations".

---

Thus said the Lord of Hosts: "The fast of the fourth month, and the fast of the fifth, and the fast of the seventh, and the fast of the tenth shall be to the house of Judah joy and gladness and cheerful feasts; but love truth and peace."
Zechariah VIII, 19.

Thus the prophet spoke regarding those who continued to bewail the fall of the old temple at Jerusalem, after the foundation had been laid for the new. Already then the views and habits of the conservative and the progressive parties seemed to collide. Dissension and discord threatened to harm the common cause. But the prophet was far from preaching peace at every price. Knowing full well that, as long as truth was not established as the basis, peace was only futile, he insisted on having truth first well grounded, and peace sought for afterwards. And these prophetical words also serve us as a motto: Truth first and then peace!

It certainly required all the boldness and original independence of mind which Einhorn possessed to proclaim the national fast, the memorial day of Jerusalem's destruction a national feast for Reform Judaism, as our prayer-book designates it; to declare that out of the fire of the conflagration of the temple Israel

Source: Kaufmann Kohler, 'Fifth Discourse' [delivered on the Fourth of July, the Sabbath after the seventeenth of Tammuz], Studies, Addresses and Personal Papers, New York, 1931, pp. 229-35.

rose rejuvenated as the Messiah of the nations. It certainly is not within everybody's reach to soar as high in the realization of a still distant future. Still every Jew to-day ought to take side with either view, the progressive or the retrogressive one, as regards the Holy Land; he must decide whether this day, as the first Sabbath between the Seventeenth of Tammuz and the Ninth of Ab, should be devoted to wailing over Jerusalem's sad fate, or, being the Fourth of July, given over to joy and thanksgiving in view of the Holy Land of Freedom and Human Rights which on this day was offered to all men and nations. In short, he must face the question, whether we [are] as Jews under the ruins of Zion, and waiting for a resurrection, or whether we are to celebrate the Fourth of July, not merely as Americans socially, but also as Jews in a political and religious sense as well, thanking the sublime Ruler of History for the new aims and prospects opened on this free soil for the realization of our Messianic expectations? For us, as Reform Jews, the question has been decided long ago. We love Jerusalem as the cradle of our national existence, but we do not long for a return. We behold in Jerusalem's overthrow, not a fall, but a rise to higher glory. For us Zion stands for fulfilment of humanity's keenest hopes and loftiest ideals, as pronounced by Israel's great seers of yore, and every "city of Brotherly Love" forms a part and link of the same. Consequently, we perceive in the jubilant tocsin peals of American liberty the mighty resonance of Sinai's thunder. We recognize in the Fourth of July the offspring of the Sixth of Sivan. We behold in the glorious sway of man's sovereignty throughout this blessed land the foundation stone for the splendid temple of humanity we hope and pray for. Why then should we lament over the fall of the old? Still it behooves us to-day to examine a little closer what the Fourth of July means to us, both as Americans and as Jews.

What the privileges are with which the Declaration of Independence endowed us as Americans, I may express in one sentence: It placed a king's crown on every human brow. It invested every human being with heaven-born sovereignty. As the Sixth of Sivan appointed Israel to be a kingdom of priests, so did the Fourth of July render the American nation a priesthood of true human royalty. *Freedom, Equality,* and *Brotherly Love* form the *three* precious jewels in the diadem of American citizenship.

Freedom is first and uppermost. No oppression from above, no compulsion from without, no obstruction by law, no barrier nor class privilege checks man in the unfolding of his power and his individuality. Free speech, free press, free exercise of all civil rights, free practice of every art and industrial vocation, free expression of thought and opinion throughout the land! What a vigorous, energetic, enterprising and noble type of mankind has this new liberty fostered and raised! What a splendid, firm and resolute spirit of enterprise and industry has it roused and cultivated! It has pushed the old world into the background. It outshines and challenges the rest of nations in inventive genius, in clearness of judgment, in practical, sound common sense.

Equality is the second. All are alike before the law. No difference of rank, of blood, class, or creed. Man alone counts. With equal rights and equal duties, each stands against the other, holding the same chance as the other. One opinion is as good as the other; one sect entitled to the same respect as the other. And behold the fruits that grow on the beautiful tree of liberty and equality! A new and decidedly better kind of humanity thrives and flourishes under our benign institutions. The exclusive and offensive particularities of the former immigrants are dropped, and broader views and finer traits take their place. All that is small, clannish and local is, by force of public opinion, pushed aside, and that which is humane and universally good and sweet brought into prominence. Human worth and dignity, human greatness and skill form the standard and object of all our endeavors in social and religious life. Great cosmopolitan aims and achievements decide on the value and success of each single effort within the great national fabric.

And here we have already included the third jewel of American life, the spirit of broad-minded liberality and brotherly love. Freedom, far from unbridling passion and selfishness in the genuine American, tended rather to bring out the nobler and tenderer qualities of man. It engendered humility and devotion in his attitude towards God, and generosity and kindness in his relation to his fellow-man. The American is profoundly devout and religious, but his religion has not the flavor of fanatical bigotry. He is by nature tolerant and philanthropic. Without inquiring after birth or creed, rank or profession, he readily and gladly lends assistance to all the suppliants and needy. Church and school, municipal and State affairs help and promote the interests of benevolence and charity. What in other countries the princes, fattened on the marrow of the people, now and then consent to do, all the industrial classes of the people, high or lowly, vie with each other in accomplishing. Liberality is one of the chief innate traits of the American people. Yes, the American people is a nation of nobel-minded sovereigns. And to spread and plant these truly Republican ideas and notions all over the globe is its glorious mission. Its seeds lie deeply imbedded in the wilderness of Sinai, in the truths revealed by our great prophets of yore; but the magnificent tree, as it stands before us to-day, overtowering all other human plantations, is to offer shadow and fruit to all the nations and kingdoms of the world. And this reminds us Americans not only of our debt of gratitude to God, but of our sacred task for future mankind.

Particularly great and solemn is our debt of gratitude and our obligation as American Jews. Not only because we enjoy comparatively greater blessings on this blessed soil of freedom than elsewhere on the globe, but because the very aims and ideas of humanity, which form the essence and soul of our religion, find here a more congenial and fertile soil than anywhere else. Here is the land where milk and honey flow for all. This is the land of promise of a great and new human race. Here the old dividing lines of race and sect are obliterated, and by natural selection a new type and standard of manhood and womanhood is developing. But then it behooves us as Jews to contemplate and to know what position we have to take in the midst of this great nation, and what the duties are which devolve upon us as the divinely chosen people of priests, as the oldest of nations among this, the youngest one in human history.

Brethren! The answer is not difficult. In order to exert our influence, in order to carry out our mission, we must first cultivate and develop the fine qualities which distinguish American life, and then enrich the world surrounding us with those treasures of the mind and the heart which we have stored up during our journey through the lands and ages. It will not do for us as teachers of humanity to remain Hebrews in garb and custom, in views and language. It will not do to offer our prayers in a tongue which only few scholars nowadays understand. We cannot afford any longer to pray for a return to Jerusalem. It is a blasphemy and a lie upon the lips of every American Jew. Neither ought we any longer to retain the Pentateuch lessons unrevised and unabridged, either in an annual or in a triennial cycle. I revere the venerable Torah scroll as our sacred palladium of the ages, for which our fathers a thousand times sacrificed their lives, and which, in fact, miraculously preserved our own, but I want to have it read, or rather the whole Bible used and perused with caution by way of wise eclecticism. If we may, in the words of Moses, the great law giver, proclaim: "Which is the people that has laws so wise and just as are ours? And which people has a God so holy and high, and yet so nigh as is ours?" we must, I am sure, bring our religion home to the understanding and appreciation of all the people. We must do away with all that detracts from the grandeur and wisdom of Judaism, and hold aloft only that which enhances its human worth and brightness. If we want to give expression and scope to the great prophetical wish and hope that our sanctuary should become "a house of prayer unto all nations," we certainly ought to render our mode of worship, all our religious observances truly attractive and impressive for all. King Solomon's dedicatory prayer, so mindful of the stranger that comes from afar to listen and to see, should ring forth its melodious sounds out of every human heart. Religion humanized and humanity religionized—that is the aim, the beginning and end of Judaism, as Reform understands and expounds it. Now the reform movement, so happily and auspiciously started in the old Fatherland, has there only too soon been interfered with and partly suppressed by the authorities of either the State or the older generation. Free America offers bright prospects for its healthy and vigorous growth and rise. Untrammelled and unimpeded by any power, Judaism may evolve all its strength and its wisdom, and it must naturally assume a really democratic, cosmopolitan character. In this atmosphere of freedom and broad humanity it cannot help becoming a free, practical, common-sense religion, able to enter the arena and compete with the great religious denominations, and striving for victory through pulpit, school, and press. But in order to win in this great prospective contest, it must throw into the background everything small, clannish, and exclusive. It must drop its Orientalism, and become truly American in spirit and form.

Mark well. We have first to use the pruning-knife and trim our own tree of life before improving those of others. We must first embellish ourselves ere we may embellish others. We must first learn from our American fellow-citizens how to blend religious devotion and piety with freedom. We must first rekindle the flame of religion in our hearts, and at our domestic firesides, before we may enlighten others. We must first awaken religious sentiment and enthusiasm in our children, and render our houses and our synagogues what they were in the dreary ghetto, sanctuaries of faith, temples of virtue and piety; we must first have again, as of yore, our domestic life hallowed by Sabbath rest and sacred festive praise and song, ere we can claim the title and name of God's holy people before the world. Much is needed to render Judaism honored, admired, and influential in our country. Many are the sacrifices we have to bring ere we have reached the standard which commands the respect of those around us. We must first succeed in opening the eyes of our own people, in familiarizing them with our priceless past and our world-redeeming truths, in inspiring our younger generations with love and zeal for our great historic mission, before we dare offer our religion as a model and a bright gem to others. It is true, nowhere has Judaism better chances of becoming the pioneer of a humanitarian religion, nowhere can the Jewish faith venture to be the advocate of the broadest truths concerning God and man, and form the golden chain to embrace all religious and sacred books, and blend them into one religion of humanity than in this blessed new world. Still this requires moral earnestness, a deep religious conviction, a positive, self-assertive faith. And this is what Radical Reform aims at, not by *destructive* measures, but by *constructive* ones, by ever new attempts at building up, just as nature works—recuperating, refashioning and putting up new tissues, while, or even before, the decaying old have begun to shrivel and fall off.

The seventeenth of Tammuz, with its sad reminiscences of Israel's tragic fate, recalls to my mind the touching words of the saintly martyr, Rabbi Hanina ben Thordion, who, having been found studying the Law in spite of the imperial interdict, was condemned to be burned together with the sacred scroll. His pupils, sorrowing witnesses of his terrible sufferings, stood aghast, won-dering at the marvellous patience and resignation which brought a smile on the face of the martyr amidst the most agonizing pains. "What seest thou, O Master, that causes thee to smile in this awful moment?" was their question. "I see the scroll of the Law consumed to ashes, but the letters, as if written in fire, rise up to heaven, as visible testimonies of the Invisible God to whose throne my soul is soaring up." הגוילין נשרפין והאותיות פורחות באויר. Indeed, this is the secret of the entire Jewish history. The outer shape is being steadily consumed, the Jewish temple, the Jewish nationality, the laws, the rites, all crumble to pieces before the storm which works destruction throughout the ages, but the vital spirit permeating the past continues, ever creating new and better forms in place of the old ones. Israel is the burning bush, and God appears in the fire that burns but consumes not. And only when the fire has spread to fill the entire world with its bright blaze of holiness, only when Israel's God will be worshipped in truth as the King of the nations and the Father of man, the full secret is revealed, the mission of the Jew fulfilled. Amen.

# This is my God

## HERMAN WOUK

In later decades of the twentieth century many of the descendants of the great wave of Jewish migrants became educated and prosperous and progressively assimilated to American ways. These developments significantly affected religious attitudes. The popular novelist, Herman Wouk, gives a rather melancholy assessment of American Judaism in 1960.

---

## Dissent: Reform

Reform Judaism began in Germany early in the nineteenth century. A movement which broke off from it in its first decades gained little ground in Germany, but took hold in America as Conservative Judaism. These denominations are today the two religious structures in Jewry outside orthodoxy.

Reform drew its energy, which was at first very high, from two sources: the new freedom of the enlightenment, and the strong stand of the rabbis against change. As thousands of Jews went streaming through the break in the ghetto wall to apostasy, some scientific scholars and leading preachers started casting about for means to harness the flood. An obvious solution was to make the religion easier and more attractive in German terms. In the teeth of all the traditionalist objections, they went boldly to work.

At the start the changes were mere touches of ritual: prayer in German, the use of an organ, uncovered heads, attractive vestments for the rabbi. But the appetite of the enlightenment was not to be appeased by such crumbs. There ensued a rapid jettisoning of laws and customs. A new credo emerged with these changes. The essence of Judaism was the worship of the one universal God. The rest of the work of Moses was temporary machinery, no longer in force in the present day. It followed that the common law too was out of date, since it rested on the Torah. On this premise, German Jewry within a single generation worked out an undemanding religion, freed of any ritual inconvenience, housed with

Source: Herman Wouk, *This is my God*, London, 1960, pp. 246-59.

elegance, and invitingly Western in tone and language. Traditional rabbis fought Reform hard, mainly with anguished emotional onslaughts. Shaken and depleted, German orthodoxy closed its ranks, but Reform won and kept a large following.

It is hard for us to imagine now the elan, the brilliant excitement, of the first years of German Reform. The brotherhood of Jew and Christian must have seemed for a while to be in sight. The Reform Jews were discarding all the distinctive ways of their old faith and merging into the manners and aesthetics of the West. Surely the German citizenry would meet them half way, and together they would usher in religious peace! The German Jews who emigrated to the United States in mid-century took Reform with them. There it chiefly survives, a stable way of life for a sizeable community. German Reform was obliterated by Hitler.

## Conservatism Overtakes Reform

Within Reform itself, early in its growth, there was a serious reaction at the immensity of the change, at the wide sweep of the knife. Major Reform scholars set themselves against the trend. They argued—anticipating ideas that are common in today's sociology—that a working faith had to be more than an abstract idea, that life went deeper than logic. They made little headway against the jubilant tide of change at first. But today Conservative Judaism has drawn abreast of Reform.

When I briefly attended a yeshiva high school around 1930, the senior students were full of dark talk about an alluring place called "Schechter's Seminary". To go there, the rumour went, was to flirt with apostasy; on the other hand, one might acquire the suave charm that would lead to a pulpit in a wealthy Conservative temple. Among the lads who intended to become rabbis, this temptation caused great soul-searchings.

Solomon Schechter, the father of American Conservatism, was a scholar of great ability. He was a disciple of the moderates in the German Reform movement: hence, the name Conservative. To this day the seminary he founded is a most conservative graduate school of divinity; not at all the glittering mixture of Monte Carlo and the Left Bank which the yeshiva lads fondly imagined it to be. The young men keep up traditional observances and forms of worship, and get a grounding in Jewish law. They are trained too in the historical criticism of religion, which was Schechter's forte.

Schechter's ideas really took hold in the early twentieth century, when the nature of American Jewry radically changed. The fugitives from the pogroms and the revolutions of East Europe, perhaps two million strong, arrived fresh from the ghetto. In the bewildering new land, many of them were not at all inclined to drop the old faith pell-mell. They rather clung to it; it was a familiar anchor in a sea of strangeness.

All the same, as they became used to America and won a place in the land, the tug between the old way of life and the new grew strong. They wanted to hold their faith, but they also wanted—somehow or other—quick relief from the strain. Reform was cold and queer to them. They could not comfortably pray in English with uncovered heads. A rabbi who ate pork, and smoked a cigar after the Sabbath service, was a shocking figure, however fine his discourse might be. They had to look elsewhere.

The disciples of Solomon Schechter offered, in their new Conservative temples, certain of the attractions of Reform. Husbands sat with wives; an organ played; English enlivened the cut-down liturgy, but there were some old familiar Hebrew prayers too. The young rabbis, smooth-shaven and well-spoken, were clearly of the new world. Immigrants who were being pushed by circumstances to break the Sabbath laws and to eat banned foods could hardly bear to face the Holy Ark and the rabbi of the synagogue. They were less uncomfortable in the temple. There they felt good about the Judaism they were managing to retain, rather than guilty about the laws they were violating. While Reform gained but a few adherents in these years, the newcomers made of Conservatism, in a decade or so, a movement equal to Reform in strength.

If the first generation could find the Conservative pattern attractive, their children naturally found it more so. The Jewish education of the young being so scanty, their ties to the old faith were largely sentimental, twined with love for their parents. Some of them were already for the step to Reform, but so long as one parent remained alive, the Conservative compromise was the clear choice. When they did join Reform temples—as many did, and are still doing—they were accustomed to more ceremony, rite, and Hebrew than they found. The Reform leaders, pledged to the doctrines of the German Enlightenment, could not acknowledge the force of the Mosaic law. But there has been a trend for some time in Reform to renewal of rites and symbols, and to a greater use of Hebrew, for cultural reasons.

## The Blurring of the Lines

So it happens that the lines between the two movements sometimes blur. In what might be called the liberal Conservative congregations, the distinction from Reform may be a matter of caps and prayer shawls for the men, and more Hebrew. We have it on the authority of *Conservative Judaism*, an able and wholly sympathetic study of the sociologist Dr. Marshall Sklare, that the observance of Sabbath, diet, and other disciplines in these congregations falls off steadily and steeply. This tends to merge the worshippers with Reform Jewry in practice.

Conservative use of Reform innovations and its own departures, like permission to drive cars to the temple on the Sabbath, are defended as minor changes adopted to save the faith. The Conservative rabbi does not smoke on the Sabbath. He observes the laws of diet, and enforces them in temple catering. In his personal life he keeps up traditional duties and customs. He is thus vulnerable to the Reform challenge that there is a double religious standard in his movement: one for rabbis, which is practically orthodox, and one for the laity, which is practically Reform. But the theoretical standard of Conservatism is the same for rabbi and laymen. The difficult lies in the facts of human behaviour. The mingling of the sexes, the playing of the organ, the permission to drive cars, and the abridged prayers somehow suggest to the laymen a general release from the ritual law. The wide differences in practice from temple to temple, and the lack of any Conservative law, make the task of correcting this impression very hard.

## Orthodoxy and Dissent

Between the dissenting movements on the one hand and the large and various bodies of orthodoxy on the other, there is at present a sort of polite peace. The anathemas of the nineteenth century have died away. Naturally the contest for minds, or at least for memberships, is keen under the amicable surface.

That there will be a major change in this picture in the near future seems unlikely. Reform cannot admit authority in the Mosaic law without vanishing. The Conservatives cannot drop their innovations without merging into orthodoxy. Both dissenting movements have nationwide plants: temples, divinity schools, Sunday schools, afternoon schools: and large bodies of members. It is not usual for an establishment to vote itself out of existence.

Will the orthodox discard their fealty to the law and acknowledge the wisdom of Reform or Conservative improvisations? The time for that would seem to have been in the nineteenth century. Orthodoxy has survived and recovered from the impact of modern dissent. Individuals, indeed, continue to drift away. There has been a well-known cascading from orthodox to Conservative, and from Conservative to Reform groups. But Reform does not swell as it might, because of attrition into disinterest and loss of identity. Nor, curiously, does orthodoxy seem to diminish. It received massive new strength from the refugees of the Hitler terror; and since then it is, if anything, on the rise. The prospect so far as the eye can see, at least in the United States, is that the three denominations will continue for a long time.

The dissenting movements can scarcely wish for the disappearance of orthodoxy. Their existence more or less depends on a main body of Mosaic followers who write the Holy Scrolls, study the classics, keep the faith at its picturesque maximum, and provide a pool of strength and renewal for the less demanding denominations. The great weakness of both Conservative and Reform Judaism—at least this is my impression—is their tendency to run down without constant infusion of orthodox-trained new blood.

It is widely argued today that both movements were shock absorbers of the enlightenment, and kept great numbers of Jews from being utterly lost to the ancient House. If, as the orthodox believe, the Mosaic law has a decisive inner force, they ought to await with tolerance and with confidence the coming return of dissenters, beginning with the most intelligent. But that is asking a lot of human nature. When a temple opens in a neighbourhood where a synagogue has reigned for a generation, and attracts away some husbands and wives who like to sit side by side, the reaction is usually less than philosophic.

The dissenters have had a very good thing in mixed seating. Against orthodoxy it has been until lately their trump card, because it is so much nearer to the manner of the American majority. For the orthodox, this detail of synagogue custom has become a rallying ground. Since the invasion has struck at them here, it is here that they dig in. It is the hallmark of the new orthodox edifices that the men and women worship separately. The issue may seem a small one on which to divide a community as ancient, and as rich in ideas, as Jewry. But one never knows in advance, marching into battle, which of the many hills on the field is going to become Bloody Nose Ridge.

## A Personal Note

I have here done my best to portray the Reform and Conservative movements candidly and accurately. My portrait should perhaps be corrected in the reader's mind by a fact that will be obvious to him; my general sympathy is with the main tradition, and so I view these movements more or less as an outsider. Individuals in these movements have contributed magnificently to scholarship, to Jewish rescue and survival, and to the physical plant of Jewry in America and in Israel. How can men who score such achievements be in error, if they are? The answer would have to lie not in any lack of wisdom or talent in them—and most certainly not in any superior insight ascribable to me—but in the large social forces that have created the movements of dissent. In the history of every people, men of the best energy and wit, and of the highest value to their fellows, have been on the wrong side in long-range issues. Perhaps the orthodox are out of step with history, not they. History will decide. My object here has not been to criticize any party in Jewry, but to tell the truth as I understand it.

The American Jewish community works together in rescue and philanthropy, whatever its religious differences. Whether the task is helping Israel, or building hospitals, or supporting community projects, the orthodox, the Conservative, and the Reform Jews fall in side by side and get at the job. Vigorous leaders often come from the dissenters, or from the large group that does not worship at all. Major service organizations like B'nai Brith and Hadassah, renowned for energy and achievement, are not committed to any one religious party. A minor point, but one that illuminates the underlying good will in the community, is this: even when unobservant Jews happen to outnumber religious ones in a project, they usually make their catered affairs kosher, sometimes at high added cost. The instinct that suggests such conduct is worth high praise, but nobody thinks much about it.

If charity, healing, rescue, and welfare work were all of Judaism, the bulk of the community would be orthodox. These things are not the whole Torah, but they are much of it. Pietists sometimes despair of American Jewry. I for one am proud to be part of the community, and I think its great days lie ahead.

## Assimilation

"The best thing we can do is intermarry and disappear," a fraternity brother said to me when I was about seventeen. It was the first time I had heard the slogan of assimilation spoken loud and clear. It froze me. I peered at him, wondering whether he could be serious. He was. The assimilators are always quite serious, though some Jews find their state of mind almost unimaginable.

Assimilation is, and for the longest time has been, a main party of dissent in Jewry. It does not seem a party, because in its nature it has no organization, no temples, no schools, and no books of doctrine. But in periods of freedom like the present—and there have been several such interludes in our history—it sometimes wins half of the Jews, and occasionally more than half.

To call the assimilators turncoats, weaklings, traitors, breakers of the faith, is to substitute abuse for the effort to think. Assimilation is not only a popular way, it has weighty logic on its side. The real surprise is that the Jews have not wholly evaporated in one of these times of tolerance. What, to be given the chance to lay down the burden of ostracism and disappear among the billions of mankind, and not to take advantage of it with a rush and a cheer? Where is the sense—in view of the sombre history of the Jews—in behaving any other way?

With all that, the assimilator seldom states his position in the cold blood of my fraternity brother. Nor does he, as a rule, plot a course of vanishing. He allows it to happen. This is achieved simply by doing nothing about being Jewish. Three or four generations, and the family ceases to count as Jews, unless bloodthirsty lunatics like the Nazis start up a grandfather hunt. Remaining Jewish in a free society takes work. If the work goes undone, Jewishness dims and dies. It is the exceptional assimilator who tries to speed the death by such devices as changing his name and obscuring or denying his background.

Assimilation, like frostbite, begins at the extremities of Jewry. Settlements far from the centres of the community almost always fade away fast. In the social body it is the wealthiest and the poorest, the best educated and the least educated, the brightest and the dullest, who tend to go first. Ignorance and low intelligence cause loss of grip on the faith. Carried along in the ghetto by the current around them, the ill-informed and the incapable drift into non-observance when cut loose, and into oblivion. Poverty drives people to suspend observance, and grinds away their identity. At the other extreme the rich and the gifted make their way swiftly into the non-Jewish world. Judaism being an encumbrance on the way, they tend to drop it. It is in the middle that Jewish identity persists longest, whether as Zionism, orthodoxy, or religious dissent.

Yet here too assimilation at last takes hold. When professors and governors, movie stars and millionaires, writers and judges openly give up their Jewish ties and ways—these in America, and their equivalents in German, Spain, Morocco, Rome, and Babylon in other days—the wonder is that anybody at all remains behind to carry on the faith. Yet a remnant always does, and Judaism in time renews itself with the greatest struggles—if only to produce, in the next age of tolerance, another wave of gifted assimilators. It is even argued that this is the true mission of the Jews, the secret of the Messiah symbol—that they must go on relinquishing to the world St. Pauls, Spinozas, Freuds, Disraelis. It is a fetching idea. One weakness of it is that if assimilation ever won a round of history the milieu and the human strain that produce such luminaries would disappear, and the world would see no more of them.

The loss of these intelligences in the van of a new assimilation surge is each time foredoomed. Quickest to see the conflicts of the old way and the new, they are the first to decide that Judaism is dated. They find in their mastery of the new life, in the welcome granted to their talents, a whole answer to existence. They create a climate in which assimilation becomes first a smart, then an ordinary course. Masses of plain people follow them without the compensations of high achievement, simply because it is always easier not to be Jewish, once the communion weakens.

The odd thing is that this momentous rejection by the able few is almost never a well-considered act. Often they are born of parents already adrift, so that they never get a chance to know Judaism. Or if they find a received form of it in their homes, it loses out swiftly to the interests generated by their special talents. By the age of fifteen they have swept into a life, and a state of mind, which exclude for ever an adult estimate of their Jewish identity. It is a freakish occurrence when—as with Heine—a man of genius has second thoughts about assimilation, reopens the case with all his energy, and reverses the verdict. And such a rare event comes too late, both for the man and for the people who have followed him.

## The Assimilator Speaks

"What you say here is quite true, and on the whole well put. I respect your knowledge of Judaism and your ability to respond to it. In an abstract way I envy you—not your life exactly, but the knowledge of a lore and the experience of a belief, which are quite strange to me. But it is out of the question for me to reopen the matter. As you know, I have never denied being a Jew, and I am proud of an ancestry which, as you say, is ancient and distinguished. I'm sorry to say the Jewish mission means nothing to me. It is a curiosity of intellectual history, no more.

"I'm well aware that my children will probably slough off their Jewish identity, and that my grandchildren most certainly will. At the risk of offending you, I have to say I think this will be a good thing for them. My talents, such as they are, have not protected me from certain stings and stabs that come a Jew's way. Life is hard enough. To forgo a disability seems sensible to me. Again, all of you who prefer to make it the core of your life have my respect and puzzled admiration. You may even have a point, in the eyes of the God you believe in and I don't. But to me you are all Quixotes, carrying on an obsolete code of honour in rusty armour on a collapsing nag, with a mad and sadly comic energy. I wish you well. If you turn out right and there is a beyond in which we will compare notes, you may have the laugh on me, assuming there is laughter there. But I do not think I will ever hear that laugh, and for the life of me I cannot change my views, which are as clear and inescapable to me as the sky above.

"You want me to re-examine my 'heritage'. Would you have me also examine in depth Mohammedanism, Buddhism, Catholicism, and Zoroastrianism? When, then, will I get my day's work done? Judaism means exactly as much to me as one of those. It is a collector's item in the gallery of comparative religion. I know its general picture: Abraham, Moses, one God, the Exodus, the Torah, no ham, all that. No, I have not studied the Talmud. But I claim to have a contemporary intelligence. If the West has put those special Jewish studies aside and taken only the Bible, that verdict must be mine. Does the Rambam have anything to say to me on the far side of Kant, Nietzsche, and Whitehead? If so, where are his discoverers? I gather he is a sort of Jewish Aquinas. Aquinas is an old story to me. My integrity requires that I know the best in current thought, and by and large I do. I will not go back to the yeshiva and sit among the boys. I am a man, doing a man's work, and I am aware of no gap in me that needs such a drastic and melodramatic repair."

I have, of course, deliberately invented a thoughtful assimilator to speak for his party. It would be stacking the cards to select a poor chap living in an echoing Tudor-style mansion in a New York suburb, who said to the visitor from the United Jewish Appeal, in a slight accent, "Who told you I was Jewish? Get out of here, please, and don't bother me again." Or the girl who sued to break her grandfather's will, which barred from his legacies any grandchild marrying outside the faith. The girl's parents had given her no Jewish training. She wanted her Gentile sweetheart, and also her ancestor's stocks and bonds, but not his awkward religion. I believe she won.

These people—the imaginary one who speaks so well, and these others whose acts speak just as eloquently—are lost from Judaism, that is all; lost down a road which has swallowed many more Jews than the Hitler terror ever did. Of course they survive as persons. But from the viewpoint of an army, it makes little difference whether a division is exterminated or disperses into the hills and shucks off its uniforms.

Our faith teaches that God can revive Judaism in a Jew to his last hour. But in the ordinary course of things, we must say of the assimilators that the nerve of Judaism is killed in them. It has happened all through our history to many people. Lack of training, lack of will, sharp changes of environment, persecution, absorbing interests, intellectual alienation—all these things can kill the nerve.

The given reason is almost always the last—intellectual alienation. But most of the time these are words that follow the events. The Spinoza figure is so rare as to be almost single—the man who plumbs Judaism and passes through a crisis of rejection. Most people lose their Jewishness because they have never had a chance to get a grip on it. The Talmud called this large group "children raised in captivity", holding them innocent of religious violations. Among these "children" in the Talmud's day were some of the most prosperous people in the Roman Empire.

## The Uncertain

There is a class of Jews just as large as the assimilators today, but wholly different. In them the nerve is damaged, but alive. They may speak and act as the assimilators do. Usually they belong to no temples, and they follow no rites. They may be eloquent in the parlour against the conformity of religion, and the supernatural God of Moses. For all that, they cannot regard with calm their own fading Jewishness. The thought that their children may be lost from the Jewish tale darkens their peace, though they cannot say why. They are almost ashamed of their own survival instinct. These are not assimilators. They are vital Jews, thrown out of orbit by the cataclysms of the past two centuries. Their retention of identity and feeling is a marvel. They testify as much as the observant to the strange endurance of the spirit of Abraham's House.

# Religion in Urban
# Industrial Society

# ❦130❧

# Perils—Wealth

## JOSIAH STRONG

Strong's critique of American society as it was being transformed by economic development focuses on the moral weaknesses being exposed in the population by opportunities to pile up wealth. But the critique arises from the paradox, as Strong sees it, that the vigour of the Anglo-Saxon character, combined with the possibilities offered in the United States, intensifies the dangers of mammonism, materialism, luxuriousness, and the congestion of wealth. For religious writers the social crises of the industrial era were initially moral crises. From that starting point they responded in a variety of ways; Strong himself moved towards progressive reform, drawing upon the vitality of Anglo-Saxon Protestantism.

A nd such wealth contains mighty possibilities, both for good and evil. Let us, in this connection, look at the latter.

1. As civilization increases, wealth has more meaning, and money a larger representative power. Civilization multiplies wants, which money affords the means of gratifying. With the growth of civilization, therefore, money will be an ever-increasing power, and the object of ever-increasing desire. Hence the danger of *Mammonism*, growing more and more intense and infatuated. The love of money is the besetting sin of commercial peoples, and runs in the very blood of Anglo-Saxons, who are the great wealth-creators of the world. Our soil is peculiarly favorable to the growth of this "root of all evil"; and for two reasons. First, wealth is more easily amassed here than anywhere else in the world, of which we have already seen sufficient proof; and, second, wealth means more, has more power, here than elsewhere. Every nation has its aristocracy. In other lands the aristocracy is one of birth; in ours it is one of wealth. It is useless for us to protest that we are democratic, and to plead the leveling character of our institutions. There is among us an aristocracy of recognized power, and that aristocracy is one of wealth. No heraldry offends our republican prejudices. Our ensigns armorial are the trade-mark. Our laws and customs recognize no noble

Source: Josiah Strong, 'Perils—Wealth', *Our Country*, New York, 1885, [1963 ed.], pp. 160–9.

titles; but men can forgo the husk of a title who possess the fat ears of power. In England there is an eager ambition to rise in rank, an ambition as rarely gratified as it is commonly experienced. With us, aspiration meets with no such iron check as birth. A man has only to build higher the pedestal of his wealth. He may stand as high as he can build. His wealth cannot secure to him genuine respect, to be sure; but, for that matter, neither can birth. It will secure to him an obsequious deference. It may purchase political distinction. It *is* power. In the Old World, men commonly live and die in the condition in which they are born. The peasant may be discontented, may covet what is beyond his reach; but his desire draws no strength from expectation. Heretofore, in this country, almost any laborer, by industry and economy, might gain a competence, and even a measure of wealth; and, though now we are beginning to approximate the conditions of European labor, young men, generally, when they start in life, still expect to become rich; and, thinking not to serve their god for naught, they commonly become faithful votaries of Mammon. Thus the prizes of wealth in the United States, being at the same time greater and more easily won, and the lists being open to all comers, the rush is more general, and the race more eager then elsewhere.

"But they that will be rich, fall into temptation and a snare, and into many foolish and hurtful lusts, which drown men in destruction and perdition." They who "will be rich," are tempted to resort to methods less laborious and more and more unscrupulous. Fierce competition is leading to frequent adulterations, and many forms of bribery. It is driving legitimate business to illegitimate methods. Merchants offer prizes to draw trade, and employ the lottery to enrich themselves and debauch the public. The growth of the spirit of speculation is ominous. The salaries of clerks, the business capital, the bank deposits and trust funds of all sorts which disappear "on 'change," indicate how widespread is the unhealthy haste to be rich. And such have the methods of speculation become that "The Exchange" has degenerated into little better than a euphemism for "gambling hell." "While one bushel in seven of the wheat crop of the United States is received by the Produce Exchange of New York, its traders buy and sell two out of every one that comes out of the ground. When the cotton plantations of the South yielded less than six million bales, the crop of the New York Cotton Exchange was more than thirty-two millions. Pennsylvania does well to run twenty-four millions of barrels of oil in one year; but New York City will do as much in two small rooms in one week, and the Petroleum Exchange sold altogether last year two thousand million barrels." Such facts indicate how small a portion of the transactions of the "Exchange" is legitimate business, and how large a proportion is simply gambling. Mammonism is corrupting popular morals in many ways. Sunday amusements of every kind—horse-racing, base ball, theaters, beer-gardens, steamboat and railroad excursions—are all provided *because there is money in them.* Licentious literature floods the land, poisoning the minds of the young and polluting their lives, *because there is money in it.* Gambling flourishes in spite of the law, and actually under its license, *because there is money in it.* And that great abomination of desolation, that triumph of Satan, that more than ten Egyptian plagues in one—the liquor traffic—grows and thrives at the expense of every human interest, *because there is money in it.* Ever since greed of gold sold the Christ and raffled for his garments, it has crucified every form of virtue between thieves. And, while Mammonism corrupts morals, it blocks reforms. Men who have favors to ask of the public are slow to follow their convictions into any unpopular reform movement. They can render only a surreptitious service. Their discipleship must needs be secret, "for fear of the" customers or clients or patients. It is Mammonism which makes most men *invertebrates.* When important Mormon legislation was pending, certain New York merchants telegraphed to members of Congress: "New York sold $13,000,000 worth of goods to Utah last year. Hands off!" The tribe of Demetrius, the Ephesian silversmith, is everywhere: men quick to perceive when this their craft by which they have their wealth is in danger of being set at naught. "Nothing is more timorous than a million dollars—except two millions."

Mammonism is also corrupting the ballot-box. The last four presidential elections have shown that the two great political parties are nearly equal in strength. The vast majority of voters on both sides are party men, who vote the same way year after year. The result of the election is determined by the floating vote. Of this, a comparatively small portion is thoroughly intelligent and conscientious; the remainder is, for the most part, without convictions, without principle and thoroughly venal; hence the great temptation to bribery, to which both parties yield. Moreover, the influence of great corporations, which so often controls legislation, is moneyed influence.

2. Again, by reason of our enormous wealth and its rapid increase, we are threatened with a gross materialism. The English epithet applied by Matthew Arnold to Chicago, "too beastly prosperous," has a subtle meaning, which perhaps was not intended by the distinguished visitor. Material growth may be much more vigorous than the moral and intellectual as to have a distinctly brutalizing tendency. Life becomes sensuous; that is deemed real which can be seen and handled, weighed and transported; and that only has value which can be appraised in dollars and cents. Wealth was intended to minister to life, to enlarge it; when life becomes only a ministry to enlarge wealth, there is manifest perversion and degradation. We may say of it as Young said of life—"An end deplorable! A means divine!" Says Mr. Whipple: "—there is danger that the nation's worship of labors whose worth is measured by money will give a sordid character to it mightiest exertions of power, eliminate heroism from its motives, destroy all taste for lofty speculation, and all love for ideal beauty, and inflame individuals with a devouring self-seeking, corrupting the very core of the national life." We have undoubtedly developed a larger proportion of men of whom the above is a faithful picture than any other Christian nation; men to whom Agassiz's remark, "I am offered five hundred dollars a night to lecture, but I decline all invitations, for I have no time to make money," is simply incomprehensible; it dazes them.

There is a "balance of power" to be preserved in the United States as well as in Europe. Our safety demands the preservation of a balance between our material power and our moral and intellectual power. The means of self-gratification should not outgrow the power of self-control. Steam-power would have been useless had we not found in iron, or something else, a greater power of resistance. And, should we discover a motor a hundred times more powerful than steam, it would prove not only useless but fearfully destructive, unless we could find a still greater resisting power. Increasing wealth will only prove the means of destruction, unless it is accompanied by an increasing power of control, a stronger sense of justice, and a more intelligent comprehension of its obligations.

There is a certain unfriendliness between the material and the spiritual. The vivid apprehension of the one makes the other seem unreal. When the life of the senses is intense, spiritual existence and truths are dim; and when St. Paul was exalted to a spiritual ecstasy, the senses were so closed that he could not tell whether he was "in the body or out of the body." A time of commercial stagnation is apt to be a time of spiritual quickening, while great material prosperity is likely to be accompanied by spiritual death. A poor nation is much more sensitive to the power of the gospel than a rich one. So Christ taught: "How hardly shall they that have riches enter into the kingdom of God!" "It is easier for a camel to go through the eye of a needle than for a rich man to enter into the Kingdom of God!" Words as true now as when they were first uttered, and having a fuller meaning in the nineteenth century than in the first.

3. Again, great and increasing wealth subjects us to all the perils of luxuriousness. Nations, in their beginnings, are poor; poverty is favourable to hardihood and industry; industry leads to thrift and wealth; wealth produces luxury, and luxury results in enervation, corruption, and destruction. This is the historic round which nations have run. "Nations have decayed, but it has never been with the imbecility of age." "Avarice and luxury have been the ruin of every great state." Her American possessions made Spain the richest and most powerful nation in Europe; but wealth induced luxury and idleness, whence came poverty and degradation. Rome was never stronger in all the seeming elements of power than at the moment of her fall. She had grown rich, and riches had corrupted her morals, rendered her effeminate, and made her an easy prey to the lusty barbarian of the North. The material splendor of Israel reached its climax in the glory of Solomon's reign, in which silver was made to be in Jerusalem as stones; but it was followed by the immediate dismemberment of the kingdom. Under all that magnificence, at which even Oriental monarchs wondered, was springing a discontent which led to speedy revolt. Bancroft has wisely said that, "Sedition is bred in the lap of luxury."

The influence of mechanical invention is to stimulate luxurious living. We are told by Edward Atkinson that by the hand looms in the South ten hours' work will produce eight yards of cloth, while in the factory of New England ten hours, work will produce 800 yards. In 1888 the steam power of the United

States was equal to the working-power of 161,333,000 men; as if one-half of all the male workmen on the globe had engaged in our service. When we remember that this machinery is an enormous producer of the necessaries, comforts, and luxuries of life, but is not a consumer of the same, we see how immensely the average consumption per caput has increased. As luxuries are thus cheapened and brought within the reach of an ever-widening circle, there is an increasing tendency toward self-indulgence. Herodotus said: "It is a law of nature that faint-hearted men should be the fruit of luxurious countries; for we never find that the same soil produces delicacies and heroes." Is there not danger that our civilization will become tropical? The temperate zone has produced the great nations, because in it the conditions of life have been sufficiently hard to arouse energy and develop strength. Where men are pampered by nature, they sink to a low level; and where civilization is of the pampering sort the tendency is the same. By means of coal, which Mr. Emerson calls a "portable climate," together with increasing wealth and luxuries, we are multiplying tropical conditions here in the North.

The splendor of our riches will doubtless dazzle the world; but history declares, in the ruins of Babylon and Thebes, of Carthage and Rome, that wealth has no conserving power; that it tends rather to enervate and corrupt. Our wonderful material prosperity, which is the marvel of other nations, and the boast of our own, may hide a decaying core.

4. Again, another danger is the marked and increasing tendency toward a *congestion of wealth*. The enormous concentration of power in the hands of one man is unrepublican, and dangerous to popular institutions. The framers of our government aimed to secure the distribution of power. They were careful to make the several departments—executive, legislative, and judicial—operate as checks on each other. An executive, chosen by the people and responsible to them, may exercise but little authority; and after a short period he must return it to them. But a money-king may double, quadruple, centuple his wealth, if he can. He may exercise vastly more power than the governor of his state; but he is irresponsible. He is not a constitutional monarch, but a czar. He is not chosen by the people with reference to his fitness to administer so great a trust; he may lack utterly all moral qualifications for it. We have indeed, some rich men who are an honor to our civilization; but the power of many millions is almost certain to find its way into strong and unscrupulous hands. Our money-king must not, after two or four years, return his power to the people; he has a life tenure of office, provided only his grip upon his golden scepter be strong. Less than thirty years ago, Emerson wrote for our wonder: "Some English private fortunes reach, and some exceed, a million dollars a year." At least one American has had an income of $1,000,000 a month; and others follow hard after him. A writer in *The Forum* gives a list of seventy names of persons in the United States, representing an aggregate wealth of $2,700,000,000, or an average of $37,500,000 each. "It would be easy," he says, "for any specially well-informed person to make up a list of one hundred persons averaging $25,000,000 each,

in addition to ten averaging $100,000,000 each. No such list of concentrated wealth could be given in any other country in the world."

Superfluity on the one hand, and dire want on the other—the millionaire and the tramp—are the complement each of the other. The classes from which we have most to fear are the two extremes of society—the dangerously rich and the dangerously poor; and the former are much more to be feared than the latter. Said Dr. Howard Crosby:

> The danger which threatens the uprooting of society, the demolition of civil institutions, the destruction of liberty, and the desolation of all, is that which comes from the rich and powerful classes in the community. . . .The great estates of Rome, in the time of the Caesars, and of France in the time of the Bourbons, rivaled those of the United States to-day; but both nations were on their way to the frenzy of revolution, not in spite of their wealth, but, in some true sense, because of it.

We have seen, in the preceding chapter, that mechanical invention tends to create operative and capitalist classes, and render them hereditary. It is the tendency of our civilization to destroy the easy gradation from poor to rich which now exists, and to divide society into only two classes—the rich and the comparatively poor. In a new country almost any one can do business successfully, and broad margins will save him from the results of blunders which would elsewhere be fatal. But, with growing population and increasing facilities of communication, competition becomes severe, and then a slight advantage makes the difference between success and failure. Accumulated capital is not slight, but an immense advantage. "To him that hath, shall be given." There will, therefore, be an increasing tendency toward the centralization of great wealth in corporations, which will simply eat up the small manufacturers and the small dealers. As the two classes of rich and poor grow more distinct, they will become more estranged, and whether the rich, like Sydney Smith, come to regard poverty as "infamous," it is quite certain that many of the poor will look upon wealth as criminal.

We have traced some of the natural tendencies of great and increasing wealth. It should be observed that these tendencies will grow stronger, because wealth is increasing much more rapidly than population. Remarkable as the growth of the latter is, it being four times the European rate of increase from 1870 to 1880, and three times that of England or Germany, the multiplication of wealth has been even more remarkable. In one generation, 1850–1880, our national wealth increased more than six fold, and, notwithstanding the growth of population, the wealth per caput increased nearly three fold. There is reason to believe that this rate of increase will be sustained for years to come. If it is, the danger from mammonism, materialism, luxuriousness, and the congestion of wealth will be a constant increasing peril.

# ❧·131·❧

# Accumulation of Riches

## GERALD HEUVER

Revulsion from some of the business practices of the new industrial order provoked, at its most conservative, an insistence on the morally responsible use of investment capital and accumulated wealth by individuals. It will be noted that the extract below offers no hint of any need for organised action to regulate the economic system, and in the writer's preference for philanthropy operating indirectly, implies a sceptical view of the moral character of the poor.

---

Acting on the principle that business is business, and that all is fair in love and in war, and that business is war, is also a great evil. It has filled our land with bitterness. It begets no end of suspicion. It kills faith. It divides class against class. It crushes the weak. It ruins souls. Modern business methods cannot possibly be reconciled with Christ's requirement. The combination of capital for the purpose of furthering self-interest, irrespective of the suffering which it entail upon those from whom the markets are taken, or those thrown out of employment; the freezing out of competitors; the pooling of interests, the shutting down of factories or mines because the profits diminish a little, when doing so causes the most acute suffering to helpless women and children, is not generous, and violates the principle embodied in Christ's saying about business loans without interest.

The third principle relating to riches, in the Sermon on the Mount, enjoins beneficence:

> Take heed that ye do not your righteousness before men, to be seen of them; else ye have no reward with your Father which is in heaven. When therefore thou doest alms, sound not a trumpet before thee, as the hypocrites do in the synagogues and in the streets, that they may have glory of men. Verily, I say unto you, they have received their reward. But when thou doest alms, let not thy left hand know what thy right hand doeth; that thine alms may be in secret; and thy Father which seeth in secret shall recompense thee. (Matt. vi. 1-4.)

Source: Gerald Heuver, 'Accumulation of Riches', *Teachings of Jesus Concerning Wealth*, London, 1903, pp. 176-85 .

This, it is true, is no command to give alms, but the endeavor to improve the practice involves the recognition of its importance.

It is interesting to notice how secret Jesus has kept his own almsgiving. The naturalness with which the eleven concluded that Judas had been directed to go and give something to the poor, when he departed from them (John xiii. 29), and the readiness with which they criticized Mary for not giving the money which she spent in anointing Jesus for swelling the poor fund (Matt. xxvi. 9), makes it clear that Jesus gave alms, and had emphasized its importance, yet no instance of it is recorded.

How full his heart was with love for the needy! "When thou makest a dinner or a supper." he says,

> call not thy friends, nor thy brethren, nor thy kinsmen, nor rich neighbors; lest haply they also bid thee again and a recompense be made thee. But when thou makest a feast bid the poor, the maimed, the lame, the blind; and thou shalt be blessed; because they have not the wherewith to recompense thee; for thou shalt be recompensed in the resurrection of the just. (Luke xiv. 12-14.)

These people need your inspiration, your sympathy, and the influence of your example and presence. Checks are not sufficient for them. They need the loving look, the touch of the hand that is friendly, and the heart that is sympathetic. It was for this reason that he ate and drank with them so often and was their companion and friend.

The story of the good Samaritan hardly needs any comment. It speaks for itself. To analyze it mars its beauty.

> And behold, a certain lawyer stood up and tempted him, saying, Master, what shall I do to inherit eternal life? And he said unto him, What is written in the law? how readest thou? And he, answering, said, Thou shalt love the Lord thy God with all thy heart, and with all thy soul, and with all thy strength, and with all thy mind; and thy neighbor as thyself. And he said unto him, Thou hast answered right: this do, and thou shalt live. But he, desiring to justify himself, said unto Jesus, And who is my neighbor? (Luke x. 25-29)

and then comes the story. It is the account of a traveler who fell among thieves, who robbed him and beat him and left him half dead, whom a Samaritan found and cared for, and putting him upon his own beast, brought him to an inn, to the keeper of which he gave the money required for the care of the sufferer.

Having told it Jesus said to the lawyer, "Go and do likewise."

One incident in this story should not be overlooked. It has often escaped the interpreter. It is that the Samaritan did not give the money to the sufferer, but to the keeper of the inn. And this suggests the important truth, that help for the needy can often be more wisely bestowed when given indirectly than directly, as when it is given to institutions which are founded for helping them.

In these days, when there are so many of these institutions, it is almost always better. Giving alms, especially to unknown men, is dangerous. Beneficence to the back-door tramps does harm. It should not be practiced, no matter how good it may feel. Money given to schools for the endowment of scholarships to assist enterprising young people; to hospitals to enable the needy to obtain good treatment at low cost; to libraries to bring downtrodden people in touch with high-minded, inspiring authors; to boards for the distribution of bibles, the establishment of churches, or to enable them to send out Christian teachers and missionaries to fire men with a realizing sense of their possibilities because of their divine sonship; does usually much more good than what is given in alms.

And may we not believe that Jesus would have viewed the investment of capital in business enterprise with the dominating thought of blessing, with great joy? Undoubtedly we may. For he who invests in plants—factories, mines, etc.—giving work to a large number of people, and paying these, not with a view to keeping the largest possible share for self, but with a view to giving the largest wage consistent with the safety of the plant, becomes exceedingly useful, and he meets the demands of Jesus as truly as if he gave largely to charities, or schools, or churches.

Warnings against the selfish use of money are contained in the following stories: There is first the story of the sad death of a rich capitalist, who enlarged his barns to enjoy the fruit of his wide acres, and suddenly died a spiritual pauper. (Luke xi. 16–21.) A second story is that of a rich man who was clothed in purple and fared sumptuously every day, but showed no concern for a pauper who lay festering in sores and hungry at his gate. "And the rich man also died, and was buried. And in Hades he lifted up his eyes, being in torments." (Luke xvi. 22, 23.)

A third story is that of the rich young man—in some respects the saddest story of them all—who was so anxious to inherit eternal life, but because he was not willing to put the interests of God's kingdom before his wealth, failed to do so. (Matt. xix. 22.)

In order to encourage the unselfish use of wealth, Jesus promised as a reward for it the treasures of heaven (Luke xii. 33), and the friendship of the saved.

> And I say unto to you, make to yourselves friends by means of the mammon of unrighteousness; that when it shall fail, they may receive you into eternal tabernacles. (Luke xvi. 9.)

Gratitude survives the grave. What a stirring thought it is, that a good man who uses his wealth to help his fellow-men will be welcomed when he enters the spirit world by those whom his benevolence blessed!

But more stirring still is the scene which Jesus portrayed, and which he says shall be seen at the judgment day. (Matt. xxvi. 31–46.) In this picture he shows us how such as have fed the hungry, clothed the naked, and visited the sick and the prisoners shall be awarded with heaven, while those who have failed to do this shall be condemned to perdition.

One almost fears to write what this story so plainly teaches. So earnestly have we been taught by catechism and teachers that salvation is of grace, and that works cannot save us, that we have almost come to believe that good works have no merit. But the teaching is so plain, so direct, that we cannot possibly mistake it. Jesus says that he is the friend of those who are his friends, the poor, the hungry, the prisoners, and the sick, and the helping these will do what doctrines, worship, church-going, and prayer will sometimes fail to do, i.e., insure one an entrance into heaven.

This truth, the importance of helping the needy, of being humane, sympathetic, tender, is another neglected truth. Everybody knows the importance of it, everybody gives assent to it, but so few act accordingly.

The people in Jesus' day knew its importance. They had the magnificent humanitarian laws and teachings of the Old Testament. But they despised the poor. (Jas. ii. 6.) They would occasionally help them, but with money which they had first extorted from them. At least this seems to be taught by the ironical remark of Jesus to the Pharisees to give alms of such things as were within their cups and platters—things that were obtained by extortion and wickedness. (Luke xi. 41.)

The people in Russia know its importance. Has not the large Greek church the beautiful teachings of Jesus? But the earthly existence of the great mass of the people of that tremendous realm is positively painful. They are hungry, filthy, oppressed, enslaved, and ignorant, and the leaders of the church mind it not.

The people of the Middle Ages knew its importance. Those warring knights and feudal lords, who were fired with zeal for the rescue of Christ's sepulcher from the hand of the Saracen infidels, but had no pity for the suffering serfs.

The people of a hundred years or less ago knew its importance. The churchmen who sent children to labor in unhealthy mines, until the knowledge of it roused Christian England's anger and stopped it, and the slave-owner who shrank not from ignoring domestic affection, selling boys and girls from out of the reach of their parent's embrace.

And we know its importance, and while a great deal has been done by us in obedience to Jesus' command, how much there yet remains to be done! What an amount of suffering there still is! What sad tales one reads with every morning paper! And if we will look for it, we might see sights that would make sadder tales still.

The Christian world is still hard on the unfortunate. If one is down he is apt to be trampled lower. Success is honored while hard words are reserved for the failures. The children of the failures are called riffraff, trash, scum, dregs. Poor things! It is well for youth to battle with difficulties, but there are some difficulties that crush. "Have not all a chance in free America?" it is asked. Not all. Such as possess a good environment and a healthy body and brain have; but the others do not. The child of the gutter has no chance. The child of shiftless, drunken, impure parents, living in overcrowded, foul-smelling tenements, has not. He cannot be anything but shiftless and drunken. To rise unaided above a debased environment and a depraved hereditary tendency is impossible. To speak of those who have had both of these disadvantages to contend against as dregs and scum, riffraff, and pariahs, is wrong. That is punishing them for what they cannot help.

For these people far more should be done than as yet has been done. There is a stirring passage in an address by the late ex-Mayor Hewitt, of New York, which he made about three years ago in New York before meeting to raise funds for the East Side work of the Episcopal Church. "The rich," he says,

> have not even begun what they ought to do. Men that I almost worship for their generosity and solicitude for those that have less, are not giving in proportion to their wealth the half that was given by their families a generation ago. Have we a right to take this wealth and do nothing to correct the evils created in its production? Can you accept these millions and shut your eyes to the evils which weave themselves about the producers? Can any one be content with such conditions? Good God! can this be the end to which we have been working all these centuries? Is this the result of our industrial development, and must our prosperity as a nation be purchased at such a staggering price? If these terrible tenements, these overcrowded districts, these dark and foul-smelling places, and all the attending miseries must go with industry, then I would to God that every industrial centre could be destroyed as were Sodom and Gomorrah of old, and men be driven back to the land where they can at least have the breezes and the green grass and the sunshine and blue of heaven to look up to. (*Outlook*, Vol. LXVII. No. 2, p. 89.)

Are these words too strong? I do not know that they are. This is sure, that far more attention will have to be paid to the redemption of these classes than there yet is, before the Christian world can expect to hear from the Judge in the final day:

> Come ye blessed of my Father, inherit the kingdom prepared for you from the foundation of the world..... Inasmuch as ye did it unto one of these my brethren, ye did it unto me.

# ⊰·132·⊱

# The Knights of Labor

## CARDINAL JAMES GIBBONS

The Catholic hierarchy in the United States was divided on the labour question in the late nineteenth century. Some bishops feared that Catholic workers' allegiance to labour organizations would draw them away from their loyalty to the Church. Gibbons, however, as a step towards a more just social order, supported workers forming their own unions. Conspicuously, he used his influence in Rome to prevent a repetition in the United States of the papal condemnation of the union organization, the Knights of Labor, which had occurred in Canada.

1 These considerations, which show that in these associations those elements are not to be found which the Holy See has condemned, lead us to study, in the second place, the evils which the association contends against, and the nature of the conflict.

2. That there exist among us, as in all other countries of the world, grave and threatening social evils, public injustices which call for strong resistance and legal remedy, is a fact which no one dares to deny—a fact already acknowledged by the Congress and the President of the United States. Without entering into the sad details of these evils, whose full discussion is not necessary, I will only mention that monopolies, on the part of both individuals and of corporations, have everywhere called forth not only the complaints of our working classes, but also the opposition of our public men and legislators; that the efforts of monopolists, not always without success, to control legislation to their own profit, cause serious apprehensions among the disinterested friends of liberty; that the heartless avarice which, through greed of gain, pitilessly grinds not only men, but even the women and children in various employments, make it clear to all who love humanity and justice that it is not only the right of the laboring classes to protect themselves, but the duty of the whole people to aid them in finding a remedy against the dangers with which both civilization

Source: Cardinal James Gibbons, 'The Knights of Labor', A Retrospective of Fifty Years, Baltimore, 1916, pp. 194-209.

and social order are menaced by avarice, oppression and corruption.

It would be vain to dispute either the existence of the evils, or the right of legitimate resistance, or the necessity of a remedy. At most a doubt might be raised about the legitimacy of the form of resistance, and of the remedy employed by the Knights of Labor. This, then, is the next point to be examined.

3. It can hardly be doubted that, for the attainment of any public end, association—the organization of all interested—is the most efficacious means—a means altogether natural and just. This is so evident, and besides so comfortable to the genius of our country, of our essentially popular social conditions, that it is unnecessary to insist upon it. It is almost the only means to invite public attention, to give force to the most legitimate resistance, to add weight to the most just demands.

Now, there already exists an organization which presents innumerable attractions and advantages, but with which our Catholic working-men, filially obedient to the Holy See, refuse to unite themselves; this is the Masonic Order, which exists everywhere in our country, and which, as Mr. Powderly has expressly pointed out to us, unites employers and employed in a brotherhood very advantageous to the latter, but which numbers in its ranks hardly a single Catholic. Nobly renouncing advantages which the Church and conscience forbid, our workingmen join associations in no way in conflict with religion, seeking nothing but mutual protection and help, and the legitimate assertion of their rights. Must they here also find themselves threatened with condemnation, hindered from their only means of self-defense?

4. Let us now consider the objections made against this sort of organization.

(a) It is objected that in such organizations, Catholics are mixed with Protestants, to the peril of their faith. Naturally, yes; they are mixed with Protestants at their work; for, in a mixed people like ours the separation of religious creeds in civil affairs is an impossibility. But to suppose that the faith of our Catholics suffers thereby is not to know the Catholic working men of America, who are not like the working men of so many European countries— misguided children, estranged from their Mother, the Church, and regarding her with suspicion and dread—but intelligent, well-instructed and devoted Catholics, ready to give their blood if necessary, as they continually give their hard-earned means, for her support and protection. And, in fact, it is not here a question of Catholics mixed with Protestants, but rather that Protestants are admitted to share in the advantages of an association, many of whose members and officers are Catholics; and, in a country like ours, their exclusion would be simply impossible.

(b) But it is asked, instead of such an organization, could there not be confraternities, in which the working men would be united under the direction of the clergy and the influence of religion? I answer frankly that I do not consider this either possible or necessary in our country. I sincerely admire the efforts of this sort which are made in countries where the working people are led astray by the enemies of religion, but, thanks be to God, that is not our condition. We find that in our country the presence and direct influence of the clergy would not be advisable where our citizens, without distinction of religious belief, come together in regard to their industrial interests alone. Short of that we have abundant means for making our working people faithful Catholics, and simple good sense advises us not to go to extremes.

(c) Again, it is objected that, in such organizations, Catholics are exposed to the evil influences of the most dangerous associates, even of atheists, communists and anarchists. That is true, but it is one of those trials of faith which our brave American Catholics are accustomed to meet almost daily, and which they know how to face with good sense and firmness. The press of our country tells us, and the president of the Knights has related to us, how these violent, aggressive elements have endeavored to control the association, or to inject poison into its principles; but they also inform us with what determination these machinators have been repulsed and beaten.

The presence among our citizens of those dangerous social elements, which have mostly come from certain countries of Europe, is assuredly for us an occasion of great regret and of vigilant precautions; it is a fact, however, which we have to accept, but which the close union between the Church and her children that exists in our country renders comparatively free from danger. In truth, the only thing from which we would fear serious danger would be a cooling of this relationship between the Church and her children, and I know nothing that would be more likely to occasion it than imprudent condemnations.

(d) A specially weighty charge is drawn from the outbursts of violence, even to bloodshed, which have accompanied several of the strikes inaugurated by labor organizations. Concerning this, three things are to be remarked—first, strikes are not an invention of the Knights of Labor, but a means almost everywhere and always resorted to by the working classes to protect themselves against what they consider injustice, and in assertion of what they believe to be their just rights; secondly, in such a struggle of the poor and indignant multitudes against hard and obstinate monopoly, outbursts of anger are almost as inevitable as they are greatly to be regretted; thirdly, the laws and the chief authorities of the Knights of Labor, far from encouraging violence or the occasions of it, exercise a powerful influence to hinder it, and to retain strikes within the limits of good order and of legitimate action.

A careful examination of the acts of violence accompanying the struggle between capital and labor last year leaves us convinced that it would be unjust to attribute them to the association of the Knights of Labor, for this association was but one among the numerous labor organizations that took part in the strikes, and their chief officers used every possible effort, as disinterested witnesses testify, to appease the anger of the multitudes, and to hinder the excesses which, therefore, in my judgement, could not justly be attributed to them. Doubtless, among the Knights of Labor, as among the thousands of other working men, there are to be found passionate or even wicked men who have committed inexcusable deeds of violence, and have instigated their associates to the same, but to attribute this to the association would, it seems to me, be as unreasonable as to attribute to the Church the follies or the crimes of her children against which she strives and protests.

I repeat that, in such a struggle of the great masses of the people against the mail-clad power, which as it is acknowledged, often refuses them the simple rights of humanity and justice, it is vain to expect that every error and every act of violence can be avoided; and to dream that this struggle can be hindered, or that we can deter the multitudes from organizing, which is their only hope of success; would be to ignore the nature and forces of human society in times like ours. Christian prudence evidently counsels us to hold the hearts of the multitudes by the bonds of love, in order to control their actions by the principles of faith, justice and charity, to acknowledge frankly what is true and just in their cause, in order to deter them from what is false and criminal, and thus to turn into a legitimate, peaceable and beneficent contest what might easily, by a course of repulsive severity, become for the masses of our people a dread volcanic force like unto that which society fears and the Church deplores in Europe.

Upon this point I insist strongly, because, from an intimate acquaintance with the social conditions of our country I am profoundly convinced that here we are touching upon a subject which not only concerns the rights of the working classes, who ought to be especially dear to the Church which our Lord sent forth to preach His Gospel to the poor, but with which are intimately bound up the fundamental interests of the Church and of human society for the future. This is a point which I desire, in a few additional words, to develop more clearly.

5. Whoever meditates upon the ways in which divine Providence is guiding mankind in our days cannot fail to remark how important is the part which the power of the people takes in shaping the events of the present, and which it is evidently destined to take in molding the destinies of the future. We behold, with profound regret, the efforts of the prince of darkness to make this power dangerous to the social weal by withdrawing the masses of the people from the influence of religion, and impelling them towards the ruinous paths of license and anarchy. Hitherto our country has presented a spectacle of a most consolingly different character—that of a popular power regulated by love of good order, respect for religion, by obedience to the authority of the laws, not a democracy of license and violence, but that true democracy which aims at the general prosperity through the means of sound principles and good social order.

In order to preserve so desirable a state of things it is absolutely necessary that religion should continue to possess the affections, and thus rule the conduct of the multitudes. As Cardinal Manning has well written, "A new task is before us. The Church has no longer to deal with Parliaments and princes, but with the masses and with the people. Whether we will or no this is our work; we need a new spirit and a new law of life." To lose influence over the people would be to lose the future altogether; and it is by the heart, far more than by the understanding, that we must hold and guide this immense power, so mighty either for good or for evil.

Among all the glorious titles which the Church's history has deserved for her, there is not one which at present gives her so great influence as that of "Friend of the People." Assuredly, in our democratic country, it is this title which wins for the Catholic Church not only the enthusiastic devotedness of the millions of her children, but also the respect and admiration of all our citizens, whatever be their religious belief. It is the power of this title which renders persecution almost an impossibility, and which draws towards our Holy Church the great heart of the American people.

And since it is acknowledged by all that the great questions of the future are not those of war, of commerce or finance, but the social questions—the questions which concern the improvement of the condition of the great popular masses, and especially of the working people—it is evidently of supreme importance that the Church should always be found on the side of humanity—of justice towards the multitudes who compose the body of the human family. As the same Cardinal Manning has wisely written,

> I know I am treading on a very difficult subject, but I feel confident of this, that we must face it, and that we must face it calmly, justly, and with a willingness to put labor and the profits of labor second—the moral state and domestic life of the whole working population first. I will not venture to draw up such an act of Parliament further than to lay down this principle. These things (the present condition of the poor in England) cannot go on; these things ought not to go on. The accumulation of wealth in the land, the piling up of wealth like mountains, in the possession of classes or individuals, cannot go on. No commonwealth can rest on such foundations. (*Miscellanies*, Vol. 2, p. 81).

In our country, above all, this social amelioration is the inevitable programme of the future, and the position which the Church should hold towards it is surely obvious. She can certainly not favor the extremes to which the poor multitudes are naturally inclined, but, I repeat, she must withhold them from these extremes by the bonds of affection, by the maternal desire which she will manifest for the concession of all that is just and reasonable in their demands, and by the maternal blessing which she will bestow upon every legitimate means for improving the condition of the people.

6. Now let us consider for a moment the consequences which would inevitably follow from a contrary course—from a course of want of sympathy for the working class, of suspicion for their aims, of ready condemnation for their methods.

(a) First, there would be the evident danger of the Church's losing in popular estimation, her right to be considered the friend of the people. The logic of the popular heart goes swiftly to its conclusions, and this conclusion would be most pernicious both for the people and for the Church. To lose the heart of the people would be a misfortune for which the friendship of the few rich and powerful would be no compensation.

(b) There would be a great danger of rendering hostile to the Church the political power of our country, which has openly taken sides with the millions who are demanding justice and the improvement of their condition. The accusation of being un-American—that is to say, alien to our national spirit—is the most powerful weapon which the enemies of the Church can employ against her. It was this cry which aroused the Know-Nothing persecution thirty years ago, and the same would be used again if the opportunity offered. To appreciate the gravity of this danger it is well to remark that not only are the rights of the working classes loudly proclaimed by each of our two great political parties, but it is not improbable that, in our approaching national elections there will be a candidate for the office of President of the United States as the special representative of the popular complaints and demands.

Now, to seek to crush by an ecclesiastical condemnation an organization which represents more than 500,000 votes, and which has already so respectable and so universally recognized a place in the political arena, would, to speak frankly, be considered by the American people as not less ridiculous than rash. To alienate from ourselves the friendship of the people would be to run great risk of losing the respect which the Church has won in the estimation of the American nation, and of forfeiting the peace and prosperity which form so admirable a contrast with her condition in some so-called Catholic countries. Angry utterances have not been wanting of late, and it is well that we should act prudently.

(c) A third danger—and the one which most keenly touches our hearts—is the risk of losing the love of the children of the Church, and of pushing them into an attitude of resistance against their Mother. The world presents no more beautiful spectacle than that of their filial devotion and obedience; but it is well to recognize that, in our age and in our country, obedience cannot be blind. We would greatly deceive ourselves if we expected it. Our Catholic working men sincerely believe that they are only seeking justice, and seeking it by legitimate means. A condemnation would be considered both false and unjust, and, therefore, not binding. We might preach to them submission and confidence in the Church's judgment; but these good dispositions could hardly go so far. They love the Church, and they wish to save their souls, but they must also earn their living, and labor is now so organized that without belonging to the organization it is almost impossible to earn one's living.

Behold, then, the consequences to be feared. Thousands of the Church's most devoted children, whose affection is her greatest comfort, and whose free offerings are her chief support, would consider themselves repulsed by their Mother, and would live without practising their religion. Catholics who have hitherto shunned the secret societies, would be sorely tempted to join their ranks. The Holy See, which has constantly received from the Catholics of America proofs of almost unparalleled devotedness, would be considered not as a paternal authority, but as a harsh and unjust power. Surely these are consequences which wisdom and prudence counsel us to avoid.

7. But, besides the dangers that would result from such a condemnation,

and the impracticability of putting it into effect, it is also very important that we should carefully consider another reason against condemnation, arising from the unstable and transient character of the organization in question. It is frequently remarked by the press and by attentive observers that this special form of association has in it so little permanence that, in its present shape, it is not likely to last many years. Whence it follows that it is not necessary, even if it were just and prudent, to level the condemnations of the Church solely against so evanescent an object. The social agitation itself will, indeed, last as long as there are social evils to be remedied; but the forms of organization meant for the attainment of this end are naturally provisional and short-lived. They are also very numerous, for I have already remarked that the Knights of Labor is only one among many labor organizations.

To strike, then, at one of these forms would be to commence a war without system and without end; it would be to exhaust the forces of the Church in chasing a crowd of changing and uncertain spectres. The American people behold with perfect composure and confidence the progress of our social contest, and have not the least fear of not being able to protect themselves against any excesses or dangers that may occasionally arise. Hence, to speak with the most profound respect, but also with the frankness which duty requires of me, it seems to me that prudence suggests, and that even the dignity of the Church demands that we should not offer to America an ecclesiastical protection for which she does not ask, and of which she believes she has no need.

8. In all this discussion I have not at all spoken of Canada, nor of the condemnation concerning the Knights of Labor in Canada; for we would consider it an impertinence on our part to meddle with the ecclesiastical affairs of another country which has an hierarchy of its own, and with whose social conditions we do not pretend to be acquainted. We believe, however, that the circumstances of a people almost entirely Catholic, as in lower Canada, must be very different from those of a mixed population like ours; moreover, that the documents submitted to the Holy Office are not the present constitution of the organization in our country, and that we, therefore, ask nothing involving an inconsistency on the part of the Holy See, which passed sentence "*localiter et juxta exposita.*" It is of the United States that we speak, and we trust that we are not presumptuous in believing that we are competent to judge about the state of things in our own country. Now, as I have already indicated, out of the seventy-five archbishops and bishops of the United States, there are about five who desire the condemnation of the Knights of Labor, such as they are in our own country; so that our hierarchy are almost unanimous in protesting against such a condemnation. Such a fact ought to have great weight in deciding the question. If there are difficulties in the case, it seems to me that the prudence and experience of our bishops and the wise rules of the Third Plenary Council ought to suffice for their solution.

Finally, to sum up all, it seems to me that the Holy See could not decide to condemn an association under the following circumstances:

1. When the condemnation does not seem to be justified either by the letter or the spirit of its constitution, its law and the declaration of its chiefs.

2. When the condemnation does not seem necessary, in view of the transient form of the organization and the social condition of the United States.

3. When it does not seem to be prudent, because of the reality of the grievances complained of by the working classes, and their acknowledgement by the American people.

4. When it would be dangerous for the reputation of the Church in our democratic country, and might even lead to persecution.

5. When it would probably be ineficacious [sic], owing to the general conviction that it would be unjust.

6. When it would be destructive instead of beneficial in its effects, impelling the children of the Church to disobey their Mother, and even to enter condemned societies, which they have thus far shunned.

7. When it would turn into suspicion and hostility the singular devotedness of our Catholic people towards the Holy See.

8. When it would be regarded as a cruel blow to the authority of bishops in the United States, who, it is well known, protest against such a condemnation.

Now, I hope the considerations here presented have sufficiently shown that such would be the effect of condemnation of the Knights of Labor in the United States.

Therefore, I leave the decision of the case, with fullest confidence to the wisdom and prudence of your Eminence and the Holy See.

## ❦ 133 ❧

# Social Realization of Democracy

## GEORGE D. HERRON

George D. Herron (1862–1925) achieved public notice in the 1890s as a Congregationalist minister and college teacher in Iowa by arguing strongly in favor of the application of Christian ethics to the system of government and to economic practices. The only Christian political system was a pure democracy, the concord of the people in righteousness, which required a drastic reform of the existing corrupt and manipulated process. The groundwork would thus be laid for social democracy, the democratic organization of production and distribution, which Herron regarded as the only morally tolerable arrangement. Such views took Herron into socialist politics when the Socialist Party was founded in 1901 and, eventually, beyond definably Christian language.

---

A Christian political philosophy will teach us how to translate Christ's law of sacrifice into economic association and political organization, into the statutes of the state; so that the state shall become the visible incarnation and expression of the invisible divine government of the world which Jesus made known and established anew.

The political realization will be a pure democracy. Christianity can realize itself in a social order only through democracy and democracy can realize itself only through the social forces of Christianity. A pure social democracy is the political fulfilment of Christianity; the political organization of Christ's law of love; the order through which faith in the right manifests itself in the freedom of man. The old Hebrew idea of God dwelling in the midst of the people constituted in a free commonwealth expresses the fact and method of democracy. The true democracy is still better defined by the apostolic term, "the communion of the Holy Ghost," by which term is meant the concord of the people in righteousness; the government of the people by a spirit of unity within, rather than by a dominion over them. History is the progressive disclosure of the self-

Source: George D. Herron, 'Social Realization of Democracy', *The Christian State*, London, 1898, pp. 74–87.

government of the people as the providential design. Christianity in its fulfilment is the self-government of the people through communion with God, through the surrender of the common will to do the righteous will expressed in Christ. It is the historical and providential idea that God shall lead the people by his Spirit of right as his sons, governing them inspirationally rather then institutionally. Institutions that are democratic in fact, will be organs that shall both inspire and obey the people, rather than organs of dominion with the people for their servants. The end of democracy is the political redemption and perfection of man in the human life revealed in Christ.

Nothing can be more presumptuous than the literature which treats of the triumph or failure of democracy. As yet democracy can scarcely be considered to have been an experiment. It has not been tried. A government of the people by the people is a dream yet to be realized. There do not exist any purely democratic institutions. Wherein democracy has been thought triumphant, it has been the triumph of expediencies substituted for democracy; wherein it has failed, something less than democracy has been the experiment.

We Americans are not a democratic people. We do not select the representatives we elect; we do not make our own laws; we do not govern ourselves. Our political parties are controlled by private, close political corporations that exist as parasites upon the body politic, giving us the most corrupting and humiliating despotisms in political history, and tending to destroy all political faith in righteousness. Our legislation is determined by a vast system of lobby. The people know, though they cannot prove, that our legislative methods have become the organization of indirect bribery and corruption. It is hardly an exaggeration to say that the chief work of both State and National legislatures in recent years has been to obstruct, defeat, or cheat the will of the people. Instead of being democratically governed, we are under the government of political and legislative bureaucracies that dominate, plunder and oppress by an indirection that conceals both the reality and the nature of the dominion, corruption, and oppression. Our American Senate, with members openly and shamelessly elected as the virtual agents of vicious corporate properties, has been seriously reminding us of the court of Louis XVI. The moral tone of our politics has become so low, and the power of immoral wealth so subtle and strong, that we have almost ceased to think of our institutions as having any relation to political morality. Though we have constitutional means of overthrowing our present system of government by political bureaucracies and corporate wealth, and realizing a true government by the people, we are scarcely trying to utter our real political thought and faith through our institutions. The politicians who control our political organizations are ignorant of what the people really think and believe. They are largely insensible to the rising tide of social feeling and purpose that will yet sweep away the foundations of political faith and order, unless recognized and received as a national regeneration. A great political uprising, like that under the leadership of Dr. Parkhurst in New York, while a cause for profound national gratitude and hope, has yet a sad significance in the fact that it is the result of an extra-governmental organization to protect the people from the official administration of an existing government. And this extra-governmental organization has been performing the highest functions of the great municipal government within which it exists. So throughout the land, organizations which are virtually governments within governments are rapidly forming to perform the holiest duties of governmental offices, which were instituted to protect the people in freedom and perfect them in justice, but have become the instruments of lawlessness and oppression. Necessitated by the surrender which the people have made of their authority and institutions to usurping political corporations, organizations are being effected by aroused citizens to protect themselves from the administration of governments which should be the organized virtue of the people.

The jobbers in politics, making the affairs of the public well-being their political stock exchange, strive to create the impression that they represent the actual political faith of the people. Through deceiving the people they have procured an increasing centralization of political power. It is this centralization of power, used mainly to serve for political and material profit the interests of privileged classes, that has caused the political degradation and indolence of the people. Only the responsibility of power educates the people to administer power, and reveals the common moral worth. Not the centralization, but the diffusion of power is the safety of the present; it is also the lesson of history and the divine method of procedure. Unbelief in God is no more fatal to freedom and progress, to justice and right, than unbelief in the people. Only through becoming the organ of the common faith and aspiration, the common life, the holy life, the moral well-being, the common wholeness, of the whole people, can the State endure the social strain and change, and prove its right to be. Such it can become only through the realization of the democracy that will politically organize the people in the order of life begun with the birth of the Christ man.

We can no more stop the progress of democracy where it now is than we can take the race back to the garden of Eden. From the idea of the absolute monarch, we have progressed to the idea of representative institutional government. But we have scarcely reached the halfway house of political progress. We shall have to move on to the goal, which is the fulfilment of democracy in the direct self-government of the people. In a pure democracy the people will be their own legislators, making their own laws directly, or through an elective and representative system that will receive and effectuate in legislation the actual will of the people. Existing representative legislation and representative government are as distinctly two forms of government as the absolute and the limited monarchy. There can be no true democracy with present systems of representative legislation. And these have accomplished the beginnings of their own doom. There have been few important measures before our state or national legislatures during the last decade which could not have been passed upon by the people themselves with intelligence and character, with thoroughness and directness, wholly beyond the moral or intellectual comprehension of the men, many of them virtually self-chosen, now legislating as the people's representatives.

A step toward the political realization of democracy would be the change of our representative system so as to secure proportional representation. Our legislative district order of representation, arbitrarily and corruptly managed in the interests of the particular politicians in power, instead of with a view to providing for the immediate and accurate expression of the will of the people, practically deprives a large proportion, often a majority, of the people of any representation in the affairs of legislation. For instance, in the State of Iowa, of which State I am a citizen, in the election of 1892, the 219,215 votes cast by one political party elected ten members to our national Congress; while the 201,293 votes cast by another party elected but one congressman; and two minor parties were without representation. Fully if not more than one-half of the people of Iowa were thus unrepresented, and doubtless misrepresented, in the popular and more democratic branch of the national legislature. The instance I have noted simply indicates — though many more glaring instances could be cited — the utter caricature of representative government which our legislative district system has procured. It has put the whole legislation of our land, both State and National, into the keeping of the political bureaucracies — the speculators who thrive and fatten through marketing the rights and well-being of the people to corporate properties, while the people are made to think themselves represented in legislation. By recent elections, more than one-half of the people in the United States are not represented in the national councils, because of our district systems and party control of legislation. Really, we are not representatively governed, and the majority does not rule. Representative legislation and government are a fiction, so far as our nation is concerned. The majority of our citizens, not far from two-thirds at present, are virtually disfranchised, and we are under the government of minorities; the majority is without power to effect legislation. Prof. John R. Commons of Indiana University, whom I regard as our most promising and divinely opportune political economist, and who has made an exact and thoughtful study of the subject of proportional representation, says:

> True representative government does not exist. We have a sham representation. It gives a show of fairness; but it is crude and essentially unfair. It does not represent the people. It represents the politicians. We are a law-abiding people. Yet our laws are made by a minority of the people, and by an irresponsible oligarchy more dangerous than that our fathers revolted against.

The only possible deliverance from this oligarchic and minority government is in some form of proportional representation that will enable all parties and degrees of political and even religious opinion, according to the votes cast by each, to be represented in National, State, and municipal councils. It is through a system of proportional representation, and the system of electing from any borough, any strong man, from any part of the United Kingdom, that England has made such strides in popular government, and that the people there have been able to effectuate their will far more accurately and immediately than the people of the United States. Through proportional representation it is now commonly agreed, the people of England are in reality altogether more democratically governed than the people of America, notwithstanding what remains to England of feudalism. In the English Parliament the Irish minority, the temperance minority, the single-tax minority, the labor minority, the Radical minority, the Roman Catholic minority, are all represented. A just proportional representation in our nation, with certain of the initiative and referendum features of legislation conjoined, would give to the people a representative system that might practically prove to be, would indeed virtually be, the direct legislation of the people for the people, and would initiate and preserve a true political democracy. Then the people would grow in political knowledge and virtue, with the purifying sense and divine moral dignity of responsibility. And the education in justice which association in democracy would give, with the continued trial of faith in righteousness which the mutualism of power would procure, would develop in the people the wisdom and forces of their common moral reason, their now waking social consciousness, which is nothing else than the intelligence of the Spirit of God, inspiring, enlightening, and directing the mind and affairs of man toward the unity of the race.

But democracy only begins its real struggle and work in becoming political; it must become social. Unless democracy retreat from the field of progress, it must take possession of the industrial world. The government of the future will be mainly concerned with the social being and industrial association of the people. Political freedom can realize itself only through freedom. The life of man is objectively an economic life. In the sphere of production and distribution is the common life fulfilled. Production is communion with God; the producer is God's co-worker. Distribution is human fellowship; it is the method by which justice unites men. Until democracy be the order of production and distribution, it will be an illusive philosophy and baffled effort, and industrial slavery will be the inevitable lot of millions. It is unreasonable, and morally intolerable; it is the social continuation of the old absolutism, that the well-being of the people should depend, as it in large measure does depend under the present economy, upon the will of the few who possess the quality of power essential to reaping the harvest of the common toil, and whose authority consists in the possession of material things. The people must finally own and distribute the products of their own labor, and economic democracy must now be the search of political wisdom that would command an intelligent respect and the social patience.

# ❦134❧

# What to Do

## WALTER RAUSCHENBUSCH

Walter Rauschenbusch (1861–1918) best embodied the passionate optimism, drawing upon belief in the ultimate perfectibility of human beings, of the Social Gospel. Ordained as a Baptist minister, he spent eleven impressionable years working amongst immigrants in working class neighbourhoods in New York before teaching aspirant ministers at Rochester. His conviction that true Christianity required cooperative social arrangements led him to proclaim the need for believers, and especially ministers, to ally with the labour movement and accept that the logical outcome of its struggles was socialism.

---

Our industrial individualism neutralizes the social consciousness created by Christianity.

## Solidarity and Communism

It is assumed as almost self-evident in popular thought that communism is impracticable and inefficient, an antiquated method of the past or a dream of Utopian schemers, a system of society sure to impede economic development and to fetter individual liberty and initiative. Thus we flout what was the earliest basis of civilization for the immense majority of mankind and the moral ideal of Christendom during the greater part of it history. Communistic ownership and management of the fundamental means of production was the rule in primitive society, and large remnants of it have survived to our day. For fifteen centuries and more it was the common consent of Christendom that private property was due to sin, and that the ideal life involved fraternal sharing. The idea underlying the monastic life was that men left the sinful world and established an ideal community, and communism was an essential feature of every monastic establishment. The progressive heretical movements in the

Source: Walter Rauschenbusch, 'What to do', *Christianity and the Social Crisis*, New York, 1907, pp. 388–415.

Middle Ages also usually involved an attempt to get closer to the communistic ideal. It is striking proof how deeply the ideas of the Church have always been affected by the current secular thought, that our modern individualism has been able to wipe this immemorial Christian social ideal out of the mind of the modern Church almost completely.

The assumption that communistic ownership was a hindrance to progress deserves very critical scrutiny. It is part of the method of writing history which exalted the doings of kings and slighted the life of the people. For the grasping arm of the strong, communistic institutions were indeed a most objectionable hindrance, but to the common man they were the strongest bulwark of his independence and vigor. Within the shelter of the old-fashioned village community, which constituted a social unit for military protection, economic production, morality, and religion, the individual could enjoy his life with some fearlessness. The peasant who stood alone was at the mercy of his lord. Primitive village communism was not freely abandoned as an inefficient system, but was broken up by the covetousness of the strong and selfish members of the community, and by the encroachments of the upper classes who wrested the common pasture and forest and game from the peasant communities. Its disappearance nearly everywhere marked a decline in the prosperity and moral vigor of the peasantry and was felt by them to be a calamity and a step in their enslavement.But we need not go back into history to get a juster verdict on the practicability and usefulness of communism. We have the material right among us. Ask any moral teacher who is scouting communism and glorifying individualism, what social institutions to-day are most important for the moral education of mankind and most beneficent in their influence on human happiness, and he will probably reply promptly, "The home, the school, and the church." But these three are communistic institutions. The home is the source of most of our happiness and goodness, and in the home we live communistically. Each member of the family has some private property, clothes, letters, pictures, toys; but the rooms and the furniture in the main are common to all, and if one member needs the private property of another, there is ready sharing. The income of the members is more or less turned into a common fund; food is prepared and eaten in common; the larger family undertakings are planned in common. The housewife is the manager of a successful communistic colony, and it is perhaps not accidental that our women, who move thus within a fraternal organization, are the chief stays of our Christianity. Similarly our public schools are supported on a purely communistic basis; those who have no children or whose children are grown up, are nevertheless taxed for the education of the children of the community. The desks, the books to some extent, the flowers and decorations, are common property, and it is the aim of the teachers to develop the communistic spirit in the children, though they may not call it by that name. Our churches, too, are voluntary communisms. A number of people get together, have a common building, common seats, common hymn-books and Bibles, support a pastor in common, and worship, learn, work, and play in common. They are so little individualistic that they fairly urge others to come in and use their property. Private pews and similar encroachments of private property within this communistic institution are now generally condemned as contrary to the spirit of the Church, while every new step to widen the communistic serviceableness of the churches is greeted with a glow of enthusiasm.

Thus the three great institutions on which we mainly depend to train the young to a moral life and to make us all good, wise, and happy, are essentially communistic, and their success and efficiency depend on the continued mastery of the spirit of solidarity and brotherhood within them. It is nothing short of funny to hear the very men who ceaselessly glorify the home, the school, and the church, turn around and abuse communism.

It can fairly be maintained, too, that the State, another great moral agent, is communistic in its very nature. It is the organization by which the people administer their common property and attend to their common interests. It is safe to say that at least a fourth of the land in a modern city is owned by the city and communistically used for free streets and free parks. Our modern State is the outcome of a long development toward communism. Warfare and military defence were formerly the private affair of the nobles; they are now the business of the entire nation. Roads and bridges used to be owned largely by private persons or corporations, and toll charged for their use; they are now communistic with rare exceptions. Putting out fires used to be left to private enterprise; to-day our fire departments are communistic. Schools used to be private; they are now public. Great men formerly had private parks and admitted the public as a matter of favor; the people now have public parks and admit the great men as a matter of right. The right of jurisdiction was formerly often an appurtenance of the great landowners; it is now controlled by the people. The public spirit and foresight of one of the greatest of all Americans, Benjamin Franklin, early made the postal service of our country a communistic institution of ever increasing magnitude and usefulness. In no case in which communistic ownership has firmly established itself is there any desire to recede from it. The unrest and dissatisfaction is all at those points where the State is not yet communistic. The water-works in most of our cities are owned and operated by the community, and there is never more than local and temporary dissatisfaction about this great necessity of life, because any genuine complaint by the people as users of water can be promptly remedied by the people as suppliers of water. On the other hand, the clamor of public complaint about the gas, the electric power and light, and the street railway service, which are commonly supplied by private companies, is incessant and increasing. While the railway lines were competing, they wasted on needless parallel roads enough capital to build a comfortable home for every family in the country. Now that they have nearly ceased to compete, the grievances of their monopoly are among the gravest problems of our national life. The competitive duplication of plant and labor by our express companies is folly, and their exorbitant charges are a drag on the economic welfare and the common comfort of our whole nation. This condition continues not because of their efficiency, but because of their sinister influence on Congress. They are an economic anachronism.

Thus the State, too, is essentially a communistic institution. It has voluntarily limited its functions and left many things to private initiative. The political philosophy of the nineteenth century constantly preached to the State that the best State was that which governed least, just as the best child was that which moved least. Yet it has almost imperceptibly gathered to itself many of the functions which were formerly exercised by private undertakings, and there is no desire anywhere to turn public education, fire protection, sanitation, or the supply of water over to private concerns. But the distinctively modern utilities, which have been invented or perfected during the reign of capitalism and during the prevalence of individualistic political theories, have been seized and appropriated by private concerns. The railways, the street railways, the telegraph and telephone, electric power and light, gas—these are all modern. The swift hand of capitalism seized them and has exploited them to its immense profit. Other countries have long ago begun to draw these modern public necessities within the communistic functions of the State. In our country a variety of causes, good and bad, have combined to check that process; but the trend is manifestly in the direction of giving state communism a wider sweep hereafter.

Private ownership is not a higher stage of social organization which has finally and forever superseded communism, but an intermediate and necessary stage of social evolution between two forms of communism. At a certain point in the development of property primitive communism becomes unworkable, and a higher form of communism has not yet been wrought out; consequently men manage as best they can with private ownership. To take a simple illustration: on the farm or in a country village the creek is common property for bathing purposes; the "swimmin'-hole" is the communistic bath-tub for all who want to refresh their cuticle. As the village grows, the march of the houses drives the bathers farther out; the pervasiveness of the "eternally feminine" robs the boys of their bath; the primitive communism of the water ceases. Some families now are wealthy enough to install private bath-tubs and have the increased privilege of bathing all the year round. The bulk of the people in the cities have no bathing facilities at all. At last an agitation arises for a public bath. A beginning is made with enclosed river-baths, perhaps, or with shower baths. At last a plunge-bath is built and opened summer and winter. The bathing instinct of the community revives and increasingly centres about the public bath. The communism of the water has returned. From the communistic swimming-hole to the marble splendor of the communistic bath the way lay through the individualistic tub of the wealthy and the unwashed deprivations of the mass. In the same way there is no need of parks in primitive society, because all nature is open. As cities grow up, the country recedes; a few are wealthy enough to surround their homes with lawns and trees; the mass are shut off from nature and suffocate amid brick and asphalt. Then comes the new communal ownership and enjoyment of nature: first the small square in the city; then the large park on the outskirts; then the distant park on the seashore or by the river and lake; and finally the state or national reservation where wild life is kept intact for those who want to revert to it. Thus we pass from communism to communism in our means of enjoyment, and that community will evidently be widest which most quickly sees that the old and simple means of pleasure are passing, and will provide the corresponding means for the more complex and artificial community which is evolving. The longer it lingers in the era of private self-help, the longer will the plain people be deprived of their heritage, and the more completely will the wealthy minority preëmpt the means of enjoyment for themselves.

Everywhere communism in new forms and on a vaster scale is coming back to us. The individualistic pump in the back yard is gone; the city water-works are the modern counterpart of the communistic village well to which Rebekah and Rachel came to fill their water-jar. The huge irrigation scheme of our national government in the West is an enlarged duplicate of the tanks built by many a primitive community. The railway train carrying people or supplies is a modernized form of the tribe breaking camp and carrying its women and children and cattle and tents to better grazing or hunting grounds. Compared with the old private vehicle, the railway carriage is a triumphant demonstration of communism. Almost the only private thing about our railways is the dividends. The competitive individualism of commerce is being restricted within ever narrower limits. State supervision and control is a partial assertion of the supremacy of communistic interests. It is probably only a question of time when the private management of public necessities will be felt to be impossible and antiquated, and the community will begin to experiment seriously with the transportation of people and goods, and with the public supply of light and heat and cold.

How far this trend toward communistic ownership is to go, the common sense of the future will have to determine. It is entirely misleading to frighten us with the idea that communism involves a complete abolition of private property. Even in the most individualistic society there is, as we have seen, a large ingredient of communism, and in the most socialistic society there will always be a large ingredient of private property. No one supposes that a man's toothbrush, his love-letters, or his shirt on his back would ever be common property. Socialists are probably quit right in maintaining that the amount of private property *per capita* in a prosperous socialist community would be much larger than it is now. It seems unlikely even that all capital used in production will ever be communistic in ownership and operation; a socialistic State could easily afford to allow individuals to continue some private production, just as handicraft lingers now amid machine production. It will never be a question of having either private property absolute or communism absolute; it will always be a question of having more communism or less.

The question then confronts Christian men singly and the Christian Church collectively, whether they will favor and aid this trend toward communism, or oppose it. Down to modern times, as we have seen, the universal judgement of Christian thought was in favor of communism as more in harmony with the genius of Christianity and with the classical precedents of its early social life. Simultaneously with the rise of capitalism that conviction began to fade out. Protestantism especially, by its intimate alliance with the growing cities and the rising business class, as been individualistic in its theories of Christian society. The question is now, how quickly Christian thought will realize that individualism is coming to be an inadequate and antiquated form of social organization which must give place to a higher form of communistic organization, and how thoroughly it will comprehend that this new communism will afford a far nobler social basis for the spiritual temple of Christianity.

For there cannot really be any doubt that the spirit of Christianity has more affinity for a social system based on solidarity and human fraternity than for one based on selfishness and mutual antagonism. In competitive industry one man may profit through the ruin of others; in coöperative production the wealth of one man would depend on the growing wealth of all. In competitive society each man strives for himself and his family only, and the sense of larger duties is attenuated and feeble; in communistic society no man could help realizing that he is part of a great organization, and that he owes it duty and loyalty. Competition tends to make good men selfish; coöperation would compel selfish men to develop public spirit. The moral and wholesome influences in society to-day proceed from the communistic organizations within it; the divisive, anarchic, and destructive influences which are racking our social body to-day proceed from those realms of social life which are individualistic and competitive. Business life to-day is organized in growing circles within which a certain amount of coöperation and mutual helpfulness exists, and to that extent it exerts a sound moral influence. In so far as it is really competitive, it engenders covetousness, cunning, hardness, selfish satisfaction in success, or resentment and despair in failure. It is a marvellous demonstration of the vitality of human goodness that a system so calculated to bring out the evil traits in us, still leaves so much human kindness and nobility alive. But the Christian temper of mind, the honest regard for the feelings and the welfare of others, the desire to make our life serve the common good, would get its first chance to control our social life in a society organized on the basis of solidarity and coöperation.

It would seem, therefore, that one of the greatest services which Christianity could render to humanity in the throes of the present transition would be to aid those social forces which are making for the increase of communism. The Church should help public opinion to understand clearly the difference between the moral qualities of the competitive and the communistic principle, and enlist religious enthusiasm on behalf of that which is essentially Christian. Christian individuals should strengthen and protect the communistic institutions already in existence in society and help them to extend their functions. For instance, the public schools can increasingly be made nuclei of common life for the district within which they are located, gathering the children for play out of school hours, and the adults for instruction, discussion, and social pleasure in the evenings. The usefulness of the public parks as centres of communal life can be immensely extended by encouraging and organizing the play of the children and by holding regular public festivals. Simply to induce the crowd listening to a band concert in the park to join in singing a patriotic song, would convert a mass of listening individuals into a social organism thrilled with a common joy and sensible of its cohesion. Public ownership of the great public utilities would be desirable for the education it would give in solidarity, if for no other reason. Even if a street railway should be run at a loss for a time under city management, it would at least draw the people closer together by the sense of common proprietorship and would teach them to work better together to overcome the trouble. Every step taken in industrial life to give the employees some proprietary rights in the business, and anything placing owners and employees on a footing of human equality, would deserve commendation and help.

The Christian spirit of fraternity should create fraternal social institutions, and the fraternal institutions may in turn be trusted to breed and spread the fraternal spirit. It is a most hopeful fact that the communistic features of our government are awakening in some public officials a whole-hearted and far-seeing devotion to the public welfare. A number of our public health officers have thrown themselves into the crusade against tuberculosis and infant mortality with a zeal more far-sighted and chivalrous than is usually called out in the ordinary doctor who cures patients on the individualistic plan. When men at the head of some department of city government realize the immense latent capacity of their department to serve the people, they are fired with ambition to do what they see can be done. Their natural ambition to make themselves felt, to exert power and get honor, runs in the same direction with the public needs. Such men are still scarce, but they are a prophecy of the kind of character which may be created in a communistic society and of the power of enthusiastic work which may hereafter be summoned to the service of people. The vast educational work done by some departments of our national government, for instance the Department of Agriculture, furnishes similar proof of what may be done when we abandon the policeman theory of government and adopt the family theory. Certainly it would be no betrayal of the Christian spirit to enter into a working alliance with this great tendency toward the creation of coöperative and communistic social institutions based on the broad principle of the brotherhood of men and the solidarity of their interests.

## The Upward Movement of the Working Class

The ideal of a fraternal organization of society is so splendid that it is to-day enlisting the choicest young minds of the intellectual classes under its banner. Idealists everywhere are surrendering to it, especially those who are under the power of the ethical spirit of Christianity. The influence which these idealists exert in reënforcing the movement toward solidarity is beyond computation. They impregnate the popular mind with faith and enthusiasm. They furnish the watch-words and the intellectual backing of historical and scientific information. They supply devoted leaders and give a lofty sanction to the movement by their presence in it. They diminish the resistance of the upper classes among whom they spread their ideas.

But we must not blink the fact that the idealists alone have never carried through any great social change. In vain they dash their fair ideas against the solid granite of human selfishness. The possessing classes are strong by mere possession long-continued. They control nearly all property. The law is on their side, for they have made it. They control the machinery of government and can use force under the form of law. Their self-interest makes them almost impervious of moral truth if it calls in question the sources from which they draw their income. In the past they have laughed at the idealists if they seemed harmless, or have suppressed them if they became troublesome.

We Americans have a splendid moral optimism. We believe that "truth is mighty and must prevail." "Truth crushed to earth shall rise again." "The blood of the martyrs is the seed of the Church." In the words of the great Anabaptist Balthasar Hübmaier, who attested his faith by martyrdom,

> Truth is immortal; and though for a long time she be imprisoned, scourged, crowned with thorns, crucified and buried, she will yet rise victorious on the third day and will reign and triumph.

That is the glorious faith. But the three days may be three centuries, and the murdered truth may come to victory in some other race and on another continent. The Peasants' Rising in 1525 in Germany embodied the social ideals of the common people; the Anabaptist movement, which began simultaneously, expressed their religious aspirations; both were essentially noble and just; both have been most amply justified by the later course of history; yet both were quenched in streams of blood and have had to wait till our own day for their resurrection in new form.

Truth is mighty. But for a definite historical victory a given truth must depend on the class which makes that truth its own and fights for it. If that class is sufficiently numerous, compact, intelligent, organized, and conscious of what it wants, it may drive a breach through the intrenchments of those opposed to it and carry the cause to victory. If there is no such army to fight its cause, the truth will drive individuals to a comparatively fruitless martyrdom and will continue to hover over humanity as a disembodied ideal. There were a number of reformatory movements before 1500 which looked fully as promising and powerful as did the movement led by Luther in its early years; but the fortified authority of the papacy and clergy succeeded in frustrating them, and they ebbed away again. The Lutheran and Calvinistic Reformation succeeded because they enlisted classes which were sufficiently strong politically and economically to defend the cause of Reform Religion. It was only when concrete material interests entered into a working alliance with Truth that enough force was rallied to break down the frowning walls of error. On the other hand, the classes within which Anabaptism gained lodgement lacked that concrete power, and so the Anabaptist movement, which promised for a short time to be the real Reformation of Germany, just as it came to be the real Reformation of England in the Commonwealth, died a useless and despised death. In the French Revolution the ideal of democracy won a great victory, not simply because the ideal was so fair, but because it represented the concrete interests of the strong, wealthy, and intelligent business class, and that class was able to wrest political control from the king, the aristocracy, and the clergy.

The question is whether the ideal of coöperation and economic fraternity can to-day depend on any great and conquering class whose self-interest is bound up with the victory of that principle. It is hopeless to expect the business class to espouse that principle as a class. Individuals in the business class will do so, but the class will not. There is no historical precedent for an altruistic self-effacement of a whole class. Of the professional class it is safe to expect that an important minority—perhaps a larger minority in our country than in any other country heretofore—will range themselves under the new social ideal. With them especially the factor of religion will prove of immense power. But their motives will in the main be idealistic, and in the present stage of man's moral development the unselfish emotions are fragile and easily chafe through, unless the coarse fibre of self-interest is woven into them. But there is another class to which that conception of organized fraternity is not only a moral ideal, but the hope for bread and butter; with which it enlists not only religious devotion and self-sacrifice, but involves salvation from poverty and insecurity and participation in the wealth and culture of modern life for themselves and their children.

It is a mistake to regard the French Revolution as a movement of the poor. The poor fought in the uprising, but the movement got its strength, its purpose, and its direction from the "third estate," the bourgeoisie, the business class of the cities, and they alone drew lasting profit from it. That class had been slowly rising to wealth, education, and power for several centuries, and the democratic movement of the nineteenth century has in the main been their march to complete ascendency.

During the same period we can watch the slow development of a new class, which has been called the fourth estate: the city working class, the wage-workers. They form a distinct class, all living without capital merely by the sale of their labor, working and living under similar physical and social conditions everywhere, with the same economic interests and the same points of view. They present a fairly homogeneous body and if any section of the people forms a "class," they do. The massing of labor in the factories since the introduction of power machinery has brought them into close contact with one another. Hard experience has taught them how helpless they are when they stand alone. They have begun to realize their solidarity and the divergence of their interests from those of the employers. They have begun to organize and are slowly learning to act together. The spread of education and cheap literature, the ease of communication, and the freedom of public meeting have rapidly created a common body of ideas and points of view among them.

The modern "labor movement" is the upward movement of this class. It began with local and concrete issues that pressed upon a given body of workingmen some demand for shorter hours or better wages, some grievance about fines or docking. The trades-unions were formed as defensive organizations for collective action. It is quite true that they have often been foolish and tyrannical in their demands, and headstrong and even lawless in their actions; but if we consider the insecurity and narrowness of the economic existence of the working people, and the glaring contrast between the meagre reward for their labor and the dazzling returns given to invested capital, it is impossible to deny that they have good cause for making a strenuous and continuous fight for better conditions of life. If Christian men are really interested in the salvation of human lives and in the health, the decency, the education, and the morality of the people, they must wish well to the working people in their effort to secure such conditions for themselves and their dear ones that they will not have to die of tuberculosis in their prime, nor feel their strength ground down by long hours of work, nor see their women and children drawn into the merciless hopper of factory labor, nor be shut out from the enjoyment of the culture about them which they have watered with their sweat.

But the labor movement means more than better wages and shorter hours for individual workingmen. It involves the struggle for a different status for their entire class. Other classes have long ago won a recognized standing in law and custom and public opinion—so long ago that they have forgotten that they ever had to win it. For instance, the medical profession is recognized by law; certain qualifications are fixed for admission to it; certain privileges are granted to those inside; irregular practitioners are hampered or suppressed. The clerical profession enjoys certain exemptions from taxation, military service, and jury duty; ministers have the right to solemnize marriages and collect fees therefore; railways give them half fares, and these privileges are granted to those whom the clergy themselves ordain and admit to their "closed shop." A lawyer who is admitted to the bar thereby becomes a court officer; the bar association, which is his trades-union, takes the initiative in disbarring men who violate the class code, and the courts take cognizance of its action; in the State of New York the bar associations have assumed some right to nominate the judges, As for the business class, it is so completely enthroned in our social organization that it often assumes that it is itself the whole of society.

On the other hand, the working class has no adequate standing as yet. It did have in the guilds of former times, but modern industry and modern law under the *laissez-faire* principle dissolved the old privileges and reduced the working class to a mass of unrelated human atoms. Common action on their part was treated in law as conspiracy. In our country they have not yet won from their employers nor from public opinion the acknowledged right to be organized, to bargain collectively, and to assist in controlling the discipline of the shops in which they have to work. The law seems to afford them very little backing as yet. It provides penalties for the kind of injuries which workingmen are likely to inflict on their employers, but not for the subtler injuries which employers are likely to inflict on their workingmen. Few will care to assert that in the bitter conflicts waged between labor and capital the wrong has always been on one side. Yet when the law bares its sword, it is somehow always against one side. The militia does not seem to be ordered out against capital. The labor movement must go on until public opinion and the law have conceded a recognized position to the labor-unions, and until the workingmen interested in a given question stand collectively on a footing of equality with the capitalists interested in it. This means a curtailment of power for the employers, and it would be contrary to human nature for them to like it. But for the working class it would be suicidal to forego the attempt to get it. They have suffered fearfully by not having it. All the sacrifices they may bring in the chronic industrial warfare of the present will be cheap if they ultimately win through to an assured social and legal status for their class.

As long as the working class simply attempts to better its condition somewhat and to secure a recognized standing for its class organization, it stands on the basis of the present capitalistic organization of industry. Capitalism necessarily divides industrial society into two classes,—those who own the instruments and materials of production, and those who furnish the labor for it. This sharp division is the peculiar character of modern capitalism which distinguishes it from other forms of social organization in the past. These two classes have to coöperate in modern production. The labor movement seeks to win better terms for the working class in striking its bargains. Yet whatever terms organized labor succeeds in winning are always temporary and insecure, like the hold which a wrestler gets on the body of his antagonist. The persistent tendency with capital necessarily is to get labor as cheaply as possible and to force as much work from it as possible. Moreover, labor is always in an inferior position in the struggle. It is handicapped by its own hunger and lack of resources. It has to wrestle on its knees with a foeman who is on his feet. Is this unequal struggle between two conflicting interests go on forever? Is this insecurity the best that the working class can ever hope to attain?

Here enters socialism. It proposes to abolish the division of industrial society into two classes and to close the fatal chasm which has separated the employing class from the working class since the introduction of power machinery. It proposes to restore the independence of the workingman by making him once more the owner of his tools and to give him the full proceeds of his production instead of a wage determined by his poverty. It has no idea of reverting to the simple methods of the old handicrafts, but heartily accepts the power machinery, the great factory, the division of labor, the organization of the men in great regiments of workers, as established facts in modern life, and as the most efficient method of producing wealth. But it proposes to give to the whole body of workers the ownership of these vast instruments of production and to distribute among them all the entire proceeds of their common labor. There would then be no capitalistic class opposed to the working class; there would be a single class which would unite the qualities of both. Every workingman would be both owner and worker, just as a farmer is who tills his own farm, or a housewife who works in her own kitchen. This would be a permanent solution of the labor question. It would end the present insecurity, the constant antagonism, the social inferiority, the physical exploitation, the intellectual poverty to which the working class is now exposed even when its condition is most favorable.

If such a solution is even approximately feasible, it should be hailed with joy by every patriot and Christian, for it would put a stop to our industrial war, drain off the miasmatic swamp of undeserved poverty, save our political democracy, and lift the great working class to an altogether different footing of comfort, intelligence, security and moral strength. And it would embody the principle of solidarity and fraternity in the fundamental institutions of our industrial life. All the elements of coöperation and interaction which are now at work in our great establishments would be conserved, and in addition the hearty interest of all workers in their common factory or store would be immensely intensified by the diffused sense of ownership. Such a social order would develop the altruistic and social instincts just as the competitive order brings out the selfish instincts.

Socialism is the ultimate and logical outcome of the labor movement. When the entire working class throughout the industrial nations is viewed in a large way, the progress of socialism gives an impression of resistless and elemental power. It is inconceivable from the point of view of that class that it should stop short of complete independence and equality as long as it has the power to move on, and independence and equality for the working class must mean the collective ownership of the means of production and the abolition of the present two-class arrangement of industrial society. If the labor movement in our country is only slightly tinged with socialism as yet, it is merely because it is still in its embryonic stages. Nothing will bring the working class to a thorough comprehension of the actual status of their class and its ultimate aim more quickly than continued failure to secure their smaller demands and reactionary efforts to suppress their unions.

We started out with the proposition that the idea of a fraternal organization of society will remain powerless if it is supported by idealists only; that it needs the firm support of a solid class whose economic future is staked on the success of that idea; and that the industrial working class is consciously or unconsciously committed to the struggle for the realization of that principle. It follows that those who desire the victory of that ideal from a religious point of view will have to enter into a working alliance with this class. Just as the Protestant principle of religious liberty rose to victory by an alliance with the middle class which was then rising to power, so the new Christian principle of brotherly association must ally itself with the working class if both are to conquer. Each depends on the other. The idealistic movement alone would be a soul without a body; the economic class movement alone would be a body without a soul. It needs the high elation and faith that come through religion. Nothing else will call forth that self-sacrificing devotion and life-long fidelity which will be needed in so gigantic a struggle as lies before the working class.

The coöperation of professional men outside the working class would contribute scientific information and trained intelligence. They would mediate between the two classes, interpreting each to the other, and thereby lessening the strain of hostility. Their presence and sympathy would cheer the working people and diminish the sense of class isolation. By their contact with the possessing classes they could help to persuade them of the inherent justice of the labor movement and so create a leaning toward concessions. No other influence could do so much to prevent a revolutionary explosion of pent-up forces. It is to the interest of all sides that the readjustment of the social classes should come as a steady evolutionary process rather than as a social catastrophe. If the laboring class should attempt to seize political power suddenly, the attempt might be beaten back with terrible loss in efficiency to the movement. If the attempt should be successful, a raw governing class would be compelled to handle a situation so vast and complicated that no past revolution presents a parallel. There would be widespread disorder and acute distress, and a reactionary relapse to old conditions would, by all historical precedents, be almost certain to occur. It is devoutly to be desired that the shifting of power should come through a continuous series of practicable demands on one side and concessions on the other. Such an historical process will be immensely facilitated if there are a large number of men in the professional and business class with whom religious and ethical motives overcome their selfish interests so that they will throw their influence on the side of the class which is now claiming its full rights in the family circle of humanity.

On the other hand, the Christian idealists must not make the mistake of trying to hold the working class down to the use of moral suasion only, or be repelled when they hear the brute note of selfishness and anger. The class struggle is bound to be transferred to the field of politics in our country in some form. It would be folly if the working class failed to use the leverage which their political power gives them. The business class has certainly never failed to use political means to further its interests. This is a war of conflicting interests which is not likely to be fought out in love and tenderness. The possessing class will make concessions not in brotherly love but in fear, because it has to. The working class will force its demands, not merely because they are just, but because it feels it cannot do without them, and because it is strong enough to coerce. Even Bismarck acknowledged that the former indifference of the business class in Germany to the sufferings of the lower classes had not been overcome by philanthropy, but by fear of the growing discontent of the people and the spread of social democracy. Max Nordau meant the same when he said,

> In spite of its theoretical absurdity, socialism has already in thirty years wrought greater amelioration than all the wisdom of statesmen and philosophers of thousands of years.

All that we as Christian men can do is to ease the struggle and hasten the victory of the right by giving faith and hope to those who are down, and quickening the sense of justice with those who are in power, so that they will not harden their hearts and hold Israel in bondage, but will "let the people go." But that spiritual contribution, intangible and imponderable though it be, has a chemical power of immeasurable efficiency.

## Summary of the Argument

We undertook in this chapter to suggest in what ways the moral forces latent in Christian society could be mobilized for the progressive regeneration of social life, and in what directions chiefly these forces should be exerted.

We saw that some lines of effort frequently attempted in the past by Christian men and organizations are useless and misleading. It is fruitless to attempt to turn modern society back to conditions prevailing before power machinery and trusts had revolutionized it; or to copy biblical institutions adapted to wholly different social conditions; or to postpone the Christianizing of society to the millennium; or to found Christian communistic colonies within the competitive world; or to make the organized Church the centre and manager of an improved social machinery. The force of religion can best be applied to social renewal by sending its spiritual power along the existing and natural relations of men to direct them to truer ends and govern them by higher motives.

The fundamental contribution of every man is the change of his own personality. We must repent of the sins of existing society, cast off the spell of the lies protecting our social wrongs, have faith in a higher social order, and realize in ourselves a new type of Christian manhood which seeks to overcome the evil in the present world, not by withdrawing from the world, but by revolutionizing it.

If this new type of religious character multiplies among the young men and women, they will change the world when they come to hold the controlling positions of society in their maturer years. They will give a new force to righteous and enlightened public opinion, and will apply the religious sense of duty and service to the common daily life with a new motive and directness.

The ministry, in particular, must apply the teaching functions of the pulpit to the pressing questions of public morality. It must collectively learn not to speak without adequate information; not to charge individuals with guilt in which all society shares; not to be partial, and yet to be on the side of the lost; not to yield to political partisanship, but to deal with moral questions before they become political issues and with those questions of public welfare which never do become political issues. They must lift the social questions to a religious level by faith and spiritual insight. The larger the number of ministers who attempt these untrodden ways, the safer and saner will those be who follow. By interpreting one social class to the other, they can create a disposition to make concessions and help in securing a peaceful settlement to social issues.

The force of the religious spirit should be bent toward asserting the supremacy of life over property. Property exists to maintain and develop life. It is unchristian to regard human life as a mere instrument of the production of wealth.

The religious sentiment can protect good customs and institutions against the inroads of ruthless greed, and extend their scope. It can create humane customs which the law is impotent to create. It can create the convictions and customs which are later embodied in good legislation.

Our complex society rests largely on the stewardship of delegated powers. The opportunities to profit by the betrayal of trust increase with the wealth and complexity of civilization. The most fundamental evils in the past history and present conditions were due to converting stewardship into ownership. The keener moral insight created by Christianity should lend its help in scrutinizing all claims to property and power in order to detect latent public rights and to recall the recreant stewards to their duty.

Primitive society was communistic. The most valuable institutions in modern life—the family, the school and church—are communistic. The State, too, is essentially communistic and is becoming increasingly so. During the larger part of its history the Christian Church regarded communism as the only ideal life. Christianity certainly has more affinity for coöperative and fraternal institutions than for competitive disunion. It should therefore strengthen the existing communistic institutions and aid the evolution of society from the present temporary stage of individualism to a higher form of communism.

The splendid ideal of a fraternal organization of society cannot be realized by idealists only. It must be supported by the self-interest of a powerful class. The working class, which is now engaged in its upward movement, is struggling to secure better conditions of life, an assured status for its class organizations, and ultimately the ownership of the means of production. Its success in the last great aim would mean the closing of the gap which now divides industrial society and the establishment of industry on the principle of solidarity and the method of coöperation. Christianity should enter into a working alliance with this rising class, and by its mediation secure the victory of these principles by a gradual equalization of social opportunity and power.

# ❧135❧

# The Industrial Revolution

## WASHINGTON GLADDEN

Washington Gladden (1836–1918) was called "the father of the Social Gospel". After youthful experience as a journalist he became a Congregational minister in industrial towns in New England and the Middle West. He combined popularisation of liberal theology with public discussion of the ethical problems of industrial life. His naturalistic ethics allowed for the justice of self-assertion, if it was blended with altruism, but this was a combination which led him to be critical of socialism as a solution to industrial conflict.

T hat the sufficient remedy for the disorders of the industrial world is the application to them of the Christian rule of life is the conclusion to which my study brought me, and the entire progress of events since that day has confirmed the judgment. But it is necessary to understand what the Christian rule of life is. The form in which it is stated in Christ's compend of the moral law is, I believe, exact and adequate; but the full force of it is not always apprehended. "Thou shalt love thy neighbor as thyself" is sometimes taken as a maxim of sheer altruism. But the fundamental obligation is rational self-love. That is made the measure of our love for our neighbor. How much shall I love my neighbor? As much as I love myself. This implies that I regard myself as a being of essential worth. I am a child of God as truly as my neighbor is; and I am bound to honor and cherish the selfhood intrusted to me. I have no more right to neglect and despise myself than I have to neglect or despise my neighbor. I ought to have some sense of the value and sacredness of my neighbor's personality. I am not to degrade or destroy myself in ministering to him, nor am I to degrade and destroy him in ministering to myself; I am to identify his interest with mine, and we are to share together the good which the divine bounty distributes to all.

This is the Christian law, as I understand it, and it gives ample room for

Source: Washington Gladden, 'The Industrial Revolution', *Recollections*, London, 1909, pp. 298-315.

that legitimate self-assertion which some moralists have failed to find in Christianity, as well as for that self-denial which restrains the excesses of self-love. In the first chapter of "Applied Christianity" this principle, as it relates to human society, is stated in words which I venture here to repeat.

> Society results from a combination of egoism and altruism. Self-love and self-sacrifice are both essential; no society can exist if based on either of them to the exclusion of the other. Without the self-regarding virtues it would have no vigor: without the benevolent virtues it would not cohere. But the combination of capitalists and laborers in production is a form of society. These two elements ought to be combined in this form of society. The proportion of altruism may be less in the factory than in the home or church, but it is essential to the peace and welfare of all of them. Yet the attempt of the present system is to base this form of society wholly on competition, which is pure egoism. It will not stand securely on this base. The industrial system, as at present organized, is a social solecism. It is an attempt to hold society together upon an anti-social foundation. To bring capitalists and laborers together in an association, and set them over against each other and announce to them the principle of competition as the guide of their conduct,—bidding each party to get as much as it can out of the other and to give no more than it must—for that is precisely what competition means,—is simply to declare war, a war in which the strongest will win.
>
> The Christian moralist is, therefore, bound to admonish the Christian employer that the wage-system, when it rests on competition as its sole basis, is anti-social and anti-Christian. "Thou shalt love thy neighbor as thyself" is the Christian law, and he must find some way of incorporating that law into the organization of labor. It must be something more than an ideal, it must find expression in the industrial scheme. God has not made men to be associated for any purpose on a purely egoistic basis, and we must learn God's laws and obey them. It must be possible to shape the organization of our industries in such a way that it shall be the daily habit of the workman to think of the interest of the employer, and of the employer to think of the interest of the workman. We have thought it very fine to *say* that the interests of both are identical, but it has been nothing more than a fine saying; the problem now is to *make* them identical.

The substance of what I have been trying to say on this subject, through all the years of my ministry, is included in this short extract. Nothing is plainer to me than that the existing system of industry, with rigid organization of employers on the one side and laborers upon the other, each determined to override and subjugate the other, is the essence of unreason. The entire attitude of both parties is anti-social. It is simply absurd to imagine men are made to live together on any such basis. They are putting themselves into deadly conflict with the primary laws of life.

In the spring of 1886, when a fierce strike had been raging in Cleveland, a philanthropist of that city conceived the idea of getting the employers and the employed to come together in a mass meeting to be addressed by some one who was supposed to be reasonably impartial in his attitude toward the contending parties. The choice fell on me, and I found myself confronted, in the Music Hall of that city, by an audience in which the laboring-class was mainly in evidence, though a sprinkling of the other class was visible. "Is it Peace or War?" was the question to which I addressed myself. The workingmen before me were evidently in a critical mood. They listened, through the first half of my address, with respect, but in silence. They had their doubts about parsons; they probably expected me to take sides with their employers. In due season they were reassured on that point; they saw that they were listening to one who was able to get their point of view, and it was pleasant to see the suspicion fade out of their eyes and the signs of appreciative interest appearing. This is part of what they heard:—

> Since this is the day and age of combinations, since capital in a thousand ways is forming combinations for its own advantage, who will deny to labor the right to combine for the assertion of its just claims? Combination means war, I admit. Combinations, whether of capital or labor, are generally made in these days for fighting purposes. And war is a great evil—no doubt of that. But it is not the greatest of evils. The permanent degradation of the men who do the world's work would be a greater evil. And if, by combination, the wage-workers can resist the tendencies that are crowding them down, and can assert and maintain their right to a proportional share of the growing wealth, then let them combine, and let all the people say Amen.
>
> The present state of the industrial world is a state of war. And if war is the word, then the efficient combination and organization must not all be on the side of capital. While the conflict is in progress, labor has the same right that capital has to prosecute the warfare in the most effective way. If war is the order of the day, we must grant to labor belligerent rights. The sooner this fact is recognized, the better for all concerned. The refusal to admit it has made the conflict, thus far, much more fierce and sanguinary than it would otherwise have been.

When the workingmen heard that, they were not silent; they gave me a rousing cheer. But they were compelled to listen to quite a number of things after that which did not make them cheer. For I did my best to bring home to them, and to the employers who sat among them, the foolishness of the enterprise in which both sides were enlisted. The utter stupidity and absurdity of an industrial system based on war; the enormous waste of the common resources which it involves; the far worse destruction of the moral wealth of the community, the good will and mutual trust in which all human welfare is grounded,—all this I tried to make plain to them. "Is not his business of war," I asked them,

> "a senseless, brutal, barbarous business, at best? Does either side expect to do itself any good by fighting the other? It is about as rational as it would be for the right hand and the left hand to smite each other with persistent and deadly enmity, or for the eyes and the ears to array themselves against each other in a remorseless feud. It is a sorry comment on our civilization that here, at the end of the nineteenth Christian century, sane and full-grown men, whose welfare depends wholly on the recognition of their mutual interests and on the coöperation of their efforts, should be ready to spend a good share of their time in trying to cripple or destroy one another. It is not only wicked, it is stupid: it is not simply monstrous, it is ridiculous."

Some very frank words were then spoken to both parties in this controversy. While I was laying down the law to the employers, the men cheered heartily;

when I began to drive home to them their own blunders and sins, they were less demonstrative, but presently evinced their fairness by cheering the points that were scored against themselves. And, at the end, after a warm appeal for peace, the prolonged applause was a most grateful testimony that the hearts of fifteen hundred workingmen were in the right place.

The next week I had an engagement to lecture in Tremont Temple, Boston. The occasion was one of some importance: Goveror Robinson, an old friend and neighbor of mine, was to preside, and the audience would be composed of some of the solid men of Boston. I determined to repeat this address, "Is it Peace or War?" Would these people, mainly of the employing class, warm up to it as the workmen had done? I had my misgivings. But the vent showed that this audience was quite as cordial as the other had been; and at the close of the address, the men on the platform, including the Governor, a member of Congress, who was also a leading manufacturer, and others, united in inviting me to return to Boston on the next Saturday night and repeat the address in the same place to the workingmen of the city, to whom the hall was to be made free. On that occasion I had with me on the platform several employers, and several labor leaders, among them the head organizer for Massachusetts of the Knights of Labor; and at the close of the address, every one of these men indorsed, without qualification, my arguement and appeal.

I have given the history of this address, because it indicates the position which I have tried to maintain, and because it shows that, at that time, the chasm between the contending classes was not so wide but that it could be spanned by reason and good will.

Another opportunity of a similar sort came to me a little later. The Ohio State Association of Congregationalists made me chairman of a committee to investigate the labor conditions of the state; and this committee arranged for two conferences between employers and labor leaders, one at Columbus and the other at Toledo. To each of these conferences a number of the most intelligent and influential employers of the neighborhood were invited, and about an equal number of the leaders of organized labor. Most of the men invited responded to the invitation. In each of the cities a day was spent in the conferences, with two sessions, afternoon and evening. A short series of very simple questions had been prepared and printed on the letters of invitation,— questions calling out the opinions of the men invited upon existing conditions in the industrial world; upon the reasons for the present conflict; upon the practicability of industrial partnership and other possible methods of promoting peace and welfare. The conference was conducted by calling first on a labor leader, and then on an employer, to express his views of the situation. Some questioning was permitted, but it was all civil and respectful; we all understood that it was not a dispute but a fair opportunity for each one to speak his own mind. There was much frankness in the utterances of opinion, but very little acerbity; it did not seem impossible that such men as were facing each other in these discussions should be able to arbitrate their differences.

I fear that the relations between the contending parties have not improved since that day. So far as I can see, the breach is widening. The fierce strike in the anthracite coal regions was the worst of our labor disputes; and, although it was amicably settled, the conditions which followed were not reassuring. The workingmen, in that case, had the sympathy of the public, and they won a notable victory; I fear it must be said that they failed to make the best use of it. Their demands grew more exacting and unreasonable; in all parts of the country there were symptoms of a discomfiture of their employers. The result of that has been a serious exacerbation of temper on the part of the employing class. Organizations of employers have arisen in late years, whose attitude toward organized labor is more hostile than anything which has been known in our history. And I fear that it will be found that there are thousands of employers in all parts of the country who, a few years ago, were disposed to be reasonable in their treatment of the labor unions, but who, to-day, are maintaining toward them an attitude of almost vindictive opposition.

The Civic Federation has done something to mitigate these antipathies, but in so doing it has gained for itself the warm dislike of the belligerent employers on the one hand, and of the fighting labor federations on the other.

What the outcome of this conflict is to be, I do not predict. The evident expectation of some of the employers that they will be able to kill or cripple the unions is hardly rational; the evident determination of some of the labor leaders to extend the use of the boycott and the sympathetic strike is not intelligent; such a conflict as both sides seem bound to invoke can result in nothing but disaster. Chronic warfare in the industrial world is intolerable, and the world is coming to understand it so. We are going to make an end of international wars very soon; the absurdity of that way of settling the disputes of nations is becoming apparent to all civilized peoples. And the foolishness of industrial strife is not less obvious. If the wage-system means perennial war, the wage-system must pass, and some less expensive method of organizing industry must take its place.

The alternative now constantly in sight is Socialism. Socialism proposes that the functions of the capitalist and the *entrepreneur* shall be merged in the commonwealth. That seems to abolish one party to the quarrel, and is indicated, in the Socialist diagnosis, as the way of peace. That it may come to this sometimes seems probable. Yet I have never been able to regard this possibility with enthusiasm. There is an old Latin proverb about making a solitude and calling it peace. The Socialistic solution, applied as a panacea, would not give us a solitude, but it might give us stagnation. It does not agree with that theory of human nature of which I have spoken; it gives no adequate play to the self-regarding motives. The present system overworks them; Socialism undervalues them. What we have to do is to coördinate them with the motives of good will and sympathy, and get the full force of both in our schemes of social construction. The gains of coöperation must not be purchased at the cost of the integrity of the individual.

We may be plunged into a Socialistic experiment at no distant day; toward that precipice our employers' associations and our labor federations seem to be driving us; but if, in our haste, we take that step, we shall find leisure to repent of it. This people is not yet, in its prevailing ideas and tempers, sufficiently socialized to work the machinery of Socialism. The testimony of one of the ablest of the Socialists is in point:

> It is well to keep in mind the entire dependence of Socialism upon a high level of intelligence, education, and freedom. Socialist institutions, as I understand them, are only possible in a civilized state, in a state in which the whole population can read, write, discuss, participate, and, in a considerable sense, understand. Education must precede the Socialist state. Socialism, modern Socialism, that is to say, such as I am now concerned with, is essentially an exposition of and training in certain general ideas; it is impossible in an illiterate community, a basely selfish community, or in a community without the capacity to use the machinery and the apparatus of civilization. At the best, and it is a poor best, a stupid, illiterate population can but mock Socialism with a sort of bureaucratic tyranny; for a barbaric population, too large and various for the folk-meeting, there is nothing but monarchy and the ownership of the King; for a savage tribe, tradition and the undocumented will of the strongest males. Socialism, I will admit, presupposes intelligence, and demands as fundamental necessities, schools, organized science, literature, and a sense of the state.

It is impossible for us to persuade ourselves that "the whole population" of the United States of America, or of any state in the Union, has attained unto any such standard as is here prescribed. With the vast illiterate and unassimilated elements of our national life, with so many millions who are separated from the commonwealth and from one another by the barriers of race and language, it would be, indeed, a mock Socialism which we should succeed, at this juncture, in setting up.

It would be a great calamity, therefore, if the intolerable strife between organized capital and organized labor should precipitate an attempt to put all our industries upon the basis of collectivism. But though we could not wisely go all the way with the Socialists, we might, safely, go part way with them. Indeed, we are already moving in the direction in which they would lead us. The Post-Office is a socialistic institution; it would be wise to extend its service, and make it the universal carrier of small parcels. That the telegraph should be added to this branch of the public service is evident; and the relation of the railways to the industries of the country is so close and vital that they, too, must soon be brought under governmental control. Doubtless we shall keep on for several years trying to regulate them, but doubtless we shall fail; the only solution of the problem is public ownership. This need not mean public management; the government may own the tracks, as most European cities own the tracks of their street railways, and may prescribe rates and regulations, and then lease them, for definite terms, to companies or syndicates to operate. The stock objection to government ownership is the danger of adding such an enormous number of employees to the civil service; but that is not a necessary condition. The power of oppression which resides in the private ownership of the means of transportation is so tremendous, and so impossible of regulation, that the people will be compelled, at no distant day, to take the business into their hands. I think that it will also be necessary for them to own the mines, and to establish a rigid supervision over the watercourses. And, in the cities, not only the water-supply, but the lighting and the transportation and the telephone service, will soon be brought under public control.

All those are steps in the direction of Socialism which we are likely to take at no distant day. All the industries which I have named are virtual monopolies, and the people must own all the monopolies. That is the essence of democracy, on the economic side. There must be no monopolies of goods or services necessary to the life of the people which the people do not themselves control. If democracy is to endure, it must assert and maintain this prerogative.

But, after this principle has been fully established, there will still remain wide areas in which private property may be recognized and private enterprise liberated,—in which individual initiative may have free play. That industrial society in the future will have large features of collective ownership and control, and alongside of them extensive and varied enterprises in which men are employing their own capital and managing their own affairs, seems to me highly probable. The main problem of statesmanship will be to draw the line between these two industrial methods, to know what industries can best be taken over th the commonwealth and what can best be left in private hands. We shall coöperate, more and more, through the state, for common purposes, and we shall make vast gains by that coöperation; but we shall still cultivate the virtues of self-direction and self-reliance, we shall still keep the privilege of choosing our own careers, and of expressing ourselves freely in our industries.

But in this coming industrial society, where freedom of occupation is protected and cherished, there will still be need of a guiding law for industry, and there can be no other law than that of the Christ. In those days as in these, the law of human association must be the law of Good Will. The good of life is not found by those who prey upon one another or plunder one another; it is found only by those who in friendship serve one another.

The existing industrial order virtually rests upon the assumption that it is every man's business in this world to get for himself—and, of course, to get away from his neighbors—as much as he legally and prudently and safely can. That principle of life, no matter how artfully disguised, nor how cautiously practiced, is sure to bring strife and poverty and wretchedness. Any organization of society which is founded on selfishness will come to grief. That is the bottom trouble with the industrial world to-day; and the only radical cure for it is a change in the ruling principle of life. The stable and fruitful social order will be that which rests on the assumption that it is every man's business to give as much as he can, prudently and safely, and with due regard

198

to his own integrity, to all with whom he deals. This does not mean that he is to cripple or impoverish himself in his giving, for his own well-being should be precious to him, and he must not give in such a way as to destroy his power to give. Cases may, indeed, arise, in which the sacrifice of all may be demanded; but the ordinary regimen of life will require him to husband his power of service.

This, as I understand it, is the meaning of Christ's law of life. It is not his law because he originated it; it is his because he most clearly taught it, and most consistently lived by it; because he made it central in morality. It rests on no man's word; it is as truly a natural law as is the law of gravitation or the laws of chemical affinity; it is an induction from the facts of human nature. Experience, if men will only pay attention to it, will prove to them that this way of living together makes for universal welfare and happiness; that the way of living which keeps self central and supreme is the way to destruction. The fundamental objection to the world's way is that it is unnatural and unscientific; it is an inversion of life; it is like an attempt to make plants grow with their roots in the air and their branches on the earth.

This is the truth which the world is beginning to see. It is only as in a blurred mirror, dimly, that most men see it yet, but never before was it visible to so many. The conviction is steadily strengthening that the one thing needful is a change in the direction of the ruling motive from self-aggrandizement to service. And to all who will carefully study the prevailing tendencies it will be clear that this is the way the world is going. "One perceives," says Mr. Wells,

> something that goes on, that is constantly working to make order out of casualty, beauty out of confusion, justice, kindliness, mercy out of cruelty and inconsiderate pressure. For our present purpose it will be sufficient to speak of this force that struggles and tends to make and do, as Good Will. More and more evident it is, as one reviews the ages, that there is much more than lust, hunger, avarice, vanity, and more or less intelligent fear, among the motives of mankind. The Good Will of our race, however arising, however trivial, however subordinated to individual ends, however comically inadequate a thing it may be in this individual case or that, is in the aggregate an operating will. In spite of all the confusions and thwartings of life, the halts and resiliences and the counter strokes of fate, it is manifest that, in the long run, human life becomes broader than it was, gentler than it was, finer and deeper. On the whole—and nowadays almost steadily—things get better. There is a secular amelioration of life, and it is brought about by Good Will working through the efforts of men.

Good Will is at work, and it is making things better. In spite of the prevailing social philosophy, it is gaining ground. Even now, with such partial, halting half-hearted recognition as we give it, Good Will is making things better. How much faster things would grow better, if all the people who call themselves Christians would accept what St. James calls "The Royal Law," and would give their lives to making Good Will regnant among men!

No matter what the form of the social organization may be, it is to this principle of Good Will, ruling the lives of individuals, that we shall owe all our social peace and welfare. Our collectivism will be confusion and a curse, where it is wanting; where it is present, our individual initiative will be beneficence and bounty.

Is it not a Utopian dream that the principle of Good Will will supplant the principle of *Laissez faire* in industrial society? Can we rationally expect that such an ingrained tendency of human nature as that which is represented by the maxim "Every man for himself," will yield to the other-regarding motive so that men will learn to identify their interests with those of their neighbors? The answer is that when men see that Good Will is the law, they will learn to obey it. Most of them have never yet clearly seen it. The maxims of business have all made self-interest supreme. The whole industrial structure has rested on that philosophy. The world is beginning to see that Good Will makes things better. That, so far as the business world is concerned, is a new revelation. It is easy enough to see that a good deal more Good Will would make things a great deal better.

That is a fact which the logic of events will force upon the convictions of men. And in the light and warmth of that knowledge the ingrained egoism of human nature will slowly melt away.

Such, then, is the substance of the social faith which I have been trying to inculcate.

I believe that monopolies, actual or virtual, which supply the primary wants of human beings, must be owned and controlled by the commonwealth.

I believe that in this way, collective ownership and control will be and should be greatly extended; that many of the industries which are now in private hands will become departments of the public service. I believe that such coöperation of all the people through the state will result in great economies, and will put an end to some of the worst oppressions.

I believe that when we have gone as far as we can safely go in this direction, there will remain large room for private enterprise which will offer a free field for the cultivation of virtues quite essential to the social welfare.

I believe that all this activity, whether organized by the state, or conducted by independent enterprise, must have as its ruling motive the principle of Good Will, the spirit of service; that the church by its ministry, and the school by its training, and the state by its legislation must inculcate and enforce the doctrine that the primary business of every man in this world is service; that the man who is here to be ministered unto, and to levy tribute on his neighbors for his own aggrandizement, is living a life of sin and shame.

When this principle of Good Will becomes regnant, shall we see wealth increasing as it has been increasing during the last four or five decades? Certainly not in the same way. In a society in which the Christian law was recognized as the practical rule, there could be no such enormous accumulations in the hands of individuals as those which have been heaped up in the last twenty-five years. Such swollen fortunes are the symptoms of social disease; they have the same relation to social health that hydrocephalus or elephantiasis has to the health of the individual, and to all sound moral vision they are not less repulsive. It is profoundly to be hoped that the day of their prevalence may quickly pass. But it is probable that the social good created under the impulse of Good Will would be far more widely diffused; that in the greatly enlarged possessions and advantages held in common, all would share; that the slums would disappear; that family life would be more secure and permanent; that the crushing burden of toil would be lifted from the shoulders of little children; that there would be leisure and comfort and happiness among men, in which faith could find root and hope get some anchorage, and in which it would not be incredible that love is indeed the greatest thing in the world.

# The Teaching of the Catholic Church

## JOHN A. RYAN

Although some earlier spokesmen for American Catholicism, such as Cardinal Gibbons, had shown deep concern about the problems of industrial society, they faced strong conservative forces in the Church before the First World War. Only with the impact of war and the need to consider reconstruction did Catholic social thought in America become truly creative, while drawing upon the social encyclicals of Leo XIII. Father John A. Ryan (1869–1945) was a major figure in this process through his writings and organizational work in what became the National Catholic Welfare Conference. He was largely responsible for drafting the 1919 document commonly known as 'The Bishop's Program'; the article below, written in 1922, is a concise expression of its principles.

W hy should the Church have anything to say about the relations between capital and labor? Are not these purely economic arrangements, and as such outside the province of a religious society? These questions imply a misconception which Pope Leo XIII noted as very common, but which he promptly rejected. In his words,

> the social question . . . is first of all a moral and religious matter, and for that reason its settlement is to be sought mainly in the moral law and the pronouncements of religion.

To any reflecting mind the truth of this statement is obvious. Industrial relations are human relations; they involve human actions: therefore, they are subject to the moral law. They are either morally right or morally wrong. Inasmuch as the Church is the accredited interpreter and teacher of the moral law, her authority and function in the field of industrial relations are quite as

Source: John A. Ryan, 'The Teaching of the Catholic Church', *Annals of the American Academy of Political and Social Science*, Vol. 103, September 1922.

certain and normal as in domestic relations, or in any other department of human life.

The principles which underlie the teachings of the Church on industrial relations are found in the Gospel of Christ and in the moral law of nature. One of these is the principle of justice. Its basis is found in Christ's teaching on personality. Every human being has intrinsic worth, has been redeemed by Christ, and is destined for everlasting union with God. In the eyes of God all persons are of equal importance. Neither in industry nor in any other department of life may one man be used as a mere instrument to the advantage of other men. Industrial, no less than all other relations, must be so organized and conducted as to safeguard personality and afford to all persons the means and conditions of life as children of God. The principle of charity or love is even more conspicuous in the teaching of Christ. If it were honestly and adequately applied in the dealings of employer with employee there would be no unsolved problem of industrial relations.

It is beyond the scope of this paper to describe the extent to which these two great principles have been developed and applied in the various forms of industrial relations since the beginning of the Christian era. By way of historical summary it will be sufficient to recall that the doctrine of the Catholic Church on this subject has exhibited great consistency and continuity throughout the whole period. The discouragement of slavery and serfdom, the insistence upon risk and labor as the chief claims to economic rewards, the doctrine of the just price, the regulations and ideas of the guilds concerning labor organization, good workmanship, reasonable hours, provision against sickness, etc., were the medieval expression of the traditional doctrine. Its first systematic adaptation to the conditions of modern capitalism occurs in the labor program of the German, Bishop Ketteler. In this program we find demands for the prohibition of child labor, of unsuitable woman labor, of unsanitary labor and of Sunday labor; for the legal regulation of working hours; for insurance against sickness, accidents and old age; for state factory inspectors; for general increases in wages; for the legal protection of workingmen's coöperative associations; and for several other industrial reforms. More than once Bishop Ketteler declared that there was nothing new in his industrial views and proposals, that he had drawn them all from the storehouse of patristic and medieval doctrine.

## Encyclical of Pope Leo XIII "On the Condition of Labor"

Less than fourteen years after the death of Bishop Ketteler, Pope Leo XIII issued his great encyclical, "On the Condition of Labor" (*Rerum Novarum*, May 15, 1891). Previously he had referred to Bishop Ketteler as, "my great precursor." The principles which the illustrious Bishop of Mainz enunciated and applied, Pope Leo reiterated, developed, systematized and brought into more specific relation to current industrial conditions, practices and institutions. While two of his three successors (Pius X and Benedict XV) have made pronouncements upon various phases of industrial relations, they have both expressly disclaimed the intention of adding anything essential. Therefore, the authoritative teaching of the Catholic Church on this subject can be found in the encyclical "On the Condition of Labor." In that document we find not only the general principles but a considerable measure of concrete application.

Having rejected and condemned socialism as a remedy for industrial ills, the Pope explicitly asserts his right and authority to lay down principles for the guidance of the two great industrial classes, "for no practical solution of this question will be found apart from the intervention of religion and the Church." This is a clear challenge to and condemnation of all those selfishly interested persons and all those sincerely ignorant persons who say or think that "the Church ought to keep to spiritual matters and not meddle with business or with industrial matters."

The Pope then takes up the social principles of the Gospel. Equality of human conditions is impossible. No kind of social organization can drive pain and hardship out of life. Capital and labor are not necessarily hostile to each other, but are mutually dependent. Religion teaches the laborer to "carry out fairly and honestly all equitable agreements," to refrain from injuring persons or property, and to avoid men of evil principles. Religion teaches the employer to respect the dignity of his employees as men and Christians, to refrain from treating them as "chattels for the making of money," to pay them fair wages, to give them sufficient time for religious duties and not to impose tasks unsuited to sex, age or strength. Those who are rich should regard themselves as stewards, charged with the duty of making a right use of their wealth for themselves and others. Those who are poor should realize that their condition was adopted and blessed by Christ Himself, and that the true worth of man lies not in his material possessions but in his moral qualities. Both classes should always bear in mind that they are children of the common heavenly kingdom.

So much for the general Christian principles. The man who considers them fairly and adequately will be compelled to answer in the affirmative the question with which Pope Leo closes this part of the encyclical: "Would it not seem that, were society penetrated with ideas like these, strife must quickly cease?" The process of "penetration" is, however, retarded by two very formidable obstacles. The first is wholly moral; the second, partly moral and partly intellectual. The practice of justice and charity in industrial relations is greatly and frequently prevented and impeded by deliberate selfishness and flagrant bad faith. More often, perhaps, the current injustice and uncharity are due to culpable or inculpable ignorance. Nay men accept the principles of justice and charity as applicable to industrial relations, but do not realize that they are violating the principles in their industrial practices. For example, an employer admits the obligation of paying "fair wages," but refuses to exceed the inadequate rate that is frequently determined by the unmoral forces of supply and demand. An employee is willing to carry out "equitable agreements," but "loafs on the job" because he thinks that his wage contract is not equitable. An employer admits that the precept of brotherly love is as pertinent to the employment relation as to the neighborhood relations, yet he exploits little children for profit or maintains an unsanitary workshop. An employee clamors for the application of the Golden Rule to industry, but does not scruple to cause his employer great inconvenience by absenting himself from work for a trivial reason. Such ignorance of the practical application and practical obligations of moral principles in the field of industrial relations is sometimes quite unconscious and unsuspected by the person whom it affects and afflicts. Sometimes it is culpable, at least to this extent: the misguided person suspects that his conduct is not entirely consistent with the general principles of justice and charity, but he fails to investigate its moral aspects because he is indifferent, or because he is afraid that the results might disturb his conscience.

This condition and this need Pope Leo meets by a fairly specific application of general principles to particular situations. "Fairly specific," because many of these declarations are still somewhat general in character. However, this was unavoidable in a document which was written for the industrial conditions of all countries, and which endeavored to treat all the great moral problems of industry within the compass of an encyclical letter. Nevertheless, the Pope's pronouncements on the most important phases and the most acute problems of industrial relations are sufficiently specific to provide clear and adequate guidance to all men of good will. The other kind of men are beyond the reach of instruction and argument. They can be moved only by fear. They will respond only to the denunciation of the prophet, or the coercive power of the State.

## Teachings of the Encyclical

The specific teaching of the encyclical can be summarized under the heads of wages, labor organization, state intervention and private property. Each of these topics will be dealt with briefly.

*Wages.*—Justice in this matter is not realized through mere freedom of contract. While worker and employer

> should, as a rule, make free agreements concerning wages, there is a dictate of nature more imperious and more ancient than any bargain between man and man, namely, that the remuneration must be sufficient to support the wage-earner in reasonable and frugal comfort. If through necessity or fear of a worse evil the workman accept harder conditions because an employer will give him no better, he is made the victim of force and *injustice*.

This is the doctrine of the living wage. Pope Leo does not say that it represents complete justice. It is merely the minimum of justice, the amount that is ethically due to every wage-earner by the mere fact that he is a human being, with a life to maintain, and a personality to develop. The special qualifications and claims which entitle men to more than the minimum of justice, such as skill, hazard, responsibility, cost of training, etc., are not formally considered in the Pope's discussion. The living wage that he has in mind is an amount sufficient not merely for the worker himself, but also for the proper maintenance of his family. Such is the law of nature, and such is the interpretation evidently put upon the phrase by Pope Leo himself.

That the living-wage doctrine continues to have great practical importance, is shown by the following deplorable facts: the majority of laborers, even in the United States, receive less than living wages; probably the majority of employers reject both the principle and its application, still adhering to the idea that wage justice is determined entirely by the operation of supply and demand; the principle was deliberately ignored by an important public tribunal, a few months ago, in fixing the wage rates of many thousands of employees on the railroads. How profoundly industrial relations would be transformed and how greatly they would be improved, if this one doctrine were universally accepted and translated into reality!

*Labor Organization.*—The Catholic Church has always regarded organization, whether of employees or of employers, as the normal condition. She has never accepted the philosophy of individualism and unlimited competition. Pope Leo deplores the disappearance of the ancient guilds, and expresses gratification over the existence of various forms of workingmen's associations; "but it were greatly to be desired that they should become more numerous and more efficient." Men have a natural right to enter them, a right which cannot be annulled by the State. "We may," says the Pope,

> lay it down as a general and lasting law, that workingmen's associations should be so organized and governed as to furnish the best and most suitable means for attaining what is aimed at, that is to say, for helping each individual member to better his condition to the utmost in body, mind and property.

On the other hand, Pope Leo denounces those societies which

> are in the hands of secret leaders, . . . who do their utmost to get within their grasp the whole field of labor, and force workingmen either to join them or to starve.

The first of the two passages just quoted implicitly, yet unmistakably, condemns the insidious "open shop" campaign, and every other movement which seeks to render the unions ineffective, by denying the right of adequate collective bargaining. In the words of the Pastoral Letter of the American Hierarchy, the workers have a right "to form and maintain the kind of organization that is necessary and that will be most effective in securing their welfare."

Pope Leo makes more than one reference to joint associations of employers and employees, "which draw the two classes more closely together." The underlying principle is exemplified in joint conferences for the establishment of trade agreements, and in shop committees, works councils and other arrangements for increasing the control of labor over employment conditions and industrial operations. Upon the application and extension of this principle and these methods depends to a very great extent the attainment of industrial peace.

*The Function of the State.*—Under this head Pope Leo lays down one general principle and several specific applications.

> Whenever the general interests or any particular class suffers or is threatened with injury which can in no other way be met or prevented, it is the duty of the public authority to intervene.

No more comprehensive authorization of State intervention could be reasonably desired. Applying the principle to industrial relations, Pope Leo declares that the poor "have no resources of their own to fall back upon, and must chiefly depend upon the assistance of the State." Continuing in more particular terms, he says that the law should forestall strikes by removing the unjust conditions which provoke them; protect the worker's spiritual welfare, and his right to Sunday rest; restrict the length of the working day, so that men's labor will not "stupefy their minds and wear out their bodies"; prohibit the employment of children "in workshops and factories until their bodies and minds are sufficiently developed"; prevent the entrance of women into occupations for which they are not fitted; and provide all classes of workers with "proper rest for soul and body." While the Pope does not explicitly declare that the State should enforce a living wage, he clearly indicates that such action should be taken in default of effective voluntary arrangements.

*Diffusion of Property.*—Those students and thinkers who believe that industrial relations will not be stabilized nor industrial peace assured until the wage-earners become to a great extent participants in the ownership of industry, will find considerable encouragement in Pope Leo's declarations on private property. To represent these as merely a condemnation of socialism, as merely concerned with the *institution* of ownership and not with its *distribution*, is highly misleading. The whole argument of the Pope on this subject manifests a strong appreciation of the benefits which private property brings to the individual workingman. Hence the policy of the State should be "to induce as many as possible of the humbler class to become owners." As a consequence, "property will become more equitably divided," and "the gulf between vast wealth and sheer poverty will be bridged over."

The Pope's observations on this subject afford little comfort to the defenders of industrial autocracy. He deplores the division of industrial society into two classes, one of which

> holds power because it holds wealth; which has in its grasp the whole of labor and trade; which manipulates for its own benefit and its own purposes all the sources of supply, and which is even represented in the councils of the State itself.

Referring to the wide extension of ownership in the later Middle Ages, the Pastoral Letter of the American Hierarchy declares: "Though the economic arrangements of that time cannot be restored, the underlying principle is of permanent application, and is the only one that will give stability to industrial society. It should be applied to our present system as rapidly as conditions will permit."

To sum up: Now as always the Catholic Church conceives her mission as that of saving souls. Men save their souls by conducting themselves righteously in all the relations of life. Among the most important of these relations are those that we call industrial. If the Church did not provide guidance in this field she would neglect one of her most important duties. If the principles and proposals contained in the encyclical, "On the Condition of Labor," were carried into effect our industrial society would be improved immeasurably.

# ❧ 137 ❧

# Judaism and the Industrial Crisis

## SIDNEY E. GOLDSTEIN

Highly trained in the social sciences, rabbi at the Free Synagogue in New York and, by the 1920s, Professor of Social Service at the Jewish Institute of Religion, Sidney E. Goldstein (1879-1955) played a prominent role in both social service organizations and government bodies concerned with the family and employment. Here he derives remarkably broad and radical interpretations from the prophets and Jewish codes for action in modern society.

---

The teachings of Judaism concerning industry and industrial problems are derived from the preaching of the prophets and also from the codes of Israel. We recognize the prophets as the earliest protagonists of social reform; but to the principles these teachers announce must be added the less known laws and commands found in the many codes Israel has constructed for guidance in the affairs of life. Both the laws of the codes and the principles of the prophets are, however, in turn the outgrowth of two fundamental facts, first, a passion for justice that is central to the faith of Israel; and second, a world experience that extends over forty centuries—an experience that has brought Israel into contact with many forms of life, nomad, agricultural and urban; with many systems of legislation, secular and sacred; with many different conceptions of civilization, in Asia, Africa, Europe and America. Out of this passion, unabated and unimpaired, enriched and intensified rather by our contacts and coöperations and conflicts with other social groups and conceptions of life, we have formulated our social program.

## Freedom

Israel began its history as a people with the Exodus. The escape from Egypt, the house of bondage, the miraculous emancipation from industrial servitude, has

Source: Sidney E. Goldstein, 'Judaism and the Industrial Crisis', *Annals of the American Academy of Political and Social Science*, Vol. 103, September 1922.
© 1922 by Sage Publications, Inc.

never faded from the heart of Israel. From year to year we recall this providential experience and reaffirm our faith in the lesson of freedom. No man shall live in slavery to his brother. Tyranny and autocracy are intolerable in human society. All men must be free, free to determine the conditions under which they are to live and to work.

The present attempt of small groups of men to deny to the mass of workers the right to organize in their own way, to elect and to speak through their own representatives, to decide for themselves the terms of employment, is violative of the elementary right of freedom. Judaism protests against the policy of the United States Steel Corporation because the chairman of the Executive Committee and his associates have established in the steel industry a state of industrial autocracy. They presume to dictate to three hundred thousand workers, over a million men, women and children, the conditions of labor and the standards of life. Judaism sympathizes with and supports the steel worker because we know from our own experience that not until the power of the Pharaohs has been broken will men be free to march forward to the land of promise. The people may perish in the wilderness, but it is far better to die in freedom than to live in slavery.

## Health

Another principal [sic] cardinal in Judaism is the sanctity of human life. This teaching is emphasized in every code and in every command. Human life must be guarded and preserved. Industry must be so organized and conducted that it will not endanger the life of men and women. Occupational diseases must be eliminated, industrial accidents must be prevented. The crippling of workers and the undermining of health is inexcusable. But more than this, industry must be so developed that it will promote and advance human life. Tuberculosis is a case in point. Tuberculosis is a disease of low resistance. The chief way to raise the resistance of men and women is to raise the standard of living. The chief way to raise the standard of living is to increase the income of the working class. The sudden drop in the mortality rate from tuberculosis during the last four years is due in part to campaigns of education, in part to reduced immigration, in part to the influenza epidemic that carried away many who would have died of tuberculosis, but the largest factor of all is the improved economic status of the laboring classes. To permit a form of industrial organization that jeopardizes life and that makes it impossible to outgrow the plagues that follow upon lowered resistance, physical and mental, is contrary to the teachings of Judaism that life is sacred and that it is our sacred duty to preserve and to promote the health of men and women and children.

## Rest

The third principle is found in the command to observe the Sabbath day and to keep it holy. In the Deuteronomic interpretation the reason given for the Sabbath is rest: rest from labor for the manservant, for the cattle and for the stranger within the gates, as well as the master of the household. But back of this Commandment there is a larger thought that is developed through the literature of Israel. Every man and woman must be assured the opportunity for rest and refreshment of both body and spirit. Judaism is not committed to the eight-hour day nor to the six-hour day, but it is committed, and this irrevocably, to the full development of all our powers, physical, mental and spiritual. No industry is properly organized that works men to the point of weariness and fatigue and exhaustion. No industry is organized in accordance with the teachings of Judaism that makes it impossible for the men engaged therein to increase knowledge and to cultivate character. The less time men spend in the darkness of the mine and the sweat of the factory and the monotony of the mill, the more time will these men have to spend in the library, the museum, the art gallery and the chamber of music. The invention of machinery must mean not greater profit for the employer and greater slavery for the worker, but the saving of hours and the release of energy for the cultivation of higher graces that come with education and culture and comradeship. These graces every man and woman should enjoy, not as a grant, but, according to the teachings of Judaism, as an inalienable and unquestioned right.

## Work

The importance and dignity of labor is the fourth thought constantly stressed in the Jewish faith. An ancient tale tells us that when God told Adam and Eve the earth would bring forth thorns and thistles they wept: when He added they would eat their bread in the sweat of their brow, they laughed and rejoiced. Nowhere is the teaching concerning the place that labor holds in the economy of human life so finely expressed as in the Apocryphal Book of Ben Sirach:

> Let us now praise famous men,
> Even the artificer and workmaster
> That passeth his time by night as by day;
> And is wakeful to finish his work.
> So is the smith sitting by the anvil,
> And considering the unwrought iron:
> The vapor of the fire wasteth his flesh,
> And in the heat of the furnace doth he wrestle with his work.
> All these put their trust in their hands,
> And each becometh wise in his own work,
> Yea, though they be not sought for in the council of the people,
> Nor be exacted in the ceremony;
> Nor shall men sojourn or walk up and down therein,

For these maintain the fabric of the world,
And in the handiwork of their craft is their prayer.

Any system of industry and industrial manangement that robs men of this sense of pride and joy in their own work and that fails to kindle in them the creative instinct and to inspire them with the service they are rendering society is contrary to the teachings of the Jewish faith.

## Fairness

The injunction against false balances, many times repeated in the codes of Israel, contains the fifth principle that applies to industry. There must be no defrauding, no exploitation, no profiteering. The consumer must be protected against the greed of the manufacturer and the merchant. The coal industry is here an illustration. It is difficult to ascertain the facts at present, but this much is clear, that those who control the mining and the transportation and the distribution of coal as a commodity have multiplied the unnecessary stages through which it must pass to such an extent that the increase in cost between the mine and the household is nothing less than exploitation and robbery. The difference between the cost of mining a ton of coal and the cost of delivery at the household cannot be explained in any other manner. It is a common excuse of the coal operators and their associates that the increase in cost is chargeable to labor. To charge the cost of coal to labor is an unwarrantable deception on the part of the operators. When labor is granted or wins an increase of 10 per cent in wages, the coal operators and the merchants add 30 percent or 40 percent to the cost of coal. A fair charge for service is reasonable and right, but an artificial and extortionate charge is a gross violation of the teaching of Judaism.

## Common Ownership

In the prophetic passage "Woe to those who join house to house and lay field unto field" is expressed the sixth principle that we emphasize. This passage is often quoted as a protest against monopoly, and that it is; but to those acquainted with the history of property and property rights in Israel, it contains a vaster message. The early Hebrews did not believe in the private ownership of land and water sources or of food supply. No individual could claim title to the pasture land, the wells and springs and the trees from which the community as a whole nourished itself. The title rested not with man but with God. The earth is the Lord's and all that is therein. Man is merely the trustee and custodian of what he holds. The resources of the world, in other words, must be used not selfishly for the enrichment of a few, but wisely in the service of all. The machinations of small groups today to control the wealth of the earth is contrary to the highest teachings of Judaism. One-tenth of the population must not possess nine-tenths of the treasures of the world. The community as a whole must own and control those great reservoirs of wealth upon which all men are ultimately dependent for their existence and progress.

A fundamental error of the present day is that we are organizing industry in accordance with the so-called laws of economics rather than in keeping with the principles of ethics. We are still under the unhappy spell of the teachings of the economists of the last generation. Francis Walker in his *Political Economy*, a book that became the economic Bible of those in control of our economic life, says quite frankly:

> The boundary line between ethical and economic inquiry is perfectly clear. The economist, as such, has nothing to do with the question whether existing institutions are right or wrong.

Judaism does not accept this teaching. We do not admit that the law of supply and demand is the last word in business and industry. It leads to unjust prices and to exploitation. No law can be final that leads to injustice. Judaism does not accept the doctrine of competition. It leads to unnecessary and unworthy struggle and strife and suffering in human relationships. Men are not to compete with each other for personal gain, but are to coöperate with each other for the common good. The whole science of economics needs to be reconstructed in accordance with ethics before it can serve as a guide in industry and commerce and finance. Judaism insists and has never ceased to teach the truth that not economics but ethics constitute the organic law of social life.

## Religion

The ultimate test of industry, Judaism teaches, is religious. How far and how fast does our present industrial system further the Kingdom of God? How fast is it inaugurating the age when injustice and oppression and misery will no longer be part of our social life? How far is it advancing the new order when every man, woman and child will rejoice in the fullness of strength, the widest development of mind and the highest cultivation of the spirit? This function industry cannot achieve until it organizes to do two things: First, to adequately maintain all those who labor, for the first charge upon industry is not dividends but the welfare of the workers; second, to serve society, for the primary purpose of industry is not to create profits but to meet the needs of men, to free them and to equip them for the larger life that is to be shared by all those who enter the Kingdom of God.

# ✥138✥

# The Workingman's Alienation
# from the Church

## H. FRANCIS PERRY

Though primitive in its methods, this survey of 1899 of the opinions of labour movement spokesmen and working people about the churches is revealing of attitudes which Social Gospel ministers were trying to overcome. The response of the ministerial author is noteworthy for its dismissal of criticisms of the churches as unjustified; he claims the workers themselves are responsible for their sense of alienation. The Social Gospel outlook was adopted by only a minority of ministers.

MY DEAR SIR: Will you do me the kindness to give me your aid in trying to solve a vexing problem? The problem is this: Why are so many intelligent workingmen non-churchgoers? It may be that the church can be of more service to the men of its community than it is at the present time. Will you please send me an answer, within a few days, to the questions submitted?

1. What reason would be given by your associates, who do not attend church, for their absence from the church?

2. What remedies would you propose to bring your associates into closer touch with the church?

Sincerely,<br>H. FRANCIS PERRY

The plan of this research has been to seek, from three classes of men, an answer to two central questions. Accordingly the above letter was sent to —

1. Representative leaders of the wage-earners.

2. Workingmen who are churchgoers.

3. Laboring men who are alienated from the church.

The response has been most cordial and gratifying. Of the three classes from which replies have been invited, I consider Class 1—the representative leaders of the wage-earners—to be the least important in reflecting the real relation of the

Source: H. Francis Perry, 'The Workingman's Alienation from the Church', *American Journal of Sociology*, March 1899.

workingman to the church, because there is here a possible professional bias.

The replies received were from Mr. Samuel Gompers, president of the American Federation of Labor; Mr. John B. Lennon, general secretary of the Journeymen Tailors' Union of America; Mr. M. M. Garland, fourth vice-president of the American Federation of Labor; Mr. John F. O'Sullivan, president of the central Labor Union of Boston; Rev. Herbert N. Casson, of the Labor Church, Lynn, Mass.; Miss Mary A. Nason, of Haverhill, Mass.; Mr. George H. Paige, treasurer of the H. & P. Engineers.

These replies offer several definite causes for the alienation in question. The most general is that the laboring man believes there is an alliance between the rich man, who oppresses him, and the church. Some comments touching this point are worth noticing:

> MR. GOMPERS.— My associates have come to look upon the church and the ministry as the apologists and defenders of the wrong committed against the interests of the people, simply because the perpetrators are possessors of wealth, . . . . whose real God is the almighty dollar, and who contribute a few of their idols to suborn the intellect and eloquence of the divines, and make even their otherwise generous hearts callous to the sufferings of the poor and struggling workers, so that they may use their exalted positions to discourage and discountenance all practical efforts of the toilers to lift themselves out of the slough of despondency and despair.
>
> MR. LENNON.—Workmen stay away from the church because their employers attend and control the church, and in their daily life, in shop and factory, the workman receives but little of Christian treatment from the employers.
>
> MR. GARLAND.—Workingmen find much difficulty in reconciling the religious fervor of the wealthy while at church with their attitude to their fellows in actual life.
>
> MR. O'SULLIVAN.—Believing, as I do, that employers are not all worth praying for, and disliking to pray for the prosperity of a "sweater," I do not go to church, even if I had the time to do so.
>
> REV. HERBERT M. CASSON.—The men who grind them in business are the ones whom they recognize in the front pews.
>
> MISS NASON.—The churches are not built by them, nor for them, but with money taken from them to be used against them.

The other causes, with explanatory extracts, follow:

> There is plenty of ecclesiasticism in churches, but there is little Christianity.
>
> MR. CASSON.—Workingmen are understanding better the teaching of Christ, and do not see any similarity between Christ and the church.
>
> MISS NASON.—Workingmen understand that Christianity is only another name for justice, love, and truth, and that churchianity is only another name for wrong, injustice, oppression, misery, and want. Then they take the two apart, and cheer the name of Jesus Christ and hiss the church, separating Christianity from churchianity; honoring the one, scouting the other.

The church is wrong in trying to reconcile present industrial circumstances with a normal and just theory of life:

> MISS NASON.—The cornerer, the syndicate, the trust, hold back the riches of earth, sea, and sky from their fellows who famish and freeze in the dark . . . . and

the effort of the church to reconcile the commercial morals of modern industrialism with the revelation of human law and life in Christ is treason to the kingdom of God in the eyes of most of my associates.

## The church does not treat living issues:

MR. CASSON —The church must base its right to existence on present usefulness, on character, and on living issues, and not on a past revelation and a future life. This we have done in our labor church, and have no trouble in reaching the masses.

## The church frowns upon trade unions:

MR. GOMPERS.—The means and methods which my associates have, by experience, learned to be particularly successful in maintaining their rights and securing improved conditions—i.e., organization of the trade unions—have been generally frowned down upon with contempt, treated indifferently, or openly antagonized by the ministers and the apparently staunch supporters of the church.

## Pew rents are an objection:

MR. CASSON.—They cannot pay for a front row pew, and are too self-respecting to take a back one.

## Church services are stale and uninteresting:

MR. PAIGE.—I don't find the average sermon preached in the churches interesting to the union workingmen. They are interested in a shorter working day, more pay for their labor, better homes to live in, and better conditions for their families and children in this world, which the church ignores.

MR. CASSON.—Church services are stale and uninteresting to practical or hungry men.

For these evils, four remedies are suggested:

The ministry must show their sympathy with the great struggling mass of workingmen. Mr. Grompers thinks that there is an honorable exception to the ministers of whom he has previously spoken in

The men who preach from their pulpits and breathe with every word their sympathy with the great struggling masses of humanity; . . . . these ministers you will find always interesting, and not only interesting, but the churches filled with the workers who go to hear them.

Mr. Lennon testifies that he himself is a churchgoer, and continues:

I believe the church will fill with workers and their families as soon as the church makes manifest its intention to help the masses to secure a better and more comfortable daily life.

## Give the workingmen the same rights and privileges which the rich enjoy:

MR. PAIGE.— If the church would let the workingmen have the same rights and privileges that the rich enjoy, the church would be too small to hold them all. Let the church help us fight some of our battles with the rich, and show it is friendly with the working classes.

Preach and study less theology and more social ethics:

MISS NASON.—Set the ministers earnestly to studying, not theology, nor creeds, but social economy and its bearing on morality . . . . until the church repents of its money-worship it is not a fit companion for the common people.

Miss Nason prescribes the last remedy suggested by the labor-leader class. It is a no less radical one than driving the rich out of the church altogether. In Miss Nason's own words she proposes

To drive the money-changers out of the temple.

Rev. Herbert N. Casson returns a reply still more startling. Mr. Casson despairs of any remedy until the church repents and is converted:

The church has nothing to give that we care to receive, and nothing to teach that we care to know. We are very well satisfied to have workingmen out of touch with the church. The church must learn before it can instruct.

The replies from workingmen who are churchgoers strike an entirely different note from the foregoing, as regards both cause and remedy. The causes assigned by this class are four in number:

1. Viciousness on the part of workingmen. A Christian workman writes:

In the present shop where I am some devote Sunday to worldly pleasure, and in the case of some it would interfere with vicious ways.

2. The result of poverty:

Some think they cannot pay for religious privileges, and cannot dress well enough to be present in the church.

3. The inconsistencies of Christian men. A deacon writes:

All that the majority of my daily associates know about the church is what they see in the lives of us who are Christians. The most frequent reason I receive for non-churchgoing is that there are as good people out of the church as in its membership. In other words, the apparent inconsistent lives of those who profess to love the church is an excuse most difficult to meet.

4. Indifference:

No real reason; they are more ready to bluff me when I invite them than to suggest any genuine reason for absence from the church.

The remedies proposed are:

More spiritual life and personal effort for non-churchgoers. Writes one correspondent:

Christians should be more spiritual in heart and life, and so be better fitted for personal effort with all classes.

Show that the church cares for the welfare of the workingman, not as a workingman, but as a man:

There is not much sympathy now between employers and employés; each is seeking to get the better of the other, and there is an impression that the church does not, as a body, care for workingmen, as distinguished from salaried men. I think if I were preaching I would not say much about classes, but of the pressing need for all men to seek salvation through Christ.

True living by Christians:

We must be sure and serve our earthly employers faithfully, not as eyeservants, but as honest Christians.

We next come to the most interesting and important evidence of all. Here we have neither the possible "professional bias" of the labor representative, nor the different point of view of the workingman within the church, but the alienated workman speaking for himself. We should here, if anywhere, strike the root of the matter.

In the replies received from this class, five causes of alienation appear: Loss of faith:

Men have grown hard under bitter conditions, and think of God as unjust and unkind, if there be any God.

Childhood training. A bookbinder replies:

Men do not go to church because they had so little training at home when they were children. If the Bible be not taught them at home and in Sunday school, they will not be found in church in later years.

Using Sunday for a rest and recreation:

It is the disposition of many to make Sunday a day of recreation.
The churches are opposed to the workingman,

writes one man,

inasmuch as the church opposes Sunday newspapers, Sunday threaters, the Sunday opening of libraries, and every other reform of the kind that would benefit the laboring class.

Too much theology and too little practical preaching:

There is too much theology and not enough plain gospel truth in the sermon. This theology is beyond the comprehension of the workingman. He has no interest in it.

Many men who do not go to church claim that it is because they honestly believe that theology is a scheme gotten up to turn the poor man's thought away from the present life to some dim, mysterious future world where all his sufferings here will be made up for, and in this way to prevent his trying to better himself and his class by overthrowing the system of slavery which our present method of business entails.

The ministers and churches have but little interest in the workingman:

Wage-earners fail to attend church because ministers of the various churches fail to visit their homes. The wage-earner has an idea that, while all ministers will be courteous to him, they give all their time to the richer members of the church. They claim that the church is doing nothing positive to help them in their difficulties.

The churches are sustained by rich men who grind their workmen.

We are interested more in the getting of food, raiment, and the paying of our rent than in the future life. We want a heaven on earth instead of a heaven after death. Jesus Christ is with us outside the church, and we shall prevail with God.

Other comments on this point are in a bitterer vein:

The church has, as an organized body, no sympathy with the masses. It is a sort of fashionable club where the rich are entertained and amused, and where most of the ministers are muzzled by their masters and dare not preach the gospel of the carpenter of Nazareth.

The unjust and inequitable manner in which the commercial class, which sustains and supports the churches for its own selfish purposes, has treated them, causes the laboring men to have nothing to do with the churches.

As one of the leaders has expressed it:

The American workingman hates the very shadow that the spire of the village church casts across his pathway.

The church is too fashionable a place for the poor clothing which I must wear,

is the conviction of another.

## Remedies

Apply the Sermon on the Mount:

Have courage to apply the Sermon on the Mount to the social order of today.

The ministers of the church must make themselves familiar with the social and economic questions of the day:

Let the ministers study economics. Let them thoroughly inform themselves upon the labor question; then let them talk upon these things and not upon dead issues, such as those concerning Jonah and Lot.

Preach Christianity instead of theology. Preach of a heaven on earth:

Advocate and teach a heaven on earth.

Let the pastor have a personal relation with the needs of labor. Be our champion. Visit the laboring man and study his needs:

Ministers should mingle more freely with the poor and less with the rich. By doing so you can come in contact with the person, and can better judge for yourself of the best way of inducing him to attend church.

Why should I wish to go into a $200,000 church and listen to a minister who gets perhaps $3,000 a year for preaching one sermon a week, denouncing the poor railroad man who is striking that his brother-worker should have $2 per day?

You must have their temporal welfare at heart and understand the great questions that interest them as nothing else can until these are settled.

Let the minister of the gospel visit the homes of the non-churchoers. I believe many fail to attend church because the ministers fail to visit their homes.

It is interesting to notice here a cry from laboring man in Newton, Mass., who echoes a sentiment we have already heard from Rev. Herbert N. Casson:

> I would propose no remedy, and have no hope of social reform through the church as it exists today.

I have thus far given in detail many of the anwers received in my research. None of the bitter things have been suppressed. The submitted declarations are a fair résumé of the opinions received. Five indictments are made against the church:

1. The church is subsidized by the rich. The minister is, consequently, tongue-tied. The rich man's influence is so powerful that anything which would arouse his conscience will never unwisely escape the preacher's lips.

While these charges are doubtless true of a few so-called churches and of a very few preachers, yet we know scores and hundreds of men who would resign a pulpit at once where there was a command, either open or implied, to padlock their lips in the presentation of truth. It is culpable beyond ordinary cowardice for a preacher of righteousness to sell his conviction for gold, and such a man would be frowned out of the fellowship of the ministers of any community.

2. The ministry discusses themes which are stale and flat. They are not living issues.

This is thoroughly false to the genuine spirit of the church. The pulpit teaches preparation for this world's conflicts and temptations, as well as safety in a future world. These themes ought not to be stale and flat to the earnest man.

3. The ministry is not well enough informed on economic and social questions.

To this we plead guilty in part. Social science is a new study, and could not be found in the college curriculum ten or fifteen years ago. To have studied economics or ethics years ago is not now to be informed in sociology. To study the labor movement as the ordinary laboring man glances at it would be far from satisfactory.

4. The workingman is not welcome in the churches of the land.

This is a mistake on the part of wage-earners. Some churches may be icy toward him, but these are the isolated exception, not the rule.

5. The church is not aggressive enough in assisting the workingman to secure his rights.

Grant all the necessary exceptions to the rule, and deduct considerable for sluggishness in the performance of duty, and even then the fact remains that most of those who unselfishly are aiding the causes of humanity are Christian men, and a large proportion of these are ministers. In considering the causes dear to the wage-earner which are left unaided by the church, the difficulty often is that the postulates of the workingman are so wide of the truth that the church cannot champion them. It is not true that men are in a prison-house and the church is holding the key. The church may be depended upon to lead in securing justice and truth. It must also warn the workingman that his alienation often results from tendencies within himself rather than within the church. The Jesus who is applauded by the average workingman is a minimized Jesus Christ, a fictitious person, not the Christ of the gospels.

## ⟨⟩·139·⟨⟩

# Great Central Parishes and their Neighborhood Ministries

## ROSS W. SANDERSON

By the 1950s, churches in the centres of cities often felt the need to justify themselves through the social services they provided and the community activities they encouraged. The structures through which they operated were often interdenominational. This trend sometimes prompted the question as to whether churches had adapted too easily to the secular demands of society in order to retain a hold on the population.

---

First of all, this study seeks to document the fact that not every central city church neglects its neighborhood, however great the temptation to do so. Not all centrally located churches are rich; many of them are without adequate endowment. A few, by reason of accumulated capital funds, are able to spend twice as much as or more than they could without such exceptional resources. Among these is a historic parish, now presented as

## Case I—Trinity Church, Boston

Among the recognizably great churches of America is Trinity Church, Boston. Always associated with the name of Phillips Brooks, is it indelibly stamped with his spirit.

In 1869, at the age of 33, Phillips Brooks came to Boston from Philadelphia to be pastor of Trinity Church. Organized in 1729, as an offshoot of King's Chapel, Trinity was worshiping at its Summer Street location, near Washington Street, in a building erected in 1829. Soon came the fire, and the move to Copley Square was accelerated. The new rector labored for years in the erection of a great building and became one of the greatest preachers in the world; but when he came to Boston, according to his biographer, A. V. G. Allen, "a significant change in his

Source: Ross W. Sanderson, 'Great Central Parishes and their Neighbourhood Ministeries',
*The Church Serves the Changing City*, New York, 1955, pp. 20–5, 39–43.

ministry" had occurred. Here "he sought to know the people to whom he preached, to study their needs, to share in their joys, to lead them into larger conceptions of the mission of a parish to the church and to the world."

A colleague "had an appointment to meet him at the rectory at eight o'clock. . . . Not until nearly eleven did Mr. Brooks return. . . . He had been detained at a hospital by a colored man who had been injured in some affray and had sent for him." When a dying colored girl sent for him on Sunday morning, an assistant was sent to explain "why he was unable to come. But the assistant returned with the message that the girl had declared she would not die until he came. When the service was over Mr Brooks himself went according to the request."

"He had a great gift for inspiriting people who were depressed or had lost heart for their work. A word from him would send them back to their tasks again with renewed energy. . . . The letters he wrote to people in affliction, if gathered together, would form a considerable volume. He seemed to attract them, as he did the poor, the sick, the outcast, by some force which he did not consciously exercise, and yet of whose existence he was aware."

That was the kind of man he was. That is the sort of tradition he left. Is it not the authentic opportunity of the church in the inner city, now as then?

Succeeding rectors have included such men as the presiding bishop of the Protestant Episcopal Church, Rt. Rev. Henry Knox Sherrill, and the present pastor (since 1942), the Rev. Theodore P. Ferris. Men like these do not merely use the Prayer Book words concerning "all sorts and conditions of men"; they tune their ministry to the needs of all those whom it is their privilege to serve, both those of the neighborhood and those of the wider community in which their leadership is exercised. Such men unavoidably become nation-wide figures. Such churches are city-wide parishes; Trinity attracts regular Sunday attendance from as far away as Providence, which is 48 minutes from Boston's South Station by the fastest New Haven train.

Roughly Trinity Parish is said to consist of three concentric circles: first, a fifth or more of the total constituency, those who live within a mile of Copley Square; second, maybe three-fifths of the total, those who live within fifteen or twenty minutes by public transportation, or less by private automobile—in Brookline, Cambridge, or other close-in communities; and third, approximately the final fifth, who reside on the outer rim—in Needham, Dedham, Wellesley, the Newtons, Wakefield, Reading, and other places just inside, outside, or astride Route 128, the circumferential highway that roughly bounds an area with a fifteen-mile radius (sometimes less) from the State House dome. By car, coming in along any one of the spokes, even from this far rim, to the center of the Hub is a matter of half an hour or so. Accordingly six or eight boys may travel twice a week to Trinity Church choir rehearsals, as well as on Sundays, from a town on the outer edge of the metropolitan district. This is a typically metropolitan parish. Then, too, at a church like this there are always a host of visitors from all parts of the nation, and of the wider world, attracted by a historic spot and a famous pulpit.

By and large, parishioners who live farthest out may have the best economic status, or at least enjoy the best living conditions for families with children. In the second or closer-in circle there are people in fine houses or comfortable and expensive apartments, and people in quite other neighborhoods, just as loyal to Trinity but materially at the other end of the spectrum. Then within walking distance there are all sorts of parishioners. Between the church and the Charles there are still some well-to-do people, but nowadays rooming houses are more characteristic of the area. Such territory houses many people who have known better days economically, now living frugally but representing all that is best in New England culture. Others are young people, mature students and couples on their way up, who in due time will arrive; for the moment, their resources are sometimes as limited as their hopes are legitimately high.

Across the tracks it may be quite different. Boston's South End is an area of vanished glory. From its earlier high residential status many a family has migrated, first to the Back Bay, later to the suburbs. Here, too, however, are many of Trinity's parishioners.

Accordingly Trinity's parish is cosmopolitan. It draws important people, "proper Bostonians," from many miles; it also serves people not yet important, including students (graduate and undergraduate) from the region's numerous colleges and universities; and it ministers lovingly too to many persons who never were important and maybe never will be, persons stranded in little urban pockets, with the great city swirling all around them. Perhaps three out of four, maybe four out of five, are persons referred to the parish by the diocese, by individuals, by groups or agencies, all of whom have come to know that Trinity is set in the heart of the metropolis to be as one who serves—or maybe they just came in on their own. Fortunately there is a modest endowment which enables the staff to be more helpful than they could be without this resource.

These days, however, such money does far more than meet the emergency needs of individuals. Trinity does not do social work that can be better done by established social agencies. What Trinity seeks to do is to become the sort of friend who can put at the command of the individual or family all the resources of a highly organized urban community. One of the clergy makes it his business to know who can help, and in what manner. Requests from Trinity can often expedite the slow process of social work or governmental agency. Sometimes a lay person or couple can provide just the lift needed—of counsel or "know-how."

In Boston everybody knows about Trinity. It has prestige. When it makes a request, it is a reasonable one, humane and understanding. It seeks not favors for its own, but assistance for those who need it. As a result, everybody lends a hand, wherever possible.

This is not the place to rehearse specific kinds of needs that Trinity has to face. Occasionally the need is just plain financial. Without help, *now*, not next week, somebody will be evicted. On their own resources alone, a couple may not be able to put a bright youngster through school. More often, even when there is economic need, the real trouble goes deeper. Personal counseling is largely used. The rector is accessible, and does his full share of this part of the parish work. When he passes a person along to a colleague, it is because in the particular instance the colleague happens to know the available resources better. Nobody gets the "run-around" if he comes in real quest of help.

Once in a while it turns out that a situation is of a sort that keeps recurring. At this point Trinity can help organize a civic force, bigger and broader than itself, inclusive perhaps of Roman Catholic and Jew, to fill a gap in the social work structure. Here Trinity has the tremendous advantage, far more important than its material assets, of being able to command some of the ablest personnel in Massachusetts as volunteers, only part of them from its own membership. Trinity has become known as a place from which new needs are seen, new agencies are incubated, new social competence is organized. In at least two cases, its sincere request for help has enabled much-needed new civic groups to get started, make a demonstration of their worth, and take their place in the fabric of the larger community life. Several other opportunities seem now to be ripening. One need may be adequately met by processes already under way; but if not and a new agency proves desirable, Trinity could spark-plug another program, during the critically determinative period of its infancy. Of course, behind all the referrals or the organization of new agencies is the long, patient, face-to-face contact of clergyman or other parish worker with parishioner—or, perhaps in four cases of five, with the stranger whose sole reason for appealing to Trinity is his sheer sense of need. The applicant may be referred to this agency or that, or to this expert or that, but always it is with the firm friendliness of a parish that seeks to be neighborly in the midst of a city's loneliness and desperate personal inadequacy.

This chapter does not attempt to tell picturesque details of what in the nature of the case is confidential. It seeks not at all to praise the work of this one parish for what it seeks to do. Trinity itself is deeply convinced that it is only trying as best it can to serve all the children of God who look to it for guidance, mindful of the fact that God loves them all, alike. Students from the ends of the earth are made welcome. Among worshipers, neither color nor status bars one from the church's ministry. Rich as it is, and famous, this is a house of God for *all* people—in deep intent and in practice recognized by all those who seek to serve humanity in this seaboard city. What Trinity seeks to do, it regards as normative for any church similarly located in any city: to minister to all who come, from wherever, for whatsoever reason.

It will be understood, of course, that these brief pages have made no effort to describe the work of Trinity's varied parish organizations, or even to present its worship and preaching ministry. As in scores of churches, in Boston and in other cities, the fact that its pulpit is literally of nation-wide significance only adds to the contribution it makes to the residents of the neighborhood. Of all that the central church does to serve its local community, no factor is more outstanding than its ability to reach people through the sermons of an able preacher. None of his Trinity staff associates would be willing to have the homiletical excellence of the rector's ministry overlooked. Dr Ferris continues a great pulpit tradition.

## Case II—The Baptist Christian Center, Milwaukee

In 1890, on Milwaukee's South Side, then an elite residential area, the largest Baptist church in the city was housed in the building now chiefly used as a Christian Center. In 1923, when the South Church moved farther out, a small group of people stayed on in the old building. From them started both the Center and the present Hulburt Church.

The State Convention helped, and the national Woman's Home Mission Society provided a worker. In 1934 Rev. C. Dwight Klinck came as director of the Center, which is located at 611 West Washington Street, at the corner of South Sixth Street. He stayed until 1946. To meet an obvious community need the church auditorium was remodeled to make both a gymnasium and a chapel. The latter was rented to the Hulburt Baptist Church, which is a separate organization, named after a state Baptist executive. In 1942 the Center was incorporated and became part of the War Chest; and in 1946 it was accepted as one of the "Red Feather" services of the Community Council of Milwaukee County. (This is placarded on the outside of the building.) Since 1942 the two budgets (church and Center) have been separated.

The membership of the Center was recently found to be

> 50 per cent Roman Catholic
> 25 per cent Lutheran
> 9 per cent Baptist
> 3 per cent Methodist
> 2 per cent Episcopal
> 6 per cent other Protestant
> 5 per cent no church preference

The Center does all it can to encourage its constituents to observe the festival days of the Christian Year in accordance with the various church connections.

The articles of incorporation provided that the purpose of the Center should be to "develop better citizenship and the more abundant life as we find it in the life and message of Jesus Christ: and to that end to provide facilities for leisure-time activities, contacts with home, a spirit of Christian friendliness and helpfulness, and community programs: and to promote interest and activity in the community, city, state, national and world affairs."

The nominees for the membership of the exceptionally strong Board of Directors must be approved by the executive committee of the Wisconsin Baptist State Convention, and at least two-thirds of them must be members of Baptist churches (Articles IV).

Article VIII provides: "The person who is appointed by the Wisconsin Baptist State Convention in conjunction with the American Baptist Home Mission Society as Director of the Milwaukee Christian Center shall have general supervision of the work for which the coporation is responsible; and such Director shall be elected a member of the Board of Directors of the corporation and shall be an ex-officio member of all its committees."

The purpose of the Center, as publicized in recent annual reports, is now formulated thus:

> 1. To develop among children, youth, and adults a sound and practical attitude toward life, and a belief and conviction that the Christian way of life is The Way of Life.
> 2. To help our members to understand what democracy means, and to give them practice in democratic living through the group process.
> 3. To provide opportunities to develop creative interests, abilities, and skills through various crafts and hobby groups, such as ceramics, wood, metal, leather, photography, cooking, sewing, and hooked rugs.
> 4. To develop the leadership abilities of our members and to show them how to use these abilities in the Center and community.

Since 1946 Rev. John A. Craig has been director; he is also pastor of Hulburt Church. Mr Craig served as a chaplain in the Marine Coprs and has had experience in a Kansas City, Missouri, Center. Associated with him are three group workers, an office secretary and several assistants, part-time and custodial personnel, and 24 volunteers, some of them students: a total of thirty persons.

The Center serves all ages, from three-year-olds up through the Golden Age Club for people over sixty years of age, which just celebrated its eighth anniversary. Six different age brackets are recognized, with different-colored membership cards for each. A busy schedule of activities features gymnasium and other classes (and weekly movies), from 3:30 (or 1:30) to bedtime, five days a week, also Saturady morning, afternoon, and evening. There are four two-week sessions of summer day camp.

The staff members visit in the churches, and church groups visit the Center. The director is active in Milwaukee social work and is studying for a master's degree in group work at the University of Wisconsin School of Social Work. The Center belongs to the National Federation of Settlements. Recent improvements in the building include two new furnaces and new basement facilities (a new game room accommodating up to 75). A new building is dreamed of, some day. If there were large-scale new housing, the whole situation might be somewhat changed.

In 1952–1953 the enrollment was heaviest in the 11–13-year bracket, and among adults:

| Years of Age | Number |
|---|---|
| 3 to 5 | 95 |
| 6 to 8 | 167 |
| 9 to 11 | 230 |
| 12 to 13 | 158 |
| 14 to 17 | 143 |
| 18 and up | 215 (chiefly adults) |

The economic status of the in-migrant residents is down, there is an increase of the "no church preference" type, and the returned copies of a monthly mimeographed "Leaf" show an increase turnover in population, or mobility rate. A weekly one-page bulletin, "The Bud," lists the gymnasium schedule for the ensuing week each Friday.

The emphasis is shifting. For example, an item in the October 1953, "Leaf" declares

### The Club Is the Thing

The days of big mass activities at our Center are over. We are placing most of our emphasis upon the friendship club. This year we have close to 30 of these group meetings each week.

This change in policy may account in part for a drop in organized club attendance, which climbed from 4,224 in 1946 to 9,991 in 1949, but dropped to 8,568 in 1951, as well as for the increase to 9,066 in 1953. (Total attendance of groups with definite enrollment amounted to 21,595; including individuals and groups without enrollment, last year's contacts numbered 64,267.)

The same issue of the "Leaf" contained the following editorial paragraph:

### Do You Teach Religion Here?

"Do you teach religion?" is a question that we are often asked. To answer such a question, we must know what the person asking the question means by religion. Does he mean some particular creed, some denominational doctrine, such as Lutheran, Methodist, Catholic, etc.? If so, the answer would be no. If the person means by religion the difference between right and wrong, that the Christian philosophy is the way of life, the rights of others, the Golden Rule, the brotherhood of man and the Fatherhood of God, then we must plead guilty. Those are the principles on which our democracy is founded. These are the principles that unite people. Our Settlement House is to help people to learn to live together happily.

The Center's treasurer reports the following main items of income for the last fiscal year:

| | | |
|---|---:|---|
| American Baptist Home Mission Society $ | 2,030.62 | ⎫ |
| Woman's Baptist Home Mission Society | 1,800.00 | ⎬ 17.5 per cent |
| Wisconsin Baptist State Convention | 1,880.04 | ⎭ |
| Rent from Hulburt Baptist Church | 450.00 | ⎫ |
| Fees and sales | 4,428.36 | ⎬ 14.9 per cent |
| Contributions | 510.85 | ⎫ |
| Contributions for specific purposes | 485.35 | ⎬ 3.1 per cent |
| Community Chest | 21,062.00 | 64.5 per cent |
| | $32,647.22 | 100.0 per cent |

It will now be of value to consider briefly the locale of this work. The Center is located in Block 23 of Census Tract 113 on Milwaukee's near South Side. To the east is Census Tract 114; to the south, 116; to the west, 112 and 117. A summary of some of the 1950 census data of these five tracts will characterize the immediate neighborhood objectively.

The total population for the five was 23,268— as a whole almost equally divided between the sexes, but with more males in Tract 113, and especially Tract 114. Foreign-born included Yugoslavs (754), Austrians (428), Germans (420), Poles (418), and Mexicans (161). In three tracts (112, 113, 114), Yugoslavs and Austrians predominated; in the other two, Germans and Poles. The number of Mexicans has increased rapidly since 1950; and these have been mostly adults, to whom a larger number of children have been born in this country.

The nonwhite population in 1950 was only 120 for the five tracts; only 12 of these nonwhites were Negroes.

# Moral Behaviour and Political Action: Religion and Prohibition

The crusade of the praying women against the saloons, Ohio, 1874

Plate 15: *The Crusade of the praying women against the saloons, Ohio*, 1874.

## ꙮ140ꙮ

# Messages to the Women's Christian Temperance Union

## FRANCES E. WILLARD

In the late nineteenth century, intemperance became the main issue of personal moral behaviour in politics; it was put there largely through the efforts of the Women's Christian Temperance Union. They pressed the view that a sober nation could be most effectively secured through legal prohibition of the sale of intoxicating liquor. Since temperance linked the condition of the family, the designated sphere of female responsibility, with politics, the temperance crusade provided a major opportunity for religious women to expand their activities in the public world. One of the most formidable of them was Frances E. Willard (1839–1898) who rose rapidly in the W.C.T.U. from 1874 onwards and who linked her temperance activities to the politics of women's suffrage. She pursued both on essentially moral and religious grounds.

---

At the convention of 1885, which was the largest and best convention which had ever been held up to that time, she again devoted a part of her address to "Our Relations to Politics,"

> Eighteen state legislatures, the majority of them Republican, have voted down the proposition of a Prohibition constitutional amendment. . . . We want the Democratic party to bite the dust and will do our utmost for its final overthrow. It is the enemy of our cause, and we pronounce upon it the "anathema maranatha" of the American home. Nor can we do less to that degenerate party which some of us once loved but of which the Brewers' League declared, "It has been in power for twenty-five years and has done for us all we have asked." In Ohio its platform would give the liquor traffic a permanent legal status; in New York it places two men formerly connected with the liquor traffic at the head of its ticket; in Pennsylvania it denies the prayer of the temperance men; in Illinois it is locked with the liquor abomination as one soul. The two old parties are nationally the two sworn allies of the saloon. The White Ribbon army is the open enemy of both,

Source: Frances E. Willard, 'Messages to the W.C.T.U.', in D. Leigh Colvin, (ed.), *Prohibition in the United States*, London, 1926, pp. 284–9.

while the new movement, which from the disintegrating forces of the old gathers out the best material for a new party, is the one that has our prayers, our hopes, our loyalty. . . .

Do we attain our object by working for something else? Does not our non-partisanship help the two old parties? Do we aid the new political movement that will tackle the liquor traffic and afterward shackle it, by remaining strictly non-partisan? If, as we have repeatedly declared by resolutions, State and National, such a movement ought to be, is it not our duty to help it to be? But the question will be asked, "Just what have we, as a National Union, done for the Prohibition party and what do we propose to do?" I answer, we have simply let it be known that we have discovered that the saloon is entrenched in politics even more firmly than in law and our sympathies, appreciation and gratitude must necessarily go with the voters who carry this issue straight to the caucus, the convention and the ballot box, voting only for men who are pledged to give us prohibition. . . .

Some of our friends urge us to be non-partisan because we have always been non-sectarian. But the cases are not parallel. We are differently related to churches from what we are to politics. Moral suasion methods alone apply to our efforts with denominations as such. Nothing in the Methodist creed antagonizes the Temperance Reform, nor does anything in the Catholic, the Universalist or Baptist. Hence we can be strictly non-sectarian and yet wholly consistent.

But something in the Democratic creed does specifically antagonize the Temperance Reform and the same is true of the Republican in the proportion that we analyze its record. There are exceptions in that party at the North as in the other at the South. But the Prohibition party creed coincides exactly with ours. Hence, we cannot, in my judgement, be consistently non-partisan, standing in an attitude of equal friendship towards politicians who deny, who ignore and who espouse the cause of Prohibition.

How could the W. C. T. U. of Ohio remain neutral when one party declared for license, another for tax and a third for prohibition; when the Democratic platform was unequivocally committed to the liquor interests and in Cincinnati six hundred saloon-keepers in convention assembled voted to support the Republican ticket? It seems to me, had the women of the Crusade kept silent, the very stones would have cried out against their inconsistency. . . .

At first we assailed the saloon itself with a directness and courage unparallelled in history. Later when we found the saloon to be entrenched in law, we followed it straight to city council room and legislative hall; and at last when its hidings of power were discovered to be in politics we followed it there, as brave soldiers always pursue their enemy even to its forts and fastnesses. We are crusaders as truly as when the outward and visible saloon itself was our objective point; only now we have grown wiser and carry our crusade straight to the brain, the heart and the conscience of the individual voter praying him to represent his home constituency and to stand at the ballot-box for prohibition first, last and always.

Again in 1886 Miss Willard in her annual presidential address said:

We are firmly persuaded that the separation of the people into distinct armies, one voting for men who will outlaw the poison curse and the other for men who would legalize it, must come and that separation cannot come too soon. Today the sheep and goats are mixed, and that is not the method of a wise shepherd. Today the temperance people are a mob and not an army, save as the drums beat, the recruiting goes forward and the battle is being set in array by our brave brothers, the political Prohibitionists. God bless them in these crucial hours! Their work is slow and hard and thankless—harder than the Crusade itself. Indeed, I think of them as the Crusaders of the present, worthy sires and sons of women brave and true.

The same pulpits and papers that were most bitter against the women in Ohio in 1874 are the bitterest against the Prohibition voters of 1886. To recruit and drill an army is the gigantic task to which they have set their heroic hands. Wisely have they turned aside from the armies of the past whose watchword is, in Pennsylvania, "Give the platform to the temperance people and the candidates to the saloons" ; and in New Hampshire and Vermont, "Favor the law but wink at non-enforcement."

An old campaigner whom I met at Lake George said, "We tried hard to get the Whig party to take up our anti-slavery cause and many of its members wanted to do so but then you see Alexander H. Stephens was a Whig." There was the whole argument in a nutshell. Let me paraphrase it. "We tried hard at the North to get the Republican party to take up our anti-slavery cause of temperance, and many of its members wanted to do so, but then, you see, Gottlieb, the brewer, is a Republican and so is Herman Raster, the politician."

Using the theme, "The New Politics," in 1887, Miss Willard in a section of her presidential address held up a standard of Christian principles in politics with a sublimity which has seldom been equalled.

Some brave men, longer in the work than we, discerned about fifteen years ago that the curse had coiled itself up in every caucus, darted its venom into every county, district, state and national political convention in all the land and had thrown the two great political parties into such abject fright that the Kingdom of Christ, "which must enter the realm of law through the gateway of politics," as our own Mary T. Lathrap has said, was effectively kept out and Satan was victoriously barred in. We then most earnestly and prayerfully studied the subject of the Christian versus the saloon politician and learned that to offset the influence and ballot of the one we must have the ballot and influence of the other. We found that legislation against the curse could never be expected from the old parties because self-preservation is the first law of nature, and each of these parties had a liquor vote large enough to defeat it at the polls. We learned that it was not enough to have a prohibitory law, the penalties of which were sufficiently heavy to make the investment in alcoholic stimulants unsafe, but we must have a judiciary that was not controlled by the saloons in its decisions, and enforcing officers who were true to the cause and to their oaths, and besides all this we must have a party in power that would defeat any officer that was false to Prohibition. We learned that as our great and lamented leader, John B. Finch, has said: "No party will do right if you give it your vote when it does wrong."

And so the cry ran all along the line, "To your tents, O Israel, come out from among them and be ye separate and touch not the unclean thing."

He who votes for the saloon politician, or the saloon politician's candidate is as bad as he who votes for the saloon itself. There are enough temperance men in America, if they will come off the sinking old hulks of the past and join the crew on our new steamship *Prohibition*, to bring us into the harbor of deliverance.

There are not enough anti-saloon Republicans in the North to carry prohibition in a single state that is now struggling to secure it, nor enough anti-saloon Democrats in the South, as has been proved in this memorable year of our Constitutional defeats, but there are enough temperance men in both to take possession of the government and give us national prohibition in the party of the near future which is to be the party of God. When will good men see their duty? When will they set their faces to the dawn? When will they heed the piteous cry from women whom they love and trust, "How long, O Lord, how long?" We pray heaven to give them no rest, to banish sleep from their eyelids and peace from their hearts until they shall forever part company with the treacherous leaders who deceive and the traitorous saloon voters who betray them, lift the white banner of the party that declares for home protection and saloon destruction, swear an oath of allegiance to Christ in politics and march in one great army "up to the polls to worship God."

The Bible is the most political of books. It recognizes more clearly than any other that God must rule in politics, else the devil surely will. I firmly believe that the patient, steadfast work of Christian women will so react upon politics within the next generation that the party of God will be at the fore; ministers will preach it from their pulpits, and Christian men will be as much ashamed to say that they never go to the caucus as they would be now to use profane language or defame character; for there is just one question that every Christian ought to ask, "What is the relation of this party, this platform, this candidate to the setting up of Christ's kingdom on earth? How does my vote relate to the Lord's Prayer?"

The answer to this question is sacred, not secular, worthy to be given from the pulpit on the Sabbath day. In the Revolutionary War, the question at issue being religious liberty, our forefathers felt that they could preach and pray about it on the Sabbath. In the Civil War, both sides, believing their cause to be holy, could do the same, and now, when it is a question of preserving the Sabbath itself and guarding the homes which are the sanctuaries of Christ's gospel, we women believe that no day is too good, no place is too consecrated, for the declaration of principles and the determining of votes.

The ascetic in the olden time shut himself away from the world and counted everything secular except specific acts of devotion. The Christian soldier of today reverses the process and makes everything he does a devotional act, an expression of his loyalty to Christ—so finding his balance in God that no sin can overcome and no sorrow surprise him. Prayer is the pulse of his life; there is no secular, no sacred, all is in God, and as the followers of Bruce enclosed that hero's heart in a silver shrine and flung it into the ranks of the enemy so that they might fly to win it back, shouting, "Heart of Bruce, I follow thee," so Christian men today take their ideal of Christ in government, hurl it into the ranks of His foes and hasten on to regain it, by rallying for the overthrow of saloon politics and the triumph of the Christian at the polls.

Our prayers are prophetic and predict the day of glad deliverance as being at the door. The man who, in presence of such possibilities, says, "I don't want to throw away my vote," is quite likely to throw away something even more valuable— and that is the voter himself. For as Miss West has said, "Today Christ sits over against the ballot-box as of old He sat over against the treasury and judges men by what they cast therein."

# ❦ 141 ❦

# Public Life and Social Reform

## JAMES CANNON JR.

James Cannon Jr. (1864-1944) was a theologically conservative southern Methodist clergyman who gave aggressive leadership to the prohibition cause in Virginia and nationally through the Anti-Saloon League. His sketch of early encounters with drunkenness is typical of the formula in much temperance literature. The young minister's sermon which represented him facing down sinful saloon keepers and drinkers illustrates Cannon's assimilation of the prohibition cause to evangelical preaching.

Through nearly fifty years of more or less troublous, tempestuous, tempting times I have been kept steady by the fact that I desired absolutely nothing in the way of political office or honor. All my work in public life has been in behalf of some social or moral reform. Such activity as I may have engaged in in the political sphere other than that which is the duty of any good citizen has been to accomplish what I conceived to be some moral purpose. When legislation has been necessary to secure the desired result, the opponents of such legislation have not hesitated to endeavor to becloud the issue, to ascribe false and selfish motives, and to go to the extreme of denunciation, abuse, slander, and even persecution.

Doubtless many mistakes have been made in the activities of these years, but notwithstanding persistent, vindictive, and fierce attacks by individuals, newspapers, hostile political and ecclesiastical groups, even with the aid of prejudiced court officials, all have utterly failed to show that I ever desired any political office or that any personal profit ever accrued to me from any of these activities in behalf of social reforms.

Rum, Romanism, and Bourbonism—the last in personal, public, and church life—at various times and in various ways have organized to defeat the work which I have tried to do, even if it involved my own personal destruction. That no one of them, nor all of them combined have been able to destroy me has not

James Cannon Jr. 'Public Life and Social Reform', *Bishop Cannon's Own Story*, Durham, N.C., 1955, pp. 108-11.

been because of my superior abilities, but because of the inability of my opponents to show at any time any motive for the work which I was doing other than the openly declared aim of that work.

While sometimes taxed to the extreme limit of financial, physical, mental, and spiritual ability, during all these years I have never had the slightest doubt as to the final outcome of these personal attacks. Knowing all the facts, I knew that the proper presentation of the facts would disprove, indeed wipe out, all the charges of my opponents. In the pages which follow I shall endeavor to present, as fairly and impartially as I can, the real facts concerning my public life and relation to social and moral reforms.

In the preceding pages the background has been given which made possible if not probable the years which were to follow. The roots which developed the fruitage of later years sprang naturally from the circumstances and associations of my childhood and youth. The barroom across from my boyhood bedroom, involving the death of my beloved uncle, the personal contact with the homes and families of drunkards, the callousness of saloonkeepers, [knowledge of] which came from going the weekly rounds with my mother in her errands of mercy; above all, the teaching and example of my father and mother—these had led me already, in my childhood and youth, to despise the liquor traffic. My experiences with drunken college classmates, my work in connection with the *Southern Crusader* in the Virginia campaign for local option, and my teaching of children in a Band of Hope at Princeton, had confirmed and strengthened the convictions of my boyhood.

But it was when I became a pastor that I was obliged to face the question of my personal responsibility, not only for the personal habits of the members of my churches but for the responsibility of those same members for the existence of the licensed liquor traffic in the community. It was easy to preach on the evils of drunkenness and the importance of total abstinence. It was not quite so easy to preach plainly and positively upon the selfish, unchristian conduct of men in selling intoxicants to steal away their neighbors' brains, especially when, in all my congregations, there were liquor sellers, members in good standing in other churches. But I did do such preaching.

I soon became convinced, however, that my responsibility did not stop with preaching against dramshops and drunkenness. Liquor licenses in the various neighborhoods where I preached were all granted at the discretion of the county judge, but he could refuse to grant a license upon the petition of the people in the neighborhood where the dramshop was to be located. I waited until I had collected my facts as to the location of the saloons in my circuit: the amount of drunkenness, the families affected, the number of church members living near each saloon, the names of the people who signed the petition to the judge for the license, and other pertinent facts.

I prepared my sermon with unusual care, writing it out in full, and, contrary to my custom, reading it word for word, that there might be no question as to exactly what I had said. I took for my text the latter part of the fourteenth chapter of Romans:

> Destroy not him with thy meat, for whom Christ died. It is good, neither to eat flesh nor to drink wine nor anything, whereby thy brother stumbleth or is offended or is made weak.

After discussing the facts of the saloons in their midst, of the drunkenness, of the families affected, of the duty of the followers of Christ to live unselfish, helpful lives, I emphasized that the members of the Church were responsible for the saloons and for all the evils wrought by them until those members had done everything they could by personal persuasion, with the saloonkeepers, and, as citizens, by a petition to the judge, to have the saloon closed.

I did not preach this sermon until near the close of the first year on my first charge, as I wanted to get the facts and an understanding of conditions. My congregations at all the churches were quite large, including the members of other churches in which there was no preaching, and, I think in every case, including the saloonkeepers. I preached the same sermon in succession at all my appointments.

I was not in the habit of reading my sermons, for, preaching freely from notes, I could watch the congregation very closely. But, being obliged to keep my eyes on my manuscript, I could not see what impression the sermon was making. I could only feel. As I advanced from point to point, the congregation became very quiet, and when I called upon them, the members of the churches, to meet their responsibility and close the saloons, there was a stillness all over the church which could be felt. The congregation remained quiet until after the benediction, but in every case, after getting outside the church, there was animated discussion in many groups.

That sermon was the first time that I ever grappled publicly with the liquor problem, and I learned then, in the first year of my ministry, some things of great importance: first, never state anything for a fact unless you are certain it is true; second, one fact is worth a page of rhetoric; third, in any discussion of a disputed matter, write what you have to say so that you cannot be misquoted; fourth, expect criticism or attack whenever you preach against the lust of the flesh, the lust of the eye, or the pride of life.

Criticism of my sermon was plentiful, the most blatant and abusive coming from some younger men who did not hear the sermon but who quoted me as saying what I had not said, and what I did not believe. I made no direct reply to those parties by name, but, with the brief statement that I had been misquoted, I published in the county paper exactly what I did say on the disputed points. While it did not soothe the lacerated feelings of the lovers of intoxicants, it effectually stopped their mouths, so far as such misrepresentation was concerned. I had planned to organize to secure the signing of petitions against the granting of a license, but at the Annual Conference session a short time later, much to my surprise, I was given another appointment, and had no opportunity to follow up my sermon.

This experience probably does not warrant the amount of space which has been given to it, but it marked the beginning of my public warfare with the liquor traffic and taught me some important lessons. The facts concerning the liquor traffic, which I tried faithfully to proclaim in that sermon, produced, as they always will, a line of cleavage in the several communities where the sermon was preached. Brother William A. Smith, my leading steward at Charlotte Court House, said to me the next morning, calling the two liquor sellers of the place by name, "They will never forgive you. They, their wives and children, were all in the congregation, and the men to whom they sell were sitting all around the church. They may come to hear you again, but if they do, they will take back seats."

# ❧142❧

# The Church and Temperance

## WALTER ELLIOTT

Catholic commitment to temperance is often overlooked. Father Mathew, the Irish temperance advocate, had a srong impact during his tour of America in the 1840s. In the 1890s Father Walter Elliott (1842–1928), active in missionary work in the United States, (still then designated a missionary zone by the Vatican) argued that sobriety was necessary for a Christian family life and that, unless widespread Catholic intemperance was overcome, a large obstacle to successful missionary work amongst Americans would remain.

These words tell us of a great natural virtue and a great supernatural society. Because temperance is primarily a virtue of the mere man—natural—and because the church is a society of men raised above nature, a supernatural organism, many Catholics, laymen and priests, find more or less difficulty in a distinctively Catholic temperance movement. Are not the supernatural virtues of Faith, Hope, and Charity enough? they ask. Do not these supernatural virtues necessarily establish temperance? Is there any holiness which cannot be found in the Catholic supernatural life? Are not the administration of the sacraments by the clergy and their devout reception by the people, attendance at Mass, and hearing the word of God—are not these enough to secure the attainment of any virtue? Are not these the *only* necessary means of securing a virtuous life, reforming men from sin, and enabling them to persevere to the end? Such are the exordium, body, and peroration of the emphatic speech so often privately spoken against our requests to form Total Abstinence Societies, or to join them when already formed.

The relation of the church to temperance, or rather to intemperance, throws us back, therefore, upon the yet more fundamental question of the relation, on the practical side of religion, of the supernatural to the natural. And I believe that the solution of the problem in hand is thus formulated: before you have the Christian you must first have the man. Or put it this way: before the grace of God can do its work well it must have good natural material to work upon.

Source: Walter Elliott, 'The Church and Temperance,' *The Catholic World*, September 1890.

Before the Holy Spirit can infuse the supernatural virtues of Faith, Hope, and Charity into the man, he must have certain natural prerequisites. One may live and die a baptized infant or idiot, and thus be saved by no co-operation of his own. But if otherwise he must have sound sense to understand the truths of faith, free will to stake his life upon them in hope of a future eternity, as well as to prefer God and his law before all things, in holy charity. Or the idea is better expressed thus: Before the supernatural virtues can do their proper work they must do a preliminary work, and that is the establishment of certain natural virtues. Of these virtues, temperance, or self-restraint, stands among the most necessary; it is one of the foremost natural virtues. The command of reason over appetite is a cardinal virtue; it is one of the hinges of the portal closing the inner and outer chambers of the human soul through which the grace of God must pass.

Take a comparison. The business of the farmer is to plough and plant and reap. But multitudes of farmers have done little more than hew down trees and grub up stumps their whole lives long; their children think them the best farmers the land has ever known. It is so with the preparation of the human soul for the supernatural life by the inculcation of the natural virtues, especially self-restraint or temperance. The more highly we appreciate the need of true manhood for a valid Christian character, the more vigorously will we attack intemperance. Whatever is the foe of man's reason is every way, supernaturally and naturally, man's worst foe; and that certainly is intemperance. The lowest degree of Christian character must start with some degree of clear manhood, of intelligence and of freedom and of affectionateness, and against these intemperance wages the most destructive war. Religion does not start with nothing; it must have a man to begin with, and what makes the man is his reason, and what unmakes the reason and the man and the Christian all at once is intemperance.

Hence, wherever the Christian pastor finds a tendency to excessive drink in his parish, he is confronted with the absolute necessity to antagonize it before he can hope to succeed in any way whatever. What he preaches; how, when, and to whom he administers the sacraments; how he shall edify by his conduct; all that he does and says, and prays and preaches must be a two-handed endeavor to place clear manhood in reach of the divine gifts on the altar. If his right hand offers the saving absolution for sin in the confessional, his left must shut the saloon door if he has absolved men addicted to drink. Drink maddens the intelligence which the faith seeks to enlighten; hence the instruction from the altar must condemn fearlessly the drink habit which is the enemy of reason's sovereignty. Drink darkens with despair the soul which hope would illumine with courage; drink demonizes the heart which love would ennoble. "Blind drunk" is the description of the fulness of the evil. Take, then, a comparison from the sorrows of the blind: "What manner of joy shall be to me," says the blind Tobias, "who sit in darkness and never see the light of heaven." What manner of supernatural faith, hope, and love shall exist in a parish darkened by intemperance and infested with saloons.

We call drunkenness a brutalizing vice. Precisely so. And men brutalized by intemperance, and their children brutalized by its heredity and by its evil example, must first be humanized before they can be Christianized. Civilize first and then Christianize, or rather civilize in the very process of Christianizing.

*Sacramenta propter homines* is a theological maxim—the sacraments are for the sake of men. Give yourself men, then, say the advocates of the temperance movement, that the sacraments may avail them. The more manly—that is to say, the more sober, intelligent, conscious of human dignity, and self-respecting your people are, the better use they will make of the sacraments. Before regeneration comes generation; men were before the sacraments. Their native virtues and excellences were bestowed upon them by God that the sacramental life might the more readily elevate them to union with the Diety. Exactly in proportion to the manhood of a people will the sacraments work a divine work among them. The church can; indeed, adjust itself to the state of savages, as it does to that of children and of the feeble-minded. But religion tends to abolish savagery just as nature tends to develop childhood into manhood. The normal work of religion is not to be sought among the weaklings of humanity, but is found among men and women of powerful intelligence and heroic will.

In view of these principles, let us look at the facts. Is the church in America seriously injured by intemperance? To answer this question intelligently, we must call up sufficient courage to face undisputed facts. Now, the Catholic Church of America is an urban institution. Its members are almost wholly residents of cities and industrial towns. If our people have any vices they are the vices of the city. Are our cities and factory towns infested with saloons and are the working people addicted to drunkenness? There cannot be the slightest doubt of it. The saloons are so numerous in such localities that in many, if not most of them, there is one for less than a hundred and fifty persons. Of these seven score and a half persons to one saloon there are fully five score who pay little, if any, tribute to the tax-gatherer behind the bar, except through their drunken husbands or fathers; all the children, more than half the women, many of the men drink little or not at all. Archbishop Ireland has estimated that the trade of less than fifty persons is the actual support of the average saloon. Drunkards of various grades there must be, then, or the saloon-keeper could not pay his rent from their trade. The number of the saloons thus proves the prevalence of drunkenness. It is the few heavy drinkers who keep up the beer and whiskey business: men who love drinking for its own sake, or who drink in parties together and are convivial drinkers; who provoke each other to drink, and to drink again and over again till they are made drunk by treating; men in whose rottenness we priests are so often compelled to dabble as we visit their families for sick-calls or on errands of charity in connection with the St. Vincent de Paul Conferences. These are the ones who mainly support the saloons, and they are drunkards.

Now comes the horrible truth. In all the cities of the Union a large proportion of these wretches are Catholics. To deny this is a great weakness; it is a folly to try to conceal it. Mr Powderly ought to know whether the working classes are given to excessive drink, and at the last convention of the Catholic Total Abstinence Union of America he affirmed that nine out of ten of the supporters of the saloon are workingmen—the very class which forms nearly the whole of our Catholic community. In many cities, big and little, we have something like a monopoly of the business of selling liquor, and in not a few something equivalent to a monopoly of getting drunk. Scarcely a Catholic family among us but mourns one or other of its members as a victim of intemperance.

This is lamentable. I hate to acknowledge it. But the concealment of such a deadly thing by us eliminates the most necessary element from the discussion—namely, the facts of the case. This would be far worse than petty vanity; for Catholics to refuse to face this fact is to withdraw, defeated, from the controversy with the rum-power. It would be a public and an official lie to conceal such a fact. The Catholic Church in America is grievously injured by drunkenness. Yet who will say that the sacraments have not been duly administered, the word of God—on the routine lines, at any rate—faithfully preached right in the very communities referred to? Yet from Catholic domiciles—miscalled homes—in those cities and towns three-fourths of the public paupers creep annually to the almshouses, and more than half the criminals snatched away by the police to prison are by baptism and training members of our church. Can any one deny this? Or can any one deny that the identity of nominal Catholicity and pauperism existing in our chief centres of population is owing to the drunkenness of Catholics? And can any one deny that this has been the horrible truth for something like thirty-five years, or ever since the Father Mathew movement began to wane? Yet no one will affirm that the cause is a lack of churches and priests, or a want of any of the supernatural aids of religion. This detestable vice has been a veritable beast in the vineyard of the Lord, making its lair in the very precinct of the buildings containing the confessional and the altar. I will give you an example. For twenty years the clergy of the parish of St. Paul the Apostle, New York, have had a hard and uneven fight to keep saloons from the very church door, because the neighborhood of a Catholic church is a good stand for the saloon business; and this is equally so in nearly every city in America. Who has not burned with shame to run the gauntlet of the saloons lining the way to the Catholic cemetery? Whether it be the christening of the infant or the burial of the dead, the attendance at the ordinary Sunday Mass or the celebrating of such feasts as Christmas and New Year's and St. Patrick's day, the weakness and the degradation of our people has yoked religion and love of country and kindred, the two most elevated sentiments of our nature, to the chariots of the god Gambrinus and the god Bacchus, whose wheels crush down into hell a thousand-fold more victims than ever perished under the wheels of Juggernaut.

We cannot claim a better clergy or people than the Irish in Ireland. Yet listen to a competent witness of the drink-evil in the Irish cities. I quote from

"Intemperance in Ireland," published in this magazine for last July:

> I was four years working as a priest among a dense and poor population, and I
> can use no language more truly descriptive of what my eyes saw than the homely
> phrase "It was a fright!" Such a tangled mass of recollections stares me in the face
> that I am afraid that I can give no order to my impressions. What was the
> occupation of the people? Some were messengers uptown; some drivers of vans;
> some engaged in the factory; some at the docks, and some were fishermen. The
> wives and daughters of many of them were washerwomen at home who did the
> laundry work of the city. Half, perhaps two-thirds, of the men themselves belonged
> to the Confraternity of the Holy Family. Their little girls went to the nuns; their
> little boys to the Christian Brothers' Schools. There was even a benefit and total
> abstinence society in the parish, and yet—drunkenness! drunkenness! The place
> was sprinkled with public houses. There was a huge distillery in full swing, giving
> employment to hundreds and destined to beggar thousands.

I positively affirm that this is a true picture of many parishes in our American
cities, the miserable simulacrum of a neglected Temperance Society included.

The regular administration of the aids of religion to a population defective
of so essential a natural virtue as restraint from excessive use of drink, is like
scattering good seed upon the matted sod of the unbroken prairie or rather upon
the ash-heaps of the foundry dump.

To attack the vice of drunkenness from an entirely supernatural point of
departure is to begin without the beginning. Intemperance is primarily a sin
against nature, and the resources of natural virtue should be first called upon
to vanquish it. A man should be sober whether he believes in God or not. To
overcome drunkenness, the only faith a man need have is belief that he is a
reasonable being; the only hope he need have is one for a tolerable existence in
this life; the only charity, self-love. Experience and observation prove that these
lowest of even the natural reasons for sobriety succeed in reforming multitudes
of drunkards of every creed. Drunkenness, therefore, is a vice to assail which
the priest must go out of the sanctuary if he would make his apostolate integral;
and to make it successful, he must associate with him persons and things not
entitled to stand in any holier place than the sanctuaries of pure and upright
nature, a happy home and a well-ordered state. The layman is the priest of
nature's shrine, which is home, and the family is his sanctuary. To him must be
yielded the first place, if he is competent to assume it, in the warfare against a
vice which is firstly against manhood, and only secondarily against the Christian
character. Yet we know that few parishes can wage a successful fight against drink
without the aid of the priest; and often without his entire supervision the whole
battle will be lost. But in that case and in every case the attitude of the priest,
although it can never lose its supernatural force, must in addition take on the
natural. As a fellow-man of the drunkard he must appeal to him, as an equal
citizen of the civil community must he antagonize the saloon-keeper, and all this
both in public and private.

I am not ordained priest to keep a laundry; but if a class of my people are too
dirty to go to church, I must set to work to get them cleaned—unless I am a

mere ecclesiastical official. So with the case in hand. I am no policeman, but if a class of my people are going to hell through the Sunday back-entrance of the corner saloon, I must at once set about becoming more than a policeman; at any rate I must be so to the keeper of that saloon.

The supernatural influences of religion, joined to the drink-wounded natural character of man, are like a noble tree whose bark has been girdled at the root. What, indeed, is the bark compared to the wood, or to the sap, or to the fruit. But the wood must die, and the sap must stop, and the fruit must rot unripe if the bark be cut away. To confine one's self to the assiduous administering of the sacraments, the faithful preaching of the ordinary Sunday sermon, and the usual sacerdotal labors for the sanctification of the people, in an average city parish of America, *without an aggressive crusade against saloons and saloon-going,* is to water and to prune a tree all day long whose bark is gnawed by a beast all night long.

Rev. Dr William Barry in a defence of his admirable paper, read at the Catholic Truth Conference in Birmingham, quotes in support of his thesis, "First Civilize and then Christianize," some words of the German explorer Von Wissmann, which apply directly to the question we are considering: "Every one who knows the Africans," says this witness of Catholic missionary wisdom,

> and, for the matter of that, who knows any savage people, will agree with me that an understanding of the religion of love is not to be expected from people in such a low state of civilization. Therefore the proper way of a mission is first to make a savage a higher being, and then to lead him to know religion. This is what the Roman Catholic missions do, by adopting the maxim *Labora et Ora,* and not like the Protestant, *Ora et Labora,* which is only suitable for a people of higher civilization.

I leave it to any priest experienced in the reform of drunkards whether the absence of the sense of right and wrong he has had to take account of, and the weakness of will he has encountered, would not be worthy of the naked savages of the dark continent. And as the Catholic missionary is successful there because he not only preaches the word, but preaches the wearing of breeches and the cultivating of the soil, so shall we be successful in many places here in America only on condition of in like manner using civilizing influences in preparation for those of the gospel.

A house may be laid upon solid foundations, built of enduring materials, proportioned and adorned by a skilful architect; but let the drainage be defective, and it is turned into a house of death in which miasmatic fevers slay the inmates. So is a city parish presided over by a priest who ignores the prevalence of drunkenness. If asked by his bishop or the missionary what are the people's chief faults, he perhaps names missing Mass, neglect of Easter duty, failure of parents to instruct their children or to send them to Sunday-school. In this he names the effects, and does not even suspect the one only efficient cause of these sins, and of the worst of the others: the drink-habit. There are not a few such good priests in America, well-educated and devout men, who have many drunkards among their people, and have never preached a temperance sermon. I am persuaded that the reason of this is a delusive idea of the all-sufficiency of the supernatural aids of religion. Such men are neither cowards nor sluggards, but are oblivious to the need of bringing into play the moral forces of nature in order to secure the fruits of supernatural religion. If asked to take a leading part in an aggressive attack on saloons and saloon-going, to organize or to reorganize a temperance society, they answer: "I really have no time to do so. I am kept too busy by my regular clerical duties—my confessional, visiting the sick, paying off my debt, etc., etc.—to attend to *outside matters* like that." They tether themselves in their sanctuaries, and go round and round their lives long with beautiful churches and fine houses, and a drunken people. The solid ground of the faith, the high privilege of the sacraments, the noble brotherhood of the Christian society—what do they avail to multitudes of the dwellers in a beautiful temple beneath which flows the miasmatic sewer of the drink-habit.

Another view of the case is that which arises from the duty the church owes to the community at large in distinction with that which she owes to individual souls. This duty has been continually insisted on by Pope Leo as, in these times especially something of the utmost importance. The farther the public life of men recedes from the morality of the gospel, the more assiduously should the church endeavor to win men back to that best guarantee of civil welfare. The Church of Christ is the only divinely appointed public guardian of the moral law, that law which is a condition of the happiness of nations as well as of men. Now, this office involves the necessity of *keeping up a good name* for the Catholic parish of every town in the land, the necessity as well as the duty. What God made the church to be to the civil community, that will the civil community instinctively demand that the church shall actually be. The parish priest has no less an obligation to win the respect and to earn the gratitude of the non-Catholic community about him than he has to break the bread of life to his own parishioners. The wise doing of the one secures the performance of the other duty. Yet how many of our priests absolutely confine their efforts, their very thoughts, to their own "ecclesiastical subjects," and that in a strictly exclusive sense. "You are the salt of the earth," applies in their view only to the Celtic or the Teutonic colony of the busy city in a corner of which they dwell; or to the "exiles" scattered throughout a smaller town. Nay, priests are sometimes found to privately sneer at the efforts of public-spirited citizens to lessen the number of the saloons, to break up gambling dens, to secure the observance of Sunday laws; and this in spite of the earnest exhortations of the American hierarchy that priests and laymen should do all in their power to aid such movements. Those who deem themselves but Celts transplanted or Teutons transplanted are too absorbed by backward glances regretfully cast across the ocean to seriously grapple with an American evil present everywhere about them. This is true also of their use of theologians. The theorizings of distant men on distant facts are respected by some priests more than the positive injunctions of the American hierarchy itself, stamped with the broad seal of

Rome; I have often been met with the allegation of customs tolerated in Europe as an answer to the express decrees of the Third Plenary Council of Baltimore. All priests who have been active advocates of the total-abstinence movement and the anti-saloon movement will tell you how often they have been knocked about with theological "stuffed clubs," stuffed with words and sentences written in "temperate wine-drinking France" or Italy, or "sober beer-drinking Germany"; as if this land were Italy, or Germany, or France; as if moral theology were not a practical application of principles; as if the bishops were not the divinely appointed legislators of the church to judge of circumstances and apply principles.

Now let me ask what use have the American people at large for Catholicity? Not one in six of them is a Catholic, nor is there much in the signs of the times to indicate that they are going to become Catholics. What use have they for our religion? Will they thank us for building big churches and convents? Do you perceive any sign of gratitude for our parochial schools? As a matter of fact, the people of the United States, though without ill-will towards us, yet look upon us as besotted with love for our faith because it is an heirloom of our race, or as men and women of little independence of character who are willing to delegate our thinking to an hierarchical caste. Our non-Catholic Americans are a kindly people, and will not molest us until sorely provoked. But, taking their standpoint to judge from, what use have they for us? The Sister of Charity is the only answer, so far given them, which they can understand. Were it not for our hospitals, asylums, reformatories, we should be without any cause at all in the court of public opinion, apart from the feelings born of personal acquaintance between members of all forms of religion among us. Our great works of charity make us good Samaritans, by proxy at any rate. Charity is always lovely, and the mere spectacle of Catholic benevolence wins honest men's hearts. In its charities, too, the Catholic Church helps to solve the most threatening of the social problems—that which is pictured by the poor man's hand stretching towards the rich man's purse. But the *faith* of the Catholic people, the *sacramental life* of them—these are things known as of use to the civil order only by whatever fruits of natural virtue they may bring forth. Industry, truthfulness, obedience to law, love of country, cleanliness, honesty, and above all sobriety, are what men outside the church look for as the signs of her utility. Without such fruits as these bare toleration is what we may count on, and that will be swept away in the first burst of passionate religious excitement. Unless a religion makes men better *men* and better citizens its insignificance must be its only enduring guarantee of perpetuity in the state.

On the other hand, show me a town in which the Catholic priest lives publicly up to the Third Plenary Council, and is the declared enemy of the saloon, and his church the shrine of a sober people: that priest is sure of the honor of his religion in public and in private. He is among the foremost citizens because he represents an organism which is a powerful conservator of the commonwealth. Whoever hurts him or his church cuts the state to the quick.

More: his church presses upon all honest minds for an answer to her claims, because those claims, if supernatural in themselves, have nature's universal credentials of validity to support them, the manly, natural virtues everywhere seen among a Catholic sober people.

"How can you expect conversions," demands Canon Murnane in his paper read to the Catholic Truth Conference at Birmingham—a most terrible because a most undeniable confession of the infection of the body Catholic with the drink-plague—"how can you expect conversions when a Catholic prison chaplain can assert that of six or seven thousand women brought into the prison yearly, more than eighty percent. are Catholics?" Can we deny this of American penal institutions? Alas! No. I remember witnessing the horror of an American bishop after a visit to such a place near one of our large cities, his horror and his shame that a prodigious majority of the inmates were unmistakably of our own people, though in population we are not one-third of the city. This moral cesspool filled from Catholic "homes" through the open sewers running from the saloons to the police courts, daily revealed in the press, is the extinction of the hope of converting the "other sheep not of this fold." What the above authority, in addition to his quoted words, says of England is true of America:

> The people of this country understand nothing of supernatural virtues, they see not the life of the soul; but they do see and do hear what takes place next door and in the street. They know and appreciate the moral virtues, temperance, honesty, etc. *These must be our motives of credibility and the notes of the true Church.* The conclusions are obvious.

No career can have so calamitous an end as that of a body of Christians tried, found wanting, and rejected by the application of its Founder's own test, "By their fruits ye shall know them." If the drunken neighborhood is the Catholic neighborhood; if the drunkards' names in the police reports are notoriously those of Catholics; if the saloon-goers and the saloonists are Catholics; if the "Boodlers" who thrive by saloon politics are Catholics; if the saloon-made paupers and tramps are Catholics, then as a moral force among men Catholicity is done for in that community; whatever individual good it may do to its members its public force for morality is nothing. Chrysostom and Bossuet, aye or Paul and Patrick, could not convert men to such a Catholicity; nor can twenty universities discover a truer test or a fairer one than that the tree shall be known by its fruits.

If drunkenness were prevalent in a bad priest's parish, "Like master like man," we could say. But the poison of the sting is that the evils we have been considering are often enough found in the parishes of our best priests, judged so by the standards of education and piety; and that in the midst of it all the sober Catholics are not led to show their hatred of drunkenness publicly. It is seldom that most of the people are drunkards; as a minority of the Catholic population support the saloons in the Catholic neighborhoods, so does a minority of wicked men blight the fair fame of the entire Catholic community. The virtues cultivated in societies and for public show are unfortunately too often exclusively such as are appreciated only by the faithful themselves, as is the case with the usual confraternities and sodalities. They are most excellent for us who have the supernatural standard to judge by; they are nothing, are generally never known, to the outside world. The case is totally different where the priest preaches openly against saloons and against convivial drinking, and gets his sermons into the daily press; where he joins reform movements, lends his name and influence to public efforts for the suppression of the drunkenness and its occasions; joins with all and any citizens, Protestants, Jews, and Gentiles, in every lawful effort for the relief of human misery and the elevation of men. In the parishes of such priests Catholic laymen take heart. They soon become conspicuous for their political virtue and public spirit. If drunken Catholics are upcast to them, they can answer by pointing to flourishing Catholic Total Abstinence Societies; they can offset the Catholic boodler with the Catholic reformer, and the Catholic saloon-keeper with the Catholic temperance hall.

The priest without a good temperance society, but a flourishing devotional society, in a parish full of flourishing saloons, is like a lawyer who has a good case but lets his antagonist get judgment by default; or he is like a certain kind of bankrupt: assets in the form of securities far in excess of debts, but the securities cannot be realized on. Show that you hate drunkenness and saloon-going publicly, for the vice is public, and the good name of a public society like the church can only be safeguarded by public conduct. If you have got good fruits of sobriety to show, show them; they shouldn't be all hustled away out of sight into pious sodalities.

The words written in this article will be hot words to some of my readers, but they will burn no one who reads them more painfully than they have burned me in writing them.

# ᛒ143ᛒ

# Pressure Politics:
# The Story of the Anti-Saloon
# League

## PETER ODEGARD

The Anti-Saloon League was the organization most active in the final push for prohibition legislation. A near contemporary account of it, written during the period of national prohibition (1918–1933), is by the political scientist, Peter Odegard. He documents the religious sectarianism and intolerance expressed during its campaign.

## Intolerance and Bigotry

A struggle so intensely emotional as that for prohibition produced its own fanaticism. People who refused to coöperate with the League were sometimes regarded as friends of all iniquity. The attitude toward the Catholic Church is in point. Although the leaders insisted that their criticism was due solely to the Church's stand on prohibition, there were extremists who desired a vigorous anti-Catholic campaign. This fact has enabled critics of the League to brand it as a spiritual confrere of the Ku Klux Klan and the heir of the A.P.A.

The Anti-Saloon League sought to meet this criticism by insisting that prohibition was not a peculiarly Protestant nostrum. It has long been able to point to Father J. J. Scurran, who for twenty-five years has been a vice-president of the National Anti-Saloon League. When in 1913 Father Patrick J. Murphy of Texas addressed the Anti-Saloon League Convention on "Why Should We Do Away with the Saloon Business," copies of his speech were widely distributed. The South Dakota League, about 1915, issued a pamphlet, *Catholic Clergy and the Saloon*, with quotations from Pope Leo XIII, Archbishop Keane, Bishop Conaty, Bishop Canevin, Bishop Monaghan, Father P. S. McKenna and Father

Source: Peter Odegard, from *Pressure Politics: The Story of the Anti-Saloon League,* New York, 1928, pp. 24–33.

J. M. Cleary, advocating prohibition. Thousands of reprints of an article by United States Senator Ransdell of Louisiana, a Catholic prohibitionist, on *Catholics and Prohibition* were circulated. The Catholic Clergy Prohibition League, was also cited. Mayor Dever, of Chicago, a Catholic, was praised for his ardent advocacy of strict enforcement.

None the less, certain extremists within the League had difficulty in restraining themselves when confronted with the indifference or active opposition of Catholics. In 1919, William H. Anderson, superintendent in New York, in a public letter denounced the views of Joseph P. Tumulty, President Wilson's secretary, thus:

> There is a pro-brewery and reactionary element within the Catholic Church which is violently anti-prohibition and it is this element that has been able to reach the President with the impression that the Catholic Church is opposed to prohibition, when the truth is that a large portion of the membership of the Catholic Church is just as strong for prohibition as the majority of the members of Protestant Churches.... It is time for someone to say, so the public will know, that a certain element of the Catholic Church in New York last fall, deliberately and stealthily went out to put over a Catholic governor by arousing religious prejudice through the systematic circulation of the mendacious falsehood that the success of the opposing candidate (a prohibition Protestant) would interfere with religious liberty and prevent the securing of wine for sacramental purposes.... The Anti-Saloon League is not anti-Catholic... but when certain wet elements in the Catholic Church... attempt to use the prohibition issue as a stalking horse behind which to put over some Catholic project, then it is the duty of the Anti-Saloon League to turn on the light and expose the proposition... The talk of running the New York Governor for President looks like these wet Catholics... having played the game successfully once, with respect of the governorship... now intend... to capture the presidency in 1920 by a secret coalition between the German brewers and certain ecclesiastics....

He concludes by calling upon all "Christian, right-thinking, patriotic, American-minded, sincere, God-fearing, man-loving Catholics" to repudiate the scheme.

Commenting upon this and similar effusions of the League's stormy petrel, Archbishop Hayes called Anderson

> This sinister figure in American politics, a sower of strife, who sinks so low as to play the un-American role of a brewer of bigotry. He seems but little concerned about the protection against unlawful search and seizure, religious freedom, free speech, free press and free legislatures. Fomenter of distrust and breeder of mischief! Better for America that he had never been born!

To this Anderson replied:

> ... if... it makes me a sinister figure, a sower of strife, a brewer of bigotry, to state the truth about the attitude of some leaders of the Catholic Church with respect to the enforcement of the prohibition amendment, then... so much the worse for these leaders.... Not even the Archbishop of New York can obscure an issue by talking about something else.... What I did say is that most of the officiary of the Roman Catholic Church in this state are in sympathy with the Tammany efforts to destroy the prohibition victory.

Even more violent was a letter to the Archbishop from the Rev. W. M. Hess of Trinity Congregational Church, New York City, defending Anderson. Portions of this letter would certainly warm the heart of the Grand Dragon of the Klan. After criticizing the Archbishop for evading the issue, Dr Hess says:

> Should not a representative of the most bigoted church in America, the Roman Catholic, make a better reply than to merely call him a "bigot" and "fanatic"? ... Will you tell me what else Tammany Hall has been during the past forty years, but a combination of Rum and Romanism? ... Why so sensitive now when William H. Anderson tells a simple truth that every intelligent person knows? Is it not about time for the real Americans to drive the low-down, grafting, Irish-Catholic rum-sellers and "rummies" out of city politics?

Catholics who feared such outbursts advised against doing anything that would justify the charge that they were defending law violation. On June 7, 1923, Father George Zucher of St. Vincent's Church, North Evans, New York, wrote "as a Catholic and a priest" requesting Governor Smith not to sign the bill repealing the state enforcement law.

> Your signing the repeal would revive, not without some shadow of truth, Burchard's slander, of Rum, Romanism and Rebellion.

Generally speaking, Catholic leaders have been a bit lukewarm toward prohibition and many have actively opposed it. In February, 1918, before Maryland had ratified, Cardinal Gibbons declared his opposition to the Eighteenth Amendment. His purpose is reflected in the assertion that

> the Cardinal's statement would have had telling effect with the people at the polls had they been permitted to vote on the measure. Those behind the amendment realized this and pushed it through an anti-Catholic legislature without consulting the people.

Archbishop Messmer of Milwaukee issued in 1918 an order forbidding any priests who visit in the archdiocese to deliver addresses in favor of prohibition or under the auspices of the Anti-Saloon League. The Catholic Clergy of Brooklyn declared that they would oppose "any candidate for public office who endorsed by the Anti-Saloon League or who endorses the League." The Rev. Dr. J. J. Cloonan, President of St. John's College, also of Brooklyn, denounced the Volstead Act as immoral and unjust. It is safe to say that, with a few exceptions, all Catholic editors repudiate prohibition.

Aside from a few individuals of the type represented by Anderson, the League officials frown on anti-Catholic propaganda. They feel that Catholics are not friendly toward the amendment, but they know that the least effective method of securing their coöperation is slander and abuse. The League is interested in making a success of prohibition. Leaders of moral crusades are often intolerant of opposition. The remarkable thing is not outbursts like those quoted, but the surprising fairness and restraint of the League leaders.

In supporting a candidate for public office the League does not inquire as to his religion. His stand on the liquor question alone determines its attitude. The

Anti-Saloon League supported Senator Ransdell of Louisiana, a Catholic. One of its outstanding friends in the United States Senate is Walsh of Montana, a well-known Catholic. Others who come to mind are Senator Ashurst of Arizona and Congressman Sinnott of Oregon.

During the latter weeks of the Senatorial fight in New York in 1926, Arthur J. Davis, superintendent of the League, received a letter from the Women's Republican Club of New York City. This letter appealed to Davis to

> throw all your weight and influence with your League... to induce them [i.e., League supporters] to vote the Republican ticket.

Among the arguments presented was a reference to

> events during the Eucharistic Congress... [which make it] seem little short of treason for Republicans not to stand together for Mills and Wadsworth.

Here then was a direct attempt on the part of a responsible Republican organization to inject a nasty religious controversy into the campaign. Davis replied:

> With all courtesy, I must decline to discuss the Eucharistic Congress in its relation to Mr. Wadsworth's campaign.

Prohibition has produced its fanatics on both sides. If some of the drys seem willing to institute a Holy Protestant Inquisition for wets, there are wets who advocate the tar barrel for drys. It is difficult to say just who, on this issue, should cast the first stone. It may be that the membership of the Ku Klux Klan sympathizes with the aims of the Anti-Saloon League, but it is certain that few League Leaders have anything but contempt for the Klan.

## Main Street Morality

It is true that the Anti-Saloon League, being a league of Protestant churches, appeals to essentially the same constituency as the Ku Klux Klan. The Protestant Church in America is overwhelmingly rural. This is true even in cities.

> The Protestant Church in American cities is largely the property and product of rural immigrants. In the larger cities it has survived from the earlier rural period of the state's development. Counts made of those attending city churches indicate that they are largely made up of rural immigrants; seventy-five percent of those present are frequently found to have been born in the country.

The rural church tends to be a center of intellectual and social life. The city church competes with movies, theaters, clubs, music halls, libraries and lectures. The rural church, particularly the Protestant Church, is ideally adapted to crusading. It is more than a place of worship; it is a meeting-house, a forum.

The rural Protestant seems to be a natural-born reformer. To him the city is a place of vice and corruption, a fleshpot to be feared. It is the home of the "foreign element" which he abhors. In the city, on the other hand, strange persons, strange ideas, and strange customs meet and mingle. A live and let-live philosophy prevails; there is less demand for conformity. The interstimulation of a variety of sects and creeds works for tolerance bordering on indifference. Any other attitude would make city life unendurable. Villagers and the inhabitants of Main Street live in glass houses; every man is his brother's keeper. The village dweller, his own life drab and uneventful, is an ideal soldier for a moral crusade. He takes literally the admonition of St. Paul,

> It is good neither to eat flesh, nor drink wine, nor anything whereby thy brother stumbleth, or is offended, or is made weak.

Reformist movements in cities emphasize the social and economic rather than the moral; prohibition has been essentially a moral movement. Its leaders used economic and political arguments, but to the rank and file it was at bottom a moral problem. Drink was not only the cause of disease, destitution and depravity; it was above all "the Great Destroyer of the Temple of the Soul," the inciter of base passions and the arch enemy of Christian virtue.

Where Protestants are in the majority, as in the rural South, prohibition sentiment is strong. There were nine Southern states which adopted prohibition prior to 1916. Table II shows them to be overwhelmingly Protestant, rural and native.

Contrast this with Connecticut and Rhode Island, the two states which failed to ratify the Eighteenth Amendment: the Catholic percentage of the total church population was 67 and 76 respectively. Without concluding too much from these figures, they help to explain the League's attitude. The League, being a league of Protestant churches, could look for small influences in the cities where the Catholics generally predominated. Sixty-five percent of the church-goers in cities of 350,000 or more are Catholics. Three-fourths of the Catholics in the United States live in the cities of 25,000 or more. In these cities they constitute one-half to two-thirds of the church-going population.

Lastly, the constituency to which the Anti-Saloon League appeals is suspicious of aliens. When the Arbeiter Bund of Michigan declared its opposition to prohibition, the *American Issue* said:

> Really, is not the country growing rather tired of having a lot of swill-fattened, blowsy half-foreigners getting together and between hiccoughs laying down definitions to Americans regarding the motive of our constitution and laws. But then we suppose that to intimate anything of this sort is A.P.A.-ism and "attempting to excite odium against foreigners".

This charge was in fact made. "This whole Anti-Saloon movement," said an opponent,

> is in reality a thinly veiled warfare on everything foreign — an outbreak of envy and jealousy, directed against the hard-fisted, hard working, money saving, child-rearing foreigner and his descendants, who in the struggle for existence are gradually crowding out the effete, bloodless, anaemic, self-righteous remnant of puritan stock which is physically too feeble to do anything but cavil and denounce.

The League's attitude is reflected in resolutions adopted in 1925 demanding the deportation of aliens convicted of violating the liquor laws.

Whatever anti-Catholic or anti-alien sentiments the Anti-Saloon League may have should not be attributed to a dislike for Catholics or aliens as such. If these groups suddenly mounted the water wagon, there is reason to believe that the League leaders would be the first to sing their praises, though the rank and file of their supporters might not do likewise.

## Pulpit Politics

The idea of the church engaging in politics filled many with alarm. "There will be few," said a writer for the German–American Alliance,

> who will not agree with me when I say that a political propaganda carried on by or under the auspices of a religious body is extremely dangerous, let the ostensible purpose for which the propaganda is made be ever so noble or meritorious.... [The church] cannot mix in these affairs itself, without thus eventually losing that hold on the faith and reverence of mankind which alone enables it to successfully do God's work on earth.

The League met the charge head on:

> The cry of politics in the pulpit has grown old and stale.... The mission of the church is to right wrongs and to establish the Kingdom of Heaven among men. Whatever will tend to these ends, it is the business of the church to promote, and the part of which the pastor should play is that of leadership. If that leadership compels him to take an active part in movements of civic reform, his duty may be in the political arena as well as in the pulpit.

Assistant Attorney General Trickett of Kansas declared:

> The Christian pulpit might properly be called the upper house in the parliament of world politics.

"Occasionally some poor specimen of humanity," said the American Issue,

> leaning over a saloon bar and looking through the bottom of a beer glass, condemns the Anti-Saloon League for its activity in politics.... Of course the Anti-Saloon League is in politics. That is part of its business. It is not playing either the elephant or the donkey as a favorite, but it is in politics to help elect good men to office and to keep bad men out of office.... It is politics to keep the brewers and liquor dealers from filling offices with their tools and from hanging a beer sign above the doors of legislative halls.

In general the League's answer has been that it would get out of politics when the liquor interests did.

# Faith in a Changing World

Plate 16: *Another Pied Piper* c. 1925.

# ❧144❧

# The Gospel for an Age of Doubt

## HENRY VAN DYKE

Although not entirely forgotten, Henry Van Dyke (1852–1933), was once a widely-read poet, Presbyterian preacher, literary critic and Christian apologist. In pages from his best known work of apologetics, he characterized the age of spiritual doubt. His theological liberalism was evident in his acceptance of the principle of freedom of investigation. Yet he also laid the basis for an attack on the pretensions of materialism and rationalism to provide total explanations. Science, he believed, could not comprehend the spiritual sphere.

---

A s soon as we step out of the theological circle into the broad field of general reading we see that we are living in an age of doubt.

I do not mean to say that this is the only feature in the physiognomy of the age. It has many other aspects, from any one of which we might pick a name. From the material side, we might call it an age of progress; from the intellectual side, an age of science; from the medical side, an age of hysteria; from the political side, an age of democracy; from the commercial side, an age of advertisement; from the social side, an age of publicomania. But looking at it from the spiritual side, which is the preacher's point of view, and considering that interior life to which every proclamation of a gospel must be addressed, beyond a doubt it stands confessed as a doubting age.

There is a profound and wide-spread unsettlement of soul in regard to fundamental truths of religion, and also in regard to the nature and existence of the so-called spiritual faculties by which alone these truths can be perceived. In its popular manifestations, this unsettlement takes the form of uncertainty rather than of denial, of unbelief rather than of disbelief, of general scepticism rather than of specific infidelity. The questioning spirit is abroad, moving on the face of the waters seeking rest and finding none.

It is not merely that particular doctrines, such as the inspiration of the Bible, or the future punishment of the wicked, are attacked and denied. The preacher who concentrates his attention at these points will fail to realize the gravity of

Source: Henry Van Dyke, *The Gospel for an Age of Doubt*, New York, 1896, pp. 6-15.

the situation. It is not that a spirit of bitter and mocking atheism, such as Bishop Butler described at the close of the last century, has led people of discernment to set up religion

> as a principal subject of mirth and ridicule, as it were by way of reprisal for its having so long interrupted the pleasures of the world.

The preacher who takes that view of that case now will be at least fifty years too late. He will fail to understand the serious and pathetic temper of the age.

The questioning spirit of to-day is severe but not bitter, restless but not frivolous; it takes itself very seriously and applies its methods of criticism, of analysis, of dissolution, with a sad courtesy of demeanour, to the deepest and most vital truths of religion, the being of God, the reality of the soul, the possibility of a future life. Everywhere it comes and everywhere it asks for a reason, in the shape of a positive and scientific demonstration. When one is given, it asks for another, and when another is given, it asks for the reason of the reason. The laws of evidence, the principles of judgment, the witness of history, the testimony of consciousness,—all are called in question. The answers which have been given by religion to the most difficult and pressing problems of man's inner life are declared to be unsatisfactory and without foundation. The question remains unsolved. Is it soluble? The age stands in doubt. Its coat-of-arms is an interrogation point rampant, above three bishops dormant, and its motto is *Query?*

## II

If we inquire the cause of this general scepticism in regard to religion, the common answer from all sides would probably attribute it to the progress of science. I do not feel satisfied with this answer. At least I should wish to qualify it in such a way as to give it a very different meaning from that which is implied in the current phrase "the conflict between science and religion."

Science, in itself considered, the orderly and reasoned knowledge of the phenomenal universe of things and events, ought not to be, and has not been, hostile to religion, simply because it does not, and cannot, enter into the same sphere. The great advance which has been made in the observation and classification of sensible facts, and in the induction of so-called general laws under which those facts may be arranged for purposes of study, has not even touched the two questions upon the answer to which the reality and nature of religion depend: first, the possible existence of other facts which physical science cannot observe and classify; and second, the probable explanation of these facts. What has happened is just this. The field in which faith has to work has been altered, and it seems to me enormously broadened. But the work remains the same. The question is whether faith has enough vital energy to face and accomplish it. For example, the material out of which to construct an argument from the evidences of final cause in nature has been incalculably increased by the discoveries of the last fifty years in regard to natural selection and the origin of species. The observant wanderer on the field of nature to-day no longer stumbles upon Dr. Paley's old-fashioned, open-faced, turnip-shaped watch lying on the ground. He finds, instead, an intricate and self-adjusting chronometer, capable not only of marking time with accuracy, but also of evolving by its own operation another more perfect and delicate instrument, with qualities and powers which adapt themselves to their surroundings and so advance forever. The idea of final cause has not been touched. Only the region which it must illuminate has been vastly enlarged. It remains to be seen whether faith can supply the illuminating power. Already we have the promise of an answer in many books, by masters of science and philosophy, who show that the theory of evolution demands for its completion the recognition of the spiritual nature of man and the belief in an intelligent and personal God.

The spread of scepticism is often attributed to the growth of our conception of the physical magnitude of the universe. The bewildering numbers and distances of the stars, the gigantic masses of matter in motion, and the tremendous sweep of the forces which drive our tiny earth along like a grain of dust in an orderly whirlwind, are supposed to have overwhelmed and stunned the power of spiritual belief in man. The account seems to me incorrect and unconvincing. I observe that precisely the same argument was used by Job and Isaiah and the Psalmists to lead to a conclusion of faith. The striking disproportion between the littleness of man and the greatness of the stars was to them a demonstration of the necessity of religion to solve the equation. They saw in the heavens the glory of God. And if man to-day knows vastly more of the heavens, does not that put him in position to receive a larger and loftier vision of the glory?

We observe, moreover, that it is just in these departments of science where the knowledge of the magnitude and splendid order of the physical universe is most clear and exact, namely, in astronomy and mathematics, that we find the most illustrious men of science who have not been sceptics but sincere and steadfast believers in the Christian religion. Kepler and Newton were men of faith. The most brilliant galaxy of mathematicians ever assembled at one time and place was at the University of Cambridge in the latter half of this century. Of these "Sir W. Thomson, Sir George Stokes, Professors Tait, Adams, Clerk-Maxwell, and Cayley—not to mention a number of lesser lights such as Routh, Todhunter, Ferrers, etc.—were all avowed Christians." Surely it needs no further proof to show that the pursuit of pure science does not necessarily tend to scepticism.

No, we must look more closely and distinguish more clearly in order to discover in the scientific activities of the age a cause of the prevailing doubt. And if we do this I think we shall find it in the fallacy of that kind of science which mistakes itself for omniscience.

What we see is the pretence of certain sciences to represent in themselves all human knowledge. And as outside of knowledge there is no longer, in the eyes of science thus curtailed, any means for man to come in contact with the realities, we see the pretence advanced by some that all reality and all life should be reduced to that which they have verified. Outside of this there are only dreams and illusions. This is indeed too much. It is no longer science, but scientific absolutism.

"The history of the natural sciences," said Du Bois-Reymond in 1877, "is the veritable history of mankind." "The world," says another, "is made of atoms and ether, and there is no room for ghosts." M. Berthelot in the preface to his *Origines de l'alchimie,* modestly claims that "the world to-days without mysteries"; meaning thereby, I suppose, that there is nothing in existence, from the crystallization of a diamond to the character of a saint, which cannot be investigated and explained by means of a crucible, a blow-pipe, a microscope, and a few other tools.

This is simply begging the question of a spiritual world in the negative. It is an immense and stupefying assumption. It is a claim to solve the problems of the inner life by suppressing them. This claim is not in any sense necessary to the existence of science, nor to any degree supported by the work which it has actually accomplished. But it is made with a calm assurance which imposes powerfully upon the popular mind; and, being made in the name of science, it carries with it an appearance of authority borrowed from the great service which science has rendered to humanity by its discoveries in the sphere of the visible.

The result of this *petitio principii* in the minds of those who accept if fully and carry it out to its logical conclusion, is a definite system of metaphysical negation which goes under the various names of Naturalism, Positivism, Empiricism, and Agnosticism. Its result in the minds of those who accept it partially and provisionally, but lack the ability or the inclination to formulate it, is the development of a sceptical temper. Its result in the minds of those who are unconsciously affected by it, through those profound instincts of sympathy and involuntary imitation which influence all men, is an attitude,—more or less sincere, more or less consistent and continuous,—an attitude of doubt. The spirit of the age tacitly divides all the various beliefs which are held among men into two classes. Those which are supported by scientific proof must be accepted. Those which are not thus supported either must be rejected, or may safely and properly be disregarded as matter of no consequence.

262

# 145

# The Inspiration of the Bible

## WILLIAM JENNINGS BRYAN

One swelling response to the age of doubt was the reassertion by conservative evangelical Protestants of their unchanging belief in the basics of Christianity. These were concretely expressed by an interdenominational and international group of conservative theologians in a series of booklets published between 1910 and 1913 under the general title of *The Fundamentals*. Important amongst them was the divine inspiration of the whole Bible and thus its inerrancy. William Jennings Bryan (1860-1925), three-time presidential candidate, Wilson's Secretary of State and, at the end of his life, participant in the trial of John Scopes for infringing a Tennessee law forbidding the teaching of evolution in the public schools, took this fundamentalist position on the Bible. He saw himself fighting the major threat to orthodox Christianity: theological liberalism and the higher criticism of the Bible. He prided himself on his close contact with ordinary Americans and believed he spoke for their convictions.

---

I s the Bible true? That is the great issue in the world to-day, surpassing in importance all national and international questions. The Bible is either true or false; it is either the Word of God or the work of man. If the Bible is false, it is the greatest impostor that the world has known. And, if an impostor, it will be dragged down from its high place and condemned to association on equal terms with the books that are the product of human minds. Worse still, if it is an impostor, the odium of indictment and conviction will sink it to a place far below the level of man-made books because, from beginning to end, it claims to be the Word of God, by inspiration given.

As there can be no civilization without morals, and as morals rest upon religion, and religion upon God, the question whether the Bible is true or false is the supreme issue among men. As the Bible is the only book known to the Christian world whose authority depends upon inspiration, the degradation of

Source: William Jennings Bryan, 'The Inspiration of the Bible', *Seven Questions in Dispute*, New York, 1924, pp. 15-26.

the Bible leaves the Christian world without a standard of morals other than that upon which men can agree. As men's reasons do not lead them to the same conclusion, and as greed and self-interest often overthrow the reason, the fixing of any moral standard by agreement is impossible. If the Bible is overthrown, Christ ceases to be a Divine character, and His words, instead of being binding upon the conscience, can be followed or discarded according as the individual's convenience may dictate.

If, on the contrary, the Bible is true—infallible because divinely inspired,— then all the books that man has written are as far below the Bible in importance as man is below God in wisdom. The only ground upon which infallibility or inerrancy can be predicated is that the Book is inspired. Man uninspired cannot describe with absolute accuracy even that which has already happened. Carlyle characterized history as "the distillation of rumour"; it has also been described as "fiction agreed upon". Wendell Phillips, whose geographical location ought to be a guaranty that he was not prejudiced towards the section in which most of our history is written, says that the people make history, while the scholars write it, part truly and part as coloured by their prejudices.

The Bible not only gives us history, and that, too, written in many cases long after the events transpired, but it gives us prophecy which was fulfilled centuries later. The language of the Bible cannot be explained by environment, for environment in most instances, was entirely antagonistic. It cannot be explained by the genius of the writers, for they were largely among the unlettered. The Bible could not have lived because of favouritism shown to it, because it has been more bitterly attacked than any other book ever written. The attacks upon it probably outnumber the attacks made upon all other books combined, because it condemns man to his face, charges him with being a sinner in need of a Saviour, indicts him as no other book does, holds up before him the highest standard ever conceived, and threatens him as he is threatened nowhere else.

And yet the Book stands and its circulation increases. How shall we account for its vitality, its indestructibility? By its inspiration and by that alone. Those who accept the Bible as true, inerrant, and infallible believe that the original autograph manuscripts which, through copies, are reproduced in the Old and New Testaments, were true, and true because divinely inspired—"holy men of God spake as they were moved by the Holy Ghost" (2 Peter 1:21). Because they were moved by the Holy spirit, they spoke with accuracy and with the truth of God Himself. There may have been mistakes in the copying, and there may have been mistakes in the translation as shown by revisions, but these do not materially change the phraseology and do not change the vital truths of the Bible. The assaults that are made upon the Bible to-day are not attacks upon the copying or upon the translation; they are attacks upon that which the Old and New Testaments offer as Divine truth. The dispute is not over the language of the Bible; it is over the inspiration that directed the utterances. The most important passages rejected are rejected not because of lack of proof that they are true, but on the ground that they cannot possibly be true, regardless of proof.

Orthodox Christians believe in plenary inspiration; that is, that all of the Bible was given by inspiration. They believe in verbal inspiration; that is, that the words used in the original manuscripts were the actual words of God as spoken by holy men of God "as they were moved by the Holy Ghost." They accept the Bible as true and divinely inspired, beginning with belief in God as Creator of all things, continuing Ruler of the universe which He made, and Heavenly Father to all His children. They believe that God is a personal God, who loves, and is interested in, all His creatures. They believe that He revealed His will unto men, and they accept the testimony of the writers of the Bible when they declare that the Holy Ghost spoke through them or through those whom they quote.

Those who deny that the Bible is true and infallible may be divided into several groups.

First: atheists reject the Bible because they deny the existence of God. Believing that there is no God, they are consistent in believing that there is no Bible or Word of God.

Second: agnostics profess ignorance; they do not know whether there is a God or not, and they consistently reject the Bible because they cannot believe there is a revealed will of God unless they believe there is a God with a will to reveal. Darwin was consistent when, in a letter written in his old age, after he declared himself an agnostic, he also declared that he believed there never had been any revelation. It is useless to argue either with an atheist or an agnostic in favour of an inspired Bible. They must first be brought to believe in a God before it is worth while to talk to them about God's word—although the Bible itself is proof of the existence of God.

Third: there are some who believe in God but do not believe that He ever revealed His will to men except through Nature. They profess to know God through what they call Nature, and through Nature alone.

## Where the Real Conflict Lies

Here are three classes made up of those who deny that the Bible is an inspired book, but they are not the ones who are to-day doing the greatest harm. The atheists are few in number, relatively speaking, and are so unreasonable as to exert little influence. Their denial of the existence of God in the face of overwhelming evidence that He does exist discredits their intelligence and reduces their influence to a minimum.

The agnostics by professing ignorance, forfeit their right to advise on the subject. They become a mere negative force, unwilling to accept the evidence in favour of the existence of God, and yet confessedly unable to furnish proof of the non-existence of God, And, as they do not attempt to prove that there is no God, they cannot consistently assert that the Bible is not the revealed will of God. They simply do not know.

And so with those who affirm belief in God but deny all revelation. Their denial of a revelation rests upon an assumption that God would not speak directly to man, which is combatted by proof that God did actually speak to man, as proved not only by the words themselves but by the influence the words have exerted on hearts and lives. The Christian need not be alarmed by any efforts that can be put forth by the members of the third class—those who deny all inspiration or refuse to believe in any inspiration.

The real conflict to-day is between those, on the one hand, who believe in God, in the Bible as the Word of God, and in Christ as the Son of God, and those, on the other hand, who believe in God but who believe that the Bible is inspired only in part—differing among themselves as to how much of it is inspired and as to what passages are inspired. The latter set up standards of their own, and there are nearly as many different standards as there are believers in partial inspiration. When they deny the infallibility of the Bible, they set up a standard that they regard either as infallible or as more trustworthy than the Bible itself. They really transfer the presumption of infallibility from the Bible to themselves, for either they say, "I believe this part of the Bible to be untrue because my own reason or my own judgment tells me that it is untrue," or they say, "I believe it untrue because So-and-so, in whose judgment I have confidence, tells me it is untrue." Whether one trusts in his own judgment as to the truthfulness of a passage, or trusts the judgment of some one else who denies the truthfulness of a passage, he is, in fact, trusting his own judgment, because if he does not rely on his own judgment in rejecting the passage it is his own judgment that substitutes the authority of the individual selected by him for the authority of the Bible.

It need hardly be added that such a rejection of the Bible, however the objector tries to limit it, is equivalent to a total rejection of the Bible as an authority, because an authority which is subject to be overruled on any point on any subject by anybody who cares to take the responsibility of overruling it, ceases to be of real value.

To illustrate: The orthodox Christian says to his child: The Bible is the Word of God. It contains the truth about the science of How to Live, and all the truth that it is necessary for one to know. Accept it and follow it, and it will be "a lamp to your feet and a light to your path." Trust it and you will make no mistake.

What is the attitude of the parent who believes that the Bible contains error? It depends upon how much error he thinks there is in the Bible—that is, how "liberal" he is. If he thinks that the errors outweigh the truth that the Bible contains, he will not care to have his child read it at all. If, like some of the modernists, he spends so much time finding fault with some of the so-called errors that he does not have time to quote the parts which he thinks probably, if not actually, true, the child will not desire to read it. By the time the child is sixteen, it may think itself able to decide Bible questions for itself and, following its parent's example, do some rejecting on its own responsibility.

A sophomore in a Georgia college informed me, at the conclusion of an address in Atlanta, that in order to reconcile Darwinism and Christianity, he only had to discard *Genesis*. Only *Genesis!* And yet there are three verses in the first chapter of *Genesis* that mean more to man than all the books of human origin: the first verse, which gives the most reasonable account of creation ever advanced; the twenty-fourth verse, which gives the only law governing the continuity of life on earth; and the twenty-sixth, which gives the only explanation of man's presence here.

The tendency of the human mind is to be consistent; therefore, when, for any reason, one eliminates a passage from the Bible, he generally proceeds to eliminate all other passages to which the same objections apply. The usual starting point, to-day, is the Mosaic account of man's creation; this is eliminated on the ground that it is inconsistent with the hypothesis of evolution, which will be considered in another article. The same reasoning eliminates the miraculous and the supernatural if carried to its logical conclusion. The Fall of man is next denied and, with it, the Atonement. Then the Virgin Birth is eliminated on the ground that it is miraculous and supernatural. By the time the modernist has brought the Saviour down to the stature of a man and then brought man down to a brute ancestry, he is ready to deny the bodily resurrection of Christ and leave Him entombed with the other dead. When the miracles and the supernatural are taken from the Bible, its inspiration denied, and its Christ robbed of the glory of a virgin birth, of the majesty of deity, and of the triumph of a resurrection, there is little left in the Bible to make it worth reading—certainly not enough to justify one in patterning his life after it or in carrying it to heathen lands.

The rejection of the doctrine of inspiration is a complacent sort of philosophy, that leaves those who adopt this view at liberty to spend upon their own pleasure time and money that they would feel it a duty to use for the spread of Christianity if they considered the Bible's message a Divine one and the world's need of Christianity an imperative need.

The Bible's inspiration is proved in many ways. Prophecies fulfilled are proof that those who uttered the prophecies were inspired. The harmony existing between Bible writers separated by centuries is proof that the same Spirit revealed to them the truths which they recorded. The truths which the Bible contains—truths vindicated in the lives of thousands of millions of people, millions of whom have died in the defense of those truths—are the strongest evidence possible.

The inspiration of the Bible is also proved by the fact that, while progress has been made along other lines, no progress has been made in the matters of which it treats. We go back to the Old Testament for the foundation of our statute law, and to the Sermon on the Mount for the rules that govern our spiritual development. The words of fishermen and others of the common people to-day outweigh in influence the teachings of Grecian philosophers and the wise men of other ancient civilizations. Why? Because they spoke as they were inspired.

Personal experience, also, testifies to the truth of the Bible. God's Word has given indomitable purpose and invincible strength to those who relied upon it; to those who trusted in it it has brought peace "that passeth understanding"; and it is the only hope of peace in the war-worn world. The Bible works miracles to-day; it lifts up the fallen and infuses a passion for service into the hearts that were before overflowing with selfishness. "By their fruits ye shall know them"; and the fruits of the Bible prove its Divine origin. It points the way to God and to Christ, and gives us the only solution of the problems that vex our hearts and perplex the world, namely: Thou shalt love the Lord with all thy heart, soul and mind, and thy neighbour as thyself.

The Bible is the only Book that gives the Christian's conception of God; it is the only Book that tells us of Christ and His mission. When faith in the Bible's veracity is destroyed, we have no God to worship or to fear, and no Christ to save by His blood and to guide by His heaven-born wisdom.

The world never needed an evangelistic Gospel more than it does to-day; and evangelism, it must be remembered, dies when the Bible ceases to be accepted as the revealed will of God.

# ❧146❧

# Science and Religion

## HARRY EMERSON FOSDICK

Harry Emerson Fosdick (1878–1969) was the best-known, self-proclaimed religious modernist in his heyday in the interwar period. A teacher at the Union Theological Seminary and pastor of the Riverside Church in New York supported by the Rockefellers, he was also a prolific author. Writing here in the aftermath of the Scopes trial, he acknowledged Van Dyke's point that the spiritual and scientific spheres were separate but explained that the continuing war between religion and science as the result of elements on both sides refusing to recognize it. The implication was up-to-date and comforting; benign reconciliation was possible from which only the immoderate would be excluded.

═══════════════════════════════

## I

The uproar about the teaching of evolution has brought back once more to the center of the stage the old controversy between science and religion. As one reads the many articles upon the subject one gets the uncomfortable impression that, while the extreme fundamentalists are unmistakably definite in their views about an inerrant Bible and the wickedness of evolution, and while the scientists are clear-cut in their attitude about the truth of evolution and the necessity of freedom in teaching it, the position of religious liberals is not being clearly put.

Some vaguely progressive minds take too much comfort in such consoling generalities as that true science and true religion cannot conflict. The proposition is so harmless that no one is tempted to gainsay it but, so far from solving any problems, it serves only to becloud the issue. The plain fact is that, however true science and true religion ought to behave toward each other, actual science and actual religion are having another disagreeable monkey-and-parrot time.

Source: Harry Emerson Fosdick, 'Science and Religion', *Adventurous Religion*, London, 1926, pp. 91–106.

That this ought not to happen, that, ideally, science and religion move in different realms and should peacefully pursue each its separate task in the interpretation of man's experience, is easy to say, and it is true. Life, like the thirteenth chapter of First Corinthians, if it is to be fully understood, needs for one thing the grammarian. He will analyze it into its parts of speech, note the differences between nouns and pronouns, verbs, adjectives, articles, and adverbs, and will formulate the laws by which they are put together to make a complex unity. That is an indispensable piece of business in the understanding of the chapter and it represents the scientist's work on the world at large. But if the chapter is to be fully known, a more comprehensive method of interpretation must be exercised upon it than the grammarian alone can be responsible for. Its meaning as a whole must be apprehended, its lessons understood, its spiritual value appropriated, its author studied through the medium of his expression. That attitude applied to life is religion. Religion is the appreciation of life's spiritual values and the interpretation of life, its origin, its purpose, and its destiny, in terms of them. The grammatical analysis and the spiritual appreciation ought not to quarrel. The appreciator ought to thank God for the grammarian whenever he thinks of him.

But, for some reason or other, making the lion and the lamb lie down in peace together has proved no more ideal a dream than getting science and religion to quit their controversy and become partners in the interpretation of life. What is the reason?

## II

In so far as religion is responsible, there are at least two explanations of this recurrent contention. One is the association of religion with an inerrant book. Every one who knows anything about the historical origins of the Bible knows how little it is an artificial product, the result of supernatural dictation, handed down from heaven, as has been taught of the Koran, or miraculously hidden and discovered, like the golden plates of Mormon. Modern scholarship has traced the progressive writing and assembling of our Scriptures with a massing of evidence which puts the general outline of the process beyond reasonable doubt. From the earliest documents, such as the war-songs of Deborah, up through the long story of growing laws, changing circumstances and customs, enlarged horizons of moral obligation, worthier thoughts of God, through the prophets and the Master's ministry to the early Christian church—stage by stage the writing and assembling of the documents which now comprise our Bible can be traced. How much of the Bible was in existence in the eighth century B.C. we know, and what each new century with its changing thoughts and insights contributed we can see.

It is obvious that this amazing literature came warmly up out of human experience. That is its glory and its strength. Touch it anywhere and you can feel the pulse of men and women in their joys and sorrows, struggles, aspirations, faiths and despairs. The whole book is "blood-tinctured, of a veined humanity". These were real folk whose spiritual life welled up in psalm and prophecy and whose life stories are told in the most rewarding narratives that literature has preserved. Here also was recorded a development of thought about God, about duty, about the significance of human life, far and away the most valuable that history records. Of course, a Christian who deeply believes God does not think it was an accident. Of course, he sees in it a revelation, an unveiling of the truth by which man's life is elevated, purified, redeemed. Of course he thinks it was inspired.

But whatever else inspiration may mean, it certainly does not mean that men in writing a sacred book are lifted out of their own day and provided with the mental thought-forms, scientific explanations, and world-views of a generation thousands of years unborn. It is that utterly fallacious and futile idea of inspiration which causes the trouble. One wonders why anybody should wish to believe it. What good does it do? What addition does it make to the inherent spiritual value of the book? Would the Twenty-third Psalm be more beautiful if the writer had had a Ph.D. from Harvard, or is the fourth chapter of Ephesians dependent for its worth upon the supposition that the writer held the Copernican astronomy.

There is no peace for religion in its relationships with science until we recognise that, of course, the Bible is not an inerrant book. As far as the physical universe is concerned, all the writers of the Bible supposed that they were living on a flat earth covered by the solid firmament of the sky, with heaven above and Sheol beneath, and fiery bodies moving across the face of the sky to illumine man. The Great Isaiah did not have to look through Galileo's telescope to write his fortieth chapter, nor would Micah's summary of the law, to do justly, to love kindness, and to walk humbly with God, have been any finer if he had been able to explain Einstein on relativity.

When, therefore, the Bible is set up in opposition to evolution, the whole issue is ludicrously false. The Bible knows nothing about evolution, just as it knows nothing about automobiles and radio. It knows no more about Darwin and his mutation of species than it does about Copernicus and his revolution of the earth. The Bible antedates all that. The first chapter of Genesis simply took the old Semitic story of creation, purified it of mythology, made it monotheistic, and set it in majestic language. It is the noblest narrative of creation in any ancient literature. But it has no possible connection with evolution, for or against. It is a picturesque presentation of creation in six literal days, each with an evening and morning. It is not proscientific; it is not antiscientific; for the simple reason that it is not scientific at all. And the absurd attempt to make Genesis mean evolution by stretching the days into eons never was dreamed of during long centuries of the Bible's existence until it was ingeniously suggested by some scribal mind, as a desperate device to insinuate geologic ages into Holy Writ.

No armistice can possibly be declared in the recurrent war between science and religion unless this elemental fact about the Bible is clear. To suppose that we must think about scientific problems in the way the Biblical writers did is incredible. Nobody does it. The most rock-ribbed fundamentalist never remotely approaches doing it. Voliva of Zion City comes nearest to it. He believes that the earth is flat. The Bible is the supreme Book of spiritual life. There we touch a valid revelation of the character and will of God. It is a fountain that never runs dry, and the better it is known the better for personal character and social progress. But to use it as a scientific text-book is perilous nonsense which does far more harm to religion than to anything else. That is indeed hoisting religion with its own petard.

## III

Religion's responsibility for the contest with science can be traced to another source. Religion may almost be said to consist in a sense of sacredness; it makes man feel that some things in his life are holy, inviolable; it reveres them, loves them, even worships before them as the symbols and evidence of God. This attitude of religion, throwing a glamour of sanctity over everything with which it is closely associated—shrines, rituals, holy persons and places, ideas and ideals—belongs to its very genius. No one would want a religion that did not do that. The cleansing of religion from superstition does not eliminate this powerful influence which inheres in the sense of sacredness; it simply detaches the feeling of sanctity from unworthy and magical objects and reorients it around moral ideals, transforms it into reverence for personality and devotion to duty seen as the will of God.

This consciousness that something in life is sacred, worth living and dying for, is one of humanity's moral indispensables, and religion is the fruitful mother of it. But it is very dangerous. It is one of the things which we cannot get on without but which it is perilous to get on with. I was talking recently with a student of sociology about the strange contrast between the eager welcome given to new scientific inventions and apathy, dislike, or active opposition that greets new suggestions in the social and spiritual realms. The automobile, the aeroplane, the radio—how instantly and avidly they are received and utilized! But to alter the ritual observances of a church, to introduce eugenic practices, to get a reformation of theology, or to organize a League of Nations to replace belligerent nationalism—what an uproar of outraged sentiment always accompanies suggested change in such realms!

The reasons for this strange inconsistency are doubtless many, but the sense of sacredness clearly plays an important part. That holds up progress indefinitely in any place where it can get a foothold. Nobody counts a bicycle sacred if he wants an automobile, or regards rowing a boat as holy if he is able to buy a motor. The sense of sanctity does not operate in such realms. We change from candles to kerosene lamps, to gas, to electricity with no struggle against the rebellious sentiment of sacredness. But in the realms of human relationships in general and of religion in particular the feeling of sanctity is one of the most powerful, restraining influences in our lives. Patriotism conceived in terms of *my country against yours* gains sanctity, and when men wish to change it to *my country with yours for the peace of the world*, aroused patriots resent the new idea as though a shrine were being desecrated. Even such unlikely things as the rules of the United States Senate can become sacred until any alteration seems sacrilege. As for religion, this truth easily explains most of its ultraconservatism. How typical of all religion it is that, long after the stone age was passed and bronze knives had come in for household purposes, the old flint knife still was used to slay sacrificial beasts! Religion had cast over the ancient implement the glamour of sanctity and it could not be changed.

The application of this to the problem in hand is clear. Whatever else religion may clothe with feelings of reverence, it is sure to do so with those forms of thought, those mental vehicles, in which it has carried the precious freight of its spiritual experience. Listen to good old Father Inchofer in 1631 as he pours out of a pious heart his outraged sense of sacrilege at the idea that the earth moves:

> The opinion of the earth's motion is of all heresies the most abominable, the most pernicious, the most scandalous; the immovability of the earth is thrice sacred; argument against the immortality of the soul, the existence of God, and the incarnation, should be tolerated sooner than an argument to prove that the earth moves.

Why this rage? Why should a gentle servant of his fellows thus boil with indignant grief at a new astronomy? The reason is precisely the same that makes the fundamentalist to-day forget the Sermon on the Mount and ransack the dictionary for something bad enough to say about the evolutionists. Father Inchofer, I suppose, had had a deep and beautiful spiritual experience. He had lived in fellowship with God and love for men. He had always visualized that relationship in terms of a stationary earth with the concentric heavens encircling it. On that mental trellis the flowers of his spirit had bloomed. It was very sacred to him. He revered it as part and parcel of his faith. We ought to sympathize with him. No wonder the idea of a moving earth seemed to him, not an advance of science, but an abyss of blasphemy.

Nevertheless, Father Inchofer was wrong and Father Inchofer's successors to-day are wrong for the same reason. They have let their sense of sacredness run away with them. Their feeling of sanctity has unintelligently attached itself to all sorts of things that are not integral parts of vital religion. A stationary earth is not sacred; a whimsical universe where miracles, not law, are the order of the day is not sacred; creation by fiat is not sacred. Religion has no inherent dependence on such outgrown ideas. Yet all these things, along with many others from the use of anesthetics in operations to acceptance of the law of gravitation, have been bitterly opposed in the name of religion as though the old science to which the religious imagination had clung, around which it had entwined itself, were a holy thing. There is no peace in sight between science and religion until religion recognizes that the sense of sanctity is too valuable to be misused in holding up scientific progress. Once many Christians were scandalized at geology just as now they are scandalized at evolution; they called it "a dark art", "dangerous and disreputable", "a forbidden province" "an awful invasion of the testimony of Revelation". How long will religious people go on making this lamentable blunder which always reacts disastrously upon the fortunes of religion itself and in the end can do nothing against the new truth?

Always the outcome has been the same: the scientific view of the world has triumphed and the seers of the spirit have found the new truth a nobler vehicle than the old for the experiences of the soul. Religion is not dependent on this scientific formulation or that. Religion moves in the realm of the spiritual values where the soul does justly, loves kindness, and walks humbly with its God. Through all the centuries, under every conceivable scientific view of the world, men have found their peace and power in that; and if to-morrow our modern view should be upset and Darwin be out-Darwined by some new discoverer, our children's children at their best would find, flowing in their new channels, the water of eternal life, whereof, if a man drink, he does not thirst again.

## IV

One does not mean that blame for the repeated contests between science and religion rests exclusively upon religion. Scientists are human; they are quite capable of making fools of themselves. Especially they display an inveterate weakness before one besetting temptation. They get a working hypothesis in some special science; they rejoice in its effectiveness; they organize by means of it the data in their particular realm; and then, infatuated by their success, they proceed to postulate the hypothesis as a complete explanation of the universe and an adequate philosophy of life. Again and again that has been done. One specialist in the effect of sunlight on life was even guilty of the ludicrous dictum: "Heliotropism doubtless wrote Hamlet". To-day some of our behaviorists in psychology are doing the same thing. One might have expected it. This overweening confidence in the adequacy of a working hypothesis in a special science to explain everything naturally emerges in the early days of the science when the new idea has just burst in all its glory on the thought of its discoverers. Behaviorism is a very valuable working method of investigation in psychology, but behaviorism is not an adequate account of personality, as some of its devotees consider it; much less does it furnish a comprehensive philosophy of life.

Religion, therefore, does have reason to be deeply concerned about some tendencies in modern science. There is a real conflict between those whom science has led to a materialistic philosophy and those who interpret life in terms of its spiritual values. But this is not a conflict between science and religion; this is a conflict between most scientists and all religionists on one side and a few scientists upon the other.

As for the issues now popularly upsetting the equilibrium of the churches in America, let fundamentalism look to itself. It is not fighting evolution with facts, which alone can be effective instruments in such a war. No one who knows the facts is against evolution. It is fighting evolution with authoritative dicta from an inerrant Book and with a horrified sense of outraged sanctity about the disturbance of an outgrown way of thinking. That sort of procedure never yet did anything but harm to religion. Meanwhile, increasing multitudes of devout Christians rejoice in the larger thought of God and the stronger faith in him which evolution has brought.

# ❧·147·❧

# The Kentucky Campaign against the Teaching of Evolution

## ALONZO W. FORTUNE

Tennessee's was the most dramatic, but the struggle over proposed or enacted laws to restrain the teaching of evolutionary theory in publicly funded education was quite widespread in the 1920s. Fortune's narrative of the controversy in Kentucky was as a contemporary witness of events from his position as professor and dean at the College of the Bible in Lexington. The documentation indicates sharp divisions between denominations over the proposed law.

The state of Kentucky has been passing through a period of intense religious discussion. In pulpit, press, schoolroom, social gathering, around the fireside, and on the street corner evolution has been the favorite topic. This controversy became state wide when a bill to prohibit the teaching of evolution was introduced in the Kentucky legislature, January 23, 1922. Inasmuch as the propaganda which is back of this bill is extending throughout the country, the religious and educational leaders of the nation have been much interested in the proceedings at Frankfort. The papers and magazines of the country have had articles and editorials on the Kentucky situation, treating it more or less lightly; but it is really a time to be serious, for what has been attempted here may be attempted in any state of the union.

The introduction of this bill was the culmination of an active campaign against the teaching of evolution which has been conducted with increasing vigor for four or five years. The colleges and public schools of Kentucky have for years been teaching the modern scientific theory of evolution, and no objection has been made. One of the colleges which is under the control of the denomination which has been the most active in this recent anti-evolution movement celebrated the birth of Darwin in 1909. About five years ago a reactionary wing

Source: Alonzo W. Fortune, 'The Kentucky Campaign against the Teaching of Evolution', *Journal of Religion*, May 1922.

in the Christian church made an attack on the members of the faculty of the College of the Bible, one of their theological institutions which is located in Lexington. Among other things these men were charged with teaching the theory of evolution as it applies to man. This opposition has continued to the present. During recent months there has been a growing sentiment against the teaching of evolution in schools supported by public funds. The Baptists have taken the lead in this opposition, but they have had the support of other communions.

The immediate occasion for the attempted legislative barrier against the teaching of evolution was the proposed enlargement of the University of Kentucky. President Frank L. McVey launched a movement during the summer to enlarge greatly the state university. It was generally understood that the theory of evolution was taught in the university, and one of the professors has engaged in newspaper controversy on the subject with Dr. J. W. Porter, who was until recently the pastor of the First Baptist Church of Lexington. Some of the professors of the university were accused of being radical in their views, and their statements and the effect of these on the faith of the students had been greatly exaggerated. This proposed enlargement of the University of Kentucky intensified the activities of those who were opposed to the teaching of evolution.

Plans were being formulated for several months for the campaign which was to drive evolution from the state. During the autumn the "Fundamentalists" held conferences in several of the important centers of the state, and much was said in these meetings about the dangers of evolution. The campaign for legislative enactment against the teaching of evolution was inaugurated by Dr. J. W. Porter, who became the leader of the movement, in a resolution which was presented to the Baptist State Board of Missions, meeting in Louisville, December 6. This resolution charged that the "false and degrading theory of Darwinian evolution is taught in textbooks" of the state university and many of the high schools throughout Kentucky. This resolution led to the appointment of a committee which was to prepare literature, launch active propaganda against the theory and to carry the matter to the state legislature for the purpose of obtaining the enactment of "laws in harmony with the resolution." This committee was charged to "look into funds going to the state university if the university does not conform to the requirements of the resolution."

Shortly after this action by the Baptist State Board of Missions, Dr. Porter preached a sermon against evolution in the First Baptist Church of Lexington. In the course of this sermon he read a letter from William Jennings Bryan, praising him for his opposition to the teaching of the Darwinian theory of evolution in the public schools. In this letter Mr. Bryan said:

> I have seen much of your activity and am gratified. You have done exactly what I think should be done and our Florida Baptists have taken the same step. I cited the action of the Baptists of your state in speaking to them here. The movement will sweep the country and drive Darwinism from our schools.

Mr. Bryan seemed to think that inasmuch as the evolutionists lacked courage it would be easy to rout them. He said:

277

The agnostics, who are undermining the faith of our students, will be glad enough to teach anything the people want taught when the people speak with emphasis. My explanation is that a man who believes that he has brute blood in him will never be a martyr. Only whose who believe they are made in the image of God will die for a truth. We have all the Elijahs on our side. Strength to your arms.

In this sermon Dr. Porter declared that "Darwinism would be run out of Kentucky if it took every cent the Baptist people of the Commonwealth had to do it." He also stated that the Lexington City Board of Education would be petitioned to discontinue the use of the present textbook on zoology because it teaches the evolution theory.

The campaign was intensified by the coming of W. J. Bryan to deliver a series of addresses in central Kentucky. He had delivered his address in Louisville in September. He spoke before the House and the Senate in joint session January 19. He denounced the evolutionists with his usual vigor and called upon the lawmakers to protect our young people. His meeting in Lexington was typical of the others. Although the price of admission was fifty cents and one dollar the auditorium was crowded to hear him. Although he bitterly denounced Darwinism he did not seem to make any definite distinction between that and other theories of evolution. He warned students against the professor who teaches the Darwinian theory as "the most dangerous man that could be met." He referred to numerous incidents in various universities to show that the teaching of evolution destroys faith in God and the Bible. He read passages on evolution from some of the textbooks used in Kentucky schools and urged that such teaching should be prohibited in schools supported by public funds. At the close of his lecture Rev. W. L. Brock, pastor of the Immanuel Baptist Church of Lexington, presented the following resolutions which were adopted by a rising vote in which a large majority of those present participated:

Whereas, Darwinian evolution, the unscientific anti-Biblical teaching that man is descended from a lower form of life, is being taught in the schools of Kentucky, supported by the taxation of her citizens, and whereas we believe this teaching to detrimental to the faith, and therefore to the morals of the rising generation; therefore, be it resolved:

1. That, while we cherish the right of every man to worship God according to the dictates of his own conscience, and while we accord to all men the right to found and maintain schools to teach the tenets of their faith, we vigorously deny the right of any set of men, whether orthodox, atheists, or infidels, to teach their own peculiar views of the Bible at state expense;

2. While conceding that state schools, on the ground of our constitutional separation between church and state, are excused from the positive teaching of the Bible, we maintain with deepest earnestness that this constitutional provision prohibits their teaching views antagonistic to the Bible—that separation prohibits alike the union of the church and state and the union of the state and atheism or infidelity;

3. In view of the above, we respectfully request presidents, faculties and trustees of state schools, municipal boards of education and trustees of public schools to co-operate in the elimination of Darwinism and similar evolution

theories, teaching that man is descended from a brute or some lower form of life, from their teaching and textbooks;

4. We earnestly appeal to the General Assembly of Kentucky for legislation prohibiting the teaching in state schools of evolution, destructive criticism and every form of atheism and infidelity whatsoever.

These preliminary steps were followed by the campaign in the legislature. This was inaugurated by the introduction in the House of a bill against the teaching of evolution. This bill reads as follows:

KENTUCKY GENERAL ASSEMBLY
1922
House Bill 191—Introduced January 23
By Representative George W. Ellis, Barren County

An act to prohibit the teaching in public schools and other public institutions of learning, Darwinism, atheism, agnosticism or evolution as it pertains to the origin of man.

Be it enacted by the General Assembly of the Commonwealth of Kentucky:

SECTION 1. That it shall be unlawful for a teacher, principal, superintendent, president or anyone else who is connected in any way with the public schools, high schools, training schools, normal schools, colleges, universities or any other institutions of learning in this Commonwealth, where public money of this Commonwealth is used in whole or in part for the purpose of maintaining, educating or training the children or young men or young women of this Commonwealth; for such teacher, principal, superintendent, president or other person connected directly or indirectly with such schools or institutions of learning to teach or knowingly permit the same to be taught; Darwinism, atheism, agnosticism, or the theory of evolution in so far as it pertains to the origin of man; and anyone so offending shall on conviction be fined not less than fifty nor more than five thousand dollars or confined in the county jail not less than ten days nor more than twelve months, or both fined and imprisoned in the discretion of the jury.

SEC. 2. If any school, college, university, normal school, training school or any other institution of learning which has been chartered by the Commonwealth of Kentucky and which is sustained in whole or in part by the public funds of said Commonwealth shall knowingly or willingly teach or permit to be taught Darwinism, atheism, agnosticism, or the theory of evolution as it pertains to the origin of man it shall forfeit its charter and on conviction shall be fined in any sum not to exceed five thousand dollars. In all proceedings of forfeiture or revocation of charter, the holder thereof shall be given thirty days notice in which to prepare for a hearing to be attended by its representative or counsel.

The Commonwealth or the accused may take such oral or written proof for or against the accused as it may deem it the best to present these facts.

This act is to be in full force and effect from and after its passage and approval as provided by law.

This was followed two days later by the introduction of a similar bill in the Senate by Senator James R. Rash, of Madisonville. This bill is as follows:

An act prohibiting the teaching of evolution in any school, college or institution of learning maintained in whole or in part in this State by funds raised by taxation and providing penalties therefor.

Be it enacted by the General Assembly of the Commonwealth of Kentucky:

1. It shall be unlawful in any school or college or institution of learning maintained in whole or in part, in this State, by funds raised by taxation, for anyone to teach any theory of evolution that derives man from the brute or any other form of life, or that eliminates God as the creator of man by a direct creative act. No textbook containing any such teaching shall be adopted for use in any such school or college or institution of learning maintained in whole or in part by funds raised by taxation in this state. Any person violating any of the provisions of this section shall be fined not less than fifty dollars nor more than one thousand dollars.

2. Any person acting as a teacher or instructor in any school or other institution of learning maintained in whole or in part by funds derived from taxation who shall teach or give instruction in any of the theories prohibited by Section 1 of this Act shall forfeit his position and place as such teacher or instructor and shall be entitled to no salary, either past or future.

Any two persons having information that instruction in any of the theories prohibited by Section 1 of this Act is being given or has been given in any school or institution of learning maintained in whole or in part by funds derived from taxation may make complaint thereof. Said complaint shall be in writing and signed by the parties making the charge and shall be delivered to the board or other persons authorized by law to employ such teacher. Within five days after the filing of such complaint said board shall call said teacher before them and shall investigate said complaint, and if the same is found to be true, said teacher shall be discharged.

The introduction of these two bills was the signal for a state-wide campaign. Most of the ministers in the state either preached against evolution, or attempted to show that it was possible for one to be an evolutionist and still be a Christian. The dailies and the county papers had articles and editorials for and against in almost every issue. Evolution was discussed by all classes wherever they met together. It was marvellous to see how proficient in scientific knowledge the average citizen of Kentucky suddenly became. The anti-evolutionists carried advertisements in the papers to further their propaganda. In these advertisements an attempt was made to discredit evolution by quoting authorities against it. The arguments that were made against evolution can be summed up under four heads. It is antagonistic to the Bible, and the teaching of it undermines faith in Christianity. It lowers man to the brute, and takes away his divine birthright. It eliminates God from creation. It justifies force as a social program.

The opponents of legislation on the subject of evolution insisted that education should be untrammeled. They urged that instead of belief in evolution destroying faith in God, it gives him a larger place. The annual council of the Episcopalian Diocese of Kentucky, which met in Louisville shortly after the introduction of the bills, unanimously passed the following resolutions:

Whereas a bill was introduced Monday, January 23, in the Kentucky Legislature against the teachings of Darwinism, atheism, agnosticism, or evolution as pertains to the origin of man in schools maintained wholly or in part by State funds;

Be it resolved by this council, representing the Episcopal Church in the diocese of Kentucky, assembled at Christ Church Cathedral in Louisville,

Kentucky, the 26th day of January, 1922, that we most urgently protest against the passage of such a bill for the following reasons:

First—The theory popularly known as Darwinism, or natural selection of evolution, is not synonymous with atheism or agnosticism, as the title of this bill seems to indicate. Some of the most scholarly, devout and eminent Christian thinkers have been and are today avowed evolutionists, notably the late Henry Drummond, Alfred Russell Wallace, the co-discoverer with Darwin, and many others.

Second—While opposing with all earnestness possible the teaching of atheism or agnosticism, yet we deprecate the attempt of a popular legislative body to decide questions concerning the curricula of our schools and colleges and our textbooks, for which task they were not selected; nor have they the time, technique or training to fit them to be judges. These questions pertain to and must be left to the decision of those chosen and fitted for this purpose, namely, our educators themselves.

The test was first made in the Senate. Senate Bill 136, which had been introduced by Senator Rush, was argued before the Committee on Kentucky Statutes February 9. The senate chamber was crowded and the hour was one of intense feeling. Any legislation on the subject under consideration was opposed by President McVey of the University of Kentucky and Dr. E. L. Powell, pastor of the First Christian Church of Louisville. Some legislation on the subject was urged by President E. Y. Mullins of the Baptist Theological Seminary, of Louisville and Dr. J. W. Porter of Lexington.

The following amended bill, which was agreed on at a meeting of Baptist ministers, was introduced at the instance of Dr. Mullins:

An Act prohibiting the teaching of anything that will weaken or undermine the religious faith of the pupils in any school or college or institution of learning maintained in whole or part in this State by funds raised by taxation and providing penalties therefor.

Be it enacted by the General Assembly of the Commonwealth of Kentucky:

Whereas a fundamental principle of the separation of church and state is organic in our American laws, and

Whereas the separation does not imply an antagonism between church and state, but rather mutual respect and relations of friendship and co-operation, and

Whereas the religious rights of our people are guaranteed to them by law, and

Whereas it is glaring violation of the principle of religious liberty when teachers in our schools, supported by our taxes, attack or seek to undermine or destroy the religious beliefs of students.

1. Now in order to safeguard the religious rights of our people and to establish more securely the principle of separation of church and state, no teacher in any department on any university, normal school, or public school in the State of Kentucky, supported in whole or in part by funds raised by taxation, who shall directly or indirectly attack or assail or seek to undermine or weaken or destroy the religious beliefs and convictions of pupils of said university, normal school, or public school shall be employed as a member of the faculty of said university, normal school, or public school by the authorities entrusted with such duties.

2. Should such teacher, by oversight on the part of the board or misrepresentation by said teacher or teachers, be employed by the governing

boards of any of said institutions entrusted with such duties, said governing boards shall duly consider any and every complaint made in writing by two persons against any teacher or teachers violating the above provisions, and if said charges are established as true, said teacher or teachers shall be immediately dismissed from the faculty of said institution.

President McVey argued that the legislation proposed "leads to a lack of personal liberty provided for under the rights of the constitution." He said, "If you can pass such an act as the one before you for consideration you would be justifiable in passing one which provides for a certain religious belief." He declared that if the proposed legislation were enacted it would be impossible to secure textbooks for the schools of Kentucky. He maintained that such legislation would force our young people to go to church schools or to the universities of other states to complete their education.

Dr. Powell argued that the proposed legislation is un-American and contrary to the fundamental principles of Protestantism. He insisted that it is unconstitutional because it interferes with the freedom of conscience.

Dr. Mullins took the position that there should be no legislation that interferes with science, but he insisted that certain conditions exist which make some legislation necessary. He said,

> I do not believe that the church shall have the power to say what shall and shall not be taught in the school, and, on the other hand, I do not believe that the state shall have the power to teach something that is a direct attack on the Christian religion.

He urged the passage of the first amendment. Dr. Porter insisted on the passage of a bill that prohibits the teaching of any theory that derives man from a lower form of life.

The committee reported out the amendment suggested by Dr. Mullins which was discussed in the Senate February 15. The Senate seemed to be about equally divided with perhaps a slight majority in favor of the bill. After much filibustering the bill was finally referred to the Rules Committee by a vote of 19 to 17. this action virtually killed the bill as far as the Senate was concerned.

People generally seemed to think that there would be no further action during the present session, and they seemed to be satisfied to call a truce in the controversy and give time a chance to throw some light on the whole situation. The question, however, was reopened when the House voted to call the Ellis bill out of the Rules Committee. Practically the entire day, March 5, was given up to a discussion of the bill with virtually the same arguments that were made before the Senate. Although this was the most objectionable of all the bills it was defeated by just one vote, the vote being 42 to 41. Thus the evolution controversy in this session of the General Assembly has ended with a slight victory for a free educational system.

# ❦·148·❧

# The Social Gospel

## JOHN HORSCH

The Social Gospel was always a minority tendency in the main denominations and, by the 1920s, it had provoked strong reactions. As this critique suggests, theologically conservative Christians saw the Social Gospel's concern with social improvement displacing the urgency of individual spiritual renewal. They attributed this to the inadequacies of the liberal theology which underpinned the Social Gospel.

The new theology rejects the Bible teaching on man's sinfulness and the biblical conception of the world. The "exceeding sinfulness of sin," the existence of Satan and his kingdom, and the need of supernatural salvation are denied. For the Bible message of *personal* reconstruction the social gospel substitutes the call to *social* reconstruction.

Not long ago the General Secretary of Home Missions of one of the more prominent evangelical denominations in a public address set forth the nature and meaning of the social gospel, he himself being an ardent advocate of it. His address in substance follows.

The main root of the social gospel goes back to the doctrine of divine immanence. If God is the immanent world energy, there is no room for moral or religious dualism.

The thought that there is a kingdom of evil besides the kingdom of God is all wrong. There is only one kingdom and every man is a citizen of it. Since there is only one immanent life force, the world is a unit and man also is a unit. There is no room therefore for the old conception of sin. Furthermore there should be no attempt made to draw a line of distinction between things religious and secular, holy and unholy, Christian and non-Christian, the church and the world. Sin is, in the last analysis, not a personal but a social evil. It is the result of improper social conditions. So long as our social order is not Christianized, sin will ever be present with us. It is impossible to lead a Christian life except in a Christianized society. Yet if we accept the thought of divine immanence, sin and evil cannot be quite so bad as they seem to be. Considered from the viewpoint of

Source: John Horsch, 'The Social Gospel', *Modern Religious Liberalism*, Scottsdale, PA, 1920, pp. 132–45.

the social gospel the thought that God would damn a man because of sin is offensive.

Since man is inherently good and all men are God's children, there is in modern religion no place for individual salvation. The divine plan of salvation of which conservatives still speak is superstition. What is needed is not individual but social salvation. For although the world is God's kingdom, it does not follow that all is developed to perfection, or is incapable of further improvement. Such a conception would not fit into the scheme of general evolution. Salvation has become a social term. It means that the world must be made better socially by reforms and social improvements of various kinds, by education and moral advancement.

In a word, the social gospel address itself to the task to make the world a decent place to live in. This is the business of the church in the new age. Considered in its true light this endeavor is essentially religious, it is the manifestation of true spirituality. What was formerly spoken of as religious is of value only in so far as it serves social ends. If my life is a unit, then all that pertains to my life is an object of the church's mission.

Such is the modern social gospel. The Biblical Gospel of salvation is "restated"; the Cross is given "a social interpretation". For true spiritual religion we are offered a substitute having no other purpose than to make the world a decent place to live in. The new gospel is the gospel of externalism. It is assumed that favorable external conditions will bring about the moral regeneration of society and that human nature will respond automatically to its better environment. Salvation is to come through civic, economic, social and political remedies. Until the individual's economic and social desires have been satisfied, they tell us, it is both useless and illogical to preach to him morality and spirituality. To Christianize the social order, rather than the individual, or in other words, to make the world a decent place to live in, is supposed to be the great task of the church.

The social gospel therefore lays enormous emphasis on a man's physical and material well-being. Religion is held to be nothing more than a plan for social welfare. Christianity is considered a scheme of social improvement. It is reduced to humanitarian and social endeavors. It is interpreted in terms of materialistic humanitarianism. Education and sanitation take the place of personal regeneration and the Holy Spirit. True spiritual Christianity is denied.

The social gospel is in fact religiously indifferent. It holds that the difference between Christianity and other religions is in degree, not in kind. Yet the social gospel comes under the cloak of religion. We are told that the spirit of loyalty and devotion shown towards modern social endeavors deserves the name of religion and Christianity. "The man who enters thoroughly into the social movements of his time," says Professor Edward Scribner Ames, of the University of Chicago,

> is to that extent genuinely religious, though he may characterize himself quite otherwise (i.e., though he may be an avowed unbeliever). Non-religious persons are accordingly those who fail to enter vitally into a world of social activities and feelings.

John Herman Randall says:

> The simple fact is, we are living in an age that is fast becoming socialized from top to bottom, and individual religion, like individual ethics, must give way to broader and more social conceptions.

"The rapid and significant development of Christianity in the interests of what is called the 'social gospel'," says Professor Gerald Birney Smith of the University of Chicago, "is really part and parcel of *a humanizing of religious interest.*"

The social gospel is proclaimed in numerous books and magazine articles as well as from many pulpits. Countless representatives of modern liberalism are defending it. "Our old religion was a process of saving a few souls here and there out of a world that we condemned as bad," says a prominent Methodist preacher of the State of New York;

> the new religion is a community affair, and we will make our towns and our cities the right kind of places so that everybody will be a Christian as a matter of course. When it used to be hard to be good, it will become difficult to be bad.

Individual salvation is practically spurned and denied. A minister of a Unitarian church in New York said recently in a sermon:

> No man is satisfactorily saved unless he is a member of a saved home; there cannot be a saved home unless there is a saved community, nor can there be a saved community unless there is a saved world.

In other words, salvation is wholly a matter of social advance.

Considering the question from the viewpoint of New Testament Christianity some fatal weaknesses of the social gospel are in evidence. The new gospel identifies essence and fruit. Making social service the most important feature of Christianity, the fruit is mistaken for the essence. In fact, the fruit is divorced from the tree that produces it. Social betterment is excellent as the outgrowth of Christianity; the attempts to make it a substitute for the Christian religion have signally failed. The social gospel overlooks the fact that man's greatest needs are of a spiritual nature, and hence the greatest service to man is to supply these needs. The new gospel ignores the vital and fundamental issues that have to do with man's spiritual well-being and true betterment. The primary duty of the church, namely, to give spiritual food to the souls of men, is set aside. It is a wholesome effort for the improvement of mankind on the surface rather than for betterment in the mainspring of the heart where the seat of evil lies.

Christianity recognizes the fact that personal reconstruction through the Gospel is the greatest factor in bringing about real and lasting social betterment in the world. John Morley, a noted British author, gives the following significant testimony:

> We all have been upon the wrong track, and the result is that the whole of us have less to show for our work than one man, Booth [of the Salvation Army]. Herbert Spencer, Matthew Arnold, Frederic Harrison, and the rest of us who have spent our lives in endeavoring to dispel superstition and to bring on a new

era, have to admit that Booth has had more direct effect upon this generation than all of us put together.

The social gospel, then, fails to distinguish between *Christian* service and *social* service. But the two are not identical. The successful business man, or laborer, is rendering valuable social service though he may not be a Christian, or he may be a Christian only nominally and hence may be lacking the Christian motive that is essential to Christian service. It is quite true that the meanest manual labor is sanctified and becomes elevating when it is done from a Christian motive, "as unto the Lord." But this does not mean that such work is in itself of equal importance with the more direct Christian work which has to do principally with leading men to Christ and caring for their spiritual welfare. The apostle Paul making tents in Ephesus did an important work. It enabled him to continue his labors to which the Lord had called him. But great would be the world's loss had Paul been of the opinion that secular work in itself is as important as the preaching of the Gospel, and had given his whole time and effort to tent making and other kinds of social service. Had Paul even devoted the entire income from his business to Christian purposes, he would have made a mistake. It was not the work to which God called him. Yet there are plenty of men who are called of God to make tents. If they do their work from the same motive as Paul did his work and are as faithful as Paul was, their reward in the day of Christ will be equal to that of Paul. Christian work done from the Christian motive must be distinguished from social service in which this motive is absent.

Another glaring weakness of the social gospel is that it does not address itself to all classes. If social service is the whole of Christianity, then those who are unable to render such service are deprived of the privilege of being Christians. The social gospel has no message for the halt and maimed, the suffering from cancer and tuberculosis; no message for the dying. To those whose souls cry out for the living God the message of the new gospel is a mockery.

Professor Thomas N. Carver, a radical religious liberal, calls attention to another flaw in the gospel of social service, namely its indefiniteness. He points out that "under the old doctrine of salvation Christian work had a definite meaning. It meant saving souls . . . bringing them into the kingdom". He says further:

> It is not enough to preach the gospel of work unless you mention the job at
> which you expect people to work. Instead of merely saying, "Work, for the
> night is coming," it is necessary to be somewhat specific and say (if the metre
> can be fixed up), "Improve this road, for the night is coming. Build this bridge,
> for the night is coming. Drain this swamp. Improve this crop, for the night is
> coming.
> In the absence of some kind of doctrine of salvation work means little more
> than persuading people to join the Church. Under these conditions, the Church
> becomes very much like an initiation society, such as you would find in many
> colleges.

The pastor of a Unitarian Church—formerly a Presbyterian minister—writes:

> Not very long ago the liveliest and most vigorous denominations had two objects, which really amounted to one, that were perfectly clear in their own consciousness and to the world,—the conversion to goodness of those who were not good, and the building up in goodness of those who had been converted. All their efforts were directed to the accomplishment of these definite ends. Their conception of what constitutes goodness and of the way to put one's self in possession of it was doubtless crude and in large measure mistaken. They had involved goodness in a network of abstruse theology. But nevertheless, sticking close to the Bible, as they understood it, they drew the people, held their grip on them, and promoted real goodness in their lives. Fundamentally these forefathers were right. And they  held the people because both they and the people knew that they were right. We *who have discarded conversion and growth in grace as outlandish absurdities, and the Bible too,* or at least have reduced them to the flabbiest kind of thing, who have left ourselves without any clear object, who are driven hither and thither by every wind of doctrine and sleight of men, *are in mortal error, and the world knows it.*

A reason why the social gospel is lacking in definiteness is that the task which it would lay upon the church is too extended in scope. Social service is a very broad term. A number of writers, as for example Professor Edwin L. Earp, of Drew Theological Seminary, are of the opinion that the church should identify herself with the Rural Life Movement. To make the country church a success, we are told, the church must make it her business to build up a prosperous farming community. The rural preacher must be an agricultural expert. He must concern himself with the problems of better seeds, better breeds, better implements, and up-to-date methods of farming. As a prominent religious periodical summed it up some years ago, a minister should be trained to "save the crops of his people, as well as their souls". There have been arranged agricultural summer courses for ministers. "It is the plan to teach the rural pastors how they may help the farmers to get better crops by applying scientific methods, "we read in a prospectus for such a course, "so that the farmers in return may learn better church-methods".

If it is the church's business, however, to teach agriculture to rural populations, can she consistently overlook the fact that the cities are teeming with those whose usefulness could be greatly enhanced by further training in the occupations which they are following, and who also should be won for the church?—For the church to accept the modern program of social service would be not merely to neglect the work to which she is called, but it would mean that she become a "Jack of all trades and master of none"—a real obstacle to general efficiency. American agriculture must be in a bad way if the farmers need the ministers to teach them how to raise pigs and grow corn.

Rejecting, in short, the Christian view of man's sinfulness and of an evil world, the social gospel prescribes reformation as the needed remedy. Reformation and man-wrought changes are believed adequate to make the individual as well as the world all that is to be desired. Now it cannot be questioned for a moment that reform is good in its place. If a thief ceases to steal and begins to work for an honest living, he is doing a praiseworthy thing. Christianity does not hold the absurd view that the vicious and profligate are as desirable members of society as they who live honorable lives. But it is the church's business to stand for Christianization in the New Testament sense, not for mere reformation. A sinner who reforms is not for that reason a Christian. Reformation will not change the human heart. Regeneration is the work of God.

Walter Rauschenbusch has written A *Theology for the Social Gospel*. The title of the book is significant. The substance of its contents is not claimed to be *the* theology but *a* theology for the social gospel. This author's primary interest was the gospel of Socialism. Theology was to him, as it is to modernists in general, quite a secondary matter. Its value is, in his view, to be measured by the possible service it could be made to render the social gospel. This new liberalistic theology is supposed to be a thing to be used rather than accepted as true. Rauschenbusch's theology is by no means the foundation for his gospel, but is itself founded on the social gospel. He admits that some other theology may be built on the principles of Socialism and he knew that the great majority of Socialists do not accept his theology. In fact nearly all the leading Socialists, following in the footsteps of Karl Marx, their greatest representative, look upon all theology with contempt. Rauschenbusch never made the claim that Socialism would not be successful without accepting his theology, but he hoped that his theology would aid the cause of Socialism by making it acceptable to professing Christians. In one instance he makes this honest confession: "Of course some of the ideas I have ventured to put down are simply a play of personal fancy about a fascinating subject." All this means that "the theology for the social gospel' is not a matter of vital concern to the cause of Socialism nor to any other cause.

"The social gospel is believed by trinitarians and unitarians alike," says Rauschenbusch, "by Catholic Modernists and Kansas Presbyterians of the most cerulean colour. It arouses a fresh and warm loyalty to Christ wherever it goes, though not always a loyalty to the Church." But since the social gospel as represented by this author, rejects the deity of Christ, it is incorrect to say that it is accepted by trinitarians. Again, deny Christ's deity, and the Jesus you have left is not a person deserving loyalty. Could you honor as a leader a mere man who said in regard to his own person what Jesus said about Himself:

> "I am the light of the world—the way, the truth and the life—the living bread come down from heaven; before Abraham was I am; all power is given unto me in heaven and on earth," etc?

Would not one saying these things about himself, unless they are true, deserve sympathy and pity, rather than honor?

Dr. Lyman Abbott in the *Outlook* recently said that church attendance is not an index to religious interest, because men read religious articles in magazines and express their worship in social service. Indeed modern church-goers are often told that such service is the leading interest of Christianity. It is generally known that in the modernized churches the emphasis is laid on social service, reform, and morality. Addresses on subjects of this nature are largely taking the place of the sermon. May not this be one of the principal causes of the decline of church attendance? A layman writing in a theological magazine complains that the attempt of the church to "Christianize the social and civil life of the world" through social service has resulted in the secularization of the church by the world. He deplores the fact that this cry of warning should come from a layman, and that of the clergymen (who, as a rule, were trained in liberalistic theology) "not one in ten" will agree with his view. He says further:

> The sacred edifice heretofore dedicated to the worship of Almighty God has now become the center of secular functions. We now go to church to hear sermons on the minimum wage, adequate housing of the poor, the regulation of moving pictures and the dance-halls, how to vote, and the latest vice-investigation report. Billiard and pool-table are being installed, dancing classes are organized, and all sorts of amusements offered to entice the youth within its sacred precincts. A child returning home from Sunday-school recently was asked by its mother the subject of the lesson. It was how to keep the streets clean. Another Sunday, kindness to dumb animals furnished the subject of the lesson, and this was a graded Sunday-school up to date. A good woman who had suffered greatly with a recent sorrow brought herself to church longing for some comforting word. She heard a sermon on the Charity Organization Society and the Visiting Nurse.
>
> Ministers of the Gospel are willing to preach on every subject under the sun except the Gospel, and when they begrudgingly mention the Gospel, they almost tell us it is not divine, but a man-made thing. They have relegated to the brush-heap most of the sacred doctrines and many of them even deny the validity of their own divine office as ministers of God. All comes from man, nothing from God. Perhaps this is the reason so many ministers look down on empty pews and complain bitterly that their members do not come to hear the sermons prepared with so much labor.

Social service as a substitute for the old Gospel message has been tried out by Unitarians and other liberal churches. There is abundant proof to show that it has utterly failed, a fact that is persistently ignored by its present advocates. The churches which have embraced the social gospel, says a writer in the *Harvard Theological Review*, "have distinctly weakened their life and influence". A writer in the *Biblical World* says:

> The secularization of the activities of the church has weakened its spiritual life and emptied its pews of devout worshipers.—Today altruism has largely superseded churchly Christianity, and social service in a very material manner has made many churches in our land a social club or an executive committee for the engineering of social activities.

A prominent Unitarian minister writes:

> During my sixty years of service in the Unitarian ranks *I have seen scores of organizations go down to defeat* because they did not make religion the one all-important element in their work and in their appeal to the public. Let me cite

instances of this kind. A minister and his wife took charge of a Unitarian church that was fairly prosperous and immediately threw themselves with ardor into every available kind of social service. Among other good things they organized an unsectarian literary club which attracted some of the best people in the city. Some years after, the minister's wife was eagerly telling me of wonderful success of the club, when I asked, "How about the church?" "Oh, that is closed", was the answer.

In another church there was a popular preacher who always drew a large congregation of people who were interested in the various radical reforms that he advocated, but his audience was a procession and not a compact congregation. As soon as the people whom he attracted became familiar with his idiosyncrasies they ceased to attend his church. He once said to me, "I have seen enough people go through my church to build a city." I repeated his remark to a brother minister who said, "And they never go to church again."

A well-known literary man said to me, "Some of us thought we could do without the church, so we met on Sunday morning and discussed literature and sociology; but after a time we learned that the church had something to give that we did not get, and so we adjourned our meetings and went to church."

Social reform, as differentiated from the social gospel, ought to be a principal concern of every government. It is in no sense a substitute for individual regeneration and for the Christian religion. Despite the most desirable reforms people may be materialistic and godless. Col. Raymond Robins, of Chicago, gives the following reports from a land which is well-known for its political reforms:

In Australia, foremost in legislation for women and children, where the eight-hour day is the universal day, where municipal ownership of railroads, trams and telephones prevails, where that whole social program has been worked out, a labor party is in full command of the three industrial states. "Surely," you say, "everything will be happy and beautiful there." Well, in the streets of Sydney I saw more drunken men and women than I ever saw in Chicago, and the whole community was getting the uneconomic mind, the something-for-nothing attitude. Why, you could see whole groups stand in line on Saturday afternoon waiting to bet a portion of their week's wages in government protected lotteries. A greater illegitimate birth rate prevails there than in any other nation of which we have record, and a lower general birth rate in the cities than of any nation of which we have a record. Why? Material prosperity. Seven million people fringed around an area as large as the United States.

Maxim Gorky, the noted Russian author, writes:

What alarms me most is the fact that the social revolution does not bring with it any sign of spiritual regeneration among men. It does not seem to be making men more honest. It is not lifting their self-esteem nor the moral value of their labor. At least one does not notice among the masses that the revolution has lifted or quickened their social conscience. Human life is appraised just as cheaply as it was before. The habits of the old regime are not disappearing. The new authorities are just as brutal as the old ones were and, in the bargain, their manners are worse. The new officials permit themselves to be bribed just as easily and they send men to prison in herds as the old did. Physical force has merely been transferred. But this does not in any way help the growth of new spiritual forces among us. The rectification of wrong can come only through the development of our spiritual forces.

Various representatives of the social gospel, among them Walter Rauschenbusch, have said, it is impossible to be a Christian so long as our social order has not been reconstructed along socialistic lines. No one can live a Christian life, we are told, in an unsocialized commonwealth. So, as concern personal salvation, the social gospel, according to its own representatives, means that we cannot hope to be Christians at the present time. Considered from a Christian viewpoint it must be said, therefore, that the social gospel brings a message of despair.

# ⚜·149·⚜

# Why Temple Baptist Church Withdraws from the Northern Baptist Convention

## J. FRANK NORRIS

J. Frank Norris (1877-1952) was a Southern Baptist fundamentalist preacher whose pastorates were in Texas and at the Temple Church in Detroit, to whose congregation this sermon is addressed. An ardent evangelist, he shared the opposition of colleagues to a social religion. What he had to say in 1935, in the context of economic depression, also registers the emergence of political conservatism in the critique of socially active religion.

---

### What Was the Purpose of the Northern Convention?

Ladies and gentlemen, I quote to you what was the purpose of the organization of the Northern Baptist Convention. This Convention was organized in 1907—what would be—7 from 35 would be 28 years ago—now there are those who say we cease to be Baptists if we withdraw from the convention—we are going to answer this question if the church votes to adopt this resolution, and I think I know what this great people will do—the deacons have already unanimously adopted it—and I am going to give you the opportunity to express yourself—to the question that we cease to be Baptists—in the first place, Baptists were here 1900 years before you ever heard of the Northern Baptist Convention. The second answer is that the charter of the Northern Baptist Convention states specifically that the purpose of the Northern Convention is for the evangelization of the world, and not to go into politics, not to regulate society and the economic life; no, but to preach the Gospel. They put it in there 28

Source: J. Frank Norris, 'Why Temple Baptist Church Withdraws from the Northern Baptist Convention', 1935, in Joel A. Carpenter, ed., *Inside Story of the First Baptist Church*, New York, 1988, pp. 224-33. © 1988 by Garland Publishing Inc.

years ago. The Northern Baptist convention was not organized for the purpose of taking over Henry Ford's plant, the Chrysler, or taking over the telephone companies or oil companies—I am not going to argue whether they ought to be taken over—the point I am making, that it is not the business of the churches to enter into business, to regulate society or enter into the field of economics. It is the scheme of the devil to sidetrack the Church of Jesus Christ from its one and only commission, yet the head of the Baptist machine of Detroit says this report is "epochal."

I think they are going to find themselves split from Maine to California.

Here is the answer—the third answer, instead of this church ceasing to be Baptist—the answer is that it has remained Baptist—and the fourth answer is that the Convention crowd, this Socialistic, unbaptistic, modernistic, compromising crowd have gone off from Baptist doctrines, It is a fulfilment of the Scripture which says, "They went out from us because they were not of us."

## "The Evangelization of the World"

This is the chartered purpose of the Northern Baptist Convention. It is found in Section 2, of the articles of Incorporation.

"The Evangelization of the World"; Beautiful and Scriptural. If the proponents and organizers of the Northern Baptist Convention had put it in the articles of Incorporation that it is the purpose and aim of the Northern Convention "to approach or regulate the social, political, economic and international" questions of this age and generation—the Convention would have died still-born.

Therefore, the church which refuses to endorse this socialistic scheme of the Northern Baptist Convention and remain true to the one and only mission of the church; namely, "The Evangelization of the World"—it is the Convention and not the true churches which has ceased to be Baptist. The Convention machine has departed from the true faith and gone off after false gods. It is the Convention, and not the churches, that is offering "strange fire." The Convention comes with the hands of "Baptist orthodoxy," but with the voice of Russian Sovietism.

"Well, now," somebody says, "look here, I am a deacon in a church and the pastor is a modernist, what can I do?"—Well, if you haven't sense enough to know what to do I couldn't advise you. (Laughter). Suppose I give you some Scripture on that—here is what it says, II Cor. 6:14-18

> Be ye not unequally yoked together with unbelievers: for what fellowship hath righteousness with unrighteousness? and what communion hath light with darkness? And what concord hath Christ with Belial? or what part hath he that believeth with an infidel? And what agreement hath the temple of God with idols? for ye are the temple of the living God; as God hath said, "I will dwell in them, and walk in them; and I will be their God, and they shall be my people. Wherefore"—what does it say? Listen—"come out from among them, and be ye separate, saith the Lord, and touch not the unclean thing; and I will receive you."

I make bold to tell you here these preachers who masquerade under the livery of heaven—I don't care how many degrees they have after names—LLds, DDs, Asses, they are infidels when they deny the Word of God. Yes, sir—I have more respect for Tom Paine in his grave, and Bob Ingersoll—at least they had self respect enough to stay out of the church and out of the pulpits—they were not like these little modernistic, lick-the-skillet, two-by-four aping, asinine preachers who want to be in the priest's office so they can have a piece of bread, and play kite tail to the Communists.

I am not going to say anything about them this afternoon, but I plan to do so sometime soon. (Laughter).

"Oh!" some sister will say, "I don't think that's the Christian spirit"—Honey, you wouldn't know the Christian spirit, any more than a bull would know Shakespeare. (Laughter).

I'll tell you the spirit we need in this compromising, milk-and-cider, neither-hot-nor-cold—you want to know the kind of spirit we need? We need the spirit of old John the Baptist when he told that Sanhedrin, "You are a generation of snakes."

We need again the spirit of the Apostle Peter when he stood before the Sanhedrin and said, "Is it right to obey man rather than God."

Talk about you Methodists, we need again the spirit of old John Wesley when he preached out of his father's church and stood on his father's slab and preached a sermon that shook the world! (Applause).

We Baptists need the spirit of Roger Williams when he walked out in the snows with the Naragansett Indians rather than to stultify his conscience.

We need again the spirit of those Baptist preachers in 1767 yonder on the Court House yard in old Culpepper, Virginia, when stripped to the waist with hands tied and held up, the strap was put on their bare backs and drops of blood fell—Patrick Henry rode up and said, "What crime have these men committed?"—When they answered, "They were preaching the Gospel of the Son of God without a license." He answered one word three times: "My God, my God, my God."

Hear me, friends, you Baptists especially, the scheme today is what? To Sovietize the Churches of America, to honeycomb the public schools, then the red propaganda can go on unmolested. They know if they can break down the voice of the pulpit—the greatest moral force time ever witnessed, they will have this whole country—yet you Baptists will go and put your money, your time, your presence into that sort of thing. You say, "What can I Do?" "Come out from among them, and be ye separate, saith the Lord."

Friends, there is going to be a separation—all present existing denominational machines are gone—you Methodists, your machine is gone too, and it ought to be gone—the truth of Jesus Christ will survive, but we are going to have a terrible conflict in this country and we had just as well face it—that bunch of atheistic, Communists have charge of this government, and it is high time we found it out. (Applause).

Now if that be treason, make the most of it!

If the laboring classes think they will solve their problems by going Communistic—Come with me down into the mines of Russia and see the condition there—if the farmers think it will solve their problems come with me and I will show you five million Kuluks, the owners, the highest class of farmers, driven from their homes to yonder cold Siberia never to return. If you think it will solve your problems, go yonder and see the greatest country in the world for resources—it is the devil's scheme to destroy this present civilization—But I believe old America will stand! (Applause.) We will meet them at Philippi!—They snatch the new born babies from their mother's arms—They don't believe in marriage—a man may be mated a dozen times—there is no regard for sex relation. This is not hearsay. I know what I am talking about. I have seen it first hand.

What shall we do? "Wherefore come out from among them, be ye separate, saith the Lord, and touch not the unclean thing; and I will receive you."

Old Amos says, "Can two walk together, except they be agreed?"

Here is the situation we are facing—I am talking about our own upheaval—we are going to let you backslidden Methodists alone while we attend to ourselves—follow me—your machinery, your leadership, your Board, your officialdom, your Detroit Baptist Union, the head of it—they come out and say, "This is our platform"—not mine. I am not going into any social, economic, political scheme instead of blood redemption. (Applause). That is what we are facing. Now whenever we render encouragement to that bunch of modernists, when we bid them Good speed, just remember what Jehu said to Jehoshaphat when he returned from battle where he had made an unholy alliance with Ahab,

> And Jehoshaphat, the king of Judah returned to his home in peace to Jerusalem, And Jehu the son of Hanani the seer went out to meet him, and said to king Jehoshaphat,—Listen to this—"Shouldest thou help the ungodly, and love them that hate the Lord? therefore is wrath upon thee from before the Lord."

Listen again to the Word of God on what we should do—Rev. 18:-5,

> And I heard another voice from heaven, saying Come out of her, my people, that ye be not partakers of her sins, and that ye receive not her plagues: for her sins have reached unto heaven, and God hath remembered her iniquities.

Now you will be glad to hear this resolution recommended by unanimous vote of the Deacons—and this is what I am going to ask everybody here this afternoon to express themselves on:

> WHEREAS, the Temple Baptist Church of Detroit, Michigan, has supported and co-operated with the Northern Baptist Convention and Baptist Convention of Michigan, by sending money to their Boards and delegates to their annual meetings;
>
> WHEREAS, June 24th, 1935, the Northern Baptist Convention at Colorado Springs forced on the churches of the Northern Baptist Convention for their consideration, adoption or rejection, the Communistic plan of Karl Marx, by the following action of the convention:

1—Received the report and authorized the General Council to make it available to individual churches for study.

2—Continued the Social Action commission for a year with the understanding that its educational program and peace plebiscite among churches be conducted only for those churches desiring them.

3—Stated that neither the whole 15,000-word report nor a part of it "shall be made a test of Baptist fellowship of service."

Let me stop here—I want to say that I can turn to fifty places in the writing of Karl Marx and find that identical expression, "Social Action Commission"—Yes, sir, and that instead of being put on the table has been forced upon the churches—that is what they propose to put over—that isn't all:

WHEREAS, the Northern Baptist Convention officially appointed the "Social Action Commission" for the avowed purpose of binding the Convention to a political and economic program which is a violation of the most fundamental doctrine held by Baptists, namely, the separation of church and state; and further the Convention by its action in receiving, authorizing and continuing the "Social Action Commission", and forcing its communistic plan upon the churches, has thereby thrust a divisive issue among all the churches;

WHEREAS, the report of the "Social Action Commission" sums up, sets forth, and advocates essentially the revolutionary, communistic plan of Soviet Russia, which is better known by its American Brand of "New Dealism";

WHEREAS, the one and only business of the church and the ministry is not to enter into or regulate the economic or political affairs of the Government, but to follow the admonition of our Lord, "Render to Caesar the things that are Caesar's, and to God the things that are God's," thereby maintaining the age-long and cherished Baptist faith of separation of church and state; that the one and only mission of the church of Jesus Christ is to preach the gospel of salvation to the individual, thereby carrying out the Great Commission, "Go preach the gospel to every creature";

WHEREAS, the leadership of the Northern Baptist Convention and the State Convention of Michigan, has departed from the age-long and Scriptural position held by Baptists, by substituting a so-called social or communistic gospel instead of the gospel of salvation for the individual soul;

WHEREAS, ten years ago the Northern Convention at Seattle, Washington, adopted what is known as the "inclusive policy", sending out both modernist and fundamentalist missionaries, and at which Convention the action adopting the inclusive policy repudiated a resolution offered by the late Dr. W. B. Hinson "requesting all the missionaries of the Northern Baptist Convention to signify their belief and acceptance of the fundamental doctrines of the Virgin Birth, the Deity of Christ, the Atonement on the Cross, the Resurrection of Christ, and the New Birth of the individual soul"

My friends, you can get the Minutes and you will find where they turned down Dr. Hinson's resolution; namely, "Requesting all the missionaries of the Northern Baptist Convention to signify their belief and acceptance of the ;Virgin Birth, the New Birth of the individual soul."—My friends, I saw that crowd of Northern Baptist modernists vote that resolution down two to one. Here is what it means: It means that the missionaries don't have any longer to believe in the Atonement on the Cross, in the New Birth, in the Deity of Christ, in the Virgin

Birth, or the Resurrection of Christ—no, they are going out under a social gospel that has dictation over the churches.

Reading on, the resolution:

WHEREAS, there has rapidly developed in the Northern Baptist Convention an unscriptural and unbaptistic, ecclesiastical, centralized dictatorship over the churches, as evidenced by many definite, concrete actions through the years, the latest of which is the action of the Northern Baptist Convention at Colorado Springs when the Convention "authorized" in the report of the "General Council" to the churches what was designated by the "15,000 word report" of the "Social Action Commission";

WHEREAS, the so-called plan of designation of mission funds is a misnomer and dishonest, because when the church designates a certain amount to a mission station the Foreign Mission Board simply decreases the appropriation to that station, thereby forcing orthodox Baptists to support, in an indirect though very definite way, the unscriptural, modernistic, socialistic leadership of the Northern Baptist Convention;

WHEREAS, the Northern and Michigan Baptist Conventions belong to, and are a part of the World Baptist Alliance, which is controlled and dominated, in the main, by modernistic leadership; and

WHEREAS, the Temple Baptist Church has been on record for several years in its stand for the historic faith once for all delivered to the saints;

THEREFORE BE IT RESOLVED, by the Board of Deacons of Temple Baptist Church, and the members of the entire church, in special called session at 3:00 p.m. Sunday afternoon, June 30, 1935, that we exercise, as a church, our inalienable, sovereign right as a body of believers, in recognizing Christ only as head over all things to the church, and reaffirming our faith in the fundamentals of the Christian faith as commonly held by Baptists; and further we reaffirm and declare it our purpose to have no part or lot with the unscriptural, unbaptistic, socialistic, modernistic Convention;

RESOLVED SECOND, in separating from these bodies, from these ecclesiastical organizations, which have departed from the faith held by Baptists, we call upon all true orthodox Baptist throughout the Northern Baptist Convention, to join with us in contending for the faith once for all delivered, and giving the gospel of salvation to the individual soul;

RESOLVED THIRD, that we reaffirm our faith in those foundation principles—freedom of speech, freedom of press, and freedom of worship;

RESOLVED FOURTH, that Temple Baptist Church urge every individual member to make regular contribution to worldwide missions; and that we support the Association of Baptists for Evangelism in the Orient, which Association of Baptists has adopted the identical Confession of Faith held by the Temple Baptist Church;

RESOLVED FIFTH, that copies of these resolutions be given to the denominational and secular press that the world may know of the uncompromising position and stand of the Temple Baptist Church against all the present day vagaries of modernism, socialism, communism, ecclesiasticism, and our positive stand for the faith in the whole Bible as our only rule of faith and practice.

## The Dishonesty, the Duplicity, and Insincerity of These Denominational Politicians

I know that this is strong language but we are performing a major, triple operation in order to save the patient.

You have noticed how these denominational politicians are saying that the report of the Social Action Commission is not communistic.

Here they are following the advice of their patron, Lenin. I can take the writings of Karl Marx and Lenin and put them beside the identical writings of the Social Action Commission.

Now, I am going to make a charge that the Social Action Commission and Russian Communism, especially two principle [sic] American branches are identical. Let me quote from the report:

> We are convinced that the economic system as it has been operated has also created serious obstacles to Christians living. There are multitudes of Christian in high and low positions in our economic and industrial life who desire to express their Christianity in these relations but who find it impossible within the system. The church has a responsibility to them. It is futile to bring up generations of youth on Christian ideals which they are compelled to discard when they go out to make a living. Christians owe it to themselves and to their fellows to work for an economic order in which Christian motives have freer chance for expression and in which Christian ideals have larger hope of realization.
>
> The possibility of change for the better must be accepted as a fact by the Christian. The economic system has been man-made and it can be changed by men. Changes must begin with the individual and an improved operation of any system rests with individuals. "No gain can be achieved by society that is not supported by human wills."
>
> In view of these conditions, what may be done by our denomination to effect the changes which are necessary to provide more opportunity and encouragement for men and women to live as Christians in their economic and industrial relations and to secure fundamental justice for all?
>
> It is clear that the denomination corporately cannot prosecute particular measures for social change. It should however have a constant program of education on these matters for its constituency which will enable them to act in accordance with Christian standards in these relations.
>
> We therefore recommend that such a program be conducted by the denomination through the local churches with the following definite objectives:
>
> I—To create social attitudes based on these fundamental considerations:
>
> II—A second definite objective of such a program of education should be to keep before our constituency certain basic issues, among them being: . . .
>
> (1)—Economic security for all. This would involve general education on the need of unemployment, sickness and accident insurance and old age pensions; assembling and distributing the facts relative to specific measures for economic security; making available lists of information sources and agencies; and co-operation with other denominations and agencies for the furtherance of economic security.
>
> (2)—Collective bargaining in industry. This would involve a program of education for a better understanding of the relative positions and problems of

employers and employees in bargaining over wages, hours and conditions of work; and further the provision for a social action committee in every church, or in co-operation with other churches, to ascertain and publish the facts in the event of conflict and to encourage the exercise of moral judgment; and finally the support of whichever party in a dispute is in the right by purchasing the products of the industry or by contributions to the needs of the workers of funds, moral encouragement and places of meeting where needed.

(3)—More adequate representation of consumer interest in the determination of economic policies. This would involve the study of how the government may safeguard the consumer and promote his welfare and how consumers themselves may be informed so as to buy for their real needs and best interests instead of being at the mercy of the producer's and seller's advertising.

(4)—Keep open the channels of discussion of controversial economic and industrial issues. This would involve the dissemination of information about anti-sedition legislation designed to prevent the discussion and advocacy of legitimate economic changes and the organization of sentiment and effort for the defeat or repeal of any such laws as infringe upon constitutional liberties. It would also involve giving moral and financial support to those who have been victims of discrimination.

III—A third definite objective of such an educational program for the denomination should be to inculcate in individuals worthy economic motives and incentives that through them the basis of the economic system may be shifted from that of acquisitiveness to that of service. . . .

IV—A fourth definite objective should be to impress upon our individual members the importance of effecting changes in the economic order by the exercise of their three-fold citizenship, political, civic and economic.

(1)—By political citizenship support should be given to whatever political party or candidate represents, on the whole, the most favorable disposition and opportunity to effect the desired changes. Since, however, the major political parties have not come to be in any considerable measure parties of clearly avowed and continuously held social principles, political effectiveness through them in the direction of the desired economic changes must involve support of smaller interest and pressure groups whose intelligent and persistent advocacy may lead to the espousing of social principles and programs from time to time by these major parties. Such pressure groups are numerous and range in point of view in our country from the American Liberty League to the League for Industrial Democracy.

## "There is Death in the Pot"

Now we have the whole thing out. Two of the principal Russian Communistic organizations in this country are "The American Liberty League" and "The League for Industrial Democracy.}

Just think of it, you Baptists, the free-est of the free people, the most patriotic! The Baptist machine authorized a committee of nine to bring in and report endorsing the two principal branches of Russian Communism!

What will you Baptists do?

What answer will you give?

So help me God, I will never bow the knee to Russian Communism in capsule form! (Applause).

Shall we sit supinely by while Lenin's Communism plays the Trojan horse act on our Baptist churches?

## Northern Modernists Control Southern Leaders

Yes, Dr. A. W. Heaven runs and controls Dr. George Truett, who is sound in the faith personally, but he runs with modernists, especially when he comes North. He was eulogized to the skies by one of the modernist pastors in the city this morning. He is President of the modernist World Baptist Alliance, which is no more and no less than a small self-appointed group of modernists, pussyfooting so-called fundamentalists down South to do their bidding—there is where the trouble comes.

Now friends we have crossed the Rubicon. We have come to a great hour in this country—everybody realizes it—in the realm of politics and business as well as in the realm of religion. We are facing Kadesh-Barnea, and I make bold to declare to you who believe in a supernatural Christ, who believe He had a supernatural birth, believe He lived a supernatural life, believe He spoke supernatural words, performed supernatural miracles, died a supernatural death, had a supernatural ascension and is coming back in supernatural glory to establish a supernatural kingdom—people who believe these things are going to get together in this country of ours! (Applause).

We are in another Reformation period like they had in the sixteenth century—let me say something—every century has witnessed a great awakening—the sixteenth century witnessed the Reformation led by Martin Luther, and other great reformers; the seventeenth century witnessed a great awakening led by the Puritans; the eighteenth century witnessed a great awakening led by Whit[e]field, Wesley and others; the nineteenth century witnessed what was known as the Oxford movement and the modern missionary movement; and the twentieth century is more than a third gone—Watchman what of the night?

## "We Will Not Serve Thy Gods"

Here is what is coming, what is happening, God's people, the "Seven Thousand" who have not bowed the knee to Baal are awakened and coming to light! We are coming to a time as witnessed in the third chapter of Daniel, when there went forth the decree from Nebuchadnezzar that all the people in every province when they heard the sound of the cornet, the flute, the harp, the sackbut, the psaltery, the dulcimer, and all kinds of musical instruments, that they should bow down and worship that image of gold 60 cubits high and six cubits wide, out in the plains of Dura; and every man that did not bow down and worship would be cast in the fiery furnace, and when the sound went forth, every prince, every sheriff, every secretary, every denominational leader bowed down and worshipped that statue of gold—except three that stood erect with heads up, and when the report was carried to this old king that these three Jews would not bow, he was filled with rage, and he called them before him while he sat on his throne, and said to them, "Is it true that you will not bow down as I commanded?" They said, "We are not careful to answer thee in this matter"—"We won't even bother to answer you. We will not put on your socialistic modernistic program." And they said, "If you put us into the fiery furnace, our God whom we serve is able to deliver us from the burning fiery furnace, and he will deliver us out of thine hand"—"But if not, be it known unto thee, O king, that"—and here is my text—"We will not serve thy gods, nor worship the golden image which thou hast set up!" "We will not submit to your ecclesiastical tyranny." (Applause).

# ⚜·150·⚜

# Radicalism and Religious Disinterestedness

## REINHOLD NIEBUHR

Neo-orthodoxy, associated with Reinhold Niebuhr (1892–1971), was a much more sophisticatedly expressed dissent from liberal religious pieties than fundamentalism. Niebuhr's refusal to abandon critical and historical methods led fundamentalists to conclude that neo-orthodoxy was irredeemably contaminated by modernism. He aimed to restate Biblical Christianity, giving the weight to human sinfulness which he believed the liberals had not, so that believers were enabled to deal with modern life. In this passage he grappled with the paradox that the religious ethic required the pursuit of the pure spirit of disinterestedness but, in the world, such a spirit was inevitably compromised. Concretely, the nearest it was possible to come to it was to embrace the interests of the underprivileged. Thus in the 1930s Niebuhr allied himself with the political Left, a position from which he retreated after World War II.

The liberal soul is pedestrian and uninspired. Its moral philosophy is always utilitarian and practical. It avoids the fanaticisms and passions of the servants of the absolute and goes about its business to tame life and bring larger and larger areas of human society into its circles of humane goodwill and prudent reciprocity. But liberalism can tame life only if it is fairly tame to begin with. It knows how to make life decent, intelligent and sociable in the comfortable atmosphere of a suburban village; and it is not unserviceable as the guiding genius of, say, an international conference on trade. In such an enterprise it softens prejudices and animosities and enhances mutual accord by considerations of prudence. But when life is not tame in the first instance, when it expresses itself in terms of tempest and fury and when it is driven by impulses arising from compelling immediate necessities or by dreams of the final good,

Source: Reinhold Niebuhr, 'Radicalism and Religious Disinterestedness', *Reflections on the End of an Era*, New York, 1934, pp. 261–73.

by hunger or by sublime passion, the liberal soul is baffled and confused. It does not know what to do with life-as-nature, except, like the Lilliputians, spin gossamer threads around the giant and be surprised when the giant brushes its little restraints aside. Nor is it any more effective with life which yearns after the absolute and seeks by some heroic adventure or by some self-denying ordinance to burst the bounds of nature and find rest in pure spirit. The liberal soul produces neither warriors nor saints, heroes nor rebels, and it is ill at ease when confronted with their fury and their passion. The manifestations of life which reveal its darkest depths and its sublimest heights leave the liberal soul in baffled confusion. The prudent and shrewd calculations of its reason are unable to cope with life when it is totally unreasonable or when it strives with imprudent passion to achieve perfect rationality and purity. Confronted with a Lenin or a Napoleon on the one hand or a Francis or a Tolstoi on the other it can only deprecate their fanaticism and regret their ignorance of the principles of sociology.

Whenever reason aspires to something more than a manipulation of the immediate impulses and processes of society and seeks to achieve perfect purity and (in the field of morals) complete disinterestedness something of the religious spirit emerges. To understand the difference between the rationality of prudence which is completely involved in the play of impulse, though it seeks to direct it, and the unprudential passion for perfect rationality is to mark the distinction between a secular and a religious ethic. Whitehead indicates the distinction, though he does not apply it to the field of morals, in the words:

> We have . . . two contrasted ways of considering reason. We can think of it as one among the operations involved in the existence of an animal body, and we can think of it in abstraction from any particular animal operations . . . The older controversies have mainly to do with this latter mode of considering reason. For them, reason is the godlike faculty which surveys, judges and understands. In the newer controversy, reason is one the items of operation implicated in the welter of the process . . . There is reason, asserting itself above the world, and there is reason as one of many factors within the world. The Greeks have bequeathed to us two figures, whose real or mythical lives conform to these two notions—Plato and Ulysses. The one shares Reason with the Gods, and the other shares it with the foxes.

When the passion for pure rationality expresses itself practically in the field of morals it issues in the demand for complete disinterestedness and insists that all life, rather than the life of the ego, be affirmed. The practical character of this demand transmutes rationality in morals into a spirituality which affects and is affected by will and emotions. Pure rationality would be confined to the field of observation. If the effort is made to isolate the rational element in the field of moral life the tendency is always to set the reason against the emotions and to divide the human psyche. This tendency is particularly obvious in Stoic and Kantian morality. In the religious morality of Jesus reason is not set against the impulses. Reason accepts the altruism which is rooted in natural impulse and transmutes, perfects and enlarges it. The human psyche is not divided against itself in the attainment of the moral ideal. Altruistic impulse and rational imperatives are united in the will.

The observation of Jesus, "If ye love those who love you what thank have ye?" grows out of a spiritual insight in which natural altruistic emotions have been heightened by rational force. Yet to see life in its total relationships is not synonymous with feeling an obligation toward the whole of life. The sense of obligation arises only when life is not only seen but felt, when reason not only observes it from the outside but transmutes it from the inside. Pure rationality in morals is therefore more accurately described as pure spirituality. The entire spirit is engaged in the achievement of pure disinterestedness. The whole of life is seen and affirmed not merely by reason but by reason, emotion and will. The comprehension of life *per se* is an emotional as well as a rational achievement because reason alone is incapable of achieving the synthesis of total reality, particularly living reality. Thus an adequate view of the whole must ultimately result in a religious appreciation of life as such in which the emotions of a living organism, which feels itself in organic contact with a living world, are combined with the more analytic insights of reason, which seeks to understand the details of this relationship.

The affirmation of all life is, even more than its comprehension, an achievement of the whole psyche and not simply of reason; for to affirm life in the absolute sense rather than the life of the ego means that the will (the organization of personality) is extended beyond itself. The force of rationality always remains the primary source of the extension but it is an effective moral force only when it remains in organic contact with the whole. If it is separated it either becomes merely an observer of life or its demands are placed into such a contradiction to the impulses that the ideal of disinterestedness is unable to draw upon those resources of altruism which are supplied not by reason but by nature (mother-love, pity, gregariousness, etc.). The ideal of pure love and disinterestedness is therefore both a rational and religious ideal. Its form is possible only where reason comprehends life beyond itself in the most inclusive terms; but the obligation to realize the ideal represents a sublimation of the will and the emotions which is religious rather than rational in character.

The obligation of pure disinterestedness is clearly the universal moral obligation (expressed in every moral system which makes altruism morally preferable to egoism) raised to the highest degree. It represents the demands of pure spirit set against the immediate impulses of life. But since it is impossible to act in the world of nature and history in terms of pure spirit it is obvious that the highest moral ideal is compromised in every realization.

The paradox in which all morality moves is that nothing short of the affirmation of the total needs of humanity can be regarded as completely moral but that this can be accomplished concretely only by asserting the interests of those who have been defrauded against the interests of those who have undue privileges. Every practical assertion of the principle of disinterestedness therefore involves the assertion of interest. It is idle to deny that the assertion of neglected interests may not lead to an undue emphasis upon them and thus betray disinterestedness. The problem of all practical morality is therefore that of revealing the spirit of justice and disinterestedness in actual life without compromising too seriously with the forces egoism and interest which express themselves in all history.

The solution of asceticism for this problem falls clearly into the category of morbid perfectionism. In asceticism the demands of pure spirit express themselves in terms so individualistic that the organic relation of the individual to society is destroyed and his perfection becomes parasitic on the "sins" of those who continue to assume responsibility for the larger relations of life. Ascetic disinterestedness is not only an irrelevance from the standpoint of the needs of an adequate social morality but it is finally self-defeating from the standpoint of its own goal. The mystic-ascetic effort to destroy egoism involves the soul in greater and greater preoccupation with the self.

The solution of orthodox Christianity is hardly less satisfactory. The validity of the absolute ideal is recognized but it is changed into a purely religious rather than ethical ideal. The tension between egoism and the obligation of disinterestedness is therefore transferred from the field of morals to that of religion. This tempts orthodox Christianity to make premature compromises with the inequalities and injustices of an established social order and to regard the assertion of neglected social interests as more sinful than the assertion of established interests. The resource of the orthodox position is that it provides insights by which the imperfections of every concrete social achievement are recognized.

In rational liberalism the demands of absolute love and disinterestedness are reduced to a prudent and utilitarian altruism. The value and inevitability of this emphasis have been previously considered. Its weakness lies in the fact that its rational disinterestedness either escapes to the vantage point of pure observation upon life (in which case it has similarities with asceticism) or it becomes involved in the play of impulse and interest without seriously checking individual or collective egoism. It is cursed by either timidity or hypocrisy. A rational-liberal adjustment of interest to interest usually means a measured but insufficient check upon the interests of the group from which the idealism proceeds. Aristotle, who is in many respects the fountain source of all liberal morals, was thus able to elaborate a political theory in which slavery and the caste system of Greek society were completely rationalized and justified. It is interesting to note that the equalitarian and universalistic elements in morality were much stronger in Stoicism than in Aristotle and the difference between the two may be due to the fact that Stoicism was a religio-rational morality. The implications of the moral ideal were therefore pressed more rigorously to their logical conclusion.

The tendency of modern liberalism to justify the interests of the socially privileged in the very act of seeming to consider the interests of all groups in impartial survey is illustrated in journalism of the type of Walter Lippmann's. Here suave and bland pretences of disinterestedness seek, with no great success, to hide a definite protagonism of the viewpoint of the present financial and industrial oligarchy. Christian liberalism, leaning on secular liberalism more than it realizes, is frequently tempted to the same sin. Its errors are doubly reprehensible because it appropriates the prestige of the religiously inspired absolute ethic of Jesus for the ideals of prudence which have developed in a commercial civilization.

Judged in terms both of its inner integrity and its social consequences a radical social ethic is the most effective manifestation of the religious and moral ideal of disinterestedness. The religious drive toward the absolute in it prevents it from suggesting merely slight modifications in the unequal social relations of a given social order in the name of the ideal of justice. On the contrary it sets the absolute ideal of equal justice into sharp and vivid juxtaposition to the injustices and inequalities of society. This policy is clearly a fruit of the religio-rational demand that all life be equally affirmed. Considerations of prudence and the practical necessities of a social order always relativize the ideal of equal justice and prove that it cannot be fully attained. This fact would seem to justify the liberal rather than the radical as the more practical statesman. But it also proves that the radical is superior in religious and spiritual insight. His ideal is in fact akin to the religious ideal of pure love. Both are unattainable and yet every historic moral and social achievement must be judged in their light.

The ideal of equal justice sets the demands of pure spirit against the facts of nature. Nature does not endow men equally; and the impulses of nature create societies in which the inequalities of endowment are accentuated because the shrewd and the strong are able to arrogate powers and privileges which enhance their strength and place the weak, the simple and the unfortunate under additional disadvantages. Every social system thus tends to create differences in strength and weakness, in wealth and poverty much greater than anything which the world of pure nature knows. Every social system endows the strong man, who is able to grasp the reins of power, with strength which is derived from society itself and is not of his own contriving. Thus the human world suffers from inequalities such as the brute world does not know.

The fact that this will be a perennial problem in every social system may prove the Marxian radical wrong in assuming that a collectivist society will finally eliminate every basis of injustice. But he is not wrong in setting the absolute demands of justice against the inequalities of the present social order nor in believing that the destruction of present disproportions of economic power through collective ownership will make for a more equal justice.

The religious character of this demand for equal justice is attested by the whole history of religion. While religion may make its demands so absolute that it despairs of realizing them in history there has always been a strain in religious thought which has insisted that love and equal justice be realized in history. Whenever religious idealism directs itself to the problems of history it dreams of the day when the mighty will be cast from their seats and those of low degree exalted, when, in other words, disproportions of power will be levelled.

If the effort is made to achieve this result in political terms, when, in other words, religious apocalypticism is changed into a political program, it becomes immediately apparent that it is no longer an expression of pure disinterestedness. As soon as a moral criticism of the undue privileges of a few becomes associated with a political policy it demands that the interests of the many be asserted against the few. There is always a possibility that in this assertion of interest against interest neglected values and interests be asserted too narrowly. Thus for instance the proletarian may neglect the legitimate interests and override the natural desires of the agrarian poor. Or both may express their protest against injustice in such vindictive terms that the highest values of society are imperiled. The dangers of corruption in radical disinterestedness are, in other words, important from the standpoint of an adequate social morality and the desire to avoid them is dictated by something more legitimate than a morbid individual perfectionism.

The dangers cannot be completely avoided in any social morality which assumes political responsibility. An organic relation to socio-political movements involves every disinterested spirit in the forces of nature which express themselves in the political world. Lest moral perfectionists become too concerned about that problem it is well to point out that every one (with the possible exception of the ascetic) is equally involved in the play of natural forces in politics. For the next decades those who desire to make a moral choice between the semi-moral alternatives of politics must make a choice between hypocrisy and vengeance. The old world which hides its injustices behind the forms of justice is embattled with a new world which expresses its protest against injustice in vindictive terms. Purer moral insights may mitigate the hypocrisy of the old order and the vengeance of the new. But they cannot eliminate these evils completely nor avoid all the perils which lurk in them. A choice has to be made and it ought to be fairly clear on which side the moralist who aspires to disinterestedness must cast his fortunes. Even when the rebels and martyrs of the radical cause are involved in the animosities of the social conflict they reveal, at their best, authentic proofs of their kinship with the children of the spirit. It must be admitted of course that radical disinterestedness may become completely engulfed by the forces of nature in history which it seeks to manipulate. It may express itself in terms so vindictive and so blind a hatred that it becomes a peril to society and to the interests of those it seeks to serve. There are always demonic forces in politics. To seek their complete elimination is a counsel of perfection. It is nevertheless important that they be restrained by those who seek to use them for moral ends.

It is necessary for this reason that radical spirituality be brought under the scrutiny of the more absolute demands and the higher perspectives which are characteristic of classical religion. The most courageous and honest effort to establish justice in history must remain under the discipline of pure spirit through which the imperfections of every historical achievement are recognized and the perils to society in every assertion of interest against interest are discovered. This is a fact which modern radicalism is bound to treat with scorn. Its Utopianism makes it incapable of recognizing the relativities in its moral attitudes and the possibilities of new tyrannies and injustices in its policies. Those who have looked more deeply into the problems of the human spirit and human society must not be deterred by this scorn from insisting that radical disinterestedness will become completely corrupted and a peril to its own ends if it cannot maintain contact with the spiritual disciplines through which the perils of anarchy and tyranny in every political movement are discovered.

A moral perspective which is high enough to discover the perils and relativities in every historic movement naturally makes demands which are not capable of complete realization in history. Pure spirit in man always suggests a realm of reality which transcends the realm of nature. It creates tensions which cannot be completely resolved in moral endeavor. Some way must be found to relax these tensions without destroying the validity of the absolute ideal or without tempting too premature compromises with historical forces. Whenever the tension between spirit and nature is fully felt the aesthetic motif in religion arises to compete with the ethical urge. Men find it necessary not only to approximate perfection ethically but to adjust themselves to an imperfect world in terms of aesthetic insights which, in classical religion, are expressed in the experience of grace. There is no place in either radical or liberal Utopianism for the "experience of grace." The hope of realizing perfection in history has made such an experience unnecessary. When the hard realities of history have once again dissipated the Utopian dreams of the present the emphasis of classical religion upon the experience of grace will find its way back again into the moral and religious life of the race.

# ⊰·151·⊱

# A Fundamentalist Sermon by a Modernist Preacher

## HARRY EMERSON FOSDICK

By the end of the interwar period, religious liberals like Fosdick appeared somewhat chastened.

═══════════════════════════════════════════════════

This sermon springs from conversations with two young men. One of them a Jew, the other a Christian, in intellect and character they represent the best we have, and in effect they said the same thing.

Said the young Jew, "Long ago I gave over orthodox Judaism and am a convinced liberal, but sometimes, worshipping in modernist synagogues, I feel that something is missing from our new Judaism which the old Jews had, and that in comparison with theirs our religious faith is thin and superficial."

The young Christian said to me: "I am a modernist. I never could force my mind back into the narrow moulds of the old theology, but sometimes, especially in crises, when one wants deep rootage, the modernist soil seems thin. There were power and depth in that old-fashioned Christianity which sometimes we modernists lack."

As I listened to those young men I thought about another Jew, also the best of his time, who long ago in a day of crisis and moral chaos said: "Ask for the old paths, where is the good way; and walk therein."

This morning I share with you the consequence of thinking about these young men. Let us say plainly at the start that the words of Jeremiah, "Ask for the old paths," are so fundamentalist in tone that one wonders whether any one except a fundamentalist has hitherto preached them. We, of course, stand stoutly here for the gains of modernism. We do not run our thoughts of God into the moulds of old world-views or identify our Christian convictions with obsolete doctrines, miracles, and Biblical inerrancies. We do not believe in the old pictures of creation behind us or of second-comings on the clouds ahead of us.

Source: Harry Emerson Fosdick, 'A Fundamentalist Sermon by a Modernist Preacher', *The Power To See It Through*, London, 1935, pp. 237–48. © 1935 by SCM Press Ltd.

We gratefully accept the new knowledge of the world and we will have our Christianity in terms of thinking that honestly belong to us as intelligent moderns or we will not have it at all. So far from singing:

> 'Tis the old time religion,
> And it's good enough for me;

we would as soon sing that the old ideas of a flat earth or old ways of getting from New York to Chicago are good enough for us. They distinctly are not. When, therefore, this morning, we ask for the old paths, we are making no recantation of modernism.

Lowell is right about that:

> ... Time makes ancient good uncouth:
> They must upward still, and onward, who would keep abreast of Truth;
> Lo, before us gleam her camp-fires! we ourselves must Pilgrims be,
> Launch our Mayflower, and steer boldly through the desperate winter sea,
> Nor attempt the Future's portal with the Past's blood-rusted key.

That is true. Nevertheless, consider that James Russell Lowell wrote that. He was a very modern man, a Harvard professor, a Unitarian, an emancipated intellectual. Where, then, was he looking for the example of the kind of spirit which he did not wish his generation to lose? Of all places, in the Pilgrim forefathers! How little he would have agreed with most of their opinions! and yet he did wish that his generation might keep something that was deep in the spirit of the Pilgrims at their best. Even he was asking for the old paths.

This, I take it, is what my young friends meant. This is what we are driving at. Old-fashioned Christianity did have in it something deep and powerful which we modernists often miss.

What we are doing, then, this morning might be summed up in some such way as this. Our religious modernism, standing for the right of the mind for freedom from the cramping limitations of obsolete theologies, has had to win its way against militant opposition. As always happens in such a case, we have had to show up the faults of the old-fashioned Christianity, take our stand against them, assail their obscurantisms and their appalling appeals to fear. In a word, modernism has been compelled to deal with the old-fashioned Christianity at its worst. To-day we are going to take a look at it its best.

That is fair. If we are to hold the allegiance of my two friends, we had better take a look at the old-fashioned religion at its best. They are right about it. Depth and power were sometimes there which our superficial modernism lacks.

Consider Martin Luther, for example. We could not go back to his theology even if we wanted to. To his dying day he thought the earth was stationary, and he even called Copernicus "a new astrologer." He thought that demons caused thunderstorms, and is reputed to have hurled his ink-pot at the devil. Any modernist can have his fill of condescension, thinking how much better informed he is than Martin Luther.

Yes, but let every modernist remember that once Martin Luther stood in the presence of the Emperor Charles, surrounded by his royal court, and, knowing that he was bringing down upon his head the combined wrath of Empire and Church, announced his dangerous convictions, saying, "Here stand I. God help me. I cannot otherwise." What a religion! It produced something that our modernism often does not produce, the unconsenting individual conscience.

If there is one thing that society has a right to expect from religion it is that. As a religious man society does not need me because I happen to believe in evolution or in a law-abiding cosmos. As a religious man society needs me because I am supposed to have an inner loyalty to something greater than kings, stronger than armies, more imperative than popular majorities. As a religious man society needs me because I am supposed to keep my moral watch, not by casual street clocks, but by sun and star time.

That is why so many religious leaders in America protested against the majority decision of the judges of the Supreme Court in the Macintosh case. So far as legal technicalities are concerned, that is their affair—we are not competent—but when Justice Sutherland for the majority and Chief Justice Hughes for the minority said what they did say concerning the effect of that decision on religion, then we men of religion knew that Chief Justice Hughes was right.

To say that no man can become a citizen of this republic without agreeing in advance to surrender his conscience to the nation in any future war is to say that citizenship in this nation involves willingness in advance to give up any real religion that he has. For a real religion always erects at the centre of a man's life an inner tribunal, his conscience before God, which he must obey rather than anything that any government or any majority may dictate to him.

Now, the old-fashioned Christianity at its best did often produce that unconsenting conscience. To be sure, our forefathers often put their stubborn conscientiousness in dour forms. John Bunyan would stay in jail for his convictions, he said, till the moss did grow upon his eyebrows. Who was it said of John Calvin that he feared God so much he feared nothing else at all? Outgrow the forms if you will: nevertheless, let it be said that old-fashioned Christianity was not emotionally sentimental and morally easy-going like much of our superficial modernism. It did at its best put granite into the characters of men, and sometimes that unconsenting conscience lifted whole groups, like the Puritan and the Pilgrims, into tremendous exploits. I suspect that one of the things which my two young friends miss in some modernism is the moral grip.

To be sure, modernists have often told them that they must clear up the social situation, rebuild the economic order, and improve international relationships. That kind of unconsenting conscience which deals with social evils in the large, modernism distinctly does possess. In that respect I imagine that we have more faith and a better kind of faith than our forefathers had. But these young people discover that in the meantime, before we have transformed the world, they have another task—to transcend the world, individually to live above it, individually to stand out from it and be superior to it, and from the low levels of its life to appeal to the inner tribunal of conscience. I call you to witness that at that point much of our broad-minded, emancipated, intellectual modernism is soft.

We had better take that truth to heart in this city. You say you never will go back to those old theologies and sectarianisms. I agree. But, my friends, they are not the essence of religion. Remember the words which Myers put upon the lips of St. Paul:

> Whoso has felt the Spirit of the Highest
> Cannot confound nor doubt Him nor deny:
> Yea, with one voice, O world, tho' thou deniest,
> Stand thou on that side, for on this am I.

That is an essential consequence of genuine religion, and for all our new intelligence we had better ask for that old path.

Again, consider a man like St. Augustine, in the fourth and fifth centuries. His theology would be impossible to us. He was so responsible for the doctrine of predestination that if in any kingdom of heaven he knows what came of it on earth he must be penitent and ashamed. Nothing would be easier than for a modernist to condescend to Augustine—until he starts thinking about Augustine's life. Running away from his boyhood's home in North Africa to Italy to escape the influence of his Christian mother, living there with his mistress, prospering as a rhetorician at the headquarters of the Empire, there at last he fell under the spell of a great Christian, Ambrose of Milan. Walking one day in his garden, at war with his own conscience, he thought he heard a voice saying, "Take up and read," and turning to the New Testament his eyes fell on this verse: "Put ye on the Lord Jesus Christ, and make not provision for the flesh, to fulfil the lusts thereof." That was to him what the Damascus Road was to Paul or a little Moravian prayer meeting in Old London to John Wesley. From that day his life ran out like an ever-deepening river through one of the most chaotic, desperate eras in history, with the Roman Empire crashing all around him until at last he died courageously in his episcopal city of Hippo while the barbarians were hammering at the city gates. And through it all runs the tremendous power of his prayers.

> Come, O Lord, in much mercy down into my soul, and take possession and dwell there. A homely mansion, I confess, for so glorious a Majesty, but such as Thou art fitting up for the reception of Thee ... Give me Thine own self, without which, though Thou shouldst give me all that ever Thou hast made, yet could not my desires be satisfied.

What a religion!—power over tumultuous passions within and desperate circumstances without. I suspect it is that kind of thing which my two young friends often miss in superficial modernism.

You see, modernism has stressed activity. We modernists are very busy. The gospel of modernism has largely concerned work. Admirable as that is, our forefathers understood that religion is not simply activity but receptivity. So at their best they struck their roots far down; at their best they dug their wells deep. They did not read so many books as we do, but those they did read they thought more about. They did not do so many things as we do, but they understood better the uses of solitude. They did not join so many committees as we do, but they understood better the meaning of prayer. Sometimes, in consequence, there emerged a personal, spiritual power that puts us to shame.

The progress of spiritual life is in this regard a good deal like the advance of an army—the objectives are ahead but the provisions come from behind. Alas for an army that is all objective and no base! A good deal of our superficial modernism is in precisely that situation to-day—excellent objective, but the lines of communication with the base of supplies cut, so that, when a crisis falls and brings the impact of its fear and its discouragement, modernism lacks reserves.

If someone says that this is an old man's point of view, I protest. Only this last week there came to see me a young man who was considering the possibility of going over from Protestantism to Roman Catholicism. Why? Because, said he, in all his youth in liberal Protestant churches he never had been taught how to pray, and now in a crisis, when things were hard outside and inside, he had found some Roman Catholic friends who knew how to pray and, trying their method, he had found power to carry on. You see, we Protestant modernists have sometimes been so anxious to be liberal that we have forgotten to be religious.

We had better take that to ourselves in this church. We never will go back to old theologies and outgrown sectarianisms. Granted! But we might well go back to One who antedates old theologies and sectarianisms, and who long ago, having to face the cross, sought the Father's help in a garden. He never would have been able to face that cross as he did face it without his experience in that garden. As we see him coming out from under the olive trees inwardly ready now for any Calvary with which the world may face him, for all our new intelligence we had better ask for that old path.

Consider again a man like John Calvin. He was too hard and metallic a soul to become fond of easily, and he so shared the intolerance of his day that some things he did, like consenting to the death of Servetus, seem to us unforgivable. As for his theology, with the damnation of non-elect infants and the rest, even fundamentalists cannot stomach that. A few years ago in this country, one of our great denominations, I am told, in convention assembled, held a debate as to whether or not they believed in the damnation of non-elect infants, and as the vote was about to be taken a professor of Greek with a sense of humour rose and said:

"Mr. Moderator, would it be possible so to phrase this motion that the effects of it would be made retroactive so that all those helpless infants who have been roasting down there for ages might be saved any further suffering?"

The assembly broke down in uncontrollable hilarity. So, nothing could be easier from the standpoint of modern intelligence than to deride John Calvin.

Nevertheless, take one good look more at that terrific theology of his with predestation, election, and eternal punishment. Of course I do not believe it. But I see that at least here was an honest man who did not propose to allow himself soft deceits about the kind of universe he lived in. Go yourself and look at an imbecile child. There is predestination for you. As another said, that child was not born but damned into the world. Look all about you at children, some of them endowed with everything that heredity and early environment give to guarantee achievement and some of them endowed with little or nothing except foretokens of failure and doom. There is election for you, some chosen and some not. Or watch the law-abiding process of this cosmos where we reap what we sow and men and nations plunge prodigiously through evil-doing into inevitable punishment. There is hell for you, observable to anyone with eyes.

The old theological forms in which our forefathers endeavoured to put such facts I take to be as dead as Sennacherib, but I call your attention to the sobering truth that in comparison with the candour and fearlessness with which the old-time Christianity faced these facts, our superficial modernism, with its singsong from Coué that every day, in every way, we are getting better and better, sounds soft and lush and sentimental.

That is why scientists of an earlier day, like Thomas Huxley, or modern agnostics like Walter Lippmann, agree in having more intellectual respect for the old Christianity than for the new, though believing in neither. Listen to Thomas Huxley:

> The doctrines of predestination, of original sin, of the innate depravity of man and the evil fate of the greater part of the race ... faulty as they are, appear to me to be vastly nearer the truth than the "liberal" popular illusions that babies are all born good ... that it is given to everybody to reach the ethical ideal if he will only try; that all partial evil is universal good, and other optimistic figments, such as that which represents "Providence" under the guise of a paternal philanthropist, and bids us believe that everything will come right (according to our notions) at last.

Indeed, in a time of storm and stress like this, we have some lamentable consequences from the soft and roseate view of the universe which too often modernism has encouraged. What a stream of individuals appear who, having maintained faith in God while everything was going well, now give it up because some things are going ill! They are fair-weather Christians. They can believe in God as long as they are comfortable, but if they are uncomfortable they give up God.

What kind of universe do they think they are living in anyway? This is a wild place. Our forefathers understood that. This is a world where Christs come and are crucified, where being disciples of Christ might mean being boiled in oil. This is a world where whole civilizations crumble into dust so that only archaeologists can read the meaning of their hopes and fears. This is a universe where an entire planet, like this earth, once having been uninhabitable, will some day be uninhabitable again, and the fairest hopes that ever stretched their sails upon the human sea can be wrecked and made hulks of by man's unwisdom and his sin. We fair-weather modernists had better salute those old-time Christians. They did not blink the facts. Instead of lying to themselves about the kind of universe this is, they achieved a faith strong enough to rise above it, carry off a spiritual victory in the face of it, and in the darkest hours that ever fell on human history they lifted high an ancient song:

> Therefore will we not fear, though the earth do change,
> And though the mountains be shaken into the heart of the seas;
> Though the waters thereof roar and be troubled,
> Though the mountains tremble with the swelling thereof.
>
>   ......
>
> The Lord of Hosts is with us;
> The God of Jacob is our refuge.

I suspect it is a realistic and courageous faith like that which my young friends too often miss in modernism, and they are right. Fair-weather Christians are not Christians at all. Look at Christ and see. Not until a man can face, as he faced, the darkest facts of life and still keep his soul unafraid does he know what it means to be a Christian.

An unconsenting individual conscience, the deep secrets of prayer, a courageous faith in God that rises above the darkest facts of life—there were depth and power in that old-time Christianity which our thin modernism often misses. If that be fundamentalism, make the most of it.

You see, we modernists have often gotten at our faith by a negative process. We do not believe this. We do not believe that. We have given up this incredible idea or that obsolete doctrine. So we pare down and dim out our faith by negative abstractions until we have left only the ghostly remainder of what was once a great religion. Then seeing how few our positive convictions are and how little they matter, we grow easy-going about everybody else's convictions, and end in a mush of general concession. Then a crisis falls upon the individual soul, upon the family, upon the world at large, where a religion that is going to amount to anything must have deep conviction in it. "The rain descended, and the floods came, and the winds blew, and beat upon that house; and it fell not: for it was founded upon the rock"—how much we need that!

Some of us have never lost that. There is no reason why a modernist should lose that. If modernism is going to make any permanent contribution to the spiritual life of man it must not lose that. Here in this church we will not stand for such thin modernism. O my soul, be broad in your sympathies, but, O my soul, go deep in your convictions!

# New Thought and
# Therapeutic Religion

# ⊱152⊰

# Science and Health

## MARY BAKER EDDY

Mary Baker Eddy (1821-1910) owed much in her philosophy to the clockmaker-healer, Phineas Quimby, who had aided her after she had experienced a period of pain and misery. None the less, it was she who became the fount of a variety of currents in American religion flowing within the same broad channel, that of New Thought. Neither mainstream revivalistic Protestantism, nor socially conscious religion, could reach all the restless Americans living in a world in flux. The Church of Christ (Scientist) was chartered in 1879 and from the 1880s onwards growing numbers of people derived comfort from Christian Science practitioners spreading out from New England. Practical application of Christian Science doctrine flowed from the basic idea expressed in Eddy's canonical text; real man, rather than 'mortal man', was an expression of God, of Mind. The everyday world experienced by mortals was thus illusory.

---

*Question.*—What is man?

*Answer.*—Man is not matter; he is not made up of brain, blood, and other material elements. The Scriptures inform us that man is made in the image and likeness of God. Matter is not that likeness. The likeness of Spirit cannot be so unlike Spirit. Man is spiritual and perfect; and because he is spiritual and perfect, he must be so understood in Christian Science. Man is idea, the image, of Love; he is not physique. He is the compound idea of God, including all right ideas; the generic term for all that reflects God's image and likeness; the conscious identity of being as found in Science, in which man is the reflection of God, or Mind, and therefore is eternal; that which has no separate mind from God; that which has not a single quality underived from Deity; that which possesses no life, intelligence, nor creative power of his own, but reflects spiritually all that belongs to his Maker.

And God said:

Source: Mary Baker Eddy, *Science and Health*, 1875, (Boston, 1917 ed.), pp. 475-77.

"Let us make man in our image, after our likeness; and let them have dominion over the fish of the sea, and over the fowl of the air, and over the cattle, and over all the earth, and over every creeping thing that creepeth upon the earth."

Man is incapable of sin, sickness, and death, The real man cannot depart from holiness, nor can God, by whom man is evolved, engender the capacity or freedom to sin. A mortal sinner is not God's man. Mortals are the counterfeits of immortals. They are the children of the wicked one, or the one evil, which declares that man begins in dust or as a material embryo. In divine Science, God and the real man are inseparable as divine Principle and idea.

Error, urged to its final limits, is self-destroyed. Error will cease to claim that soul is in body, that life and intelligence are in matter, and that this matter is man. God is the Principle of man, and man is the idea of God. Hence man is not mortal nor material. Mortals will disappear, and immortals, or the children of God, will appear as the only and eternal verities of man. Mortals are not fallen children of God. They never had a perfect state of being, which may subsequently be regained. They were, from the beginning of mortal history, "conceived in sin and brought forth in iniquity." Mortality is finally swallowed up in immortality. Sin, sickness, and death must disappear to give place to the facts which belong to immortal man.

Learn this, O mortal, and earnestly seek the spiritual status of man, which is outside of all material selfhood. Remember that the Scriptures say of mortal man:

As for man, his days are as grass: as a flower of the field, so he flourisheth. For the wind passeth over it, and it is gone; and the place thereof shall know it no more.

When speaking of God's children, not the children of men, Jesus said, "The kingdom of God is within you;" that is, Truth and Love reign in the real man, showing that man in God's image is unfallen and eternal. Jesus beheld in Science the perfect man, who appeared to him where sinning mortal man appears to mortals. In this perfect man the Saviour saw God's own likeness, and this correct view of man healed the sick. Thus Jesus taught that the kingdom of God is intact, universal, and that man is pure and holy. Man is not a material habitation for Soul; he is himself spiritual. Soul, being Spirit, is seen in nothing imperfect nor material.

Whatever is material is mortal. To the five corporeal senses, man appears to be matter and mind united; but Christian Science reveals man as the idea of God, and declares the corporeal senses to be mortal and erring illusions. Divine Science shows it to be impossible that a material body, though interwoven with matter's highest stratum, misnamed mind, should be man,—the genuine and perfect man, the immortal idea of being, indestructible and eternal. Were it otherwise, man would be annihilated.

# ·§·153·§·

# Christian Healing and the People's Idea of God

## MARY BAKER EDDY

Christian Science's great attraction was not its metaphysics but its claim to be a science of health. Eddy and the practitioners she trained, including many women, interpreted scripture as giving the key to individual healing of sickness, anxiety, and sin. When the mind of the individual attained harmony with that of God, then Mind, Truth cast out error and banished sickness and anxiety. Individuals could thus gain Truth and prosper; conventional medical practitioners were irrelevant, if not harmful. By the 1930s Christian Science, the best organized of the forms of New Thought, had reached membership of over a quarter of a million.

God is All, and in all: that finishes the question of a good and a bad side to existence. Truth is the real; error is the unreal. You will gather the importance of this saying, when sorrow seems to come, if you will look on the bright side; for sorrow endureth but for the night, and joy cometh with the light. Then will your sorrow be a dream, and your waking the reality, even the triumph of Soul over sense. If you wish to be happy, argue with yourself on the side of happiness; take the side you wish to carry, and careful not to talk on both sides, or to argue stronger for sorrow than for joy. You are the attorney for the case, and will win or lose according to your plea.

As the mountain hart panteth for the water brooks, so panteth my heart for the true fount and Soul's baptism. Earth's fading dreams are empty streams, her fountains play in borrowed sunbeams, her plumes are plucked from the wings of vanity. Did we survey the cost of sublunary joy, we then should gladly waken to see it was unreal. A dream calleth itself a dreamer, but when the dream has passed, man is seen wholly apart from the dream.

We are in the midst of a revolution; physics are yielding slowly to

Source: Mary Baker Eddy, *Christian Healing and the People's Idea of God*, 1909, (Boston, 1917 ed.), pp. 10–13.

metaphysics; mortal mind rebels at its own boundaries; weary of matter, it would catch the meaning of Spirit. The only immortal superstructure is built on Truth; her modest tower rises slowly, but it stands and is the miracle of the hour, though it may seem to the age like the great pyramid of Egypt,—a miracle in stone. The fires of ancient proscription burn upon the altars of to-day; he who has suffered from intolerance is the first to be intolerant. Homoeopathy may not recover from the heel of allopathy before lifting its foot against its neighbor, metaphysics, although homoeopathy has laid the foundation stone of mental healing; it has established this axiom, "The less medicine the better," and metaphysics adds, "until you arrive at no medicine." When you have reached this high goal you have learned that proportionately as matter went out and Mind came in as the remedy, was its potency. Metaphysics places all cause and cure as mind; differing in this from homoeopathy, where cause and cure are supposed to be both mind and matter. Metaphysics requires mind imbued with Truth to heal the sick; hence the Christianity of metaphysical healing, and this excellence above other systems. The higher attenuations of homoeopathy contain no medicinal properties, and thus it is found out that Mind instead of matter heals the sick.

While the matter-physician feels the pulse, examines the tongue, etc., to learn what matter is doing independent of mind, when it is self-evident it can do nothing, the metaphysician goes to the fount to govern the streams; he diagnoses disease as mind, the basis of all action, and cures it thus when matter cannot cure it, showing he was right. Thus it was we discovered that all physical effects originate in mind before they can become manifest as matter; we learned from the Scripture and Christ's healing that God, directly or indirectly, through His providence or His laws, never made a man sick. When studying the two hundred and sixty remedies of the Jahr, the characteristic peculiarities and the general and moral symptoms requiring the remedy, we saw at once the concentrated power of thought brought to bear on the pharmacy of homoeopathy, which made the infinitesimal dose effectual. To prepare the medicine requires time and thought; you cannot shake the poor drug without the involuntary thought, "I am making you more powerful," and the sequel proves it; the higher attenuations prove that the power was the thought, for when the drug disappears by your process the power remains, and homoeopathists admit the higher attenuations are the most powerful. The only objection to giving the unmedicated sugar is, it would be dishonest and divide one's faith apparently between matter and mind, and so weaken both points of action; taking hold of both horns of the dilemma, we should work at opposites and accomplish less on either side.

The pharmacy of homoeopathy is reducing the one hundredth part of a grain of medicine two thousand times, shaking the preparation thirty times at every attenuation. There is a moral to this medicine; the higher natures are reached soonest by the higher attenuations, until the fact is found out they have taken no medicine, and then the so-called drug loses its power. We have attenuated a grain of aconite until it was no longer aconite, then dropped into a tumblerful of water a single drop of this harmless solution, and administering one teaspoonful of this water at intervals of half an hour have cured the incipient stage of fever. The highest attenuation we ever attained was to leave the drug out of the question, using only the sugar of milk; and with this original dose we cured an inveterate case of dropsy. After these experiments you cannot be surprised that we resigned the imaginary medicine altogether, and honestly employed Mind as the only curative Principle.

What are the foundations of metaphysical healing? Mind, divine Science, the truth of being that casts out error and thus heals the sick. You can readily perceive this mental system of healing is the antipode of mesmerism, Beelzebub. Mesmerism makes one disease while it is supposed to cure another, and that one is worse than the first; mesmerism is one lie getting the better of another, and the bigger lie occupying the field for a period; it is the fight of beasts, in which the bigger animal beats the lesser; in fine much ado about nothing. Medicine will not arrive at the science of treating disease until disease is treated mentally and man is healed morally and physically. What has physiology, hygiene, or physics done for Christianity but to obscure the divine Principle of healing and encourage faith in an opposite direction?

Great caution should be exercised in the choice of physicians. If you employ a medical practitioner, be sure he is a learned man and skilful; never trust yourself in the hands of a quack. In proportion as a physician is enlightened and liberal is he equipped with Truth, and his efforts are salutary; ignorance and charlatanism are miserable medical aids. Metaphysical healing includes infinitely more than merely to know that mind governs the body  and the method of a mental practice. The preparation for a metaphysical practitioner is the most arduous task I ever performed. You must first mentally educate and develop the spiritual sense or perceptive faculty by which one learns the metaphysical treatment of disease; you must teach them how to learn, together with what they learn. I waited many years for a student to reach the ability to teach; it included more than they understood.

Metaphysical or divine Science reveals the Principle and method of perfection,—how to attain a mind in harmony with God, in sympathy with all that is right and opposed to all that is wrong, and a body governed by this mind.

Christian Science repudiates the evidences of the senses and rests upon the supremacy of God. Christian healing, established upon this Principle, vindicates the omnipotence of the Supreme Being by employing no other remedy than Truth, Life, and Love, understood, to heal all ills that flesh is heir to. It places no faith in hygiene or drugs; it reposes all faith in mind, in spiritual power divinely directed. By rightly understanding the power of mind over matter, it enables mind to govern matter, as it rises to that supreme sense that shall "take up serpents" unharmed, and "if they drink any deadly thing, it shall not hurt them". Christian Science explains to any one's perfect satisfaction the so-called miracles recorded in the Bible. Ah! why should man deny all might to the divine

Mind, and claim another mind perpetually at war with this Mind, when at the same time he calls God almighty and admits in statement what he denies in proof? You pray for God to heal you, but should you expect this when you are acting oppositely to your prayer, trying everything else besides God, and believe that sickness is something He cannot reach, but medicine can? as if drugs were superior to Deity.

# ❦154❧

# The New Alinement of Life

## RALPH WALDO TRINE

Ralph Waldo Trine (1866–1958) also propounded a variety of New Thought intended to energize individuals by allowing them to recognise God as the Life Force 'back of all' and within themselves. Believing that the competing structures of organized religions hid this basic truth common to all of them, he foresaw a worldwide spiritual awakening cutting across previously entrenched divisions and made extensive use of the media to try to achieve it.

It is the difference between coming to God as a spiritual mendicant, in a we-poor-miserable-sinners, we-who-are-about-to-die attitude, or as children would naturally come to a loving Father.

The world of thinking men and women is rapidly dividing now upon this very question. We have reached the place where it is necessary to choose between an old theology based upon the inherent sinfulness and degradation of man, who is condemned by the combined fact of original sin and his own *natural* depravity and sinfulness, unless he accept the means of escape through a vicarious atonement that became a part of God's system—for us—on account of Paul's building his own conception of the mission of Jesus into a system that, through Rome, has come down to us as the orthodox Christian religion of our day. It is a system, it is but just to say, which on the way down has been the cause of bitter dissensions and persecutions, and of differences that have resulted in many splits and divisions which have been the cause of the innumerable sects and denominations that are among us; and all of them have been directly caused by the dogmas which it has carried with it.

It is this, on the one hand, compared to the simple, open sky, hillside teachings of Jesus as given *directly by himself*, and that come with the same authority to-day and as they came to those to whom he more immediately addressed them, because they appeal to our own inner consciousness as truth, even as they appealed to theirs. As we understand him and his own direct

Source: Ralph Waldo Trine, from *The New Alinement of Life*, London, 1913, pp. 146–51.

message in this way, truly we can say as did his Galilean hearers—Never man spake as this man.

It is a teaching of the Divinity of man as opposed to the degradation of man. It is the teaching of our at-one-ness with Creative Life, Divine Being, God the Father, if you choose, through our recognition of the fact that He is essentially the Life of our life, and, therefore, in Him we live and move and have our being. It is living continually in this realisation and thinking and acting always from this conscious Centre. It is that love of God that is so all-absorbing as Jesus said, that we have no other desire or will than that the Divine Life manifest itself continually in and through us. It is likewise that love of the neighbour of which Jesus spake, that springs naturally forward and sits enthroned in the human heart, when once we realise that we are all parts of the one great Whole, in slightly differing degrees of enfoldment, indissolubly linked together, and that the welfare of the one is to be found always and only in the welfare of the Whole. It is a belief that Jesus knew whereof he spoke and also that he intended to say exactly what he did say in his conclusion: "On these two commandments hang all the law and the prophets."

It is a Life Foundation that will never have to shift its base in order to conform itself to advancing science, so as not to outrage the innate sense of reasonableness or of probability in the minds of men. It is in alinement with the findings of modern science and research, in that through the operation of the laws of Evolution—through which God is continually working—we are gradually evolving from the lower to the higher, and eventually from the material into the spiritual.

It is a religion of the spirit, leading men and women to a direct, personal, intimate relationship with the Father, where the element of immediacy is primal, and not through the intermediary of some other person or agency. It is truly a religion of redemption, for redemption takes place immediately when the Spirit of God takes possession of the mind and heart and permeates the daily life even to its minutest details. It actualises the divine sonship, "For as many as are led by the Spirit of God, they are the Sons of God."

This truth is also appealing to men because by virtue of it their religion does not have to rest upon an historical basis, which can never give anything that is certain or final. Independently of Jesus' direct reaching—though by no means independently of his influence on the world's thought—some of our ablest minds have come back to this central truth of Jesus' life, and have built upon it some of the most vital and practical, although we call them idealistic, philosophies that we have yet known.

Every man, whether he realises it or not, has in his life some basis of religion, some elements of philosophy To give these a continually greater conscious form, that they may become active and even creative forces in his life, becomes the source of an ever greater gain. Each of us, whether he admit it or no, stands— and always must stand—in some conscious relation to his Maker, the Source of his life—God. God to me is that Spirit of Infinite Life and Power that is back of all, working in and through all—the life of all. To realise it as the source of our own very life and power, and to live daily more and more consciously in this realisation, brings into activity a latent spiritual or life force—an interior illumination and wisdom and power—that will bring inevitably in its train, and to any human soul, peace and power and plenty. It is none other than the finding of that Kingdom of God and his righteousness which will be the cause, as the Master said, of all other things being added.

It brings also a real, vitalising, a practical everyday religion; for the basis, indeed the sum and substance of all religion is this consciousness of God in the soul of man. It is the spiritual, if not indeed the scientific basis of that priceless truth as enunciated by the great seer: "Thou wilt keep him in perfect peace whose mind is stayed on thee."

The great soul-cry of this changing age with which we are already face to face is for a real, vitalising, everyday religion, a religion that will make pregnant the spiritual energies that are potential within us, and that this insurgence of the Divine vitalises into an active force. The basis of all growth and health and strength, physical as well as mental and spiritual, as well as a continually higher attainment and satisfaction in the individual life, is consciously to establish and then to keep one's conscious connection with the great Source whence issues all life.

It is this new alinement of life that is the great fact of our day. This lifting of men's souls up to the Divine is bringing beauty, and faith, and hope, and through them a greater vigour of life to continually increasing numbers—literally a new birth for countless numbers.

# ❦ 155 ❧

# Doorways to a New Life for You

## NORMAN VINCENT PEALE and
## SMILEY BLANTON

Particularly after the Second World War, Norman Vincent Peale (b. 1898) successfully blurred even further for a vast readership the already hazy distinction in New Thought between spiritual and worldly comfort. Peale began as Methodist but, by the time he took over the Marble Collegiate Church on Fifth Avenue in New York in 1932, denominational limits were unimportant to him. He retailed the ingredients of successful living in a series of best selling therapeutic manuals and also collaborated with the psychiatrist, Smiley Blanton (1882–1966), in a clinic affiliated to his church in promoting mental equilibrium as the basis of success.

---

Successful living hinges on the capacity to believe. The unconquered and unconquerable of this world are those who have mastered the art of faith. They draw constantly on this inner source of strength, for they have acquired and hold ever fresh in their hearts an abiding faith in a Higher Power, and in their own destiny. Without such faith they are defenceless before the inevitable difficulties that all must face; with it they are armoured against even the most cruel of adversaries.

No age has a monopoly on misery, although our own can claim more than its full share, and, at that, misery of a most particular kind. For in the midst of economic plenty we starve spiritually. Surrounded by unmatched potentialities for the good life, we are overwhelmed by the deadly fear that all is lost!

Then the ironic fact emerges that physical medicine, which has triumphed over so many of the bodily diseases that once scourged mankind, has proved utterly inadequate in the treatment of the maladies that canker the modern soul. Hosts of emotional ills gnaw at the roots of our serenity and health, and plague us with shadowy terrors.

But certainly the appearance betrays the reality. Everything is not lost, as one would think! The persistence of such happy affirmations as young people

Source: Norman Vincent Peale and Smiley Blanton, 'Doorways to a New Life for You', *The Art of Real Happiness*, London, 1951, pp. 1–21.

falling in love and, thereby, renewing man's perennial lease on Eden; of teachers unfolding new wonders, and perpetuating old ones, in the minds of youth; of parents nurturing children through unsung years of patience and sacrifice—all of these are the unanswerable rebuttal to the "all is lost" school of thought. All of these and ten thousand other yes-saying acceptances of life reassure us that there is an inexhaustible reservoir from which the human race can draw sustaining strength and hope.

Recently Captain Eddie Rickenbacker, one of the outstanding heroes and leaders of our time, was talking to a group of airmen in a veterans' hospital. The veterans were all men who had been seriously wounded and were, many of them, badly shaken psychologically.

Captain Rickenbacker is a man of inspired and demonstrated faith, and in the midst of his talk he paused, and then said earnestly: "If there is any one of you who has not yet had an experience of God, my advice to him is to go out after it and get it." There was a hush in that hospital room. They knew that he had uncovered to them the secret that had brought him to safety. They realised that this flying ace had pointed out to them the surest way out of their uncertainty and despair.

Rickenbacker does not say such words idly. He does believe that faith is the key to life. "Think postively and masterfully, with confidence and faith," he has said,

> "and life becomes more secure, more fraught with action, richer in achievement and experience. This is the sure way to win victories over inner defeat. It is the way a humble man meets life or death."

But unfortunately all too many of us have erected barriers in our everyday lives to the operation of belief, to the acquisition of this power-giving faith. A perverse blockage dams the flood of energy that should flow with irresistible force into the healthy heart. What stops this flow? What diverts this stream of hope and belief and confidence that should irrigate the dry and hopeless hearts of men?

These are the questions that are a challenge to every clergyman, to every teacher, to every physician (and especially to every psychiatrist) in our society. Neither are they academic questions. With mounting insistence they enter the lives of troubled human beings who, dangerously close to the breaking-point, are unable to live happily in this world until their emotional problems are solved.

In quiet rooms in the Marble Collegiate Church, shut off from the brawling traffic of New York's Fifth Avenue, is a clinic where religion and psychiatry have, we believe, been welded into a powerful therapy for the ills that wrack the human spirit. Here, under the joint direction of a clergyman and a psychiatrist, many harrowed men and women are learning to break down the barriers that keep them from living successfully. Here, day after day, the anxious and the depressed, the worried and the frightened, are gaining the priceless secret of inner peace.

This book is an effort to tell how it is being done.

The clinic of the Marble Collegiate Church was founded more than ten years ago by a minister and a psychiatrist, the authors of the present book. Each of us, in our own professional work, had long been familiar with the tragedy of those who, with the capacity to stand upright, yet crawled through life on their hands and knees. Despite their wish to move forward joyously, they were tormented with the secret thought, repeated like the ominous ticking of a clock: "I should have done ... I ought not to have done." With no place to turn for guidance, no ear to listen to their grief, they naturally became filled with panic and with despair. And for such as these the clinic of the Marble Collegiate Church was established. It originated in our mutual conviction that a new approach was need to the personal difficulties that beset modern man.

A great adventure began for us. In our minds we dedicated the clinic to a theory, to a dream if you will, that together religion and psychiatry might accomplish more than either could alone. The dream has become reality; the theory we believe, a proved fact. The techniques which we have worked out together can, as we believe we have demonstrated time and again, regenerate a person, bring him into touch with his own creative forces and, in turn, with the infinite forces of the universe. This faith-restoring process brings a power and a joy to the individual which he had never dared to hope was possible.

We realised quite early that the people who came to us were a cross section of the troubled millions who, Sisyphus-like, push the cruel stone of anxiety up an endless hill. Most of them had, potentially, the ability to be reasonably content. They were intelligent, well disposed persons who had tried earnestly to follow their best ideals. They were not devoid of religious faith: they prayed; they made us of the sacraments humbly and regularly. But somehow their religion had failed them; it had ceased to be for them a dynamic way of life. In the deepest sense they were cut off from that healthy savour of life, and from a vibrant faith that would give them confidence in themselves and trust in their Creator.

Not only did they lack a sound faith; they lacked self-knowledge. The well-established psychiatric fact that the human mind operates on two levels, the conscious and the unconscious, came as a shocking surprise to many of them. The "mind", as they conceived it, was the uniquely human organ that enabled them to remember facts, make decisions, order a dinner, or understand a book. Those and many other functions of the mind were apparently clear to them. But they failed to realise that the conscious part of their minds was merely the uppermost layer of a depthless ocean. They were slow, sometimes unwilling, to accept the fact that most of their mental life was taking place, and most of their behaviour was motivated, in these profound depths termed by psychiatry the "unconscious".

The first work of the clinic was to acquaint them with the forces that exist in these depths. Step by step they were shown how conflicts hidden there,

330

particularly those between love and hate, begin in childhood and are often repeated in later life. And it was necessary to explain to them over and over again how these hidden conflicts are reflected on the surface of the mind in the disguised forms of fear, worry, depression, and, significantly enough, a weakening of faith.

It is no accident that loss of faith accompanies other neurotic symptoms. Faith flows from the capacity to love, and this capacity to love may be dulled, or even destroyed entirely, by the bitter struggle between conflicting feelings in the unconscious mind.

An illustration is the story of a young architect who came to the clinic suffering from a profound sense of impending disaster. He lived in the shadow of an unrelenting anxiety. He could not understand it! Its cause did not exist in the outside world: nothing actually threatened him, except his inner sense of dread.

He was the son of domineering and changeable father, who had persistently frustrated his son's need for love all during his childhood. He recalled one day when his father had promised to spend all Saturday afternoon walking with him in the woods. He was just a little fellow, and this had seemed an occasion of great importance. But, when the day came, his father gathered up his golf-bag and started off to the country club. When the small boy cried, his father scolded him and called him a cry-baby and a nuisance. This episode had been symbolic of all their relationships: one day sympathetic playfulness; the next selfish indifference.

His ability to love anyone or anything was greatly impaired, and he carried this impairment of one of the most vital of all human functions into all his later love relationships. By the time he came to the clinic he believed that he had even lost faith in God. "God is a delusion," he said, angrily, during the first interview.

As he gained insight into the true nature of his problem, a burning but hitherto completely repressed and hidden anger towards his father, a powerful mental catharsis took place. The rage that had been poisoning his mind was dissipated. And, after some religious guidance which revitalised his atrophied capacities for love, he not only shook off the painful anxiety which had tormented him since childhood, but he was also enabled to regain his lost faith in God and in mankind.

The first step, then, towards the restoration of faith is to exorcise the devils of submerged emotional conflict. Once the psychiatrist with this specialised skills begins the task of removing these neurotic barriers built of hate, resentment, fear, and anxiety, religious guidance then stimulates an influx of healing faith in the ultimate power and rightness of God.

This, in essence, is the driving force that motivates our entire programme at the Marble Collegiate Church clinic.

It may be difficult for some to accept the fact that feelings of which they are completely unaware can distort their lives. Many people actually doubt the existence of these unconscious primitive motivations. They find it difficult to believe that an angelic child, or a mild-mannered man or woman, can harbour the most savage, amoral, and anti-social passions. Since these unconscious impulses are generally exhibited in masked form, it is natural to assume that they are not there. And pleasanter! But the evidence of their existence is overwhelming and, *until they are accepted in all their intensity as one of the facts of life, it is impossible to deal realistically with the spiritual anguish which they can cause.*

In his sleep, when the unconscious takes over, man re-lives in dream form these earliest longings and desires. He re-experiences his old loves, and hates, and fears. During the enigmatic episodes of his dreams, which psychiatry can fully explain only after long study, he expresses the deepest and sometimes the most primitive wishes of his unconscious mind. In these night-time fantasies he often does not hesitate to love illicitly, or even to kill.

In one of his most celebrated short stories, Robert Louis Stevenson gave the English language a symbol for this basic duality of human nature. But in real life there is no need for a magic elixir such as turned the amiable London physician, Dr Jekyll, into his primitive counterpart, the bestial Mr Hyde. To show his teeth, all the average person needs is frustration, sometimes even the most apparently trivial sort. Then suddenly the gunpowder of unconscious rage, stored up in the timeless unconscious, is detonated. The tantrum of the small child, whose scooter is snatched away by an older brother, comes out in the rage of an adult baseball fan screeching at an umpire who has called an obvious ball a strike; or in the disproportionate fury of the housewife beating a maid who has broken her favourite piece of bric-à-brac. But there is, you say, no mayhem here, no actual lusting Mr Hyde? Of course. As the child represses the murderous content of his rage, so does the frustrated adult. Having learned that society, and his own conscience, demand at least the appearance of self-control, he confines his anger to a burst of temper. He merely blows off steam.

Sometimes these grown-up angers are expressed in very revealing terms. The baseball fan, his eyes popping, screams: "Kill the umpire!" And the housewife, telling her husband about the careless maid, declares casually, "I could have killed her". Such common expressions, not intended literally, actually do reflect the feelings and desires far more accurately than most of us would suspect. Sigmund Freud has described in blunt, and scientifically substantiated terms, the Hyde-like aspects of the average person. "In our unconscious," Freud wrote,

we daily and hourly deport all who stand in our way, all who have offended or injured us. Indeed, our unconscious will murder even for trifles. And so, if we are to be judged by the wishes of our unconscious, we are, like primitive men, simply a gang of murderers. It is well that these wishes do not possess the potency which was attributed to them by primitive man; in the cross-fire of mutual maledictions mankind would long since have perished, the best and wisest of men and the loveliest and fairest of women with the rest.

We are, of course, morally responsible only for what we think and do consciously. We cannot be held accountable for wishes buried so deeply in our unconscious minds that we are only dimly, it at all, aware of them. But even though we do not translate these wishes into action, they still exist and are able to exert a strong influence on our state of mind.

Psychologically speaking, many people are in an almost constant state of inner warfare without realising it. Strong, often violent, impulses of a sort absolutely alien to their conscious concept of ethical behaviour well up from the "depthless ocean" of the unconscious mind. Their conscious mind rejects them, or represses them as the psychiatrist would say, before they are even fully apprehended. And, through this almost immediate repression, the most painful anxiety arises.

Psychiatry's objective is to enable man to modify and control this primitive side of his nature so that it can be bent to the will, and channelled into useful purposes. It strives to bring a cessation of inner conflict and so restore peace of mind, and to make the reasoning, adult, ethically conscious mind the master of the whole personality.

With methods differing through the centuries, this has been the great task of religion also. The Church, too often regarded as an institution removed from the main stream of life, is on the contrary a scientific laboratory dedicated to the re-shaping of men's daily lives. Its great principles are formulae and techniques designed to meet every human need. The minister, no less then the psychiatrist, is a scientist who works with the human soul. The pulpit behind which the pastor stands is a sacred desk, but it is also a laboratory table on which are performed experiments in the laws of human nature and in the application of spiritual truths.

The New Testament is his textbook of laws: spiritual laws as specific as the laws of physics or chemistry, and compiled by the most subtle and skilled students of behaviour. Gathered together in this book the revelation of Jesus Christ is, in simple codified form, a power-releasing mechanism of surpassing therapeutic strength.

As a matter of fact, a re-evaluation of the New Testament in relation to modern psychiatric findings proves it to be beyond question one of the most profoundly astute books on human nature ever written.

Innumerable parallels can be drawn between the fundamentals of the two disciplines. Psychiatry postulates the unconscious, in which it finds not only savage impulses that give rise to fear and anxiety, but also those strivings which are the source of faith, and hope, and of courage, as well as the basis of creative strength. Religion postulates the soul. Charged with evil, this deepest recess of man's being drags him down; but once attuned to God's power, it is the well-spring of his moral strength.

Psychiatry lays bare the innate self-centredness of the new-born infant. Man, Theology says, is born in sin. And the ethical precepts of religion play an important rôle in so modifying the child's self-centredness that he can become a healthy adult, functioning within the social group.

Love and hate are primary concerns of both sciences. Psychiatry says that it is inner conflict, kindled by hatred, which destroys faith. Christianity counters hate with love, instructing that under God all men are brothers and that we should love our neighbours as ourselves.

Religion and psychiatry alike direct their healing skill towards the release of those inner powers which are possessed by all. The psychiatrist knows that a person can revitalise his whole life once he re-directs and alters the character of his disturbing unconscious drives. The concept of change, of spiritual regeneration, is basic to all theory of human behaviour. "Do not be satisfied with what you are," the pastor tells his congregation. "Do not give up your dreams of what you may become," says the psychiatrist.

One great scriptural verse which, in many respects, is the very heart of the Christian faith, declares: "If any man be in Christ, he is a new creature: old things are passed away; behold all things are become new." That is to say that if any man fills his mind with Christ's spirit, talks with Him, prays with Him, lives with Him, that man may be completely sure that the old things that have defeated and harassed him shall pass away and all things shall become new.

Modern, dynamic psychiatry has learned that not only can man change through the solution of neurotic conflicts, but that once it is done he can also draw on energies the presence of which he hardly suspected. The clergyman directs himself to the release of man's inner powers: "The Kingdom of God is within you." Through faith in Christ you can attach yourself to the flow of Divine power. "Behold," we read in a great text from St Luke's Gospel, "I give unto you power to tread on serpents and scorpions, and over all the power of the enemy: and nothing shall by any means hurt you."

It is just such an endless list of parallels between psychiatry and religion that makes the alliance between them so natural and fruitful. At the clinic they are the basis for what we believe is amazingly effective team-work. Once the psychiatrist has diagnosed the psychic ailment and given his treatment, the minister is enabled to take from the great medicine-chest of the Christian faith that remedy best suited for its cure.

The technique of administering the cure is of particular importance. The failure of the Church has often been that it tells persons to pray, but does not tell them how. It encourages them to have faith, but does not give them specific techniques for acquiring it. It tells them to practise love, but gives no detailed methodology for the practice of it in their lives. At the clinic, the important word is HOW.

But before any programme for cure can be prescribed, it is necessary to give the person some knowledge of the emotional patterns underlying his behaviour. And we encounter some very strange patterns indeed! Perhaps the commonest and most distinctive of these is the feeling of guilt, born of the unconscious desire to injure or kill some other person for wrongs suffered at their hands. This guilt frequently takes the form of anxiety. It is not uncommon for people to come into the clinic sweating and trembling with a fear the origin of which they do not understand.

Such was the case of a young businessman, who complained of a constant sense of fear which was making his life "just plain torture". It made no sense, he told us, but it was there and he could not shake it off. During several interviews it became obvious that his trouble stemmed from a childhood, and lifelong, hatred of his older brother, who had been consistently held up to him as a model. His hatred was so intense that, unconsciously, he wished for his brother's death. This had brought a persistent, overwhelming unconscious fear of being punished.

A staff minister, informed of the exact nature of his problem, was able to show him how to allay his anxiety and regain his faith through prayer. "You must consciously cultivate just ordinary affection for your brother!" he was told.

> No matter how hard this may seem, you will have to do it in order to combat the suppressed hatred and anger which has done you so much harm.
> But in order to do that, you will have to change the whole pattern of your thinking. Love, and the faith that flows from it, cannot penetrate your mind while it is suffused and choked by the anxiety you have felt for so long. I am going to give you what I call a prescription to drive out the fear the lies in your mind like a poison. Here is a text from the Scripture. Take it. Repeat it to yourself over and over again, until your mind is completely possessed with it. Conceive of it as a medicine dripping into your mind, and it will spread a healing influence that will give you an immunity from this fear.

As he prayed for this deliverance, he was asked to believe that he received it not at some far off time in the future, but now, immediately!

Inasmuch as the first thing he had to do was get a new spirit in his mind, a spirit of love that would drive out the fear, he was given, as his first text: "Perfect love casteth out fear." He was to use that several times daily for the first week. The second week he was to add another: "I sought the Lord, and He heard me, and delivered me from all my fears."

The next week: "What things soever ye desire, when ye pray, believe that ye receive them, and ye shall have them." The following week: "I will fear no evil: for Thou art with me," to remind him that he was not alone in this fight, but that God was with him, and that God was all-powerful to take away his fears. And still another: "Thou wilt keep him in perfect peace, whose mind is stayed on thee."

This process continued over a considerable period, each week a new text.

He was asked to keep an actual record of how often he repeated each one of the texts the pastor gave him, and he reported later that it was often scores of times in a single day. Gradually, almost like a powerful drug dissipating a centre of pain, the religious "prescription" dissolved his fear.

"It's amazing," he told the minister one day. "I've found that those texts are not just words, nor combinations of words! They are power, distilled power."

He was discovering the old truth: that the words of Jesus do indeed have an active healing power; that they are surcharged with light and healing radiance when they are used in a simple forthright way. He found the old truth, also, of the passage in the New Testament: "If ye abide in me, and my words abide in you, ye shall ask what ye will, and it shall be done unto you."

As his anxiety lessened, and his belief in the power of religious faith was gradually restored, a remarkable change came over him. His depressed and beaten look was replaced by one of buoyant self-assurance. later he told us that his work was very much improved, and that his relationship with his wife and children had become richer and deeper than ever before. A feeling of affection towards his brother, replacing the old antagonism, had laid the ground-work for a new, rewarding friendship. He was, he said, at last finding out what life could really be like.

In the beginning, it was our belief that the association of religion with psychiatry would serve other useful ends beside actual therapy. It has. It has helped to dispel the commonly held notion that psychiatry is in some way unwholesome or connected only with the abnormal side of life. Then, too, many persons earnestly desiring psychiatric help hesitate to seek it for fear of meeting with an attitude of indifference, or even antagonism, to their religious beliefs. Our clinic, of course, solves this dilemma. Here all can be sure of finding psychiatrists who have integrated their medical work with a religious point of view.

We believed it would be a tremendous advantage to have the clinic situated in the church buildings; and such has been the case. The Church stands for an ancient tradition of love, forgiveness, strength, and protection. In such an environment feelings of guilt tend to be rapidly reduced, which opens the way to a frank discussion of doubts and fears. The church background creates an atmosphere of such trust and confidence that acceptance of the counsellor's authority, a vital point in all psychotherapy, is more easily and quickly achieved.

Under these favourable circumstances, recovery from emotional disturbance can often be gained with a rapidity not possible in any other kind of clinic. For example, a woman came to the church in a state of extreme despair. She had a sense of sin so great that it seemed almost to have destroyed her.

This was her story. Five years ago she had become pregnant; a short while later her husband went into the army leaving her along with her three young children. Financially hard pressed, and emotionally unable to face the responsibility of another child, in her desperation she made the mistake of submitting to an abortion. Although at first in her warped thinking this seemed justified to her, her wrong-doing eventually began to prey on her mind. Regret for her act became an obsession with her. She lost weight, suffered from insomnia and finally began to neglect her children.

Had she prayed for forgiveness? "Yes. I have asked God for forgiveness thousands of times, but all my prayers have fallen dead," she answered.

The logic of common sense, which told this woman that her inability to adjust to this past wrong act which she now sincerely repented was abnormal, had no force with her. it was necessary to meet this disability with another technique.

During the conferences it was learned that when she was five years old she had felt a desperate jealousy of a new-born sister, whom she considered to be a dangerous rival for her parents' love. An unconscious wish for her sister's death had stimulated a conscious act and she had tried to injure the baby by jamming a ring down its throat. She was caught in the act and severely punished.

At that moment there was planted in her mind a deep sense of guilt over this wrong-doing, which time had neither removed nor even softened. The true significance to her of the abortion in later years could now be understood. The guilt over the desire to be rid of her own child was reinforced in her unconscious mind with the old infantile wish to destroy her baby sister. And when the old guilt attached itself to the new, her feeling was of such an intensity that no reasoning, nor even the power of prayer and confession, could alleviate it.

Her anguish already somewhat quieted by the confidence instilled by the atmosphere of the church clinic, she was eventually able to accept this explanation. In fact she had an almost immediate sense of release. And when she followed the method of prayer given her, she was finally able to accept the feeling of God's forgiveness that had been denied her for so long. Now, she was able to forgive herself. The change in the woman was amazing. In two months she gained fifteen pounds. She looked much younger and had a joyous contentment which seemed to radiate all about her.

There was one scriptural passage which had proved especially helpful to her: "... forgetting those things which are behind," said St. Paul, "and reaching forth unto those things which are before, I press towards the mark." To a person suffering from a sense of guilt, no sounder psychiatric advice can be given.

When we began the clinic, we believed that the fellowship of the church and the value of common worship, a resource not available to the ordinary clinic, would be of great benefit. It has worked out that way. The church is the centre of a broad programme of social activities; and so when a person comes to us suffering from depression, for example, with a deep need for friendship, and for a real contact with the world, we are able to relate him in a creative way to some group that can fulfil this need. We not only counsel him on his inner problem; we can actually put him in touch with the confidence-inspiring companionship of persons who, like himself, believe in the religious way of life. We can help him integrate his emotional, and spiritual, and social self.

Sometimes this integration is the most important factor in the healing process. We recall a woman who came to the clinic because she felt that her life was empty, without meaning and without hope. A rather pathetic person, with a listless manner and an extraordinarily drab and untidy appearance, she said the she was on the edge of a "nervous breakdown".

Two facts about her eventually came out which, to the untrained eye, might have seemed unconnected, but which actually gave the clue to her basic problem. First: some years before, her father, a querulous, complaining man, had retired and come to live with her, and ever since then she had waited on this demanding slave-driver hand and foot, to the point where there was no time in her life for even the slightest sort of relaxation. She maintained a conscious attitude of almost morbid dedication to the unrewarding task of caring for him. And she had resigned herself, as well, to the necessity of becoming a frustrated old maid.

Questioned, she said yes, of course she loved her father, even though he was difficult and cranky. She obeyed the Biblical injunction: "Honour thy father and thy mother". At least she had convinced herself that she did. Actually, though, as she was eventually able to see, she had only succeeded in bottling-up a seething anger at her father because he was limiting her life so cruelly. She had done so complete a job of this that she was absolutely unaware of her real attitude towards him.

The second pertinent fact revealed was that at the place where she worked she was continually having accidents. As we have said, it is a common trick of the mind to drive back into its unconscious depths ideas and feelings which are repugnant or frightening. In her unconscious mind, however, the suppressed rage had aroused an appalling sense of guilt. The guilt, in turn, had taken the not unusual form of self-punishment.

"Self-punishment?" She looked puzzled.

"Of course," the counsellor told her. "Don't you see? Those accidents you have been having really are self-inflicted punishment for your hostile feelings towards your father."

Insight into the true nature of her buried emotions was half the battle. With understanding of it, her hostility and the accompanying guilt began to melt away. She was then able to develop a more normal attitude towards her father, to say a firm but loving "no" to his excessive demands on her. Her anxiety lessened and the accidents eventually stopped altogether.

Meantime, she was advised to give some well considered attention to her appearance, her clothes, and her hair, and to learn the art of judicious make-up. It was arranged to get her launched in the social life of the church. And subsequently she met a suitable young man, fell in love, and was engaged to be married. In brief, every aspect of her life was changed.

The technique which has been developed at the clinic varies only in detail: the broad principles are by now well established. The staff has necessarily grown, until now it includes seven consultants. The first interview may be with either a minister or a psychiatrist, more or less by chance. The main course of the therapy may be directed more or less equally by both, or almost entirely by either one, all depending on the exact nature of the problem. Sometimes a single interview is sufficient; more often several are required; occasionally a great many.

There is no claim made, of course, that every troubled person can be basically affected by this combined therapy. Some mental and emotional disturbances are so deep-seated that they can be remedied only the by the most prolonged psychiatric treatment. Others are such that they yield quite rapidly to religious guidance alone. But in countless cases of persons who worry and fret and feel inadequate to the fulfilment of their desires, the alliance between the two disciplines has a marvellous effectiveness.

The child, said Wordsworth, is father to the man. And for many persons, reeling under the shock of life in this age, this parentage is their undoing; for the shackles of unresolved conflicts placed upon them in childhood remain to enslave them in their adult life. Our hopeful message is that a way is at hand to help remove these fetters. They can, we believe, be most effectively struck off by the combined blows of modern dynamic religion, and of psychiatry.

In succeeding chapters we shall try to tell the whole story of what is being accomplished; of how the principles and methods that are worked out in the clinic can be of direct benefit. Perhaps in these pages you may find the answer to our problem or to the problems of those dear to you. The minister and the psychiatrists of your clinic, joined in a common love of people, unitedly assert to all who sense failure in their lives that it is never too late to find through faith the sources of power which give man courage; never too late to acquire faith in one's self, in other people, other causes, and other ideals; and, above all, never too late to find a creative faith in God.

# Black Churches and Sects

Plate 17: Walker Evans, *Country Church, South Carolina*, 1936.

# ❧·156·☙

# The Function of the Negro Church

## W. E. B. DU BOIS

W. E. B. Du Bois (1868-1963) was the outstanding African-American intellectual of the early twentieth century. He was always concerned in his work as historian, sociologist, essayist and editor of the N.A.A.C.P.'s journal, *The Crisis*, to investigate and value the distinctive features of African-American culture as well as to demand civil and political equality for blacks. He recognised the importance of the church in black life and gave an account of its organisation and workings in one old African-American community in his study of Philadelphia (1899).

---

The Negro church is the peculiar and characteristic product of the transplanted African, and deserves especial study. As a social group the Negro church may be said to have antedated the Negro family on American soil; as such it has preserved, on the one hand, many of tribal organization, and on the other hand, many of the family functions. Its tribal functions are shown in its religious activity, its social authority and general guiding and co-ordinating work; its family functions are shown by the fact that the church is a centre of social life and intercourse; acts as newspaper and intelligence bureau, is the centre of amusements—indeed, is the world in which the Negro moves and acts. So far-reaching are these functions of the church that its organization is almost political. In Bethel Church, for instance, the mother African Methodist Episcopal Church of America, we have the following officials and organizations

| | |
|---|---|
| The Bishop of the District ................................. | |
| The Presiding Elder............................................ | } Executive |
| The Pastor ......................................................... | |
| The Board of Trustees ...................................... | Executive Council |
| General Church Meeting ................................... | Legislative |

Source: W. E. B. Du Bois, 'The Function of the Negro Church', *The Philadelphia Negro*, Philadelphia, 1899, pp. 200-7.

| | |
|---|---|
| The Board of Stewards ..................................... | ⎫ |
| The Board of Stewardesses .............................. | ⎬ Financial Board |
| The Junior Stewardesses ................................. | ⎭ |
| The Sunday School Organization ........................ | Educational System |
| Ladies' Auxiliary, Volunteer Guild, etc. ............... | Tax Collectors |
| Ushers' Association ......................................... | Police |
| Class Leaders ................................................ | ⎫ |
| Local Preachers ............................................. | ⎬ Sheriffs and Magistrates |
| Choir .......................................................... | Music and Amusement |
| Allen Guards ................................................ | Militia |
| Missionary Societies ........................................ | Social Reformers |
| Beneficial and Semi-Secret Societies ..................... | Corporations |

Or to put it differently, here we have a mayor, appointed from without, with great administrative and legislative powers, although well limited by long and zealously cherished custom; he acts conjointly with a select council, the trustees, a board of finance composed of stewards and stewardesses, a common council of committees and, occasionally, of all church members. The various functions of the church are carried out by societies and organizations. The form of government varies, but is generally some form of democracy closely guarded by custom and tempered by possible and not infrequent secession.

The functions of such churches in order of present emphasis are:

1. The raising of the annual budget.
2. The maintenance of membership.
3. Social intercourse and amusements.
4. The setting of moral standards.
5. Promotion of general intelligence.
6. Efforts for social betterment.

1. The annual budget is of first importance, because the life of the organization depends upon it. The amount of expenditure is not very accurately determined beforehand, although its main items do not vary much. There is the pastor's salary, the maintenance of the building, light and heat, the wages of a janitor, contributions to various church objects, and the like, to which must be usually added the interest on some debt. The sum thus required varies in Philadelphia from $200 to $5000. A small part of this is raised by a direct tax on each member. Besides this, voluntary contributions by members roughly gauged according to ability, are expected, and a strong public opinion usually compels payment. Another large source of revenue is the collection after the sermons on Sunday, when, amid the reading of notices and a subdued hum of social intercourse, a stream of givers walk to the pulpit and place in the hands of the trustee or steward in charge a contribution, varying from a cent to a dollar or more. To this must be added the steady revenue from entertainments, suppers, socials, fairs, and the like. In this way the Negro churches of Philadelphia raise nearly $100,000 a year. They hold in real estate $900,000 worth of property, and are thus no insignificant element in the economics of the city.

2. Extraordinary methods are used and efforts made to maintain and increase the membership of the various churches. To be a popular church with large membership means ample revenues, large social influence and a leadership among the colored people unequaled in power and effectiveness. Consequently people are attracted to the church by sermons, by music and by entertainments; finally, every year a revival is held, at which considerable numbers of young people are converted. All this is done in perfect sincerity and without much thought of merely increasing membership, and yet every small church strives to be large by these means and every large church to maintain itself or grow larger. The churches thus vary from a dozen to a thousand members.

3. Without wholly conscious effort the Negro church has become a centre of social intercourse to a degree unknown in white churches even in the country. The various churches, too, represent social classes. At St. Thomas' one looks for the well-to-do Philadelphians, largely descendants of favourite mulatto house-servants, and consequently well-bred and educated, but rather cold and reserved to strangers or newcomers; at Central Presbyterian one sees the older, simpler set of respectable Philadelphians with distinctly Quaker characteristics—pleasant but conservative; at Bethel may be seen the best of the great laboring class—steady, honest people, well dressed and well fed, with church and family traditions; at Wesley will be found the new arrivals, the sight-seers and the strangers to the city—hearty and easy-going people, who welcome all comers and ask few questions; at Union Baptist one may look for the Virginia servant girls and their young men; and so on throughout the city. Each church forms its own social circle, and not many stray beyond its bounds. Introductions into that circle come through the church, and thus the stranger becomes known. All sorts of entertainments and amusements are furnished by the churches: concerts, suppers, socials, fairs, literary exercises and debates, cantatas, plays, excursions, picnics, surprise parties, celebrations. Every holiday is the occasion of some special entertainment by some club, society or committee of the church; Thursday afternoons and evenings, when the servant girls are free, are always sure to have some sort of entertainment. Sometimes these exercises are free, sometimes an admission fee is charged, sometimes refreshments or articles are on sale. The favorite entertainment is a concert with solo singing, instrumental music, reciting, and the like. Many performers make a living by appearing at these entertainments in various cities, and often they are persons of training and ability, although not always. So frequent are these and other church exercises that there are few Negro churches which are not open four to seven nights in a week and sometimes one or two afternoons in addition.

Perhaps the pleasantest and most interesting social intercourse takes place on Sunday; the weary week's is done, the people have slept late and had a good breakfast, and sally forth to church well dressed and complacent. The usual hour of the morning service is eleven, but people stream in until after twelve. The sermon is usually short and stirring, but in the larger churches elicits little response other than an "Amen" or two. After the sermon the social features begin; notices on the various meetings of the week are read, people talk with each other in subdued tones, take their contributions to the altar, and linger in the aisles and corridors long after dismission to laugh and chat until one or two o'clock. Then they go home to good dinners. Sometimes there is some special three o'clock service, but usually nothing save Sunday-school, until night. Then comes the chief meeting of the day; probably ten thousand Negroes gather every Sunday night in their churches. There is much music, much preaching, some short addresses; many strangers are there to be looked at; many beaus bring out their belles, and those who do not gather in crowds at the church door and escort the young women home. The crowds are usually well behaved and respectable, though rather more jolly than comports with a puritan idea of church services.

In this way the social life of the Negro centres in his church—baptism, wedding and burial, gossip and courtship, friendship and intrigue—all lie in these walls. What wonder that this central club tends to become more and more luxuriously furnished, costly in appointment and easy of access!

4. It must not be inferred from all this that the Negro is hypocritical or irreligious. His church is, to be sure, a social institution first, and religious afterwards, but nevertheless, its religious activity is wide and sincere. In direct moral teaching and in setting moral standards for the people, however, the church is timid, and naturally so, for its constitution is democracy tempered by custom. Negro preachers are often condemned for poor leadership and empty sermons, and it is said that men with so much power and influence could make striking moral reforms. This is but partially true. The congregation does not follow the moral precepts of the preacher, but rather the preacher follows the standard of his flock, and only exceptional men dare seek to change this. And here it must be remembered that the Negro preacher is primarily an executive officer, rather than a spiritual guide. If one goes into any great Negro church and hears the sermon and views the audience, one would say: either the sermon is far below the calibre of the audience, or the people are less sensible than they look; the former explanation is usually true. The preacher is sure to be a man of executive ability, a leader of men, a shrewd and affable president of a large and intricate corporation. In addition to this he may be, and usually is a striking elocutionist; he may also be a man of integrity, learning, and deep spiritual earnestness; but these last three are sometimes all lacking, and the last two in many cases. Some signs of advance are here manifest: no minister of notoriously immoral life, or even of bad reputation, could hold a large church in Philadelphia without eventual revolt. Most of the present pastors are decent, respectable men; there are perhaps one or two exceptions to this, but the exceptions are doubtful, rather than notorious. On the whole then, the average Negro preacher in this city is a shrewd manager, a respectable man, a good talker, a pleasant companion, but neither learned nor spiritual, nor a reformer.

The moral standards are therefore set by the congregations, and vary from church to church in some degree. There has been a slow working toward a literal obeying of the puritan and ascetic standard of morals which Methodism imposed on the freedmen; but condition and temperament have modified these. The grosser forms of immorality, together with theatre-going and dancing, are specifically denounced; nevertheless, the precepts against specific amusements are often violated by church members. The cleft between denominations is still wide, especially between Methodists and Baptists. The sermons are usually kept within the safe ground of a mild Calvinism, with much insistence on Salvation, Grace, Fallen Humanity and the like.

The chief function of these churches in morals is to conserve old standards and create about them a public opinion which shall deter the offender. And in this the Negro churches are peculiarly successful, although naturally the standards conserved are not as high as they should be.

5. The Negro churches were the birthplaces of Negro schools and of all agencies which seek to promote the intelligence of the masses; and even to-day no agency serves to disseminate news or information so quickly and effectively among Negroes as the church. The lyceum and lecture here still maintain a feeble but persistent existence, and church newspapers and books are circulated widely. Night schools and kindergartens are still held in connection with churches, and all Negro celebrities, from a bishop to a poet like Dunbar, are introduced to Negro audiences from the pulpits.

6. Consequently all movements for social betterment are apt to centre in the churches. Beneficial societies in endless number are formed here; secret societies keep in touch; co-operative and building associations have lately sprung up; the minister often acts as an employment agent; considerable charitable and relief work is done and special meetings held to aid special projects. The race problem in all its phases is continually being discussed, and, indeed, from this forum many a youth goes forth inspired to work.

Such are some of the functions of the Negro church, and a study of them indicates how largely this organization has come to be an expression of the organized life of Negroes in a great city.

# The Changing Church

## CHARLES S. JOHNSON

Charles S. Johnson (1893–1956) was active from the end of the First World War in Chicago race-relations bodies and was director of research and then founding editor of its magazine, *Opportunity* (1923–29). As professor of sociology at Fisk from 1928 onwards and member of various national and international committees on social and racial issues, Johnson was a major analyst of black life in the 1920s and 1930s. A fundamental precept of his social analysis was that it was first necessary to see the world through his subjects' eyes before drawing conclusions. This makes his description of a black church in the rural South in the early 1930s particularly valuable.

The sixtieth anniversary of the Macedonia Baptist Church was the occasion for a retrospective comparison of the church since slavery. Although not a regular service, it afforded interesting documentation of the changing mores. There was a program with announced papers, but the older members who took part in the celebration simply accepted the stilted announcement of a paper to be presented as an opportunity to talk. The minister had tried hard to introduce a note of formality into the ceremonies, with indifferent success. It was an artificial performance challenged by one exasperated old member who frankly stated her fear of the disintegration of the institution as a force in the life of the community. She was realistic and accurate in her appraisal, which provoked general irritation. The chairman made her sit down.

> We are celebrating our sixtieth anniversary today. . . . Don't talk. Some of you school girls back there are talking. . . . We are celebrating. . . . We asked all of you ladies to dress in white. Some of you all had old white dresses and some of you all coulda got them. Of course all of them didn't know about it is excused. All you members who wore white dresses take the front seat We going to be hard on them that knowed and didn't. You could take thirty cents and buy one. You can make a dress out of three yards, and you can get goods for ten a yard. . . . All the members take the middle aisle. We are asking everybody

Source: Charles S. Johnson, 'The Changing Church', *Shadow of the Plantation*, Chicago, 1934, pp. 170–79. © 1934 by University of Chicago Press.

to write your name on an envelope. There will be a secretary to take it 'cause everybody can't read everybody's writing. . . . Everybody haven't got sixty cents put in a quarter or dime, and if you ain't got one borrow one. We are going to be hard. We can't whip you but we can make you feel mighty bad.

We are going to have two subjects today. The first is going to be delivered by one I have known all my days. He's been our superintendent of Sunday school for years. His subject is "Difference in Spiritual Progress in the Church Now and Twenty-five Years Ago. "

The superintendent arose and put on his glasses to speak. He said:

I can't say so much about the difference in the church twenty-five or thirty years ago but I know it is a big difference. My mother used to take me by the hand and lead me to church and Sunday school. They used to have midweek meetings and Saturday-night meetings, and men and women was converted by prayer meetings. We don't take the time now to have meetings like they used to have twenty-five or thirty years ago. I believe, though, that times will be better to come. Used to be my mother and your mother would start shouting soon as they got in the door of the church. Now you might think it a little different, but we are serving the same God today as we did thirty years ago. Everything in the world has changed. In those days people had to go to the graveyard, and 'less'n you told a great long tale about a dog or something else you couldn't be let in. We don't do that now. We know that Jesus Christ is right here and you can get him anywhere if you got the love of God in your heart. Now let us try to serve God pure and honest; let us begin singing, preaching, or whatever we do—serve him with a pure heart.

> Lordy, won't you hear me pray;
> I want to be holy every day.
> Lordy, won't you hear me pray
> I want to be more holy every day.

The minister proceeded with the program:

Next subject on hand to be delivered [under his breath he muttered] ain't but one thing 'bout it he is able to do and I want to ask him to cut it sorta short. His subject is: "My Vision of the Future Church," by Deacon A.M. Turner.

Deacon Turner strove to be correct in every detail:

MASTER OF CEREMONIES, MEMBERS, PASTOR, AND FRIENDS: One way we will have a future church will be the way we lead our lives daily and give the folks what they need. I am not a preacher; I was only called to be a deacon. Ain't very much work I can do. I might say something here he wouldn't like, yet he and I work together; if we fall out nobody won't know it but us. Every church that ever been organized or come up rested on that Book there. If we ever be anything in the future we got to come out to church; that is our only hope. People that got children ought to bring them to the Sabbath school or send them. When you fail to bring your child up in the Sunday school you have just failed. Train your child in the way you would have it to go; when it get old it won't depart from you. Young people is our only hope. You try to break a old dried-up stick and it will break every time. I am scared of the man or woman who won't let their children be brought up in the Sunday school. I mean from the Deacon Board on down. You can't just turn them loose. If we never have no prayer service here we don't know whether our boys can sing or not. We got to quit so much frolicking.

Your son and daughter gonna do and say just what you do. You want your child to be able to say, "I want to be like mother or father." Our only hope is to bring them to the Sabbath school, have prayer services so that child will be able to take care of the future church.

> Look 'way down that lonesome road,
> Look 'way down that lonesome road,
> Look 'way down that lonesome road,
> I see trouble down that road,
> I see trouble down that road,
> I see trouble down that road,
> Lord been here and blessed my soul,
> Lord been here and blessed my soul,
> Lord been here and blessed my soul,
>
> I ain't gonna lay my religion down,
> I ain't gonna lay my religion down,
> I ain't gonna lay my religion down,
> Look 'way down that lonesome road,
> Look 'way down that lonesome road,
> Look 'way down that lonesome road.

Amen, Amen.

At this point one of the older members of the church, a woman, got up and began talking, even though she was not on the program. "The future church gonna be worser than that what is past. Now all the chillun think 'bout learning is the 'black bottom' and all other devilment." The master of ceremonies began to ring the bell for her to sit down, but she was indifferent to it.

> We was scared to do anything. Just much difference in Sunday school now and then as day and night. Everybody is learning things now what they ain't got no business. They won't even go to school. I am the mother of this church, and I will say what I please. This is my old stand and I'll say what I please. Boy come long and say he believe the Lord done pardoned his sins and if you don't watch him he will be back in thirty days saying he needs 'ligion. If you don't change the church is lost. Listen, I'm gonna talk but I ain't gonna say nothing out of school. They must be educated in the heart first. Look up and love God in his heart. "Seek ye first the kingdom of Heaven and all these things will be added." You got to move, you can't do nothing with a educated heart only, you got to be educated in your hands next, then you must be educated in you feet and in your eyes. That's what it takes for the future church.

The master of ceremonies began tapping the bell with force, and continued until she finally sat down. He said in apology:

> Brothers, I know you all honor Sister Moore. Course our time is short but she has acted as a mother to me when I used to go to school here. Any time old folks get up I give way to them. I'm 'fraid of old folks till today. If we had space we would have some more. I am satisfied our boys can put it over.

The chief sermon was to be delivered by the pastor. He came forward bustling and earnest giving orders to the congregation between the lines of the introduction to the sermon.

My friends, we are happy to be here. Come to the front, ladies. You all must take turn about and help find these ladies seats, and you all must help keep order. Now we are praising God today and in our praises don't forget the sixty years God has been with us. I must mention here, before I forget it, that Brother Boyd has asked for our prayers, and when you all pass there go and ask how he is getting along, but don't go in and talk to him for he is mighty sick and don't have strength to talk. Come right on down to the front, ladies. Bring them right on down this way, brother. Make believe you love them; that's the way to do. When you go to First Baptist they always make you welcome, and they make you feel at home. I am glad to have our members and friends here, and I wish we had time to hear them all. Ladies are not wearing the short dresses now and they can take front seats. Thank the Lord they are letting them down and they won't have to be ashamed to take the front seats. Don't talk, don't talk, please.

There is quite a change in now and years ago. There is quite a change in everything. I want my son to be a partner with me. I want to take him along by my side and let him tell me what he thinks. When you knock them down now you may not get off so light. You know folks used to knock and beat their children around, but you can't do it so well now. Our old folks got afraid from slavery. I want my boy to talk to me and not feel he is afraid of me. He talked to me not long ago. He said, "Papa, I believe the Lord got something to do with this thing." He wanted a job and couldn't get it, and wanted a new suit; that was why he was talking so to me. Whatever my business may be I want my son to know about it. If I got a dollar I want him to have one, but let him work for it, and get it like I did. A man that haven't got a dollar and can't get one ain't much of a man. It takes a hustler to get one. If I couldn't get a dollar I would go to Europe or somewhere else and get one. I ain't gonna stay no where I can't get a dollar. Some of us ain't got nothing and don't want nothing. When he gets to the place where he doesn't want nothing he is in a bad fix.

I want to preach thirty minutes, and want to be through in that time. I believe I want to hear you all sing a verse, just a verse:

> I heard the voice of Jesus saying,
> "Come unto me and rest.
> Lie down, thy weary one, lie down,
> Thy head upon my breast."

I been here twenty years, going on twenty-one, and I never smelt a drop of whiskey on one of my deacons' breath, and they ain't never offered me one. I ain't never told them to tell a woman no secret and they ain't never told me one. If they ever had any bad tricks they never told me. We have been straight and fair with each other these twenty-one years. You ought to say "AMEN." They treat me with the highest respect; yes, they have. They must be all right, ain't they? I am going to give them credit.

The text I am gonna take is just two sentences. The first is "I have fought a good fight"; second, "I have kept the faith".

I have fought a good fight; I have kept the faith. The Scripture designates just as our leader, as our captain of soldiers; before a man or woman can make a good soldier he must realize that life in this battle cannot be lost; he must believe that he is gonna win. We lost soldiers in France but the United States conquered. Jesus Christ died but he brought life by dying. Some people think the church is something to be played with. A man goes out on the battlefield and goes out there to win. It takes a brave person to be a good soldier. That is why they give so much praise to the man who volunteers to go to the army. We had boys in the last war to volunteer; and that's what we want in the church. I am ready to serve,

351

not have to persuade folks to do anything. That's the kind of religion we ought to have. I never give a dime for a man who never do nothing in the church. A man that won't do nothing in the church ain't much to him. You say "Amen" mighty dry. Any man that won't serve needs a changed heart. When a man's heart is changed he is willing to serve. You don't have to ask if he belongs to church; you know it by how he goes about his work.

Any attack on the traditional ways is hazardous, and this minister approached the issue with some misgivings.

You can't hardly change an old man from his ways; he is stubborn as the devil. You can change young folks. An old man is set in his ways. Brother, I am preaching now; you all better say "Amen." I been talking this way for twenty years and I ain't been put out yet. They might cuss me out, but they ain't put me out. I will be like the monkey—"ain't gwine nowhere." I'm telling you now I ain't gwine nowhere. Get this rich thought I am giving you this morning. It isn't money— any fool know money will last only a short time. In his soul religion ought to be the strongest thing. Get love in your hearts. Wake up, Brother Swenny, you know you can't sleep over me. You got to go somewhere else to sleep, 'cause I'm gonna wake you up. A man who can serve and won't serve just needs to be born again, that's all.

The illuminating byways of the sermon illustrate the manner in which new ideas enter. He is bringing to them new ideas about education, consolidation of effort for efficiency, race spirit, and he is well aware that his high mission of instruction is encountering the doubt and dismal conversation of the group.

We don't want no deacons on the board who won't serve. I am thinking the time is gonna come when these churches have got to double up. Ain't no need of all these churches around here. Railroads are going together and banks are going together. A colored man don't like to think; a white man thinks in terms of millions; not only the white man but the intelligent Negro. You just as well get ready to think. You fool around and don't educate your girls and boys, but he got to pay for it. I had rather be dead and in my grave than have my children come up ignorant. If I had a child and couldn't school him, I had rather go somewhere and fight. Some of you say you can't do without them, but you would do without them if they would die. You can get along without them all right if you just try sending them away to school. O Lord, everything is all right, ain't it? I know you all don't like it, but I don't care if you don't. Don't talk, don't talk. Christ shed much blood and had great suffering. You all haven't suffered. You are getting along fine. A man that is a good Christian don't have a hard time. I tell you, my friends, we can say I have fought a good fight and I have kept the faith. Let us go on. I told you the church back yonder had to face a terrible crisis but we have to die to conquer. What does it mean to die? If a man got to die to win, let him die. The boys over in France brought the bacon home and Uncle Sam is doing what he can for them now. Our girls have got to have courage to go on. Matthew was put to death by the point of a sword; next Mark was tied to a wild beast and drug through the streets of Alexander. Preachers used to wear long-tailcoats and beaver hats, but now they wear whatever they want. I am going to wear the kind of hat and shoes, too, I want to wear. There ain't no need to be dead. I wouldn't give a dime for a teacher who come to class all drawn and dead. We want plenty of pep in them. I believe that teachers who teach our children ought to be Christians. I believe a man teaching Sunday school ought to be a

Christian and a man teaching psychology or anything else ought to be a Christian. About sixty-some-odd years ago we didn't have teachers like we do now. You folks back there will have to be still and quit getting up and going out. . . . I can't preach with all that noise.

James was crucified with his heels up and head down. Luke was hanged to an olive tree. You can't mean much unless you suffer for the church. We have as much devilment as white folks; it's tit for tat. I have often heard it said, "Be careful how you promote a colored man, because after you promote him he goes crazy." He got crazy 'bout automobiles but he done quit; now they all standing under sheds. You used to be able to hear a "chuck, chuck, chuck" everywhere. But they are driving wagons now. Every man that don't volunteer in the army ain't a coward, but if he enters he can be helped and can be made strong where he is weak. I am preaching now; you ought to be up shouting. My daddy was a soldier in the Revolutionary [Confederate] Army. As long as the drums tapped he was encouraged to go. You can say, "I will love Jesus"; you ought to be encouraged to go on. There is somebody crying for the word of God; you ought to be willing to go.

I have fought a good fight. I am nearly through, my friends. Be a soldier in the army. Well, what you gonna fight this army with? Prayer is the first weapon; a man that won't pray won't make a good soldier. The man who won't love the church is not a good soldier. A man that is born again will be brave; a man can't mean much in the army if he ain't got that weapon. I don't care what you do, but pray. God Almighty will hear your prayers if you just call him right. Joshua was in a mighty battle and he called on God, and he reached out his mighty hand and stopped the sun. . . . Wake up, sister!

My friends, by faith the children walked down in the Red Sea on dry ground. Any man won't hear him ain't got faith. God called Abraham to offer his son Isaac on the altar as a sacrifice. He just went right on and obeyed God. He told his son to get ready to go on over the mountain. He was obeying God. My friends, don't set down; go to work and God will make you well. You quarrel about what you can't do; nothing is impossible with God. Get prepared. When Abraham was about to kill his son God sent a message to him not to strike. God can do anything. Adam just done what God told him not to do. After a while, my friends, God will come back. I want to ride up one of these mornings; I want to say I've kept the faith. I wonder if the church will meet me on that morning? Since that time sixty years ago somebody has said, "I have kept the faith." I got a mother over yonder, and I hope to meet her some day.

> Father, I stretch my hands to Thee,
> No other help I know, etc."

There began a low moaning all over the church at this point, and it was impossible to hear everything the preacher was saying at the time; but it lasted only a few minutes.

We thank thee, our Heavenly Father, for sparing us. We are glad to meet at church one more time again on this side of death. Many who started with us is deprived of this privilege of being here this morning. You being God, you know the secret of every man and woman's heart. We know that you know all about us, Heavenly Father. You know every turn we make and kept our bed from being a cooling-board this morning, and we was able to look upon a day that we never will forget as long as we live. We have kept our feet in the paths of righteousness. I once was lost but now I'm found, was blind but now I see. Bless the people of this congregation. When we stack up our books and Bible; got to stoop down and unlace our shoes, take us home in thy Kingdom, for Christ's sake. AMEN.

> *What kind shoes I'm gonna wear? Golden slippers.*
> *What kind shoes I'm gonna wear? Golden slippers.*
> *Golden slippers I'm bound to wear.*
> *Yes, yes, yes, my Lord, I'm a soldier of the cross.*
> *Yes, yes, yes, my Lord, I'm a soldier of the cross.* [Repeat.]

> *What kind crown I'm gonna wear? Starry crown.*
> *What kind crown I'm gonna wear? Starry crown.*
> *Starry crown I'm bound to wear.*
> *Yes, yes, yes, my Lord, I'm a soldier of the cross.*
> *Yes, yes, yes, my Lord, I'm a soldier of the cross.* [Repeat.]

Now we are going to open the doors of the church. If anyone like to join the church, come right on up.

> *This heart of mine, this heart of mine,*
> *When Jesus fixed, when Jesus fixed this heart of mine.*

> *One day, one day I was walking along*
> *When Jesus fixed, when Jesus fixed this heart of mine.*

> *All night long, down on my knees,*
> *When Jesus fixed, when Jesus fixed this heart of mine.*

I haven't got time to tell you what I want to tell you; seem like you all are in a hurry. I hope the rain will run you all back in. Don't nobody leave till we show them what Macedonia folks can do.

The connection between the ceremonial function of the church and the basic religious sentiments of the people is not clear. Nor is it apparent how closely these religious sentiments apart from the church are related to individual social conduct. Not all religious sentiment was related to the church, and not all reactive church members gave expression to religious sentiments. A woman who felt a friendlessness for which the social church was responsible could say: "I ain't got nobody, nobody but Jesus. I know I got Jesus." A man who acknowledged profound belief in God said: "But I ain't got time to be going to all these here church processions." There is, moreover, a pervasive skepticism of the pretensiveness of the church which has little relation to religion.

> They turn you out sometimes for playing ball. They don't want you to play cards either. They don't want you to do nothing but work and give them money to set down on in this country.
> The church don't give you nothing; but they rob you, though. They come after every chicken you got.

There were persons who disliked the church, and those who merely disregarded all its attempted regulations, but nowhere was there observed anything approaching religious skepticism. Imperfect understanding of the Bible extended at times to the ludicrous, as, for example, in the serious expostulation of one man: "Cain found his wife in the land of Nod, and she was a monkey."

The dominant attitude was one of unquestioning belief in and reliance upon God as a protection against everything that was feared, and an answer to everything that could not be understood.

In so simple a society the range of the unknown fell far into the field of ordinary experience. Just as God brought droughts, rain, pestilence, disease for a purpose both local and inscrutable, there was no appeal from his elections, whether with respect to the incidence of contagion or the exigencies of the cotton crop. All is mystery colored by a faith and fatalism which tended to dull both striving and desire. The conventional response to a death in the family, to the acuteness of hard times, to tragedy, and to the prospect of personal death and damnation is "seeking." And such seeking partakes of all the fears which make up life. It probably accounts for the frequent "visions" and dreams so colored by the workaday world, and for the ecstasies of the release. It seems just as true of the religious experiences of this group as of other similarly naïve Negro groups of which it has been observed that they were not converted to God, but converted God to themselves.

# ᚛158᚜

# Middle Class Religion

## HORACE CAYTON and ST. CLAIR DRAKE

By the 1940s, urban African–American communities had developed social hierarchies built on income, property and education. Social hierarchy was registered in differences of cultural style and institutional, including church, attachment. Cultural characteristics were consciously articulated as confirmations of difference. Here is an account of middle-class black religion, and of middle-class perceptions of the relation of social class to religion, from a classic study of Chicago in 1945.

When a person in Bronzeville says that he is "sanctified" or that he attends a Spiritualist church or one of the "cults," he is immediately marked down as "low-status." We have referred in the preceding chapter to the fact that the members and preachers of these churches are well aware that they are "looked down on." If a man says he's an Episcopalian or a Congregationalist, Bronzeville thinks of him as "dicty" or a "strainer" or "striver." But if he says he's Baptist or Methodist or Catholic he can't be "placed" until he tells what specific congregation he belongs to. Some entire denominations are "class-typed," but among the larger denominations there are "class-typed" congregations *within* the group. There are, for instance, one or two Methodist and Baptist churches that have the reputation of "catering to high-toned people," and there are scores of churches that are of very low status—usually store-fronts.

If we examine what the opponents of store-fronts have to say about them, we get some clues as to what makes a church low-status. A rather comfortably situated Catholic housewife comments on her religious preferences as follows:

> I like good music, but I don't like the songs that these gospel choirs in the store-fronts sing—these jazz tunes. I think it is heathen-like to jazz hymns. Another thing about these store-fronts is all these funny isms —like giving a person a rose that's been blessed with the idea of bringing good luck. Some people actually believe these fool things.

Source: Horace Cayton and St. Clair Drake, 'Middle Class Religion', *Black Metropolis*, London, 1946, pp. 670-85.

A young high-school graduate who wants to go to college pays his respects to the store-fronts:

> I've stood outside these store-fronts a lot of times and listened to the people sing and dance. In my opinion that kind of service has done more than anything else to cheapen the feeling people once had for the church. When I stand and listen to them I say to myself, Why should I pay to see a show when these people are putting one on free?

A postal employee who is thinking of joining the Catholic Church comments:

> No wonder white people laugh at colored people and their peculiar ways of worship. Just look at these store-fronts. I don't believe in shouting and never did. I like a church that is quiet. I just can't appreciate clowning in any church.

Occasionally the store-front preachers are assailed:

> There's a store-front everywhere you turn. I think these people at the head of all these store-fronts are just in the churches for what they can get out of them. I know some of them may be in earnest, but since there is a church everywhere you turn, it makes me wonder if the people who are starting them are sincere.

> I don't know much myself, but I feel that people in the pulpit and schoolroom should be trained to lead other people. Some of these men and women take preaching for a racket—just to raise money in an easy way. Some of them preach one thing and live another.

A railroad porter, living in the high-status Rosenwald Apartments, was very definite in his opposition to store-fronts:

> I'm not in favor of these store-front churches. I think they give all churches a bad name. From what I know of them, the store-fronts are composed of people who have very little education, and their type of service is the kind that has made our people a laughing-stock for years. I may be too severe, but I think that everything people do ought to be done in an intelligent way.

Other persons interviewed were not so careful about being "severe." For instance, a young Presbyterian minister shelved his Christian charity to denounce them:

> I am certainly very much against store-fronts. They are demoralizing to our race. The field is overwhelmed with them. The lower class of people support them and I feel they are just another place to go to express their pent-up emotions. They encourage "jumping-jack" religion. I think those people are in the first stages of insanity.

A Congregational pastor, however, was somewhat more moderate in his appraisal:

> There is no doubt that some "jack-leg" preachers are charlatans, but some aren't. A good many of them are ministering to folks that I just couldn't minister to.... The folks a "jack-leg" preacher has to handle are in such a socio-economic and educational position that they just wouldn't understand me. They need an outlet for their embittered emotions. Their lives are pretty much disorganized. The "jack-leg" preacher fills a need. He may be ignorant and utterly uninformed in the respects that we think a preacher should be trained, but he has a useful role.

Even while justifying the existence of the store-front, however, this minister reveals the class gulf between his upper-middle-class congregation and lower-class church people.

If we analyze the complaints which middle-class people make against store-fronts, it is obvious that is not *size* alone that repels them. They are reacting against the type of religious *behavior* which goes on in most store-fronts—and this behavior is not confined to such churches. There are at least three Baptist churches seating over 2,000 members which have the reputation of being "shouting churches," as well as several Methodist churches. Two or three Holiness congregations and one Spiritualist church also have large edifices in which the members praise the Lord with gusto. One young lady, high-school-trained, belongs to one of these Baptist churches:

> I belong to the —— Baptist Church. Rev. —— is my pastor. He is certainly a good man and a soul-stirring preacher. The only thing I dislike about the church is the shouting of its members. It seems like Rev. —— never wants to end a sermon until his flock gets happy. The men as well as the women have outbursts. They run up and down the aisles shaking and yelling, overcome as it were with emotion. I get happy to the point of wanting to cry and sometimes do, but I have known the sisters and brother to become so happy that persons around them are in actual danger of getting knocked in the face. They might even get their glasses broken sometimes if the "nurses" didn't watch out for them.[1]

The woman just quoted has remained in her church, but many people of her type either move to some other quieter denomination or a quieter church within the denomination. The split between "shouters" and "non-shouters" often reflects an age division as well as a class division. Both middle- and lower-class people in the older age groups lean toward the "old-time religion"; the younger people of both classes, toward "refined," "fashionable," or even "high-toned" religion.

One minister in a church where objections to shouting had been raised stated:

> I try to preach to the old as well as the young. You know most of the older people have worked hard to help us, and they just want a little consideration. I think every church should remember that the older people struggled to help get us where we are. Some preachers just push the older people out of the picture. I don't have much of a shouting crowd, but they know they can shout if they want to. You know young people are educated so far above the older people that the older people feel out of place in some of our churches.

Preachers of this type, concerned with holding the allegiance of "shouters" and "non-shouters, "face a problem. Out of their attempts to meet it have arisen the "mixed-type" or "mass" churches, in which the tone is set by people with middle-class aspirations, but in which some concession is made to the "shouters". These churches, with memberships ranging from a thousand to five or six thousand, tie together people of all social levels into a functioning unit. This is done by having a variety of organizations and activities, and by modifying the ritual so as to put the older middle-class people and the lower-class members at ease. The pastor of such a church is usually a college-trained, middle-class man, who consciously manipulates the status system to get the maximum in co-operation. He even turns class divisions into an asset by organizing competition between groups of differing class levels in money-raising campaigns, always taking care, of course, to moderate and control the rivalry so that it does not flare into open antagonism. Occasionally, however, a church will "split" if the pastor is not skillful; some of his lower-class members may desert to the storefronts or to a large "shouting church," or some of his middle-class members may transfer to a "dicty" congregation or a high-status denomination.

## The Mixed-type Church

Most of Bronzeville's middle-class church people belong to what one student has called the "mixed-type" congregation, one that incorporates both lower-class and middle-class features in its rituals and its pattern of organization. Most of the very large congregations and many of the medium-sized churches try to hold together in one congregation the people who like "rousements" and "shouting," as well as those who prefer a more restrained service. The pastor of a large church must cater to those who like the "old-time religion" as well as to the more modern members. Such ministers become adept at keeping the allegiance of both groups.

To satisfy middle-class members, an astute pastor of a mixed-type church will present a "prepared message" with moral and ethical exhortation and intelligent allusions to current affairs; but he will also allow his lower-class members to shout a little. Such shouting is usually rigidly controlled, however, so that it does not dominate the service. Since most of the pastors of the larger churches are seminary-trained men with a middle-class orientation, and some are university men with advanced degrees, they do not want to be classed as "ignorant" or "uncultured," nor do they wish to alienate professional and businessmen, or young people who reject the "old-time religion."

So a skillful pastor will rigorously control the emotional display by changing the tone of his sermon at strategic points to stimulate shouting, shutting it off before it gets out of hand. Thus, one very astute performer shouts his audience violently and then suddenly stops, with a remark such as the following:

> My, I forget where I was this morning. I musta thought I was still down between the plow-handles and not here in a Chicago pulpit. Lemme get back to this paper [manuscript]. I forgot I had these educated folks in here. But I'm not ashamed of my Jesus! [There will be a chorus of "*Amens*" and some laughter, and the shouting will be over for a while.]

When Baptist and Methodist conventions and conferences are in session, even a "dicty" middle-class church may become the scene of considerable shouting. On one occasion when the pastor of a local Methodist church shouted the congregation at the annual conference, a woman sitting next to the participant-observer remarked, "I declare, you would think we were in Reverend

Cobb's [Spiritualist] church, the way these people are acting tonight." When asked, "Don't they shout at the regular service?", the woman answered, "No, but you know there are people here from "all over" tonight." The preacher was aware of the possible criticisms that might be leveled at him by some of his members and tried to head it off. Clapping his hands and walking to and fro, he cried out pointedly: "We don't have conferences like this up here in the North. These are the kind we have down home!" An evangelist who followed him on the program also made a defensive statement:

> I don't know about you, but I feel all right. I don't believe in being a fool, but I am a fool for God. All over everywhere folks are fools for the Devil. A couple of years ago, at the annual conference, many men turned away from me because of my "foolishness." They said, "You are going crazy." But the spirit moved me. If you ever have "it" really happen to you, you can't forget it. Sometimes, I like to turn loose. I want everyone to know I'm a fool for God.

Another familiar device for establishing rapport with the lower class in a mixed church is "talking down"—using dialect or broken English or referring to aspects of lower-class life. Talking down ranges from quiet statements of sympathy with the trials and tribulations of the lower class to a very secular, and even joking, attitude toward lower-class "sins." Pastors of mixed-type congregations also occasionally play up to their lower-status members by putting the higher-status members in their places. This is usually done by direct allusions to the "sinfulness" of the proud or to the "pretensions" of the educated. The lower-class members of the congregation will always say *"Amen"* with fervor when a preacher modernizes a Bible story in the following manner:

> Jesus was standing by the temple, trying to teach the people. Here come the scribes and the Pharisees in their long robes, trying to catch him, trying to set a trap for him. One of them says, "Rabbi, is it right for us to pay taxes to Caesar?" They thought they had him in a hole. But my Jesus asked one of the disciples to give him some money; then he held it up and asked them, "Whose picture do you see on there?" One of them said, "Caesar's." "Well," my Lord said, "render unto Caesar the things that are Caesar's and unto God the things that are God's." That fixed 'em—all those Ph.D.'s in their long robes and mortarboard hats, all puffed up with their education. With all their degrees and learning, they couldn't trick the Son of the Living God!

Higher-status members understand the necessity of this type of appeal to the uneducated, even if it is at their expense. Instead of being insulted, they are more likely to smile and say, "Rev. —— knows his psychology."

Other features of a Sunday worship service than the sermon have this dual class appeal. All of Bronzeville's churches have an adult or senior choir, and many have a junior choir. These present ordinary hymns and anthems. Some are highly trained choral groups. But, in addition to these choirs, most large Bronzeville churches also have one or two "gospel choruses"—a concession to lower-class tastes. A gospel chorus is not highly trained, but it is usually loud and spirited. The gospel chorus specializes in spirituals and revival songs. Chorus members often shout while they sing. In many lower-class churches there is no choir other then the gospel chorus. The choruses are very popular throughout Negro America and have an independent national organization known as The National Convention of Gospel Choruses and Choirs, the president of which is a Bronzeville musician. (In the course of his presidential address in 1939, he referred to the opposition that gospel choruses encounter from "hightoned" people who think that "God just wants to hear anthems and arias.")

The "Order of Sunday Worship Service" as printed in one Baptist church newspaper reveals the place assigned to the gospel chorus:

> 10:45 A.M.—Organ Prelude
> 11:00 A.M.—Processional—"*All Hail the Power*"
> Chant—Congregation—"*Holy, Holy, Holy*"
> Scripture Reading
> Chant—"*Let the Word of My Mouth*"
> Morning Hymn—"*Keep Me Every Day*"
> Invocation
> Song—Gospel Chorus
> Consecration and Meditation
> Anthem—Choir
> Tithes and Offerings
> Song—Choir
> Sermon
> Invitation—Gospel Chorus
> Special Offering
> Doxology—Benediction

The weekly calendar of this same church also indicates "concessions" to the lower-status members in the form of midweek vespers and a visit on Wednesday to a Spiritualist church:

SUNDAY:
> 9:15 A.M.—Church School—"Take my yoke, learn of me."
> 11:00 A.M.—Worship Service—"O Come! Let us bow before Him."
> 3:00 P.M.—Pastor to preach at Morning Star, "Love ye one another."
> 6:00 P.M.—BYPU—A Christian Program for Young and Old.
> 8:00 P.M..—Holy Communion—"This do in remembrance of Me!"

MONDAY:
> 12:00 Noon—Housewives' Hour—"Church Women and Their Work."
> 2:00 P.M.—Missionary Society.
> 7:30 P.M.—Progressive Young Women Meeting.
> 8:00 P.M.—Calendar Social

TUESDAY:
> 8:00 P.M.—Midweek Vespers—Meditation, Bible Study, Prayer, Song—Sermonette.

WEDNESDAY:
> 8:00 P.M.—Pastor to preach at 1st Deliverance, Spiritualist.

THURSDAY:
> 8:00 P.M.—Mortgage-Burning Meeting, Educational Movies Program, Christian Social.

FRIDAY:
> 12:00 Noon—Mothers' Annual Dinner.

The same issue of the church paper announced "PRIZES AWARDED FASHION-SHOW TICKET-SELLERS" and carried a half-page of ads from Negro businesses.

Faced with the competition of secular organizations, and constantly needled by businessmen and Race Leaders, the pastors of Bronzeville's larger churches can attract and hold middle-class members only by making some concessions to their standards, too. For the Baptist and Methodist churches there is always the competition of the Presbyterians, the Congregationalists, the Episcopalians, the Christian Scientists, and the Lutherans, who offer what is called colloquially a more "high-toned" service. Yet an appreciable number of people with a middle-class orientation (including a great many young people who have attended or finished high school) do not leave the churches in which they were raised for the less emotional denominations.

Appeals to the middle-class members, as previously said, take the form of "good" music rendered by a well-trained choir singing anthems and other classical religious works. The ministers take some care, too, to prepare intelligent sermons and to deliver at least a part of the message in such a form as not to alienate the "educated" members. They refer frequently to "advancing The Race," and mention with praise individuals who are away at school and those who are Race Leaders. They also handle their services in such a way as to signify that they appreciate the "higher things of life." It is not at all unusual to hear a minister make a remark such as, "All this hollering and shouting isn't religion."

The large "mixed type" church is an institution with members of diverse class levels under the leadership of a middle-class preacher who skillfully attempts to gradually reshape lower-class behavior into a middle-class mold. Meanwhile, the institution provides meaningful activity for people of diverse social levels. The medium-sized and large churches are very complex institutions with a variety of sub-organizations and activities. This permits the voluntary segregation of persons within the church according to class lines. Individuals gravitate to those organizations in which people like themselves are in the majority. Thus, weekly prayer meetings tend to have a lower-class pattern and to attract the older people who wish to sing, pray, and shout. Missionary societies tend to organize middle-aged and older women who do not have a social-club pattern or civic interests. Here they may gain prestige from money-raising and from participation in the larger state and national conventions. Mothers' boards also function to make a place for the older women of lower- or middle-class rank. There is a tendency for upper middle-class people to assume the positions of financial leadership within the larger churches and to take over all posts which require some training, such as the direction of the choral groups or the keeping of records. A large church duplicates the pattern of social stratification in the outer world.

## The Preacher as a Race Leader

The ministry is not a very popular profession with Negro college graduates. Yet enough young Negro men enter the ministry to provide a group of well-trained ministers for the larger mass churches and for the few high-status churches. These ministers, on the whole, tend to be theologically conservative, at least in their public utterances. An interview-study of the 51 most prominent Bronzeville preachers made in 1935 indicated that on such matters as the Virgin Birth and orthodox conceptions of sin and salvation and Biblical authority, the majority claimed to be dispensers of "sound doctrine." This same group of ministers was sophisticated enough to have doubts about miracles and to profess an interest in squaring religion with science. Yet, paradoxically, they were on the whole very conservative when asked about certain church procedures. The overwhelming majority believed that people needed "individual conversion" in order to be saved, and that "Christian education" (moral instruction) was no substitute for a "second birth." They thought, too, that preaching was the most important function of the church and that the Bible should be the center of Sunday School instruction. A surprisingly large number claimed to believe that church property was sacred and that preparing people for Heaven was the churches' main business.

The latter responses are interesting in view of the facts that Bronzeville's large churches are anything but other-worldly institutions, and that their pastors concern themselves with all sorts of community matters, including politics. It seems likely, however, that these ministers feel that they must stress religion as the *raison d'être* for their churches even while they make them community institutions. This is their sole claim to leadership as they face the competition of secular leaders.

These pastors of middle-class churches may say they believe that their primary job is "to prepare people for Heaven," but they are very this-worldly. The Negro church is a "Race institution" and the preachers, in their sermons and through their support of Negro politicians and professional and business men as well as in their connections with organizations like the NAACP and the Urban League, display a lively interest in "advancing The Race." In fact, not a few ministers dabble in business ventures or serve on boards of Negro business enterprises. The following life history of the pastor of a large Baptist church illustrates the type of preacher who is likely to get ahead as the pastor of a middle-class church. He is considered "a progressive young man," a "go-getter," and is interested in labor activities as well as in Negro business.

> I was born in 1904 on a farm in Mississippi. I went to a rural school until I was sixteen and had completed the fifth grade. I then left home to work on the railroad as a water boy, section hand, and track man. I made $21 a week, plus overtime. When I was nineteen, I returned home. Father gave me a horse which I immediately tried to sell, but I couldn't get enough money for him. Finally, I found a man who traded his mule colt for my horse. I then sold the colt for $50 and with

this money decided to go to Jackson, Mississippi, and enter school: My father gave me $20 more. At this time I was a big, overgrown boy, countrified, nineteen years old and had only been to fifth grade. I enrolled in the public school, but the kids all laughed at me so I quit.

I then went to Jackson College [a boarding school] and talked with the president. He was a very kind man and encouraged me to enter special classes for overgrown students. I studied hard and in two and a half years completed the eighth grade. While in school I worked at the best hotels as porter, elevator operator, bus boy, clothes-presser, and waiter. I am an expert waiter.

I came to Chicago in April of 1926. My first job was as a waiter. I entered Wendell Phillips High School, graduating in three and a half years with an average of nearly 90. While attending high school, I worked at night at the stockyards and at a hotel. The white woman who ran the hotel was a good, understanding friend.

In 1930, I registered at a law school. One day on my way to class I had what I term a mystical experience. I was not led to take law, but to register at the Moody Bible Institute and to prepare for the ministry. I graduated from there. I took a general course and a special course in archeology. In my class were 150 students, the largest ever to graduate. I was the only Negro in the class.

For two years after finishing the Bible School, I worked at a law firm as an all-round man. I served warrants and was a general investigator. My average salary was $80 a week. In 1934 I entered the Baptist Theological Seminary, graduating with a Th.B. There were two Negroes in my class. I have since registered at Northwestern University and have done all my B.D. work except one year of Greek and the writing of a thesis. I hope to start work on my Master's in the fall.

In 1930, while attending law school, I opened a grocery store and school supply store. I sold it in 1931 for $900 cash. I also worked for a while as a clothing salesman. I preached my first sermon on Easter in 1932. My subject was "The New Birth." That same year, I went into the undertaking business, and five months later was called as "supply pastor" to the Solid Rock Baptist Church. After supplying for three months, they called me to the pastorate.

I married in 1927. My wife is a preacher's daughter and has had two years of high school. She is now taking nursing. She is rather quiet and reserved, easy to get along with, and understands a minister's work; she's not jealous.

Since I took this church we have enrolled 2,400 members. I have baptized 1,000 myself. We have an active membership of 700. We have built and paid for the first unit of our church. It was a storefront, at first, you know. It seats 500 now. We are only $400 in debt, and we hope to complete building next year.

In our church we have adult education classes—sewing, business administration, and reading and writing—all sponsored by the WPA. We also have a benevolent society connected with the church, of which I am president. This society charges 10 cents to join and a 10 cents weekly fee. We give a $2 sick benefit and a $90 burial. We have a welfare center and a free employment agency. In the last two years we have placed 187 people on jobs. I also have assigned to my supervision a number of boys from the juvenile court, and six men from Pontiac and Joliet [state prisons].

I am a part of every organization in the Baptist church and am secretary of my association, which consists of more than 70,000 members. I am secretary of the Apex Funeral Parlor, Inc., and I own a half-interest in the business and the funeral cars. I am a Mason, and also the sponsor of a Boy Scout troop.

I own a three-flat building and a vacant lot. I also have a two-car garage. I might add that I carry $5,000 in straight life insurance and a $1,000 sick and accident policy. I own a good car.

My salary from the church is $35 a week. They pay me, too—not *promise* to pay!

Middle-class people (and Bronzeville in general) expect the ministers to be interested in "advancing The Race." Ministers accept this as one of their functions, and during the Depression years the pastors of all of the larger churches were active in campaigns for better housing, more adequate relief, and health programs.

The way in which "advancing The Race" becomes an integral part of church dogma may be illustrated by an excerpt from a pamphlet written just before the CIO drive in the late Thirties by the pastor of one of Bronzeville's highest status churches.

### The Great Opportunity of the Negro Church

Dr George E. Haynes of the Federal Council of Churches [a Negro] advanced the idea that, as the Negroes are not organized in labor units, as 85 per cent of them are in industrial or domestic occupations, and as the Negro church is the largest organized unit of Negro life, the Negro Church today faces a most unusual opportunity to overcome an uneconomic and unsocial past. The building up of a moral reserve, the securing of Negro workmen's living standards, the saving of body along with soul, is the big job for Christianity today. All inter-racial contacts must point to deep understanding of the problems of living which all must face, especially Negroes. The problem of Christianity among the 13,000,000 Americans of African descent is more or less contingent upon the Christian solution of the problem here. Chicago, one of the greatest racial laboratories of the world, faces. because of its very constitution and problem, an opportunity and a challenge that are unique.

Pastors of the large mass-churches are less erudite in their formulation of the problem and are sometimes very blunt in their statement of what they think the Black Ghetto needs in the way of social reform. They have a tendency, too, to stress individual salvation as well as social service. The comments of the pastor of one very large church during Negro Health Week will illustrate this type of straight talk:

I think it would be a good thing for everyone in this church—visitors, friends, and members alike—to go out and find a child and put him in the Bible Study School of this church. We have a certain definite program that we are going to carry out in an effort to try to save our race. Sometimes a good talk is better than a sermon. The world is laughing at us. Do you know that venereal diseases are eating us up? That a very large percentage of syphilis and gonorrhea is found among our little children of five, six, and ten years old? Out of a corrupted mess like that we cannot hope to do anything.

Anticipating middle-class resentment and embarrassment, and lower-class disapproval of injecting such worldly matters into a sermon, the minister continued:

It may not sound right to speak about this on Sunday, but it is something that we suffer for on Monday. Unless the Negro churches will get busy and help to save them you—as a race—are damned forever. Get out in these alleys and get these children who need guidance and help.

Middle-class people seldom respond to these exhortations to do missionary work among the lowers, but they, as well as church-people of all social levels, are continually talking about "saving the youth" of Bronzeville.

## Saving the Youth

Bronzeville's devouter church people are almost unanimous in their belief that "our young people are on the road to Hell." They see the youngsters streaming to the movies and taverns and dance-halls—even on Sunday, for Sunday School and young people's societies are unable to compete with the city's more exciting leisure-time pursuits. They know that the lower-class world provides even more sinister enticements and that the preacher's pleas, the teacher's admonitions, and their own whipping and counseling do not hold the children in line. Older people in Bronzeville, like oldsters everywhere, spend a great deal of their time shaking their heads and denouncing the younger generation. Most of them feel that the church ought to do something about it.

In analyzing the problem of juvenile delinquency, Bronzeville's middle-class ministers usually exhibit an interesting blend of theology and sociology. One minister began a sermon by insisting that "we can't have peace until sin is conquered," and then proceeded to say that "Christian people must help to fight down some of the things in our community that cause our boys and girls to go astray." He gave his prescription as follows:

> I tell you I am getting quite alarmed about our young people. I was called into a private meeting with some of the city officials. They told me that the Negro youth of Chicago were committing more crimes than ever in the history of Chicago. They wanted to know just what is the cause. I could only give this solution—wipe out vice and give my people jobs!

In the final analysis, all preachers blame the home. One minister did so before a statewide Baptist convention by saying:

> We must have Christian fellowship in the home. Boys don't want to be bad, but economic conditions compel them to be so. One parent has to get up at one hour; another at another hour; and one may work at night. There is no more of that set time for devotion in the home. This has caused the home to be upset. What to do about it? Re-establish family altars. . . . Bring the young people into the church.... Make your children comrades. . . . The home has fallen short of what it should do. You can never have right homes unless they are built on this book [the Bible].

He compared the Baptists and Methodists with the Catholics and Jews who

> come closer to saving their young people by not letting outsiders get to them. Wherever you find a Jewish synagogue or Catholic Church, you find their school right along with it. If you can't make a program to interest them you can't hold the young people. If you can't hold the young people, what of the future?

The larger Baptist and Methodist denominations have their hands tied, however. In the first place, "sound doctrine" does not permit dancing and card-playing under secular auspices. It absolutely forbids any such activities under church control. Attempts to plan community recreational programs therefore do not have the wholehearted support of most older church people except among Congregationalists, Episcopalians, and Catholics.

The feeling that they are losing the youth leads many ministers to assail the Catholics and other churches that do not denounce card-playing and dancing. One minister commented: "You've got a proposition on your hands with the Catholics. They say these things are all right if you go to Mass afterwards." Several conferences have been held in Bronzeville during the last few years to discuss ways and means of saving Protestant youth from the Catholics. At one such conference a preacher advised, "Have a program so interesting that the Catholics will come *here*." But he had no practical suggestions. Another minister said, "If the Catholics encourage them with plays and parties, so can we." He then mentioned an attempt to poll some youngsters in his church as to what they did at the last party they attended. They answered, "We talked a while, played cards, and danced." An elderly delegate to the conference shouted out, "That's all they want to do—play cards!" This particular meeting closed with another statement of generalities:

> You can't tell young people to come back to the church because your parents go to this church. Youth must have recreation. The church alone can't do the job, but there should be a set-up made of half adults and half youths to make a program for young people under the right direction where they can function at our own churches.

## Note

1. Some of these churches have a white-uniformed nursing corps to take care of the shouters.

# ⌇159⌇

# Hoodoo in America

## ZORA NEALE HURSTON

The African–American novelist, Zora Neale Hurston (1901?–1960), grew up in an all-black town in Florida where she was familiar with African–American folk religious beliefs. Her formal education culminated in graduate work in folklore at Columbia University during which she did the field work reported in this paper. Her work confirmed her view of the distinctiveness and vitality of popular religious beliefs and practices as elements in constituting the culture of black communities. What she found here owed little to mainstream Christianity.

---

## Ruth Mason

Ruth Mason is a well-known hoodoo doctor of New Orleans, and a Catholic. It was in October, 1928, when I was a pupil of hers that I shared in a hoodoo dance. This was not a pleasure dance, but ceremonial. In another generation African dances were held in Congo Square, now Beauregard Square. Those were held for social purposes and were of the same type as the fire dances and jumping dances of the present in the Bahamas. But the hoodoo dance is done for a specific purpose. It is always a case of death-to-the-enemy that calls forth a dance. They are very rare in New Orleans now, even within the most inner circle, for they are forbidden by law and the noise of the drums is certain to reach some policeman's ear. So on the rare occasions when one is held, no drum is used. Hand-clapping and foot-patting take the place of other music.

The neighborhood of the Bayou, St. John, is a very modern suburb now, so hoodoo dances are out of the question in that former stronghold of the great Marie Leveau.

This is how the dance came to be held. I sat with my teacher in her front room as the various cases were disposed of. It was my business to assist wherever possible, such as running errands for materials or to verify addresses; locating

Source: Zora Neale Hurston, from 'Hoodoo in America', *Journal of American Folklore*, Oct.–Dec. 1931. © 1931 by The American Folklore Society.

materials in the various drawers and cabinets, undressing and handling patients, writing out formulas as they were dictated, and finally making "hands". At last, of course, I could do all of the work while she looked on and made corrections where necessary.

This particular day, a little before noon, came Rachael Roe. She was dry with anger, hate, outraged confidence and desire for revenge. John Doe had made violent love to her; has lain in her bed and bosom for the last three years; had received of Rachael everything material and emotional a woman can give. They had both worked and saved and had contributed to a joint savings account. Now, only the day before yesterday, he had married another. He had lured a young and pretty girl to his bed with Rachael's earnings; yes, had set up housekeeping with Rachael's sweat and blood. She had gone to him and he had laughed at his former sweetheart, yes. The police could do nothing, no. The bank was sorry, but they could do nothing, no. So Rachael had come to Ruth.

Did she still love her John Doe? Perhaps, she didn't know. If he would return to her she should strive to forget, but she was certain he'd not return. How could he? But if he were dead she could smile again, yes—could go back to her work and save some more money, yes. Perhaps she might even meet a man who could restore her confidence in menfolk.

Ruth appraised her quickly. "A dance could be held for him that would carry him away right now, but they cost something."

"How much?"

"A whole lot. How much kin you bring me?"

"I got thirty-seven dollars."

"Dat ain't enough. Got to pay de dancers and set de table."

One hundred dollars was agreed upon. It was paid by seven o'clock that same night. We were kept very busy, for the dance was set from ten to one the next day, those being bad hours. I ran to certain addresses to assemble a sort of college of bishops to be present and participate. The table was set with cake, wine, roast duck and barbecued goat.

By nine-thirty the next morning the other five participants were there and had dressed for the dance. A dispute arose about me. Some felt I had not gone far enough to dance. I could wait upon the altar, but not take the floor. Finally I was allowed to dance, as a delegate for my master who had a troublesome case of neuritis. The food was being finished off in the kitchen.

Promptly on the stroke of ten Death mounted his black draped throne and assumed his regal crown, Death being represented by a rudely carved wooden statue, bust length. A box was draped in black sateen and Ruth placed him upon it and set his red crown on. She hobbled back to her seat. I had the petition and the name of the man written on seven slips of paper—one for each participant. I was told to stick them in his grinning mouth. I did so, so that the end slip protruded. At the command I up-ended nine black tapers that had been dressed by a bath in whiskey and bad vinegar, and bit off the butt end to light, calling upon Death to take notice. As I had been instructed, I said: "Spirit of

369

Death, take notice I am fixing your candles for you. I want you to hear me." I said this three times and the assembly gave three snaps with the thumb and middle finger.

The candles were set upside down and lighted on the altar, three to the left of Death, three to the right, and then three before him.

I resumed my seat, and everyone was silent until Ruth was possessed. The exaltation caught like fire. Then B. arose drunkenly and danced a few steps. The clapping began lightly. He circled the room, then prostrated himself before the altar, and, getting to his hands and knees, with his teeth pulled one of the slips from the jaws of Death. He turned a violent somersault and began the dance, not intricate, but violent and muscle-twitching.

We were to dance three hours, and the time was divided equally so that the more participants, the less time each was called upon to dance. There were six of us, since Ruth could not actively participate, so that we each had forty minutes to dance. Plenty of liquor was provided so that when one appeared exhausted the bottle was pressed to his lips and he danced on. But the fury of the rhythm more than the stimulant kept the dancers going. The heel-patting was a perfect tom-tom rhythm, and the hand clapping had various stimulating breaks. At any rate no one fell from exhaustion, though I know that even I, the youngest, could not have danced continuously on an ordinary dance floor unsupported by a partner for that length of time.

Nearly all ended on the moment in a twitchy collapse, and the next most inspired prostrated himself and began his dance with the characteristic somersault. Death was being continuously besought to follow the footsteps of John Doe. There was no regular formula. They all "talked to him" in their own way, the others calling out to the dancer to "talk to him". Some of the postures were obscene in the extreme. Some were grotesque, limping steps of old men and women. Some were mere agile leapings. But the faces! That is where the dedication lay.

When the fourth dancer had finished and lay upon the floor retching in every muscle, Ruth was taken. The call had come for her. I could not get upon the floor quickly enough for the others and was literally hurled before the altar. It got me there and I danced, I don't know how, but at any rate, when we sat about the table later, all agreed that Mother Ruth had done well to take me.

I have neglected to say that one or two of the dancers remained upon the floor "in the spirit" after their dance and had to be lifted up and revived at the end.

Death had some of all the food placed before him. An uncorked pint of good whiskey was right under his nose. He was paid fifteen cents and remained on his throne until one o'clock that night. Then all of the food before him was taken up with the tablecloth on which it rested and was thrown in the Mississippi River.

The person danced upon is not supposed to live more than nine days after the dance. I was very eager to see what would happen in this case. But five days after the dance John Doe deserted his bride for the comforting arms of Rachael and she hurried to Mother Ruth to have the spell removed. She said he complained of breast pains and she was fearfully afraid for him. So I was sent to get the beef heart out of the cemetery, and John and Rachael made use of the new furniture bought for his bride. I think he feared that Rachael might have him fixed, so he probably fled to her as soon as the zest for a new wife had abated.

Ruth began by teaching me various ways of bring back a man or woman who had left his or her mate.

# 1. Love

*a.* Use six red candles. Stick sixty pins in each candle—thirty on each side. Write the name of the person to be brought back three times on a small square of paper and stick it underneath the candle. Burn one of these prepared candles each night for six nights. Make six slips of paper and write the name of the wanderer once on each slip. Then put a pin in the paper on all four sides of the name. Each morning take the sixty pins left from the burning of the candle. Then smoke the slip of paper with four pins in it in incense smoke and bury it with the pins under your door step. The piece of paper with the name written on it three times (upon which each candle stands while burning) must be kept each day until the last candle is burned. Then bury it in the same hole with the rest. When you are sticking the pins in the candles, keep repeating: "Tumba Walla, Bumba Walla, bring (name of person desired) back to me."

*b.* Write the name of the absent party six times on paper. Put the paper in a water glass with two tablespoons full of quicksilver on it. Write his or her name three times each on six candles and burn one on a window sill in the daytime for six days.

*c.* (For a man only): Write his name three time. Dig a hole in the ground. Get a left-foot soiled sock from him secretly. His hatband may be used also. Put the paper with the name in the hole first. Then the sock or hatband. Then light a red candle on top of it all and burn it. Put a spray of Sweet Basil in a glass of water beside the candle. Light the candle at noon and burn until one. Light it again at six P. M. and burn it till seven. (Always pinch out a candle—never blow it.) After the candle is lit, turn a barrel over the hole. When you get it in place, knock on it three times to call the spirit and say: "Tumba Walla, Bumba Walla, bring (name) home to me."

*d.* Use nine red candles. Write the absent name on each candle once. (Use a needle to write on candle.) Write it three times on paper. Put the paper in a cup. Put Van-Van in the cup on the paper and dress all the candles (wash them) with Van-Van. Burn one of these candles every day, beginning at a good hour.

*e.* To rule a man head and feet: Get his sock. Take one silver dime, some hair from his head or his hatband. Lay the sock out on a table, bottom up. Write his name three times and put it on the sock. Place the dime on the name and the hair or hatband on the dime. Put a piece of "he" Lodestone on top of the hair and sprinkle it with steel dust. As you do this, say, "Feed the he, feed the she." That is what you calling feeding the Lodestone. Then fold the sock heel on the toe and roll it all up together tight. Pin the bundle by crossing two needles. Then wet it with whiskey and set it up over a door.

f. For fussy husbands: Put a medal of St. Benedict up over your door and he will become as sweet as a lamb.

g. If you and your husband are at a balance (out), take the following mixture and sprinkle it over nine lumps of loaf sugar: essence of Van-Van, essence of geranium, essence of lavender. Go nine blocks from the house and turn around and drop one lump of sugar in each block all the way back to the house, and he will make up with you.

h. To change a man's mind about going away: Take the left shoe, set it up straight, then roll it one-half over first to the right, then to the left. Roll it to a coming-in door and point it straight in the door, and he can't leave. Hatband or sock can be made into a ball and rolled the same way; but it must be put under the sill or over the door.

i. To make one love you: (1) Take nine days—wait till you see the new moon to begin. Take one teaspoon of your own urine each day and put it in his tea or coffee or anything, and you can lead him by the nose.

(2) Soak your foot in warm water and scrape it and put the scrapings in water and put the water in his food, and you can be the boss. Scape from the toe to the heel—that's coming to you all the time. Do this on the new moon.

j. To make a man come home: Take nine deep red or pink candles. Write his name three times on each candle. Wash the candles with Van-Van. Put the name three times on paper and place under the candles, and call the name of the party three times as the candle is placed at the hours of seven, nine or eleven.

k. To make people love you: Take nine lumps of starch, nine of sugar, nine teaspoons of steel dust. Wet it all with Jockey Club cologne. Take nine pieces of ribbon, blue, red or yellow. Take a desert spoonful and put it on a piece of ribbon and tie it in a bag. As each fold is gathered together call his name. As you wrap it with yellow thread call his name till you finish. Make nine bags and place under a rug, behind an armoire, under a step or over a door. They will love you and give you everything they can get. Distance makes no difference. Your mind is talking to his mind and nothing beats that.

l. To break up a love a love affair: (1) Take nine needles, break each needle in three pieces. Write each person's name three times on paper. Write one name backwards and one forwards and lay the broken needles on the paper. Take five black candles, four red and three green.

Tie a string across the door and from it suspend a large candle upside down. It will hand low on the door; burn one each day for one hour. If you burn your first in the daytime, keep it on in the day; if at night continue at night. A tin plate with paper and needles in it must be placed to catch wax in.

When the ninth day is finished, go out into the street and get some white or black dog dung. A dog only drops his dung in the street when he is running and barking, and whoever you curse will run and bark likewise. Put it in a bag with the paper and carry it to running water, and one of the parties will leave town.

(2) Mix together two tablespoons cayenne pepper, three tablespoons black pepper, three tablespoons ground guinea pepper, three tablespoons ground mustard, and three tablespoons dirt dauber nest. Write the person's name as before, once with red ink and once with green. Put the mixture in a dirty tin can and write the name on a slip of paper three times. Put the paper in the bottom of the can. Set the can in the chimney and burn four red candles for war and burn also five green candles for separation. When you have it set, and burning, make your wish. Say, "I want fighting and destruction and perfect disgrace." To make sure, write B, Y, E, U, T on the paper with the names. These are the names of the spirits that will make them fight.

## 2. Court Scrapes

*a.* Take the names of all the *good* witnesses (for your client), the judge and your client's lawyer. Put the names in a dish and pour sweet oil on them and burn a white candle each morning beside it for one hour, from nine to ten. The day of the trial when you put it upon the altar, don't take it down until the trial is over.

Take the names of the opponent of your client, his witnesses and his lawyer. Take all of their names on one piece of paper. Put it between two whole bricks. Put the top brick crossways. On the day of the trial set a bucket or dishpan on the top of the bricks with ice in it. That's to freeze them out so they can't talk.

*b.* Take the names of your client's lawyer, witness and the judge. Write them on white cotton with pen and ink. Sprinkle steel dust in the cotton and wear it in the shoe till the case is over.

Write the names of your opponent and his witnesses and lawyer on paper. Buy a beef tongue and split it from the base towards the tip, thus separating top from bottom. Put the paper with names in the split tongue along with eighteen pods of hot pepper and pin it through and through with pins and needles. Put it in a tin pail with plenty of vinegar and keep it on ice until the day of court. That day, pour kerosene in the bucket and burn it, and they will destroy themselves in court.

*c.* Put the names of the judge and all those *for* your client on paper. Take the names of the twelve apostles after Judas hung himself and write each apostle's name on a sage leaf. Take six candles and burn them standing in holy water. Have your client wear six of the sage leaves in each shoe and the jury will be for him.

Write all the enemy's names on paper. Put them in a can. Then take soot and ashes from the chimney of your client and mix it with salt. Stick pins crosswise in the candles and burn them at a good hour. Put some ice in a bucket and set the can in it. Let your client recite the One Hundred Twentieth Psalm before court and in court.

Never begin any of this work until the subpeona is served on your client.

d. One spool of No. 8 white thread. Wind all the thread off the spool, tangle it all up and pin it in your bosom under your clothes. It will be thrown out of court.

e. Use the one hundred fiftieth psalm. Write the judge's name and your lawyer's. Write all together on the same piece of paper.

Now the ones that's against you, you write their name and the seventh psalm. Write one line of the psalm, then the enemy's name on a slip of paper. Make eighteen of these every day for nine days and each day nibble it up fine and curse the enemy as you throw the finely torn paper into the fire and burn it. They will fuss in the court and destroy themselves with the judge.

f. To keep police away: Take flaxseed and brown sugar and mix it, and throw it at the four corners of the block and officers will never come.

## 3. Business Success

a. To bring a crowd: (1) Burn lump incense, dragon's blood, bay leaves and sugar together. Put the ashes in the corners of the room.

(2) Powdered sulphur, sugar, black pepper (ground), and ground cinnamon. Mix well together and put it corners or sprinkle in the rug.

(3) Get Van-Van, essence of geranium, essence of lavender. Mix them together, sprinkle it in the house. If a prostitute, sprinkle the bed.

b. Prayer for money: Say, "I am money, I am love, I am the father's son." Say this at good hours for gamblers. Never gamble at bad hours.

c. To rent a house: Have a picture of St. Roque tacked up over the door, and burn a candle in the middle of the floor to match his mantle, sleeves, etc., (dark blue, brown and pink).

d. To pull a crowd in business: Boil one quart of water, put in a dime's worth of honey, ten cents of Japanese Fast Luck. Take one cup every morning (or twelve at night), and throw it at the gate, and you will have great crowds.

e. Powder to pull business to your door: Get the bark off the sun rise side of a sycamore tree and dry it in the sun, and make a powder. Strow it. First mix sand and sugar and strow it over the floor. Then sprinkle the sycamore powder mixed with Japanese Fast Luck.

f. To make an employer have firm confidence: Take the name of every member concerned. Use steel dust and powdered cinnamon. Take a bottle, put their names in it and put an A. H. A. Say, "In the name of Aha I bind you to me in spirit and in truth."

g. To fix a creditor: You take fresh ground coffee that ain't been used and the same amount of sugar. Get a new bottle cork that ain't never been used—a large one. Get nine new needles, nine new pins, stick'em all round in dat cork. Set dat cork in dat cup wid dat coffee grounds and sugar. Then you say EEL, call the person's name and say, "EEL, keep my creditors safe and quiet till I return." When he calls, he will put it off without speaking to you.

h. To make a sale: Use three teaspoons of sugar, three of molasses, three teaspoons of gum incense and three of black incense. Put all on a tin plate and burn it in the street and cause the smoke to go towards the house, and you will have customers by the dozen.

i. To make a person progress: Take the names of all who he is going to buy from, or deal with, and the accounts they will have and just put 'em under a light—three white, (peace); three blue, (true); three pink, (success). If it's a man, you burn the light to St. Anthony; if a woman, you burn to St. Ramond. If there is any competitor who tries to hurt you, take a fresh black hen's egg, make a hole big enough to get the egg out and take the names, pepper sauce and mustard and fill the egg up and soak it in War Water for nine days and throw it over the house, and it will cross the house and they will have to move away.

j. To hold a congregation together (for a preacher): Take Shia seeds, mustard seeds, nine spoons of powdered sugar. Put in deep plate. Put blue candle in plate and put Shia seeds with sugar and mustard and burn one candle every day for three days, and put it at the four corners of block and people will flock there and never notice nothing he has done.

k. To buy when the owner doesn't want to sell: Take they name, the person who owns the place and the person who wants to buy. Take three candles, blue, white or pink. Put the names in cup or saucer and pour Van-Van on them and burn candles in cup for seven to nine days. Then go to the person and they will agree.

## 4. To Give People Work

a. Nine crumbs of bread, three slices of garlic, some steel dust and lodestone. Put that in a bag and give it to them to wear on the person. They cannot be refused a job.

b. If you are afraid the boss-man will fire you, write his name seven times on a piece of white cotton and wear it in your shoe, and he can't go against you.

## 5. To Plant Yourself at a Place
### (If another conjure doctor is working against you.)

Take a three-edged file and a yard of linen tape and write his name seven to nine times on the tape. Wrap that tape around the file and bury it under a door or a step where you have to walk over it. Walking over it brings him under your control.

## 6. To Move Neighbors

*a.* Buy War Water and break it at a person's door at twelve o'clock, day or night, and they will surely move.

*b.* Write the name of the person you want to move eight times on paper. Put it in a dark bottle and add four tablespoons of vinegar, one tablespoon of whole black pepper, one guinea pepper, one cayenne pepper and hang the bottle where the sun can rise and set on it. They will move quickly.

*c.* Sweep behind an undesirable roomer every time he goes out, or put hatred powder in the hatband and it will give him a wandering mind.

*d.* Take their shoe and throw it in the graveyard—an abandoned graveyard. They will wander about and no one will pay any attention to them.

## 7. To Make Sick or Punish An Enemy

Take a soiled undergarment of theirs, hang on a bare rafter and get some hackberry switches and whip the garment. They will be so sore they can't get out of bed.

## 8. To Break a Friendship

Take three lemons and cut stem end off (squeeze some juice out). Write one name eight times one way on the paper and the other eight times across it. Roll it up and poke in the lemon, one in each lemon. Bury those lemons in the yard where the sun rises and sets on them. Every day at one o'clock pour one-half cup vinegar on the lemons. Those people will fight and part.

## 9. To Keep a House Empty

*a.* Tie nine red peppers on a string and hang them up the chimney.

*b.* Nine ten-penny nails driven in sill of the door.

## 10. To Make the Rectum Sore

Take dung of victim. Mix it with plenty of red pepper and turpentine and keep a slow fire under it for eight or nine days.

## 11. To Set Crazy

Cut the seat of the victim's underwear (or sanitary napkin, or hatband). Cut jet black rooster or hen open in the breast and put the piece of underwear in its breast and sew it up. Don't feed it and tie it to a fence. Chicken will get light, so will victim.

## 12. To Stop a Man from Wandering

Take a Barred Rock rooster, name it after the man and tie it with a long rope to the fence and shorten it by one foot every day, and feed him there. Start with a five-foot rope and shorten it to a yard. Feed the chicken three days there at one yard, and the man will never wander.

## 13. To Uncross

Put some whole cloves and whole spice and some lump incense into a saucer and smoke the party every morning for nine mornings. (Set the saucer on the floor and have him stand in the smoke.) Give a bath of bark cinnamon (brewed) before the smoke. This is the treatment for lack of friends or lack of attention from the other sex.

## 14. To Find Out Secret Enemies
### (People who try to trip you.)

a. Take a new white plate. Make twenty-one marks on the inside and fifty on the bottom outside. Put the plate where no light don't shine. If there is an enemy laying wait to trip you, the plate turns dark. Make marks with very small brush and lamp black. (This is for bootleggers or anyone hiding from the police.)

b. If you want to know if a man friend is coming back or wishes to send anything, take a white saucer and treat as the plate, and it will work on the mind and cause them to do what you want.

For a woman you use a cup.

## 15. To Run a Person

a. Take the names, make seven slips. Take a toad when the moon is wasting. Roll those up in a small ball and give to the toad. Take the toad in a box over into another town and the person will leave and never return.

b. Treat a rabbit the same way, but slit his skin, insert the half of paper and sew up the slit.

## 16. To put worms, caterpillars, etc., in one

Feed the eggs in already cooked foods.

## 17. To Discover Poison

Either put a piece of silver money in the mouth of the patient or bind it on the flesh. If it turns black he is poison. If so, take a file and file some silver off the money and give it to him to drink in white rum or milk from a red or black cow. Their milk is strongest.

## 18. To revenge yourself upon a man

Hold a slice of onion on the tongue during intercourse. This will give the man bad disease. Then throw slice away and it will come.

## 19. To Keep Your Husband Home

*a.* If a man tends to wander, hang one of his shoes behind the door and it will tie him home.

*b.* Tie a stock in a knot and hide it under a rug and it will keep your husband home.

## 20. To Kill

*a.* Take the intended victim's name eighteen times, eighteen red peppers, eighteen pins, eighteen needles, eighteen brass tacks, one round steak. Put the name on a steak and add the peppers; stick pins, needles and tacks through paper and peppers and fold steak over. Take one yard of new black calico and tie steak and all in it like a bundle. Knot it nine times. Take it to an old cemetery and throw it in broken grave with either a bottle of whiskey uncorked or fifteen cents, and ask the spirit in there to follow them for you. Say, "Spirit, I am paying you to follow that person."

*b.* Put a beef heart in a pot with cloves and spice and let it keep hot till sundown. Put the name, pins, peppers, tacks, one big nail driven through the heart, or through a tongue or steak. Tie in black calico as above and bury in an open grave. Just as you wrap up the heart, light the black candle and let it burn out. The victim will live from one to six months.

*c.* Get a tin-type picture of the person you want to hurt and bury it head down in a graveyard, and it will kill.

## 21. Working Hours

The time of day that work is done is very important. Some hours are beneficent and some are evil.

| Good | Bad |
|---|---|
| Two o'clock | Eight o'clock |
| Four o'clock | Three o'clock |
| Five o'clock | Ten o'clock |
| Six o'clock | One o'clock |
| Seven o'clock | |
| Nine o'clock | |
| Eleven o'clock | |
| Twelve o'clock | |

### Hours for Spirit Mediums

| | |
|---|---|
| Six a.m. to twelve m. | One to six p.m. |
| Six to seven p.m. | Seven to two p.m. |
| Three to four, any time | Five to six a.m. |

## 22. Colors of Candles for Love Cases

Red is the strongest to bring love back.
 Pink is the strongest to make them love you.
 Green is the strongest to drive them off.

## 23. Luck Pieces
### (To carry on the person or keep in the house).

1. John de Conquer.
2. Kings root—he and she.
3. Snake root.
4. Violet root.
5. Devil's Shoe Strings (a root).

## 24. To Set a Feast

Have chicken, goose, coffee, tea, crackers and cheese and fried plantains, fried bananas, sweet and Irish potatoes, eggs. Have plenty of people invited at four A.M. New Year's morning. If you want the spirit to work with you never eat meat except at twelve noon—eat as little meat as possible. Keep fruit in house and on first of month buy plenty of fruit.

## 25. Dance

Place a gig bottle in the centre of the floor with holy water and Jockey Club perfume, and give it out after the dance. Take a broomstick and tap a circle around the bottle four or five times—then dance. Sing:

*John O, John O, John O,*
*I'm going away to leave you*
*John O, dance, John O.*

## 26. Mental Powers

Repeat: *a.* I sincerely send to you the thoughts of my forces at this hour (nine o'clock).

 *b.* I sincerely send you my mental influence that I can overcome all obstacles and gain what I desire in all influence.

 Sit down at nine every morning and speak these thoughts. Close the eyes five or ten minutes—fingers on forehead, thumb on cheek bone. (Nine in the morning and seven at night—then you have one million to help you.)

## 27. War Powder

Ground flax seed, gumbo filet, copperas, blue stone, ground black pepper, ground guinea pepper, cayenne pepper and graveyard dirt, brimstone and gunpowder; beat it all up together.

## 28. Beliefs

a. The spirits: There are seven spirits on the face of the earth.

b. Always keep black hen's eggs, garlic and parsley around to cure folks that's poisoned.

c. Snakes don't help in conjure.

d. Cut broomsticks in foot lengths and gild them and cross them on the wall. Keep plenty flowers and lights.

e. St. Roque church down at Raquet Green, where all the hoodoo dances used to be held, is a good place to burn candles for what you want. But you must walk down and back.

# ❈160❈

# 'There Goes God!' The Story of Father Divine and His Angels

## CLAUDE McKAY

A black-led cult which attracted a great deal of attention in the 1930s was Father Divine's Peace Mission. Its leader, George Baker, later Father Divine (1878?–1965), had various cultic pastorates in the South and Long Island before arriving in Harlem in 1931 where he expanded his influence amongst both blacks and whites during the Depression. His cult drew upon different strands of religious belief. Proclaiming himself the incarnation of God, he brought heaven down to earth by providing feasts free, or at minimum cost, to adherents. He saw sin and sickness as the product of a lack of true faith. But the Peace Mission was also worldly enough actively to oppose war and racial discrimination.

---

The most African characteristic of Harlem, after the color of its people, is the multitude of amazing cults. Native African churches (so-called), groups of Negro-Jews, and a host of straight Christian and revival sects pullulate in Harlem. To say that there is a cult to every block would be no exaggeration.

It is through religion, more than any other channel, that primitive African emotions find expression in our modern civilization. Indoors and along the pulpit pavements of Harlem, black men and women, some singularly robed, ecstatically prance and reel and writhe with a fervor that is tolerated simply because their exhibitions bear the label of religion. No Negro cabaret or Negro theater could permit the display of such very African antics.

Returning to Harlem after three years spent in North Africa, I had a queer, topsy-turvy sensation when I mingled with folk who were so similar physically to those of North Africa (and from the same cause—miscegenation) but in spirit so different, though they have precisely the same strenuous preoccupation with religion. My arrival in Harlem coincided with a big religious parade. The streets

Source: Claude McKay, '"There Goes God!" The Story of Father Divine and His Angels', *The Nation*, 6 February 1935. © 1935 by *The Nation*.

are massed with marching people, led by bands of music, shouting, singing, bearing banners proclaiming "Father Divine Is God," "God Almighty Is Father Divine." Automobiles loaded with enthusiastic disciples were bright with pennants praising Father Divine. Spectators jammed the pavements. Excited black and brown faces, framed in appartment windows, beamed down on the scene. Suddenly an airplane droned through the clouds, and looking up the people shouted: "God! God! There goes Father! Father Divine is God! The true and living God." Never had I seen such excitement in Harlem except in the days of Marcus Garvey's Back-to-Africa movement.

Father Divine is God! With that one phrase Father Divine stands out above all the other leaders and their cults. God, who was invisible to all before, is now personified in him. He has created "Kingdoms" of Heaven in Harlem and elsewhere. "He is sweet, so sweet," chant his "angel" followers, "God, so sweet, Father Divine." According to them Father Divine is the source of all things. He gives his "angels" work, health, food, happiness, prosperity—everything. Accepting nothing, he gives all, being God.

Father Divine was a name unknown to the large public a little more than two years ago. As the leader of a holy-rolling kind of black-and-white cult, he was known only in Sayville, Long Island. There Father Divine had acquired property, upon which he had built a house. The house was called a "kingdom." He had lived there for about ten years. Actually he was supposed to be in retirement after many years of preaching. But some of his faithful white and colored disciples, mainly from New York, continued to visit him, eating, sleeping, and worshiping in his house. As their numbers increased, their presence disturbed the respectable white residents, and Father Divine was prosecuted for maintaining a public nuisance. That colored and white persons of both sexes were united under a Negro leader seemed particularly to incense the presiding judge. In his preliminary examination of Father Divine he laid special emphasis upon that fact.

Meanwhile the case had attracted wide attention, especially among Negroes, because of its white-with-black feature. A clever Negro lawyer with some political influence offered his services free to Father Divine. In Harlem his followers organized large protest meetings. At one of these meetings, held at the Rush Memorial Baptist Church, a leading disciple exhorted the assembled congregation to hold together and be not dismayed, for their Father Divine would sentence the judge to death if the judge dared to sentence him to prison.

The court was unable to elicit anything about the antecedents of Father Divine, since he insisted that he had been divinely projected into existence and had no record of his life. Thereupon the judge committed him to jail, to obtain further information and to have his mental condition determined by a psychiatrist. When the case came up for final trial, the judge sentenced Father Divine to a year in prison and $500 fine. Curiously, three days after the sentence the judge died suddenly. He was very old and had been stricken by heart disease. To the Divine disciples the hand of their Father had struck the judge dead. They even reported that Father Divine had said that he regretted having to make an example of the judge. The news spread through the country.

Father Divine's attorney appealed the sentence. The verdict was reversed by the Brooklyn Supreme Court, which ruled that the presiding judge had injected prejudice into the minds of the jurors. Upon being released, Father Divine entered into his apotheosis. Overnight his following had developed into a vast army. The man who had retired to Sayville emerged as God. He came to New York again and thousands flocked to the Rockland Palace to hear him speak.

"Peace!" he cried to them; "Good health, good appetite, prosperity, and a heart full of merriness. I give you all and everything." And his people responded: "God! It is wonderful! I thank you, Father." Such is the essence of the Divine message and the response it calls forth. And so greatly grew that response that Father Divine alone could not handle it as he had done at Sayville. More and greater "kingdoms" had to be created. Father Divine declares, and his followers believe, that he is in all of them at the same time. "I am here and I am there and I am everywhere," he says, "I am like the radio voice. Dial in and you shall always find me."

Fifteen Divine kingdoms are maintained in New York City alone. In fine buildings all. The finest is the former bath premises in 126th Street, now known as the Faithful Mary Kingdom. Other kingdoms are in Jamaica, Brooklyn, and White Plains, in New Jersey and Connecticut. From Washington, D.C., to Seattle, Washington, centers have been established by Father Divine enthusiasts. Headquarters Kingdom, where Father Divine has office and residence, is in 115th Street. In whichever "kingdom" he eats, Father Divine himself serves the flock. The food goes through his hands before it is served. He pours and passes the coffee and cream in the grand style of a maître d'hotel. And he has more dignity and naturalness doing that than when he is haranguing an audience.

The kingdoms are sanitary and apparently well managed. They pay their way. The secret of their financing is Father Divine's. Rooms are rented to individuals at a dollar a week, but there is more than one person to a room. In the restaurants meals are served for ten and fifteen cents. The food is good and plentiful. A good piece of meat and two vegetables cost ten cents; a piece of cake or ice-cream, five cents; coffee or soft drink, three cents. There are separate kingdoms for men and women. For in the kingdom sex is proscribed.

The decorative motif of all the kingdoms is the apotheosis of Divine. His enlarged photographs dominate the walls. Large posters with black and red lettering proclaim his virtues: "Father Divine is God." "Father Divine is the living Tree of Life, Father, Son, and Holy Ghost." "We all may take of the words of Father Divine, eat and drink and live forever." Other posters make a queer melange of social and religious statements. They reveal that Father Divine is aware of social problems and that he has a special approach to them. Framed newspaper clippings advertise Father Divine's letters to firms doing business with him, from which he solicits jobs for his people. Also displayed are letters to the mayor referring to Father Divine's secret service, which is investigating racial and color discrimination and segregation in New York City institutions. One poster reads:

> We the Inter-racial, International, Inter-denominational and Inter-religious Coworkers . . . as being called Father Divine's Peace Mission Workers . . . do demand the release through commutation of the life sentence of the Scottsboro boys, and other means of releasing the nine boys. And also we demand freedom, and extermination of the mistreatment of the Jews in Germany and all other countries, and we demand the equal rights and religious liberty according to our Constitution.
> I thank you, Father.

Enthusiastic masses of colored people, with a sprinkling of whites, West Indians, and Latin Americans, make up the kingdoms. Women predominate, forming about three quarters of the whole number. It is largely a middle-aged crowd. No prayers are said at the meetings. Praise has taken the place of prayer in Father Divine's religion. He often quotes: "Prayer is the heart's sincere desire, unuttered or unexpressed." And instead of praying, his people testify, praising and thanking him. Of music and singing and dancing there is no end—a riotous, prancing, antic performance that "it is wonderful" indeed to see and to feel. Loosely the women fling themselves about, with a verve and freedom that would startle a cabaret. They toss up their skirts and contort their limbs, dancing and singing to Father Divine:

> I don't know why, I don't know why,
> I don't know why you love me so . . .
> You put your arms around me and you took me in. . . .

With nervous, petulant gestures they turn from the men, the forbidden, and dance extravagantly with one another, colored with colored and colored with white. After they are exhausted from singing and dancing in chorus, they give individual testimony—amazing testimony, whether openly given in the kingdoms or privately related.

At Headquarters Kingdom I saw a little, wiry black man cleave through the jam to reach and kneel a moment against the back of Father Divine's chair. Standing up again with uplifted hand he cried: "Peace—O Father, thank you, Father, for what you have done for me. Father, I used to think I was smart. But I was all wrong and bad. I used to take the Jew man's furniture and then change my address and sell it. But Father, you showed me where I was wicked and I don't do that any more. And I mean to pay back all what I stole. And Father, I used to make the women pay. I was a mean feller, Father. Until I find one woman what was different and wouldn't pay off. And I wanted her, Father. And wanted her that bad I couldn't help falling for her. But I had to take it the way she wanted to give. And she made me go housekeeping together like an honest couple and I changed my ways and worked like a man. Then we both heard about you, Father. And we came to you. And you stopped us from living in sin, thank you, Father it is wonderful. Peace. And you put me in one kingdom, Father, and put her in another. And you did right, for Father Divine is always right. But oh, Father, she been coming to my room every night in my dreams. It was powerful awful, Father, and I was afraid and asked you to guide me. I concentrated on your spirit, Father, and last night when I was dreaming she coming again and all at once you just descended into the room like a lightning bolt between us. Oh, thank you, Father. It was wonderful."

"It is wonderful!" everybody echoes and joined in singing: "All hail the power of Father's name, let angels prostrate fall."

From a mulatto young woman standing behind Father Divine's chair escaped a frightened yell. "Father, you did call me," she cried, "call me all the way from Seattle, Father, let me confess the truth that I had sinful thoughts about you, sinful, deceitful woman as I am. Imagined that you were just another colored minister. I said, Father can't be so different, he is just another one. For I have lived my life, Father, as a sample and example of a free woman among men and counted my victims. All the long way from Seattle I came, Father, thinking evil. And when I entered your presence and tried to fix you, you fixed me instead. You saw straight through me, Father, the lust that was in me, and you drove it out of me into the Gadarene swine. And, oh, Father, you were God in the place of the man I was looking for. You put your spirit in me and made me pure, one of your angels, Father. I thank you, Father. It is truly wonderful."

California and other points west have supplied most of the white followers. An old man in his sixties said that he had left California doubting that Father Divine could be more than a prophet, because there is a passage from the Bible which says that no man can look upon God and live. But as soon as he saw Father Divine he was convinced that he was in the presence of God. And he immediately experienced a transformation from a mortal to an angel. He lives now in one of the kingdoms.

The skeptic part of Harlem's population, whatever its opinion of Father Divine, is excited over his success and the financing of it. Unlike other evangelists Father Divine never collects any money at his meetings; he delights in making a mystery about the source of the funds he uses to run his Divine Trust of large, well-appointed kingdoms, cheap restaurants (where hundreds of hungry out-of-work persons are fed free daily), and the splendid buses and automobiles which convey his disciples from kingdom to kingdom. He waxes sharply waggish when inquires are made. He told a group of white parsons, professors, and students that he got his money from the Treasury in Washington, just like other people. At his meetings he jokes with his followers about "people who want to know where I get my money." "They want to know how I get my money. But you all know I take absolutely nothing." "Right, Father! Yes, Father!", the people cry. "I give everything because I am omnipotent. I give you plenty of good food, clothes, shelter, work. And you are fat and merry" "Yes, Father! Thank you, Father!" the people shout. "It is wonderful!"

Graciously granted an interview, I could not ask Father Divine how he got his money. His white secretary had explicitly stated to be beforehand: "Father Divine does not accept money from his followers. Rich people interested in his work have offered large sums of money which Father Divine has refused, because he does not want to be limited in the conception of his work." The secretary also intimated that inquiries about the source of his income were annoying to Father Divine. I said that primarily my interest was in Father Divine's work.

In his sumptuous living quarters, African in the gay conglomeration of colors, Father Divine in a large easychair appeared like a slumping puppet abandoned after a marionette show. He seemed shrunk even smaller than his five feet four, which is not unimpressive when he is acting. He pointed to a seat near him , and said he thought he had said enough at his meetings to give me an idea of his work and mission. I told him that I was interested mainly in his ideas about social problems and interracial relations and would like a special pronouncement from him as a Negro leader and pacifist. Father Divine replied: "I have no color conception of myself. If I were representing race or creed or color or nation, I would be limited in my conception of the universal. I would not be as I am, omnipotent."

I said that I accepted his saying that he was above race and color, but because he happened to have been born brown and was classified in the colored group, the world was more interested in him as a Negro. And I asked him what was his plan for the realization of peace and understanding between the masses and the classes. Father Divine said: "I am representative of the universal through the cooperation of mind and spirit in which is reality. I cannot deviate from that fundamental. The masses and the classes must transcend the average law and accept me. And governments in time will come to recognize my law."

I drew his attention to an editorial in the *Daily Worker* referring to the demonstration against war and fascism, in which the Communists had paraded in company with Father Divine at the head of thousands of his people carrying banners bearing Divine slogans. The editorial was an explanation to critical readers of the necessity of cooperating with Father Divine and his followers, "carrying such strange and foolish placards." Father Divine said that he was always willing to cooperate in his own way with the Communists or any group that was fighting for international peace and emancipation of people throughout the world and against any form of segregation and racial discrimination. But what the Communists were trying to do he was actually doing, by bringing people of different races and nations to live together and work in peace under his will. He had come to free every nation, every language, every tongue, and every people. He did not need the Communists or any other organization, but they needed him. For he had all wisdom and understanding and health and wealth. And he alone could give emancipation and liberty, for he was the victory. I thanked Father Divine for the interview, and he dismissed me with the gift of a pamphlet.

The followers of Father Divine are always ready to testify to his divinity, the glory of the kingdoms, and the sweetness of the fellowship, and the wonders of his works. But ask a pertinent question about the Divine finance and immediately they clamp their lips. That is something as taboo with them as it is with Father Divine.

Some cabalistic thing, such as exists in a secret society, may be at the bottom of this. The Divine disciples are called "angels." And Father Divine has said, "Denial of money is Angelship degree." Even those who have ceased to be followers will not discuss it. There is a story of a Negro petty shopkeeper who disappeared taking $1,500 of his own money. Investigating, his wife discovered him in one of the kingdoms, but without the money. Finally he was persuaded to return home. But neither he nor his wife will discuss the incident or what has become of the money.

Perhaps a clue to the Divine method of finance may be found in Faithful Mary. She was the first disciple of Father Divine. At all his big meetings she sits at his right. In striking contrast to him, her brown-moon face shines with a disarming otherworldliness. She is middle-aged, a fine-fleshed, compact, and balanced motherly woman. She testifies that she had been insane from drink for ten years, had been discharged from hospitals as incurable. She was living soddenly in the gutters of Broome Street in Newark, eating out of garbage cans, when she heard about Father Divine. She concentrated upon him, believing that he was God. He lifted her up and cured her. And now she belongs to God. Faithful Mary's sincerity strikes you; her story is convincing.

Father Divine's little white secretary, who unlike Father Divine does talk about the material side of the Peace Mission, had this to say of Faithful Mary:

> She is blessed with the love of the people and they give her great gifts. They have given her houses to be converted into kingdoms, clothes, and automobiles. The largest kingdom in 126th Street was given to her.

If Father Divine as God takes absolutely nothing, his first disciple, Faithful Mary, is not like him. And she declares that she belongs to God.

"It is truly wonderful," even as the "angels" of Harlem sing-song, this frantic, prancing expression of black emotionalism in the heart of the great white city.

# ✠161✠

# The Moorish Science Temple

## ARTHUR HUFF FAUSET

The Moorish-American Science Temple, founded by Noble Drew Ali (1866-1929) in New Jersey in 1913, spread to a number of other cities in the 1920s and outlived its founder's death, as this report from 1944 indicates. It supplied recruits to Garveyism, the black nationalist movement of the 1920s, and later for the Nation of Islam. Ali believed that African-Americans were the descendants of North Africans and of Asiatic origin. His version of Islam was consciously represented as the black man's religion, clearly distinct from the white man's faith, Christianity. As the description of the service reveals, however, the ritual of the group was culturally eclectic.

T he first page of the *Holy Koran* contains a picture of Noble Drew Ali. We see a tall, slender, dark Negro, with rather pronounced qualities of the dreamer suggested in his physiognomy. He is clad in dark trousers, dark shoes, a white robe and sash, collar and necktie, and fez. His right hand, which is distinguished by long lender, sentient fingers, is stretched across his breast. Under the picture is the sub-title:

THE PROPHET AND FOUNDER OF THE MOORISH SCIENCE
TEMPLE OF AMERICA, TO REDEEM THE PEOPLE
FROM THEIR SINFUL WAYS.

On the second page is a portrait of a Mohammedan priest or sheik, with title:

SULTAN ABDUL AZIZ IBU SUAD
THE DESCENDANT OF HAGAR, NOW HEAD OF THE
HOLY CITY OF MECCA

Then follows an introductory page of instructions.

The introductory page of instructions indicates clearly certain outlines in the beliefs of the Moors:

Source: Arthur Huff Fauset, 'The Moorish Science Temple', *Black Gods of the Metropolis*, Philadelphia, 1944, pp. 46–9. © 1944 by University of Pennsylvania Press.

1. Although they are a Moslem sect, Jesus figures prominently.

2. The cult is secret.

3. Noble Drew Ali is a prophet ordained by Allah.

4. Allah is God, and He has ordained His prophet, Noble Drew Ali, to divulge His secrets to the dark folk of America.

5. Moslems (i.e., people of dark hue) belong to certain areas of the world including the American continent.

6. The guiding spirit of the universe is love.

After the introductory page, there follow many pages containing apocryphal chapters from the life of Jesus, and further pages of instruction, admonition, caution, warning, and reference to the rôle of the dark races in the world's development.

The concluding chapters, which are numbered 45-48, treat of the divine origin of Asiatic nations, the beginning of Christianity, Egypt as the capital empire of the dominion of Africa, and the End of Time and the fulfilling of the prophesies. In these chapters many of the racial principles of the cult are expounded.

On the inside of the back cover are these words:

The fallen sons and daughters of the Asiatic Nation of North America need to learn to love instead of hate; and to know of their higher self and lower self. This is the uniting of the Holy Koran of Mecca, for the teaching and instructing of all Moorish Americans, etc.

On the back cover occur the following words:

THE HOLY KORAN
OF THE
MOORISH SCIENCE TEMPLE
OF AMERICA
KNOW YOURSELF AND YOUR FATHER
GOD ALLAH
THAT YOU MAY LEARN TO LOVE INSTEAD OF HATE
EVERYMAN NEED TO WORSHIP UNDER HIS OWN
VINE AND FIG TREE
THE UNITY OF ASIA

## Beliefs

The charter of the Moorish Science Temple came from the great capital empire of Egypt.

Before you can have a God, you must have a nationality.

Noble Drew Ali gave his people a nation (Morocco).

There is no Negro, black, colored, or Ethiopian — only "Asiatic" or Moorish-American.

Ethiopian signifies a division.

Negro (black) signifies death.

"Colored" signifies something that is painted.

For the above reasons, the term Moorish–American must be used, and not other, opprobrious terms.

The name means everything; by taking the Asiatic's name from him, and calling him Negro, black, colored, or Ethiopian, the European stripped the Moor of his power, his authority, his God, and every other worth-while possession.

Christianity is for the European (paleface); Moslemism is for the Asiatic (olive-skinned). When each group has its own peculiar religion, there will be peace on earth.

Nobel Drew Ali is a kindred personage and spirit to Confucius, Jesus, Buddha, and Zoroaster.

Marcus Garvey was to Noble Drew Ali as John the Baptist was to Christ.

## Ritual

### Typical Service

At 8 P.M. promptly, the leader, who sits at the front of the temple facing the congregation, begins to chant a hymn softly, and this is taken up by the members of the congregation. Unlike the singing in many Negro services, the chants of the Moors are very soft. Next the leader reads from the *Holy Koran* of Noble Drew Ali, and his voice is very low, scarcely above a whisper. When he has finished his reading, he makes a brief discourse to the members. He reminds them that they are the descendants of the Moabites and Canaanites, that they have a charter and that this charter was procured in the great capital in Eygpt, and that it entitles the Moors to possession of northwest and southwest Africa. He emphasizes that Egypt is a greater capital than Washington. He reminds his followers that there is no Negro, black, colored, or Ethiopian, and that before they can have a God they must have a nationality. He proclaims the reincarnation of their Prophet, Noble Drew Ali, and states that he is in reality Mohammed III, who gave them a nation which he called Morocco.Christianity, he tells them, is the religion for the Europeans, but Islam is the religion for the Asiatics. When Europe and Asia each has its own religion, then there will be peace.

Christianity, he continues, is a European religion which was founded in Rome. The Romans killed Jesus, who was a Canaanite, and following the death of Jesus there was peace for a time. But Mohammed II came, and then there was no longer any peace. The name means everything, and by taking away the name of the Moors the palefaces stripped the power, authority, God, and everything from the darker peoples. Thus the Europeans have taken away their flag, their land, their God, their name — everything. The Moors must struggle on, establishing a world in which love, truth, peace, freedom, and justice will flourish. Always there must be peace, and although the Moors are hostile to the palefaces there must be no question of obedience to the American flag and loyalty to the United States.

After the leader has spoken, an elder reads the special laws of the temple which are in the questionary, and which also hang in a frame on the wall. This copy he takes down from the wall and reads. The elder man makes comments as he goes along, similar to the remarks already made by the grand sheik. After he has concluded his reading, the leader again rises and picks up the *Holy Koran*, and invites members to come forward and speak. One after the other they approach the front, take the *Holy Koran* to testify. Each begins by saying,

> I rise to give (do) honor to Allah, and to his Holy Prophet, Noble Drew Ali, Reincarnated, who gave to us this *Holy Koran*.

Then follows reading from the *Koran* and a talk in the same vein as the one given by the leader. The individual talks will bear testimony to the efficacy of the spirit of Noble Drew Ali, Reincarnated, and how that spirit, or perhaps an actual word from the living prophet, has illuminated the life of the follower. Frequent reference is made to the fact that the prophet has removed the stigma of color and of race.

At 9:30 promptly, several members move forward with collection plates; the leader begins a chant, which is taken up quietly by the followers. Usually the chants are ordinary hymn tunes set to words which conform to Moslem teaching. For example:

> *Give me that old time religion . . .*

becomes:

> *Moslem's that old time religion . . .*

The collection takes about fifteen minutes, after which the followers continue to come forward, reading from the *Koran* and testify until, exactly at 10 P.M., the leader gives a signal, everyone stands, faces east, raises the arms horizontally, with first and second fingers of the right hand uplifted, and says,

> Allah, the Father of the Universe, the Father of Love, Truth, Peace, Freedom and Justice. Allah is my Protector, my Guide, and my Salvation by night and by day, through His Holy Prophet, Drew Ali. Amen.

# Religion and Race Relations

Plate 18: The March on Washington, August 1963.

# ❧162❧

# Methodists' Opinions
# on Segregation

## DWIGHT L. CULVER

This analysis of the results of a survey conducted in the Methodist Church on the eve of the civil rights era illuminates a number of issues: the extent to which southern white believers differed from co-religionists in other regions about racial segregation in the Church; the tension between segregationist practices in the Church and the idea of spiritual equality; the nature of rationalization for opposing or limiting change. It should, of course, be remembered that many African-Americans worshipped in separate denominations which they had formed of their own volition, as well as belonging to all-black congregations in the Methodist Church through the operation of Jim Crow policies.

The statement A Christian goal is a nonsegregated church and a nonsegregated society is as limited to value judgment as any that could be chosen on the subject. It is certainly more free from considerations of fact than are the other statements of the questionnaire. The predicate is taken from the Federal Council statement which pledged the Council and its constituent denominations to "work for" such a church and society. As used here, however, it is simply a statement of an unqualified ideal with no implications regarding implementation. Of the white superintendents, 54 per cent agree with the statement, 26 per cent disagree, and 20 per cent leave it unmarked. Agreement is higher, but not complete, on the part of the other ministers. The segregationists position is not taken by Southerners only, although a sectional comparison indicates important differences. Three-fourths of the superintendents replying from the Western and the two Northern jurisdictions agree with the statement and one-tenth disagree. In the two Southern jurisdictions, 37 per cent agree, 41 per cent disagree. Negroes unanimously approve nonsegregation as a Christian goal.

Dwight L. Culver, 'Methodists' Opinions on Segregation', *Negro Segregation in the Methodist Church*, New Haven, 1953, pp. 22-41.

Whatever their own accommodation to the present patterns of segregation, they are not satisfied with the situation, and they think there should be a change. In holding this position, Negroes contradict the whites who report that Negroes are completely satisfied and that segregation is "accepted by them as best for all concerned." It should be remembered in this connection that these are not only Northern Negroes speaking but Southern Negroes as well. Whites may be more or less divided sectionally in their valuations and opinions on segregation, but these Negroes of The Methodist Church are united in their belief that segregation must go.

When the generalized goal is narrowed to the statement *Services in Christian churches should be open to all regardless of color* the whites appear more liberal. Almost half of the Southern white superintendents and ministers agree, and 90 per cent of those in the North are willing to accept the principle of interracial worship. All but 6 of the 60 white superintendents who do not accept the statement are in the Southern jurisdictions. The unanimity of the Negroes is again impressive. Only 2 feel that services should not be open to all regardless of color, and 2 others failed to respond, making a total of only 3 per cent who do not agree.

In the responses to the statement *Membership in Christian churches should be open to all regardless of color* there is only a slight shift from the percentages on the preceding statement about permitting attendance. Twelve of the superintendents (5 per cent) agree that services should be open to all but disagree that membership should likewise be open. Two Negroes take a similar position. In the study of practices in the local church in Chapter IV it will be seen that this distinction between attendance and membership in the church is even more important in practice than it seems to be here in theory.

*Negroes attending church with whites should sit in separate sections* is a statement describing a former widespread pattern in Southern churches, a pattern still followed in theaters and public meetings over large parts of the South. Almost 70 per cent of the white superintendents and ministers disagreed with the statement, as do 93 per cent of the Negroes. The 5 Negroes who approve the statement are all in the South, as are all but 4 of the 49 superintendents who similarly approve. The correlations between responses on this statement and those on the question of opening services to all show some shifts of opinion. Of the 185 white superintendents who thought services should be open to all regardless of color, only 147 oppose separating Negroes from whites in the service. Of the 60 white superintendents who opposed opening services at all, almost half (29) would keep Negroes separate when they do come. The rest apparently agree with the superintendent who said:

"If the Yankees want them in your churches you had better sit beside them."

*Negroes should be excluded from social events (like suppers) in white churches* is included to test the extent to which the word "social" influences Methodist thinking on race. The parenthetical "like suppers" is also intended to secure an affirmative response from those who fear to break the taboo against interracial eating. Each group of respondents is slightly more willing to exclude Negroes from social events than to make them sit separately from whites at services. Sixty-four of the 273 white superintendents who returned the questionnaire think that Negroes should be excluded from social events (like suppers) in their white churches. More than one-third of these who find eating with Negroes an impossible or impractical situation are nevertheless willing to sit with them in the church service. This supports Myrdal's "scale of friendliness toward the Negro" and indicates that some superintendents would favor a limited fellowship if it could be arranged.

In the statement *I fear the increase of intermarriage will be a result of interracial worship* the word "fear" was used in order that the emotions of the informant might be recorded rather than simply a belief regarding a factual situation. Thus the statement is "loaded" to secure an affirmative response from segregationists. Twenty-five per cent of the white district superintendents fear that intermarriage will be a result of interracial worship, the corresponding percentages for North and South being 13 per cent and 34 per cent, respectively. Judging from the interviews for the present study, a large majority of white ministers are influenced by a basic fear of intermarriage, although not more than one-fourth of them express that fear with regard to the particular situation involved in interracial worship. Negroes generally regard intermarriage with the "high indifference" which characterizes the integrationist position. Many of the Negroes interviewed mentioned the sexual exploitation of Negro women by white men as being in large part responsible for the whites' fear of intermarriage. They feel, as does Myrdal, that there would actually be less miscegenation if intermarriage were legal in all states.

There has been a recent tendency to consider the question of intermarriage a "red herring." The topic is often used to disrupt a discussion of justice for the Negro. Yet, despite the unrealistic way in which the clichés about intermarriage are often used, miscegenation is probably a genuine fear of most whites. Though the aversion toward miscegenation is sometimes withheld in casual conversation, it was discovered in the interviews that all but a few whites will admit such fears after sufficient questioning. Some well-known leaders in the move to eliminate segregation in The Methodist Church say they hope there will be no increase in intermarriage between Negroes and whites. For the most part, these same leaders are uncertain whether or not interracial worship will lead to intermarriage. One Northern white superintendent asked for information concerning a Negro minister in his city. The main thing he wanted to know was whether or not the Negro would "preach intermarriage." Another superintendent in the North writes:

> In this entire problem there is just one thing that troubles me. I do not want intermarriage and am not sure whether a free mingling of the races in the church would lead to it or not.

Without giving up his valuation, this same man adds that he has an open mind concerning the probable results: "I think the cases would be so few as to be negligible."

The opposition to intermarriage, expressed in many letters, is best summarized in the following excerpt from a letter which elevates the fear to a conviction, gives religious sanction to the valuation, and justifies "any device" that may be judged to reduce intermarriage.

> You speak of fear of intermarriage, if certain barriers were removed. With me it is not a matter of fear, it is a matter of conviction. Holding the belief that God made man and made him of different colors and of racial characteristics, it is fundamentally wrong for the races to amalgamate. I think each race should develop all of its God-given powers without mixing with any other. And any device that reduces intermarriage to a minimum is at least a less sin than wholesale racial amalgamation. (Georgia)

The preoccupation with the question of intermarriage serves to obscure the fact that social segregation operates to discriminate against Negroes in the interests of white people. Whites are in general reluctant to discuss any sexual basis of race prejudice and discrimination. Some insist that sex relations of white men with Negro women are a "thing of the past" and therefore play no part in race relations of the present. Most view a ban on intermarriage as the only necessary means of preventing an undesirable "mixing." Many whites are not aware of the extent of intermixture already accomplished. Others believe seriously that whites are not responsible for such crossing. One superintendent writes:

> Our people in this section are for segregation. The Negro race is not pure in this section. They have been guilty of illicitly crossing with white blood.

Some careful observers and analysts may recognize that equal treatment will at some time lead to an end of segregation, to interracial friendships, and thereby to occasional intermarriage. The process may be simplified in their summary:

> Equal treatment and integration lead to intermarriage.

If, however, they have a low estimate of the time required for the predicted result, an unusually high estimate of the number of probable intermarriages, and, especially, if they "fear" that result, there would seem to be ground for the suspicion that the belief, or fear, is opportune. This suspicion is strengthened when the fear of intermarriage is linked with other beliefs that are more obviously opportunistic in the interest of white defenders of segregation. Myrdal finds that

> The great majority of non-liberal white Southerners utilize the dread of "intermarriage" and the theory of "no social equality" to justify discriminations which have quite other and wider goals than the purity of the white race. Things are defended in the South as a means of preserving racial purity which cannot possibly be defended in this way. To this extent we cannot avoid observing that *what white people really want is to keep the Negroes in a lower status.* "Intermarriage"

itself is resented because it would be a supreme indication of "social equality" while the rationalization is that "social quality" is opposed because it would bring "intermarriage".

In this sense the fear of intermarriage appears to be one of the rationalizations for the segregationist opinions on the five preceding statements. Although it is used more with reference to the problem in society as a whole than to the situation in the church, it is worthy of note that there is a high correlation between those who fear intermarriage will be a result of interracial worship and those who agree with the next three statements, which can likewise be considered as, at least in part, opportune beliefs of the segregationist.

As on most of the opinions, there is a significant difference between the North and the South in responses to the statement that Negroes can be treated fairly without eliminating the practice of segregation. For example, 72 per cent of the white superintendents in the South agree with the statement, while in the North 35.5 per cent agree. Less than 17 per cent disagree with the statement in the South, while almost half their Northern brethren disagree. Negro disapproval of the statement is considerably greater, with 71 per cent of the superintendents and 88 per cent of the other ministers disagreeing. Thus most Negroes disagree with that half of the white group which thinks Negroes can be treated fairly without eliminating segregation.

The idea that Negroes can be treated fairly without eliminating segregation is denied by integrationists and accepted by some, if not most, segregationists. An affirmative response comes both from those who are indifferent to the injustices suffered under segregation and from those who, knowing these injustices, have some reason for compromising with the system and defending it. The latter mention that opportunities are offered to the segregated group which they could not secure without segregation. There are "gains" to the Negro from a segregation system, and these are recognized by sociologists and other students of race relations. However, only a few types of examples or illustrations of this theory were made by those asserting it in this opinion study. One is that the whites will give direct financial aid to a segregated Negro church. This is, however, less an argument for segregation than it is an explanation of a mode of social control by which whites can stifle Negro protest against segregation. Negro churchmen have already developed a degree of self-sufficiency so that they are not so dependent upon the financial assistance of a white paternalism as they once were. Help is appreciated, but there is no indication that it could not be given more freely and received with better feeling in an integrated system. A second illustration of the opportunity offered by segregation is that Negro leadership can develop better when separated from whites. . . .The final illustration is that, in the specific case of The Methodist Church, equal representation is offered by national boards and in the General Conference because there is a separate Negro body from which to draw a numerical quota.

The three opportunities—financial aid, development of leadership, and representation—are the only concrete illustrations given to show how Negroes can be treated fairly under a system of segregation. Each of these opportunities can be shown to be limited by the segregation which, it is claimed, makes them possible. Their logical inadequacy does not prevent these examples from being widely used throughout the church and especially in discussions of the Central Jurisdiction of The Methodist Church. However, they are always used in a general sense, and concrete instances are seldom mentioned in which individual Negroes or the Negro group as a whole have been aided by segregation.

Statements from both whites and Negroes throw light on the extent to which the belief that fair treatment is possible within a system of segregation may be opportunistic. Segregationist whites maintain that segregation is fair because it operates on both groups. Superintendents in North Carolina and Missouri, respectively, write:

> I dislike the use of "segregation" as referring to Negroes alone. One might as well refer to segregation of white. Negroes should be given every advantage and opportunity afforded to white people, but under present conditions and for a long time to come, the two separate cultures should be developed separately.

> The Christian ideal is no difference in race, but I am quite sure America is not ready for it. It is no more segregation of Negroes than it is of whites for them to have their own church.

Others who are not so sure that segregation works both ways agree, nevertheless, with the statement under discussion in this section. The explanations of their position are based on the idea that Negroes are not now being treated as fairly as possible under segregation, and that, therefore, improvement is possible without attacking the system. The segregationist district superintendent whose letter is quoted at the beginning of the chapter provides an illustration on this point. Two other whites write, as he did, that Negroes should have the right to build in the more desirable subdivisions of their respective cities, but that this should be possible without "taking away the rights and privileges of the majority race to enjoy the benefits that come from the exclusion of those who have been found objectionable." *How* this could be arranged "fairly" is not suggested.

A Texas district superintendent supports the segregationist position with the assertion that segregation "does not mean that they are not to be treated fairly and just." Another Texan puts it more bluntly: "We help the Negro here and that is all they want and best." From Arkansas comes the opinion that there is no race problem "and will be none if negroes and whites are permitted to work out their own problems." This last statement ends with the idea which is so hard for integrationists to understand—that less contact means more co-operation.

> I think that more and better co-operation between the races will obtain when each is permitted to work out its problems with the sympathetic understanding but not with the interference of the other.

An Alabama Negro minister disagrees:

> You can't like a fellow or have any special regard for him unless you can get close enough to him to know him. In my section, whites and negroes live as though they inhabit different worlds. They pay no attention to each other. Business is their only contact. Religion is no factor in bringing them together.

The idea that *Colored Methodists prefer to worship in churches separate from whites* was volunteered by whites in interviews more frequently than any other possible justification of the separation of churches on racial lines. When used on the opinion questionnaire it was found that, of the white superintendents, 71 per cent agree with the statement, 6 per cent disagree, and 23 per cent leave it unmarked. Agreement is not quite so great on the part of the other ministers, although approximately half agree with the statement. An analysis of the superintendents' responses by sections shows that even in the North only 10 per cent disagree.

In the interviews the "voluntary segregation" implied by the idea that colored Methodists prefer to worship in churches separate from whites is described in terms of a simple preference of Negroes for association with "their own kind." Sufficient basis for this assertion is alleged in the fact that Negroes are together in communities and churches. Because they are segregated and no protest is heard, it is assumed that Negroes prefer segregation. Only a small proportion of whites interviewed and a few of those writing letters on the subject mentioned that the preference of Negroes for each other's company might be because of discrimination at the hands of whites. On the other hand, every Negro interviewed who agreed with the statement added some word of qualification. All but a few of those reached by mail wrote some notation to the effect that Negroes prefer their own churches because they feel unwelcome in white or mixed churches. They know that their preference in the matter will be used to justify segregation, and they feel that this is unfair.

Having made these qualifications regarding the statement, a majority of Negroes agreed that colored Methodists prefer to worship in churches separate from whites. Whites use the same statement without qualification to justify segregation in the church. Myrdal's brief comment on this is supported by the present study.

> If this moral problem of American Christianity has not become more conspicuous and troublesome for white people's conscience, the explanation is that probably most Negroes—the caste situation being what it is—prefer to worship in Negro churches, even if they are against church segregation in principle.

As one minister in Detroit says,

> It's not that they are unwelcome—or that they want to be separate. But they like to be alone partly because their culture is not on a level with a white's. However, it is more because they recognize that the churches' policy is segregation and they don't like to take a chance. They don't know when they will be at home and when they will be rebuffed. They stay away not because they don't want to come, but because they are afraid.

Only a few of the other white ministers interviewed have this understanding. Some cite the fact that Negro ministers sit together at joint meetings of white and colored ministerial associations as proof that "They like to be by themselves." In every city visited there were reports that Negroes in mixed meetings group themselves together, supposedly indicating a significant preference for separation. As an argument for segregation this appeal to Negro preference is weakened by contrary evidence in the same cities, and sometimes in the same interviews, that Negroes are "offensive" at mixed meetings because they "force" themselves on whites by sitting scattered throughout the auditorium. An Alabama superintendent writes his view and belief:

> In the South it is better for Negroes and whites in the Methodist Church to worship in their own houses of worship. I think the Negroes prefer to worship to themselves.

A more dogmatic statement comes from South Carolina:

> We are separated in our churches for the sole reason that neither one of the races care [sic] for it to be otherwise.

A white minister in Baltimore says:

> The colored people no more want to worship in white churches than white people dislike having them.

Occasionally Negro preferences for separation is described more ambiguously. For example, Mason Crum of Duke University, in a book circulated widely and studied by women's groups in The Methodist Church, asserts that

> there seems to be a sort of autonomous principle of separation at work which is due as much to the Negroes as to the whites.

Conceivably Crum might mean by this that, while Negro preference for separation may be a historically conditioned response to *original* discriminations on the part of whites, the historical background may for certain purposes be ignored and the Negro preference taken as an independent factor. However, this may be giving Crum too much credit, especially since he bypasses another opportunity for analysis at this level: He later dismisses a complex problem with a disappointingly casual and obscure phrase when he says that one of the two forces working against . . . a truly integrated Methodism" is "the powerful racial pull toward segregation."

Other whites are undecided on the question of Negro preferences. Their comments on the statement explain that "some do" and "some don't"; that is, some Negroes prefer to worship in churches separately from whites and some oppose segregation in the church. The ministers who respond in this way probably realize that the statement which they were asked to check is a question of fact, and one on which they do not have sufficient information to answer. Only two mention that they have asked Negroes about their preference. Both of these are Southerners who report that they have not found a single Negro who is in favor of the combined worshipping of white people and Negro people in the same congregation.

Negroes, asking the question "Why are race churches necessary?" are letting it be known that they do not prefer such separation. Bishop Jones, writing in 1916, had said:

> Admitting that there were certain social conditions in the past that from a human standpoint justified churches built upon race lines, present day indications are that that day is passing, if not indeed already passed and gone.

In 1947 Negro ministers commented as followers on the statement that Negroes prefer to worship in separate churches.

> Whilst most Negroes prefer their own churches, segregation in all churches should be abolished. There should be no law, written or unwritten, that prohibits any person from attending any church. There would be a real Christian atmosphere in such a situation. As is, the Church situation here is unchristian. (Mississippi)

> While there is a sense of unity and at-home-ness on the part of the average Negro in a purely Negro organization that is not felt in a predominantly white organization; I think he nevertheless desires and deserves that sense of freedom to worship wherever the Spirit might direct him at any given time. I seriously doubt, however, that Negroes will ever turn in mass to churches other than their own, no matter how great the incentive to do otherwise. (Indiana)

> [The Negro] wants equal opportunities to work, worship and education and he does know the white people have the best facilities, and he feels that in as much as he or she can nurse, cook, sew, wash and iron, and keep their houses for them, surely he can study and worship with them. (Texas)

> My place in the Methodist Church is the place any Methodist minister would expect. I am not permitted to preach to every creature if I can only preach to my race. I want the opportunity to preach to all nations, races, kindred and tongues. (Texas)

> I believe that all Christians should be as one in Christ. I am not in favour of any discrimination in the Church. I really think something should be done about it. (Mississippi)

A majority of whites agree with the next statement that *The religious needs of Negroes are best served by separate racial churches.* They explain that the Negro is at a different cultural level from whites, and that Negroes have a greater need for "emotional arousements." The minority of Negroes agreeing with the statement do so for different reasons. The Negro superintendents are about evenly divided on the statement, and other Negro ministers are opposed two to one. Negroes generally stress the idea that it is impossible to worship in a place where you feel unwelcome. In interviews it was necessary to ask several questions about "religious needs of Negroes" before securing any response at all. Far from feeling that separate services are needed because the Negro is more emotional, the Negro ministers seem to take pride in the steps they have taken toward a more formal type of service and to think that more interracial worship would help the trend away from emotionalism in worship. They do not deny that the average Negro worship service is more emotional than the average white service, but they point out that a fair ranking of Negro and white churches on this characteristic would slow much overlapping. Negroes also tend to make a distinction between needs for emotional expression and "religious needs," a distinction which whites usually fail to make when discussing Negro worship.

The white responses to this statement are very closely correlated with those on the preference of Negroes. Only 6 per cent of all the whites shifted from an affirmative response on the statement that Negroes prefer separate churches to a negative response on this statement that their religious needs are best served by such churches. The shift in Negro responses on these two statements is much larger. Of the 75 Negroes who think colored Methodists prefer separate churches, 33 (44 per cent) also think that their religious interests are *not* best served in separate churches. There is only an 11 per cent shift in the other direction. Comparing the whites' responses on the statement with the same individuals' responses on the first statement discussed in this section, we find that, of the 148 superintendents who consider a nonsegregated church and society to be a Christian goal, only 35 (24 per cent) take the position that the religious needs of Negroes are not best served by separate racial churches. The corresponding figure for the entire white group is 22 per cent. Thus less than one-fourth of those who view nonsegregation as a Christian goal deny this supposed benefit of segregation in the church. Of the 71 superintendents who disagree that nonsegregation is a Christian goal, all but one think the religious needs of Negroes are best served by separate racial churches.

*Jesus' teachings demand the elimination of segregation* states an interpretation held by all but 5 of the 144 Negroes who checked the questionnaire. It is not possible to discuss this statement very carefully with Negroes because they give an affirmative response so readily and hasten on to other topics. They are so certain that the teachings of Jesus are opposed to segregation that they see no need to discuss it at length. Whites, likewise, do not discuss this question very fully, although in some cases the reasons might not be the same. Some of the whites' reluctance in connection with Jesus' teachings may be due to a sore conscience at this point. In Embree's words:

> Segregation in Christian churches is an embarrassment. In a religion whose central teaching is brotherly love and the golden rule, preachers have to do a great deal of rationalizing as they expound their own gospel.

Almost 60 per cent of the whites who checked the questionnaire think Jesus' teachings demand the elimination of segregation. Most of these persons also agree that a Christian goal is a nonsegregated church and a nonsegregated society. As in the case of this earlier statement, their agreement on the nature of Jesus' teachings is not necessarily a commitment to put those teachings into practice. Yet it must be concluded that there are some grounds for expecting improvement in race relations since this 60 per cent can be presumed to feel some degree of tension between their Christian ideal and the present social order with its system of segregation.

There remain one-fifth of the white ministers and superintendents who find religious sanction for segregation. A negative answer to the statement that Jesus' teachings demand the elimination of segregation appears to be an opportune belief, the more so because of the high correlation of such an answer with an affirmative response to the three statements discussed immediately above. The 77 whites who do not think that Jesus' teachings demand the elimination of segregation do think that (1) Negroes can be treated fairly without eliminating the practice of segregation; (2) colored Methodists prefer to worship in churches separate from whites; and (3) the religious needs of Negroes are best served by separate racial churches. (There are but ten exceptions to all these statements combined.)

Those who attempt to explain their negative responses to the statement of Jesus' teachings do so in three different ways. Several claim that the elimination of segregation is a negative goal, whereas Jesus' goals are positive. Using the word "positive" in its meaning as opposed to "privative," they add an emotional value to the term which is carried over into a condemnation of the original statement. A second explanation of disagreement with the statement on Jesus' teachings is that these teachings were not "positive," in the sense of being explicit or definite with regard to segregation. The third segregationist interpretation of the statement of Jesus' teachings is that Jesus would not use "force" to bring social changes. Four superintendents thought that "demand" was the wrong word to use in connection with Jesus. They explained that "force" will bring more harm than good when used in race relations. Eager to make this point, they avoided answering the question of whether or not Jesus' teachings are incompatible with a philosophy of segregation.

The negative answer to this statement on Jesus' teachings is the major appeal to theological and religious sanctions in support of segregation. Only a few other appeals are made. An earlier quotation on the question of intermarriage has presented the idea that God created separate races and the *non sequitur* that therefore man must keep them separate. A white Methodist bishop made the same point in an interview, by quoting the appropriate Biblical passage in full with a meaningful stress on the last clause:

> God hath made of one blood all nations of men to dwell upon the face of the earth *and hath appointed the bounds of their habitations.*

He added that racial differences may not coincide exactly with class and cultural differences, but that race lines are still the most adequate guide to follow in keeping groups "in their proper places." A Cincinnati minister made a statement which identifies God's will with the white man's in a revealing way.

> The need is for education of the Negro to help him understand how the white man feels about it. There are racial instincts. Or if not, at least whites think there are, so Negroes should be taught to act accordingly. God wills these differences. He set up the barrier. Why should we tear it down?

"*Outside interference.*" In addition to the basic valuations and the beliefs disclosed in the opinion questionnaires, statements were returned in connection with an inquiry on practices which throw some light on Methodist attitudes and opinions with regard to segregation. For example, 11 of the 317 white superintendents who responded mentioned as their "major problem in race relations"—"*outside interference!*" This is the phrase most of them use and the way they emphasize it, but there are these variations:

> The Negroes and the whites understand each other in the South and get along nicely together except when some Yankee tries to tell the Negro that he is being mistreated. A Negro man told me recently that Mrs Roosevelt had done the Negro race *more harm than slavery every did*. (Kentucky)

> If you Christians in the North will convert the Jews, Communists and Foreigners in your midst we Christians in the South will get along with our Negroes in a most glorious way. There is no trouble between the Christian Whites and Blacks in this part of the Country. (Alabama)

> Every place you have put the word "Negro" [on the questionnaire on segregation practices in the church] I wish you would put the words, "Jews," "Communists," "Foreigner," then answer as you have indicated and send it back to me. Thanks. (Alabama)

> We have more negroes in —————— County than we have whites but we have no problems. The blacks and the whites in this area know every much better how to work out our relationship than the people away from here, and if both races are let alone to work out their salvation we will do it well. (Virginia)

> Some of the Northern Brethren never see but one color in the Race Relation— Come down South and you will find we get along better than you Yankees with the Negro. They like and respect us better. (Texas)

> The negroes and whites understand each other and get along fine. Only trouble is when somebody from the north *meddles*. (Kentucky)

Several Northern ministers, apparently forgetting the many Negro Methodists in the North, suggest that the problem of segregation belongs to the South, and Northerners should not say or do anything about it lest progress in the South be impeded. The election campaigns of Bilbo and Talmadge focused national attention on the alleged part played by Northern "agitation" in the election of these Southern politicians. Many white ministers and three Negroes suggest that Northerners were to blame for the election of racist politicians. Other Negroes point out that, if Southern whites are so ashamed of their politicians that they have to blame the North for them, we are perhaps making some progress in political life, if not in race relations.

Two white ministers in Border sections claim that there is no problem, by which they seem to mean that they favor the continuance of segregation.

> Let the few agitators stop talking about race relations and it will take care of itself. (Washington D.C.)

> [The church should] cease the irritating and foolish discussion of the subject. Let us all go our way in peace without so much fault finding. The present study of

the matter, and the agitation, is creating a sense of dscrimination that is not truly found in areas where there are enough of both colors to make possible separate churches. My voice would be for cutting out this continuous discussion of the race issue. (Baltimore)

*Segregation as transition.* Others in the South are less irritated but more concerned. About 10 per cent of Southern ministers feel that the Christian ideal challenges the present situation, and they desire to see change. However, they fear to move too rapidly. They defend segregation only as a transition to a more perfect system, the only possible justification of race parallelism with which the integrationist can sympathize. A few statements of this position are presented here to show that there are Southern whites whose Christian ethical thinking is not completely accommodated to a system of segregation.

> Keeping in mind the time element, the south at present, simply will not tolerate indiscriminate mixing of the races in churches, theatres, or otherwise. I wish that the relations were much further advanced than they are, but this intermixing must of a necessity be gradual. (Georgia)

> While I am in sympathy with all efforts to eliminate discrimination, injustice and segregation as a Christian goal, I am not sure that we are ready for a complete application of this principle in all particulars. Maybe this goal can be reached most surely if not pressed out of proportion to its importance. (Tennessee)

> I am not contending that Christ approves of these conditions nor of the Southerners' attitude regarding such. I am sure He does not, nor does He approve of conditions which seem to prevail in other sections. Let us hope and pray and work for the day when the "mind of Christ" shall be in complete control throughout the universe. (North Carolina)

> I am of the opinion that one of the best ways to ruin what is being done in a very fine and constructive way is for the matter of entire nonsegregation to be pushed vigorously at this time. (Kentucky)

> I think it is not expedient that these things be done [services and membership opened to Negroes] until we have won more white people. I can't see that we will gain adherents, particularly in the South, from either race by this procedure. (Arkansas)

> The character of the Negro is not yet ripe enough to properly use the social and religious advantages for which a few of them are now asking. (Pennsylvania)

> I do not know how this tragic dilemma is to be met, but I have the gravest misgivings about the consequences of trying to change the plan [of Methodist unification] suddenly. Those who think otherwise should at least seek to gauge the average attitudes with which we have to deal all the time. There surely must be a more constructive and more hopeful approach than that of violent assault. (Alabama)

There are not more than ten whites who, in the course of the interviews or through correspondence related to this study of Methodist opinion, suggested that segregation in the church should be eliminated even at the cost of white membership. More would probably answer "yes" to a direct question on this, but since no such question was included, it would be impossible to say how many would take a radical position. Certainly no large number of white Methodists is ready to advocate that the church abolish segregation if it means losing large numbers of whites.

*Conflict of valuations.* The findings discussed on the preceding pages suggest a basic conflict in valuations, in part a conflict between individuals but also a conflict within individuals. Two major opposing values emerge from the analysis of the opinions: *integration* and *opportunity.* Both values have the support of organized Christianity. The integration value is that of "brotherhood" and "fellowship," the "of one blood" part of the familiar Biblical quotation. Also in the churches, and especially in The Methodist Church, there has long been a recognition of the necessity of helping the Negro and providing opportunities for his development. The segregationist claims that the value of opportunity can best be served by limiting integration through a system of segregation. The integrationist feels that the value of integration is on a higher plane, so that when segregation is eliminated, opportunity will still be provided and in a fuller measure.

In the examination of the practices of The Methodist Church with regard to segregation, it will be seen that the opportunity value has been served much more consistently than has the value of integration. Most whites are rather easily persuaded by appeals based on the opportunity valuation. Some Negroes are also swayed by the opportunities offered them under segregation. However, Negro ministers are coming to an increasing conviction that fullness of opportunity in the church and society will be denied them until segregation can be eliminated. They see more clearly than do the whites that this value conflict must be faced squarely in the church if it is to be resolved successfully in society as a whole. As one of the Negro bishops of The Methodist Church said recently,

> We want opportunities to develop leadership, of course, but when that opportunity is provided only by limiting fellowship, I don't want it. *Without fellowship, there is no church!*

The emphasis upon the nature of the church as a fellowship of believers offers the best hope of resolving the apparent conflict between the values of integration and opportunity.

Guidance to the integrationist and to all those who are seeking a more Christlike approach to problems of race is offered by a statement adopted by the Federal Council of Churches, explaining the relation of ultimate goals to practical social action. Having affirmed that:

> In God all men are brothers regardless of the accidents of antecedents, entitled to equal and unsegregated opportunity for self-development without distinction either in law or fact on account of race or nationality. . . . In facing the issues of race, therefore, we associate ourselves with the declaration of the Cleveland Conference on world order: "Christians must act in situations as they exist and must decided what God's will demands of them there. At all times they must keep the ultimate goals clearly in view but they have equal responsibility to mark out attainable steps toward these goals, and support them. An idealism which does not accept the discipline of the achievable may lose its power for good and

ultimately lend aid to forces with whose purpose it cannot agree. If we accept,, provisionally, situations which fall short of our ultimate objective, we cannot be morally bound to sustain and perpetuate them. That would be stultifying. It is the possibility of change which is the bridge from the immediate situation to the Christian ideal. That possibility is an imperative for Christians, who must constantly maintain tension with any secular order."

In the spirit of this declaration it is in order to examine now the practices of Methodists with regard to segregation, to learn what progress they are making toward their goals. A study of the history of racial patterns within the denomination, of the jurisdictional system, of the denominational boards and institutions, and of the local churches of The Methodist Church may reveal gaps between their goals and present practices.

# ❦·163·❦

# Race and Racial Tension in the Church

## T. B. MASTON

Particularly after the successful Montgomery bus boycott (1955–56), led non-violently by Martin Luther King, Edgar Nixon and other black ministers and securing much of its organizational strength from religious networks amongst African-Americans, it was clear that in denominations with both white and black members, or in situations when white and black Christians met regularly, white church members could, and black church members would, no longer avoid relating their faith to their practice in race relations. The gradualist programme from 1957 is a response to rising tensions in the churches.

## Within the Church

The church is a creator of tension and is involved in that tension. The message it proclaims is a factor of considerable importance in the creation of racial tension. Among the underprivileged the gospel contributes to tension by the high value it places upon the individual. Being created in the image of God, he is of greater worth than all things material. He is lifted above the animal level. Through the acceptance of Christ he comes into the family of the heavenly Fathers; "he is a child of a king." He learns that his Father is no respecter of persons; that in his presence the privileged and powerful are on the same level as the under-privileged and oppressed. This creates within the hearts of the disinherited greater self-respect and a deepened, although somewhat restrained, dissatisfaction with the inequalities of life. The consequent pressure toward the equalizing of opportunities may be eased somewhat by the "other-worldly" emphasis which is innate, to a degree, in the gospel.

The message of the gospel would restrain one from selfishly seeking through

Source: T. B. Maston, 'Race and Racial Tension in the Church', *Christianity and World Issues*, New York, 1957, pp. 96–99; 110–15.

revolution improved status for himself, but it would and does inspire him to seek in Christian ways improved status for others. The gospel also creates tension, if taken seriously, within the minds and hearts of the privileged. It may be that the church is "the author of social refinement," is very conservative and sometimes remains "among the stubborn strongholds of racialism"; but the gospel it preaches and teaches is always more challenging than the one it practices. Paradoxically, the Christian church, which is usually a defender of the *status quo*, is, through the message it proclaims, the source of much if not most of the pioneering spirit that provides leadership for social and moral advance along many lines, including the racial. The church, which inspires through its message social and spiritual pioneers, frequently ostracizes and persecutes as heretics the same pioneers. In other words, many of the heretics of the Christian faith have simply been those courageous souls who took seriously the ideals and purposes mediated to them by the church. Because many of those inspired by the church no longer feel free within the church, they frequently give themselves to leadership of movements outside the church, but movements which may represent advanced Christian positions. This is one of the reasons that the church is in constant danger of losing her moral and spiritual leadership. That leadership is threatened in the area of race. This threat is one of the factors in the growing tensions within the church.

The progressive steps taken by the church also contribute to heightened tension within the church. For example, the disapproval of segregation by the Roman Catholic Church and by the Federal Council of the Churches of Christ in America stirred the minds and challenged the consciences of many church groups and individual Christians. The wave of pronouncements on the race question by various Christian groups is both an evidence and a creator of increasing tension. These pronouncements, at times, may come close to being hypocritical, are frequently "couched in such general terms of sweet moralizing that they mean little in the practical world," and tend to skirt "around important matters." On the other hand, they may and often do represent real progress. At least they are used by the social pioneers of the church as a beachhead for additional exploration and advance.

## Within the Individual

The church as an institution not only faces the problem of tension within the church body but also within the minds and consciences of its members. "It is as a moral issue that the problem presents itself in the daily life of ordinary people." This war within the Christian conscience is between the Christian ideal and the very imperfect practice of that ideal. There is always a danger that the failure to narrow the gap between an ideal and its practice may lead one to doubt the validity of the ideal. Frustration concerning the application of the ideal to real life situations may and frequently does lead to moral cynicism. Some seek to escape the moral demands and the social implications of the Christian faith

411

by a "high indifference." But psychology and psychiatry have taught us that one does not solve one's problems by pushing them out of the conscious mind. In the subconscious they tend to create tensions and complexes that may be very damaging to one's personality.

The conscientious Christian faces over and over again the whole matter of the best Christian strategy. Is it wisest and best for him to seek to apply fully the Christian ideal now or to move gradually toward that ideal? If he does not apply it fully now is he failing to do so because he is honestly convinced that such represents the most effective strategy, or is it because he is a moral coward, afraid to face the consequences of full application? These are questions that more or less constantly disturb the socially and morally sensitive Christian; the more sensitive he is, the more he is under constant tension. This is a type of tension which cannot be understood by those who have not had to answer those and similar questions in an environment where whatever strategy one follows would seem to involve some evil as well as good. The sensitive Christian souls, who have a constant inner struggle between the demands of the Christian ideal in their lives and in their world and the very imperfect realization of that ideal, are the very ones who are the chief hope for progress in the application of the Christian spirit and Christian principles to every phase of our common life. The preceding correctly implies that there is no easy and universally applicable answer to the question of Christian methodology or strategy.

Tensions are felt not only by individuals of the majority race but also by those of the minority group. One writer suggests that the Negro "feels guiltless with regard to the racial situation." This may be true of most Negroes, but it does not relieve them of inner conflicts because of racial situations. The Negro, as is true of others in minority groups, has to fight against fear and hate, which are self-defeating and are contrary to the Christian spirit. He has to battle against a tendency to lose his faith in the Christian ideal and particularly in the efficacy of established Christian methods for the attainment of the Christian ideal. And "the minority man, when he abandons his ethical standards . . . is tempted to find refuge either in other-worldliness or in some brand of fanaticism." There is a disturbing element of truth in Gallagher's suggestion that "for the minority man or for the Caucasian, failure to resolve the inner conflict of conscience leads through uncertainty about ethical ideals to an open doubting of them, and finally to the abandoning of ethical standards in favor of some more easily sustained position."

Of course, there will not and cannot be a perfect realization of the Christian ideal in the area of race or any other realm of life. The test is not have we arrived at perfection, but are we working toward perfection. This is the test in our individual lives and also in the world. There is no progress toward the ideal without pressure toward or tension in regard to that ideal. This means that a certain amount of tension within the individual, the church, and the world is a healthy sign. It is one evidence that there is a pull or a struggle toward a higher, a better, a more ideal way of life. We should not be too worried about the prevalence of racial tension; we should be concerned about our response and the response of others to that tension.

## Relieve the Pressure Areas

There are two general ways that pressure may be relieved. The individual or the group may become convinced that the existing situation is more or less inevitable, and adjust to it or accept it. The other method is to attempt to remove, as far as possible, the occasions for the pressure. In the case of race relations, the latter method may be utilized by the minority or by the majority group. When it is a part of the strategy of the minority it is hard to keep it from increasing tension, at least for the time being, rather than decreasing it.

This method for the release of tension, if used by those of the majority group, would operate somewhat as follows: Let them examine the areas where those of the minority group are exerting the greatest pressure, and see if anything can be done to relieve the pressure in such areas. For example, if the main problem is segregation and particularly legal segregation, could the segregation laws be repealed? To answer the question wisely one would have to consider the effect of such repeal on the majority and on the entire racial situation. It is possible that the elimination of all "racial laws" would not change noticeably the relation of the races. The main thing, however, is that an honest effort to do something about any source of tension is a necessary step in its release. This is just as true of a group as it is of the individual. There must be a clear conscience, if such is ever entirely possible. At least there must be an honest effect to do something constructive.

## Education and Release.

Education in a number of ways and in several areas can contribute considerably to the release of racial tension. The lifting of the general educational level of both the majority and the minority groups, at least in the long run, will help. It may tend to increase the pressure by the minority for improved status; but even this increased pressure may be an element in the solution of the problem, and ultimately it may reduce the tension.

There is also needed a specialized program of racial education. This is particularly important for the majority. An intelligent approach to the racial issue will help to reduce the restraining pressure of the majority, and hence it will reduce some of the existing tension. It will enable the majority to keep in step, to a greater degree, with the pressure exercised by the better educated of the minority, and this will reduce the friction between the two groups. Among the important purposes of an effective "racial education program" are the following: to help people to get away from their prejudices and to change their habit of stereotyping races and individuals; to lead them to think of people as human beings rather than as members of a race or a class; and "to substitute

413

new indoctrinations for old."

If the educational program is to be adequate it must utilize many different educational agencies, instruments, and procedures. It must include more than the public school. The education received at the public school "is only a small part of that larger education which men receive from direct contact with the world." It is even possible, as Montagu suggests, that men do not really believe what they are taught in school, and they act only on that which they believe. An effective racial educational program must include not only the more or less formal educational institutions such as the home, the school, and the church; but it must include also the tremendously important informal and more or less incidental educational agencies such as the daily newspaper, magazines, the motion picture, the radio, and the television.

All of these agencies, if they are to make an effective contribution to the releasing of racial tensions, must give some attention to techniques, to strategies, to programs of action, as well as to the dissemination of information and the formulation of basic principles. This emphasis is particularly needed by the church. The church seems to have a weakness, although it is not peculiar to the church, to think that it solves a problem when it makes a pronouncement concerning it, or sets out in a very general way moral and spiritual principles applicable to the problem. The latter is tremendously important and should not be belittled, but the church must go beyond such generalizations if it is to be a constructive educational agency in the field of race relations. This does not mean that the church should identify itself with any organization or program of change. It does mean that it should do something within the framework of its own organization and program.

As a part of its educational approach to the race problem the church can and should utilize every educational agency that it has. The programs of these agencies should be used not only to inform the people but also to challenge the prejudices of the people. The agencies also can maintain mutually helpful contacts with those of other racial groups, entering into cooperative services with them. In addition, church members should be led to understand and to cooperate discriminatingly with agencies working for better race relations in the community.

In the whole program of education for better race relations, the Christian college maintains a difficult but strategic role. Logically the Christian college should blaze new trails in social strategy; it should provide much of the leadership for social and moral advance. It seems on the surface that Christian colleges should be the first to open their doors to all qualified young people regardless of their race. Under the pressure of legal action the tax-supported colleges and universities have been forced to receive as students those of the minority group. The problem of the church-related college is not so much with its faculty or its students as with its board of trustees and its constituency in general. The more directly these schools are controlled by the denomination owning them, the more difficult it seems to be for them to break with traditional

414

patterns. This should be understood by those who tend to be unduly critical of the social conservatism of so many church-related colleges.

There is a possibility, however, that the opening of its doors to Negro students will not be the main contribution of the Christian college to the releasing of racial tension. The Christian college should pass on to its students a Christian philosophy of life, a Christian interpretation of all of life. It should seek to build into their lives basic Christian principles and send them out into the world with a genuine Christian spirit and a driving passion to dedicate themselves to God and his will and way among men. If the Christian college can do that, those young people will make a definite and distinctive contribution to the righting of wrongs of our society, and hence they will be factors in the releasing of the tensions of society. Such, conceivably, might increase considerably the tension between such Christian-motivated young people and their friends and elders. This is the price frequently paid by social and moral pioneers. But the glorious thing is that this fact will not increase inner tension if one is conscious of working within the will of God and can hear his "Well done."

## Religion and Release

The church is both a creator and a reliever of tension. It is the church's responsibility to create tension in any area of life that does not conform to the Christian ideal. The religion which the church proclaims also possesses the most effective resources for the release of conflicts and tensions. It contains a message of sin and judgment, but also of repentance and forgiveness. It should be remembered, however, that true repentance is accompanied by an honest effort to overcome sin, to correct any wrong spirit or attitude, to make things right with those sinned against. In other words, repentance will not relieve tension in any area unless we attempt to do something about the conditions that have created out inner dissatisfaction and tension.

Unfortunately, however, the sincere Christian is frequently caught in a frustrating dilemma. For example, he may be convinced that if he goes too far right now in applying consistently the Christian ethic to race relations, or to other pressing social problems, he may lose all opportunity to serve. In other words, the tension may become too great between him, his friends, his neighbors, his community, and even his church. This posits a threat for him, but even worse for his family. He may find himself frustrated on every side. He wants to go all the way right now in applying the Christian ethic, yet he feels that he must compromise, to a degree, or be crucified; and he is not ready to be crucified. And what is more significant, he is not sure whether his crucifixion would serve the kingdom of God better than for him to relax the pressure a little, but to see that the tension is maintained in the right direction.

The Christian religion has a message that will give some relief to such frustrated individuals. It seems that they must maintain, in a sense, a constant interplay of action and repentance. They can be assured that God will graciously forgive and will give the sustaining grace and wisdom that is needed for the next advance. All of us can hope and believe that God will judge us not so much by our attainment as by the direction of our lives and by the rate of our progress to his ideal for us and our world.

Some may contend that the above represents a compromise, and that it is not true to original Christianity. Those who make such suggestions, in the main, have failed to read discriminatingly their New Testament, particularly its teachings concerning slavery. Furthermore, in the main, they are not involved personally in the most crucial phases of social conflicts such as the race problem. It is comparatively easy for a person to work out a theoretical solution for the most complex problems of life, so long as he does not have to apply his theory to actual situations. An understanding of some of the problems faced and some of the inner struggles of soul by many sincere Christians, particularly in the South, would mean more Christian charity by those who are not so directly involved in the conflict.

The church not only needs to deliver a message that will relieve the tension within the minds and hearts of its members, it also needs to do something to relieve the tension within the church as an institution. Churches have attempted to satisfy their consciences by making pronouncements, some quite liberal, on race relations. While pronouncements can and do make some contributions to the release of racial tension, yet they have inevitable limitations. The church cannot permanently pacify its conscience by beautiful generalities. The church as an institution, just as is true of its individual members, must undertake a consistent, constructive program to implement the ideals expressed in its pronouncements.

> The profound hunger of out time is not for brotherly words, but for brotherly deeds, not for the publishing of brave resolutions, but for the launching of brave experiments.

Such a program of action will create, at least in many churches, friction and tension. But the only hope for permanent relief is through such a program. The church should remember that any effective program of action involves more than moralizing, which Gallagher suggests is only the beginning of strategy. An effective program involves social engineering, and social engineering will require the cooperation of the church with those who have the social skills required to cope with racial pressure and problems.

A constructive program of action must also include the disinherited masses. The message of the church contains a vital word for the underprivileged and the dispossessed or, as Thurman expresses it, those "who stand with their backs against the wall." Jesus had a message for these; he was particularly interested in them.

> Wherever his spirit appears, the oppressed gather fresh courage; for he announced the good news that fear, hypocrisy, and hatred, the three hounds of hell that track the trail of the disinherited, need have no dominion over them.

The Christian religion can give to the oppressed and disinherited inner peace and victory. They can be assured that if they will, God can and will be their heavenly Father; that he looks on the heart and not on the outer conditions and circumstances. If God is a living reality within them, his presence will give them release from the inner tensions that are so destructive of all that is highest and best. It will prevent them from contending for the right in the wrong spirit. It will enable them to recognize the inequalities of life without hate. It will save them from frustration, because they can have a deep conviction that their heavenly Father will be on their side, will keep them from frustration, if their goals are within his will and their spirit is right. They can be assured that ultimately love and truth will triumph because God is truth; he is love; he is sovereign.

## The Individual's Responsibility

The church, through the gospel it proclaims, may offer release to whites and Negroes who are under tension; but they, if they are to have release, must appropriate the message delivered. Even the Lord himself cannot help an individual or a group that does not want to be helped.

This message of individual responsibility is in accord with the basic nature of the Christian gospel. Its word is addressed primarily to individuals; men as individuals are judged and redeemed. Furthermore, as individuals, men and women are held accountable by God, and if accountable unto God, then man "is not a slave to his environment." The Christian, as a citizen of two worlds, must not only answer to the mores but also to the Master.

It is the conflict between his environment, which would restrain and limit him, and the Christian message, which would lift and challenge him, that creates for the socially and spiritually sensitive soul his keenest and most distressing inner conflict. The main hope of progress, however, is in this tension, and the most reliable assurance of an easing of the tension is a movement toward the Christian ideal coupled with a genuine sense of humility and a continuing spirit of repentance and renewal of fellowship with God, who has "made from one every nation of men to live on all the face of the earth."

# ❧·164·❧

# Pilgrimage to Nonviolence

## MARTIN LUTHER KING

The leadership of Martin Luther King (1929–1968) in the civil rights struggle is identified with the method of non-violent direct action. For King it was not merely a tactic but arose from his appreciation of the spiritual force of Gandhi's ideas in the campaign for Indian independence and from his conviction of the persuasive and essentially religious power of redemptive suffering, expressed in the American context through non-violence. Non-violence also guaranteed that purity of spirit would suffuse the means to a pure end since it offered a disinterested Christian love even towards opponents. King and his associates were not devoid of hard, tactical calculations but his style of leadership expressed his religious vision.

First, it must be emphasized that nonviolent resistance is not a method for cowards; it does resist. If one uses this method because he is afraid or merely because he lacks the instruments of violence, he is not truly nonviolent. This is why Gandhi often said that if cowardice is the only alternative to violence, it is better to fight. He made this statement conscious of the fact that there is always another alternative: no individual or group need submit to any wrong, nor need they use violence to right the wrong; there is the way of nonviolent resistance. This is ultimately the way of the strong man. It is not a method of stagnant passivity. The phrase "passive resistance" often gives the false impression that this is a sort of "do-nothing method" in which the resister quietly and passively accepts evil. But nothing is further from the truth. For while the nonviolent resister is passive in the sense that he is not physically aggressive toward his opponent, his mind and emotions are always active, constantly seeking to persuade his opponent that he is wrong. The method is passive physically, but strongly active spiritually. It is not passive non-resistance to evil, it is active nonviolent resistance to evil.

A second basic fact that characterizes nonviolence is that it does not seek to

Source: Martin Luther King, 'Pilgrimage to Nonviolence', *Stride Toward Freedom*, London, 1959, pp. 96–101. © by Laurence Pollinger and the Estate of Martin Luther King.

defeat or humiliate the opponent, but to win his friendship and understanding. The nonviolent resister must often express his protest through noncoöperation or boycotts, but he realizes that these are not ends themselves; they are merely means to awaken a sense of moral shame in the opponent. The end is redemption and reconciliation. The aftermath of nonviolence is the creation of the beloved community, while the aftermath of violence is tragic bitterness.

A third characteristic of this method is that the attack is directed against forces of evil rather than against persons who happen to be doing the evil. It is evil that the nonviolent resister seeks to defeat, not the persons victimized by evil. If he is opposing racial injustice, the nonviolent resister has the vision to see that the basic tension is not between races. As I like to say to the people in Montgomery:

> The tension in this city is not between white people and Negro people. The tension is, at bottom, between justice and injustice, between the forces of light and the forces of darkness. And if there is a victory, it will be a victory not merely for fifty thousand Negroes, but a victory for justice and the forces of light. We are out to defeat injustice and not white persons who may be unjust.

A fourth point that characterizes nonviolent resistance is a willingness to accept suffering without retaliation, to accept blows from the opponent without striking back. "Rivers of blood may have to flow before we gain our freedom, but it must be our blood," Gandhi said to his countrymen. The nonviolent resister is willing to accept to violence if necessary, but never to inflict it. He does not seek to dodge jail. If going to jail is necessary, he enters it "as a bridegroom enters the bride's chamber."

One may well ask: "What is the nonviolent resister's justification for this ordeal to which he invites men, for this mass political application of the ancient doctrine of turning the other cheek?" The answer is found in the realization that unearned suffering is redemptive. Suffering, the nonviolent resister realizes, has tremendous educational and transforming possibilities. "Things of fundamental importance to people are not secured by reason alone, but have to be purchased with their suffering," said Gandhi. He continues: "Suffering is infinitely more powerful than the law of the jungle for converting the opponent and opening his ears which are otherwise shut to the voice of reason."

A fifth point concerning nonviolent resistance is that it avoids not only external physical violence but also internal violence of spirit. The nonviolent resister not only refuses to shoot his opponent but he also refuses to hate him. At the center of nonviolence stands the principle of love. The nonviolent resister would contend that in the struggle for human dignity, the oppressed people of the world must not succumb to the temptation of becoming bitter or indulging in hate campaigns. To retaliate in kind would do nothing but intensify the existence of hate in the universe. Along the way of life, someone must have sense enough and morality enough to cut off the chain of hate. This can only be done by projecting the ethic of love to the center of our lives.

In speaking of love at this point, we are not referring to some sentimental or affectionate emotion. It would be nonsense to urge men to love their oppressors in an affectionate sense. Love in this connection means understanding, redemptive good will. Here the Greek language comes to our aid. There are three words for love in the Greek New Testament. First, there is *eros*. In Platonic philosophy *eros* meant the yearning of the soul for the realm of the divine. It has come now to mean a sort of aesthetic or romantic love. Second, there is *philia* which means intimate affection between personal friends. *Philia* denotes a sort of reciprocal love; the person loves because he is loved. When we speak of loving those who oppose us, we refer to neither *eros* nor *philia*; we speak of a love which is expressed in the Greek word *agape*. *Agape* means understanding, redeeming good will for all men. It is an overflowing love which is purely spontaneous, unmotivated, groundless, and creative. It is not set in motion by any quality or function of its object. It is the love of God operating in the human heart.

*Agape* is disinterested love. It is a love in which the individual seeks not his own good, but the good of his neighbor (I Cor. 10:24). *Agape* does not begin by discriminating between worthy and unworthy people, or any qualities people possess. It begins by loving others *for their sakes*. It is an entirely "neighbor-regarding concern for others," which discovers the neighbor in every man it meets. Therefore, *agape* makes no distinction between friend and enemy; it is directed toward both. If one loves an individual merely on account of his friendliness, he loves him for the sake of the benefits to be gained from the friendship, rather than for the friend's own sake. Consequently, the best way to assure oneself that Love is disinterested is to have love for the enemy-neighbor from whom you can expect no good in return, but only hostility and persecution.

Another basic point about *agape* is that it springs from the *need* of the other person—his need for belonging to the best in the human family. The Samaritan who helped the Jew on the Jericho Road was "good" because he responded to the human need that he was presented with. God's love is eternal and fails not because man needs his love. St. Paul assures us that the loving act of redemption was done "while we were yet sinners"—that is, at the point of our greatest need for love. Since the white man's personality is greatly distorted by segregation, and his soul is greatly scarred, he needs the love of the Negro. The Negro must love the white man, because the white man needs his love to remove his tensions, insecurities, and fears.

*Agape* is not a weak, passive love. It is a love in action. *Agape* is love seeking to preserve and create community. It is insistence on community even when one seeks to break it. *Agape* is a willingness to sacrifice in the interest of mutuality. *Agape* is a willingness to go to any length to restore community. It doesn't stop at the first mile, but it goes the second mile to restore community. It is a willingness to forgive, not seven times, but seventy times seven to restore community. The cross is the eternal expression of the length to which God will go in order to restore broken community. The resurrection is a symbol of God's triumph over all the forces that seek to block community. The Holy Spirit is the continuing community creating reality that moves through history. He who works against community is working against the whole of creation. Therefore, if I respond to hate with a reciprocal hate I do nothing but intensify the cleavage in broken community. I can only close the gap in broken community by meeting hate with love. If I meet hate with hate, I become depersonalized, because creation is so designed that my personality can only be fulfilled in the context of community. Booker T. Washington was right:

> Let no man pull you so low as to make you hate him.

When he pulls you that low he brings you to the point of working against community; he drags you to the point of defying creation, and thereby becoming depersonalized.

In the final analysis, *agape* means a recognition of the fact that all life is interrelated. All humanity is involved in a single process, and all men are brothers. To the degree that I harm my brother, no matter what he is doing to me, to that extent I am harming myself. For example, white men often refuse federal aid to education in order to avoid giving the Negro his rights; but because all men are brothers they cannot deny Negro children without harming their own. They end, all efforts to the contrary, by hurting themselves. Why is this? Because men are brothers. If you harm me, you harm yourself.

Love, *agape*, is the only cement that can hold this broken community together. When I am commanded to love, I am commanded to restore community, to resist injustice, and to meet the needs of my brothers.

A sixth fact about nonviolent resistance is that it is based on the conviction that the universe is on the side of justice. Consequently, the believer in nonviolence has deep faith in the future. This faith is another reason why the nonviolent resister can accept suffering without retaliation. For he knows that in his struggle for justice he has cosmic companionship. It is true that there are devout believers in nonviolence who find it difficult to believe in a personal God. But even these persons believe in the existence of some creative force that works for universal wholeness. Whether we call it an unconscious process, an impersonal Brahman, or a Personal Being of matchless power and infinite love, there is a creative force in this universe that works to bring the disconnected aspects of reality into a harmonious whole.

# ⚵·165·⚵

# The Voodoo Cult
# [Nation of Islam] among
# Negro Migrants in Detroit

## ERDMANN DOANE BEYNON

The interest of this near contemporary account of the beginnings of the
'Nation of Islam' is that it provides some detail on W. D. Fard, the
mysterious initial prophet, and on some of the early difficulties and schisms
of the cult.

The Negro sect known to its members as the "Nation of Islam" or the
"Muslims," but to the police as the Voodoo Cult, has significance for social
research because of its synthesis of heterogeneous cultural elements and partly
because of its unique expression of race consciousness. If the movement be
viewed as the life-cycle of a cult, however, its various phases tend to show an
orderly progression through which the attitudes of its devotees were molded to
a common pattern. There developed among them a way of living which isolated
them to a certain extent from all persons not members of their cult, even though
they themselves remained scattered among an urban population of their own
race and color. In their trade relations the members of this cult have continued
to live, like other Negroes, within the ecological organization of the Negro
community of Detroit. Their principal occupational adjustment has been factory
labor, and thus the cult members have maintained a functional relationship with
the metropolitan economy outside of the Negro community. At the same time,
however, they have severed contacts with the social organization of the
community in which they live, so that they have gained isolation almost as
effectively as did the members of agricultural religious communities who
migrated to new homes.

Source: Erdmann Doane Beynon, 'The Voodoo Cult [Nation of Islam] among Negro Migrants
in Detroit', *American Journal of Sociology*, May 1938. © 1938 by University of Chicago Press.

## The Beginning of the Movement

The prophet and founder of the cult made his first appearance among the Negroes of Detroit as a peddler. Like other Arab and Syrian peddlers, he went from house to carrying his waves.

> He came first to our houses selling raincoats, and then afterwards silks. In this way he could get into people's houses, for every woman was eager to see the nice things the peddlers had for sale. He told us that the silks he carried were the same kind that our people used in their home country and that he had come from there. So we all asked him to tell us about our own country. If we asked him to eat with us, he would eat whatever we had on the table, but after the meal he began to talk: "Now don't eat his food. It is poison for you. The people in your own country do not eat it. Since they eat the right kind of food they have the best health all the time. If you would live just like the people in your home country, you would never be sick any more." So we all wanted him to tell us more about ourselves and about our home country and about how we could be free from rheumatism, aches and pains.

At the stranger's suggestion a group of people was invited to one of the houses visited by him, so that on a particular evening they all might hear the story in which all alike were so much interested. Accustomed as these people were to the cottage prayer meetings of the Negro Methodist and Baptist churches they found no difficulty in holding informal meetings in their homes.

The former peddler now assumed the role of prophet. During the early period of his ministry he used the Bible as his textbook, since it was the only religious book with which the majority of his hearers were familiar. With growing prestige over a constantly increasing group the prophet became bolder in his denun-ciation of the Caucasians and began to attack the teachings of the Bible in such a way as to shock his hearers and bring them to an emotional crisis. Brother Challar Sharrieff told of the crisis through which he himself passed after hearing the prophet's message:

> The very first time I went to a meeting I heard him say: "The Bible tells you that the sun rises and sets. That is not so. The sun stands still. All your lives you have been thinking that the earth never moved. Stand and look toward the sun and know that it is the earth you are standing on which is moving." Up to that day I always went to the Baptist church. After I heard that sermon from the prophet, I was turned around completely. When I went home and heard that dinner was ready, I said: "I don't want to eat dinner. I just want to go back to the meetings." I wouldn't eat my meals but I goes back that night and I goes to every meeting after that. Just to think that the sun above me never moved at all and that the earth we are on was doing all the moving. That changed everything for me.

The report of the prophet's message spread through the Negro community. Many of those who heard him invited their friends and relatives to come to the meetings, appealing either to their curiosity or to deeper interests. The attendance at the house meetings increased so much that the prophet was compelled to divide his hearers into several groups, the members of each of which were permitted to hear his message only at the time assigned to their group. The inconvenience was so obvious that the prophet's followers readily contributed money sufficiently to hire a hall which was fitted up as the Temple.

## The Prophet

Although the prophet lived in Detroit from July 4, 1930, until June 30, 1934, virtually nothing is known about him, save that he "came from the East" and that he "called" the Negroes of North America to enter the Nation of Islam. His very name is uncertain. He was known usually as Mr. Wali Farrad or Mr. W.D. Fard, though he used also the following names: Professor Ford, Mr. Farrad Mohammed, Mr. F. Mohammed Ali. One of the few survivors who heard his first addresses states that he himself said:

> My name is W.D. Fard and I came from the Holy City of Mecca. More about myself I will not tell you yet, for the time has not yet come. I am your brother. You have not yet seen me in my royal robes.

Legends soon sprang up about this mysterious personality. Many members of the cult hold that the prophet was born in Mecca, the son of wealthy parents of the tribe of the Koreish, the tribe from which Mohammed the Prophet sprang, and that he was closely related by blood to the dynasty of the Hashimide sheriffs of Mecca who became kings of the Hejaz. He is said to have been educated at a college in England, in preparation for a diplomatic career in the service of the kingdom of the Hejaz, but to have abandoned every thing to bring "freedom, justice and equality," to "his uncle" living "in the wilderness of North America, surrounded and robbed completely by the Cave Man."

There has grown, however, among the members of the cult a belief that the prophet was more than man, as Brother Yussuf Mohammed claimed:

> When the police asked him who he was, he said: "I am the Supreme Ruler of the Universe." He told those police more about himself than he would ever tell us.

## The Negroes who heard the "Call"

Not all who attended the meetings and heard the stranger's message accepted him as a prophet. Many ridiculed his attack against the Caucasians and were angered by his criticisms of the churches and the preachers. During the four years of his ministry, however, approximately eight thousand Negroes in Detroit "heard the call" and became members of the Nation of Islam. Interviews with more than two hundred Moslem families showed that with less than half-a-dozen exceptions all were recent migrants from the rural South, the majority having come to Detroit from small communities in Virginia, South Carolina, Georgia, Alabama, and Mississippi. Investigations of cult members by the Wayne County Prosecutor's office also indicated the same origin. The interviews disclosed that the Moslems not only had migrated recently from the South, but also had visited their old homes in the South one or more times after their migration and before they had come into contact with the Nation of Islam. Through these visits they had become more conscious of race discrimination on the part of the Caucasians. After their brief sojourn in the North they tended to reinterpret with sinister implications incidents of race contact in the South. They began to realize that lynchings and the indignities of the Jim Crow system were perpetrated by Caucasians who worshiped the same God as they did and worshiped Him in the same way. In many of its parts the Secret Ritual of the cult reflects the aroused feelings with which these Negroes returned from their visits to the South.

> Me and my people who have been lost from home for 379 years have tried this so-called mystery God for bread, clothing and a home. And we receive nothing but hard times, hunger, naked and out of doors. Also was beat and killed by the ones that advocate that kind of God.

The illiteracy of the southern Negroes now seemed due to Caucasian "tricknollogy."

> Why does the devil keep our people illiterate? So that he can use them for a tool and also a slave. He keeps them blind to themselves so that he can master them.

Awakened already to a consciousness of race discrimination, these migrants from the South came into contact with militant movements among northern Negroes. Practically none of them had been in the North prior to the collapse of the Marcus Garvey movement. A few of them had come under the influence of the Moorish–American cult which succeeded it. The effect of both these movements upon the future members of the Nation of Islam was largely indirect. Garvey taught the Negroes that their homeland was Ethiopia. The Noble Drew Ali, the prophet of the Moorish–Americans, proclaimed that these people were "descendants of Morrocans [sic]." The newer migrants entered a social milieu in which the atmosphere was filled with questions about the origin of their people. Long before their new prophet appeared among them they were wondering who they were and whence they had come.

The migrants did not find life in the North as pleasant as they had expected it to be , when first they came to the "land of hope," as the North was known in Negro poetry and song. The depression deprived them of their means of livelihood, and they suffered their first experience of urban destitution. Though public relief came to their rescue, the attitudes shown by the welfare agents increased their hatred of the Caucasian civilization. Forced to stand waiting for hours to receive their dole, these people began to believe that race discrimination was evident in the North as well as in the South. The welfare workers—including those even of their own race—became symbolic of all that these people hated.

> An Asiatic trend among Negro dole recipients of the Elmwood district, noted at the time as a passing whim, to-day came back with horror to two women welfare workers on learning that the fanatical Robert Harris had intended them for human sacrifices as infidels . . . . Harris stated to the police that each of these was a "no good Christian," and that they would have been sacrificed if he knew where he could have found them.

A further disillusionment came from their own physical discomfort resulting from the life in crowded quarters in a northern city. Unaccustomed to the climate of the North, and especially to its winters, these people soon developed many bodily ailments. Their condition is described by the Prophet Fard in his teaching:

> He had fever, headaches, chills, grippe, hay fever, regular fever, rheumatism, also pains in all joints. He was disturbed with foot ailment and toothaches. His pulse beat more than eighty-eight times per minute: therefore he goes to the doctor every day and gets medicine for every day in the year: one after each meal and three times a day, also one at bedtime.

The migrants realized that they suffered much more physical pain than they had in their old homes. They connected this suffering with the civilization of the white man to whose cities they had come. Even before they met the prophet, they had begun to blame the Caucasian for their aches and pains.

Maladjusted migrant Negroes came into contact with the prophet at the informal meetings in their own homes. With the change to temple services the movement took on a more formal character. The teaching became systematized. Membership was recognized and "registered." The movement itself became organized in a hierarchical manner.

The prophet's message was characterized by his ability to utilize to the fullest measure the environment of his followers. Their physical and economic difficulties alike were used to illustrate the new teaching. Similarly, biblical prophecies and the teaching of Marcus Garvey and Noble Drew Ali were cited as foretelling the coming of the new prophet. As additional proofs of his message, the prophet referred his followers to the writings of Judge Rutherford, of Jehovah's Witnesses, to a miscellaneous collection of books on Freemasonry and its symbolism, and to some well-known works, such as Breasted's *Conquest of Civilization* and Hendrik van Loon's *Story of Mankind*. Since many of these people were illiterate, it became necessary to organize classes in English so that they might be able to read "the proofs about themselves." They were also instructed to purchase radios in order that they might listen to the addresses of Judge Rutherford, Frank Norris, the Baptist fundamentalist, and others. The prophet explained to the people that the recommended books and addresses were symbolic and could be understood only through the interpretation which he himself would give at the temple services. The Koran itself was soon introduced as the most authoritative of all texts for the study of the new faith. The prophet however, used only the Arabic text which he translated and explained to the believers. Here too they were completely dependent upon his interpretation.

To give more systematic character to his teaching, the prophet himself prepared certain texts which served as authoritative manuals of the religion and were memorized verbatim by all who became members of the Nation of Islam.

The prophet's teaching was in substance as follows:

426

The black men in North America are not Negroes, but members of the lost tribe of Shebazz, stolen by traders from the Holy City of Mecca 379 years ago. The prophet came to America to find that to bring back to life his long lost brethren, from whom the Caucasians had taken away their language, their nation and their religion. Here in America they were living other than themselves. They must learn that they are the original people, noblest of the nations of the earth. The Caucasians are the colored people, since they have lost their original color. The original people must regain their religion, which is Islam, their language, which is Arabic, and their culture, which is astronomy and higher mathematics, especially calculus. They must live according to the law of Allah, avoiding all meat of "poison animals," hogs, ducks, geese, 'possums and catfish. they must give up completely the use of stimulants, especially liqor. They must clean themselves up—both their bodies and their houses. If in this way they obeyed Allah, he would take them back to the Paradise from which they had been stolen—the Holy City of Mecca.

Those who accepted this teaching became new men and women, or, as the prophet expressed it, were restored to their original and true selves. As a mark of this restoration the prophet gave them back their original names which the Caucasians had taken from them. Since a sum of money—usually ten dollars— was required to secure the original name, this work must have been extremely profitable to the prophet. Each new believer wrote a separate letter asking for his original name, which the prophet was supposed to know through the Spirit of Allah within him. Examples of the changed names are:

Joseph Shepard became Jam Sharrieff
Lindsey Garrett became Hazziez Allah
Henry Wells became Anwar Pasha
William Blunt became Sharrieff Allah.

Apparent mistakes sometimes occurred when three or more brothers applied for new names, neglecting to mention in their letters that they were blood brothers. Thus, despite his omniscience, the prophet once gave the surnames of Sharrieff, Karriem, and Mohammed to the three Poole brothers. The prophet explained this seeming mistake as due to his divine knowledge of the different paternity of the three brothers.

The people who secured the new names value them as their greatest treasure.

"I wouldn't give up my righteous name. That name is my life."

They became so ashamed of their old slaves names that they consider that they could suffer no greater insult than to be addressed by the old name. They sought to live in conformity with the Law of Islam as revealed to them by the prophet, so that they might be worthy of their original names. Gluttony, drunkenness, idleness, and extra-marital sex relations, except with ministers of Islam, were prohibited completely. They bathed at least once a day and kept their houses scrupulously clean, so that they might put away all marks of the slavery from which the restoration of the original name had set them free.

The rapid increase in membership made necessary the development of a formal organization. Subsidiary organizations had been established as the need for them arose. Chief of these was the University of Islam to which the children of Moslem families were sent rather than to the public schools. Here they were taught the "knowledge of our own," rather than the "civilization of the Caucasian devils." Courses were given in "higher mathematics," astronomy, and the "general knowledge and ending of the spook civilization." That women might keep their houses clean and cook food properly, there was established the Moslem Girls, Training and General Civilization Class. Fear of trouble with the unbelievers, especially with the police, led to the founding of the Fruit of Islam—a military organization for the men who were drilled by captains and taught tactics and the use of firearms. Each of these organizations was under the control of a group of officers trained specially by the prophet for their task. Finally the entire movement was placed under a Minister of Islam and a corps of assistant ministers, all of whom had been selected and trained by the prophet. Within three years the prophet not only began the movement but organized it so well that he himself was able to recede into the background, appearing almost never to his followers during the final months of his residence in Detroit. This was undoubtedly an important factor in the cult's survival after the prophet's departure.

Inherent apparently in the prophet's message were certain teachings which, from the very beginning of the movement, led to schisms within the membership of the cult and to persecution from without.

The prophet proclaimed that his followers did not belong to America. They were citizens of the Holy City of Mecca and their only allegiance was to the Moslem flag. Their children must be removed from the public schools and sent to the University of Islam. In revolt against this position, Abdul Mohammed, one of the first officers in the temple, seceded and organized a small Moslem group of his own in which the cardinal principle was loyalty to the Constitution of the United States and to its flag. The attendance officers of the Board of Education and the police attempted to break up the University of Islam and to compel the children to return to the public schools. This led to a severe riot in which the members of the cult tried to storm the police headquarters. Fearful of race riots, the judges of the recorder's court released with suspended sentence almost all of the rioters. Since that time the University of Islam has continued its classes.

More serious difficulties arose over the question of human sacrifice. The prophet's position on this question was never made clear. He taught explicitly that it was the duty of every Moslem to offer as sacrifice four Caucasian devils in order that he might return to his home in Mecca. The prophet also taught that Allah demands obedience unto death from his followers. No Moslems dare refuse the sacrifice of himself or of his loved ones if Allah requires it. On November 21, 1932, the people of Detroit became conscious of the presence of the cult through its first widely publicized human sacrifice. A prominent member, Robert Harris, renamed Robert Karriem, erected an altar in his home at 1249 Dubois Street and invited his roomer, John J. Smith, to present himself

428

as a human sacrifice, so that he might become, as Harris said, "the Saviour of the world." Smith agreed, and at the hour appointed for the sacrifice—9:00 A.M.—Harris plunged a knife into Smith's heart. After constant recurrences of rumors of human sacrifice or attempted sacrifice, on January 20, 1937, Verlene McQueen, renamed Verlene Ali, brother of one of the assistant ministers, was arrested as he prepared for the ceremonial slaying and cooking of his wife and daughter. This sacrifice was, as he said, to have "cleansed him from all sin."

These cases of human sacrifice have directed to the cult much attention from the Police Department so that the cult has been forced to pursue many of its activities in secret. The question of sacrifice has led also to serious internal clashes. "Rebels against the Will of Allah," as they are called, have left the Temple and organized another Temple of Islam, desiring to remain within the framework of the cult but to avoid human sacrifice, the necessity of which as an expiation of sin forms one of the most hotly debated subjects among the cult members.

Persecutions and schisms alike have tended to increase the cultural isolation of the members of this group. The effect of the schisms was selective, leaving within the parent organization those who were bound together by common attitudes and common loyalties. Attacks made on the cult by the Police Department have been instigated usually by the leaders of Negro organizations. These persecutions have led naturally to a greater solidarity among the cult members and to a constantly increasing isolation of the Moslems from the other residents of the Detroit Negro community.

## Efforts to Exploit the Movement

The solidarity and cultural isolation of the Moslems have rendered ineffectual the various attempts made by interested parties to redirect the activities of the cult in order to further their own particular purposes. The first of these efforts was made by the Communists in 1932, but the cult members rebuffed their appeal. Then came Major Takahashi, a reserve Japanese officer, who sought to lead the Moslems to swear allegiance to the Mikado. Only a small minority of the members followed him into the new movement he organized—The Development of Our Own. With his deportation, this schismatic movement came to nought. An Ethiopian, Wyxzewixard S. J. Challouehliczilczese, sought in June, 1934, to reorganize the movement as a means of sending financial support to Ethiopia. This too, was unsuccessful. At present the members of the cult have come under the influence of certain anti-Union interests and talk violently of the war of the C.I.O. against Allah, and the need of removing from the Planet Earth all Union organizers. While this trend seems very pronounced at present, it is unlikely to leave any permanent impression upon the movement, and still less likely to detach from the Nation of Islam any of its members.

## Adjustments of Cult Members in the Urban Economy

At the time of their first contact with the prophet, practically all the members of the cult were recipients of public welfare, unemployed, and living in the most deteriorated areas of Negro settlement in Detroit. At the present time there is no known case of unemployment among these people. Practically all of them are working in the automobile and other factories. They live no longer in the slum section around Hastings Street, but rent homes in some of the best economic areas in which Negroes have settled. They tend to purchase more expensive furniture, automobiles, and clothes than do their neighbors even in these areas of higher-class residence. This improved economic adjustment is due, doubtless, partly to postdepression conditions of employment and to the increased hiring of Negroes as a result of recent labor troubles. The members of the cult, however, claim that they have secured work much more easily than have other Negroes. They offer thanks to Allah for this evidence of his favor. To some extent their claim appears to be justified, though no statistical study has yet been made of comparative unemployment of cult members and other recent Negro migrants. Through the Nation of Islam they have gained a new status and a new confidence in themselves. When they meet Caucasians, they rejoice in the knowledge that they themselves are superiors meeting members of an inferior race. Employment managers tend to accept more readily persons whose appearance gives evidence of clean living and self-reliance, than those who show the marks of debauchery, defeat, and despair.

The ascetic manner of life of the Moslem also has contributed to their economic improvement. No money whatever is spent by them on liqor, tobacco, or pork. Their one meal of the day consists almost entirely of vegetables and fruits. Consequently their expenditure on food is significantly smaller than is that of other Negroes in Detroit. This economy in consumption, howver, is not extended to visible marks of status, such as houses, automobiles, and clothes. The prophet taught them that they are the descendants of nobles in the Holy City of Mecca. To show their escape from slavery and their restoration to their original high status, they feel obliged to live in good houses and to wear good clothes. Despite their expenditure of these items, members of the cult constantly declare that they are ashamed that they have not been able to purchase better commodities or to rent finer homes.

> This furniture is the best we could afford to buy here in the wilderness of North America, where we have to live other then ourselves. When we go home to Mecca, we will be able to get really good furniture, just like all our people who live there use.

## Relation to other Negro Cults

The story of the Nation of Islam cannot be considered as complete in itself. Militant and cultist movements among migrant Negroes in the cities of the North have formed a sort of tree. After one branch has grown, flourished, and begun to decay, another shoots up to begin over again the same cycle, though always with an increasing degree of race-consciousness and anti-Caucasian prejudice.

Out of the wreck of the Marcus Garvey movement, there sprang Phoenix-like the Moorish–American cult of which the prophet was Noble Drew Ali. After this prophet's disappearance and the stabilization of the movement as a formally organized denomination, there sprang up the Nation of Islam. Although the cultural isolation of the members of this cult has not declined during the three years of their prophet's absence, there are many evidences of the loss of militant aggressiveness which once characterized this group. The organization also is tending to become more amorphous. From among the larger group of Moslems there has sprung recently an even more militant branch than the Nation of Islam itself. This new movement, known as the Temple People, identifies the prophet, Mr. W. D. Fard, with the god Allah. To Mr. Fard alone do they offer prayer and sacrifice. Since Mr. Fard has been deified, the Temple People raise to the rank of prophet the former Minister of Islam, Rlijah Mohammed, now a resident of Chicago. He is always referred to reverently as the "Prophet Elijah in Chicago." A former assistant of his, the Haitian Theodore Rozier, has become the minister and director of the new movement.

Thus continues the chain of these movements, each running through its cycle of growth and decay and all of them interwoven as strands of a web. Fundamental to them all is the effort of migrant Negroes to secure a status satisfactory to themselves after their escape from the old southern accommodation of white and Negro.

# ⊰166⊱

# The Black Revolution

## MALCOLM X

Fard's successor in the Nation of Islam was Elijah Muhammad whose emergence is recorded in the immediately preceding source. Elijah's teachings were much more widely spread once Malcolm X become a prominent minister in the Nation of Islam in the 1950s. Malcolm X (1925–1965), born Malcolm Little, had a Garveyite father; Malcolm was converted to the Nation of Islam while in prison and as part of a process of self-education and self-realization. Here he enunciates some of the Nation's core doctrines and presents Elijah Muhammad's version of Islam as an instrument of liberation and African–American dignity.

There are just some quick questions that I think will provoke some thoughts in your minds and my mind. How can the so-called Negroes who call themselves enlightened leaders expect the poor black sheep to integrate into a society of bloodthirsty white wolves, white wolves who have already been sucking on our blood for over four hundred years here in America? Or will these black sheep also revolt against the "false shepherd," the hand-picked Uncle Tom Negro leader, and seek complete separation so that we can escape from the den of the wolves rather than be integrated with wolves in this wolves' den? And since we are in church and most of us here profess to believe in God, there is another question: When the "good shepherd" comes will he integrate his long-lost sheep with white wolves? According to the Bible when God comes he won't even let his sheep integrate with goats. And if his sheep can't be safely integrated with goats they certainly aren't safe integrated with wolves. The Honorable Elijah Muhammad teaches us that no people on earth fit the Bible's symbolic picture about the Lost Sheep more so than America's twenty million so-called Negroes and there has never in history been a more vicious and bloodthirsty wolf than the American white man. He teaches us that for four hundred years

Source: Malcolm X, 'The Black Revolution', 1964, in Benjamin Goodman, ed., *The End of White World Supremacy: Four Speeches by Malcom X*, New York, 1971, pp. 68–71.

432

America has been nothing but a wolves' den for twenty million so-called Negroes, twenty million second-class citizens, and this black revolution that is developing against the white wolf today is developing because The Honorable Elijah Muhammad, a godsent shepherd, has opened the eyes of our people. And the black masses can now see that we have all been here in this white doghouse long, too long. The black masses don't want segregation nor do we want integration. What we want is complete separation. In short, we don't want to be segregated by the white man, we don't want to be integrated with the white man, we want to be separated from the white man. And now our religious leader and teacher, The Honorable Elijah Muhammad, teaches us that this is the only intelligent and lasting solution to the present race problem. In order to fully understand why the Muslim followers of The Honorable Elijah Muhammad actually reject hypocritical promises of integration it must be first be understood by everyone that we are a religious group, and as a religious group we can in no way be equated or compared to the nonreligious civil rights groups. We are Muslims because we believe in Allah. We are Muslims because we practice the religion of Islam. The Honorable Elijah Muhammad teaches us that there is but one God, the creator and sustainer of the entire universe, the all-wise, all-powerful Supreme Being. The great God whose proper name is Allah. The Honorable Elijah Muhammad also teaches us that Islam is an Arabic word that means "complete submission to the will of Allah or obedience to the God of truth, God of peace, the God of righteousness, the God whose proper name is Allah." And he teaches us that the word Muslim is used to describe one who submits to God, one who obeys God. In other words a Muslim is one who strives to live a life of righteousness. You may ask what does the religion of Islam have to do with the American so-called Negro's changing attitude toward himself, toward the white man, toward segregation, toward integration, and toward separation, and what part will this religion of Islam play in the current black revolution that is sweeping the American continent today? The Honorable Elijah Muhammad teaches us that Islam is the religion of naked truth, naked truth, undressed truth, truth that is not dressed up, and he says that truth is the only thing that will truly set our people free. Truth will open our eyes and enable us to see the white wolf as he really is. Truth will stand us on our own feet. Truth will make us walk for ourselves instead of leaning on others who mean our people no good. Truth not only shows us who our real enemy is, truth also gives us the strength and the know-how to separate ourselves from that enemy. Only a blind man will walk into the open embrace of his enemy, and only a blind people, a people who are blind to the truth about their enemies, will seek to embrace or integrate with that enemy. Why, Jesus himself prophesied. You shall know the truth and it shall make you free. Beloved brothers and sisters, Jesus never said that Abraham Lincoln would make us free. He never said that the Congress would make us free. He never said that the Senate or Supreme Court or John Kennedy would make us free. Jesus two thousand years ago looked down the wheel of time and saw your and my plight here today and he knew the tricky high court, Supreme Court, desegregation decisions would only lull you into a deeper sleep, and the tricky promises of the hypocritical politicians on civil rights legislation would only be designed to advance you and me from ancient slavery to modern slavery. But Jesus did prophesy that when Elijah comes in the spirit and power of truth he said that Elijah would teach you the truth. Elijah would guide you with truth and Elijah would protect you with truth and make you free indeed. And brothers and sisters, that Elijah, the one whom Jesus has said was to come, has come and is in America today in the person of The Honorable Elijah Muhammad.

This Elijah, the one whom they said was to come and who has come, teaches those of us who are Muslims that our white slave masters have always known the truth and they have always known that truth alone would set us free. Therefore this same American white man kept the truth hidden from our people. He kept us in the darkness of ignorance. He made us spiritually blind by depriving us of the light of truth. During the four hundred years that we have spent confined to the darkness of ignorance here is this land of bondage, our American enslavers have given us an overdose of their own white-controlled Christian religion, but have kept all other religions hidden from us, especially the religion of Islam. And for this reason, Almighty God Allah, the God of our forefathers, has raised The Honorable Elijah Muhammad from the midst of our downtrodden people here in America. And this same God has missioned The Honorable Elijah Muhammad to spread the naked truth to America's twenty million so-called Negroes, and the truth alone will make you and me free.

The Honorable Elijah Muhammad teaches us that there is but one God whose proper name is Allah, and one religion, the religion of Islam, and that this one God will not rest until he has used his religion to establish one world—a universal, one-world brotherhood. But in order to set up his righteous world God must first bring down this wicked white world. The black revolution against the injustices of the white world is all part of God's divine plan. God must destroy the world of slavery and evil in order to establish a world based upon freedom, justice, and equality. The followers of The Honorable Elijah Muhammad religiously believe that we are living at the end of this wicked world, the world of colonialism, the world of slavery, the end of the Western world, the white world or the Christian world, or the end of the wicked white man's Western world of Christianity.

# ❧167❧

# Letters from Abroad

## MALCOLM X

Malcolm broke from the Black Moslems in early 1964 because of constraints imposed on his speech by Elijah Mohammad and because he wanted a more direct political engagement with the struggles of both African–Americans and the people of the colonial and ex-colonial world. He travelled to Africa and the Middle East, converted to what he now understood as true Islam and published letters about his experiences. In them he hinted at changing attitudes toward the relation of religion to race, changes which foreshadowed on his part a willingness to contemplate alliances with white radicals.

Jedda, Saudi Arabia
April 20, 1964

Never have I witnessed such sincere hospitality and the overwhelming spirit of true brotherhood as is practiced by people of *all colors and races* here in this ancient holy land, the home of Abraham, Muhammad and all the other prophets of the Holy Scriptures. For the past week I have been utterly speechless and spellbound by the graciousness I see displayed all around me by people *of all colors.*

Last night, April 19, I was blessed to visit the Holy City of Mecca, and complete the "Omra" part of my pilgrimage. Allah willing, I shall leave for Mina tomorrow, April 21, and will be back in Mecca to say my prayers from Mt. Arafat on Tuesday, April 22. Mina is about twenty miles from Mecca.

Last night I made my seven circuits around the Kaaba, led by a young Mutawif named Muhammad. I drank water from the well of Zem Zem, and then ran back and forth seven times between the hills of Mt. Al-Safa and Al-Marwah.

There were tens of thousands of pilgrims from all over the world. They were *of all colors,* from blue-eyed blonds to black-skinned Africans, but were all participating in the same ritual, displaying a spirit of unity and brotherhood

Source: Malcom X, 'Letters from Abroad', 1964, in George Breitman, ed., *Malcolm X Speaks*, New York, 1965, pp. 59-63. © 1965, 1989 by Betty Shabazz and Pathfinder Press.

that my experiences in America had led me to believe could never exist between the white and non-white.

America needs to understand Islam, because this is the one religion that erases the race problem from its society. Throughout my travels in the Muslim world, I have met, talked to, and even eaten with, people who would have been considered "white" in America, but the religion of Islam in their hearts has removed the "white" from their minds. They practice sincere and true brotherhood with other people irrespective of their color.

Before America allows herself to be destroyed by the "cancer of racism" she should become better acquainted with the religious philosophy of Islam, a religion that has already molded people of all colors into one vast family, a nation or brotherhood of Islam that leaps over all "obstacles" and stretches itself into almost all the Eastern countries of this earth.

The whites as well as the non-whites who accept true Islam become a changed people. I have eaten from the same plate with people whose eyes were the bluest of blue, whose hair was the blondest of blond, and whose skin was the whitest of white—all the way from Cairo to Jedda and even in the Holy City of Mecca itself—and I felt the same sincerity in the words and deeds of these "white" Muslims that I felt among the African Muslims of Nigeria, Sudan and Ghana.

True Islam removes racism, because people of all colors and races who accept its religious principles and bow down to the one God, Allah, also automatically accept each other as brothers and sisters, regardless of differences in complexion.

You may be shocked by these words coming from me, but I have always been a man who tries to face facts, and to accept the reality of life as new experiences and knowledge unfold it. The experiences of this pilgrimage have taught me much, and each hour here in the Holy Land opens my eyes even more. If Islam can place the spirit of true brotherhood in the hearts of the "whites" whom I have met here in the Land of the Prophets, then surely it can also remove the "cancer of racism" from the heart of the white American, and perhaps in time to save America from imminent racial disaster, the same destruction brought upon Hitler by his racism that eventually destroyed the Germans themselves. . . .

Lagos, Nigeria
May 10, 1964

Each place I have visited, they have insisted that I don't leave. Thus I have been forced to stay longer than I originally intended in each country. In the Muslim world they loved me once they learned I was an American Muslim, and here in Africa they love me as soon as they learn that I am Malcolm X of the militant American Muslims. Africans in general and Muslims in particular love militancy.

I hope that my Hajj to the Holy City of Mecca will officially establish the religious affiliation of the Muslim Mosque, Inc., with the 750 million Muslims of the world of Islam once and for all—and that my warm reception here in Africa will forever repudiate the American white man's propaganda that the black man in Africa is not interested in the plight of the black man in America.

The Muslim world is forced to concern itself, from the moral point of view in its own religious concepts, with the fact that our plight clearly involves the violation of our *human rights*.

The Koran compels the Muslim world to take a stand on the side of those whose human rights are being violated, no matter what the religious persuasion of the victim is. Islam is a religion which concerns itself with the human rights of all mankind, despite race, color, or creed. It recognizes all (everyone) as part of one human family.

Here in Africa, the 22 million American blacks are looked upon as the long-lost brothers of Africa. Our people here are interested in every aspect of our plight, and they study our struggle for freedom from every angle. Despite Western propaganda to the contrary, our African brothers and sisters love us, and are happy to learn that we also are awakening from our long "sleep" and are developing strong love for them.

Accra, Ghana<br>May 11, 1964

I arrived in Accra yesterday from Lagos, Nigeria. The natural beauty and wealth of Nigeria and its people are indescribable. It is full of Americans and other whites who are well aware of its untapped natural resources. The same whites, who spit in the faces of blacks in America and sic their police dogs upon us to keep us from "integrating" with them, are seen throughout Africa, bowing, grinning and smiling in an effort to "integrate" with the Africans—they want to "integrate" into Africa's wealth and beauty. This is ironical.

This continent has such great fertility and the soil is so profusely vegetated that with modern agricultural methods it could easily become the "breadbasket" of the world.

I spoke at Ibadan University in Nigeria, Friday night, and gave the *true* picture of our plight in America, and of the necessity of the independent African nations helping us bring our case before the United Nations. The reception of the students was tremendous. They made me an honorary member of the "Muslim Students Society of Nigeria," and renamed me "Omowale," which means "the child has come home" in the Yoruba language.

The people of Nigeria are strongly concerned with the problems of their African brothers in America, but the U.S. information agencies in Africa create the impression that progress is being made and the problem is being solved. Upon close study, one can easily see a gigantic design to keep Africans here and the African–Americans from getting together. An African official told me,

> When one combines the number of peoples of *African descent* in South, Central and North America, they total well over 80 million. One can easily understand the attempts to keep the Africans from ever uniting with the African–Americans.

437

Unity between the Africans of the West and the Africans of the fatherland will well change the course of history.

Being in Ghana now, the fountainhead of Pan-Africanism, the last days of my tour should be intensely interesting and enlightening.

Just as the American Jew is in harmony (politically, economically and culturally) with world Jewry, it is time for all African-Americans to become an integral part of the world's Pan-Africanists, and even though we might remain in America physically while fighting for the benefits the Constitution guarantees us, we must "return" to Africa philosophically and culturally and develop a working unity in the framework of Pan-Africanism.

# ❦168❦

# We are God's Chosen People

## ALBERT B. CLEAGE JR

Albert B. Cleage (b. 1911) was pastor of the Shrine of the Black Madonna in Detroit when he delivered a number of sermons speaking directly to African-Americans of the Black Nation as God's chosen people and seeking to convince them that a revolutionary struggle to maintain their dignity was God's will. The only criterion for right action was that it should make black people proud.

A s black people, we don't have a lot of separate dignities. We have one dignity. If you mess it up, you mess it up for all of us. Or you see our black kids acting a fool out on the streets. They are messing up *our* dignity. You know why they are doing it? Because they don't understand. Because they are living in a world in which they have been shattered—leaning walls, tottering fences. So they are out there fighting back in their own little way, making a fool of themselves for the man.

We have got to find dignity somewhere because we will never be a Nation until we can first build a sense of dignity. That means that anywhere, on the job, on the bus, on the street, there are certain things that the man is not going to make you do. What can he give you if he takes your dignity? Nothing he has is worth it. You say, "I've got to eat." And I say, "Eating is not that important." You say, "I've got a wife and children." I am not going to tell you that they are not that important. I am going to say that they *are* that important. They don't want a clown feeding them, and if you feed them, acting a clown, you are destroying them at the same time. "They only tear him down from his dignity." The Psalmist analyzed it all a long time ago, and he knew that it was possible to take a man and make a clown out of him.

John O. Killens means the same thing when he says the white folks took a black man and made a Nigger out of him. They robbed him of his dignity. The children of Israel remembered this one thing, and struggled to keep their dignity.

Source: Albert B. Cleage Jr, 'We are God's Chosen People', *The Black Messiah*, Kansas City, 1968, pp. 52–9. © 1968 by Sheed and Ward.

They remembered that God had chosen Israel.

Don't laugh at that because *we* are God's chosen people. You don't fully recognize yet what that means. When we talk about the Black Nation, we have got to remember that the Black Nation, Israel, was chosen by God. Out of the whole world God chose Israel to covenant with, to say,

> You will be my people and I will be your God.

What else does a man need for dignity? He didn't go to the big nations with their big armies. He went to this little nation and said,

> You are my chosen people.

Perhaps if we could just remember that we are God's chosen people, that we have a covenant with God, then we would know that God will not forsake us. Even in the midst of violence and oppression, we would know that we are God's chosen people. We could look the white man straight in the eye and say,

> There is nothing you can do to destroy us, and you cannot take from us our dignity.

The concept of the Nation must include the basic truth that the Nation consists of God's chosen people. Don't be afraid to say that the word "God" because this is the 20th Century. You know what God means. It means that somebody is taking care of us. Don't try to make something selfish out of God. Don't try to use God to get something for *you* that *you* want. Understand that God is going to take care of *us*, the Black Nation, because we are God's chosen people. Because of this simple fact, the enemy is not going to destroy us. The time of our greatest strength (I am talking now about black people in this country) has not been in recent years, when we have had jobs and money and the illusion of being accepted. The time of our greatest strength was back in slavery when our slave forefathers believed that God was going to do something for them. They didn't just sit down because they believed this and wait for God to free them. The Underground Railroad was possible because black men and women were willing to take risks to get free. These black men and women were willing to go back into slave territory to bring out their people.

Nat Turner's faith in God did not stop his insurrection, nor thousands of slave insurrections all over the South. Every time a black man led an insurrection, he knew that he was doing the will of God. When you fight, you must believe that you are doing the will of God. Just being mad is not enough. That is the trouble with most of our rebellions. We get mad because somebody did something we didn't like, and we start throwing Molotov Cocktails and breaking windows. This isn't enough. We must believe that our struggle is a revolutionary struggle designed to change the world and to establish us in our rightful position. We must have faith that we are doing the will of God who created us in his own image.

Anything that destroys a black man's dignity is bad. This is our yardstick. Just ask yourself, "Is this building a black man's dignity?" Then it is good. If it is destroying a black man's dignity, then it is bad. That is the only yardstick there is. It doesn't make any difference how much money is involved. Anything you do that makes black people proud, that is good. Anything that makes black people ashamed, that is bad. That is why so many black preachers in pulpits throughout this country are bad. They use the name of God but what they are doing is bad because they make black people ashamed. That is why Muhammad Ali is good, because what he did makes us proud. So he is good. What Muhammad Ali did and is doing is the will of God. You know how we know? Because it makes black people proud. That is God's will, but what preachers are doing in so many pulpits is bad. It doesn't make any difference how many times they say God on Sunday morning, or how big their Bible is, or how many songs they sing about what God is going to do in the great bye-and-bye. It is bad because they are destroying our dignity, and even the little children sitting in these churches are getting to the point where they are ashamed. It is bad, it is not the will of God.

Don't be afraid to try to figure it out in terms of the will of God. God wants us to be men. If he had wanted us to be something else, he would have made us snakes or bears. He made us men; he expects us to be men. We tend to forget. Back in slavery our people remembered. We look back and think that this is the time we would like to forget. But we must never forget it because back there we had men and women with dignity. In the midst of the most difficult conditions, they had dignity. There were men and women that Ole Massa couldn't break. That was what he was trying to do. The things he did were not only designed to make him money, but to break black men.

That is still what the white enemy is trying to do today, to break you. That is why he is happy to get Clara Ward and her singers to shuffle for him. That is why he is happy when he can get Roy Wilkins to issue ridiculous statements. He knows that he is making us ashamed. If he can take our little children and make them think that being a pimp is the greatest thing in the world, he is happy. He is breaking us, making us ashamed.

Everything he has done to us was intended to make us ashamed, to destroy our pride. Why do you think he gives black children second-class schools which teach white supremacy? Because he knows that this is one certain way to keep a people down, by robbing them of pride. It is a miracle that we have a Black Nation today, that so many black men and women and children believe that they are somebody, after the systematic effort that has gone into breaking us. But millions of us are bewildered and confused, not even understanding that the man is deliberately trying to break us by robbing us of our dignity.

I was talking to a friend of mine in the barber shop the other day. He means well. He bought a house out there where some of you are trying to buy or have already bought. He lived around the corner for a long time, but when he started making a little money he wanted something better for his children. He wanted good schools for them and a good neighborhood. So he took his children out of public school and put them into a Catholic school. He was getting the best for them. There were only a few black children in the school or in the neighborhood. Everything was so fine. He was telling me about his son.

I said, "You are destroying that child." He loves that boy more than anything in the world. He works 12 hour a day trying to do his best for the boy.

He said, "How am I destroying the child? Everything I do is for that boy. That's why I took him out there so he wouldn't be with these..."

"That is the first wrong thing, telling him that you took him out there so that he wouldn't be with us."

"But I look out on 12th Street at night and see little children running up and down the street. I don't want that for my children." So I said, "If I had to choose, I'd choose one of those running up and down 12th Street, because if he comes out of it alive, he is going to have some sense of identity with his own people. Out there where your child is, you have destroyed that possibility. How is he going to get it in a white Catholic school, in a white neighborhood? What can you say to him?"

"I tell him to stay in school and he will get a better job. He won't be like..."

"There you go again — won't be like *them*. That is what you are trying to say. You can get a better job, you can live in a white neighborhood, you can send your children to a white school, that is what you are trying to tell him. You are separating him from the Black Nation. You whole way of life is designed to separate him from his own people."

He said, "Oh, no, he knows he's black, he has pride in being black."

"Does he know that white people are his enemy?"

"That isn't so, white people are not his enemy," he said. "Let me give you a little illustration. My little boy and another little boy play together, and there is a little white girl who lives across the street. So my little boy and the boy he plays with were talking to the little white girl, and they asked her which one she liked the best. The little white girl said that she liked the other little boy best. She didn't like my boy best, yet the little boy she picked is darker than my little boy."

I said, "Now how about *that*. Do you think you have really proved your point? Don't you know that they were both little 'Niggers' to that little white girl, and don't you see what you have done? You've got your little black boy out there in a white neighborhood, begging a little white girl to say that she likes him. Now there's no hope for either one of you."

The important thing is that this black father doesn't see anything wrong with his little boy trying to get a little white girl across the street to say that she likes him.

I asked, "How many times have they called your little boy 'Nigger' in school?"

Now he was getting defensive, "Not much, just once or twice, that's all."

"Do you think that being called 'Nigger' once or twice a day is doing him a whole lot of good?" I asked. "And do you think that all these white folks teaching him all about white supremacy are really going to make him a better black man? Don't you think that all of this will ruin his mind?"

442

"No," he replied, "what he is learning is good. He's in the best school that I can afford."

I asked, "Don't you think that when he gets through the day with all those white teachers, priests, and nuns, he must hate you when he comes home because you are black and inferior?"

"Oh, no, you don't understand," he protested, "I am protecting him from all that. I will give you another illustration. You know all these slick-headed 'processes' that the boys wear in black neighborhoods? Well, out in our neighborhood, he never sees one. Well, the other day a teen-age black boy came to pick up a maid from across the street and he had a 'process.' He is nine years old and he had never seem a process, isn't that good?"

I said, "I'm on the verge of tears, go on with your story."

"Well, that night when I came home, he told me that he would like to have his hair fixed like that so it would be long and slick and shiny. He didn't know what to call it, but he wanted one."

I asked, "What did you think about that?"

He said, "I was glad that he won't see that kind of thing very often out where we live."

I said, "Aren't you worried about the fact that the very first time he saw a black boy with a 'process' he wanted one? Why do you think he wanted it? Can't you see that your little boy is ashamed of being black with kinky hair, and he wants to be white?"

He said, "Oh, no, it just shows what a little bad influence can do to a child."

There we have poor little black boy being torn to pieces by white people—or as the Psalmist says, "being shattered." And his poor father, thinking that he is doing the best thing for his child, sacrificing, working himself to death, and his wife working herself to death, and this poor little black boy going straight to hell. By "hell" I mean the place where a man has no dignity and no respect for himself.

We have only one basis for judgment. If anything gives a black man a sense of pride and dignity, it is good. If it destroys his pride and dignity, it is bad. Remember this when you get ready to buy a house in a white neighborhood. Is it going to give your child a sense of pride to be out there in an all-white school where he is despised by teachers and students alike? The public schools are not good and the fight to improve them seems almost futile, so you are going to send him to some Lutheran or Catholic school and destroy him completely. Many black people see other black people only through the white man's eyes. The white man has completely destroyed their love of self. They have no sense of pride. They are actually afraid of us and of our influences upon their children.

We are going to hurt their little children. From the front steps of the Church everyday, I see hundreds of little children who live in our neighborhood. They are all better off than this black child in his better white neighborhood. They look around and everybody is black. I may scream at them for throwing stones through the back windows, but I scream at them because I am concerned about them. I don't want them tearing up our Church building, but I don't hate them and I don't despise them. I can't tell them "Nigger" because they are part of me. And that is the way everybody else is, up and down the street. But out in my friend's better white neighborhood, his little boy isn't part of anything, and he knows it. He can walk up and down the street and ask little white girls whether or not they like him, but every day his dignity is slipping away and self-hate is taking its place.

Those of us who are in the Black Nation realize that we are God's chosen people. No matter what the enemy does to us, we are God's chosen people and we must love each other. We fight together against a common enemy, confident of ultimate victory because we are God's chosen people.

> How long will you set upon a man to shatter him, like a leaning wall, a tottering fence? They only plan to tear him down from his dignity.

# ⚛169⚛

# The Sources of Black Theology

## JAMES H. CONE

More explicitly than other religious spokesmen committed to Black Power, Cone tried to construct a theological basis for his position. In arguing that Black Power was consistent with the gospel, he claimed that theology must take seriously, and give meaning to, the black experience of oppression, pride in being black and the history of black resistance. A theology fit for African-Americans had to speak of a God completely in tune with their community.

## What are the Sources in Black Theology?

1 *Black Experience.* There can be no Black Theology which does not take seriously the black experience—a life of humiliation and suffering. This must be the point of departure of all God-talk which seeks to be black-talk. This means that Black Theology realizes that it is man who speaks of God; and when that man is black, he can only speak of God in the light of the black experience. It is not that Black Theology denies the importance of God's revelation in Christ; but black people want to know what Christ means when they are confronted with the brutality of white racism. The black experience prevents us from turning the gospel into theological catch phrases and makes us realize that they must be clothed in black flesh. The black experience forces us to ask, "What does revelation means when one's being is engulfed in a system of white racism cloaking itself in pious moralities?" "What does God mean when a policeman whacks you over the head because you are black?" "What does the Church mean when white churchmen proclaim they need more time to end racism?"

The black experience should not be identified with inwardness, as implied in Schleiermacher's description of religion as the "feeling of absolute dependence." It is not an introspection in which man contemplates his own ego. Black people are not afforded the luxury of navel gazing. The black experience is the

Source: James H. Cone, 'The Sources of Black Theology', *A Black Theology of Liberation*, Philadelphia and New York, 1970, pp. 54-61.

environment in which black people live. It is the totality of black experience in a white world where babies are tortured, women are raped, and men are shot. The black poet Don Lee puts it well:

> The true black experience in most cases is very concrete ... sleeping in subways, being bitten by rats, six people living in a kitchenette.

The black experience is existence in a system of white racism. The black man knows that a ghetto is the white way of saying that black people are sub-human and fit only to live with rats. The black experience is police departments recruiting more men and buying more guns to provide "law and order," which means making the city safe for white people. It is politicians telling blacks to cool it *or else*. It is George Wallace, Hubert Humphrey, and Richard Nixon running for President and Nixon winning. The black experience is college admin-istrators defining "quality" education in the light of white values. It is church bodies compromising and debating whether blacks are human. And because Black Theology is a product of that experience, it must talk about God in the light of it. The purpose of Black Theology is to make sense of black experience.

The black experience, however, is more than encountering white insanity. It also means black people making decisions about themselves which involve white people. Black people know that white people do not have the last word on black existence. This realization may be defined as Black Power, which is the power of the black community to make decisions regarding its identity. When this happens, black people become aware of their blackness; and to be aware of self is to set certain limits on other people's behavior toward oneself. The black experience means telling whitey what the limits are.

The power of the black experience cannot be overestimated. It is the power to love oneself precisely because one is black and a readiness to die if white people try to make one behave otherwise. It is the sound of James Brown singing, "I'm Black and I'm Proud" and Aretha Franklin demanding "Respect." The black experience is catching the spirit of blackness and loving it. It is hearing black preachers speak of God's love in spite of the filthy ghetto, and black congregations responding, "Amen," which means that they realize that ghetto-existence is not the result of divine decree but of white inhumanity. The black experience is the feeling one has when he strikes against the enemy of black humanity by throwing a live Molotov cocktail into a white-owned building and watching it go up in flames. We know, of course, that there is more to getting rid of evil than burning buildings, but one must start somewhere.

Being black is a beautiful experience. It is the same way of living in an insane environment. Whites do not understand it; they can only catch glimpses of it in sociological reports and historical studies. The black experience is possible only for black people. It means having natural hair cuts, wearing African dashikis and dancing to the sound of Johnny Lee Hooker or B. B. King, knowing that no matter how hard whitey tries, there can be no real duplication of black soul.

Black soul is not learned; it comes from the totality of black experience, the experience of carving out an existence in a society that says you don't belong.

The black experience is a source of Black Theology because the latter seeks to relate biblical revelation to the situation of black people in America. This means that Black Theology cannot speak of God and his activity in contemporary America without identifying him with the liberation of the black community.

2. *Black History.* Black history refers to the way black people were brought to this land and the way they have been treated in this land. This is not to say that only the American white man participated in the institution of slavery. But there was something unique about American slavery, namely, the white man's attempt to define black people as nonpeople. In other countries the slaves were allowed community, and there were slave rights. Slaves were human beings, and their humanity was protected (to some degree) by certain civil laws. Black history in America means the white people used every conceivable method to destroy black humanity. As late as 1857 the highest court of this land decreed that black people "had no rights which the white man was bound to respect." The history of slavery in this country reveals the possibility of human depravity; and the fact that this country still in many blatant ways, perpetuates the idea of the inferiority of black people shows the capabilities of human evil. If Black Theology is going to speak to the condition of black people, it cannot ignore the history of white inhumanity committed against them.

But black history is more than what whites did to blacks. More importantly black history is black people saying No to every act of white brutality. Contrary to what whites say in *their* history books, Black Power is not now. It began when the first black man decided that he had had enough of white domination. It began when black mothers decided to kill their babies rather than have them grow up to be slaves. Black Power is Nat Turner, Denmark Vesey, and Gabriel Prosser planning a slave revolt. It is slaves poisoning masters, and Frederick Douglass delivering an abolitionist address. This is the history that Black Theology must take seriously before it can begin to speak about God and black people.

Like Black Power, Black Theology is not new either. It came into being when black churchmen realized that killing slave masters was doing the work of God. It began when black churchmen refused to accept the racist white church as consistent with the gospel of God. The organizing of the African Methodist Episcopal Church, The African Methodist Episcopal Zion Church, the Christian Methodist Church, the Baptist Churches and many other black churches is a visible manifestation of Black Theology. The participation of the black churches in the black liberation struggle from the eighteenth to the twentieth century is a tribute to the endurance of Black Theology.

Black Theology focuses on black history as a source for its theological interpretation of God's work in the world because divine activity is inseparable from the history of black people. There can be no comprehension of Black Theology without realizing that its existence comes from a community which looks back on its unique past, visualizes the reality of the future, and then makes decisions about possibilities in the present. Taking seriously the reality of God's involvement in history, Black Theology asks, "What are the implications of black history for the revelation of God? Is he active in black history or has he withdrawn and left black people at the disposal of white insanity?" While the answers to these questions are not easy, Black Theology refuses to accept a God who is not identified totally with the goals of the black community. If God is not for us and against white people, then he is a murderer, and we had better kill him. The task of Black Theology is to kill gods who do not belong to the black community; and by taking black history as a source we know that this is neither an easy nor a sentimental task but an awesome responsibility.

3. *Black Culture.* The concept of black culture is closely related to black experience and black history. We could say that the black experience is what the black man feels when he tries to carve out an existence in dehumanized white society. It is black "soul," the pain and the joy of reacting to the whiteness and affirming blackness. Black history is the record of the joy and the pain. It is those experiences that the black community remembers and retells because of the mythic power inherent in the symbols for the present revolution against white racism. Black culture consists of the creative forms of expression as one reflects on the history, endures the pain, and experiences the joy. It is the black community expressing itself in music, poetry, prose and other art forms. The emergence of the concept of the Revolutionary Black Theatre with writers like LeRoy Jones, Larry Neal, Ed Bullins, and others is an example of the black community expressing itself culturally. Aretha Franklin, James Brown, Charlie Parker, John Coltrane, and others are examples in music. Culture refers to the way a man lives and moves in the world; it controls his thought forms.

Black Theology must take seriously the cultural expressions of the community it represents so that it will be able to speak relevantly to the black condition. Of course, Black Theology is aware of the danger of identifying the word of man with the Word of God, the danger Karl Barth persuasively warned against in the second decade of this century.

> "Form," he writes, "believes itself capable of taking the place of content. . . . Man has taken the divine in his possession; he has brought him under his management."

Such a warning is necessary in a situation alive with satanic creatures like Hitler, and it is always the task of the church to announce the impending judgement of God against the power of the state which seeks to destroy the weak. This is why Bonhoeffer said, "When Christ calls a man, he bids him come and die." Suffering is the badge of true discipleship. But is it appropriate to speak the same words to the oppressed? To apply Barth's words to the black–white context and interpret them as a warning against identifying God's revelation with black culture is to misunderstand Barth. His warning was appropriate for the situation in which it was given, but not for black people. Black people need to see some correlations between divine salvation and black culture. For too long Christ has been pictured as a blue-eyed honky. Black theologians are right: we need to dehonkify him and thus make him relevant to the black condition.

# ❧170❧

# Black Power

## MARTIN LUTHER KING

By 1967 King's vision and methods were seriously under challenge in some black communities. He claimed to recognize the psychological roots of Black Power and to value some expressions of it. His crucial criticism, however, was that its advocates failed to recognize its destructive capacities if it was divorced from Christian love. What is particularly striking, none the less, is that King's argument with Black Power was mostly conducted in non-religious language, as if the audience for which he contended, mostly young and urban, might be less drawn by religious language.

---

Black Power, in its broad and positive meaning, is a call to black people to amass the political and economic strength to achieve their legitimate goals. No one can deny that the Negro is in dire need of this kind of legitimate power. Indeed, one of the great problems that the Negro confronts is his lack of power. From the old plantations of the South to the newer ghettos of the North, the Negro has been confined to a life of voicelessness and powerlessness. Stripped of the right to make decisions concerning his life and destiny, he has been subject to the authoritarian and sometimes whimsical decisions of the white power structure. The plantation and the ghetto were created by those who had power both to confine those who had no power and to perpetuate their powerlessness. The problem of transforming the ghetto is, therefore, a problem of power—a confrontation between the forces of power demanding change and the forces of power dedicated to preserving the status quo.

Power, properly understood, is the ability to achieve purpose. It is the strength required to bring about social, political or economic changes. In this sense power is not only desirable but necessary in order to implement the demands of love and justice. One of the greatest problems of history is that the concepts of love and power are usually contrasted as polar opposites. Love is identified with a resignation of power and power with a denial of love. It was

Source: Martin Luther King, 'Black Power', *Chaos or Community?* London, 1967, pp. 36-41; 44-57. © by Laurence Pollinger and the Estate of Martin Luther King.

this misinterpretation that caused Nietzsche, the philosopher of the "will to power," to reject the Christian concept of love. It was this same misinterpretation which induced Christian theologians to reject Nietzsche's philosophy of the "will to power" in the name of the Christian idea of love. What is needed is a realization that power without love is reckless and abusive and that love without power is sentimental and anemic. Power at its best is love implementing the demands of justice. Justice at its best is love correcting everything that stands against love.

There is nothing essentially wrong with power. The problem is that in America power is unequally distributed. This has led Negro Americans in the past to seek their goals through love and moral suasion devoid of power and white Americans to seek their goals through power devoid of love and conscience. It is leading a few extremists today to advocate for Negroes the same destructive and conscienceless power that they have justly abhorred in whites. It is precisely this collision of immoral power with powerless morality which constitutes the major crisis of our times.

In his struggle for racial justice, the Negro must seek to transform his condition of powerlessness into creative and positive power. One of the most obvious sources of this power is political. In *Why We Can't Wait* I wrote at length of the need for Negroes to unite for political action in order to compel the majority to listen. I urged the development of political awareness and strength in the Negro community, the election of blacks to key positions, and the use of the bloc vote to liberalize the political climate and achieve our just aspirations for freedom and human dignity. To the extent that Black Power advocates these goals, it is a positive and legitimate call to action that we in the civil rights movement have sought to follow all along and which we must intensify in the future.

Black Power is also a call for the pooling black financial resources to achieve economic security. While the ultimate answer to the Negroes' economic dilemma will be found in a massive federal program for all the poor along the lines of A. Philip Randolph's Freedom Budget, a kind of Marshall Plan for the disadvantaged, there is something that the Negro himself can do to throw off the shackles of poverty. Although the Negro is still at the bottom of the economic ladder, his collective annual income is upwards of $30 billion. This gives him a considerable buying power that can make the difference between profit and loss in many businesses.

Through the pooling of such resources and the development of habits of thrift and techniques of wise investment, the Negro will be doing his share to grapple with his problem of economic deprivation. If Black Power means the development of this kind of strength within the Negro community, then it is a quest for basic, necessary, legitimate power.

Finally, Black Power is a psychological call to manhood. For years the Negro has been taught that he is nobody, that his color is a sign of his biological depravity, that his being has been stamped with an indelible imprint of inferiority, that his whole history has been soiled with the filth of worthlessness. All too few people realize how slavery and racial segregation have scarred the soul and wounded the spirit of the black man. The whole dirty business of slavery was based on the premise that the Negro was a thing to be used, not a person to be respected.

The historian Kenneth Stampp, in his remarkable book *The Peculiar Institution*, has a fascinating section on the psychological indoctrination that was necessary from the master's viewpoint to make a good slave. He gathered the material for this section primarily from the manuals and other documents which were produced by slaveowners on the subject of training slaves. Stampp notes five recurring aspects of this training.

First, those who managed the slaves had to maintain strict discipline. One master said, "Unconditional submission is the only footing upon which slavery should be placed." An other said, "The slave must know that his master is to govern absolutely and he is to obey implicitly, that he is never, for a moment, to exercise either his will or judgment in opposition to a positive order." Second, the masters felt that they had to implant in the bondsman a consciousness of personal inferiority. This sense of inferiority was deliberately extended to his past. The slaveowners were convinced that in order to control the Negroes, the slaves "had to feel that African ancestry tainted them, that their color was a badge of degradation." The third step in the training process was to awe the slaves with a sense of the master's enormous power. It was necessary, the various owners said, "to make them stand in fear". The fourth aspect was the attempt to "persuade the bondsman to take an interest in the master's enterprise and to accept his standards of good conduct." Thus the master's criteria of what was good and true and beautiful were to be accepted unquestioningly by the slaves. The final step, according to Stampp's documents, was "to impress Negroes with their helplessness: to create in them a habit of perfect dependence upon their masters."

Here, then, was the way to produce a perfect slave. Accustom him to rigid discipline, demand from him unconditional submission, impress upon him a sense of his innate inferiority, develop in him a paralyzing fear of white men, train him to adopt the master's code of good behavior, and instill in him a sense of complete dependence.

Out of the soil of slavery came the psychological roots of the Black Power cry. Anyone familiar with the Black Power movement recognizes that defiance of white authority and white power is a constant theme; the defiance almost becomes a kind of taunt. Underneath it, however, there is a legitimate concern that the Negro break away from "unconditional submission" and thereby assert his own selfhood.

Another obvious reaction of Black Power to the American system of slavery is the determination to glory in blackness and to resurrect joyously the African past. In response to the emphasis on their masters' "enormous power," Black

Power advocates contend that the Negro must develop his own sense of strength. No longer are "fear, awe and obedience" to rule. This accounts for, though it does not justify, some Black Power advocates who encourage contempt and even uncivil disobedience as alternatives to the old patterns of slavery. Black Power assumes that Negroes will be slaves unless there is a new power to counter the force of the men who are still determined to be masters rather than brothers.

It is in the context of the slave tradition that some of the ideologues of the Black Power movement call for the need to develop new and indigenous codes of justice for the ghettos, so that blacks may move entirely away from their former masters' "standards of good conduct." Those in the Black Power movement who contend that blacks should cut themselves off from every level of dependence upon whites for advice, money or other help are obviously reacting against the slave pattern of "perfect dependence" upon the masters.

Black Power is a psychological reaction to the psychological indoctrination that led to the creation of the perfect slave. While this reaction has often led to negative and unrealistic responses and has frequently brought about intemperate words and actions, one must not overlook the positive value in calling the Negro to a new sense of manhood, to a deep feeling of racial pride and to an audacious appreciation of his heritage. The Negro must be grasped by a new realization of his dignity and worth. He must standup amid a system that still oppresses him and develop an unassailable and majestic sense of his own value. He must no longer be ashamed of being black.

## II

Nevertheless, in spite of the positive aspects of Black Power, which are compatible with what we have sought to do in the civil rights movement all along without the slogan, its negative values, I believe, prevent it from having the substance and program to become the basic strategy for the civil rights movement in the days ahead.

Beneath all the satisfaction of a gratifying slogan, Black Power is a nihilistic philosophy born out of the conviction that the Negro can't win. It is, at bottom, the view that American society is so hopelessly corrupt and enmeshed in evil that there is no possibility of salvation from within. Although this thinking is understandable as a response to a white power structure that never completely committed itself to true equality for the Negro, and a die-hard mentality that sought to shut all windows and doors against the winds of change, it nonetheless carries the seeds of its own doom.

Before this century, virtually all revolutions had been based on hope and hate. The hope was expressed in the rising expectation of freedom and justice. The hate was an expression of bitterness toward the perpetrators of the old order. It was the hate that made revolutions bloody and violent. What was new about Mahatma Gandhi's movement in India was that he mounted a revolution on hope and love, hope and nonviolence. This same new emphasis characterized the civil rights movement in our country dating from the Montgomery bus boycott of 1956 to the Selma movement of 1965. We maintained the hope while transforming the hate of traditional revolutions into positive nonviolent power. As long as the hope was fulfilled there was little questioning of nonviolence. But when the hopes were blasted, when people came to see that in spite of progress their conditions were still insufferable, when they looked out and saw more poverty, more school segregation and more slums, despair began to set in.

Unfortunately, when hope diminishes, the hate is often turned most bitterly toward those who originally built up the hope. In all the speaking that I have done in the United States before varied audiences, including some hostile whites, the only time that I have been booed was one night in a Chicago mass meeting by some young members of the Black Power movement. I went home that night with an ugly feeling. Selfishly I thought of my sufferings and sacrifices over the last twelve years. Why would they boo one so close to them? But as I lay awake thinking, I finally came to myself, and I could not for the life of me have less than patience and understanding for those young people. For twelve years I, and others like me, had held out radiant promises of progress. I had preached to them about my dream. I had lectured to them about the not too distant day when they would have freedom, "all, here and now." I had urged them to have faith in America and in white society. Their hopes had soared. They were now booing because they felt that we were unable to deliver on our promises. They were booing because we had urged them to have faith in people who had too often proved to be unfaithful. They were now hostile because they were watching the dream that they had so readily accepted turn into a frustrating nightmare.

But revolution, though born of despair, cannot long be sustained by despair. This is the ultimate contradiction of the Black Power movement. It claims to be the most revolutionary wing of the social revolution taking place in the United States. Yet it rejects the one thing that keeps the fire of revolutions burning: the ever-present flame of hope. When hope dies, a revolution degenerates into an undiscriminating catchall for evanescent and futile gestures. The Negro cannot entrust his destiny to a philosophy nourished solely on despair, to a slogan that cannot be implemented into a program.

The Negro's disappointment is real and a part of the daily menu of our lives. One of the most agonizing problems of human experience is how to deal with disappointment. In our individual lives we all too often distill our frustrations into an essence of bitterness, or drown ourselves in the deep waters of self-pity, or adopt a fatalistic philosophy that whatever happens must happen and all events are determined by necessity. These reactions poison the soul and scar the personality, always harming the person who harbors them more than anyone else. The only healthy answer lies in one's honest recognition of disappointment even as he still clings to hope, one's acceptance of finite disappointment even while clinging to infinite hope.

We Negroes, who have dreamed for so long of freedom, are still confined in a prison of segregation and discrimination. Must we respond with bitterness and cynicism? Certainly not, for this can lead to black anger so desperate that it ends in black suicide. Must we turn inward in self-pity? Of course not, for this can lead to a self-defeating black paranoia. Must we conclude that we cannot win? Certainly not, for this will lead to a black nihilism that seeks disruption for disruption's sake. Must we, by fatalistically concluding that segregation is a foreordained pattern of the universe, resign ourselves to oppression? Of course not, for passively to cooperate with an unjust system makes the oppressed as evil as the oppressors. Our most fruitful course is to stand firm, move forward nonviolently, accept disappointments and cling to hope. Our determined refusal not to be stopped will eventually open the door to fulfillment. By recognizing the necessity of suffering in a righteous cause, we may achieve our humanity's full stature. To guard ourselves from bitterness, we need the vision to see in this generation's ordeals the opportunity to transfigure both ourselves and American society.

In 1956 I flew from New York to London in the propeller-type aircraft that required nine and a half hours for a flight now made in six hours by jet. Returning from London to the United States, the stewardess announced that the flying time would be twelve and a half hours. The distance was the same. Why an additional three hours? When the pilot entered the cabin to greet the passengers, I asked him to explain. "You must understand about the winds," he said. "When we leave New York, a strong tail wind is in our favor, but when we return, a strong head wind is against us." The he added, "Don't worry. These four engines are capable of battling the winds."

In any social revolution there are times when the tail winds of triumph and fulfillment favor us, and other times when strong head winds of disappointment and setbacks beat against us relentlessly. We must not permit adverse winds to overwhelm us as we journey across life's mighty Atlantic; we must be sustained by our engines of courage in spite of the winds. This refusal to be stopped, this "courage to be," this determination to go on "in spite of" is the hallmark of any great movement.

The Black Power movement of today, like the Garvey "Back to Africa" movement of the 1920's, represents a dashing of hope, a conviction of the inability of the Negro to win and a belief in the infinitude of the ghetto. While there is much grounding in past experience for all these feelings, a revolution cannot succumb to any of them. Today's despair is a poor chisel to carve out tomorrow's justice.

Black Power is an implicit and often explicit belief in black separatism. Notice that I do not call it black racism. It is inaccurate to refer to Black Power as racism in reverse, as some have recently done. Racism is a doctrine of the congenital inferiority and worthlessness of a people. While a few angry proponents of Black Power have, in moments of bitterness, made wild statements that come close to this kind of racism, the major proponents of Black Power have never contended that the white man is innately worthless.

Yet behind Black Power's legitimate and necessary concern for group unity and black identity lies the belief that there can be a separate black road to power and fulfillment. Few ideas are more unrealistic. There is no salvation for the Negro through isolation.

One of the chief affirmations of Black Power is the call for the mobilization of political strength for black people. But we do not have to look far to see that effective political power for Negroes cannot come through separatism. Granted that there are cities and counties in the country where the Negro is in a majority, they are so few that concentration on them alone would still leave the vast majority of Negroes outside the mainstream of American political life.

Out of the eighty-odd counties in Alabama, the state where SNCC sought to develop an all-black party, only nine have a majority of Negroes. Even if blacks could control each of these counties, they would have little influence in over-all state politics and could do little to improve conditions in the major Negro population centers of Birmingham, Mobile and Montgomery. There are still relatively few Congressional districts in the South that have such large black majorities that Negro candidates could be elected without the aid of whites. Is it a sounder program to concentrate on the election of two or three Negro Congressmen from predominantly Negro districts or to concentrate on the election of fifteen or twenty Negro Congressmen from Southern districts where a coalition of Negro and white moderate voters is possible?

Moreover, any program that elects all black candidates simply because they are black and rejects all white candidates simply because they are white is politically unsound and morally unjustifiable. It is true that in many areas of the South Negroes still must elect Negroes in order to be effectively represented. SNCC staff members are eminently correct when they point out that in Lowndes County, Alabama, there are no white liberals or moderates and no possibility for cooperation between the races at the present time. But the Lowndes County experience cannot be made a measuring rod for the whole of America. The basic thing in determining the best candidate is not his color but his integrity.

Black Power alone is no more insurance against social injustice than white power. Negro politicians can be as opportunistic as their white counterparts if there is not an informed and determined constituency demanding social reform. What is most needed is a coalition of Negroes and liberal whites that will work to make both major parties truly responsive to the needs of the poor. Black Power does not envision or desire such a program.

Just as the Negro cannot achieve political power in isolation, neither can he gain economic power through separatism. While there must be a continued emphasis on the need for blacks to pool their economic resources and withdraw consumer support from discriminating firms, we must not be oblivious to the fact that the larger economic problems confronting the Negro community will only be solved by federal programs involving billions of dollars. One fortunate thing about Black Power is that it gives priority to race precisely at a time when the impact of automation and other forces have made the economic question fundamental for blacks and whites alike. In this context a slogan "Power for Poor People" would be much more appropriate than the slogan "Black Power."

However much we pool our resources and "buy black," this cannot create the multiplicity of new jobs and provide the number of low-cost houses that will lift the Negro out of the economic depression caused by centuries of deprivation. Neither can our resources supply quality integrated education. All of this requires billions of dollars which only an alliance of liberal-labor-civil-rights forces can stimulate. In short, the Negroes' problem cannot be solved unless the whole of American society takes a new turn toward greater economic justice.

In a multiracial society no group can make it alone. It is a myth to believe that the Irish, the Italians and the Jews—the ethnic groups that Black Power advocates cite as justification for their views—rose to power through separatism. It is true that they stuck together. But their group unity was always enlarged by joining in alliances with other groups such as political machines and trade unions. To succeed in a pluralistic society, and an often hostile one at that, the Negro obviously needs organized strength, but that strength will only be effective when it is consolidated through constructive alliances with the majority group.

Those proponents of Black Power who have urged Negroes to shun alliances with whites argue that whites as a group cannot have a genuine concern for Negro progress. Therefore, they claim, the white man's main interest in collaborative effort is to diminish Negro militancy and deflect it from constructive goals.

Undeniably there are white elements that cannot be trusted, and no militant movement can afford to relax its vigilance against halfhearted associates or conscious betrayers. Every alliance must be considered on its own merits. Negroes may embrace some and walk out on others where their interests are imperiled. Occasionally betrayals, however, do not justify the rejection of the principle of Negro–white alliance.

The oppression of Negroes by whites has left an understandable residue of suspicion. Some of this suspicion is a healthy and appropriate safeguard. An excess of skepticism, however, becomes a fetter. It denies that there can be reliable white allies, even though some whites have died heroically at the side of Negroes in our struggle and others have risked economic and political peril to support our cause.

The history of the movement reveals that Negro–white alliances have played a powerfully constructive role, especially in recent years. While Negro initiative, courage and imagination precipitated the Birmingham and Selma confrontations and revealed the harrowing injustice of segregated life, the organized strength of Negroes alone would have been insufficient to move Congress and the administration without the weight of the aroused conscience of white America. In the period ahead Negroes will continue to need this support. Ten percent of the population cannot by tensions alone induce 90 percent to change a way of life.

Within the white majority there exists a substantial group who cherish democratic principles above privilege and who have demonstrated a will to fight side by side with the Negro against injustice. Another and more substantial group is composed of those having common needs with the Negro and who will benefit equally with him in the achievement of social progress. There are, in fact, more poor white Americans than there are Negro. Their need for a war on poverty is no less desperate than the Negro's. In the South they have been deluded by race prejudice and largely remained aloof from common action. Ironically, with this posture they were fighting not only the Negro but themselves. Yet there are already signs of change. Without formal alliances, Negroes and whites have supported the same candidates in many *de facto* electoral coalitions in the South because each sufficiently served his own needs.

The ability of Negroes to enter alliances is a mark of our growing strength, not of our weakness. In entering an alliance, the Negro is not relying on white leadership or ideology; he is taking his place as an equal partner in a common endeavor. His organized strength and his new independence pave the way for alliances. Far from losing independence in an alliance, he is using it for constructive and multiplied gains.

Negroes must shun the very narrow-mindedness that in others has so long been the source of our own afflictions. We have reached the stage of organized strength and independence to work securely in alliances. History has demonstrated with major victories the effectiveness, wisdom and moral soundness of Negro-white alliance. The cooperation of Negro and white based on the solid ground of honest conscience and proper self-interest can continue to grow in scope and influence. It can attain the strength to alter basic institutions by democratic means. Negro isolation can never approach this goal.

In the final analysis the weakness of Black Power is its failure to see that the black man needs the white man and the white man needs the black man. However much we may try to romanticize the slogan, there is no separate black path to power and fulfillment that does not intersect white paths, and there is no separate white path to power and fulfilment, short of social disaster, that does not share that power with black aspirations for freedom and human dignity. We are bound together in a single garment of destiny. The language, the cultural patterns, the music, the material prosperity and even the food of America are an amalgam of black and white.

James Baldwin once related how he returned home from school and his mother asked him whether his teacher was colored or white. After a pause he answered: "She is a little bit colored and a little bit white." This is the dilemma of being a Negro in America. In physical as well as cultural terms every Negro is a little bit colored and a little bit white. In our search for identity we must recognize this dilemma.

Every man must ultimately confront the question "Who am I?" and seek to answer it honestly. One of the first principles of personal adjustment is the principle of self-acceptance. The Negro's greatest dilemma is that in order to be healthy he must accept his ambivalence. The Negro is the child of two cultures— Africa and America. The problem is that in the search for wholeness all too many Negroes seek to embrace only one side of their natures. Some, seeking to reject their heritage, are ashamed of their color, ashamed of black art and music, and determine what is beautiful and good by the standards of white society. They end up frustrated and without cultural roots. Others seek to reject everything American and to identify totally with Africa, even to the point of wearing African clothes. But this approach leads also to frustration because the American Negro is not an African. The old Hegelian synthesis still offers the best answer to many of life's dilemmas. The American Negro is neither totally African nor totally Western. He is Afro–American, a true hybrid, a combination of two cultures.

Who are we? We are the descendants of slaves. We are the offspring of noble men and women who were kidnaped from their native land and chained in ships like beasts. We are the heirs of a great and exploited continent known as Africa. We are the heirs of a past of rope, fire and murder. I for one am not ashamed of this past. My shame is for those who became so inhuman that they could inflict this torture upon us.

But we are also Americans. Abused and scorned though we may be, our destiny is tied up with the destiny of America. In spite of the psychological appeals of identification with Africa, the Negro must face the fact that America is now his home, a home that he helped to build through "blood, sweat and tears." Since we are Americans the solution to our problem will not come through seeking to build a separate black nation within a nation, but by finding that creative minority of the concerned from the ofttimes apathetic majority, and together moving toward that colorless power that we all need for security and justice.

In the first century B.C., Cicero said: "Freedom is participation in power." Negroes should never want all power because they would deprive others of their freedom. By the same token, Negroes can never be content without participation in power. America must be a nation in which its multiracial people are partners in power. This is the essence of democracy toward which all Negro struggles have been directed since the distant past when he was transplanted here in chains.

Probably the most destructive feature of Black Power is its unconscious and often conscious call for retaliatory violence. Many well-meaning persons within the movement rationalize that Black Power does not really mean black violence, that those who shout the slogan don't really mean it that way, that the violent connotations are solely the distortions of a vicious press. That the press has fueled the fire is true. But as one who has worked and talked intimately with devotees of Black Power, I must admit that the slogan is mainly used by persons who have lost faith in the method and philosophy of nonviolence. I must make it clear that no guilt by association is intended. Both Floyd McKissick and Stokely Carmichael have declared themselves opponents of aggressive violence. This clarification is welcome and useful, despite the persistence of some of their followers in examining the uses of violence.

Over cups of coffee in my home in Atlanta and my apartment in Chicago, I have often talked late at night and over into the small hours of the morning with proponents of Black Power who argued passionately about the validity of violence and riots. They don't quote Gandhi or Tolstoy. Their Bible is Frantz Fanon's *The Wretched of the Earth*. This black psychiatrist from Martinique, who went to Algeria to work with the National Liberation Front in its fight against the French, argues in his book—a well-written book, incidentally, with many penetrating insights—that violence is a psychologically healthy and tactically sound method for the oppressed. And so, realizing that they are a part of that vast company of the "wretched of the earth," these young American Negroes, who are predominantly involved in the Black Power movement, often quote Fanon's belief that violence is the only thing that will bring about liberation. As they say,

> Sing us no songs of nonviolence, sing us no songs of progress, for nonviolence and progress belong to middle–class Negroes and whites and we are not interested in you.

As we have seen, the first public expression of disenchantment with nonviolence arose around the question of "self–defense." In a sense this is a false issue, for the right to defend one's person when attacked has been guaranteed through the ages by common law. In a nonviolent demonstration, however, self–defense must be approached from another perspective.

The cause of a demonstration is the existence of some form of exploitation or oppression that has made it necessary for men of courage and goodwill to protest the evil. For example, a demonstration against *de facto* school segregation is based on the awareness that a child's mind is crippled by inadequate educational opportunities. The demonstrator agrees that it is better to suffer publicly for a short time to end the crippling evil of school segregation than to have generation after generation of children suffer in ignorance. In such a demonstration the point is made that the schools are inadequate. This is the evil one seeks to dramatize; anything else distracts from that point and interferes with the confrontation of the primary evil. Of course no one wants to suffer and be hurt. But it is more important to get at the cause than to be safe. It is better to shed a little blood from a blow on the head or a rock thrown by an angry mob than to have children by the thousands finishing high school who can only read at a sixth-grade level.

Furthermore, it is dangerous to organize a movement around self-defense. The line of demarcation between defensive violence and aggressive violence is very thin. The minute a program of violence is enunciated, even for self-defense, the atmosphere is filled with talk of violence, and the words falling on

460

unsophisticated ears may be interpreted as an invitation to aggression.

One of the main questions that the Negro must confront in his pursuit of freedom is that of effectiveness. What is the most effective way to achieve the desired goal? If a method is not effective, no matter how much steam it releases, it is an expression of weakness, not a strength. Now the plain, inexorable fact is that any attempt of the American Negro to overthrow his oppressor with violence will not work. We do not need President Johnson to tell us this by reminding Negro rioters that they are outnumbered ten to one. The courageous efforts of our own insurrectionist brothers, such as Denmark Vesey and Nat Turner, should be eternal reminders to us that violent rebellion is doomed from the start. In violent warfare one must be prepared to face the fact that there will be casualties by the thousands. Anyone leading a violent rebellion must be willing to make an honest assessment regarding the possible casualties to a minority population confronting a well-armed, wealthy majority with a fanatical right wing that would delight in exterminating thousands of black men, women and children.

# Eastern Religions in America

# ❦ 171 ❧

# Japanese Buddhism in Hawaii

## KIYOSHI K. KAWAKAMI

The chief early source of Buddhism on American territory was Japan, in the form of Japanese plantation workers in the Hawaiian Islands. It then spread with Japanese immigrants to the West Coast. The disenchanted view of Buddhist missionaries offered by Kiyoshi Kawakami (1875-1949), a Tokyo-born journalist who pursued his career from an American base, arose from his sense of the difficulty of maintaining toleration of religious and cultural pluralism amongst Americans if religious groups behaved in an aggressively separatist fashion.

Closely connected with the educational question is the question of Buddhist activities. Not only have the Buddhists established temples in cities and on plantations, but they have also established many schools throughout the archipelago. In travelling through the back country by train the first thing one notices from the car is the Buddhist temple rearing its quaint roof above the huts of plantation labourers. With the exception of the residences occupied by plantation managers these houses of worship are the only structures which break the monotony of the vast cane fields dotted here and there with clusters of camp houses. In comparison with the dismal structures surrounding them, these temples present an imposing appearance. Small wonder that the Japanese labourers point to them with a sense of pride. Even the natives and Portuguese labourers look upon them as a mark of superior civilization.

The attitude of Christian workers in Hawaii towards Buddhist propaganda is characterized with broadmindedness and leniency. They unreservedly admit that the Buddhist has the right to propagate his doctrines in Hawaii just as the Christian has the right to preach the Gospel in Japan. The only apprehension they entertain is that some of the Buddhist priests and the teachers of Buddhist schools are inclined to inspire loyalty to Japan as a means of propagating Buddhism. How far this apprehension is true I am not ready to determine, but that it is not without foundation no one can gainsay.

Source: Kiyoshi K. Kawakami, from *Asia at the Door*, New York, 1914, pp. 229-33.

The Buddhist schools seem to be one of the means of propagating Buddhism. Aggressive and enterprising, the Buddhist workers are often a disturbing element in plantation camps. They would go forth and establish a school where there is already a non-religious school, and where no other school is needed. Trouble immediately begins, for the Buddhists resort to all means in trying to take pupils out of the non-religious school and enrol them in their own. When I was in Hawaii Island the Japanese Vice-Consul at Honolulu was making a tour of the island with a view to finding the way out of this perennial trouble. It was the Vice-Consul's opinion that where there was school trouble the blame was usually to be placed at the door of the Buddhists. The Japanese Consul-General, upon receipt of the Vice-Consul's reports, formulated a plan to organize an education committee by which all the Japanese schools in the islands were to be supervised. The committee was to consist of leading Japanese business men, editors, teachers, and Christians and Buddhists, as well as a few Americans in Honolulu. The committee thus organized was to be absolutely non-sectarian, and the schools under its supervision were likewise to be non-sectarian. Such a plan would seem to me the only feasible one which would remove the present school troubles. At this writing, however, the plan is not yet put into execution.

In spite of the large number of adherents the Buddhists claim to possess in the islands it is highly doubtful if they are achieving much in the world of the spirit. It seems to be the universal opinion among the Japanese of the educated class that the Buddhist priests are in Hawaii mainly for their own material gain. They seem to be concerned chiefly with the collection of offerings from their parishioners. If a priest stays in Hawaii four or five years, he usually amasses what he considers a competence. Unlike American missionaries in the foreign fields these Buddhist priests are not paid from their headquarters in Japan. All Buddhist missions are self-supporting, and the priests in charge of them get what stipend they can make out of the votive offerings of their parishioners. In Hawaii I noticed each priest had five or six camps in his charge. In the evening he goes out on a pony and pays a visit to the camp, where he says a few comforting words to the labourers and recites the stereotyped sutras, and receives offerings from his pious audience. As he visits all camps alternately, one each evening, his evenings are pretty well occupied, repeating sermons and collecting offerings.

That the Japanese people are intensely religious there is no room to doubt, but that they are in urgent need of sound guidance is also evident. The corruption of the Buddhist hierarchy in Japan is proverbial. The Hongwan-ji temple at Kyoto is the hotbed of financial troubles and factional feuds. Water cannot rise above its source, and it is small wonder that the Buddhist priests, with a few notable exceptions, are men without inspiration or ideals. It is very well for Hongwan-ji to send priests abroad, but unless its system and methods of propaganda are completely reformed, the presence of such priests in such countries as Hawaii can do more harm than good. The erecting of temples and the maintenance of the priests entail no small financial burden on the plantation hands. That the burden is borne cheerfully and willingly is no justification of the imposition. Up to the time of the Japanese strike of 1909 the Japanese labourers had already contributed $100,000 for the restoration of Buddhist temples alone. When I was in Hawaii in 1912 the Buddhists had just decided to build a new temple at Honolulu at a cost of $100,000. Not only have the Japanese in Hawaii to bear such heavy burdens, but they are even required to make occasional contributions to Hongwan-ji at Kyoto. A few years ago a special emissary of Hongwan-ji came to Hawaii and collected $50,000 for a festival which was to be held in Kyoto. The emissary, encouraged by his unexpected success in Hawaii, came to California with the intention of collecting more contributions from the Japanese there. But here he met his Waterloo, for the Japanese on the Coast proved far more clear-sighted and well-informed than their brothers in Hawaii. The Japanese newspapers there raised a storm of protest against him, and the envoy had to leave San Francisco under very awkward circumstances.

On the mainland, too, the Christians have strong rivals in Buddhists. In Vancouver, Seattle, Portland, Fresno, and Los Angeles, the Buddhists have established respectable headquarters which are used both as places of worship and as dormitories for Japanese young men. In San Francisco they are also planning to erect a building much larger than those in the other cities. If the purpose of the Buddhists were to propagate the teachings of Buddha, pure and simple, the American people, I am sure, would have little to complain of. Much to our regret, we find some of the Buddhist priests are inclined to link Buddhism with patriotism to Japan, knowing that this method of propaganda appeals to the ignorant masses. I do not see why the Japanese Buddhists could not be broad-minded enough, and clear-sighted enough, to see the folly of such a policy. Out of my sincere respect for their character and ideals I prefer to believe that the Buddhist leaders themselves are absolutely innocent, and positively disapprove such unscrupulous means as have been resorted to by their followers. It is also regrettable that the Buddhists keep aloof from the Christians and apparently have no desire to coöperate with them. Perhaps the Christians themselves are to blame. Both Christianity and Buddhism, however different from each other in essential teachings, aim at the promotion of the spiritual well-being of humanity. In the field of practical social reform, therefore, they ought to be co-workers, not antagonists. To bring this about both Christians and Buddhists must first of all abandon their narrow views of religion.

# ❧172❧

# Institutional Religion and the Children of Asian Immigrants

## WILLIAM CARLSON SMITH

By the late 1930s, the descendants of Asian immigrants had adopted religious attitudes which diverged from, and at times were in tension with, the outlook of older generations. The survey extracted below assumes a framework of Americanization based upon the English language and Christianity. It indicates interesting variations amongst the younger generations in the relation of identity to religious attitude.

The contacts made by the children of oriental parentage with organized religion have conditioned their adjustment to American life. Some have lived in homes and in communities where the old-world religion has been predominant while others have made practically all their contacts with western Christianity.

## Children Vary from Parental Religion.

The American-born children of oriental immigrants tend to differ markedly from their parents in religion. Under American influences they cannot possibly assume the characteristic parental attitudes. As the children enter school and become acquainted with American pupils, some join Sunday-school classes in Christian churches. Here they are further imbued with the idea that everything American is best. Since the majority of white Americans are nominal Christians at least, Christianity comes to be associated with a superior status; the religion of their parents comes to be part and parcel of a position of inferiority. Consequently to enjoy the good things of life and to be Americans of some consequence, the parental religion is set aside in favor of Christianity—the American religion. To them the Christian religion is an integral part of

Source: William Carlson Smith, 'Institutional Religion and the Children of Asian Immigrants', *Americans in Process*, Ann Arbor, MI., 1937, pp. 141–57.

Americanism; it does not even occur to them that there is an alternative.

Several factors have attracted the children to Christianity. Some have been drawn by the English language. In the main, they can carry on the common every-day activities in the parental languages, but do not understand the concepts used in a discourse on religion. Their ideas are more occidental than oriental. Hence, they have great difficulty in understanding a sermon which is cast in the thought forms of the Orient. These differences in language and point of view separate the children from the religion of their parents. This situation led some to choose English-speaking churches before they began to feel conscious of racial differences. To offset this, a number of oriental churches are experimenting with English services, but as yet this has not been entirely successful. The young people are usually critical of the English used by the ministers reared in the Orient. White ministers often talk down to them in what one young man called "a sort of baby talk"—and this creates a revulsion. The Buddhists in Hawaii have sensed the situation more thoroughly than the Christians and have begun to use the English language with good results. Some pupils in school have studied Christianity because they did not wish to confess ignorance if questions should be asked about the Bible or the Christian religion. Some have turned to Christianity in the hope that relations with the white group would be more satisfactory. A number have considered attendance at American churches advisable because they might become acquainted with the best people of the community and thus have an opportunity to learn many things of value.

Contacts with these various influences have weaned the younger group from the parental religion. Some inwardly make light of the old religion, but remain silent out of regard for their parents. Some even go through certain ceremonies in order to please them. Others, who cannot appreciate the point of view of the older generation, ridicule the religious practices of their parents. A college boy in Hawaii relates his experience.

> As I grew older and grasped more of the occidental civilization I began to lose my oriental traits. Last summer I attended a Buddhist ceremony back home. I had no intention of going, but just to satisfy my dear mother I went. My two younger sisters, both in high school, were with me. When the ceremony began I could hardly keep myself from laughing, since the priest's chanting sounded so funny. I saw my two sisters giggling with their handkerchiefs against their mouths to avoid any distraction. I had better sense than to laugh, but I laughed within. I couldn't stand it. This shows how much we American-born Japanese are losing the customs of our forefathers.

It is not always a matter of holding the parental practices up to ridicule; the young people are at times placed in embarrassing situations. A high school boy in Hawaii reveals his embarrassment.

> On one occasion, after I had attended a Christian boarding school for one year, I went to a Japanese temple. Since I was the eldest boy in the family, I was morally obligated to attend the ceremony. The first thing I knew the older people were on their knees in a meditative mood before the altar illumined with a score

of candles and decorated with fruits, candies, and offerings of all kinds. I felt foolish in kneeling down before the altar without knowing what to do, but before I knew it I had gone through the formalities. I felt the icy-cold perspiration streaming down my back. That was probably the most embarrassing situation that I was ever in because my parents' customs and ideas differed from mine.

A college girl in Hawaii gives us further insight.

Unfortunately, to say the least, my mother is still unconverted. We have tried our best to make a Christian of her, but her faith in Confucius is too strong for any one to change her. I have always condemned her worship and offerings. She spends quite a sum of money for these things and sometimes I have made fun of my smaller brothers. She forces them to bow before the incense and my fifteen-year-old brother has stopped because, when he was about thirteen years old, I called him a "heathen Chinese" after he had bowed. I do not know whether I should be ashamed of myself for not respecting my parents' religion, but I have been very much embarrassed by it. We live in a district that has no other Chinese family and sometimes when it's full moon or some other festival day, mother pops fire crackers and burns incense. Some of my neighbors have teased me and I do not find it pleasant to have my friends see the little shrine that she has built in the kitchen. In this day and age, if your parents are not Christians, they are not much respected by our friends.

These experiences tend to develop religious ideas and attitudes which set the younger generation off from their parents.

## Effect of Community on Religion

The communities in which the young people live condition their attitudes. If a boy grows up in an isolated community where Buddhism is strong, he has no opportunity to make contacts with Christians. Hence he has no basis for comparison. Hence he will not think much about religion but will follow the customs of his group and will not be embarrassed by their practices. In such communities, a minority group of Christians often finds itself at a disadvantage; their children are practically outcasts. A college boy in Hawaii presents the situation.

The children of Christian parents in my home town were not treated in a friendly manner by the children of Buddhist parents. They were looked upon as "sissies"; they had to endure being teased and called "Christo" and they were excluded from participation in many of the children's activities. Somehow I managed to pass through my childhood years without being subjected to these discriminating actions. I mixed with the Buddhist children; I played with them; I talked with them; I joined their pranks. It seems that I was well liked by them. I was quite athletic and agile for my size and build and could do what most of the other children did—in many instances I did better. I could play ball fairly well, I could run fairly fast, I was virtually a monkey on a tree. I was about fourth in boxing ability among the boys of the town, and in other ways I could "hold my own" with the boys in most activities. These factors must have influenced their attitude toward me, I am sure. Furthermore, I believe that the status of my parents in the estimation of the townspeople helped me a great deal. My parents are kind, humble and sympathetic to the people of the town and vicinity, regardless of

470

religious differences. they are thus respected by them.

Sometimes a move from one area to another brings a decided change. In a community that was predominantly Christian, a boy was afraid to profess that he was a Buddhist lest he be considered a pagan. The new environment into which he moved was more favorable to Buddhism and his hesitancy disappeared.

## Parental Attitudes and Religion of Children

A liberal attitude on the part of the Japanese parents has made the situation favorable to the adoption of Christianity by the children. On the whole, it would appear that the devotees of Shintoism or Buddhism tend to be more broad-minded than members of the Christian churches. Some Christians of oriental ancestry are quite bigoted and look askance at other religions.

Many Orientals hold to their old-country religion, but have concluded that this is not suited to their children who have grown up in America. Some non-Christian parents encourage their children to attend Christian churches and Sunday schools, and even to become Christians. A Japanese college boy has revealed his father's attitude.

My parents came from Japan to Hawaii almost twenty-five years ago. When they came here, they brought their customs, traditions, and religion with them. They were Buddhists in Japan and they are still strong Buddhists. Once a year my parents pay homage to the shrine of their faith. Sometimes the children accompany them. When I was a child, it was one of the great events in my life to go out in an automobile and travel a great distance to visit this temple. This annual event was kept up until I was fourteen.

When my elder brother was about seven, he was given the duty of lighting the lanterns of the gods. He continued to do so, until I became seven. At seven I was instructed to perform this duty—to light the lanterns every night. I did it for three years, when my younger brother succeeded me.

One day it happened that a friend of ours took me to a Christian Sunday school, four miles away from home. My father raised no objections. I continued to go to that Sunday school for a year. That was when I was ten. The next year a Salvation Army officer came to our community and I attended his meetings. My sister and I were quite regular pupils. At each meeting we received little cards. We gave the cards to our mother and she kept them for us. Sometimes, my sister and I came home a little too late in the night and for that reason we were punished. Father never objected to our attendance at the Sunday school.

A strange thing occurred in my life when I was thirteen. I had just completed my seventh grade and was working in the cane fields for my vacation. One night my father confidentially asked me if I would like to go to Honolulu for my education. I was very pleased to hear this. ... I had heard a lot about the Hongwanji Boarding School. I heard that the attendance at Japanese school was compulsory. I hated the Japanese school and for that reason I asked my father where he wanted me to stay. When he replied, "You will be in the Christian dormitory," my heart leaped with joy. I was the happiest of all persons then!

A year passed by and I completed the eighth grade. To my father I was a good boy for I had made good in the language school and gotten by in the grammar school. He sent me to O—'s again. I went to high school a year. I came up to the expectations of my parents; so I was sent to O—'s for the third year. I then finished my sophomore year and went home to spend the summer.

One night as my father and I were together, he asked me if I was a baptized Christian, to which I answered in the negative. He paused for a minute and spoke up as if something were troubling him. He said, "Why don't you be a good Christian—be baptized and become a Christian. You are going to make your living in Hawaii and Christianity is the religion to follow. Society and the business world call for Christians." This remark struck my innocent mind. I returned to O—'s for the fourth time when school opened. On April 1, 1928, I was baptized by Rev. T. O— at the Japanese church.

I have often wondered why my father took such an attitude in regard to my religious affiliation. To say what made him do so is a difficult story. However, there are two or three definite things that I could relate which have influenced him to have such an attitude. First of all, come the books. He read literature of all sorts, both Christian and Buddhist. His only recreation after the day's work was reading the *Nippu Jiji* and some sort of biography, novel, or essay. Secondly, his friend Mr. H—, a Christian, influenced him much. Mr. H— was a product of the O— dormitory and his conduct among men was a radiant example of higher living. The Reverend O— visited my father twice and he, too, influenced my father. ... My father met other Christian people who influenced him in the Christian ideas. Thirdly, it was my own self that made him say that I ought to be a Christian. I had been much of a rascal at home, but after three years in the dormitory my actions were quite different. My parents both testified that I was getting better, and my father took the opportunity to advise me to be a Christian. My father respects Christianity. As I say grace at supper, he pauses and pays reverence. If I forget to do so, he reminds me. There is no question in his mind as to the value of Christianity in Hawaii.

The Chinese in the main, seem to be less liberal in their attitudes toward Christianity then the Japanese. A Chinese college graduate presented the situation as it exists among his people in Hawaii.

I was baptized in my home town. When I told my father, he fairly "blew up" and declared that he would cast my bones outside the ancestral burying ground. When I went away to the University, however, and made a good record he became more favorably disposed, but in spite of this he was enraged when I was baptized at the age of eighteen. I have observed that many Chinese parents do not hesitate in permitting their children to attend Christian Sunday schools when they are young because they have control over them and can pull them back at any time. So long as no positively harmful effects are evident, there is no hesitation. Since I had been working my way through school, I have felt rather independent and took the step of being baptized even though I knew my father would object.

Nevertheless there have been many instances of genuine religious toleration among the Chinese where the children have felt perfectly free to make their own choices.

Living in an atmosphere of comparative tolerance in religious matters, the children have tended to develop a tolerant spirit and sometimes an attitude that all religious faiths are equal.

## Disillusionment and Christianity

When some, who have accepted Christianity as part and parcel of Americanism, meet with rebuffs and discriminations, they become bitter. They say this "brotherhood stuff" that Christians talk so much about is all humbug; they will have nothing more to do with it. As they go through the process of disillusionment, they gradually give up Christianity and revert to the religion of their parents. They cannot return to it completely, but they become more sympathetic toward the whole parental culture system. A Japanese college boy in Hawaii exemplifies the process through which many go.

My mother was very religious and she had taught me to worship God, for without his help we would not be able to get along. As it is the custom of the Japanese people to light little lamps and burn incense before the shrine and image of Buddha we lighted our little lamps every morning and every evening. The duty, and privilege perhaps, fell upon me for I was the eldest son, and I really did have a feeling of worship in doing this with hands washed and mouth cleansed.

In high school I became interested in Christianity. Its teachings seemed good to me. I began to reason and doubt the workability of the gods in the religion of my father and mother. It began to hurt my conscience to stand before the image of Buddha or the shrine and light the little lamps of worship. I had my younger brother about twelve years old do that thereafter. My mother noticed the change in me and urged me over and over again to hold to the religion of my ancestors. She was suspicious of Christianity about which she did not know a thing other than that Jesus was crucified, and she believed that Christianity taught one to get rid of all his belongings and make himself poor. She was afraid that Christianity meant doing away with all the ceremonies observed for the happiness and peace of the dead, which was sacrilegious and would surely bring disaster to the family. However, I firmly believed Christianity to be the right religion and I consoled her by telling her that I would do all homage to the memory of any ancestors even though I should become a Christian. Since then she made no attempt to hold me to her faith. I was baptized and after baptism I taught Sunday school and worked diligently to bring my best friend and my other friends to Christ, which very happily, with the aid of others, was successfully done. I was very happy and for a time I wondered if those who were not Christians were ever as happy, so completely did I lean on the wonder-working power of Christ and his teachings.

When June came I graduated; I was happy that the days of schooling were over. I wanted to get a job and have my father ease up a bit in his work which was getting harder with the advance in years. I tried to get a job in the office of one of the big firms in town but without success, therefore I picked up odd office and selling jobs. My folks were very considerate and did not grumble even when I did not earn any money. During this year of disappointments I became interested in college. I wanted to be better prepared. It was difficult for me to ask my father to send me through school. I was afraid to ask him to let me go to college, let alone his support. I had thought this way and that way why I should like to go to school. But after further thought, I made up my mind that it was unreasonable of me to continue my schooling. I would try harder than ever to get a real job and help my father support the family. I was restful for a while but as I met with further disappointments, the wish to go to college was revived. One day when mother was alone I told her my intention. It was her earnest desire that I be sent to college, but that was not easy since we were poor. Furthermore she wondered if a college education would bring proportional financial returns. I told her that I would work my way through if I could be spared a few years more. My father did not object. He wanted to give me all the education possible. I resolved to make good and repay my parents and the rest of the family for their sacrifice. I registered at the University in the fall of 1922, as a commerce student..

My determination to work my way through school was one thing but doing it was another. I got a job to work a few hours every night but it did not bring enough to support myself. I picked up whatever odd job I could to make good my promise, but I was not altogether successful. But my father and mother were always kind to me and gave me every encouragement to keep on.

Every summer since my graduation from the grammar school I worked for the Hawaiian Pineapple Company. I have come to realize during these years the effect of environment upon the behaviour of people. Everybody seemed to have the impression that polite manners are for school or some other uses, but certainly not to be used in the pineapple cannery. At least, I myself have felt free from convention, to some extent, while there. Also a sort of dissatisfaction a rose within me. We worked under a contract system that called for the greatest of physical endurance. but because we worked with our hands our bonus was 10 per cent. If we had worked in white shirt and clean collar we might have received 50 per cent or more like the office workers. I became dissatisfied with the distribution of wealth—or rather the discrimination shown—and at the same time I began to get suspicious of the sincerity of the people who preached equality and brotherhood.

In my second year I got a job as assistant playground director which I have kept ever since. Beside helping through school, it played a great part in my change of course from commerce to education. There were other reasons, too, but I shall not go into them here.

Strange to say, about this time I began to lose the faith I had in Christianity. There are other sides to every story even in religion. There are unbelievable revelations of the presence of God as taught by the priests of the shrines and of the temples as well as by the Christian ministers. I have heard and have seen persons not Christians die with revelations of heaven before them. Can not all religions be teaching the same God? I began to see sincerity in the religious worship of others and it also became unbearable to have any person condemn as idolatry any worship other than Christianity. I attend church services regularly, but I fear the constant knocking down of the religion of my ancestors by the superintendent of my Sunday school is arousing antagonism within me and drawing me farther and farther away from Christianity.

The language school question, the Japanese exclusion, the discrimination in the administration of justice, the widespread use of bribery, catering of the law makers to the rich at the expense of the needy, are live questions of the time. I wonder if I am not coming to feel that Mr. — was right when he said in his newspaper column that money can buy anything from the legislature to the police court. But this last year in the University I was living over the experiences of the high school. I am beginning to move into the circle of wider association. My outlook on life is a little less pessimistic. Brotherhood is impossible, but we might learn to understand each other better.

## Effect of Contact with Church People

The methods employed by many church workers have played an important rôle in causing a break with Christianity. For some time, Christian work has been carried on among the oriental groups in America, but the results of Protestant activity, in particular, are open to question. Church officials, in their annual statistical reports, must show good results for the money expended. Hence they have adopted methods which promise the largest immediate returns for the energy expended, without considering the ultimate outcome. The method has been to allure individuals here and there. Children have been most readily won in this way, but this has pulled them away from their families. A number of parents, aware of the situation, have become resentful. A certain Japanese in Hawaii, who had never been strongly opposed to Christianity, offered a number of pertinent criticisms. On one occasion he quoted the Biblical passage (Ephesians 5:31) which says that a man must leave his father and mother, and made the comment that Christianity had pulled children away from their parents and had broken families. When some of the young people begin to reflect and begin to develop a more sympathetic attitude toward the parental cultural system, they conclude that the Christians have not played the game fairly, either with themselves of with their parents.

In a certain sense, the children have been "bought" by the Christian group. In the immigrant homes there was usually a constant struggle to make ends meet. Hence anything additional from an outside source would be greatly appreciated. Material rewards of different kinds, such as candies, cards, free moving pictures, and Christmas gifts have induced many to go to Sunday school and church. The experience of a Japanese high school boy in Hawaii is to the point.

> When I was a "kid" I had to go to the Buddhist temple, but after some time I revolted against that and spent my time playing baseball with the boys. As we were playing ball one Sunday morning, a tall, blond Haole missionary came along and rounded us up telling us he would give us some sticks of candy it we would come to his Sunday school. We went, and at the end of the hour we would get each a stick of candy. Usually through the whole period I would be thinking of the candy. We would sing the songs very lustily as we hoped to get more candy if we sang loudly. We sang "Jesus Loves Me This I Know," and I have never forgotten that song. At times some of the boys in the gang would get tired before the end of the hour and run out.
>
> They wouldn't, of course, get any candy then. Oftentimes, during the Sunday school hour we would gamble away the sticks of candy we were to get; some of us would then have several sticks and some would have none. At times we would stay for the communion service which lasted about fifteen minutes. We would kneel near the front of the room. For this each would get an extra stick of candy. We would usually get our candy about eleven o'clock. It had a very good taste then, for it was the time we were getting hungry. There were two gospel houses, one on each side of the street, that were competing for us. One held services at ten o'clock and the other at three. On some Sundays we would go to both and get candy at both places. That, however, depended on whether or not we wanted to play baseball or go swimming.

In some instances these methods have brought good results; the children have developed habits which have been valuable to them in later life. In many cases, however, the young people have seen the superficiality and have become disgusted.

Another method is that of making promises to the children; at least they are made by implication, while no attempt is made to correct the impression. Much is said about "brotherhood," "loving one another," "there is no color line in heaven," *et cetera*, and while the children are young they are accepted by the white group in many churches and Sunday schools. This acceptance makes them feel superior to their parents. This is accentuated by the fact that all too often they are made to feel ashamed of the religion of their parents. When they become self-conscious and the white group fails to cash at face value the implied promises, many revert to the parental group and become more interested in its religion.

Certain zealous religious leaders try to produce results through compulsion. Since it is difficult for students to find suitable boarding places in the cities of Hawaii, they avail themselves of a number of private dormitories. The managers, all too often attempt to force their type of religion upon the boarders. In some cases it works, but in all too many instances the results are not gratifying. A number become rebellious and break off from all religious activities at the earliest opportunity. The results are much the same be it Buddhist or Christian dormitory. At times, however, the required attendance upon religious services has worked out satisfactorily. This compulsion has given the initial impulse to an acquaintance with and finally an acceptance of the Christian religion, the outcome of which has been a wholesome life organization.

In addition to the revulsion against compulsory participation, some young people react strongly against bigotry and narrowness in religious leaders. Since they make contacts with several religions and thus examine them, cursorily at least, they are in a position to make their own choices. Many see good in the several religions and when some zealot criticizes another religion too severely there is often a reaction against this. Oftentimes their studies of history and science in the schools cast grave doubts over certain teachings received in church or Sunday school. After some reflection on the dogmatism of the religious teachers, their influence is negated, no matter whether the bigotry be found among Christians or Buddhists.

In the main, the operation of church machinery in typical American fashion has been not highly successful in Hawaii so far as the younger group is concerned. Organizations and methods quite foreign to those with entirely different backgrounds have been introduced bodily. No adequate study has been made of the conditions in order to adapt programs to actual needs. As a consequence, the Christian agencies are not highly efficient in the service they are rendering in this period of transition and are unable to elicit the whole-hearted allegiance of the younger generation.

Some young people turn against Christianity on account of unfortunate experiences with church members, chiefly with those of the Caucasian group. White people are considered members of the Christian group and, since Christianity has been highly extolled, they expect much from them. Under such circumstances the experiences leave a taste which is all the more bitter. In some instances they conclude that such are weaknesses common to all humanity and that all men, whether Buddhists, Christians, Confucianists, or what not, have these failings. Some are highly sensitive and misconstrue many actions to be discriminations against themselves on account of race. They take the position that they are American-born children of oriental parentage and as such are entitled to special consideration. Probably they are unaware of the fact that even Anglo-Saxons often receive unjust treatment.

## Other Contributing Factors

According to a second generation Chinese, the third generation in Hawaii is not turning to Christianity in the same measure as his group did. The second generation Chinese as youths were sensitive to opinion of the white group and this had an influence upon their religious affiliations. The third generation is less sensitive to pressure from this source, because the Chinese community is now of such importance that recognition and status gained in this group are sufficient. Hence they evince less interest in the Christian churches. A number of Hawaiian-born Japanese men, who in their early years and while on the mainland in college and professional schools considered themselves Christians, have given up all connections with the Christian churches after returning to practice their professions. These professional men as yet have to depend largely on their racial groups for patronage. Since the purse strings are yet largely controlled by the immigrant Japanese, who in the main are Buddhists, it is economically profitable to ally themselves with the adherents of this religion. For many this is not a difficult step to take, especially after they have gone through a process of disillusionment with reference to the Christian religion.

## Resultant Syncretistic Religion of the Younger Group

The children of oriental ancestry who come into contact with a variety of religious beliefs and practices have no single pattern to follow. In most localities with any number of Japanese residents, there is a Buddhist temple or church and also a Christian church of some denomination. Usually both conduct Sunday schools and very often parents send their children to both. Since there is considerable difference between these religions, perplexity and confusion often result which at times leads to an indifference to both. In some families this results in a heterogeneity of religious beliefs. A college boy in Hawaii reported that his father was a Shintoist, his mother a Buddhist, his elder sister a Christian, his elder brother claimed to be an atheist, while he himself "being in such a situation never did take religion seriously."

Almost invariably the religion of the younger generation of oriental ancestry will differ markedly from that of others; it will not be a Confucianism of China, a Buddhism of Japan, or a Christianity of America, but in many instances there will be a syncretism of elements from the several religions with which they have made contacts. A college girl in Hawaii has given an insight into her religious life.

In my early days I believed what my parents believed. My father is a Confucianist while my mother is a pagan. I am both and more, for I have a touch of Christianity in me. My religion is of my own making and my God is my own creation. I was superstitious and I had great faith in the curing and avenging powers of my mother's pagan gods. I burned incense and kowtowed to them in submission. As I grew older and came into contact with more people, I began to see things with a clearer vision. I realized that these gods did not meet my needs and all my previous superstitions were unreal, unscientific and of no value to me. My life has been molded by my religion. I dared not to do anything that would offend my god. When I am sick, I always look to my God to cure me. My concentration on his power of healing is so strong that I usually see favorable results. Confucius' teachings guide me in my moral actions, in my relationship between various social groups. Christianity teaches me to be loving and forgiving. Idols of paganism are really the policemen of my behavior. I am afraid of them for I believe that my misfortunes are brought by them as forms of punishment for my wrong-doings. Then I look upon my own created God to heal me. He is my judge, my savior.

# ✥173✥

# What Vedanta Means to Me

## DOROTHY F. MERCER

The interest of this personal narrative of involvement with Vedanta is two-fold. It links the author, through her mother, with the earliest important missionary of Hinduism in the United States, Swami Vivekananda (1862–1902). He created the Vedanta Society in 1897. The account also illustrates how Vedanta could be harmonized with strands in western religious and philosophical thought.

—————————————————————

I was born into the Vedanta. No searching brought me to it. No disillusionment with other faiths, with man, or with my own particular position in time or place. I was never a materialist nor did I ever go through the agony of losing my religion.

Until I reached a questionable maturity, the world to me consisted of three kinds of people: men, women, and swamis. The men and women had desires and ambitions like me. The swamis were without either; they sprang full-grown. They taught me Vedanta philosophy, and were themselves, quite naturally I thought, embodiments of it.

Some time before I was born, my mother and father heard Swami Vivekananda speak in San Francisco. My mother's enthusiasm was not peculiar, for Vivekananda's lectures and tour across the continent were triumphant. I can remember hearing about one of her friends addressing Vivekananda with envious admiration, "India must be a *wonderful* country."

"Madam," flatly retorted India's great representative, "all Hindus are not like me."

My mother's subsequently taking lessons from Swami Trigunatita, who had come to San Francisco in 1903, was not surprising. She had heard Vivekananda; she was enamoured of the Vedanta-influenced Ralph Waldo Emerson; and she had been without ardour interested in the neo-Emersonian movement called New Thought.

Source: Dorothy F. Mercer, 'What Vedanta Means to Me',
in J. Yale, ed., *What Vedanta Means to Me*, London, 1961, pp. 68–78.

One of my father's numerous cousins thrice removed had given up her solid, militant, and generations-old Presbyterianism to become a Vedantist. "The Easterners" (my mother's name for my father's Pennsylvania-bred family) were taken aback. With a long and stalwart line of American ministers, missionaries, and schoolmasters, the Presbyterian family stronghold never understood the iconoclasm.

My mother's family, on the other hand, had long since given up denominational religion. Ostensibly Protestant, they, like many San Franciscans of the time, were not so much anti-religious as without interest in religion. A worldly, cultivated people, religion would have been a supernumerary for them socially (except for weddings and funerals), and aesthetically, economically, and politically it was unnecessary. For the most part successful businessmen, they saw no real need for God.

Even so, my mother's action in getting "mixed up" with a Hindu was criticized—put down as another instance of her proclivity for acting strangely. Because of my father's illness and consequent inability to earn the money which marked success and the standard success imposed, my mother was already a rebel. She saw no reason for being ashamed or abashed before her relatives, and attributed her predicament to false social and money values, marriage, and the unfair burden placed on women—all of which had put her in her unenviable position. The most important light in her moral and spiritual struggle was Swami Trigunatita.

How great that light was is difficult for me to estimate. She must have been early established in meditation because as long as I can remember she retired into her room every morning from ten to eleven. Although her outward life was unrewarding, she was essentially a happy woman—as she brought to my attention a few years before she died. The only subjects of interest to her in my University work were feminism and mysticism. She was visibly exalted through reading Plotinus' *Enneads*, which I brought home one day, and said she understood them because she "too was once admitted and entered into union ... by ways of meditation ... to the first and all-transcendent God".

As soon as I was old enough, I went with her weekly from our home in Mill Valley to San Francisco, to the Hindu Temple (still standing and still in use) and Swami Trigunatita. To others, Swami's office was cluttered up; to me it was finely ordered. There were stereopticon slides, a revolving globe of the world, Swami's resplendent watch fob, a roll-top desk piled high with papers; and no "don't touch" admonitions. There was a round, red, stained-glass window opening on the street which, on our last visit to his office, Swami told me was a motion picture.

This was my first verbal and still unlearned lesson in the Vedanta. I can remember insisting that it was the street, not a motion picture. But I was puzzled. Swami had never, as my dear father had on occasion, via a ruse given me castor oil.

480

Around 1913 Swami started a community project in Concord, Contra Costa County, for devotees. Because of my father's increasingly bad health and my mother's interest in the Vedanta, it was decided that we should move to Concord. I was disconsolate. Except for the shadow of my father's health, I had been a happy child in the lovely, wooded, mountain town, playing wildly with my maternal first cousins, living a life of high fancy with the fairies and elves most certainly there if I just could find them, and imitating Greek gods and goddesses with my schoolmates.

My paternal forty-second cousins who were fond of children visited us once in a while. Their advent always brought excitement, particularly as my mother's sarcasm started heated arguments when the missionaries recounted their "good works" in the Orient. Too, I was surrounded by loving and loved maternal aunts and uncles who were highly critical of what they considered bad notions to implant in a child's mind. Against their untimely criticism I vigorously defended, without understanding, my mother's attitude towards life and Swami Trigunatita.

Once Swami came to see us without warning. He knew we lived in Mill Valley but not precisely where. It seemed perfectly normal to me that he should find his way by mentally calling my brother's name: Emerson, my brother, was then two years old. It was fortunate that we lived only about a mile from the railway station.

Concord, comparatively, was desolate. There were no hills to climb, flowers to pick, friends to play gods and goddesses with, or place for fairies and elves in its flat expanse. Our relatives seldom visited us; there were no heated arguments; and I felt my life was as uninteresting as the terrain. So I determined to run away from home—back to the red-wooded beauty of the Marin hills, another Rima without the incomprehensible encumbrance of the lover. Of course I knew such thoughts were naughty; I was not, therefore, unduly surprised when my mother said I would be punished if I ran away. Swami, whom I had not seen for some time, had told her what I was contemplating.

Materially, this Vedanta Brook Farm was not successful, partly because Swami Trigunatita was killed by a religious fanatic during one of his sermons in San Francisco. The last time I can remember seeing him was in our Concord cabin sitting in a rocking-chair too high for his short legs and talking to my mother about the extensive war the United States had just entered. "Women will be in a better position as a result of it," he told her.

A few years after Swami's death in 1914 we returned to San Francisco. Although my father's health was greatly improved, we had even less money than we had had when we moved to Concord. As a consequence, it was decided to send me to business college and then to work. Nothing could have worked out better. For I skipped high school, and whatever intellectual curiosity I had was entirely absorbed by the Vedanta and Swami Abhedananda, who came to San Francisco in 1918.

En route to India from New York, where he had been since 1897, Swami

Abhedananda was urged by my mother and other old students of Swami Trigunatita to stay in San Francisco, at least for a short time. He stayed for about two and a half years, lecturing twice a week and giving a class once a week.

Swami Abhedananda was tall, handsome, austere, and of commanding presence. An eloquent, scholarly, and well-organized lecturer, he addressed hundreds every week, including many eminent San Franciscans. Even a maternal aunt and her husband went to hear him, not because they were eminent nor because they felt any religious need, but because Swami Abhedananda was one of the finest lecturers in the Bay Area. In a social group he was quiet and reserved, taking each man's measure.

I can remember one occasion when a prominent and rightfully considered great San Francisco doctor was facetiously holding forth on the yogis' ridiculous claim to psychic power. Knowing intuitively the doctor's own psychic power, Swami Abhedananda rhetorically questioned, "You do not go out mentally to your sleeping patients at night?"

Not only did I go to all of Abhedananda's lectures and classes, but during this period I read Swami Vivekananda assiduously. I too wanted to be a philosopher, a sannyasin no less. "Strike off they fetters! Bonds that bind thee down, Of shining gold. ..."

That I had no "shining gold" to "strike off" did not deter me from marching right along—in imagination. In reality I was working from nine to five and unhappy.

After Swami Abhedananda left San Francisco, I decided to go to night school, save, and matriculate into the University. My early undergraduate days were miserable. I was behind my class and had neither time nor money for social life. Intellectually too I was out of step. This was the cynical late post-war era: religion was the opium of the people, the United States was the greatest show on earth, and libidos were knowingly discussed. Once, having relieved myself vociferously in a wholesale denunciation of Marx, Mencken, and Freud to the greater glory of the Vedanta, a friend, whose mother was a Vedantist, took me aside.

"I'd drop the Vedanta, if I were you. They'll think you're 'queer'."

Since by this time I thought I was queer—how else could I account for my misery?—I resolved I'd say nothing more about the Vedanta.

If I were to lose my faith, I should have lost it at this time. For the next semester Swami Bodhananda spoke in San Francisco, my dearly beloved brother died, I fell in love, saw beauty, and made a scholarly discovery based on the Vedanta—in that order.

I do not know to this day why Swami Bodhananda made an impression on me. He was not fatherly as Swami Trigunatita had been, nor had he the commanding presence of Swami Abhedananda, nor did he speak eloquently. He said nothing that I had not heard time and time again. But I was uplifted for quite a period—long enough to face my brother's death with an equanimity which astonished my mother. I had so obviously adored my brother—his light-hearted gaiety, social aplomb, handsome nonchalance which kept my girl friends at his feet—that my mother thought she had a cold-hearted daughter instead of an emotional one.

I never faced another death with the same equanimity. I think now my attitude had something to do with my brother himself. After his death when my mother could talk about it without giving way to grief, she told me that years before she had asked Swami Trigunatita what her children's destinies would be. "Dorothy will be protected by the goddess of learning; Emerson is my child," Swami had told her.

Then I thought nothing of Swami's prophecy; now I wonder. I wonder not only about my brother whom I frequently meet in warning dreams but also about myself. Because when Swami Trigunatita made his prediction, I was a harum-scarum child of six not paying any attention to school and living in a world of fantasy.

Love and art came to me simultaneously. I had always liked to read, mainly for the story but also, and especially in poetry, for the moral which I thought to emulate. Now—

> . . . I too have seen
> My vision of the rainbow Aureoled face
> Of her whom men name Beauty: proud, austere:
> Divinely fugitive, that haunts the world.

From that vision I have never been able to extricate myself, nor have I tried. I am marvellously raised and elevated by words. For that reason I enjoy teaching and doing research. Not creative, I worship through the form of appreciation enhanced as I try to impart it. Not naturally a researcher, I am nagged by wanting to find out why love, art, and mysticism are tied up together. Who was it that said, "Whenever I open a door, I meet Plato coming out?"

But I am not a mystic. The best I can do is to recognize one. During my junior year I took a course in the lyric and read *Leaves of Grass* because as an American I thought I should. Coming from Vivekananda to Walt Whitman I had a strange feeling: it was not only the many parallel ideas extracted from mid-nineteenth-century American-scene imagery; it was the tone and dynamic strength. Whitman is a poet; Vivekananda a prose writer. But some of Whitman's poetry could be put into prose form, and Vivekananda's prose at its best could be written as free verse. The invigorating, energizing, freeing effect is the same.

At the University was one of the West's most notable Sanskrit scholars— Arthur W. Ryder. He had small respect for Western philosophy—Plato and Kant were the only two he acknowledged—but great respect for Eastern. He himself was a follower of Sankhya rather than Vedanta; however, he was fair to the Vedanta and used to lecture on its "splendid lift and sweep." He had also known Swami Trigunatita and was perfectly agreeable to my using Vivekananda and Abhedananda as two authorities on the Vedanta.

Another professor, John S. P. Tatlock, worried me. He was a "fact" man, philosophically naïve, and considered by students in literary criticism as "difficult." What were my relief and astonishment to find that he had known Abhedananda at Harvard and respected his judgement. (Swami Abhedananda had written me after the subject of my dissertation had been accepted: "Walt Whitman . . . must have studied the Bhagavad Gita, for in his *Leaves of Grass*, one finds the teachings of Vedanta. . . . The 'Song of Myself' is but an echo of the sayings of Krishna.")

When I went to Oxford University, Dr. S. Radhakrishnan was Spalding Professor of Eastern Religions and Ethics. To my ears he was giving a course on the Vedanta. Had it not been that I was more interested in an aesthetic application of the Vedanta than in its ethical or metaphysical aspects, I would have requested him as my tutor. For he was a great lecturer, the greatest at Oxford. Never using a note, he lectured week after week in such a thoroughly organized and fluent fashion that it seemed as though there had been no interruption between lecturers. He was pleased and, I think, surprised at my saying after I met him that I had been taught the Vedanta by swamis of the Ramakrishna Order.

I was fortunate in having as my tutor the most remarkable man in the English School, Humphry House, when I returned to Oxford after World War II. He had taught for a brief period at Calcutta University and was generally unhappy about India. When I mentioned the Ramakrishna Order, however, his expression changed. "The Ramakrishna Order? Well, that is another story. Its reputation is excellent, and it has the respect of everyone in India."

As my work progressed from the Oxonian Collingwood, through Plato and Aristotle, and eventually to the great Christian mystic, Jacob Boehme, the old wonder of the University of California graduate days returned. I was intensely happy in my work and discovered for myself the perennial philosophy.

Theoretically, the perennial philosophy was not new to me. Swami Abhedananda at the close of each lecture had offered a prayer: "May He who is the Father in Heaven of the Christians, Allah of the Mohammedans, Divine Mother of the Hindus, grant unto us all peace and blessing." He had pointed parallels in Christian and Hindu Scripture, and had quoted from the Sufis. *The Washington Star* in reporting on his book *Great Saviors of the World* had said: "These studies are scholarly and comprehensive reviews of historic fact. ... The author's attitude is reverent towards all ... a good study fitted to open the heart and liberalize the mind." Too, I knew Sri Ramakrishna had experientially proved the common result of various religious disciplines, including Christian. And I had myself read extensively in the literature of mysticism. But I had never before made an intensive study of any mysticism other than the Vedanta.

Plato was a great experience for me. Although I already had some knowledge of him as do most college students in the United States, his mysticism had never been emphasized. I can remember in my freshman year reading *The Republic* and noting Vedanta similarities; the philosophy professors were either not interested or, more likely, my exposition was not clear. (Thanks to Swami Prabhavananda, I have recently read E. J. Urwick's *The Message of Plato* which ably points the astonishing parallels.) Whether because I was reading in the English School at Oxford, or because by now I was a mature student, or because I had such an extraordinary tutor, I was encouraged to do intensive work on Plato.

I owe Jacob Boehme also to Oxford although indirectly. One of the most difficult of the Christian mystics, Boehme was for me a profound and psychologically astute teacher after I had begun to understand his alchemical terminology and to accept rather than be impatient with his repetitions and unintelligible scientific references. Too, his qualities of humility and sincerity endeared him to me: a tiny twig in God's vast vineyard, he characterizes himself; better known is the great personal sacrifice he made in standing against the vested authority of his time without fanfare.

What has Boehme or Plato to do with the Vedanta? Nothing and everything. Leaving me free, the Vedanta has held me fast. It has not bothered me with dogma; it has never said, "Don't touch." I can read Boehme and Plato and know their truth is the truth of the Vedanta; nay, *the* truth which sages variously name. I can join the celebrants on Corpus Christi Day at St. Paul's Outside the Gates in Rome, or listen to the choristers at King's College Chapel, Cambridge, or sit in silence with the Quakers in their bare meeting-room at Oxford. Wherever God is worshipped there He resides was too early implanted in my mind for me to have any doubts. And why should I? "The nearest gnat is an explanation, and a drop or motion of waves a key."

For this breadth of outlook, I owe a debt of gratitude to my mother and to the swamis of the Ramakrishna Order which can neither be adequately expressed nor adequately paid. The faith in mysticism which they gave me has, needless to say perhaps, been a bulwark in facing emotional crises. Not so evident or so universally acknowledged is the appeal mysticism makes to the imagination.

And intellectually advaita Vedanta has stood the tangible test of two Vedanta-based dissertations: one for the B. Litt. degree at Oxford University and another for the Ph.D. degree at the University of California. I can remember the exasperation of one of my examiners faced for the first time with Shankara and his distinction between the Higher and Lower Brahman. In trying to break down one of my comments and being met at every turn with the Higher Brahman, my examiner threw up his hands: "This Higher Brahman, I must say, is very convenient." Although satisfying me emotionally, imaginatively, and intellectually, experiencially, I am ashamed to admit, I know nothing about mysticism.

"God dwells in all things; nothing comprehends him unless it be one with him" is Boehme's statement of *Tat tvam asi*. Many great mystics have repeated this ancient "Know Thyself"—repeated it so often as to be in danger of tediousness. But is there any mystic of stature who has not warned that reading about God is worth very little, at best a donkey's occupation?

No true lover of learning or of the beautiful, I have squandered a rich heritage which would have given me eternal nourishment rather than an occasional glimpse of a fugitive divinity. Frequently discouraged, I have more often than not lost my passion in routine, in duty, in petty ambition, petty appreciation, petty effort to conform to petty standards. A soul in travail, I have not been married to true being, nor have I had the hardihood to pursue the beautiful unconcerned with its many particulars. I have allowed myself to be "cheated by the magic veil of shows."

As Plato says in *The Republic* before one of his great postulations of absolute Good: "Then shall we not make a reasonable defence when we say that the true lover of learning naturally strove towards what is, and would not abide by the many particulars that are believed to be, but went forward undiscouraged, and did not cease from his passion until he grasped the nature of each reality that is, with that part of his soul which is fitted to lay hold of such by reason of its affinity with it; whereby being near to and married with true being, and begetting reason and truth, he came to knowledge and true life and nourishment, and then, and only then, ceased from the travail of his soul."

Why should not the small hope I have had after every fleeting glimpse of true being sustain me now in a larger hope? Can I not too be nourished? Am I not a legitimate child of the Divine Mother as Sri Ramakrishna reminded his devotees? I have hope, therefore (a good Christian virtue), that some day I shall be able to look out of the window and in place of seeing only the street's passing traffic know, as Swami Trigunatita so long ago told me, that what I am seeing is not Reality but a motion picture—TV he would probably say today, for he was not one to discount modern gadgets.

# ❧174❧

# Beat Zen, Square Zen, Zen

## ALAN WATTS

Alan Watts, an English-born populariser of Zen Buddhism in the decades after World War II, was particularly widely read in countercultural circles in the 1960s. Zen's stimulus to deep exploration of the self and the sense of oneness which it gave with an unchanging universe were attractive to young people alienated from a technological society riven with conflict. Zen Buddhism could also be a transient cultural fad. A lasting legacy of Zen's sense of the interconnectedness of things was a strand in the modern environmentalist movement that emerged in the 1960s.

A bove all, I believe that Zen appeals to many in the post-Christian West because it does not preach, moralize, and scold in the style of Hebrew-Christian prophetism. Buddhism does not deny that there is a relatively limited sphere in which human life may be improved by art and science, reason and good will. However, it regards this sphere of activity as important but nonetheless subordinate to the comparatively limitless sphere in which things are as they are, always have been, and always will be—a sphere entirely beyond the categories of good and evil, success and failure, and individual health and sickness. On the one hand, this is the sphere of the great universe. Looking out into it at night, we make no comparisons between right and wrong stars, nor between well and badly arranged constellations. Stars are by nature big and little, bright and dim. Yet the whole thing is a splendor and a marvel which sometimes makes our flesh creep with awe. On the other hand, this is also the sphere of human, everyday life which we might call existential.

For there is a standpoint from which human affairs are as much beyond right and wrong as the stars, and from which our deeds, experiences, and feelings can no more be judged than the ups and downs of a range of mountains. Though beyond moral and social valuation, this level of human life may also be seen to be just as marvellous and uncanny as the great universe itself. This feeling may become particularly acute when the individual ego tries to fathom its own nature,

Source: Allan Watts, 'Beat Zen, Square Zen, Zen', *This Is It*, London, 1961, pp. 87-91.

to plumb the inner sources of its own actions and consciousness. For here it discovers a part of itself–the inmost and greatest part–which is strange to itself and beyond its understanding and control. Odd as it may sound, the ego finds that its own center and nature is beyond itself. The more deeply I go into myself, the more I am not myself, and yet this is the very heart of me. Here I find my own inner workings functioning of themselves, spontaneously, like the rotation of the heavenly bodies and the drifting of the clouds. Strange and foreign as this aspect of myself at first seems to be, I soon realize that it *is* me, and much more me than my superficial ego. This is not fatalism or determinism, because there is no longer anyone being pushed around or determined; there is nothing that this deep "I" is not doing. The configuration of my nervous system, like the configuration of the stars, happens of itself, and this "itself" is the real "myself."

From this standpoint–and here language reveals its limitations with a vengeance–I find that I cannot help doing and experiencing, quite freely, what is always "right," in the sense that the stars are always in their "right" places. As Hsiang-yen put it,

> There's no use for artificial discipline,
> For, move as I will, I manifest the ancient Tao.

At this level, human life is beyond anxiety, for it can never make a mistake. If we live, we live; if we die, we die; if we suffer, we suffer; if we are terrified, we are terrified. There is no problem about it. A Zen master was once asked, "It is terribly hot, and how shall we escape the heat?" "Why not," he answered, "go to the place where it is neither hot nor cold?" "Where is that place?" "In summer we sweat; in winter we shiver." In Zen one does not feel guilty about dying, or being afraid, or disliking the heat. At the same time, Zen does not insist upon this point of view as something which one *ought* to adopt; it does not preach it as an ideal. For if you don't understand it, your very not-understanding is also IT. There would be no bright stars without dim stars, and, without the surrounding darkness, no stars at all.

The Hebrew–Christian universe is one in which moral urgency, the anxiety to be right, embraces and penetrates everything. God, the Absolute itself, is good as against bad, and thus to be immoral or in the wrong is to feel oneself an outcast not merely from human society but also from existence itself, from the root and ground of life. To be in the wrong therefore arouses a metaphysical anxiety and sense of guilt–a state of eternal damnation–utterly disproportionate to the crime. This metaphysical guilt is so insupportable that it must eventually issue in the rejection of God and of his laws–which is just what has happened in the whole movement of modern secularism, materialism, and naturalism. Absolute morality is profoundly destructive of morality, for the sanctions which it invokes against evil are far, far too heavy. One does not cure the headache by cutting off the head. The appeal of Zen, as of other forms of Eastern philosophy, is that it unveils behind the urgent realm of good and evil a vast region of oneself about which there need be no guilt or recrimination, where at last the self is indistinguishable from God.

But the Westerner who is attracted by Zen and who would understand it deeply must have one indispensable qualification: he must understand his own culture so thoroughly that he is no longer swayed by its premises unconsciously. He must really have come to terms with the Lord God Jehovah and with his Hebrew-Christian conscience so that he can take it or leave it without fear or rebellion. He must be free of the itch to justify himself. Lacking this, his Zen will be either "beat" or "square," either a revolt from the culture and social order or a new form of stuffiness and respectability. For Zen is above all the liberation of the mind from conventional thought, and this is something utterly different from rebellion against convention, on the one hand, or adapting foreign conventions, on the other.

Conventional thought is, in brief, the confusion of the concrete universe of nature with the conceptual things, events, and values of linguistic and cultural symbolism. For in Taoism and Zen the world is seen as an inseparably interrelated field or continuum, no part of which can actually be separated from the rest or valued above or below the rest. It was in this sense that Huineng, the Sixth Patriarch, meant that "fundamentally not one thing exists," for he realized that things are *terms*, not entities. They exist in the abstract world of thought, but not in the concrete world of nature. Thus one who actually perceives or feels this to be so no longer feels that he is an ego, except by definition. He sees that his ego is his *persona* or social role, a somewhat arbitrary selection of experiences with which he has been taught to identify himself. (Why, for example, do we say "I think" but not "I am beating my heart?") Having seen this, he continues to play his social role without being taken in by it. He does not precipitately adopt a new role or play the role of having no role at all. He plays it cool.

# ✥175✥

# The Real Threat of the Moonies

## HARVEY COX

Harvey Cox, a professor of religion, tried to get behind the controversies over the alleged right-wing politics and psychological programming of the Rev. Sun Myung Moon's Unification Church. Does it pose a serious theological challenge to traditional American Christians by confronting them with other spiritual traditions? Cox also suggests that, as it seemed to him in 1977, the Church's political outlook was more complex than had been supposed. What was the nature of its appeal, particularly to the young?

---

The Boston Headquarters of the Unification Church is an elaborately constructed old mansion on Beacon hill, occupied during the Gilded Age by the family of the founder of the Jordan Marsh department store. From its steep windows and grilled balconies the members of the Reverend Sun Myung Moon's organization can gaze at a plaque erected on the Common in 1930 during the administration of the late Mayor James Michael Curley to commemorate the 300th anniversary of the founding of the City of Boston. The plaque carries part of the famous sermon of Governor John Winthrop, preached on board the *Arabella* just before landing, in which he declared the settlers had been called by God to "build a city set upon a hill," a new commonwealth which, under God's providence, would establish his righteous reign in the virgin wilderness.

There is something singularly appropriate about this juxtaposition, for in the Unification Church an old idea that both Winthrop and Curley believed in their own different ways has returned like the Ghost of Christmas Past. The idea is simply that God has a special purpose in mind for America, and that if America misses its destiny, it will be an affront to the very nature of God. For Winthrop this providential vision was derived from a stoutly Calvinistic belief that God's hand had guided the settlers to the new world. For Curley it was a hope, sprung no doubt from his Catholic parish and parochial school training, as well as from his own experience as an Irish–American, that America should

Source: Harvey Cox, 'The Real Threat of the Moonies', *Christianity in Crisis*, 14 November 1977.

be the place where what he called "the newer races" would find a place in the sun. That badly battered idea, called by some the "American civil religion" and recently seen to be faltering, is back again in a surprising new form in the teaching of Moon, a former Calvinist and a member of what Curley would surely have thought of as one of his "newer races."

Earlier this fall I attended one of those notorious Moonie weekend workshops, held in this headquarters building. Friends and family bade me farewell, some joking about how long they should wait before dispatching a deprogrammer, others voicing mild or serious misgivings about whether I should get involved with such people. My reason for wanting to go was mainly curiosity. I teach one course at Harvard on new religious movements and another on heresy, and the Moonie movement seemed to be a fine example of both. Also, I had heard and read a lot about the Reverend Moon, his Unification Church and the weekend workshops where innocent young post-adolescents were allegedly brainwashed into docile robots. I had done a lot to oppose the deprogrammers. Now I wanted to see for myself; so I called the local Unification Church headquarters and registered for a weekend.

The workshop began with a supper of hamburger and noodles. While we ate, some of the brothers and sisters in the "family" sang several songs. I noticed a high proportion of young people of Oriental background (almost all Japanese, it turned out) among the singers and hosts. Later, when the 23 people who had gathered introduced themselves, we discovered that we represented seven different countries including Germany, Kenya, Japan, England and Jamaica. Most of the people were already members. Only about eight were new recruits. One workshop attender was a sympathetic mother whose son had joined the church a few years before and who had joined it herself recently. The master of ceremonies was a lively, sharply dressed, young Japanese who first introduced a sextet and then a sister who sang "Green Fields." Then he himself sang the theme song from Exodus. After a few more songs sung by the whole group, some sisters emerged from the kitchen carrying trays of banana splits.

## Uniting Religion and Science

While we ate, the director of the center, an Irish–American, gave a lecture on the Divine Principle. His approach was cheerful, confident and articulate. He explained that this lecture was "only a taste," a sample designed to persuade those still undecided to attend the workshop which was then beginning. (Only later did I learn what a small taste his lecture was and how gigantic a full helping can be.) His main argument seemed to be that we can no longer perpetuate the division between science and religion, but that religion must be brought up to date in order to meet the intellectual and social challenges of the modern world. He added that although in some movements one goes off to meditate alone in order to meet the divine, here, since people are created in the image of God, we meet the divine by meeting each other. He did not ask for questions and none were asked. After a few more songs we were asked to get to bed—it was already 11:45—and to be up for group exercise at 7 a.m. The men and women were ushered off to different floors.

At 7 a.m. the chords of a Bach fugue swelled through the building and the participants tumbled out onto the linoleum floor of a large room on the second floor to exercise. After 20 minutes of stretching, we breakfasted on orange juice, fried eggs, sliced tomatoes and toasted rolls. The morning session began at about 9:30 with more songs led by the energetic MC. Then the director began another lecture on the Divine Principle.

The lecture was unbelievably complex, elaborate and long. After an hour and 20 minutes my head began to ache; my buttocks had already gone numb. We had heard about the negative and positive valences of atoms and molecules; the feminine and masculine aspects of plants and animals; the need for a new development in Christianity; the pattern of Creation-Fall-Restoration-Last Days-Resurrection; the duality of God's being; the similarities and differences between Oriental philosophy and the Divine Principle. Were people actually listening? Although they seemed to be, I could not help wondering where minds were wandering. When I began to look a little tired after nearly two hours of the lecture, the Japanese woman seated next to me smiled and began to pound lightly on the back of my neck and massage my shoulders, apparently in a sisterly effort to keep alert.

At about noon, after I had almost given up hope that the lecture would ever end, the director announced a coffee break (not lunch) after which the "second part of the lecture" would begin.

We were back in the lecture room by 12:30 and at 2:30 the lecturer was still going strong. My stomach was screaming for lunch. I wondered how people were bearing it. Long before this, my own students would have reminded me that we had gone on far too long. The "Four Position Foundation," the "Three Blessings," the relation of the spiritual to the physical world, the reasons for the failure of Christianity to bring in the Kingdom of God, the need to establish a newly perfected family—it all poured out in cascades of words, analogies, biblical quotations and scientific allusions. I wondered what had ever happened to the "brainwashing," the group pressures, the subtle indoctrination. To me it seemed like a clear example of philosophical overkill. At first I was totally unable to recognize what the appeal could possibly be.

But appeal there is—and it is in large measure a theological-intellectual one at that. In his book, *Sun Myung Moon and the Unification Church*, Frederick Sontag has tried to discern what the appeal is. In order to do so he spent an entire year traveling and studying the Unification Church in Europe, the US and the Orient. His book is almost obsessively "objective," setting forth the roots of the Moon movement in Korea, its amazing growth in Japan, Europe and America, the teachings of the Divine Principle, the brainwashing and deprogramming controversy and the future prospects of the movement. Sontag relies very heavily—perhaps too much so—on interviews with a large number of church members, including early disciples in Korea. His book also includes a lengthy interview with the Reverend Moon. It does not probe very deeply beneath the replies.

What Sontag glaringly leaves out is any reference to the cloud of political accusations that have hung over Moon almost since his arrival in the US. Some readers will find this to be a fatal flaw in the book. I did not, however. There is very little hard evidence to be found, and at the time Sontag wrote the book the Fraser Committee's investigations of South Korean influence peddling (which, in any case, have not yet turned up much on Moon) had not even begun.

## A Three-Tiered Challenge

Whether or not these investigations turn up evidence about Moon himself, I do not believe the whole movement is merely a political front. In fact, I believe some of the liberal critics of the Moon movement do us all a great disservice by seeing the Moonies *entirely* in terms of a political threat (which they may in fact be), thus failing to come to terms with the genuine *theological* challenge the movement poses. I think this theological challenge comes at three levels, no one of which can be dealt with by attempting to reduce the appeal of Unification to behavioral control or political subterfuge. These three levels are: (1) Unification's bid to transcend the particularism of historical Christianity and combine the great religious traditions into one; (2) Its programmatic effort to go beyond the dichotomy between religion and science; and (3) Its vision of a *novus ordo seculorum* guided in its economic and cultural life by religious teachings.

(1) *Beyond traditional Christianity.* One of the things about the Unification Church which most confuses and angers traditional Christians is that it claims to be a Christian church—thus meriting membership in the National Council of Churches—and at the same time a movement which goes beyond Christianity to a higher stage of spiritual development, a stage it claims the human race is now ready for. This is not a new challenge. Mormons, Christian Scientists and others have made it in the past. But the threat it poses to almost all present forms of theology is a formidable one. The question, simply put, is: Can there be new revelations, or are all such revelations *ipso facto* heretical? Pastor John Robinson in his farewell sermon to the Pilgrims declared that "God has yet new light to break forth his Holy Word." The underlying question of what "new light" is and how it relates to the "Holy Word" has never been solved. Catholics have generally been a bit more open to progressive revelations than have strictly *schriftmassig* Protestants. Witness the evolution of Marian devotion and the revelations at Lourdes and Fatima. But Christians who emphasize the Holy Spirit more than either Catholics or Protestants do have tended to be even more open to religious ideas not derived solely from the original revelation. Lamentably, the failure of orthodox theology to deal with the claims of the Unification Church betokens a larger puzzlement about the independent churches of Africa and the burgeoning Pentecostal movements. Maybe that is why the National Council of

Churches' recent critique of the Divine Principle sounds so implausible at many points. At least the Moonies, performing the historic function of heresies, have forced the NCC to make its theology a bit more explicit. The problem is: Now that it's explicit, how adequate is it?

I have no doubt that at the core of Unification's appeal to many young people is its claim to permit them to remain Christian, but to subsume the particularity of Christianity in a larger and more comprehensive world faith. Moon's teaching combines such characteristic Oriental elements as Yin and Yang, a kind of modified version of karma called "indemnity," the role of the guru and— especially—the centrality of the family in transmitting a spiritual tradition. The volumes of Dr. Yung Oon Kim, the principle theologian of the movement, deal in a fundamentally sympathetic way with the major spiritual traditions of the world. In the research I did for *Turning East* I ran across hundreds of young people who wanted to be religious, even Christian, but who felt both attracted by Oriental ideas and practices and at the same time confused by the bewildering plethora of religious claims around them.

I do not believe Christian theology can continue to dodge this challenge of global religious pluralism much longer. Unification theology is surely not the answer, but until Christian theology comes up with a religious vision that transcends the particularism (if not parochialism) by which it is currently harnessed, nothing is to be gained by condemning Unification thought, because it tries to cope with one of the major facts of life in the late 20th century: global religious pluralism.

(2) *Beyond the conflict between religion and science.* Why did two dozen reasonably intelligent people, including a nuclear engineer from MIT and a graduate fellow in physics from Harvard, sit through those interminable lectures at the weekend workshop I attended? I think the reason is that the Divine Principle was presented not just as an authoritative religious teaching but as a system of ideas substantiated by modern science. Time after time I was reminded of the books of Teilhard de Chardin. Many of the ideas are similar: a frank acceptance of evolution, a fascination with the "inside" and the "outside" of all phenomena (called "sung sang" and "hyung sang" in Moon's theology), the notion that we stand today at a crucial turning point in the unfolding of human consciousness.

## Dubious Analogies

As the lectures proceeded, the appeals to science came less frequently, and there was even an occasional tendency to resort to proof-texting. I am not saying the appeal to science was persuasive. It was not, at least not to me, although I do not have much scientific training. Also, the science-oriented people present seemed quite unsophisticated in the problems related to the analogical applications of biological or chemical theories to other fields. Consequently they seemed more persuaded by the lectures than I thought they should be.

494

Still it made me wonder about how much theology has ducked the issue of scientific reasoning recently by accepting this division of realms, while many young people want to find a single holistic approach to all questions. In any case, the lecturer continually stressed the need to bring religion and science back together, and his listeners obviously liked the idea and believed it would be possible if worked at assiduously enough.

This aspect of Moon's teaching explains to some extent why he is willing to expend such huge amounts of time and money on the annual International Conference on the Unity of Science which is scheduled to take place this year in San Francisco and will concentrate on the "search for absolute values." The roster of this year's conference includes the usual number of Nobel laureates, as well as one prominent Marxist philosopher, Adam Schaff. I have been invited to attend this controversial and lushly arranged gathering nearly every year since its inception and have always turned it down, in part because like many others I have been suspicious of its actual intent. As I have looked into the Moon movement more carefully, however—and this observation is sustained by Sontag's more thorough study—I have come to believe that the Science Conference, though it obviously produces a large public relations pay-off, is not just a front or a subterfuge. Moon and his followers devoutly believe that science, ethics and religion must be brought back together. Although I have alerted uninformed colleagues in the past about the sponsorship of the conference and have urged them not to go unless they knew what they were doing, it seems to me improbable that it is mere window dressing.

In fact, reading this year's program makes me wonder why churches are not sponsoring more conversations on similar themes. Theologians may believe they have left the battle between science and theology far behind, but many young people—and many, many scientists—do not believe it at all. The turn of recent theology toward religious experience on the one hand, and social issues on the other, has left the vital issue of the relation between theology and science relatively unattended. Only the process theologians are pursuing it with much vigor. If the Moonie attempt to bridge the gap seems inept and heavy-handed, it should receive at least some credit for making the try. The only way to refute it is to do it better.

(3) *Spiritually guided secular order*. The critics of the Moonies are entirely right when they describe it as a political movement. Unification thought insists that its most important contribution is the idea of the "restoration" of God's original plan and the building of the Heavenly Kingdom on earth. It is a "social gospel" with a vengeance, based on a millenarian assurance that we are now living in the last days and a firm conviction that the Messiah will return when human beings have done their part to prepare the way. In Moon's theology the key institution in the transformation of any society is the *family*, since it forms the link between the individual and the larger institutions of a culture. Moonies believe that by purifying themselves and building new and holy families they are contributing to the reform of the whole. The restoration then proceeds to

clan, tribe, nation and the world.

The question is, of course, about the ideological content of the Unification "social gospel" and the theory of social change underlying its teaching. Here Moon makes no secret of his position. He is a militant anti-communist, a South Korean patriot who avidly defended Richard Nixon and a man who has publicly stated that one of his main reasons for coming to the US is to warn us about the Red Menace. Readers of the Unification Church's daily newspaper, *The News World*, can hardly miss its right-wing slant, its fondness for Ronald Reagan and its tendency to support conservative causes. On the weekend I was at the workshop the newspaper carried a letter to the editor demanding Carter's impeachment because of his pro-communist policies, and columns by such predictables as Michael Novak (supporting capital punishment) and Phyllis Schafly (denouncing the Panama Canal "giveway"). Another Moon-sponsored publication, *The Rising Tide*, is even more vehemently right-wing. The August 1977 issue featured a front-page photo and article on Dr. Fred Schwartz, director of the Christian Anti-Communist Crusade. The cartoon depicted North Korean soldiers helping to get an American soldier out of Korea. The publisher of *The Rising Tide* is Neil A. Salonen, who is also president of the Unification Church of America.

## "True Socialism"

Admittedly, this does not seem a very promising social gospel. My own experience with the Unification Church, however, suggests that its political profile may be a bit more complex than these facts suggest. Remember that Ted Patrick, the famous deprogrammer, made his original case against the Moonies by insisting that they represented a communist plot to subvert the youth of America. The lecturer at the workshop I attended frequently referred to capitalism as an example of the institutionalized selfishness which the Divine Principle is designed to eradicate. (His comment on communism: It's better than capitalism "in principle" since it looks to the whole rather than the individual, but its advocates have used "wrong methods" to introduce it, i.e., force.) The lecturer often used the term "true socialism" to describe the coming Kingdom of God on earth. The workshop attenders I talked to did not appear to be devout anti-communists. They seemed politically naive and not very well informed. A lovely African Moonie woman told me that although she came from Kenya, she actually preferred the "African socialism" of Tanzania as a more ideal social order. The main political errors of the Moonies are confusion, ignorance and innocence. Like most mainstream Americans, they are against communism and pornography, for the family and God. Making all the connections is left to someone else.

The Moon movement has been accused of being fascist or proto-fascist. Since these terms are often used very loosely, it is hard to be sure just what the accusation means. If it refers to avid anti-communism, an authoritarian ethos and blatant kind of patriotism, then those ingredients are surely there. But there are other parts of the Moon organization and ideology which do not fit into any recognizable profile of "fascism." Moon himself says the two Americans he admires most are George Washington and Martin Luther King, Jr., one because he brought freedom to America, the other because he wanted to make America a place where all colors and nationalities could unite to form a world culture. The "God Bless America Rally" in Washington in 1976 ended with a tableau including a living Statue of Liberty—who was black. Unification thought is passionately anti-racist. Many of the marriages the leaders arrange among the members are across Oriental-Occidental lines, symbolizing the coming unification of East and West. A favorite Unification hymn puts it this way:

> Hope of a New Age is the power of the world
> Song of establishing the true ideal
> Resounding all over the world
> Eastern and Western together hand in hand
> Let us accomplish a united world.

The real political challenge of the Moonies is not, I believe, that they are a proto-fascist movement or a secret part of a vast right-wing conspiracy. Those would be relatively easy to deal with. The real challenge is that Unification presents to idealistic young people a social vision aimed at peace, racial amity, ecological balance and economic justice based on stories and symbols drawn directly from the biblical sources they have heard since they were young and from the American civil religion that still—despite Watergate, Viet Nam and all the rest—maintains a grip on their imaginations. This seems especially telling since sociologists who have studied the Moon movement tell us a large proportion of its adherents come from second-generation American families where the American dream is still more vital than it is in other sectors. Furthermore, this vision of a Heavenly Kingdom that will start in America is presented as something the members can begin to work and sacrifice for right now. And they do.

I believe the attraction of the Moon movement to naive idealistic youth is not a result of sinister brainwashing but an inevitable consequence of the utter vacuum that now exists on what might be called the "Christian left." The theory that the only things young people are interested in today are beer-guzzling and careerism is simply untrue. Many are looking for a credible, religiously grounded social vision. But little is offered them. The black movement, though it now appears to be stirring again, for years has seemed to be either moribund or suspicious of non-black participation. The peace movement is dead. Feminism, which has a powerful appeal to many women, hardly presents an inclusive social program. Everywhere else we see only fragmentation, confusion and appeals to support revolutions in the Third World, which—as essential as these revolutions are—rarely give a young person something to do here and now for a just and peaceful world. Moon offers toil and martyrdom for a world that must be built anew. The mainline churches seem to offer school and career in a world expected to stay pretty much the same.

I am convinced that the only real "answer" to the Unification religious/political challenge is to provide something better. It must be a political vision based on Judeo-Christian values, open to insights from the Orient, aware of the critical factor of class (which is rarely mentioned by the Moonies) and willing to utilize Marxist analyses without falling into sectarian bickering or authoritarianism. It is time for a rebirth of a biblically based socialism with a real program. Young people whose parents and older brothers and sisters marched at Selma and flocked to the mass peace rallies search in vain for comparable opportunities to invest their energies today. Moon's appeal is a reflection of the death of social action in churches and synagogues and the failure of theology to provide a credible basis for the struggle for the Kingdom. We should not underestimate youth's willingness to accept sacrifice and discipline in the interest of an ideal.

## Beyond Ideology

At about 10 o'clock Saturday night, as the lecturer was finishing his presentation, he began talking—apparently with great feeling—about the "heart of God," a central symbol in Unification thought. "God," he said, "is a brokenhearted God, one who has suffered for thousands of years, waiting for us to do our part to serve him and build the Kingdom." And he began to weep. Soon most of the young Moonies around me were also praying and weeping, asking God to forgive them for contributing to his suffering, dedicating themselves to him anew.

At this point, in an atmosphere that reminded me of pentecostal and charismatic meetings, I became aware that the appeal of the Moon teaching is not *just* ideological. There is a part of it which does not come through in Sontag's book and is even more badly overlooked by press reports about brainwashing. The full name of the group is, after all, the Holy Spirit Association for the Unification of World Christianity. Here is a movement which manages to combine religious universalism, pentecostal immediacy, warmly supportive "family" and a program for allegedly building the Kingdom of God on earth. Such a potent admixture cannot be dismissed lightly.

I left the workshop early Sunday afternoon. The door was open. No one tried to keep me from leaving. I had not been brainwashed; in fact, if anything, I had been a bit bored. My hosts and hostesses seemed genuinely sorry to see me go, but I attribute this to the kind of affection which always develops among people who spend a weekend together, not to some insidious strategy of deception. It was clear after the hours of lectures and discussions that Moon's theology is not my cup of ginseng tea—something I had really known all along. Still, as I looked at the other churches grouped around the Boston Common—Congregational, Catholic, Unitarian, Episcopal—I could not help wondering what, if anything, they would do that day to offer a discipline, a vision, a devotion and a strategy to the millions of young contemporaries of those I left behind at the Unification headquarters. I am still wondering.

# Modern Evangelism, Radical and Conservative Christianity

# ✤176✤

# We Need Revival

## BILLY GRAHAM

Billy Graham (b. 1918) has achieved world-wide prominence as a revivalist since the late 1940s and has become the unofficial Primate who presides on national religious occasions in the United States. After conversion experiences he was ordained a Baptist minister in his native South. Early in his career he was associated with the Moody Bible Institute and began to make adept use of the mass media. He achieved national fame at the Los Angeles revival of 1949 from which this sermon is taken, a revival representing a conscious return to old-time religion but with its precepts applied to the perceived evils of modern urban society.

I want to speak on the subject, "The Choice that is Before Los Angeles During these Next Three Weeks." Remember the verse we just read,

> Except the Lord of hosts had left unto us a very small remnant, we should have been as Sodom, and we should have been like unto Gomorrah.

I have been in Europe six times since the war and have seen devastated cities of Germany and the wreckage of war. I believe the only reason that America escaped the ravages and destruction of war was because God's people prayed. Many of these people believe that God can still use America to evangelize the world. I think that we are living at a time in world history when God is giving us a desperate choice, a choice of either revival or judgment. There is no other alternative! And I particularly believe this applies to the city of Los Angeles—this city of wickedness and sin, this city that is known around the world because of its sin, crime and immorality. God Almighty is going to bring judgment upon this city unless people repent and believe—unless God sends an old-fashioned, heaven-sent, Holy Ghost revival.

How desperately we need revival! Think, for a moment, of some of the dreadful things happening throughout the western world. On Friday morning the entire world was shocked. (Sept. 23, 1949). Across Europe at this very hour there is stark, naked fear among the people, for we all realize that war is much

Source: Billy Graham, 'We Need Revival', *Revival in Our Time*, Wheaton, 1951.

closer than we ever dreamed. The people of Europe stand on the threshold of the unknown. Our President, at the same time as did Prime Minister Clement Attlee in London, announced to the startled world that Russia has now exploded an atomic bomb. An arms race, unprecedented in the history of the world, is driving us madly toward destruction! And I sincerely believe that it is the providence of God that He has chosen this hour for a campaign—giving this city one more chance to repent of sin and turn to a believing knowledge of the Lord Jesus Christ.

Recalling again our subject, Los Angeles' choice, see the need for a decision in the philosophical realm. The era of Materialism, Paganism and Humanism has been emphasized in the educational circles of this country. Man has steered our course. We have been humanizing God. Throughout our land we have denied the supernatural, outlawed the supernatural, and said that miracles are not now possible. We are taken up with *things* rather than with the *Spirit of God*.

Then look at our moral standard. There was a time a few years ago, which most of you with gray hair can remember, when this country claimed the Ten Commandments as the basis for our moral code. That is no longer true. Last year we had one divorce to every three-and-a-half marriages. Thirty years ago we had one divorce to every twenty-five marriages. The home, the basic unit of our society is breaking and crumbling, and the American way of life is being destroyed at the very heart and core of society.

At the same time we see an unchecked crime wave in this country. Your mayor recently told the editors of *Quick* magazine that crime in Los Angeles is out of hand. For the first time in many years a great metropolitan city has asked the Federal government to take over because there is so much crime. We need revival! Eight hundred per cent increase in crime in the last ten years in Los Angeles.

Look at the problem of sex. Everywhere, but especially emphasized and underscored here, we see sex placed before American young people. If we want to sell even a motor car tire, we have to use sex to do it. As a result, our high school and college young people are going to the dogs morally—encouraged by the press and radio across this Nation. We need a revival!

At the same time, gambling is going on from one end of this city to the other. Behind locked doors, there is wide-open, flagrant disobedience to the laws of this city. Our young people are gambling and being instructed in it every hour of the day. We need a revival!

The mayor has said that one of the problems in this town is too many cocktail bars—there are more cocktail bars than there are policemen in the city of Los Angeles. He said, "We don't have enough policemen to check on the liquor situation and, as a result, our city is drinking its way to destruction." Think of that! Three million chronic alcoholics in America today—thousands of them in the city of Los Angeles. We need a revival!

Let's turn to the teen-age delinquency problem. Do you know the age group having the greatest number of arrests last year? The greatest number of arrests last year in the city of Los Angeles was of seventeen-year-old boys and girls.

Let us look for a moment at the political realm. Let's see what is happening—not only in the city of Los Angeles, but in the western world. The world is divided into two sides. On the one side we see Communism; on the other side we see so-called Western culture. Western culture and its fruit had its foundation in the Bible, the Word of God, and in the revivals of the Seventeenth and Eighteenth Centuries. Communism, on the other hand, has decided against God, against Christ, against the Bible, and against all religion. Communism is not only an economic interpretation of life—Communism is a religion that is inspired, directed and motivated by the Devil himself who has declared war against Almighty God. Do you know that the Fifth Columnists, called Communists, are more rampant in Los Angeles than any other city in America? We need a revival.

Now for the first time in the history of the world we have the weapon with which to destroy ourselves—the atomic bomb. I am persuaded that time is desperately short! Three months ago, in the House of Parliament, a British statesman told me that the British government feels we have only five to ten years and our civilization will be ended. That was before he heard that Russia has the atomic bomb.

Recently I saw an educational film entitled "No Place to Hide." It is a picture story of what would happen if the germ bombs and poison bombs and atomic bombs were loosed on civilization. There would not be much left after such a bombing! We need a Holy Ghost, heaven-sent revival!

Let us look at the religious world for a moment. In this city Satan has succeeded in working his favorite strategy—counterfeiting the true gospel of our Lord Jesus Christ. We find more false prophets and cults than in any other place in all the world. The god of this age is blinding people. Demon power is felt as you walk down the streets of this city. A Gallup poll shows that 95% of the people of Los Angeles say they believe in God, but do you know how many are identified with any church? Twenty-seven per cent of the people of Los Angeles County identify themselves with a church. Do you know how many go to church more than once a year? Only eight per cent. Ninety-five per cent believe in God! Only eight per cent go to church more than once a year! There is desperate need of evangelism and prayer that God will send a revival so that people may become conscious of the tremendous issues that face us today. We need revival!

I wish we had time to go on with other statistics, but I do want to say that underlying every word I have to say is the basic law of God—"The wages of sin is death." If Sodom and Gomorrah could not get away with sin; if Pompeii and Rome could not escape, neither can Los Angeles! Judgment is coming as sure as I am standing here! Unless God's people turn to Him and the city repents, we are going to see the judgment of God come upon us.

A great many pastors tell me that, while they can't explain it or understand exactly why, they sincerely believe that this great united effort is God's plan for the city of Los Angeles. They feel that if we do not repent of sin and turn to Him while there is time, there will be no other great opportunity like this. Our responsibility as Christians during these days is tremendous! I have prayed more, and have spent more time with God than I ever have in any other city; and I am asking God's people to pray; to be faithful in attending these services and to bring others that many may come to believe in the Lord Jesus Christ.

This may be God's last great call! Look at the cities of the past that had their opportunities. The antediluvian civilization heard Noah as he stood and preached repentance. For 120 years people scoffed and did not repent. You know what God said? "My Spirit shall not always strive with man." And He said, "It repented me that I ever made man." Then judgment came upon the great civilization of Noah's day.

The peoples of Sodom and Gomorrah heard Abraham and Lot ask them to repent. But they refused and fire and brimstone from the hand of God rained down upon those cities.

Nazareth had the opportunity of hearing the most blessed and most wonderful Spirit-filled Preacher of all time—the Lord Jesus Christ. But because of the unbelief and sin of the people, He did no great works, in Nazareth. Many people of that day died and went to hell.

One day the Apostle Paul passed by the city of Pompeii. The sin and immorality of Pompeii was known throughout the Roman Empire. Pompeii would not listen nor repent; and God caused Vesuvius to erupt. The city was destroyed and every living thing in the city.

God spared not those great cities. Neither will God spare this city! I warn you to repent of sin and turn to Jesus Christ as a city before it is too late. Do you know what God is going to do? One of these days—it may not be this year, it may be a hundred years from now, I do not know the time, but I do know this— unless we have a revival, one of these little tremors that you call an earthquake may shake every building in Los Angeles. Under the judging hand of God, a tidal wave may sweep across this city, unless we repent of our sin. Do you know the area that is marked out for the enemy's first atomic bomb? New York! Secondly, Chicago; and thirdly, the city of Los Angeles! We don't know how soon, but we do know this, that right now the grace of God can still save a poor lost sinner. We know that the gates of heaven are still open to those who will repent and believe that Jesus is God's Son and our Saviour.

Somebody asked me the other day whether I think we can have a revival. What a foolish question! Some people say that apostasy is too deep, the picture is too black, and it is impossible to have a revival. They say that sin is too rampant, that a revival in 1949 is impossible.

I tell you, beloved, it was a dark day and a mighty dreary picture when Jonah went to Nineveh. The sins that I have mentioned this afternoon existed in the city of Nineveh; but Nineveh repented and the judgment of God that was about to fall, was held back. Nineveh was spared the judgment of Almighty God.

In this moment I can see the judgment hand of God over Los Angeles. I can see judgment about to fall. If we repent, if we believe, if we turn to Christ in faith and hope, the judgment of God can be stopped. From the depths of my heart, I believe that this message is God's word today.

It was a dark hour when Elijah climbed to the top of Mount Carmel—all the prophets of Baal were against him, the king and queen opposed him, the army was his enemy: he was alone! There were 7,000 people that did believe, but they were hiding in caves, afraid. Only one man dared to believe God would send a revival. Seven thousand people said, "It can't be done." "Everything and everyone is against you!" they told Elijah.

People, often God's children, say the same thing today. Let me tell you that nothing is too hard for our God!

But they had a revival in Elijah's day! On top of Mount Carmel the prophets of Baal called on their god. There was no response—he was off on a fishing trip and couldn't hear them, or he had gone off somewhere else and couldn't hear. Elijah called upon God to rain down fire. The fire fell, and revival came to the men of Israel. In a few days, Ahab and Jezebel were taken from the throne and God was given His rightful place in the land of Israel.

Look at the day when Hezekiah came to the throne. Old Ahaz his father was walking around like he owned the world. His shoulders were thrown back; he was proud and cocky, a fellow who believed in idols and who worshipped the god of the trees and the god of the sun; a fellow that had set up other gods and had denied the Lord God of Israel. Then Hezekiah came to the throne; called upon the people to repent and to turn to God. Revival took place in a dark and black hour in the history of Judah.

It was a dark hour when John Wesley and George Whitefield preached the gospel, but England had a revival! That country was saved from the fate of the French Revolution.

God said,

> "If my people, which are called by my name, shall humble themselves, and pray, and seek my face, and turn from their wicked ways; then will I hear from heaven, and will forgive their sin, and will heal their land" (II Chron. 7:14).

Do you believe that? I believe that we can have revival any time we meet God's conditions. I believe that God is true to His Word, and that He must rain righteousness upon us if we meet His conditions.

What are His conditions? First, realization of need and a desire for revival. I am talking to Christians now. Do you want a revival today? Would you like to see this city moved from center to circumference? Would you like God to bless us and people turn to Him? Would you like Hollywood to be so shaken that it might influence the world for Christ? Would you like the Spirit of God in our midst as He has never been before? We can have it! I say we can have it, if we meet God's conditions!

The second condition for revival is repentance. Scripture says, "If I regard iniquity in my heart, the Lord will not hear me" (Ps. 66:18). Do you know what repentance is? Repentance is confession of sin, repentance is sorrow for sin, and repentance is renouncing sin. Many people say they believe God's Word and accept Christ's sacrifice, but they have never been truly repentant! If they were, their lives would show it.

And then the third thing is to pray. Revival never comes except in answer to prayer. A few months ago the city of Augusta, Georgia, was moved upon by the Spirit of God. Do you know why? Before we ever arrived, there were 13,000 prayer meetings held in that city. god was moving before we got there, in answer to prayer.

Do you know what prayer implies? Prayer implies that we must be in one accord. That means we can't have divisions among us. That means that if I am a Presbyterian or you are a Baptist, or if I am a Baptist or a Pentecostal, regardless of denomination, we have to forget our differences—forget any minor points of argument and join together around the cross of the Lord Jesus Christ. We must unite in prayer and supplication to the Lord, and God will send a revival. That means that we have to love one another, and our hearts must be bound together. When we love one another, there won't be any pride. When we love one another, there won't be any jealousy. When we love one another, there won't be any envy. When we love one another, there won't be any gossip. When we really love one another, there won't be any of these sins, because love binds us together and presents us to God in the purity of Christ.

Fourth, in order to have revival we must have faith. Unbelief is a sin that keeps back revival in city after city because people will not believe God's Word and take Him at His word. God says if we meet certain conditions, He *will* send a revival; He *will* send the blessing, and sinners will turn to Him. We have to take God at His word and not doubt Him. We need revival!

Now, what are the results of revival? The church will be on fire, burning with a desire to serve Him. Christians will be compelled to bring others to know Him.

There will be a new missionary emphasis in the church. We will turn our eyes on a world that is lost and dying and going to hell because these souls have not accepted God's plan. Prayer meetings will be jammed, people will love the hour of prayer and spend time in communion with God. The church will add new members. I believe that any work, any campaign, any evangelistic effort that is not contributing to the church is not building a lasting foundation in that place. God has approved the organization of the churches, and we are praying that thousands of people will be swept into the church during the days while we are here.

Wouldn't it be great to see the members of the church filled with the Holy Ghost? They will be if revival comes. "Ye shall receive power, after that the Holy

506

Ghost is come upon you" (Acts 1:8). Not only will the church members be revived, but many more will accept the Lord Jesus Christ.

Fourteen years ago, down in the city of Charlotte, North Carolina, the ministers of our town forgot their differences; the laymen, together with the ministers, held a city-wide evangelistic campaign. Do you know one of the things that attracted me? I saw the people who, a few days before, had been quick to argue with one another, now joined together around the cross of Jesus Christ. I said, "If that is taking place, there must be something to Christianity." I went to the services and was converted in an old-fashioned revival meeting just like this. When we join hands and the gospel is preached under the anointing and power of the Holy Ghost, revival comes and souls will turn to believe on the Lord Jesus Christ.

Finally, a revival brings tremendous social implications. Do you know what came out of past revivals? The abolishment of slavery came out of revival. When the Wesleys preached in England, people were working ninety hours a week! As a result of that revival, sixty working hours became standard, and our great trade unions were organized. Did you know that the Y.M.C.A., the Salvation Army, most of our charity organizations, many of our educational institutions, slum clearance programs, the Sunday School, Christian reform and Women's Suffrage are revival results?

Now, in closing, to you Christians, you that profess the name of the Lord Jesus Christ—if this is going to be just another campaign, if we are going to take it half-heartedly, we might as well stop right now. But this may be God's last call to Los Angeles! I am going to ask you to make your business secondary, to make your family secondary, to make everything else secondary for three weeks. Try God, believe God, prove God and come to these meetings. Pray and work as if your life and soul depended on it. Then watch God work during these days, that this opportunity given to Los Angeles—the choice of accepting or rejecting Christ—may not be in vain.

This same choice must be made by every person here this afternoon without Christ. Your choice can be one of two decisions—accept Christ and believe Him, or die without Him and suffer judgment at the Great White Throne Judgment. At that time God says those whose names are not written in the Lamb's Book of Life will be cast into the lake of fire.

What can you do? Right now you can turn to Jesus. Let Christ come into your heart and cleanse you from sin, and He can give you the assurance that if you died tonight, you would go to heaven. We call this belief in Christ salvation—*anyone* can be saved by simply believing that the Lord Jesus Christ suffered and died for his sin. Right now you can know that you are going to heaven. Will you accept Him?

# ⚜·177·⚜

# Radio—'The Lengthened Reach'

## TORREY JOHNSON and ROBERT COOK

Billy Graham got his start as an agent of the Youth for Christ movement attached to the National Association of Evangelicals. Youth for Christ, under the guidance of Torrey Johnson in Chicago, made effective use of the air waves. The extract describes and gives an example of a broadcast, an early stage in the contemporary symbiotic relationship of television and evangelical religion in America.

"From Orchestra Hall ... CHICAGOLAND YOUTH FOR CHRIST!" This "punchy" announcement by Torrey Johnson introduces the half-hour broadcast from Orchestra Hall every Saturday night. During the seconds before we go on the air, the pitch has been given from the organ, the audience has been rehearsed in their part, and now, the moment Johnson has given his announcement, the audience—three thousand strong—joins in singing,

> Christ lifted me, Christ lifted me!
> When no one else could help, Christ lifted me.

The familiar theme with the words of "Love Lifted Me" continues through a verse and two choruses, and the broadcast is on its way. Beverly Shea, announcer and soloist extraordinary, gives the "commercial" while the audience is singing our sign-on theme.

The "flavor" of "Chicagoland Youth for Christ" broadcast comes not only from the personality of Master-of-Ceremonies Torrey Johnson, but also from the timing and pacing of the entire period. For instance, no time lag is allowed between numbers. The moment one is finished the next one is announced with very little unnecessary wordage. Emphasis is laid on *more* numbers with *fewer* stanzas, rather than more stanzas and fewer numbers.

Every announcement is "punchy" and has to do with the *significance* of the item to which it applies, as well as the *title*. This puts meaning and force in all that is said.

Source: Torrey Johnson and Robert Cook, '"Radio—'The Lengthened Reach"', *Reaching Youth for Christ*, Chicago, 1944, pp. 44–9.

Highlight of the first part of the broadcast is the section given over to testimonies, where two or three outstanding young Christians are invited to give their personal witness for Christ. These testimonies are limited to forty-five seconds, and must be written out beforehand. This is a wise expedient because of the fact that in forty-five seconds, *ad lib*, the average person gets precisely nowhere. Testimonies written out in full insure accuracy and a minimum of stumbling.

Care is exercised to make these testimonies outstanding in every way. For instance, the testimony of a service man must come from one who has seen some special service or experience; the testimony of a medical man must represent noteworthy medical achievement; and the testimony of some person in ordinary life must represent one whose work as a layman has been characterized by unusual achievement for the Lord Jesus Christ. This precaution takes the testimonies out of the realm of mere talky-talk and insures listener interest.

Another musical number or two follows, then a five to seven-minute message by Director Torrey Johnson. His messages very frequently use some event of the day as a springboard. One of the most successful radio talks that Johnson ever gave, many think, was his message based on the "Red Cross." It starts by citing the experience that eight German Red Cross nurses had when, after their capture by the Allies, they were carted back across No Man's Land in an ambulance and returned to the German lines. Meanwhile, all shell fire ceased and the entire progress of the war waited upon the delivery of these Red Cross nurses safely back to their base. The similarity between the Red Cross and the Cross of the Lord Jesus Christ was graphically and forcefully presented that night. Other messages follow different leads, but every one of them has a true-to-life approach and a tremendous gospel appeal. Very frequently the gospel invitation is extended after one of these radio messages.

Sign-off chorus is the tender refrain of "I Surrender All." Many have said that it leaves the listener with the sustained impression of the pleading of the Holy Spirit.

If there is any secret of success in the radio portion of "Chicagoland Youth for Christ," it is that every split second of the time is made significant in the light of a ministry to souls. Songs are "blood-gospel" songs, testimonies are strictly salvation testimonies, the message is a salvation message, everything is keyed to a salvation standard, and the appeal is straight-forward and direct.

This word about "commercials": They ought to be written so that the reader of the announcement will find no hissing sibilants or awkward phrasing, and they ought to be commercial in the best sense of the word; that is, that they help to "sell" the broadcast and the ministry to the radio audience.

*The following radio messages by Torrey Johnson demonstrate the kind of impact your unseen audience must receive: brief, simple, direct, and always, crystal-clear gospel.*

# Problems Not Solved By Science
## June 3, 1944

One hundred years ago Samuel Morse sent the first message by telegraph. We celebrated the anniversary a few days ago. This was the first message—"WHAT HATH GOD WROUGHT."

I wish it were possible tonight to bring Samuel Morse to Chicago and have him with us on the platform of Orchestra Hall. I would like to have him look at the amplification system we have for this auditorium. I would like to have him speak into this microphone that carries my voice across the hundreds of miles and into the thousands of homes where people are listening tonight.

I wish he might hear the ring of a telephone, pick up the receiver, and hear a message from someone abroad ship at sea, someone in a plane in the air, someone in a submarine under the sea, someone from some other part of the world. I would like him to step down a few doors into the lobby of a hotel and put ten cents into a box. He would see before him marvelous things on the screen. While he looked, and listened and took in all of those things, I would like to ask, "Samuel Morse, what do you think about all that has been wrought in these one hundred years since that day you first sent that message across a few miles of these United States?"

Having presented to him that picture, I would take him across the avenues of Chicago to the courts of our city, to the courts of our county, and even to the Federal Court that is here in Chicago. As he stands there in those court rooms, I would have him listen to the description of the crimes that are being committed every day by teenage young people. I would take him into a divorce court and explain to him how during the month of May there were three divorces for every seven marriages here in the City of Chicago—three out of every seven marriages at the present time going on the rocks! I would take him into the Federal Court, and I would have him listen to the record of crimes and offenses that are being committed against the finest government in all the world.

Having first seen all the marvels of this mechanical age, and then having gone into the court room to hear the categories of crime that have been committed, I would ask, "Samuel Morse, what do you think about all of this?". He would come to the same conclusion that every thinking man nowadays comes to and it is this:

While we are living in the most marvelous mechanical age such as this world never before has known, at the same time we are living in the midst of sin, of trespasses, and of offenses of every kind, never before catalogued in all the ages of human history.

There are still three problems today that are not solved by science. The first is the problem of SIN, the second is the problem of the SOUL, and the third is the problem of ETERNAL DESTINY.

I am glad that I can say that the problem of sin was settled nineteen hundred years ago when Jesus Christ died for sin upon the Cross of Calvary. With outstretched hands, He says tonight, "Him that cometh unto me, I will in no wise cast out." "I am the way, the truth, and the life: no man cometh unto the Father but by me."

The second problem is the problem of the soul. I testify to you that all the research and all the good things that science has brought to us can never satisfy the soul of man. But Jesus Christ *can* satisfy the soul, as you heard from the testimonies of these three young friends a few moments ago.

Then I think of the problems that come to us day by day. I am glad that Jesus not only saves, He not only satisfies, but He also solves all the problems that we meet along life's way.

A young woman several weeks ago gave her heart to Jesus Christ. She took her engagement ring from her finger and laid it on the altar of the church and said within her heart, "I cannot marry that man. He is not a Christian. I will not marry him until he puts his trust in Jesus Christ." She wrote him a letter that she had accepted Jesus Christ and also told of her decision about their engagement. He came to the city of Chicago to see what was wrong. He saw her on Saturday. They were up late into the night. The following morning he continued again and throughout the day—he was going to straighten that girl out—but it was to no avail. She had found that Jesus Christ, when she placed her trust in Him, settled the question of sin in her life. She had found that Jesus Christ satisfied her soul as nothing else in all the world. She had found that Jesus Christ could solve all the problems that she met on life's way.

Toward the evening of Sunday, the young man was giving up, more or less, being discouraged and disgusted. The young woman said to him, "Come to the church where I was, listen to the man to whom I listened, and see if he has not something for you." They went into a certain church and there heard a young man preach. At the close of the message that night, her friend lifted his hand and said, "I want to take Jesus Christ into my heart and into my life. If Jesus Christ can take away the sin out of a life of the girl who has been my companion, if Jesus Christ can satisfy the longings of her soul, and if she has found in Him a friend that never fails, I too want Jesus Christ."

Several weeks went by, and there came a letter to the pastor of that church. In the letter was a sum of money, and also a notice that the man and this young woman had been united in marriage as a Christian young man and as a Christian young woman, establishing a Christian home. They also wrote, "We are sending this gift along, and we want you to know that this thing worked for one, and now it has worked for the other. We believe it is going to be good for our home in the days that lie ahead."

I wonder, my friend, in the midst of all the scientific inventions and all of these conveniences that we have today, whether you have settled the sin question. I wonder whether your soul is satisfied. I wonder about all your problems of life. Let me say to you tonight that Jesus Christ is adequate to meet every need for time and for eternity. While this company of friends blend their voices in singing, will you not trust yourself to Jesus Christ and accept Him as your personal Saviour from sin?

# ❧178❧

# Declaration at St. Louis of the Assemblies of God

## WILLIAM W. MENZIES

The Assemblies of God was established in 1914 as an umbrella organization for a variety of Pentecostal congregations. They emerged from the Holiness revival movement, with its striving for perfection, largely within late nineteenth-century Methodism. The Pentecostals, however, were especially distinguished by the baptism of the Holy Spirit expressed in speaking in tongues. They have a strong belief in divine healing, a rigorously austere personal morality, and a conviction that believers are living in 'end times': that the Second Coming is near. This premillennialism means that saving those who can be saved is the highest priority for the Assemblies of God and social responsibilities, though recognized, are of secondary importance.

---

Recognizing the end times in which we live and the evident hand of God which has rested upon the Assemblies of God for these times, and having engaged together in prayerful study in this Council on Evangelism concerning God's purpose in the world today and our place in His purpose, we make the following declaration.

## Declaration

Because the Assemblies of God came into being as the Holy Spirit was poured out in prophetic fulfillment at the turn of the century and a body of like-minded Pentecostal believers voluntarily joined together in worship, ministry, and service; and

Because the Assemblies of God has accepted the Bible as the inerrant Word of God and has declared it as the whole counsel of God, giving emphasis to the full gospel; and

Source: William W. Menzies, *Anointed to Serve: The Stories of the Assemblies of God*, Springfield, Mo., 1971, pp. 391–5.

Because the Assemblies of God has grown rapidly both at home and abroad and has continued to experience the blessing of God as it has sought to do His will and to be an instrument of divine purpose; and

Because the Assemblies of God determines to remain a body of believers responding fully to the divine working in these last days; therefore, be it

*Declared,* That the Assemblies of God considers it was brought into being and built by the working of the Holy Spirit as an instrument of divine purpose in these end times; and be it

*Declared further,* That the Assemblies of God recognizes God's purposes concerning man are:

    1. To reveal Himself through Christ to seek and to save that which is lost,
    2. To be worshiped in spirit and in truth,
    3. To build a body of believers in the image of His Son; and be it

*Declared further,* That the Assemblies of God recognizes that its mission is:

    1. To be an agency of God for evangelizing the world,
    2. To be a corporate body in which man may worship God,
    3. To be a channel of God's purpose to build a body of saints being perfected in the image of His Son; and be it

*Declared further,* That the Assemblies of God exists expressly to give continuing emphasis to this mission in the New Testament apostolic pattern by encouraging believers to be baptized in the Holy Spirit, which enables them:

    1. To evangelize in the power of the Holy Spirit with accompanying supernatural signs,
    2. To worship God in the fullness of the Spirit,
    3. To respond to the full working of the Holy Spirit in expressing His fruit and gifts as in New Testament times, edifying the body of Christ and perfecting the saints for the work of the ministry.

## Response

LEADERS: In response to this declaration of mission of the Assemblies of God, we affirm that God is not willing that any should perish but is revealing Himself through Jesus Christ and is seeking to save the lost, calling man to Himself in Christ.

CONGREGATION: *This we affirm!*

LEADERS: We affirm that God desires to build a body of believers in the image of His Son, separating them unto Himself.

CONGREGATION: *This we affirm!*

LEADERS: We give ourselves to be an agency of God for evangelizing the world through Jesus Christ.

CONGREGATION: *We give ourselves to Him for this mission.*

LEADERS: We give ourselves to be a spiritual body in which man may worship God in the beauty of holiness and may be separated unto Him.

CONGREGATION: *We give ourselves to Him for this mission.*

LEADERS: We give ourselves to build a body of saints being perfected in the image of His Son, conforming unto Him.

CONGREGATION: *We give ourselves to Him for this mission.*

LEADERS: We dedicate ourselves to Spirit-filled living and teaching, to encourage believers likewise to be baptized in the Holy Spirit, knowing this will enable us to evangelize in the power of the Spirit with signs following.

CONGREGATION: *We dedicate ourselves to this mission.*

LEADERS: We dedicate ourselves to be filled with the Spirit so we will worship God in the fullness of the Spirit and minister before Him in spirit and in truth.

CONGREGATION: *We dedicate ourselves to this mission.*

LEADERS: We dedicate ourselves to respond to the full working of the Holy Spirit, praying He will use us mightily even as He worked in the New Testament Church, granting expression of fruit and gifts and ministries for the edifying of the body of Christ.

CONGREGATION: *We dedicate ourselves to this mission.*

LEADERS: This purpose of God and this mission of the Assemblies of God we affirm this day, and to this mission we dedicate ourselves, praying always to be kept in the faith, to evangelize in the power of the Spirit, to worship in spirit and in truth, and to conform to the image of His Son—so help us God!

CONGREGATION: *To this purpose of God and to this mission of the Assemblies of God we give ourselves this day—so help us God!*

## A Statement of Social Concern

THE ASSEMBLIES OF GOD recognizes with growing solicitude the grave crises existing in every segment of our contemporary society. In order to relate our church meaningfully to its social responsibilities to men as well as its spiritual obligations to God, we make the following affirmations:

As members of the evangelical Christian community, we believe that the Church has a unique and indispensable contribution to make in the current efforts at improving human conditions. We oppose the social ills that unjustly keep men from sharing in the blessings of their communities; and we abhor the moral evils that destroy human dignity and prevent men from receiving the blessings of heaven.

As sons of God as well as citizens on earth, we reaffirm the Biblical view that man is a sinner and inclined to evil by his nature; that crises in human affairs are produced by selfishness and pride resulting from separation from

God; and, that the spirit of alienation, rebellion, and racism is a universal human weakness reflecting the native spirit of fallen humanity.

Because of this Biblical view of the human race, we neither believe that alienations are healed by devised confrontations between those alienated, nor that revolution is the key to social progress. Community-betterment projects and legislative actions on social improvement may alleviate the symptoms of a fundamental human problem (and by all means they should be prominent in our society); but the human solutions of social problems are not enough. Man's greatest need is his need of God; and without God he can hope for no just and equitable society.

It is here that the Church makes its most significant social contribution. this contribution is not of goods and services only, however urgent may be the need for economic justice. And this contribution is not all good will and recognition merely, however alienated and oppressed any people may be. A sin-sick world needs the salvation of God. The first and foremost obligation of the Church to society is to preach publicly in every community the Biblical gospel of the Lord Jesus Christ.

We of the Assemblies of God intend as citizens to make our influence felt where concrete social action is justified in areas of domestic relations, education, law enforcement, employment, equal opportunity, and other worthwhile and beneficial matters. However, we reaffirm our deep conviction that the greatest need for man is for personal salvation through Jesus Christ, and we give this spiritual need its due priority. It is only as men become right with God that they can truly become right with one another.

As a community of Christians we labor to *win* men, not merely to move men. We are called to accomplish our objectives not by coercion, but by conversion. It is not in clashes and confrontations that we manifest God to the world, but it is in demonstrating the power of the Holy Spirit to change men's lives.

In these matters the world does not write our agenda. Nor do the circumstances of our times dictate our mission. These are given to us by God. Our calling is to be faithful to Him.

WE THEREFORE PLEDGE to humble ourselves before God, to pray, and to seek the power of the Holy Spirit to change the lives of men; and

We further PLEDGE to give ourselves in the Biblical way to meet today's challenge by a renewed dedication to proclaim the fullness of the universal gospel of Jesus Christ both at home and abroad without respect to color, national origin, or social status!

WE FURTHER PLEDGE to exert our influence as Christian citizens to justifiable social action in areas of domestic relations, education, law enforcement, employment, equal opportunity, and other beneficial matters.

# ⟨⟩179⟨⟩

# The People's Temple and Commitment to Change

## JOHN V. MOORE

In 1978 the Rev. Jim Jones and his followers in The People's Temple horrified the world by committing mass suicide at Jonestown in Guyana. These excerpts were written by a relative of a young woman who died at Jonestown. Though they may idealize the settlement and ignore the evidence that some who wished to leave were prevented, yet they bring out the alienation of Jones and his followers from American society expressed first in protest and then in withdrawal into their own community. Jones exemplified the charismatic prophet in relation to his followers. Did he, living through 'end times', anticipate the millennium and the rising again of the saints when he commanded the self-destruction at Jonestown?

A month after the Jonestown suicides, John wrote a letter to James Wall, editor of *The Christian Century*, describing some of the activities on which the group had worked.

> . . . Jim Jones and Peoples Temple were deeply involved in the dominant movements of the Sixties. According to the retiring executive of the F.O.R. [Fellowship of Reconciliation], while he was pastor in Indianapolis, Jim Jones integrated the Methodist Hospital overnight. Peoples Temple was an integrated church from the beginnings when other churches were trying to become integrated. When the perspective on integration changed, Peoples Temple continued as an integrated community. Consequently it came under severe criticism from those who felt that black people needed black leaders.
>
> Peoples Temple created and sustained a community during those years when the young especially were looking for new forms of communal life. The tide of new communities cast upon the shore all kinds of communes, including Christian communities. Peoples Temple was a heterogeneous community. Its simple life style attracted middle class white people who were unsatisfied with our affluent society.
>
> Peoples Temple welcomed men and women from the drug scene. Rehabilitation

Source: John V. Moore, from *The Jonestown Letters,—Correspondence of the Moore Family, 1970-1985*, Lewiston, NY, 1986, pp. 134-6, 240-8. © 1986 by Edwin Mellen Press.

of people injured by drugs was not its central concern. In this it was different from Synanon and local drug abuse centers. Peoples Temple did provide a community which enabled many to bring order out of their chaotic lives, but this number was few compared with the membership.

Peoples Temple was never simply a community concerned with itself. It was concerned with civil liberties as it was with civil rights. Long before *The Christian Century* or *New Republic* or the ACLU became concerned with Senate Bill #1 [legislation introduced in 1975 which would have increased federal police powers and infringed upon the Bill of Rights], Peoples Temple was sounding the alarm. Jones and his community were always concerned with legislation.

Jim Jones, who for a time worked with the poor in Brazil, identified with the struggles of the oppressed in Latin America. He shared the outlook, although not the stability, which comes from biblical rootedness, of the people of Solentinam and their priest. Peoples Temple always identified with the poor. Most members had always been poor. More than any other movement, the civil rights movement was of and with the poor. The loss of hope of the poor accounts in part for the attraction of Peoples Temple, and the migration of more than a thousand people to Guyana.

## II

John's "Notes and reflections on our trip to Guyana, particularly our three days at the Peoples Temple Cooperative Agricultural Project" was the most detailed and understanding account of any that described life in Jonestown. It was also the last before the tragedy.

May 1978

"Impressive" was the first word to come to mind when I was asked what I thought of the project. The clearing of more than eight hundred acres from the midst of the jungle, and the planting of crops is impressive. To imagine more than a thousand Americans migrating to Guyana and working on the project is impressive. Every aspect of the work and life there I found impressive.

As we rode into the area of the buildings, we saw Annie and Kimo. Carolyn was quickly there. They took us for a tour of the area. Senior citizens were engaged in calisthenics under the direction of a young woman. We walked to the nursery where infants and toddlers were being cared for.

Later in the day, probably early in the evening, we visited the clinic and talked with Larry (M.D.) who is obviously exceptionally bright. He showed slides and pictures of some of their work. He has equipment for cellular studies, tests, and a new portable X-ray. Two X-ray technicians are there. Two or three nurse practitioners, with varying specialties, and five or six R.N.'s (or more) round out the medical staff. Annie, in addition to nursing, is in charge of medical supplies. They provide family planning for members of their own community. Clinic hours on Sundays for residents of the region were posted at the entrance to the Project. However, they treat people whenever they come.

They are in instant communication with a network of physicians through amateur radio operators. Larry has consulted with specialists a number of times, including his delivery of twins by caesarean section. They have been visited by the president of a medical association which provides consultative services by radio, and have his full support.

Two Guyanese dentists have held clinics at the Project. Upon one occasion the dentist found only two cavities among the children. This is probably attributable to diet. I think that there are more than forty pre-schoolers living there, in addition to other children of all ages.

The educational program is accredited by the government department of education. I think that they have had, this year, classes through junior high, with high school work being offered in the fall. The teachers are enthusiastic, for they are able to do some of the things they've always wanted to do in teaching, but have never been free to do. They make their own educational tools, as well as a variety of play toys. Classes are offered for people of all ages including reading and writing, as well as current events. The p.a. system keeps the people abreast daily of events throughout the world. Both dramatic and educational films are shown every evening. "The Heart Is a Lonely Hunter," and a film on the status of women in the Soviet Union were shown one night we were there.

Our first evening at the project, a Friday, people gathered to listen to the band and enjoy the entertainment. The band has performed in Georgetown and has received good press coverage. They play jazz, soul, rock, etc. A seventy-five-year-old woman did her "Moms Mabley" routine, and a preacher the same age sang and danced. A twelve-year-old boy sang a solo. A Guyanan from that region brought his flute, played and sang. It was good entertainment.

Single people live in dormitories while families live in houses. One older woman wanted her own house, so they constructed a tiny house for her. The elderly live close in where they are checked daily to ascertain the status of their health. The buildings are simple, with wood siding and sheet-metal roofs. Throughout Trinidad and Guyana, the roofs were of sheet-metal. There was running water in the guest house, and I presume in the dorms and houses. Showers and toilet facilities are in separate buildings.

All of the cooking is done in a central kitchen on wood stoves. Imagine serving three meals a day to more than a thousand people! People are free to eat in a small dining area or take their food wherever they choose. All of the buildings, except where people sleep, have open sides. Some of the meeting areas are covered with heavy tenting, still open sided. What is needed is protection from sun and rain with structure for circulation of air to keep cool. There is no need for fuel for heat. We ate well. Most of the food has been grown or produced on the land there. They are not producing enough rice or potatoes for their use. Cassava is a tuber which is used for flour for bread, and I suspect hotcakes, as well as for feed for the animals.

They grow cassava (and use both leaves and tubers), custard apple, citrus, pineapple, coconut, bananas ... eddoes, cutlass beans and corn. They are still working on dry farming of rice. (Guyana is a rice exporting nation.) Starting with 12 seeds of the winged bean, which is 38% protein, they hope to plant eight or ten acres this fall. They produce their own eggs and frying and stewing chickens, as well as pork. They have some cows, and soon will have modern dairy equipment.

Their first priority is to become self-sufficient. I think that their major cash outlay is for animal feed, fertilizer, and petroleum for generating electricity. Of course they must pay cash for medical equipment and supplies. They have a 60-foot trawler which they use to haul in supplies and equipment to Port Kaituma, and they sometimes take pay loads, as they do with a truck in Georgetown. One of their members travels up and down the river engaging in barter.

They have a nutritionist who is engaged in continuing research. They have found some ways to use plants that have been considered inedible. The AmerIndians share their wisdom with the people about food and medicinal herbs. They have their own herb garden, as well as a smoke house. They are excavating for underground cold-cool storage.

518

They have a machine shop with a tool-and-die maker teaching younger people to do the work of machinists. They have a mill where they can cut material and erect a house in a day. They are making furniture and toys. They, of course, maintain all of their equipment. They are constructing a windmill which they hope may help with some generating power.

We heard after we returned that the President and Prime Minister of Guyana, and the Prime Minister of Surinam visited the project unannounced. Officials of the U.S. Embassy have visited, as well as officials in the departments of health, education and agriculture (Guyanese). The Guyanese have a vital interest in developing the interior of the country. The people live on the coastal plains. If the Peoples Temple Agricultural Project can become self-sufficient, it has significant implications for the nation as well as similar countries.

I have never been anyplace where I saw the older people so much a part of the community. We have visited P.T.'s homes for the elderly, infirm, and retarded in the U.S. Those homes were superior. In Jonestown, the elderly receive superior health care. One woman was out hoeing her own little garden. Others had picket fences around their houses. I know of no retirement home which provides better food and health care and a more wholesome environment. They are part of a community with babies and children as well as of young people and adults. This fact is a two-way street, benefiting the young as well as the old. When I saw the woman hoeing, I thought of Micah's words, "... they shall sit every one under his vine and under his fig tree, and none shall make them afraid ..." The fears that are a part of city life are gone.

The Project has expertise and inexperience. They are proceeding by trial and error. They have had serious accidents, but no fatalities. (Jim Jones' mother died and is buried there.) An agronomist, with a B.S., supervises their farming. They turn to the best advice they can find in Guyana and outside for assistance. A man from an urban area is in charge of the piggery. Another man with no experience is in charge of the chickery. In both instances they have been successful and are learning. Young people who have never had opportunities to learn trades or skills are being given these opportunities now.

The morale is high. There is no possible way for this Project to succeed apart from high morale. No one is paid anything. Everyone eats the same food and sleeps in comparable quarters. Everyone is expected to work. Workers were in the fields early in the morning. They do a lot of work with manual labor, even while they are bringing in some labor-saving devices. There is no way they could have done what they have done apart from hard work on the part of many men and women. I was asked by a reporter if I had asked people if they were happy. As I thought about that question later, it seemed like asking people celebrating at a party if they were happy, or coming down out of the stands and asking members of the team who were moving the ball toward a touchdown if they were happy.

Some parents have charged P.T. with brainwashing their children (who are in their twenties and older) and holding them against their will. We saw nothing to suggest any truth in this. Furthermore, I am much more ready to believe that P.T. would expend energy to facilitate unhappy people leaving the Project rather than expending energy to restrain people. In my judgment, they simply do not have the luxury of using any energy to restrain and coerce people. They need all of the energy they can muster devoted to their common task of developing that land and becoming self-sufficient.

The project is entitled "Peoples Temple Cooperative Agricultural Project." The people working in specific areas meet regularly, sometimes daily, to discuss their work. Suggestions and criticisms are encouraged.

The Project provides an opportunity for some to use education and skills, and for others the opportunity to try new things. The man in charge of the piggery is from Chicago. An attorney is developing the winged bean and citrus crops. Young people for whom doors in the city were closed are learning mechanical and agricultural skills.

I would add to the paragraph on the cooperative the following. There is a sense of ownership which is not present under private ownership. I suspect that this same sense of ownership is often absent even where the legal ownership is corporate, including the workers. The people give themselves in hard work, in part because it is their project. All share the same food and housing. I think that all spend some time in manual labor.

I had a feeling that everybody was somebody. I thought of Israel's understanding of herself, and later the church's self-understanding: "We who were nobody are now God's people." Being somebody is more than corporate identity. People in the Project give the feeling that they are somebody, not simply because they identify with the Project, but in their own right. One woman has the house of her dreams. Other older people tend their own gardens, sing and entertain. While we were in Georgetown, an older woman with a speech impediment, perhaps from a stroke, was waiting eagerly to go to Jonestown. She flew in with us. That night during the entertainment she was keeping time to the music with her cane and swaying. A boy of nine or ten flew in with us. He had been in Georgetown while his artificial leg was lengthened. We met his brother in Jonestown. He is bent with a disfigured spine. In the States, he knew ridicule of playmates. Here there's a different sensitivity. An accountant is using his experience in the business affairs of the church. A lawyer is teaching. Young adults who've come through the drug scene are engaged in significant work. I think that it was Dostoevsky who said that a society could be measured by the way it treats people in prison. Surely the humaneness of any community is to be seen in part by its inclusion of the children and the elderly, the infirm and those of limited abilities. . . .

John V. Moore

520

# ❦180❧

# Consensus Society!
# Consensus Church?

## PHILIP BERRIGAN

The multiple dimensions of crisis in the United States in the 1960s—combining race, war, the perceived failure of American institutions, moral turmoil—polarized Americans. Polarization, which extended beyond the decade, was made explicit in the politics of religious figures, radical and conservative. Philip Berrigan, a Catholic priest engaged in anti-war activity, drew on critics such as Herbert Marcuse to characterize America as a technological society swamped by material consumption and maintaining its economy through war and preparation for war. He believed it denied real human needs. The Church thus betrayed its true nature unless it challenged the society radically. But religious bureaucracies behaved in ways similar to secular ones and gained benefits from the state in doing so. Berrigan's hope was that Christians as individuals and in small, just communities would bear witness and aid the victims of society.

This subtle and creeping totalitarianism can be regarded through another lens. By any sort of absolute right, a man's needs cease beyond what is required to make life livable: food, shelter, clothing (in a wealthy economy like our own, adequate education, decent income [guaranteed, if necessary], security in sickness and in old age). Ideally, society owes its members a reasonable share of what it can produce for their human enhancement as free, responsible citizens. They in turn have the obligation to see that their society remains responsible and free.

"Free" becomes, in such a discussion, a critical concept and a practicality. In American society freedom is somehow separated from humanism. Freedom is somehow separated from an education calculated to prepare one to serve life rather than to serve a system. Freedom is somehow separated from a view of

Source: Philip Berrigan, 'Consensus Society! Consensus Church?', A Punishment for Peace, London, 1969, pp. 9-25.

people as people rather than as stereotypes of class or race. Freedom is somehow separated from the mysterious chemistry that makes a man—truth, justice, compassion, integrity.

Quality and universality are dangerously reprobate as human attributes, since one has to be lonely and exposed to cultivate them. Though one can follow an individual and largely solitary course to cut through the turgid conformism of establishment habits, the social cost is enormous.

"Freedom," under analysis, rather means the pressures exerted from childhood toward the creation of a passive and somewhat stupefied agent of a mechanically dominated society. "Freedom" means victimization by a value system projected from every conceivable institution and experience: family, school, church, government, profession or job, recreation, press and television. "Freedom" means the repetitious and lifelong acceptance of determining and dominating forces that tend of necessity to suffocate or eliminate qualitative choice and movement.

If one is free to choose at all, it is within areas defined by a consumer-war economy: schools more or less inferior; draft, reserve, or education until over-age; one occupation or another whose benefit is more operational than human; suburban boxes and squares of lawn or apartment ghettos in the central city; this or that vacation, depending on one's status; cars obsolescent before they are driven; and on and on. Freedom is reductively the suck and shove to become the tiny edition of larger society, to be mediocre or to excel in pragmatism, power sensitivity, neuroses, prejudices, moral confusion, and unconscious hypocrisy.

The value attached by Americans to such "freedoms" can be judged both by the near obsessiveness with which they are discussed and by the quality of discussion. On the human level "freedoms" are preponderantly dealt with in terms of threats to them, such as poor and black people, Communist belligerence, De Gaulle's ingratitude, unrest over delayed victory in Vietnam, black anarchy in the Congo. On the material level "freedoms" center on the relative merits of split-level or ranch house, country club or public course, or a choice of deodorant, bourbon, and laundry soap. The real world suffers constantly a torturous molding into the world of affluence, it is accpeted if it enhances affluence, rejected if it does not. Yet convictions persist that this is freedom, this is life, and these "things" are the stuff of life.

Consequently, domination is not applied by conventional means of state control, not by inhibiting speech, censoring the press, restricting association and religious practice. Repressions of social creativity and true individuality are far more scientific, and effective. Government controls (conventional totalitarianism), technological controls, are covert and imperceptible. Marketing techniques aim to articulate superfluous needs as real needs, false needs as necessities. Marketing appeal is aimed at illusions of health, appearance, acceptability, status, and solidarity, reinforced by a value network that makes the appeal reasonable, persuasive, and credible. If the result is a kind of pandering, this is justified through references to the good of the whole, with its impressive achievements of prosperity and power, its ability to compete with other societies, and so forth.

The marketing message deals blatantly with human needs as though they had no limit, as though, indeed, needs should be expanded as far as advertising genius can take them, as far as claims for them can be made credible. The object of sales is clearly to save people from thinking and, moreover, to have them feel dissatisfaction with present ownership, or absence of ownership. The pitch is then made in such a way that, implicitly, a better version of life arrives with possession of the product.

In terms of control or attempts to control, the technological process (research, production, and sales) is obviously not involved in a conspiracy to rob people of their humanity. Scientists, production-line chiefs, and Madison Avenue executives hardly consider the good or ill impact of their product upon the consumer. The net effect, however, is control of the public, since profit motivation verges on obsession, and obsession shows itself in the disavowal of moral responsibility beyond the product itself.

The regulation of people is, consequently, implicit in the need capitalism has to disgorge its overproductivity upon an already overfed, overclothed, overapplianced, and overstimulated market. To keep people buying, extremes of absurdity and bad taste become commonplace—in fact, the whole intellectual and moral desert of television is intended to condition buying. Profits are America's golden calf, and nothing short of an earthquake or God's judgment must interfere with them.

This is not to suggest that irresponsibility in this matter is a one-way street, and that the consumer is a passive, guiltless victim. On the contrary, Americans are enthusiastic buyers; the marketing world is precisely designed to exploit their joyful and virtuous delight in goods. They are also tireless, if unconscious, salesmen; no little portion of their waking hours is spent defending or selling their possessions to their friends. What women wear, what men drive, what unusual sense experience has been recently undergone, all are subjects of interminable and exhaustive conversations. "Things," it is generally assumed, have much to do with making a person, a society, a nation—America is great precisely because it has used its wealth ("things") generously and boldly.

Consumer buying or salesmanship, however, causes more than profit for the wider society. It promotes an identification with both product and producer—in fact, with both the rationale and the machinery of the industrial society. Social psychologists would call this phenomenon mimesis, or a feeling of oneness with mass production, mass distribution, and mass consumption. A claim has been put upon the entire person, even upon those mysterious inner spaces that a man usually reserves for himself and for God. These have been invaded and reduced, so that identification is made not with oneself but with society as a whole, with the technological monolith. One does not become a spectator to its complexity or an awestruck and horrified judge; one becomes instead a microcosm of it—a servant-promoter, if you will.

Such intense and undiscerning involvement militates against the development of critical reason and keeps it immobile at infantile levels. Reason, judgment, volition, and emotional life are kept at a plateau of bondage to establishment values and mores, and appeals neither to reason nor morality are likely to disturb their fixations. It is utterly consistent, therefore, that the public accepts packaging as more important than content in food, rust on a year-old car as reason to get a new one, or an influx of Negroes as an automatic threat to property rights.

Essentially, the problem becomes one of violence, a systematic offense against truth and justice. Violence bombards individuals from most quarters of society and during most of one's waking hours. It is received, assimilated, and returned again to its source. Yet it leaves its mark, and its damage can take the form of indifference, boredom, sporadic use of time and effort, uncertainty, inability to foster an enduring friendship, periodic or habitual misuse of others. Social patterns have become personal patterns, leaving society further entrapped and leaving persons further baffled, ineffective, and despairing.

The human product is, to use Herbert Marcuse's apt description, one-dimensional man, who expresses himself in one-dimensional thought and behavior. Vertical relationships to God and self have all been subsumed by a horizontal relationship to industrialized society which controls one as cog and patron. Within such limits, if concepts are not pragmatic and operational, if they do not serve established systems, they tend to face rejection, on one extreme as subversive or "communistic" and on the other, as simply useless.

Two examples of the tyrannical control of system over thought come to mind. The first involves a suggestion by me to a Congressman friend that testimony by economists be given before the Senate Foreign Relations Committee regarding: (1) the real extent of American economic presence abroad; (2) the proportion of the gross national product dependent upon such investments; (3) alleged collusion between investments and American militarism in these areas.

Such a request seemed both logical and necessary, since military–industrial alliances consume about seven-tenths of tax dollars, and since it is predictable that a wedding so mutually satisfactory in America be energetically consummated abroad as well. In a word, if America must have markets for its surpluses and must have foreign resources and labor to feed a mounting desire for profit and prosperity, it must have a political policy to favor such interests, and arms to defend them.

The Congressman answered in typically sympathetic and forthright fashion. He agreed with the necessity for such investigation, and to substantiate his own awareness, recalled a visit he made to Peru, where some four hundred American corporations had holdings. Yet he reluctantly refused to be involved in overtures to the chairman of the committee, Senator J. William Fulbright. There were the congressman's own preoccupations, to be sure, but he thought the enterprise too "explosive" and felt that it would hardly be regarded as otherwise by Fulbright.

Another example was a recent "think tank" sponsored by the American Friends Service Committee in Philadelphia. A good representative spectrum of liberal Democrats was there: a governor (other politicians invited declined the risk of appearance), two former ambassadors (one American and one foreign), several important editors and commentators, a former head of a major civil-rights organization, a priest, a minister, and a rabbi. In a word, progressive elements of the establishment were in attendance, and all were involved in opposition to the Vietnam war.

It soon became apparent that little agreement reigned as to the significance of this war to Vietnam, to America, and to the world. In characteristically human fashion, the tragedy of Vietnam was laid on the table not in its own terms or in terms of the broader danger to mankind, but according to personal experience and position within the power structure. Few comprehended, apparently, the human factors of the war: What were Vietnamese rights? Why did America need this war? What moral and legal obligations bound this country in light of possible wider war, and World War III? Because no priority was given moral and human concerns, there could be no talk of unilateral withdrawal, of civil disobedience, or revolution. In the end two measures were adopted, both of them framework policies. The first was to attempt to establish a news agency intended to supply communications media with a truer version of Vietnam realities than that supplied by the government. The second aimed through political organization to preserve the Democratic Party in power and to produce a peace candidate, ending the war that way.

Not so strangely, the only people present who questioned such provisions on the ground that they did not meet issues were those who had served the black and the poor in radical movements, who knew something of human rights and what an adequate response to those rights should be, who had felt the black (now the Vietnamese) plight under American castes of privilege. True, a day-long conference was too short a time to plunge into complicated and elusive issues. Yet I am fairly convinced that time was not the problem; attitudes were. Most men there had an unconscious yet complete commitment to functional codes, and it made hardly any difference that their interpretation of such codes tended to be liberal.

There are many reasons why men mobilize, many causes around which they can be mobilized. Hate, love, fear, greed—any combination of these or a combination of all—inspire causes that testify to life or bring it to ruin. It is really quite simple: Give men a cause, prod their noble or base emotions, and one has a movement, or a war. Technological society, however, mobilizes through plenty and the defense of plenty, becoming in the process not only the welfare, but the warfare, state as well. Patterns of mobilization follow these rough lines: Produce consumer products as extravagantly as possible in order to sell them extravagantly (free enterprise); match overproduction with overadvertising to cause overconsumption; hunt markets overseas to unload surpluses; exploit foreign labor and resources to feed the native industrial maw; meanwhile, articulate a threat to both foreign aggrandizement and home prosperity (Communism), and build a military machine to meet it.

Loyalty, fear, and greed are alternately stimulated by encomiums to national prestige, by revelations of enemy efforts to outstrip us, by promises of more prosperous conditions. (Rival powers, with aspirations and ideologies more or less similar to our own, follow the same general course.)

Thus it becomes possible for the Administration and most major American institutions to justify this country as the innocent object of world envy and hate, though we have no territorial designs and "want nothing for ourselves," though we fought two great wars for justice and peace, though peace would be impossible without our nuclear power and without our firmness against "aggression" in Vietnam. We are infinitely more sinned against than sinning, the panegyric goes, we who have given most generously to poor nations, who have sent our youth abroad to "help" them. Now we are beleaguered by Communist obsessions with world domination and by the greed of all men. So the Rightist press would have it, so also most official rhetoric by former President Johnson or Dean Rusk.

At any rate, the net result is repression of the individual by society, a type of sublimated slavery. Most men believe what they need, it seems, and needs have been well defined and firmly implanted.

Technical progress and Communism, the plus and minus of control, are both pursued with clear purpose, sometimes with fanaticism. They are apparently enough to produce the profound cohesion and consensus which distinguish our society. Allow Madison Avenue to manipulate individual and group needs; keep the middle class and the rich content with preferential concern for business; silence the poor with periodic and overpublicized bits of social legislation—result, a welfare state. Seek foreign markets first by a colonial, and later by an imperialist, design; identify competitors as "enemies"; create an ideology to confront enemy "propaganda"; arm as a gesture of "defense"; keep hot and cold-war situations various and turbulent—result, a warfare state. In operation and in effect the two are complements, halves of the same coin. One needs the other; one would suffer widespread, even violent, change without the other.

Together, they can mobilize men, institutions, and a nation, purge traditional trouble spots, eliminate historical grievances, smother opposition and dissent, keep a relative and ominous peace. Of its own kind, it is an astounding achievement, but under Christian judgment it is so destructive of human values that it is like a horror film shown too fast and enticingly to be understood.

The main dynamics and trends of producing conformity through socio-economic processes are destructive enough to be delineated again. Mythologize national needs as being identical with big-business needs; encourage industrial cartels through numberless mergers; absorb labor into management by giving labor its demands, and sometimes more; provide capital with investment outlets through worldwide systems of economic and military pacts, monetary arrangements, and assistance programs; allow a free press that censors itself through devotion to national purpose; buy the ghetto off by "pacification" money in the hot summer and by allowing it to destroy itself at other times; use churches and synagogues to moralize the grandeur of a "free" society and the "integrity" of national interest; invade homes and classrooms with mass communications and with conformist public opinion; poll the public on key establishment concerns, then react to polls instead of human needs; standardize leisure and recreation as conditioners for contentment and happiness; assimilate leadership into business, government, and church; keep dossiers on troublemakers, and keep them under discreet surveillance; employ military indoctrination as another species of thought-control, and entrust to the military abroad the same function given the police at home.

There is much more, if one intends to bore or stun a reader. But it should be made clear that such analysis is not part of a "hate America" campaign. Rather, it can be applied with slight variations to Great Britain, France, West Germany, Italy, even to the Soviet Union. In Russia direct political controls are being noticeably relaxed in favor of technological controls, the controls of an affluent society. In France and Italy two of the strongest Communist parties in the world choose to play parliamentarianism, not as a waiting game, but in direct admission of capitalist power to assimilate them and condemn them to the nonradical.

America, however, is far and away the pattern and outstanding example. The technological and cultural influences we export are received with mixed emotions in the most remote tribal villages, in the most antagonistic Communist countries. To paraphrase Herbert Marcuse, two antithetical propositions are now being clarified: (1) Technological society is capable of containing qualitative change indefinitely. (2) Technological society has within itself forces of violence which can tear it apart. We may never know which of the two wins out, for a third possibility may intrude, World War III.

To say that the Church is sharing man's crisis today is a generous claim, true only to a point. To state that the Church perceives the nature of man's crisis, and enters it in faith and service, is to risk absurdity. Such an observation, of course, is not meant to demean millions of believers whose honest desire is to implant Christ's kingdom and His justice in man's family. It is merely to insist on their failure (and one's own) to do so.

Many Christians take heart from signs of Church renewal, and they point with eagerness and relief to better qualities of training, liturgy, social sensitivity, service, authority, and *conscience*. Openness to other Christians, to Jews, humanists, and unbelievers, is a remarkable and encouraging commonplace. Christians are even talking to Communists, and finding the experience full of common concerns and anxieties.

One might venture, however, that such criteria of "progress" miss the mark and even become delusions in themselves. It is of little immediate purpose or ultimate consequence to reflect on where we were and the distance we have traversed. Such reflections lead us to forget the fact that the Church is under judgment from both the Gospel and the world, and to neglect them while concentrating on the energies and ingenuities expended in "renewal" is a dangerous ingroup pastime.

The Gospel indicts us because we do not believe its words and therefore cannot take it seriously. Part of that dilemma is that we cannot imagine it "working," which is to say that there is no point in practicing it until all men practice it. Since that eventuality is unlikely, one is discharged from responsibility. Arguments amassed to justify our version of Christianity even become startling replicas of contemporary thinking; contradictory proportions are the favorite tool of such reasonableness. So Christians will say, "Defensive wars can be fought because the gospel doesn't outlaw them." Or they will say, "Men are warlike, war is inevitable, so we support war!" And Americans will say, "Peace is war—both Vietnam and overkill prove it!"

The world indicts us because we have little concern for it, little allegiance to its aspirations and interests, little time for its plight. The world we fear and ostracize—containing the greater portion of men—is one of hunger and suffering, one of awakening consciousness, one of gathering bitterness and hate. It is a world whose cry is "revolution" and whose desire is to cast off its chains and destroy its guards, or to die trying. Ironically enough, it is a world that Christians are commanded to enter, whereas they are equally commanded to leave the world of privilege in which they live. And since they neither know this new world nor sympathize with its agony (having no intention of abandoning their privileges), there can be no reconciliation expected from them. How could there be? Presence and prophecy must precede reconciliation; but when these preliminaries are neglected, personal integrity in Christians becomes as unlikely as the just social order that flows from it.

More and more, people speak of revolution "within" this country, and though disagreements might arise about its causes and nature, few will deny its likelihood and threat. Granted, therefore, the probability of revolution, what course will it take? Nonviolent revolution is impossible without Christians; it is also impossible with Christians as they are. Violent revolution, then, becomes very nearly inevitable.

But we are attempting here to understand the Church in a technological society. One can begin such a discussion by theologizing about the Church as a community of faith and service; then one can speculate about a technocracy and the distinctive society it builds; and finally, one can judge how the two interact and influence one another. Nevertheless, our object will be to venture that a technocracy and a church are institutionally compatible, but that it is virtually impossible for an institutional church to be a Christian community under a technocracy.

It is a fact of existence that the Christian Church must live under worldly power; it is also a fact that it lives at peace with this power more often than not. Power in the United States (the epitome of Western capitalist technocracy) is an institutional triumvirate: the military, economic, and political bureaucracies. Political design, whether domestic or foreign, stems from these three bureaucracies which in turn stem from a mass-production, mass-consumer society that now welcomes war-making as an integral operation. Which is to say that our free-enterprise technocracy has now overproduced for its domestic and foreign markets, and consequently must have war-making as a new market, as an imperial protection for foreign markets, and as a safety valve for its inherent violence. It seems safe to conjecture, therefore, that war-making is here to stay for the immediate future, because our capitalism simply cannot discard it as a rising portion of the gross national product.

To put it differently, war-making carries the built-in waste-making of mass consumerism to an ultimate logic. Planned obsolescence in autos, appliances, and buildings makes more rational (or irrational) the combat waste of war material and the phasing-out of this material for faster and more deadly equipment. Add to this our assault upon space, and its connection with arms research and development.

In addition, war-making as a quasi-marketable function gives credence to our ambition to conduct the world's business. It intimidates the poor, pressures them to become and/or remain our customers, sobers their rage and unrest. If war-making fails in this regard, we have a Vietnam; if it succeeds, we have counter-insurgency, teamed with political scientists and their conflict-management. Whatever the case, however, war-making is a profitable item of the economy, a factor of planned waste, an investment that pays for itself in rising prosperity and foreign profits.

This triumvirate of military, economic, and political bureaucracies runs America. In spite of disclaimers, moreover, its policy and operation make clear its intention to run the world. It is a coalition that is interdependent and interlocking, as sensitive to reciprocal needs as it is jealous of its power. Its weaknesses baffle its friends and enrage its critics; its aims affect hundreds of millions; its excesses frighten men everywhere. It is a coalition imperial in design and ambition, arrogant, ruthless, cohesive in organization, and awesome in military might. It is instrumental in making America what is perhaps the last of history's many empires.

The Church should be the adversary of this dizzying concentration of power, yet it is not. The Church should be challenging its moral relativism, its anticommunism and antirevolutionary ideology, its imperial economics, ambiguous racism, hot and cold warring, its mounting control over a passive and neurotic citizenry, its thing-obsession and people-domination. The Church should understand that this society is engaged in a fearful race between violence-production and violence-management, that it is now an obstacle to human progress and a threat to mankind. And yet it does not understand, does not challenge.

To expect it to understand, to challenge, to become an adversary of such massive and coordinated injustice is perhaps to expect too much. It is perhaps to lay too great a public burden upon the Church. Perhaps. But where do allegiances lie, except to Christ and to man? And where does hope lie? If the Church does not withstand power's authority to plunge deeper into the doomsday race, to escalate further the insanity in Vietnam, to such excessive profits from the Third World, to allow our cities to verge on explosion, what moral authority does the Church possess? If these crimes are not immoral, what is morality? If the Church does not assert that the overlords of this nation have clearly lost the right to public jurisdiction over Americans in many areas of policy dealing with war, race, and war taxes, what is the substance of its gospel? If the Church judges divorces, uncelibate priests, couples practicing birth control, clerical revolutionaries, and Marxists as morally irresponsible, why should it not judge those who make, administer, and profit from war as criminally irresponsible? Obviously, the War Crimes Tribunals, called twice at Stockholm and Copenhagen, should have been sponsored jointly by the Vatican and the World Council of Churches.

Christians should have refused to send their young men to war, refused to pay war taxes, and refused to work in defense industries. Christians should have led draft protestors into jail, with bishops and Head Clerks in the vanguard. Christians should have disrupted military bases nonviolently; they should have, with total respect for conscience, encouraged refusal of Vietnam service and even desertion from the military. Christians should have attempted to close down war production and to destroy war machinery as a means of protecting the lives of those who operate it. Christians should have synthesized an economics that would save their countrymen from becoming the commercial rapists of the world. In a word, Christians should have fought with the weapons of their witness to make this nation honest, to force conformity with its Declaration of Independence, its commitment to the United Nations Charter, its rhetoric about self-determination. But because they have not, honest men deride the Church or courteously ignore it while, more dangerously still, the masters of society favor and commend it.

Assuredly, such acts would be a public burden upon the Church. But what of its gospel and calling? Because it has adulterated both to shameful degrees, it has helped to push America to the brink of violent revolution, and it has helped to set the world aflame. In point of fact, Christian hypocrisy has helped to stage a scenario of tragic dimensions, a whirlwind that mankind is just beginning to reap. Which says something about the price that will be paid for Christian wealth, comfort, and arrogance.

It may now be apparent that certain factors intervene to make the Church an ally of power bureaucrats instead of, given the need, their moral critic and adversary. Apart from certain historical-religious influences that have shaped American Christianity, it may be far more important to stress the impact of bureaucracy upon the Church. One can give endless attention to these influences: the Puritan ethic, the Calvinist impact on economics, missionary efforts at home and abroad (parallels to economic expansionism), denominational differences and similarities, the Catholic assimilation of immigrants, the "separation" of Church and State, patriotism as an ethical tax. But in measure of influence, much of the above has been superseded by Christian unanimity favoring institutionalism—what critics call the bureaucracy of moralism.

By way of style and operation, bureaucracies tend to concentrate on indigenous purposes and objectives. In a general manner, therefore, business focuses on profits; government legislates local, national, and international commonweal (American economic health); defense protects our freedom (American economic freedom); education gives people marketable skills; church lends to all its weight of moral approval. In a very real sense their value system is the same and their language similar, as is their attraction for administration and their appreciation of power. And at their summit are the men who run and rule the country, the men whom C. Wright Mills called "The Power Elite."

Since bureaucracies share a common power base—citizen, businessman, ex-serviceman, Christian—and since this power base provides a common point of departure into specific enterprises, harmony becomes an operational necessity and dialogue a necessary tool. Bureaucrats therefore think it essential to know the main interests and directions of other bureaucrats, and this they accomplish by maintaining an active presence within several key bureaucracies. A case in point would be the local tie-ins between manufacturing, sales, news media, finance, law, insurance, and church. One man can be an insurance executive, sit on the board of a bank, hold stock in local TV, and be on the vestry of his church or serve as an adviser to his bishop. Meanwhile, he remains active in the Rotary or the Chamber of Commerce, eats lunch and drinks cocktails with his peers.

Expand such allegiances to a national level, and one has a coalition of military, industrial, and political interests that have instant and easy access to one another, simply because the coalition's members understand that their personal and bureaucratic viability depends upon the oil in a wider machinery. Such men have transcendent loyalties, and these are not to God.

What results is a symbiotic relationship. Bureaucratic purposes are harmonized, streamlined, and widened; the links between them are firmed and strengthened. The product is a force of single-minded purpose, complex efficiency, and massive power—grudging of freedom, lavish in reward, ruthless to outside threat.

A Christian can allow much more entrenchment in secular institutions than in his church, since he knows that their different covenants ought to foster different types of power. He knows that historically, industrialization helped to make bureaucracies inevitable, even as technology now makes them larger and more complex. but he also knows that his church is a community, not a bureaucracy; that it is in fact very nearly a community *against* a bureaucracy. Obviously, it may institutionalize, but when that choice makes the Gospel an ersatz code, a Christian institution has become bureaucracy. In effect it has lost its freedom to be Christian—and human.

When that happens, the Church speaks the language of officialdom, the ethical equivalent of propaganda. It moralizes in a casuistic, neutral fashion, betraying where, in fact, its values lie. And they lie with its own bureaucracy, with its contributing members and its public image, with the tolerant credence it can arouse in other circles of power. The dynamics of its system lead it to the assumption that survival and growth require neutrality toward injustice, and once the assumption is accepted, neutrality becomes a price quite eagerly paid.

Which is to say that the Church responds with what the secular establishment asks: with a caliber of speech which clothes the atrocities of power in white garments of probity, which obscures the violence of technological materialism, which offers a superstitious palliative to the fierce tensions of technological life, and which makes one form of unreality more liveable by substituting another. The message has little to do with real life but much to do with support of life as it is led. It substitutes confidence in power for faith, or it helps to make the two one.

The public position of religious bureaucracy follows its speech consistently. If honest speech is to be shunned, so too is honest witness. In frequent contrast, secular power may conclude that a "liberal" position on human rights is to its interest. But this is not necessarily true of the Church, whose response is first to its institutional base—making it more inbred than social, more operational than ordained to a larger service of men. On the other hand, both government and business must sometimes be sensitive to their constituency and market—survival and sales sometimes demand a kind of group-interest altruism.

If Vietnam became a gut issue by endangering the Church's bureaucracy, the present neutrality would dissolve. Bishops would become doves, chanceries would sponsor draft counseling and would house deserters, clerics would minister to prisoners from within jails. But since little prospect of such a threat exists, since the war does not affect the Church's property, income, investments, membership, or privileges to any noticeable degree, silence and inaction become (and remain) policy. Given these realities, it is indeed possible to imagine the Church doing business as usual while 1984 or the first nuclear exchange is upon us.

By the same token, urban turmoil is not seen by the Church's bureaucratic vision as directly "its" issue. Church members live outside the ghetto for the most part, and those who do concern themselves with urban problems do not seriously negate the rule. The value system, dynamics, and machinery of the Church are not primarily directed toward blacks. If one were to except their motivation for a moment, both the Government and business exhibit far more honest concern in the Riot Commission Report (March, 1968) or in employment efforts than does the Church.

Briefly, the similarity of view and action between church and secular bureaucracies is brought about not so much because there is a moral vacuum created by the Church and exploited by the Government (though there is some truth in that), or because Washington must load its propaganda with moralism to advance credibility (some truth in that also), but because bureaucracies are at heart the same, and they are the same because a harmony or an interdependence of interest prevails between them. In a largely unconscious and unarticulated display of mutual concern, both the Church and the State promote the national purpose. And if their visceral reasons for doing so vary, the net result is substantially the same.

Let no one be surprised, therefore, that in exchange for being left alone by the Church in political and commercial "overreach" like nuclear-arms escalation, "rollback" foreign policy, Vietnam, the CIA, and economic invasions of both developed and developing countries, Washington grants immunities and privileges to the Church—tax exemptions, clerical dispensations from military service, grants for education and research, and consistent official approval. There is no overt contract for such mutual back-scratching, but there is a covenant lying soddenly in the guts of bureaucracies, a covenant to which all spouses are blasphemously faithful.

The covenant between bureaucracies indicates, by and large, their response to one another. The Church responds much as it is expected to, at least on leadership levels. Officially, it does let the Government alone, thereby giving huge tacit support as well—and on occasion, enthusiastic affirmation—to domestic and foreign policy. Herein lies its tragedy and the price of its betrayal. It gives support to power at the expense of conscience. Many of its members would be more Christian without it.

What is the future of religious bureaucracy? It is difficult and sobering to say. Bureaucracy can feel little urgency for change, nor can it accuse itself of massive complicity in America's crimes. But this much seems somewhat clear. It is breaking up—ponderously, incredulously—all forms of Christian and Jewish adherence. The fresh air that Pope John let into the Catholic Church is now blowing through the whole believing world, scattering before it the religious trash of centuries, leaving the faithful less and less to work with except man and his agony.

As long as retrenchment goes on, as long as renewal means only better housekeeping, as long as justice is neither spoken nor lived, the base of the religious establishment will erode like the feet of a huge clay god. Honest people will go their way and pursue their consciences, much as though church and synagogue did not exist. Clergymen will reject authoritarianism, middle-class dishonesty, and social irrelevance to leave the ministry. The best of the young, meanwhile, will hunt for substitutes, refusing affiliation with a structure so impervious to change, so immune to suffering, so contradictory to itself.

And this is a hopeful trend, because from it will come new Christian communities, small, poor by choice, passionate for justice, revolutionary, losing themselves among the victims of man's greed. They will be, above all, communities of the Spirit, Who calls to them whom He will, that the redemption of Christ might go on in a world torn by movements of hope and catastrophe.

# ❧181❧

# Letter from a Baltimore Jail

## PHILIP BERRIGAN

In his opposition to the war in Vietnam, Berrigan took symbolic direct action with friends to manifest the kind of just community in which he had hope. His justification encompassed the meaning of being 'Christ's man', the inadequacy of 'legitimate' dissent and the distorted priorities he believed many Americans had been induced to accept.

There was no conspiracy, as the government suspected. There was only a group of friends, trying to validate themselves as a community, by a decision for peace.

I make no pretension in calling this a "Letter from a Baltimore Jail." Many of you remember Martin Luther King's "Letter from a Birmingham Jail." Together we cherish the man and the martyr. As I recall, Dr. King's letter silenced his critics, most of whom were Christians and some of whom were Catholics. I do not intend that, nor do I hope for it. I ask you merely to ponder events with me and then to make whatever response you choose. As our President says, "Let us reason together." So, a letter from a Baltimore jail, written with all the esteem and love I can muster.

Many of you have been sorely perplexed with me (us); some of you have been angry, others despairing. (One parishioner writes of quarreling with people who thought me mad.) After all, isn't it impudent and sick for a grown man (and a priest) to slosh blood—wasn't it duck's blood—on draft files; to terrorize harmless secretaries doing their job; to act without ecclesiastical permission and to disgrace the collar and its sublime office? And then, while convicted and awaiting sentence, to insult a tolerant government by bursting wildly into another draft board with a larger troop of irresponsibles—forcibly seizing the records, forcibly carrying them outside, there to burn them with napalm? With smiles and jubilation? Disgusting, frenzied, violent; many of you wrote or told us that.

Source: Philip Berrigan, 'Letter from a Baltimore Jail', *Prison Journals of a Priest-Revolutionary*, New York, 1970, pp. 14-20.

You had trouble with blood as a symbol—uncivilized, messy, bizarre. *Time, Newsweek,* and the Catholic Church lent their impressive authority. You had trouble with the war—had it really gotten so bad that men had to do that? You had trouble with departures from legitimate dissent, from law and order itself. You had trouble with napalm as a symbol—what's that got to do with it? You had trouble with us calling violence nonviolence, and the press calling nonviolence violence. You had trouble with destruction of property; with civil disobedience; with priests getting involved, and getting involved this much. Let's face it: Perhaps half of you had trouble with us acting at all.

You'll forgive me for interpreting, but it has a certain legitimacy here. My friends and I have had long dealings with the press, and we think it generally reflects the attitudes of the people. We have read our mail and have spoken to—and listened to—hundreds of audiences around the country. We have talked to congressmen, cabinet members, military and intelligence men in Washington, and to state and local officials. We have spoken to servicemen on trains, buses, and planes; we have written to relatives in Viet Nam. We have experienced war firsthand, several of us; we have served Church and country abroad, several of us. And one of us (my brother) spent a week in Laos and another in Viet Nam negotiating the release of three American fliers. We have learned, finally, from the peace movement—its rhetoric, aims, convictions, criticisms of us. Pardon us for interpreting.

Let me share with you an analogy to introduce mutual concerns. Imagine, if you will, a tiny community of sixteen people, relatively isolated, exclusive, and self-sufficient. Its leader is leader for the simple reason that he owns more than the rest put together. Because he does, the others work for him, making him richer as they make themselves poorer. Naturally there is fear on his part, discontent on the others'. The rich man hires guards and intelligence; he resolves to protect his person and property. He often exhorts them, telling them of the honor of their role, carefully avoiding terms like "mercenary" and "spy." When unrest develops, it is ferreted out, condemned as godless, subversive, and hostile to law and order. Then it is crushed.

## A Wealthy and Powerful Nation

Another analogy, if you please. A nation that counts its wealth in dollars had two billionaires, six half-billionaires, and 153 multimillionaires with more than one hundred million each. Paradoxically, this nation had also many poor—ten million who hungered, twenty million inadequately fed. Many of the rich, thinking undoubtedly of other services to the nation, pay no taxes, while the poor pay upwards of fourteen percent (I must banish this dirty thought resolutely: If the rich do not draft the law, they certainly apply it!) And the citizens' attitude toward dollars is so curious that in their land of freedom and equality, five percent of the people control twenty percent of the wealth; at the other end, twenty percent control five percent. And that's what somebody calls the symmetry of injustice.

Need I remind you that my clumsy analogies depict—as through a glass darkly—our beloved country, abroad and at home? Need I remind you that wealth can be legislated abroad—NATO, SEATO, CENTO, OAS—as it is at home in graduated income tax, oil-depletion allowance? And if legislation fails, unrest can be militarized: Viet Nam, the Dominican Republic, Newark, Detroit. Need I remind you that wealth is such a priority with us that we both add to it by war production (defense budget, eighty billion dollars plus) and protect it by war (Viet Nam, Thailand, Laos, Guatemala, Bolivia, Peru)?

Need I remind you that the United States maintains its wealth by an imperial economy—foreign investments totaling seventy billion dollars in 1967, eighty percent of all the foreign investments in the world? (Another dirty thought that I must banish resolutely: Empires have always valued power more than wisdom, survival more than justice.)

Need I remind you that law legislated for the few equals lawlessness for the many, and that lawlessness rests not so much on crime in the streets as on crimes at the top? Need I remind you that conscription reflects national injustice more than the ghetto, simply because it plays a more deadly deceit upon its victims. "Tell my soldiers what they really fight for," said Frederick the Great, "and the ranks would be empty in the morning."

As for the blood, it was ours: the FBI made sure of that. Our greatest mistake was technical incompetence, not getting enough of it. You showed an odd fascination with blood, my friends. You worried the point as a puppy worries a rubber bone, and with as much profit. Surely men foolhardy enough to do such a stunt would be foolhardy enough to take their own blood?

We were painfully educated by people concentrating on blood while neglecting its meaning. Blood is life—the Bible says so; lose enough or shed enough, and death results. Blood is redemption (freedom) also, depending on how it is shed; the contrast between Cain and Christ shows that. Our point was simply this: We could claim no right to life or freedom as long as the Viet Nam war—U Thant calls it one of the most barbarous in history—deprives Americans and Vietnamese of life and freedom. If we said no to the war, we could say yes to its victims, and to sharing their predicament.

What of official disobedience, you wonder, and disgrace to the priesthood? The answer depends on one's frame of reference, I suppose. Is a Christian Christ's man, or the state's; is the Church a community of belief or a spiritual spa? If the first in both cases, I have honored the priesthood and have been obedient to the Church. One must deal, it seems, with two realities—the Church as Christ's body, and the Church as the body of man. Which has the higher reality? If you say the first, then the first must be the benchmark, and the other found and served. One cannot interpret Christ by interpreting man. One rather says what man can be because of what Christ is.

You claim we disregard legitimate dissent at the expense of law and order. Quite the contrary. My brother and I have had experience with legitimate dissent for ten years, the Melvilles nearly as long in Guatemala, Tom Lewis and David Eberhardt nearly as long. We have seen legitimate dissent first ridiculed, then resisted, then absorbed. To become, in effect, an exercise in naïveté.

## The Uselessness of Legitimate Dissent

If society can absorb lawlessness, or protests against lawlessness, without redress, it suggests its own insensitivity to injustice. Law and order tend to become a figment because law and justice become harder to attain. With ineffectual grievance machinery, there is little hope of redress. Which may explain why legal scholars say the Constitution must allow civil disobedience to check itself in keeping with the balance it constructs among the three branches of the federal government.

In point of fact, we have experienced intimately the uselessness of legitimate dissent. The war grows in savagery, more American coffins come home, Vietnamese suffering would seem to have passed the limits of human endurance. Astute and faithful men, including congressional doves, say we can't win in Viet Nam without World War III. Others disagree, saying that World War III has begun, that it is merely a question of time before one side or the other employs nuclear weapons. We have nuclear weapons in Viet Nam; we have carried them over the Chinese mainland; China is a nuclear power; Russia and China have not dissolved their mutual-defense treaty. These are not debatable items by either side.

In face of these facts, for some Americans to ask others to restrict their dissent to legal channels is asking them to joust with a windmill. More than that, it is to ask them for silent complicity with unimaginable injustice, for political unrepresentation, for voicelessness in the fate that threatens everyone. God would never ask that of any man; no man can ask it justly of other men.

In turn, we destroyed property; indeed, the people's property. Ah, there's the rub. The Jews had their golden calf, Americans have their own property. Its misuse and disparity is our most sinister social fact; its international pursuit has brought us to grips with the world. Scripture calls the love of money the root of all evil, a judgment true enough to require respectful attention. The Lord said that renouncing possessions and following Him were the two criteria of discipleship, so mutually reliant in fact that the absence of one cancels the other. In contrast, no people have cherished and celebrated property as we have, even to the point of obsessions and orgy.

Americans would not quarrel with destroying German gas ovens or the Nazi and Stalinist slave camps. We would not quarrel with violent destruction of war matériel threatening us. But let the issue become nonviolent destruction of "weapons for defense"—hydrogen bombs; germ cultures at Fort Detrick, Maryland, cluster-bomb units, Stoner rifles, Selective Service files—and the issue suffers an abortive death. Americans know, with a kind of avaricious instinct, that property like this serves as insurance policy to private property. As our

President says, "They want what we have, and we're not going to give it to them."

Friends, countrymen, such is our case. It may be over-assertive and presumptuous in spots. That is for you to judge. But here it is, and here we take our stand, because, obviously, it is the best one we have. Disagree as you might, one thing you must acknowledge—our stand disrupts our lives, removes our liberty, exiles us for a considerable time from our friends, our communities, our country, our church—from everything we love so passionately. What of your stand? It costs most of you neither risk nor loss, except perhaps your integrity, your country's welfare, your Christianity. Perhaps your immediate gain may be your long-term loss.

In closing, there is one request we make. We can fairly predict that our government will show flexible leniency if we prove ourselves contrite. We can't be contrite at this point, not seeing reasons to be so. For you to point out our errors firmly and patiently would be a great service, truly in the spirit of the Gospel. It could restore to us confidence in our government and our church, and could return us to our families, friends, and assignments. It could as well allow us a constructive part in building the Great Society—instead of a destructive share in tearing it down. In all humanity, we plead for your help.

# ᛭182᛭

# Letter to the Weathermen

## DANIEL BERRIGAN

Daniel Berrigan, Philip's brother, shared his convictions. He spent a period underground and was a participant in one of the several resistance court trials of the period. In a febrile time, the Weathermen, a faction that had broken away from the Students for a Democratic Society to use sabotage and revolutionary violence, appeared significant both to the state and to other radicals. The interest of Berrigan's attempt to reach them is in what it indicates about the boundaries of his kind of radical Christianity, both in his mode of address to them and in the substance of his discussion of violence.

Dear Brothers and Sisters,
Let me express a deep sense of gratitude that the chance has come to speak to you across the underground. It's a great moment; I rejoice in the fact that we can start a dialogue that I hope will continue through the smoke signals, all with a view to enlarging the circle. Indeed the times demand not that we narrow our method of communication but that we enlarge it, if anything new or better is to emerge. (I'm talking out of a set of rough notes; my idea is that I would discuss these ideas with you and possibly publish them later, by common agreement.)

The cold war alliance between politics, labor, and the military finds many Americans at the big end of the cornucopia. What has not yet risen in them is the question of whose blood is paying for all this, what families elsewhere are being blasted, what separation and agony and death are at the narrow end of our abundance. These connections are hard to make, and very few come on them. Many can hardly imagine that all being right with America means that much must go wrong elsewhere. How do we get such a message across to others? It seems to me that this is one way of putting the very substance of our task. Trying to keep connections, or to create new ones. It's a most difficult job, and

Source: Daniel Berrigan, 'Letter to the Weathermen', *America is Hard to Find*, London, 1973, pp. 92–8. © 1972 by S.P.C.K.

in hours of depression it seems all but impossible to speak to Americans across the military, diplomatic, and economic idiocies. Yet I think we have to carry our reflection further, realizing that the difficulty of our task is the other side of the judgment Americans are constantly making about persons like ourselves. This determination to keep talking with all who seek a rightful place in the world, or all who have not yet awakened to any sense at all of the real world—this, I think, is the revolution. And the United States perversely and negatively knows it, and this is why we are in trouble. And this is why we accept trouble, ostracism, and fear of jail and of death as the normal condition under which decent men and women are called upon to function today.

Undoubtedly the FBI comes with guns in pursuit of people like me because beyond their personal chagrin and corporate machismo (a kind of debased esprit de corps; they always get their man), there was the threat that the Panthers and the Vietnamese have so valiantly offered. The threat is a very simple one; we are making connections, religious and moral connections, connections with prisoners and Cubans and Vietnamese, and these connections are forbidden under policies which J. Edgar Hoover is greatly skilled both in enacting and enforcing. They know by now what we are about, they know we are serious. And they are serious about us. Just as with mortal fear, for the last five years they have known what the Vietnamese are about, and the Brazilians and Angolese and Guatemalans. We are guilty of making connections, we urge others to explore new ways of getting connected, of getting married, of educating children, of sharing goods and skills, of being religious, of being human, of resisting. We speak for prisoners and exiles and that silent, silent majority which is that of the dead and the unavenged as well as the unborn. And I am guilty of making connections with you.

By and large the public is petrified of you Weather People. There is a great mythology surrounding you—much more than around me. You come through in public as embodiment of the public nightmare, menacing, sinister, senseless, and violent: a spin-off of the public dread of Panthers and Vietcong, of Latins and Africans, of the poor of our country, of all those expendable and cluttering, and clamorous lives, those who have refused to lie down and die on command, to perish at peace with their fate, or to drag out their lives in the world as suppliants and slaves.

But in a sense, of course, your case is more complicated because your rebellion is not the passionate consequence of the stigma of slavery. Yours is a choice. It's one of the few momentous choices in American history. Your no could have been a yes; society realizes this—you had everything going for you. Your lives could have been posh and secure; but you said no. And you said it by attacking the very properties you were supposed to have inherited and expanded—an amazing kind of turnabout.

Society, I think, was traumatized by your existence, which was the consequence of your choice. What to do with Vietcong or Panthers had never been a very complicated matter, after all. they were jailed or shot down or disposed of by the National Guard. but what to do with you—this indeed was one hell of a question. There was no blueprint. And yet this question, too, was not long in finding its answer, as we learned at Kent State. That is to say, when the choice between property and human life comes up close, the metaphor is once more invariably military. It is lives that go down. And we know now that even if those lives are white and middle-class, they are going to lie in the same gun sights.

The mythology of fear that surrounds you is exactly what the society demands, as it demands more and more mythology, more and more unreality to live by. But it also offers a very special opportunity to break this myth that flourishes on silence and ignorance and has you stereotyped as mindless, indifferent to human life and death, determined to raise hell at any hour or place. We have to deal with this as we go along; but from what values, what mentality, what views of one another and ourselves? Not from a mimicry of insanity of useless rage, but with a new kind of anger which is both useful in communicating and imaginative and slow-burning, to fuel the long haul of our lives.

I'm trying to say that when people look about them for lives to run with and when hopeless people look to others, the gift we can offer is so simple a thing as hope. As they said about Che, as they say about Jesus, some people, even to this day; he gave us hope. So my hope is that you see your lives in somewhat this way, which is to say I hope your lives are about something more than sabotage. I'm certain they are. I hope the sabotage question is tactical and peripheral. I hope indeed that you are uneasy about its meaning and usefulness and that you realize that the burning of properties, whether at Catonsville or Chase Manhattan or anywhere else, by no means guarantees a change of consciousness, the risk always being very great that sabotage will change people for the worse and harden them against enlightenment.

I hope you see yourselves as Che saw himself, that is to say as teachers of the people, sensitive as we must be to the vast range of human life that awaits liberation, education, consciousness. If I'm learning anything it is that nearly everyone is in need of these gifts—and therefore in need of us, whether or not they realize it. I think of all those we so easily dismiss, whose rage against us is an index of the blank pages of their lives, those to whom no meaning or value has ever been attached by politicians or generals or churches or universities or indeed anyone, those whose sons fight the wars, those who are constantly mortgaged and indebted to the consumer system; and I think also of those closer to ourselves, students who are still enchanted by careerism and selfishness, unaware that the human future must be created out of suffering and loss.

How shall we speak to our people, to the people everywhere? We must never refuse, in spite of their refusal of us, to call them our brothers. I must say to you as simply as I know how; if the people are not the main issue, there simply is no main issue and you and I are fooling ourselves, and American fear and dread of change has only transferred itself to a new setting.

Thus, I think a sensible, humane movement operates on several levels at once if it is to get anywhere. So it says communication yes, organizing yes, community yes, sabotage yes—as a tool. That is the conviction that took us where we went, to Catonsville. And it took us beyond, to this night. We reasoned that the purpose of our act could not be simply to impede the war, or much less to stop the war in its tracks. God help us; if that had been our intention, we were fools before the fact and doubly fools after it, for in fact the war went on. Still we undertook sabotage long before any of you. It might be worthwhile reflecting on our reasons why. We were trying first of all to say something about the pernicious effect of certain properties on the lives of those who guarded them or died in consequence of them. And we were determined to talk to as many people as possible and as long as possible afterward, to interpret, to write, and through our conduct, through our appeal, through questioning ourselves again and again to discuss where we were, where we were going, where people might follow.

My hope is that affection and compassion and nonviolence are now common resources once more and that we can proceed on one assumption, the assumption that the quality of life within our communities is exactly what we have to offer. I think a mistake in SDS's past was to kick out any evidence of this community sense as weakening, reactionary, counter-productive. Against this it must be said that the mark of inhuman treatment of humans is a mark that also hovers over us. And it is the mark of a beast, whether its insignia is the military or the movement.

No principle is worth the sacrifice of a single human being. That's a very hard statement. At various stages of the movement some have acted as if almost the opposite were true, as people got purer and purer. More and more people have been kicked out for less and less reason. At one remote period of the past, the result of such thinking was the religious wars, or wars of extinction. At another time it was Hitler; he wanted a ton of purity too. Still another is still with us in the war against the Panthers and the Vietnamese. I think I'm in the underground because I want part in none of this inhumanity, whatever name it goes by, whatever rhetoric it justifies itself with.

When madness is the acceptable public state of mind, we're all in danger, all in danger; for madness is an infection in the air. And I submit that we all breathe the infection, and that the movement has at times been sickened by it too.

The madness has to do with the disposition of human conflict by forms of violence. In or out of the military, in or out of the movement, it seems to me that we had best call things by their name, and the name for this thing, it seems to me, is the death game, no matter where it appears. And as for myself, I would as soon be under the heel of former masters as under the heel of new ones.

Some of your actions are going to involve inciting and conflict and trashing, and these actions are very difficult for thoughtful people. But I came upon a rule of thumb somewhere which might be of some help to us: Do only that which one cannot not do. Maybe it isn't very helpful, and of course it's going to be applied differently by the Joint Chiefs of Staff and an underground group of sane men and women. In the former, hypocritical expressions of sympathy will always be sown along, the path of the latest rampage. Such grief is like that of a mortician in a year of plague. But our realization is that a movement has historic meaning only insofar as it puts itself on the side of human dignity and the protection of life, even of the lives most unworthy of such respect. A revolution is interesting insofar as it avoids like the plague the plague it promised to heal. Ultimately if we want to define the plague as death (a good definition), a prohuman movement will neither put people to death nor fill the prisons nor inhibit freedoms nor brainwash nor torture enemies nor be mendacious nor exploit women, children, Blacks, the poor. It will have a certain respect for the power of the truth, a power which created the revolution in the first place.

We may take it, I think as a simple rule of thumb that the revolution will be no better and no more truthful and no more populist and no more attractive than those who brought it into being. Which is to say we are not killers, as America would stigmatize us, and indeed *as America perversely longs us to be*. We are something far different. We are teachers of the people who have come on a new vision of things. We struggle to embody that vision day after day, to make it a reality among those we live with, so that people are literally disarmed by knowing us; so that their fear of change, their dread of life are exorcised, and their dread of human differences slowly expunged.

Instead of thinking of the underground as temporary, exotic, abnormal, perhaps we should start thinking of its implication as an entirely self-sufficient, mobile, internal revival community; the underground as a definition of our future. What does it mean literally to have nowhere to go in America, to be kicked out of America? It must mean—let us go somewhere in America, let us stay here and play here and love here and build here, and in this way join not only those who like us are kicked out also, but those who have never been inside at all, the Blacks and the Puerto Ricans and the Chicanos.

Next, we are to strive to become such men and women as may, in a new world, be nonviolent. If there's any definition of the new man and woman, the man or woman of the future, it seems to me that they are persons who do violence unwillingly, by exceptions. They know that destruction of property is only a means; they keep the end as vivid and urgent and as alive as the means, so that the means are judged in every instance by their relation to the ends. Violence as legitimate means: I have a great fear of American violence, not only in the military and diplomacy, in economics, in industry and advertising; but also in here, in me, up close, among us.

On the other hand, I must say, I have very little fear, from firsthand experience, of the violence of the Vietcong or Panthers (I hesitate to use the word violence), for their acts come from the proximate threat of extinction, from being invariably put on the line of self-defense. But the same cannot be said of us and our history. We stand outside the culture of these others, no matter what admiration or fraternity we feel with them; we are unlike them, we have other demons to battle.

But the history of the movement, in the last years, it seems to me, shows how constantly and easily we are seduced by violence, not only as method but as end in itself. Very little new politics, very little ethics, very little direction, and only a minimum moral sense, if any at all. Indeed one might conclude in despair: the movement is debased beyond recognition, I can't be a part of it. Far from giving birth to the new man, it has only proliferated the armed, bellicose, and inflated spirit of the army, the plantation, the corporation, the diplomat.

Yet it seems to me good, in public as well as in our own house, to turn the question of violence back on its true creators and purveyors, working as we must from a very different ethos and for very different ends. I remember being on a television program recently and having the question of violence thrown at me, and responding—look, ask the question in the seats of power, don't ask it of me, don't ask me why I broke the law, ask Nixon why he breaks the law constantly, ask the Justice Department, ask the racists. Obviously, but for Johnson and Nixon and their fetching ways, Catonsville would never have taken place and you and I would not be where we are today; just as but for the same people SDS would never have grown into the Weather People or the Weather People have gone underground. In a decent society, functioning on behalf of its people, all of us would be doing the things that decent people do for one another. That we are forbidden so to act, forced to meet so secretly and with so few, is a tragedy we must live with. We have been forbidden a future by the forms of power, which include death as the ordinary social method; we have rejected the future they drafted us into, having refused, on the other hand, to be kicked out of America, either by aping their methods or leaving the country.

The question now is what can we create. If feel at your side across the miles, and I hope that sometime, sometime in this mad world, in this mad time, it will be possible for us to sit down face to face, brother to brother, brother to sister, and find that our hopes and our sweat, and the hopes and sweat and death and tears and blood of our brothers and sisters throughout the world, have brought to birth that for which we began.

Shalom to you.

# ⊰183⊱

# The Chicago Declaration, 1973

## ERLING JORSTAD

By the 1970s organizations of evangelical Christians were frequently identified with economic, social and political conservatism. Recognizing this, a younger group met in 1973 in Chicago to try to revitalize a socially progressive evangelicalism. They issued the Declaration below but the political current continued to flow away from them.

---

As evangelical Christians commited to the Lord Jesus Christ and the full authority of the Word of God, we affirm that God lays total claim upon the lives of his people. We cannot, therefore, separate our lives in Christ from the situation in which God has placed us in the United States and the world.

*We confess* that we have not acknowledged the complete claims of God on our lives.

*We acknowledge* that God requires love. But we have not demonstrated the love of God to those suffering social abuses.

*We acknowledge* that God requires justice. But we have not proclaimed or demonstrated his justice to an unjust American society. Although the Lord calls us to defend the social and economic rights of the poor and the oppressed, we have mostly remained silent. We deplore the historic involvement of the church in America with racism and the conspicuous responsibility of the evangelical community for perpetuating the personal attitudes and institutional structures that have divided the body of Christ along color lines. Further, we have failed to condemn the exploitation of racism at home and abroad by our economic system.

*We affirm* that God abounds in mercy and that he forgives all who repent and turn from their sins. So we call our fellow evangelical Christians to demonstrate repentence in a Christian discipleship that confronts the social and political injustice of our nation.

Erling Jorstad, 'The Chicago Declaration, 1973', *Evangelicals in the White House,* Lewisham, NY, 1973, pp. 153-4. © 1981 by Edwin Mellen Press.

*We must attack* the materialism of our culture and the maldistribution of the nation's wealth and services. We recognize that as a nation we play a crucial role in the imbalance and injustice of international trade and development. Before God and a billion hungry neighbors, we must rethink our values regarding our present standard of living and promote more just acquisition and distribution of the world's resources.

*We acknowledge* our Christian responsibilities of citizenship. Therefore, we must challenge the misplaced trust of the nation in economic and military might—a proud trust that promotes a national pathology of war and violence which victimizes our neighbors at home and abroad. We must resist the temptation to make the nation and its institutions objects of near-religious loyalty.

*We acknowledge* that we have encouraged men to prideful domination and women to irresponsible passivity. So we call both men and women to mutual submission and active discipleship.

*We proclaim* no new gospel, but the gospel of our Lord Jesus Christ, who, through the power of the Holy Spirit, frees people from sin so that they might praise God through works of righteousness.

By this declaration, we endorse no political ideology or party, but call our nation's leaders and people to that righteousness which exalts a nation.

*We make this declaration* in the biblical hope that Christ is coming to consummate the Kingdom and we accept his claim on our total discipleship till he comes.

# ↤184↦

# God's Own Network: The T.V. Kingdom of Pat Robertson

## DICK DABNEY

Conservative evangelicals have shown themselves adept at using the evolving mass media to deliver their message. Most recently, the phase of the 'electronic church', television has been a sufficiently powerful instrument to create national reputations for a number of preachers, Pat Robertson amongst them. His success has enabled him to launch an explicitly conservative political movement based in Protestant Fundamentalism.

Out to sea that morning, from the direction the Lord would appear when He returned, the big oil tankers were moving into the mouth of Chesapeake Bay, from right to left across the motel's plateglass window. We were a mile down the beach from where the Jamestown settlers had landed in 1607 and set up a cross in the sands and dedicated this country to the glory of God. On the color video in the motel room were all the X-rated movies you would ever want to watch. All you had to do was pick up a phone and give the desk your selection, and it would pop up on the screen and be put on your Visa or Master Card. Across the street at the Beach Theater, the marquee advertised a double feature: *Jesus Christ, Superstar* and *American Gigolo*.

I got in my car and followed the wide, crawling net of expressways out to the Christian Broadcasting Network's headquarters, where I was supposed to talk with Pat Robertson, who was being called "the Christian Johnny Carson" by the national media, and whose talk show, "The 700 Club," was seen by more people, worldwide anyway, than Carson's. This headquarters, which had cost $20 million, was located in a pine forest just off a cloverleaf. Surrounded by tall trees were two large, handsome brick buildings—one housing CBN's studios and corporate offices, the other, a new graduate school offering degrees in Christian communication. Both buildings were done in the colonial Georgian style, so as

Source: Dick Dabney, 'God's Own Network: The T.V. Kingdom of Pat Robertson', *Harper's Magazine*, August 1980. © 1980 by *Harper's Magazine*.

to be as much like Williamsburg as possible. They were fashioned out of half a million handmade bricks laid in Flemish bond, and they got you to thinking not so much about Jesus but about Patrick Henry or Thomas Jefferson.

To get to the main building you had to go through a recently planted alley of matched oak trees and crepe myrtles that had been designed "to create a cathedral effect" maybe fifty years from now—a plan that was puzzling when you remembered that Robertson was telling his millions of followers that Jesus would probably be back in 1982.

On the other hand, if Jesus tarried it was going to be pretty pleasant around here from a landscaping point of view, as one saw long hedges of Japanese holly and panels of green lawn adjacent to the vivid reds of the brick sidewalks, and the brick arches to the side of the buildings accentuated by full-grown native American holly and Southern magnolia—while along the walkways there were the Natchez White crepe myrtles set in pleasant beds of ivy and periwinkle. Even the trees around this place were, in the words of Keats, "dear as the temple's self," and interspersed with the native pines were dogwood, forsythia, magnolia, azaleas, hemlock, carnelia, juniper, October Glory maple, boxwood, star and saucer magnolia, and viburnum, to say nothing of petunias, geraniums, and chrysanthemums. The new, red dump trucks of the First Colonial Construction Corporation were hauling fresh topsoil into the place for more landscaping. CBN was currently taking in more than $1 million a week, and could afford it.

There was a low, squat guard bastion at the entranceway, half Monticello and half Leavenworth, where a uniformed security officer stepped suddenly in front of the car and asked what my business was. He had a .45-caliber police special on his hip, and there was another guard inside, also watching, to back him up. While phone inquiries were being made, the first officer stood close to the car window, watching me. At last, a visitor's badge was provided and I was told to go directly to the entrance of the main building, where I would be met. I was given to understand that they could see me every foot of the way from this checkpoint to there, and I was told that under no circumstances was I to swerve from the path laid out for me, nor to go anywhere on the property without a certified guide and proper authorization. It was a beautiful day and the bright red trucks were coming in and you had the feeling something was building here that was more than just architecture.

## Enlightened Entertainment

I had first seen Pat Robertson in 1976, a weekday morning. He popped up on the television screen in my living room, smiling and likable, with a voice whose upper ranges crackled with a homespun reasonableness like that of Jimmy Stewart. He was talking about the "chicken hawks" of America's big cities, who operated from downtown street corners recruiting runaway boys into homosexual prostitution, and selling them to men whose late-model automobiles slid up to the curbs under cover of darkness. This, Robertson said, in a commonsense voice, was *wrong*. And that was one of the damnedest things I'd ever heard on TV. For in spite of the fact that I, too, suspected it was wrong, I had never heard such a view publicly expressed.

Of course, the main-line clergymen, who conducted the sleep-inducing discussion groups on Sunday morning television, had addressed that topic. And, as with most other things they discussed, they had admitted that it surely was a "problem"—their favorite word. After that, predictably, they had turned the matter over to a psychiatrist to get some "insight." But here was Robertson saying it was *wrong*.

Now, this was a radical point of view in my town—Washington, D.C.—where you were thought to be crude in the extreme if you had an answer to anything, and where, as in many other metropolitan areas of our country, a certain section of downtown (in our case, near the Justice Department) was set aside for the chicken-hawking, the reigning motif of civic morality having long ago been reduced to the commonsense maxim of "Everything in its place." But Robertson wasn't going along with that.

His was—at least in its early days—a humble and unassuming talk show, with the usual format. The host, Marion Gordon (Pat) Robertson, handsome and boyish at forty-six, was seated behind a desk like Johnny Carson's, and with guest chairs strung out to the side—one of which was occupied by the co-host, a six-foot-four black man named Ben Kinchlow, who was the laugher, applauder, and all-purpose target of restrained kidding. And there was an orchestra—this one scruffy, puffy-faced, and poor-looking, and given to chartreuse colors and rhinestones, with a chubby leader whose prime function seemed to be that of taking mirthful abuse from Robertson. Maybe it was "Christian" abuse, too, in that it wasn't risqué; but there was a hum of "The Tonight Show" vibes to it— the poised, hip king reigning by subtle abuse, and representing in his transcendent self a golden mean between tight-assed parochialism on the one hand and bohemian whoopee on the other.

## The Secular Enemy

Even so, the show's merits were considerable, because often the guests were intelligent, likable, and well-informed. And Robertson himself was a more interesting man than Johnny Carson—more enterprising, more complex, and less anxious to amuse than to persuade. There was more steel to him. He was not an entertainer, but a nineteenth-century entrepreneur who had founded, out of an initial capital of $3, the big growing television network he was president of. He did not come on like a preacher at all; he was no thundering sermoneer nor twittering-birds smirker, but a reasonable and educated man, with a unified point of view that was especially intriguing to intellectuals. Although, as for that, his appeal was broad, and he had the Grand Ole Opry crowd as well.

He was alarmed, he said, about the condition of this country—threatened from without by a murderous Communist colossus and from within by unprecedented moral decay. The family, he said, was under attack: by homosexuals, who had been allowed to become too vocal, hostile, and publicly lubricious; by that coalition of raunchy women, greedy abortionists, liberal politicians, and psychotic Supreme Court justices, who were murdering a million unborn infants each year; and by aggressive feminists—women trying to be men.

Moreover, he said, radical change, most of it malefic, was ripping America apart. And the conspicuous outward sins—pornography, public irresponsibility, and a bloated consumerism—were only the outbreakings of an inward philosophical disease that had gone down so deep into the nation's bones that it would take some kind of miracle to cure it. The name of that disease, which advertised itself as mere modernity, was secular humanism. And it was this, his attack on secular humanism, that was at the heart of most of his shows.

Secular humanism, he said, is the notion that God either doesn't exist or is irrelevant, and that man, or the government, is God. And from it came moral relativism, the pursuit of selfish pleasure, and the sort of hopelessness that resulted from having no one to appeal to. Secular-humanist educators, who'd had nothing better than John Dewey to stuff their peppers with, had extirpated prayer from public schools, undermined the character of the young through humanist propaganda courses in sex education and "values clarification," and spread moral relativism through an official view of evolutionism that encouraged children to believe that they were merely animals, and hence justified in living as amorally as animals.

Worse still were the liberal, main-line churchmen, who, having had their minds darkened with the Higher Criticism, taught their unfortunate flocks that the Bible wasn't really God's word but a bunch of old fables, including that tall tale about Jesus rising from the dead. And these, in the name of a self-worshipping intellectuality, were removing the only hope of mankind. Liberal Christianity, Robertson thought, boiled down at last to evil Christianity, and nowhere was this more manifest than in the acts of the World Council of Churches, which, in the name of the new, liberation theology, had funded the terrorists who were butchering Christian missionaries in Zimbabwe.

Other villainous servants of secular humanism, he believed, were liberal politicians and comfortable bureaucrats, who, living in unwholesome symbiosis, sought to deify government as teacher, provider, and ultimate guarantor of happiness. Thus these manipulators robbed the working class to create for themselves a huge constituency of debased, supine, vicious lumpen, whose very existence was destructive to the country.

But the prime purveyors of secular humanism, according to Robertson, were the huge national broadcasting networks and big newspapers and magazines that peddle culture-destroying vulgarity as entertainment, catastrophe chronicles as news, and humanist propaganda as objectivity. Moreover, the media had an iron, ugly law of censorship that the name of God was never to be mentioned in public save as a mild epithet, or as a patronizing anthropological description of what other people believed.

In a nation permeated with such deep philosophical lies, Robertson believed, it was not wonder people were confused, that the divorce rate was hitting up toward 50 percent, that suicides were everywhere, crime was on the rise, and that homosexuality, prostitution, and kiddie porn had vogue. This, he said, is what happened to nations who deserted God to run after Baal, Mammon, and Astarte, who sought to sate soul-cravings with money, carnal pleasure, self-worship, and self-indulgent ease. No wonder then, that people, in their frantic search for answers, were turning to transactional analysis, transcendental meditation, scream therapy, and est—or to Satan's lores: astrology, numerology, palm reading, witchcraft, black magic, and ritual murder.

The thing to do, he said, was to turn one's life over to Jesus, who would come in and give the believer eternal life, and who would even in this world, make all things new, comprehensible, and better. And so, in each program, and in a low key, he would invite people to pray with him and be reborn.

If it was the old-time religion, Biblical fundamentalism with a stiff jolt of speaking in tongues mixed in, it was presented not in any stupid or even ignorant way but as the centerpiece of a remarkably sophisticated, unified view of modern life.

But it was easy to see why people had reservations about Robertson. For instance, some Christian critics objected to the way he "brought people to the Lord," on a trip as smooth as a Disneyland kiddie ride, and on which any bumps that might be caused by some old-fashioned repentance had been engineered out. And indeed, those altar calls did seem to have a cloying sweetness about them, and to contain assurances that were nowhere in the Bible.

According to Robertson, it seemed that Jesus would run you like a placid robot, rather than let you take control of your own life and live it according to his teachings. Moreover, Jesus would provide you with all kinds of worldly bonanzas, rather than the tribulation promised in the Bible. When you got right down to it, Robertson said, the Lord would even find parking spaces for you, a chore he had performed for Robertson himself any number of times.

However, and in spite of his trivialization of the gospel, it was easy to see why Robertson was well-liked and massively followed: he was an intelligent and deeply likable man, and his diagnosis of what is wrong with America was becoming ever more plausible as catastrophic events, the national drift, and the growing sense of an impending doom became thick in the air.

But Robertson, not one for deferring Jesus' rule to any millennium, had an earthly program too. He believed it was necessary for Christians to take back public education from the secular humanists, and to support Christian schools by fighting government efforts to impose "unrealistic" racial quotas on them. Moreover, since the main-line churches were not preaching the true gospel, he thought that real Christians ought to leave those in favor of Bible-believing, blood-washed, and spirit-filled churches. And, since the media were controlled by secular humanists—and often homosexual secular humanists at that—it was necessary for Christians, at whatever financial sacrifice, to have their own media, and especially their own television network. This, in Robertson's scheme of things, would be CBN. And finally, as a more comprehensive solution, he thought it necessary for conservative Christians—whose numbers have been put as high as 80 million—to take over the government of the United States.

Useful in encouraging Christians to become more politically active, as Robert-son saw it, would be the Christian Broadcasting Network, which would mobilize the faithful. And so, over the years, "The 700 Club" has become increasingly politicized and serious—even grim. The band still plays, but is tucked away out of sight, and even the bantering with Kinchlow begins to seem forced as the tone of the show has become as tense as that of an emergency room. And one begins to hear talk in evangelical circles—although never from Robertson himself —that he is using the resources of CBN to run for president of the United States.

I discounted such talk when I heard it, and thought that if he did run, even for U.S. senator from Virginia, he'd not stand much chance of winning—so far out to the right was he. But I liked the new version of his show better than I had the old one. Before, there had been more of the smirking, patronizing, positive-thinking industrial Christian madonnas huckstering books on how to live; yowling, wet-eyed slime balladeers who'd sought to be inspirational; and the occasional psychotic missionary from Borneo or Cincinnati who claimed to have personally raised a thousand people from the dead or to have stopped an oncoming typhoon by prayer (a feat pretty thoroughly believed in by Robertson, by the way, who also claimed to have stopped a typhoon). There were fewer of those Dacron Christian insurance salesmen coming on to tell about how Jesus had got them that extra-pink Cadillac—a species of testimony not uncongenial to Robertson either, but which he delivered regularly enough himself, anyway, by telling viewers about how God had got him the television network.

## Bread Upon the Waters

Closely shepherded by the public-relations man, I walked between the forty-ton limestone columns into the lobby of the CBN headquarters building and across an immense white marble floor that was covered in part by a magnificent Persian carpet. Here and there, corporate-looking men, well- and conservatively dressed, were talking in small groups, either standing under the crystal chandelier or sitting on the beautiful, well-tended antique furniture. The place had that hushed sense of spirituality one feels in a bank. The marble floor was the most beautiful and the purest white I had ever seen. The building, without its expensive furnishings and equipment, cost $20 million; the television facilities it housed were more elaborate, modern, and expensive than those of the CBS affiliate in Los Angeles. Not long ago, Robertson had been called the "Billy Graham of tomorrow." But now tomorrow was here.

The PR man guided me to the quiet elevator that went up to where

Robertson's private offices were.

"If you want to go to the bathroom," he said, "we can do that now." Evidently, anything you did at CBN had to be supervised.

Robertson's spacious outer office was even more handsome than the lobby, with antique wood floors that looked as if they'd been burnished with care for a couple of hundred years before being lifted from an old mansion and brought here. There were beautiful antiques, too, of lambently glowing old wood, and another magnificent rug. The place was not garish like Las Vegas, either.

A corporate meeting, high-level, was taking place on the other side of those mahogany doors. At last a duo of well-dressed, well-spoken young executives came out, shook hands, smoothly explained that they were busy, and hurried away from the door, leaving Pat Robertson standing there alone, looking at me with the good-old-boy droop above eyes that were still, at fifty, those of that boxer, Marine combat captain, and general hard-ass he had once been. He had told all about that on TV, too, and you could believe it when you saw the eyes, which, though wreathed with an ingratiating friendliness, still had the afterglow of fierceness in them—a fire banked by time and policy.

He was six-foot-one, half a foot taller than he looked to be when side by side with the Wilt Chamberlain—like Kinchlow, and thin. Though his handshake was firm, the body behind it was limp, and he flopped when I shook him, as if he'd been made over cooked spaghetti. It occurred to me that he might be fasting. He did a lot of that, and told about it on TV. Or maybe it was fasting and hard work both. After all, the Washington for Jesus March, of which he was one of the prime organizers, was only a month away, and there would be a lot of work to do on that. In fact, I, too, had been thinking about that march, having just received a newsletter from the organizers carrying ads that gave me the opportunity to buy a Sackcloth and Ashes Lapel Pin for only $5, or a $10 tinted picture of Jesus healing the crack in the Liberty Bell.

I followed him into his office, where the furniture was the finest of all—an eighteenth-century sofa, butler's table, two armchairs, a round dark table, also eighteenth-century, that was his desk, and a tall, beautiful secretary breakfront against the wall. The PR man came in too. This was the standard practice. After all, you never could tell when some reporter might twist what you said, and you couldn't be too careful.

Robertson seemed worn out, and he moved in slow motion, like a man walking under water. This brought to mind other stories he'd told about himself on TV: of epic fasts, long nights praying alone on mountaintops, or all-night wrestlings with God on his study floor. Perhaps without meaning to, he'd made these things sound like fun, and I tended to believe that they had actually taken place. For I was from the South, too, and had known any number of men like him—known them, anyway, in their early twenties, before the wild idealism got transmuted into a capacity for the kind of sustained hard work that would make them successful and isolate them—as I surmised he must be isolated now. But if I thought I could break through all that, I was mistaken, and when I asked him what he did for kicks, he seemed offended.

"Not much of anything," he said. "You see, I give so much of myself to this ministry that when the week's over, all I want to do is walk around in the woods and rest." Then, as if reading my mind, he added that it was impossible to have friends anymore, like those back in the old days. Now, almost everybody he knew worked for him, and it could not be that way.

"Actually," he said, "I'm just a servant of Jesus Christ. A slave, actually." And I sat there on that soft, elegant sofa, looking at the rich drapes, the fine carpet, and the beautiful old furniture, restraining the impulse to say, "Horseshit," and wondering at the same time whether all these things, and the $1 million a week, could make you drunk, and how that felt.

At last, I began to ask him questions about where his own money came from, and how much more there was of it. He replied that he did not have any money to speak of, that in twenty years he had given back as much to CBN as he had taken out. This was puzzling, because it did not add up. He had, on conversion, given all his worldly goods to the poor. After that, according to him, he had given all his income to CBN. And yet he'd been eating and he had sent his four children to college, and he lived in a house that was furnished about as well as this office was, and he owned an expensive Trakehner stallion, which had to eat, too. It was hard to see how he had done all this on nothing.

So I pressed him. But he shied off. He seemed pained by questions about money, and had often said, on camera, that it was the only thing the secular press was interested in, and not in how many people got saved, or healed, or helped. Moreover, his manner seemed to say, questions about money were not the sort of thing one gentleman asked another.

When I asked him about his money-raising techniques, which have been described as a subtle, white adaptation of those employed by the Reverend Ike, he was equally standoffish. And when I asked him whether "The 700 Club" constituted a video cult, he was shocked, as if he had never heard the question raised—although it had been the subject of a recent intense discussion on the "Donahue" show, and in other places as well.

When the conversation shifted to politics, however, he seemed more comfortable, and began to talk animatedly. He believed that we were on the edge of a catastrophic depression, and maybe close to World War III, and that the End Times were near, when Jesus was coming back. This, of course, raised certain questions about the expensive permanence of this place. But by now it was evident that there would be no use in asking those, and he went on with politics.

Jimmy Carter, for whose election he and other evangelical television preachers had done everything this side of breaking FCC regulations, had deceived him, he said. It was impossible that a man could do as Carter had done, and truly be born again. For he had compromised the national defense, caused the depression we were about to enter, and surrounded himself with ungodly counselors like Hamilton Jordan, Peter Bourne, Andrew Young, and Bella

Abzug.

"I wouldn't let Bella Abzug scrub the floors of any organization I was head of," he said. "But Carter put her in charge of all the women of America. And used our tax funds to support that [radical feminist] convention in Houston. But I sensed something was wrong when I interviewed him for our show. There was this wonderful exterior charm to him. But underneath, terrible coldness. It was frightening."

After that, Robertson began to talk about the Rockefellers and the Trilateral Commission. That organization, he said, was trying to take over the world, and to destroy democracy and Christianity. Its influence was everywhere. It controlled the media, the liberal churches, the educational system, and the federal government. It had elected, or named, the past several presidents of the United States and all their major counselors, and it set policy. In effect, it was ruling the country already. It had already picked out the man it wanted elected in 1980–George Bush. (Robertson and some other evangelical leaders evidently prefer Ronald Reagan.)

When I stood up to go, I told him that there were a couple of things that bothered me. The first was his frequently repeated assurance to his viewers that if two or three Christians agreed together, they could have *anything* they asked for in prayer. Did he really believe that? And what would be the likely result if he and a few of his Christian friends were to pray for all the children in all the hospitals to be cured?

"They wouldn't be cured, of course," he said.

Then I told him about an elderly friend of mine, who lived on Social Security and had pledged her rent money to CBN–in response to repeated Robertson appeals to "give out of your need."

"If you'd been a friend of hers," I asked, "would you have advised her to give the money, or not?"

"Not," Robertson said.

This was why I liked him, and had not been able to believe that he was crooked. Because in his talks with me, both over the phone and now, he'd shown remarkable flashes of straightforwardness. On the other hand, if he did not believe in the things he said over 150 television stations and 3,000 cable systems, why did he persist in saying them?

"One more thing," I said. "Would you use CBN to run for political office?"

There was a long pause. "Let's put it this way," he said. "In the event of a major breakdown, the country might turn to us."

"But you regard such a breakdown as certain."

"Well," he said, "everything is going to be shaken."

## Dial a Prayer

Banks of volunteer-manned phones have been a prominent part of "The 700 Club" set all along. Robertson calls attention to them at the start of each show, and invites those who are unsaved, anxious, sick, crazy, lonely, or broke to call in for "prayer counseling."

"People who care about you are waiting to take your call!" he says—and a number flashes on the screen. These phones keep ringing throughout the show, and are manned twenty-four hours a day. There are more than eighty CBN telephone prayer-counseling centers spread around the country. And no matter what species of distress people call in with, the sovereign remedy, true to that old-time religion, is prayer—even when what they need is money. Because in the world of evangelical telecasting, money flows only one way.

Many people get hooked into that phone network, and hence into CBN's fund-solicitation list, through Robertson's adroit use of Scripture, because after issuing the altar call and welcoming the saved into the Kingdom of God, he adds a proviso: "It's not enough just to believe," he says. "You have got to confess Him with your *mouth*. Because the Bible says that if you don't confess Jesus before men, He won't confess you before his Father in Heaven. So call in! Prayer counselors are waiting to rejoice with you!"

And they are waiting, too, to get callers' names on the fund-solicitation list, or to get them to join the "700 Club"—so named because Robertson, in the early days of his ministry, had called on 700 viewers to give $10 a month. By now that's gone up to $15, and there are hundreds of thousands of members, some of whom give thousands of dollars a month, and all of whom receive in return what CBN executives, in the privacy of their offices, call the "pretty-pretties." These include a gold-plated lapel pin announcing "700 Club," a "700 Club" bumper sticker and auto decal, a certificate of membership suitable for framing, a monthly copy of Robertson's newsletter, which advertises itself as giving a "Biblical perspective" on current events, and a series of teaching tapes on Biblical subjects.

Robertson's newsletter, *The Perspective*, champions conservative political causes. And although the detailed financial and political advice it gives is heavily laced with apocalyptic predictions of an imminent Armageddon in the Middle East, it is sometimes hard to guess just where in the Bible Robertson managed to find such explicit instructions on what God's wishes are on the Equal Rights Amendment or Salt II. But the truly serious "700 Club" member need not trouble himself with details if he doesn't want to, for the cassette teaching tapes sent out to members tell them to "have no mind of your own." And all this put together—the selling of miracles, "turning over one's life," "having no mind of one's own," and the political causes presented as God's will—raises the question of whether the "700 Club" might not be a video cult.

At one time, perhaps, this would have seemed more farfetched than it does now, for it's difficult to see how a man on television could achieve a Jim Jones closeness of control over television cultists' lives. Because of that, Robertson's critics have tended to regard him as merely a religious hustler who doesn't care what his followers do, so long as they cough up the money. On the other hand, however, others have argued that he is using the huge amounts of cash he gets to achieve, through right-wing politics, exactly that kind of control. And if that is true, he's not alone in the effort, but merely the first among equals among evangelical TV superstars, who, being uniformly right-wing, have common cause politically. In terms of sheer dollar success, there are other Pat Robertsons. His former employee Jim Bakker, currently under investigation by the FCC, runs the nationally broadcast "PTL Club" out of Charlotte, North Carolina, and the Reverend Jerry Falwell of Lynchburg, Virginia, a star of the widely seen "Old Time Gospel Hour," is head of a vigorously active ultraconservative group that he calls "the Moral Majority."

Both Bakker and Falwell are currently taking in more than $1 million a week, too—and pushing the same political causes. And so the "Electric Church" has come a long way from its beginnings as a fifteen-minute radio broadcast on Pittsburgh's KDKA back in 1921. By now, there are about fifty Christian television stations, and more than 1,300 Christian radio stations, plus hundreds of "ministries," many of them small and scuffling, that buy commercial time. The dozen leading ministries are currently taking in more than $600 million a year. So what has arrived is not the Lear-like ravings of Father Coughlin, but a group of well-financed men who intend to achieve political power.

That takes a lot of money, of course, and what has got Robertson that—beyond his own considerable charm and ability—is his manipulation of the viewers' needs, to serve CBN's, through the "Kingdom Principles."

These Kingdom Principles are given the hard sell on telethons and during the miracle-service segments of the regular shows, wherein Robertson will switch smoothly from leading a learned discussion of, say, national defense or mythic themes in contemporary American literature, to conducting a fervid pentecostal prayer meeting—down on his knees, hands raised to Heaven, leading his people in passionate pleas for God to miraculously intervene in human events. "O Lord, heal cancers right *now*! Mend broken homes *now*! Cure madness right *now*! *Thank* you, Jesus. *Thank* you, Lord. Supply financial needs right *now*, in the name of *Jesus!* Thank you, Lord!"—then a pause, and intense excitement in the studio, as "the Word of Knowledge" comes over him, and he begins to have visions, personally vouchsafed to him by God, of miracles happening "all over the nation."

"I have a Word of Knowledge," he'll say. "There is a woman in Kansas City who has sinus. The Lord is drying that up right now. Thank you, Jesus. There is a man with a financial need—I think a hundred thousand dollars. That need is being met right now, and within three days, the money will be supplied through the miraculous power of the Holy Spirit. Thank you Jesus! There is a woman in Cincinnati with cancer of the lymph nodes. I don't know whether it's been diagnosed yet, but you haven't been feeling well, and the Lord is dissolving that cancer right *now*! There is a lady in Saskatchewan in a wheelchair—curvature of the spine. The Lord is straightening that out right now, and you can stand up and walk! Just claim it and it's yours. Stand up and walk. Thank you, Jesus! Amen, and amen!"

Already, the phones will be alight with people calling and claiming those miracles. But if prayers don't work either, Robertson is able to show the viewer a more excellent way, through the "Kingdom Principles," which are a kind of trick the clever Christian plays on God.

Crudely put, the Bible, according to Robertson, teaches that the more cash you give to Jesus, the more cash he will give right back to you. Every time, you will profit. And Robertson suggests that the most effective way to give to Jesus is to give to his slave, Pat Robertson. Viewers, then, are encouraged to believe that they can buy miracles, just as many of the faithful in the Middle Ages bought indulgences. Television has been transmuted by Robertson into a miracle machine that can be rigged in the viewer's favor. Moreover, he says, anybody can play and win, because if you're broke, you ought not to hesitate to send in rent money, food money, or whatever you've set aside for the children's clothes—there is more power to the trick if you "give out of your need." If you can do that, Robertson says, you can expect some really stupendous results. And on the telethons, and in the money-raising segments of the regular shows, he works smoothly with Kinchlow, driving this point home, as exemplified by this episode:

"Pat, here is a report from a woman in California," Kinchlow said, dashing up with a message just taken by one of the phone counselors. "She's on a limited income, and with all sorts of health problems, too. She decided to trust in God and to step out in faith on the Kingdom Principles. She was already giving half her disability money to the 700 Club to spread the gospel of Jesus Christ. But just last week, she decided to go *all the way*, and to give God the money she spends for cancer medicine—$120 a month. And three days later—get this!—from an entirely unexpected source, she got a check for *three thousand dollars!*"

"*Praise God!*" Robertson said. "*Let's give God a hand!*" And as the studio audience broke into loud applauding, he looked confidingly into the camera and said, "And I won't be surprised if God doesn't do something about that cancer, too. You there at home, if you want miracles, just step out in faith on the Kingdom Principles, and see what God is willing to do for you."

"You can't outgive God!" Kinchlow said.

"That's right," Robertson said. "And did you ever think of this? We're actually doing people a favor, by giving them a chance to give to God, and to open up the windows of his blessings."

After that, they went over to the easy chairs and led a discussion on the moral decay in this country.

I forget which celebrities they had on that day. But they do raise money in that manner, and frequently they have Christian celebrities on to back them up in the business about the Kingdom Principles. In a way, all these Christian superstars—Pat Boone, Colonel Sanders, Dale Evans and Roy Rogers, Eldridge Cleaver, Chuck Colson, Efrem Zimbalist, Jr.—are interchangeable. You can see them on all the regular Christian talk shows telling how they had not really known true success until they had discovered the Kingdom Principles.

When they are saying things like that, the $100,000 computerized color cameras will pan around the studio audience. It is very strange. Most of these people, presumably, are living ordinary lives. But the Christian celebrities tell them that an ordinary life is contemptible, and that there is a magical way out.

## The Fruits of Prayer

Ever since the seventeenth century, teaching Americans how to be successful through magical means has been good business, and Virginia Beach is a center of cults—among them, the Edgar Cayce Foundation and assorted Satanist organizations. The local residents I talked to seemed to casually regard the 700 Club as just one more manifestation of that kind of industry. For instance, the college student at the front desk of the motel said that CBN was a powerful tourist attraction, and brought in people from all over the country. But after scanning my lapels for pins with pious mottoes, he added that he did not respect Robertson.

"Why not?"

"Because he makes his living off of old ladies," the clerk said. "And it's not that I'm such a great Christian myself, either. But I can't respect anybody like that." Later that morning, another resident of Virginia Beach told me something I already knew—that CBN had a department devoted in part to relieving believers of their jewels—and added that his invalid aunt, who had made the mistake of sending in a sizable check, was being vigorously hounded by these people, who used lots of breath freshener and were in the habit of reminding her of life's shortness and of the desirability of salting away treasure upstairs.

But the proprietor of Dave's Filling Station thought Robertson was first-rate.

"Listen here," he said. "That fellow brings in a lot of money to this area. And the people you hear criticizing him don't make a tenth of what he does."

The day after the Robertson interview, I took my wife and children back to CBN headquarters to see a "700 Club" show. As we were approaching the reception desk, the PR man murmured, "Let's get together afterward. I have something that might interest you." Then he went over to the desk, to check off my name, my wife's, and those of my children, aged nine and ten.

As he tarried, we wandered into the circular prayer chapel, and there, at the center, was a table with a sheaf of wheat on it to symbolize the harvest of souls, and a big, black King James Bible open to the twenty-ninth chapter of Proverbs— from which I read the twenty-fourth verse, which seemed to be an appropriate text for the day.

The table rested on a stout pillar, and inside that was microfilm, inscribed with the names and secret wishes of thousands of believers. That had been another pitch for money, working like this: The viewer was encouraged to write down his "Seven Lifetime Prayer Requests"—the really big ones—and mail these to CBN. Whereupon, if he had remembered to put at least $100 in the envelope, those requests, together with his name, would be put on microfilm and interred in the pillar, where they would be "surrounded by prayer" twenty-four hours a day until Jesus came back. And this meant, presumably, that they would be close to whatever magically good emanations came from the fifty-four prayer-counseling booths located just above the chapel on the second floor, next door to the modern makeup and wardrobe rooms, and to the Christian hairstyling salon, which was equipped with modular tables, three chairs, six deluxe hair-dryers, and two shampoo basins—all of which made it possible for the talent to have their hair shampooed, cut, set, and plasticized on the premises, and in the proximity of good vibes.

Pat and Ben had worked together smoothly in raising money through the Lifetime Prayer Requests, and managed to bring in many extra dollars. And back then, before the pillar was sealed, it had been a rare morning when an eager Ben Kinchlow hadn't come excitedly up to Pat—on camera, of course—with some wonderful report on how splendidly, miraculously well it was all working.

"We have a report just in from Charlottesville, Virginia," Ben said. "a lady with an ingrown toenail sent in $100 along with her Seven Lifetime Prayer Requests. Within a week—get this—*three* of those *lifetime* prayer requests have been answered!"

"Praise God!" Pat said.

"And that's not all! The toenail was miraculously healed the *very next day!*"

"Praise God!" Robertson said. You know, you can't outgive God."

I was standing there thinking about that, and looking up at the huge wooden cross that had been hung from the ceiling as if it had been garroted, when the PR man came scurrying in. His face was ashen.

"I was afraid you all had wandered off," he said. Escorting us closely now, he led the way into the lobby, where he turned us over to the Christian usherette who would take us into the studio and watch us.

## God's Commercial Network

It was a big, modern television studio, with tiered seats for about 400 people. Down on the studio floors, which were resin-based and hence almost perfectly level, the three RCA TK-47 computerized color cameras were ready for business. These are the most expensive on the market, and can set up in thirty-five seconds—readjusting color, focus, and registration—and reset themselves by a touch of a button. The show would be live to Washington, Los Angeles, and a host of other big cities, and recorded for other markets on the new one-inch videotape machines, which were also the most modern and expensive that money could buy. The set was illuminated by a overhead lighting system—winch-operated, motorized, and computerized with a logic memory. All of this had been paid for by Christians who had been told that their money, or jewels, or whatever else CBN had been able to get out of them would be used to spread the Gospel of Jesus Christ.

Recently, however, Robertson had created, out of CBN funds and equipment, a wholly owned subsidiary called the Continental Broadcasting Network that would sell commercial products like Wheaties, General Motors cars, and

Tampax. Dedicated to this purpose would be the four television stations in Portsmouth, Dallas, Atlanta, and Boston that had been owned and operated by CBN, together with their six radio stations.

Evidently, there were still some technicalities to clear up. But the FCC had told me that what Robertson was about to do was legal. And he himself had told me that no Christian need have any concern about how his money was being spent, since the purposes of the new commercial network would also be Christian ones, and the new network would present "a wholesome view of American life." There would be none of the negativity and murmuring one saw over the big networks, and there would be Christian news, Christian variety shows, and even Christian soap operas. Moreover, there would be Christian public-affairs programs that took the right view of political events. And when I suggested that some Christians might be put out at having the money they'd given to spread the gospel used to extol the virtues of breakfast food, Robertson reminded me that the few hundred dollars I'd given to CBN, compared with the entire dollar volume, was exceedingly small. And this, of course, was true.

There the familiar "700 Club" set was, as I'd so often seen it, now irradiated with the sharp penetrating glitter of TV lights—a couple of swiveling easy chairs in front of a big mural that showed the U.S. Capitol dome being shattered to smithereens, with a motto that read, "CHRIST OR CHAOS!" And here we were, in the pleasant, friendly-looking audience of folks from all over the United States.

It was nearing air time now, and tense in that room, when suddenly Robertson entered stage left, forced a quick smile at the waiting audience, and stood there on the raised stage with a wrathful scowl on his face. He was planted, immobile, like a yard-playing child who's suddenly been told "Freeze!" with one arm straight out like a traffic cop's pointing angrily toward the banks of telephones where the prayer counselors were already taking calls. He was not looking in the direction he was pointing, either, but glaring straight ahead at the harassed floor manager, who finally saw him and scuttled quickly over to tell the prayer counselors to cool it with the volume and the babbling in tongues—which gets pretty fervent when the hard cases start calling in, and which Robertson doesn't like polluting the high political dialogue that was about to take place. For although he vigorously advocates speaking in tongues, and practices it in the heroic all-night wrestlings with God, he does not practice it on TV because it comes on as cornball or zany, and saps the show of that intellectual seriousness he wants it to have. At last, mollified by the respectful, tense silence, he took his chair and was fussed over by the makeup man—and suddenly the show was on the air.

He began by referring to our conversation of the day before. A writer from *Harper's* had come to him, he said, to ask, "What about America?" Now, I had asked no such thing, and for a moment I felt caught up in the war he'd been fighting with himself for years. He would alternately snarl at the media and sidle up to be petted. He wanted his audience to think that the humanists, having reached the dead end implicit in their assumptions, were flocking to him for advice. Thus he himself was as much under media control as he claimed America was.

A film clip came on first–a taped interview with the religion editor of a national magazine, who told the "700 Club" reporter that he thought the upcoming Washington for Jesus March was a crock. As this was being played, the first guest took the chair opposite Robertson. He was an important Atlanta preacher with a big church on Peachtree Street and a reputation for being patriotic, and for finding out when anybody else wasn't. He was a handsome, fortyish man of executive mien, with the kind of blue business suit that the ordinary banker cannot afford. He began to preen himself. Carefully, without speaking to Robertson, he began to adjust the length of his coatsleeves, the precise wrist position of his gold watch, and the exact angle at which his shoelaces fell across the wonderfully polished leather of his shoes. He made sure that his hair, which looked to have been sprayed on, was perfectly in place, and checked to ensure that his tie was in the right relation to his collar. This went on for seven minutes.

When the live part of the show came on, this preacher excoriated the media for vicious humanist stupidities, plugged his own patriotic books, said that born-again Christians had to take over the government, shook hands coldly with Robertson, and left in a grim scurry. Presumably he had other Christian talk shows on which to plug the patriotic books. It was not necessary that host and guest like each other. For the inner, affectional unity of these evangelicals is not so solid as they want you to believe. Earlier that week, the PR man for another evangelical superstar had told me, "We put our boy on 'The 700 Club' to get our message across. So we use Pat Robertson. But we don't like him."

The next guest, an earnest, plainly dressed young lawyer, was a pornography expert, and he told Pat that if he wanted to know how truly depraved the secular media are, he ought to consider the snuff films, in which the actresses were killed with chain saws. This, he said, was the ultimate expression of the humanist mentality that had set itself in opposition to the Washington for Jesus March. And sitting in the audience I thought to myself, it is no wonder they watch writers so closely.

After the show was over, I stood on the other side of the armed guards, who had sidled up inconspicuously to shield Robertson, and listened while the young lawyer, who appeared to be down on his luck, talked earnestly to him.

"Actually," the young man was saying, "I am something of an expert on foreign affairs, too. A kind of Renaissance man. So if you want to have me on another one of your shows ... you see, I'm thinking of writing a book."

The PR man shepherded us out into the lobby, where he drew me to one side.

"I can tell we think alike, Dick," he said. "So I am going to give you a real opportunity. You see, I represent the Brunswick Corporation, as well as CBN. That's the bowling people. They are some very fine, Christian people. Then he told me how I could help him get some stories planted about the Bowlers'

Convention that Brunswick would be sponsoring in Washington some weeks hence, and how they were some fine, appreciative, Christians people, if I knew what he meant.

As he was going through all this, my nine-year-old daughter, who was passionately bored, began to skip back and forth across the lobby—coming almost immediately athwart the path of that patriotic Atlanta preacher, who was headed across those white marble floors like the arrow of righteousness, surrounded by well-wishers. She impeded his progress, and for an instant he was forced to break step. As he did, and looked down at her, a look of hatred came over his face. Possibly he thought she was an agent of the Trilateral Commission.

Later on, back in the motel room, I thought to myself that being a patriotic, born-again superstar must be a pretty swell job, because you get to wear good clothes, and the righteousness standards were not high enough to make you uncomfortable. All you had to do was restrain whatever impulses you had toward chicken-hawking or making snuff films, and after that you could go around saying who was a good American and who wasn't and selling your books and getting the good parking spaces. Come to think of it, I had got a good parking place that day myself. It was just a few feet away from CBN's two big, white satellite dishes, which were aimed at the RCA Satcom I and the Western Union Westar, invisible above us in space and broadcasting the Kingdom Principles twenty-four hours a day to people who fervently hope that Jesus would get here before the Bomb did.

## Holy Ghost-writers

As the date of the Washington for Jesus March drew nearer—April 29, when Robertson and the other leaders of that extravaganza had called for one million born-again Christians to converge on Washington to repent and to beg Almighty God to heal the country—I kept in touch with the "700 Club" only in an offhand way. One morning, there was Robertson, live from Jerusalem and in the Upper Room, where he washed the feet of a couple of bystanders—a ceremony that was marred somewhat by his annoyance at having his sports jacket stained with dust when he put it aside to carry out those ablutions.

Then, several days later, there was a show on which his wife appeared, plugging her newly published soybean cookbook and all those scrimping recipes that had enabled the Robertsons to endure the years when they were living in the Bedford-Stuyvesant section of Brooklyn on nothing more than Kingdom Principles. But that show, too, took on a certain awkwardness when it turned out that she didn't know the recipe for "Self-Denial Chili,"—a circumstance attributable to the book's having been ghosted by a "wonderful Christian writer." This particular show, however, was saved somewhat by Pat's enthusiastic account of a recent flying trip to Washington, during which he had stood fervently in prayer with one arm around Anwar el-Sadat, and the other around

Warren Burger—to which a rapt Ben Kinchlow responded, "Oh, wow! 'And you shall walk upon the high places of the earth.' Just like it promises in the Bible, eh?"

And it was at about this time that I made several visits to the CBN's Washington prayer-counseling center, located in three tiny rooms in a grungy basement just across the Potomac in Virginia. It was a cramped, ugly, sweaty little place. An oily film of dirt coated the acoustical tile that lined the tiny phone cubicles, the heaps of tracts, and even the computer forms that the secretaries were busy filling in, from other filled-in standardized forms given them by the prayer counselors—so many "salvations," "financial problems," "sex problems," "suicidals," "Holy Spirit baptisms," and the like. These would be fed into the big computer down in Virginia Beach headquarters, which had much more comfortable quarters than did these mere volunteers, whose ancient, battered cars with the "700 Club" and "I Found It" bumper stickers were parked outside as rusty evidence of their not having yet become so adroit or fortunate with the Kingdom Principles as Pat Robertson was.

It was just before air time as I came in, and the atmosphere of the place was dank with sweat and Evening in Paris toilet water in about equal amounts—cut through by the high-pitched gabbling of these Christian women, most of whom were in the fullness of middle age and whose amplitude was accentuated by the tight, pastel-colored trousers they wore. As I walked in, a dozen smiling faces swiveled around and chorused, "Praise the Lord!" But some shield, or hood, fell over their countenances when I did not say "Praise the Lord!" right back.

One of the women, a nurse I'll call Greta, came up to talk to me. She was friendly and likable, and although somewhat younger than the rest, she had a strained, ravaged face, with eyes that seemed faraway and misty, like those from technicolor religious ecstasies starring Charlton Heston and produced by moguls who never had ecstasies over anything but money. She said "Praise the Lord" a lot and said that she would like to tell me what the "700 Club" had meant to her. But I was uncomfortable with those "Praise the Lords," and was yet to catch on to the evangelical lexicon, which featured familiar words used in slightly unfamiliar ways—words like *burden, fellowship,* and *shared.* Thus, in the evangelical jargon you never wanted to send some Bibles to the Indians, but "had a burden for the Indians," and you never just plain got together with other Christians, but "fellowshipped" with them, and you never flat-out told anybody anything, but "shared," as in "Floyd shared what Jesus did for his hemorrhoids."

Suddenly the telephones were beginning to light up, as the "700 Club," vibrant with energy, slipped out onto the videowaves, and in that wretched little basement, what had been a neighborhood hen party became an embattled crisis pit, as that jolted, menaced, answerless, uprooted, salvation-hungry city out there began to go ape into the horn. Bleeping like that of an outraged heart monitor came spilling out of the recorded-message machine that took the overflow.

Greta and the other smiling counselors were into it now, toiling for Jesus, leaning forward into the two-foot-wide tiled cockpits, praying and exhorting, as the desperate called in: the suicidal, drunk, drugged, anxious, and demon-possessed. Their spouses had cheated on them, they were afraid of the Bomb; they were full of cancerous lumps. They had been saved, they had been filled with the Holy Spirit, or they hadn't been, and wanted to be. They were looking for love and a better job and they wanted to step out in faith on those Kingdom Principles and send in the rent money, but were afraid to. And these counselors, with Bibles open, and turning through the thumb-indexed CBN Counseling Manuals that gave answers for every situation, were into it with them—advising, pleading, praying in tongues, hands held up to the oppressively low ceiling—and from time to time checking off the appropriate boxes on the forms—Salvation Forms, Answers-to-Prayers Forms, Holy Baptism Forms, Money Gift Forms—that the systems-analysis experts of Virginia Beach had devised for them, and that would later be fed into the computers, along with the caller's name and address. Above them, from the small television set high on a shelf, Efrem Zimbalist, Jr., was explaining urbanely to Robertson how empty his life had been before he'd found Jesus on Christian TV, and been born again, slain in the Spirit, and given the gift of speaking in tongues.

## Hearing Confession

Later, in McDonald's, where we'd gone for a cup of coffee, Greta said, "It's on those phones that Jesus' work gets done. It's the privacy, you see. They tell us things they'd never tell anybody else. It's like a confessional."

Privacy, too, was why we had come to McDonald's in the first place. She was afraid that the director would see her talking to the press and get the wrong idea. They kept pretty close tabs on you, she said, and she was anxious not to be "disfellowshipped," because she thought that the phone counseling was more important than the other things she did—full-time nursing at a home for the terminally ill, and voluntary nursing in her spare time among elderly members of her pentecostal church.

It has not always been thus. In earlier days she had been a boozer, a doper, and a low-level prostitute. She'd had an arrangement with some cab drivers, and in the mornings before the trade came would sit in front of TV with vials of sleeping capsules on the table beside her, trying to work up enough nerve to check out. Then one morning she'd tuned into the "700 Club," and Robertson was saying that there was a woman about to kill herself who thought that no one loved her. But Jesus loved her, he said, and she was not to kill herself, nor reproach herself anymore for what she had not been able to help.

After that she'd wept, and accepted Christ into her heart, and he had made all things new.

"I saw what a selfish person I'd been," she said. "And how hopeless life is without God."

Since then, everything had been different; life had been full and satisfying, and she'd had answers to things—not Robertson's answers, especially, since the

"700 Club" was primarily for intellectuals, and she wasn't one of those. But the Bible's answers—she had those, and the fellowship of people who believed as she did. And as for the criticism of Robertson, she'd heard all that, too, and all she knew was that he had led her to the Lord. And if he wasn't perfect, tough. Nobody expected Johnny Carson to be perfect, did they?

Through her, I got to meet other members of the "700 Club", most of whom belonged to the local fundamentalist and pentecostal churches and met together in each other's homes. They were as likable as she was, and had a strength, serenity, and wisdom about them that seemed genuine.

In short, they confounded my expectations and left everything up in the air. I liked these people, liked them a lot, and felt myself to be one of them. I was living an ordinary life just as they were, and I believed in Jesus just the way they did; and I was convinced that they were the real thing; certain that the help they gave over those phones was real.

And it was at about this time, by chance, that I got to talk to one of the Christian intellectuals who are so taken with the "700 Club". I got a call from an old college friend who had heard what I was doing and wanted to see me. He was a professor at a local university, and I assumed he was doing a paper on evangelicals. He was a member of the "700 Club", however, and he told me in an offhand way that in Christ he'd found the answers he'd been looking for all along. Not only that, he had been delivered from anxiety attacks, too.

He wasn't an adroit testifier, though, and told me these things with all the enthusiasm of a nun repeating some lubricious profanity. He kept a scowl on his face that seemed to be trying to say that he was still the guy I'd always known, and nobody's fool. When I asked him what church he went to, he said, no church.

"All that gives me the creeps," he said.

Television, then, was his church, and he wasn't apologetic about it, either. I told him that it all sounded pretty easy. He didn't have to visit orphanages, fold church programs, or get along with the parish faithful. All he had to do was flip on Channel 20 when he felt like it and maybe mail out a check from an air-conditioned room now and again.

"Yeah," he said. "But you see, I tried church." He went on to say that he wasn't as bitter as he once had been, either.

But I could feel in him the same seething, chronic anger he'd had as a young man. Back then, it had been random, like that of a snake that would strike at a stick. But now it was honed in, as Robertson's anger was, on the secular humanists. And he could hardly wait until November, when Ronald Reagan would be elected and the snide homosexuals, Russia-lovers, welfare chiselers, and child-killers would get theirs. Although it was, of course, too late.

"Too late for what?" I asked.

He shrugged. "It's all going up," he said. "Henry Adams was right. And it's too late for anything." We were walking past the White House when he said this. "Personally," he went on, "I keep enough sleeping pills around the house to kill my wife and children in case of bad radiation burns. And myself, of course. And I believe in Jesus. Reason sucks. And that's everything I know."

Shortly after that, I wrote a brief article for a local magazine about these "700 Club" members—one that was more favorable than not. But since it was not 100 percent favorable, I got an astonishing amount of hate mail. Some of the letters arrived on cheap lined paper, in crabbed pencil scrawls. Others were neatly typed and of a fine literary form. Most were agreed that I was "demon-possessed." That was what made the media run: demons.

## An Occasion for Repentance

The Washington for Jesus March took place in an atmosphere of imminent crisis and impending national collapse. On the night of April 28, when many of the young people were listening to Pat Boone et alii sing at RFK Stadium, images of charred helicopters down in an alien, pagan desert were coming in over the videowaves. And some evangelicals out in that rain-drenched stadium said that those downed planes were the Abomination of Desolation Standing in the Unclean Place that had been foretold by the prophet Daniel and by Jesus—a sign of the End. And as a gray, overcast Washington dawn greeted the day of the march itself, other news broke: Cyrus Vance had resigned, and a few antiwar demonstrators, Philip Berrigan among them, were throwing blood on the walls of the Pentagon—while the Hunt brothers were refusing to appear before a House committee that wanted to ask whether they were trying to get a monopoly on the world's silver and what they intended to do if they got it.

Among the tinier events of the day was a *Washington Post* column of mine about the march, which was mostly favorable but unfortunately made the mistake of suggesting that the evangelical movement, as led by the Electric Church, was in some respects similar to the Islamic fundamentalism currently sweeping Iran. As a result, I got a born-again threatening call before the day was out.

It was easy to understand the evangelicals' anger. The media did not seem to know what to do with the Washington for Jesus March—although they had been pretty sure of themselves today in strewing blossoms over the Pope's visit the previous October, and were sure of themselves today in dealing with the Pentagon blood-throwers: conducting reverential interviews with the leaders and giving the two dozen rioters about equal coverage with the 500,000 Christians who gathered on the mall. Newspapers and television news programs alike kept raising the question of whether the gathering wasn't essentially "political"—with the implication being that if it was, it was wrong. However, they did not accuse the Christian blood-throwers at the Pentagon of being political. And under the circumstances, it was understandable how those evangel-icals could be sore at the press, and why Robertson himself spent the day strenuously maintaining that it was a religious gathering. They hadn't come to point the finger at anybody, he said, but to repent themselves. And in doing so, they were relying on the Scripture that said, "If my people, which are called by my name, shall humble themselves, and pray, and seek My face, and turn from their wicked ways; then I will hear from Heaven, and will forgive their sin, and will heal their land." That's what they were here for, he said: *they* would repent.

In the meantime, in the crowd itself, one got jolted by excitement that could not be transmitted by any television camera. You felt it thick all around you, people raising hands to God and praying for him to spare the country, and singing the old, soul-stirring hymns, not through a little speaker on a TV set, but from all around you. And as in a good rock concert, you knew that no television set could ever convey the way this thing felt, with all the power around you exceeding the wattage being put forth up there on the platform, where a succession of born-again superstars were waiting to come on and give sermons.

Before that, Robertson introduced a big, heavyset black preacher from the West Coast to give the prayer, and conferred on him the highest praise he could think of, that "*Time* magazine has named him as one of the ten best preachers in America!" Again, that ambivalent attitude toward the press.

This black man, whose deep voice and rhythmic cadences reminded one of King, started off slowly in lowered tones, began mightily to pray, passionately, and with the volume ever increasing, prayed powerfully for the good of the country and for everything to be all right again. And from around you in the crowd there shone this powerful religious feeling, as all sorts of people were praying together, many of them weeping from the power of the moment. And, feeling all this, I began to think, *anything is possible.*

Just maybe, I thought, Robertson means what he says about the repentance and is up there at this moment repenting of the way he wreaks those infernal Kingdom Principles on poor and helpless people. And if that was the case, I thought, then a whole lot of other things could be possible, because a Pat Robertson purged of the itch for corporate expression, self-righteousness, and the lust for political power really would be formidable. With his great ability, he might just trigger that third great awakening that so many Christians were calling for but that had not come close to happening yet. But I understate it by saying "just maybe," because the power of the experience, and this overwhelming feeling that these people were good, whether their leaders were or not, washed over me, and I went away from there feeling that it probably *had* happened, Robertson's repentance. And I was still in that frame of mind when he phoned me later that afternoon.

He was still backstage, and from behind him came the thumping gospel music and shouts of that great crowd, that at day's beginning had numbered some 250,000—out-of-towners, mostly—and that by now had doubled, with many of the newcomers, I suspect, being native Washingtonians drawn to the power of the event. Robertson, who had been counting the house, was thrilled by those numbers, and he began talking exultantly to me about how beautiful everything was, and how the Lord was doing a great work.

"Everybody is repenting, eh?" I said.

"That too, Dick. And praising the Lord. There is just such a beautiful spirit in this place."

"A lot of people," I said, "might think that evangelicals have nothing to repent of."

"Sure they do," he said. "You know, we have this Treasure in earthen vessels. There are the little sins, and so forth. But you ought to be here. It's beautiful what the Holy Spirit is doing."

"Institutions, too," I suggested, "might have something to repent of."

This brought silence at the other end of the wire.

"What about CBN?" I asked. "Does CBN have anything to repent of?"

And that did it, as Robertson's wrath toward the media, which had abated somewhat in my case, on a trial basis, exploded into the horn.

"Listen here," he said. "I'm not going to get into that with you! The very idea, asking a question like that, at a time like this. Here we are praising God, and you. ..." It was just too much; these prying, destructive, Jesus-hating humanist smart-asses, who came on as objective and were only out to do a job on you.

"*I'm not going to get into that with you,*" he said. This was understandable, because whatever CBN had to repent of was none of my business. I never heard from him again. Although I kept hearing from the PR man about the Brunswick business.

## By Their Fruits

Later that day, the threatening call came. And still later, a phone call from my brother—a radio journalist, and a recent Christian convert. He'd had a wonderful time in that crowd, he said, and had not been ashamed to lift his hands to Jesus and pray along with all the rest. And he even thought he could go to a real church now and get a lot out of it—preferably a pentecostal church, where everybody was as warm as they had been on the mall.

"But a funny thing happened," he said. "I had these interviews scheduled with some of the leaders, and I went behind the stand, to the speakers' area. And it was different there."

"How?"

"It was cold," my brother said. "And hard-bitten. There were security guards all around, everywhere. More than I saw that time I went to the White House. They were mean-looking and followed you everywhere. Even after you had been checked through security and had your badge, one of them went with you everywhere you went. It's hard to describe. All that good feeling out front, while backstage. ... Put it this way: If they'd been wearing swastikas, you wouldn't have been surprised. Or maybe I'm going crazy."

I did not think he was going crazy. But having already said too much about a dangerous subject, I said nothing now.

"Listen," my brother said at last. "What do you suppose Pat would think, if he knew about that?"

All I knew was what it said in the Bible: "By their fruits you shall know them." And in the case of Robertson, it was a matter of mixed fruits. For there was much to like about the man, and his diagnosis of the evils wrought by secular humanism was, to my way of looking at it, essentially correct. And even if it wasn't, it was a viewpoint damn well worth listening to, and one that made the "700 Club"—at times, anyway—one of the best shows on the air.

On the other hand, however, he did seem to be raising money by selling miracles—and hard-selling them especially to the poor, the ill, and the desperate. He spent a lot of that money surrounding himself with grandeur. He equated New Testament Christianity with the worship of success. He made those who were not successful believe that God did not care about them. He boasted of his own spiritual prowess. He presented his personal political views as Biblical truth. He fostered the notion that those who disagreed with him were not only wrong, but evil. And he equated tolerance with moral drift.

I predict that his power will wax. The times are propitious for that, the national breakdown he profits from is real, and a sense of oncoming cataclysm is keenly felt by more people than just Christians. And secular humanism is fully as destructive as he says it is. But the question is whether a slick commercial Christianity is any better.

# ❧ 185 ❧

# Jerry Falwell on Armageddon

## GRACE HALSELL

Jerry Falwell was originally ordained as a Baptist minister but is much better known for his television preaching and the founding of Moral Majority to which President Ronald Reagan turned a receptive ear in the 1980s. His pre-millennialist vision, drawing on Revelation, foresees the imminent Second Coming of Christ after Armageddon in which the Antichrist—in the 1980s the Soviet Union—was to be destroyed by nuclear war. True believers, however, were to be instantaneously spirited away from destruction in the Rapture.

---

Jerry Falwell prefers the topic of Armageddon to almost any other subject. In a December 2, 1984, sermon, he began by reading Revelation 16:16—which gives us the first and only biblical mention of Armageddon, and then proclaimed:

> The word strikes fear into the hearts of people! There will be one last skirmish and then God will dispose of this Cosmos. The Scripture tells us in Revelation, chapters 21 and 22, God will destroy this earth—the heavens and the earth.
> And Peter says in his writings that the destruction will mount as with a fervent heat or a mighty explosion.

In the "holocaust at Armageddon," Falwell continues,

> the Antichrist will move into the Middle East and place a statue of himself in the Jewish temple, the holy of holies, and demand that the whole world worship him as God ...
> Millions of devout Jews will again be slaughtered at this time (Zechariah 15:8) but a remnant will escape (Zechariah 13:9) and God will supernaturally hide them for Himself for the last three and a half years of the Tribulation, some feel in the rose-red city of Petra (located in Jordan). I don't know how, but God will keep them because the Jews are the Chosen People of God.

The battlefield for Armageddon, says Falwell, quoting Zechariah 12:11 and

Source: Grace Halsell, 'Jerry Falwell on Armageddon', *Prophecy and Politics*, Bulsbrook, Australia, 1987, pp. 30–5.

Revelation 16:16, as well as Isaiah 34:35-36 and 36:1

> will stretch from Megiddo in the north to Edom on the south, a distance of about 200 miles. It will reach from the Mediterranean Sea on the west to the hills of Moab on the east, a distance of almost 100 miles. It will include the valley of Jehoshaphat—read Joel 3:2 and verse 12 as well. And the plains of Jezreel and the center of the entire area will be the city of Jerusalem—according to Zechariah 14, verses one and two.
>
> Into this area the multiplied million of men at Armageddon—they will doubtless be approaching 400 million in number—will crowd in for that final holocaust of humanity and Joel 3:14 says the kings with their armies will come from the north and the south and the east and the west. In the most dramatic sense this will be the valley of decision for humanity, with a great wine press into which will be poured the fierceness of the wrath of Almighty God referred to in Revelation 19:15.
>
> Why will they be fighting there? Why is the Antichrist leading the armies of the world against Lord Jesus?
>
> Number one, because he hates the sovereignty of God. The battle had always been Satan versus Christ. That's the issue. Secondly, because of the deception of Satan, these nations will come. Third, because of the hatred of the nations for the Lord Jesus Christ. Some things will happen during that battle. The Euphrates river will dry up (Revelation 16:12) and the destruction of Jerusalem will occur.

Meanwhile, continues Falwell, quoting John's Revelation again, "all the fowls that fly in the heaven" will be feasting themselves on

> the flesh of kings, the flesh of captains, the flesh of mighty men, the flesh of horses and their riders, and the flesh of all men, both free and slave, both small and great.

"John saw a beast in his dreams," Falwell concludes, and the kings of the earth with their armies gathered to make war against the Lord Jesus Christ, who, in John's vision, is a man sitting on a white horse.

As Armageddon draws to a close, with millions lying dead, the Lord Jesus will throw the beast and the false prophet (the Antichrist) "into the lake of fire that burns with brimstone." And the Lord Jesus will slay all His other enemies who somehow survived Armageddon.

Falwell had portrayed a horrifying picture of the end of the world. But he did not seem to be sad or even concerned. In fact he concluded this sermon by giving us a big smile and saying:

"Hey, it's great being a Christian! We have a wonderful future ahead!"

After listening to that sermon, I played tapes of "Dr. Jerry Falwell teaches Bible Prophecy" issued by the Old Time Gospel Hour in 1979. On these tapes Falwell says:

> So you see, Armageddon is a reality, a horrible reality. But, thank God, it's the end of the days of the Gentiles, for it then sets the stage for the introduction of the King, the Lord Jesus, in power and in great glory.
>
> Almost all Bible teachers I know are anticipating the Lord's imminent return. And I do believe myself that we are a part of that terminal generation, that last generation, that shall not pass until our Lord comes.
>
> There are some very recent developments in Russia, predicted by the prophet

Ezekiel, which point up the soon return of our Lord. These communists are God-haters, they're Christ-rejecters, and their ultimate goal is world conquest. Some 26 hundred years ago, the Hebrew prophet Ezekiel prophesied that such a nation would rise to the north of Palestine just prior to the Second Coming of Christ.

In Ezekiel, chapters 38 and 39, we read that the name of this land would be Rosh—that's Ezekiel 38, verse 2 in the American Standard Version—Rosh, R-O-S-H. He (Ezekiel) continues by mentioning two cities of Rosh. These he called Meschech and Tubal. That's all in verse 2, as well. The names here are remarkable similar to Moscow and Tubolsk, the two ruling capitals of Russia today. Also, Ezekiel wrote that the land would be anti-God—verse 3—and therefore God would be against it. He also said that Russia or Rosh would invade Israel in the latter days—that's verse 8—then he said this invasion would be aided by various allies of Rosh—verses 5 and 6.

He named those allies: Iran (which we have in the past called Persia), South Africa or Ethiopia, North Africa or Libya, Eastern Europe (called Gomer here in Ezekiel 38), and the Cossacks of southern Russia, called Togarmah in this chapter. In 38:15 of Ezekiel, the prophet describes the major part of horses in this invasion.

The Cossacks of course have always owned and bred the largest and finest herd of horses in history. The purpose of this invasion, Ezekiel said, was to take a "spoil,"—verse 12, chapter 38. If one but removes the first two letters of this word "spoil" he soon realizes what Russia will really be after—obviously, oil. And that is where we find ourselves today. This, then, is Ezekiel's prophecy concerning Russia.

In spite of the rosy and utterly unrealistic expectations by our government (on the Camp David accords involving Israel and Egypt), this treaty will not be a lasting treaty. We are certainly praying for the peace of Jerusalem. We certainly have the highest respect for the Prime Minister of Israel and the President of Egypt—great men, no doubt about that. And they certainly want peace—I am convinced that is true. But you and I know that there's not going to be any real peace in the Middle East until one day the Lord Jesus sits down upon the throne of David in Jerusalem.

That day is coming. And for sure, you and I are going to be a part of it. But until then, there is not going to be any peace on this earth until the Prince of Peace, our Savior, returns.

Armageddon was much on Falwell's mind when he gave an interview, published March 4, 1981, in the *Los Angeles Times*, to reporter Robert Scheer. Their conversation went like this:

Scheer: "Turning to the future—in your pamphlet on Armageddon, you prophesy nuclear war with Russia."

Falwell: "We believe that Russia, because of her need of oil—and she's running out now—is going to move in on the Middle East, and particularly Israel because of their hatred of the Jew, and that it is at that time when all hell will break out. And it is at that time when I believe there will be some nuclear holocaust on this earth, because it says that blood shall flow in the streets up to the bridle of the horses in the Valley of Esdraelon for some 200 miles. And it speaks of horrible happenings that one can only relate in Second Peter 3, the melting of the elements, to nuclear warfare. But I think, at the end of the church age, when the church is Raptured, as we use the word, or cached out, then uninhibited hostilities will occur on this earth."

Scheer: "And Russia will be—"

Falwell: "And Russia will be the offender and will be ultimately totally destroyed."

Scheer: "Well, the whole world will, won't it?"

Falwell: "No, not the whole world, because then our Lord is coming back to the earth. First, He comes to take the church out. Seven years later, after Armageddon, this horrible holocaust, He's coming back to this very earth so it won't be destroyed, and the church is coming with him, to rule and reign with Christ on the Earth for a thousand years. And then comes the new heavens and the new earth and eternity. That's all in that book on Armageddon—that is just an outline."

Scheer: "But will it be possible for Russia to be destroyed with nuclear weapons without it destroying the world?"

Falwell: "Yes, I don't mean that every person—Russia has many wonderful Christians there, too. The underground church is working very effectively in Russia, Red China. They're going to be taken out in the Rapture ... It (the war) will come down out of the North—that has to be the Soviet Union—upon the midst of the Earth—Israel and the Middle East—and so we believe the hostilities will be initiated by the Soviet Union. That's why most of us believe in the imminent return of Jesus Christ. We believe we're living in those days just prior to the Lord's coming."

Scheer: "By imminent, you mean a year or how long?"

Falwell: "Nobody is willing, of course—we're warned by the Lord not to set dates. The Lord said, 'No man knows the day or the hour.' Every religious group or leader who has ever set dates, I think, has dishonored the Lord and embarrassed themselves. It could be 50 years. I don't think so. I don't think we have that long. I think we're coming to an impasse. All of history is reaching a climax and I do not think, I do not think we have 50 years left. I don't think my children will live their full lives out ..."

In a tract, "Nuclear War and the Second Coming of Jesus Christ," published in 1983 by the Old-Time Gospel Hour, Falwell writes:

> The Tribulation will result in such bloodshed and destruction that any war up to that time will seem insignificant.

In a chapter entitled "The Coming War with Russia," Falwell predicts a Soviet invasion of Israel followed by the annihilation of Soviet forces "on the mountains of Israel."

> At the conclusion of this battle, Scripture tells us that five-sixths (83 percent) of the Russian soldiers will have been destroyed (Ezekiel 39:2). The first grisly feast of God begins (Ezekiel 39:4, 17–20). A similar feast would seem to take place later, after the battle of Armageddon (Revelation 19:17–18; Matthew 24:28). The communist threat will cease forever. Seven months will be spent in burying the dead (Ezekiel 39:11–15).

# Index of Writers, Documents, Artists and Illustrations.

# Index to Writers and Documents, Illustrations and Artists

Entries for writers and documents are listed by volume [I, II, III] and chapter number. Illustrations and artists are listed by volume and plate number. Please refer to the Table of Contents and Lists of Illustrations for page numbers.

## Writers and Documents

## Artist and Illustrations